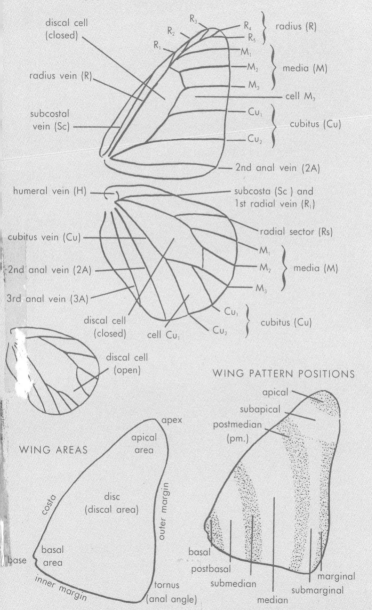

WING VENATION

discal cell (closed)

radius vein (R)

subcostal vein (Sc)

$R_3$
$R_2$
$R_1$
$R_4$
$R_5$ } radius (R)
$M_1$
$M_2$ } media (M)
$M_3$
cell $M_3$
$Cu_1$
$Cu_2$ } cubitus (Cu)
2nd anal vein (2A)

humeral vein (H)
subcosta (Sc) and 1st radial vein ($R_1$)
radial sector (Rs)

cubitus vein (Cu)
$M_1$
$M_2$ } media (M)
$M_3$

2nd anal vein (2A)

3rd anal vein (3A)
$Cu_1$
$Cu_2$ } cubitus (Cu)

discal cell (closed)
cell $Cu_1$

discal cell (open)

WING PATTERN POSITIONS

apical
subapical
postmedian (pm.)

WING AREAS

apex
apical area

costa

disc (discal area)

outer margin

base
basal area

inner margin

tornus (anal angle)

basal
postbasal
submedian
median
submarginal
marginal

# THE PETERSON FIELD GUIDE SERIES
*Edited by Roger Tory Peterson*

1. Birds — *R. T. Peterson*
2. Western Birds — *R. T. Peterson*
3. Shells of the Atlantic and Gulf Coasts and the West Indies — *Morris*
4. Butterflies — *Klots*
5. Mammals — *Burt and Grossenheider*
6. Pacific Coast Shells (including shells of Hawaii and the Gulf of California — *Morris*
7. Rocks and Minerals — *Pough*
8. Birds of Britain and Europe — *R. T. Peterson, Mountfort, and Hollom*
9. Animal Tracks — *Murie*
10. Ferns and Their Related Families of Northeastern and Central North America — *Cobb*
11. Trees and Shrubs (Northeastern and Central North America) — *Petrides*
12. Reptiles and Amphibians of Eastern and Central North America — *Conant*
13. Birds of Texas and Adjacent States — *R. T. Peterson*
14. Rocky Mountain Wildflowers — *J. J. Craighead, F. C. Craighead, Jr., and Davis*
15. Stars and Planets — *Menzel and Pasachoff*
16. Western Reptiles and Amphibians — *Stebbins*
17. Wildflowers of Northeastern and North-central North America — *R. T. Peterson and McKenny*
19. Insects of America North of Mexico — *Borror and White*
20. Mexican Birds — *R. T. Peterson and Chalif*
21. Birds' Nests (found east of Mississippi River) — *Harrison*
22. Pacific States Wildflowers — *Niehaus and Ripper*
23. Edible Wild Plants of Eastern and Central North America — *L. Peterson*
24. Atlantic Seashore — *Gosner*
25. Western Birds' Nests — *Harrison*
26. Atmosphere — *Schaefer and Day*
27. Coral Reefs of the Caribbean and Florida — *Kaplan*
28. Pacific Coast Fishes — *Eschmeyer, Herald, and Hammann*
29. Beetles — *White*
30. Moths — *Covell*
31. Southwestern and Texas Wildflowers — *Niehaus, Ripper, and Savage*
32. Atlantic Coast Fishes — *Robins, Ray, and Douglass*
33. Western Butterflies — *Tilden and Smith*

# A Field Guide to
# Western
# Butterflies

**James W. Tilden**
*and*
**Arthur Clayton Smith**

*Photographic Illustrations by*
**Terry M. Smith** *and*
**Arthur Clayton Smith**

*Drawings by*
**Gene Christman** *and*
**Barbara Young**

*Sponsored by the National Audubon Society
and National Wildlife Federation*

HOUGHTON MIFFLIN COMPANY · BOSTON
1986

**Library of Congress Cataloging-in-Publication Data**

Tilden, James W. (James Wilson), 1904–
    A field guide to western butterflies.

    (The Peterson field guide series)
    Bibliography: p. 334
    Includes index.
    1. Butterflies — West (U.S.) — Identification.
    2. Insects — Identification.   3. Insects — West (U.S.) —
    Identification.   I. Smith, Arthur Clayton, 1916–
    II. National Audubon Society.   III. National Wildlife
    Federation.   IV. Title.   V. Series.
    QL551.W3T55   1986       595.78′90978       85-30501
    ISBN 0-395-35407-2
    ISBN 0-395-41654-X (pbk.)

Printed in the United States of America

V  10  9  8  7  6  5  4  3  2  1

# Editor's Note

Butterflies, the bright wings of summer, give beauty and movement to the gardens, roadsides, and woodland trails. Like the birds, they are a litmus of the environment, sending out signals when things are out of kilter. They are an early warning system; thus the butterfly watcher inevitably becomes an environmentalist.

In North America, north of the Mexican border, there are about 763 species of butterflies. This is roughly equal to the number of birds found in North America (if we exclude the accidentals from Asia, Mexico, and the sea). As the authors of this new Field Guide point out, the number of butterfly species west of the 100th meridian is greater than the number found to the east. Here again, we find the proportion almost equal to that of the birds (nearly 20 percent more in the West). This is because the West is more complex in its terrain, with a variety of habitats — higher mountains, lower valleys, humid regions, arid deserts.

It is with alarm that we note that in the western states there are more butterflies on the endangered list than in the East. Several species have already become extinct and a number of others are endangered, most of them in California — the western state that has been subject to the greatest human pressures. One of the extinct species, the Xerces Blue, has been chosen as the symbol of the Xerces Society, a group of lepidopterists who make butterfly counts or censuses each July throughout the country and who are concerned with conservation.

Because of the relatively high reproductive potential of butterflies, collecting, except for the rarities, does not seem to have an appreciable effect on their populations. The critical factor in conserving these fragile insects is preservation of the habitat.

However, if you do not collect butterflies, you can still enjoy them as one would enjoy birds — to be looked at and watched as vibrant, colorful expressions of life, or, if you are an environmentalist, as indicators of the health of the land.

Some flower lovers plant their gardens not only with traditional favorites such as roses and tulips but also with zinnias, buddleias, and other plants whose nectar is attractive to passing butterflies. Outside my studio my wife Virginia has planted a garden for butterflies that has attracted nearly 30 species.

If collecting is not your main thrust you might try photography. I find butterfly photography a lot of fun — not only in the tropics,

131757

where butterflies can be found in almost endless variety — but also in the fields, roadsides, and trails close to home. The equipment I use is a battery of Nikon cameras outfitted with Micro Nikkor lenses. These macro lenses allow a very close focus, so that the butterfly fills a large part of the frame. Of course, if I were to approach too closely the butterfly almost certainly would take wing. So the two lenses I find most useful are the Micro Nikkor 105 mm and the Micro Nikkor 200 mm. Most butterflies when actively nectaring will allow one to approach closely enough with either of these two lenses before taking wing. Because of the relatively long focal length of these lenses, the depth of field is rather shallow, and as a result the otherwise confusing background blurs out rather pleasantly. However, the shallow depth of field does pose a problem. In order to keep the whole insect in sharp focus, a butterfly must be shot either with its wings closed in profile or spread open, as viewed on one plane. Flash equipment can be used, but is seldom necessary, because most butterflies prefer the sunlight rather than the shadows.

This new *Field Guide to Western Butterflies* by James Wilson Tilden and Arthur Clayton Smith has been long awaited. Regardless of whether you have a specialist's interest in butterflies or that of a generalist, ranging the broad spectrum of nature, take this guide with you on your field excursions. It will enable you to put names to some of the gentler inhabitants of the fields and airways and will give you further insights about our natural world. If only butterflies could sing!

ROGER TORY PETERSON

# Acknowledgments

In preparing this book, we consulted many volumes and articles and formed a card file, giving the original citation, the type locality (if stated), the food plant(s) if known, the general distribution, and other pertinent data for each species. In addition, we assembled a collection of representative specimens for illustration. These things could not have been done without the generous assistance of numerous friends and colleagues. However, the final decisions rest with the authors, who take the responsibility for all errors of commission or omission. We wish to thank all who contributed material or information, of whom the following were particularly helpful:

Dr. Paul H. Arnaud, Curator, and the California Academy of Sciences, for the use of the library, loan of specimens, and many other favors; the late Mr. James H. Baker, Baker, Ore., for specimens and field assistance; Mr. David L. Bauer, South Lake Tahoe, Calif., for help with Militaeinae; Dr. F. Martin Brown, Colorado Springs, Colo., for information, counsel, and specimens; Dr. John M. Burns, National Museum of Natural History, Washington, D.C., for information on Hesperiidae, especially *Erynnis;* Mr. Curtis J. Callaghan, Rio de Janeiro, Brazil, for Riodinidae; the late Dr. Harry K. Clench, Carnegie Museum, Pittsburgh, Pa., for Lycaenidae; the late Dr. Clarence Cottam, Rob and Bessie Welder Wildlife Foundation, Sinton, Tex., for the use of facilities; Dr. Gene R. DeFoliart, University of Wisconsin, for specimens; Mr. Thomas E. Dimock, Ventura, Calif., for genus *Vanessa;* Dr. Julian P. Donahue, Asst. Curator, and the Los Angeles County Museum for the loan of specimens; the late Dr. Ernst J. Dornfeld, Corvallis, Ore., for specimens and literature; Mr. Cyril F. dos Passos, Mendham, N.J., for many helpful suggestions; Dr. John C. Downey, University of Northern Iowa, for Lycaenidae; Mr. J. Donald Eff, Boulder, Colo., for numerous specimens; Dr. Paul R. Ehrlich, Stanford University, for literature; Dr. Thomas C. Emmel, University of Florida, for *Cercyonis;* Mr. Paul C. Engelder, San Jose, Calif., for records from San Bernardino County, Calif.; Mr. William D. Field, Smithsonian Institution, for literature and determinations; Mr. Hugh A. Freeman, Garland, Tex., for literature, determinations, helpful information, many specimens, and close cooperation; the late Mr. Perry Glick, Brownsville, Tex., for specimens; Mr. Carll Goodpasture, Pasadena, Calif., for information on blues of the genus *Icaricia;* Mr. L. P. Grey, Lincoln, Me., for *Speyeria* determinations; Mr. John H. Heitzman, Independence, Mo., for rare and much-needed specimens; the late Mr. Peter Herlan, Nevada State Museum, for specimens and much-needed information; the late Dr. William Hovanitz, Arcadia, Calif., for information on the genus *Colias;* Mr. Raymond Jae, Denver, Colo., for specimens; Dr. J. W. Kamp, Vancouver, B.C., for field assistance; Mr. and Mrs. Roy O. Kendall, San Antonio, Tex., for cooperation in many ways, including specimens and numerous food plant records; Mr. Everard Kinch, Fort Worth, Tex., for specimens; Mrs. Kimiko Fujii Kitayama, Homestead, Fla. and her mother, the late Katsu Fujii, Hayward, Calif., for translation from the Japanese of a species account on *Papilio xuthus;* Dr. Alexander Klots, American Museum of Natural History, New York, for needed information; Mr. John Lane, Santa Cruz City Museum, Calif., for field records and critical specimens; Mr. Robert L. Langston, Kensington, Calif., for information on the genus *Philotes* and specimens; the late Mr. Wilbur S. McAlpine, Union Lake, Mich., for metalmarks of the genus *Calephelis;* Mr. Paddy McHenry, Burbank, Calif., for literature references; Dr. C. Don MacNeill, Oakland Museum, Calif., for specimens and information on Hesperiidae; the late Mr. Lloyd M. Martin, Associate Curator Emeritus, Los Angeles County Museum, for suggestions, distributional records, and specimens; Mr. Stirling O. Matoon, Chico, Calif., for information on collecting localities; Dr. Lee D. Miller, Allyn Museum of Entomology, Sarasota, Fla., for literature and critical suggestions; the late Arthur H. Moeck, Milwaukee, Wisc., for specimens and literature on *Speyeria;* the National Park Service and many of its naturalists and rangers, for collecting permits and numerous courtesies in Big Bend, Crater Lake, Grand Canyon, Lassen, Olympic, Sequoia, and Yosemite National Parks; the late Mr. E. J. Newcomer, Yakima, Wash., for specimens and information; Dr. Paul A. Opler, for information on genera *Euchloe* and *Apodemia;* Mr. Larry Orsak, Xerces Society, Dept. of Entomology, University of Georgia, Athens, Ga., for critical reading and advice on butterfly conservation; Dr. Jerry A. Powell, University of California, Berkeley, for literature and helpful suggestions; Dr. E. J. Reinthal, Knoxville, Tenn., for determinations in the genus *Asterocampa;* Dr. Charles L. Remington, Yale University, Conn., for literature and helpful information; Dr. Frederick H. Rindge, American Museum of Natural History, New York, for literature; Mr. Kilian Roever, Phoenix, Ariz., for the loan of many much-needed specimens; Dr. James C. Scott, Lakewood, Colo., for specimens, literature, and records; Dr. Harvey I. Scudder, California State University, Hayward, for information and assistance; the late Dr. Oscar E. Sette, Los Altos, Calif., for the exchange of ideas, records, and field assistance; Dr. Jon H. Shepard, Nelson, B.C., for data on *Boloria* and *Parnassius;* Mr. John T. Sorenson, University of California, Berkeley, for specimens; Mr. Oakley Shields, Mariposa, Calif., for field records and specimens; Mr. Edgar A. Smith, Alexandria, Va., for specimens; Mrs. Renee Campbell Smith, Fremont, Calif., for photographic assistance; Mr. Don B. Stallings, Caldwell, Kans., for literature and specimens; Dr. Ray E. Stanford, Denver, Colo., for scarce and much-needed specimens; Mr. Ralph G. Swanson, U.S. Fish and Wildlife Service, Endangered Species Office, Sacramento, Calif., for critical reading and advice on endangered species; Mr. J. Eric Thiel, San Lorenzo, Calif., for specimens; Mr. Fred T. Thorne, El Cajon, Calif., for information, locality records, and specimens; Mr. Kenneth Tidwell, Salt Lake City, Utah, for information and specimens; Dr. Edward G. Voss, University of Michigan, for literature and information on Hesperiidae. To these and to many others not specifically mentioned by name, our sincere thanks.

Our special thanks go to our wives, Hazel M. Tilden and Eileen B. Smith, for patience, understanding, and assistance in every way possible over the years.

Finally, we wish to thank all the staff members at Houghton Mifflin who have assisted in the production of this field guide. We wish to express our appreciation for the early interest and encouragement by Roger Tory Peterson and Paul Brooks, and early much-needed advice and assistance from Helen Phillips and Morton H. Baker; for much guidance from Virginia Ehrlich, James Thompson, and Lisa Gray Fisher; and for the monumental final effort on the part of Harry Foster, Barbara Stratton, and Diane Taraskiewicz in seeing the book through to completion.

James W. Tilden
Arthur C. Smith

# Contents

# ILLUSTRATIONS

48 color and black-and-white plates,
in an insert following p. 176.

16 black-and-white figures, scattered throughout the text.

# A Field Guide to
# Western
# Butterflies

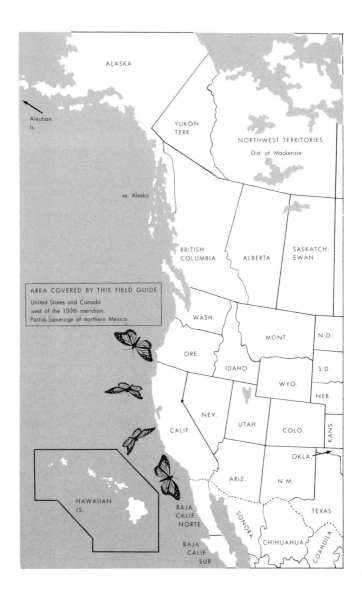

ALASKA

Aleutian
Is.

se. Alaska

YUKON
TERR.

NORTHWEST TERRITORIES

Dist. of Mackenzie

BRITISH
COLUMBIA

ALBERTA

SASKATCH-
EWAN

AREA COVERED BY THIS FIELD GUIDE

United States and Canada
west of the 100th meridian.
Partial coverage of northern Mexico.

WASH.

ORE.

IDAHO

MONT.

WYO.

N.D.

S.D.

NEB.

NEV.

CALIF.

UTAH

COLO.

KANS.

OKLA.

ARIZ.

N.M.

HAWAIIAN
IS.

BAJA
CALIF.
NORTE

SONORA

TEXAS

BAJA
CALIF.
SUR

CHIHUAHUA

COAHUILA

# 1

# How to Use This Book

In 1951 *A Field Guide to the Butterflies,* by Dr. Alexander B. Klots, was added to the Peterson Field Guide Series. Designed for use by beginner and specialist alike, it is a major contribution to the literature on American butterflies. At that time Dr. Klots could say, "During the last generation we have found out a great many new facts about our butterflies." In subsequent years work on butterflies has continued, and the users of this western guide will find that many changes have been made in classification. Name changes are numerous at both the genus and species levels. A few new species have been discovered. For many species, known ranges have been extended and more has been learned about life histories.

The sequence of families and genera given in the 1964 *Synonymic List of Nearctic Rhopalocera* by Cyril F. dos Passos began with the giant skippers and ended with the satyrs, which is the reverse of most former lists. We thought it better to use the same sequence of families used by Klots, so that the two books might be more easily compared. The sequence of genera and species, however, is somewhat different. Scientific names, with but a few exceptions, follow the 1983 *Check List of the Lepidoptera of America North of Mexico* edited by Ronald W. Hodges, *et al.,* with butterfly and skipper sections by Lee D. Miller and F. Martin Brown.

**Identification:** Butterflies are best identified and studied by examining actual specimens. Chapter 2 gives information on how to catch and examine or collect and preserve specimens. As experience and skill grow, the beginning collector will modify techniques and devise new ones. Except for certain endangered populations (see p. 21), you usually need not worry that collecting will seriously reduce a species. Most kinds of butterflies have large populations. However, any endangered, threatened or rare species should *not* be collected. Any butterfly that appears on an official state or federal list with such a designation is fully protected by law (see list on pp. 22–23).

We hope that you will take this *Field Guide* with you on your trips. The more distinctive species may be recognized readily by checking them against the illustrations. First, try to decide on the family and, if possible, the group to which your specimen belongs. Then check the plates and note the field marks indicated by the arrows that point to physical details, most of which can be seen with the naked eye. Some features can be distinguished more easily with the aid of a hand lens. Field marks are usually based on variations in the shape, color, and pattern or markings of the upper or underside of the front and hind wings. Sometimes species are distinguished by details of the antennae, legs, or body. One or two such distinguishing characters are pointed out on the plates with arrows and briefly described on the legend page. Other field marks that will assist you in identifying butterflies are included in the species accounts.

When you find a butterfly illustration in your guide that seems to match the specimen in hand, turn to the text and read carefully the description and the comparison with similar species, if any. Most of the species listed under the similar species heading will be very close relatives, such as different species in the same genus (Great Spangled Fritillary, Aphrodite), but in some cases they will be in another genus in the same family (Lorquin's Admiral, Sister) and in a few instances from a different family (Red-spotted Purple, Pipe-vine Swallowtail). Compare the size (measured wingtip to wingtip and given as a range of figures, since individuals vary) and check the months listed as the flight season for the species under consideration. It is also important to check the range to see if that species would normally occur in the locality where you collected your specimen.

Often these steps will lead to a clear-cut decision. However, in cases where you have some doubt, you may need to set a specimen aside and try again later. Some butterflies are very difficult to identify, not only for the amateur but also for the professional, and within some genera or families of butterflies misidentifications of species are frequent. The serious student often may obtain help from reference books in libraries, from more experienced collectors, from colleges and universities, and from large museums. With experience you will learn to recognize the families, the major groups, and many of the genera. At first the technical terms may seem strange, but with practice you will soon become familiar with them. The front endpapers illustrate many of the terms used in this guide. Terms are also defined in a Glossary, which begins on p. 330.

**Species included:** The 1964 dos Passos checklist included 682 species for the United States and Canada. The 1981 Miller and Brown checklist records 763 species for the same geographical area. The number of butterfly species in North America west of the 100th meridian is greater than the number east of it. Except for certain endemic species, most eastern butterflies also occur in the West, especially northward. In addition, there are extensive groups, such as the parnassians *(Parnassius)* and the green hairstreaks *(Callophrys),* that are mostly or entirely western. Of necessity, then, the number of species treated in the *Field Guide to*

*Western Butterflies* (512) is greater than in the *Field Guide to the Butterflies* (436).

**Area covered:** This guide covers species found in North America west of the 100th meridian, from the far north to the U.S.–Mexican boundary and Hawaii. Butterflies known to occur regularly in this area are described in the species accounts. Species recorded only once or occasionally are discussed in an appendix (see Casual and Stray Species, p. 319).

**Illustrations:** All but a few species are illustrated with photographs, either in color or in black and white. Color prints were made from Vericolor IIS negatives shot with a 4×5 Linhof with a Voigtländer Apo-Lanthar 150 mm lens using a 120 roll film back. Illumination was provided by two Vivitar 273 electronic flash units. Ilford FP4 and Kodak Plus-X Pan negatives for black-and-white prints were made with the same procedures and equipment.

In most cases both wing surfaces of the specimen are shown, with the upperside on the left, and the underside on the right. The underside is labeled "UN." Where there are major visual differences in the sexes, both male and female are shown.

No species in our area has been omitted intentionally; every attempt has been made to check records for accuracy. Recent work through 1983 has been included where possible. The authors would appreciate readers bringing errors or omissions to their attention.

**Measurements:** Size is given in both inches and millimeters. One inch equals 2.54 centimeters or 25.4 millimeters. The measurements represent the distance from wingtip to wingtip of the forewings and show the normal range of variation within the species. An inch/millimeter scale is included below and on the back cover for your convenience.

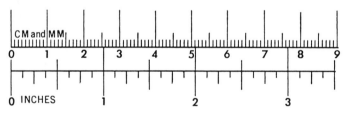

**Early stages:** Descriptions of larvae (caterpillars) are kept to a minimum. The host plants given are larval food plants, not flowers that attract adults. Some butterfly species use only a single plant species for food, while others eat plants of one genus or feed on many members of an entire plant family. Some feed on a variety of plants in several families.

**Adults:** Dates of adult emergence vary greatly with elevation or with the north-south distribution of each species, so this information often cannot be given for all localities. The flight period is given in months.

**Range:** The range given is the entire range of the species. For species that range beyond our area, the total range is given in addition to the range within our area.

**Habitats:** Most terrestrial habitats are home to at least some butterflies, and different habitats may have a variety of species, some of them unique to a single habitat. Sample as many kinds of habitats as possible. Since different butterflies may fly in the same habitat at different seasons, try to visit each place at different times of the year. A listing of some habitats and the butterflies associated with them appears on p. 6.

**Nomenclature:** Many species of butterflies have been divided into subspecies. Some populations long considered distinct species are now considered subspecies, and some former subspecies are now considered full species. Of these, many are very different in appearance from one another. For brevity, the type locality (TL) and a line of description are given for some subspecies, with the approximate extent of the range, if known. No attempt is made to assess the validity of the various subspecies. However, the most visually distinct subspecies are mentioned and the others are spoken of as weakly differentiated. In cases where a species has a very large number of subspecies, space has not permitted consideration of each one. Form, variety, and brood names are used only in those exceptional cases where differences in appearance are considerable and the names are in general use. These instances are few. Synonyms are not given except in a very few cases where they have had common or recent use, or may be better known than the name now considered valid. Common names are those in general use where such names exist. Some less well-known butterflies do not have any generally accepted common name; in a few cases, common names were coined.

**Abbreviations and symbols:** We have used a few abbreviations and symbols in this guide to facilitate the presentation of data in the species accounts. They are: FW = forewing(s); HW = hind wing(s); pm. = postmedian (see front endpapers); TL = type locality, the place where the first specimens of a species or subspecies were taken; ab. = aberration (see Plates); ♂ = male; ♀ = female; in. = inch; mm = millimeter; cm = centimeter; mi. = mile; km = kilometer.

# 2

# Learning About Butterflies

Until very recently the butterfly student has been synonymous with the butterfly "chaser," catching specimens with a net. Bird guides of an earlier day took it for granted that a shotgun would accompany the bird student in the field and pointed out that in many cases the bird must be shot to be identified. Identification was based primarily on the characteristics of the dead bird. Museum specimens still have an important place in scientific ornithology, but for many years now birdwatchers have identified birds by distinctive field marks, characteristic behavior patterns, and recognizable songs and notes. Similarly, those interested in the butterflies have begun to observe and study living butterflies in the field without making museum specimens of them.

Concern for the preservation of all forms of life has arisen in recent years throughout much of the world and is now a factor in the thinking of some entomologists, particularly the lepidopterists. As a result, amateur interest has tended to focus less attention on collecting and more on observation. At the same time, research lepidopterists, in common with most other biologists, have turned major attention to studies in the ecological and physiological aspects of the subject as well as the taxonomic. Taxonomic studies based on extensive museum collections will continue to be necessary; indeed, books such as this one could not be written without such studies. However, with these changes in emphasis it is possible to derive much satisfaction from studying butterflies without collecting them. The amateur as well as the professional may make valuable contributions to science through observations of butterfly habits, behavior, and life history.

## WATCHING BUTTERFLIES

**When to watch.** Best watching is on a warm, sunny, calm day. On windy or overcast days many butterflies take shelter. The period of greatest activity is generally between about 9:00 a.m. and 4:00 p.m. This varies somewhat with early morning and late afternoon temperatures, wind, cloud cover, and other local conditions.

## Some Butterfly-watching Locations

| | |
|---|---|
| Hilltops. | Columbian Skipper (p. 240), swallowtails (p. 113), admirals (p. 63), ladies (p. 73). |
| Mud puddles, stream banks, pond edges, sandbars. | Swallowtails (p. 113), blues (p. 187), whites (p. 124), sulfurs (p. 129). |
| Sap oozing from trees and shrubs; also honeydew. | Red Admiral (p. 74), leaf-wings (p. 58), angle-wings (p. 69), hackberry butterflies (p. 60). |
| Lippia or clover lawns in bloom. | Crescents (p. 94), coppers (p. 180), blues (p. 187), skippers (p. 203), and others. |
| Garden flowers or shrubs in bloom. | Orange Sulfur (p. 131), Cabbage Butterfly (p. 128), Mourning Cloak (p. 68), Red Admiral (p. 74), West Coast Lady (p. 75), Gulf Fritillary (p. 58), swallowtails (p. 113), many others. |
| Larval food plants. | Many species, especially females. Look for Gulf Fritillary (p. 58) on passion vines; *Euphilotes* blues (p. 197) almost exclusively on their food plants (*Eriogonum* species); Pygmy Blue (p. 187) on saltbushes; Zelicaon Swallowtail (p. 118) at sweet fennel; Monarch (p. 56) at milkweeds, etc. |
| Rotting fruit on the ground. | Red Admiral (p. 74), Lorquin's Admiral (p. 66), California Sister (p. 67), Buckeye (p. 76), others. |
| Carrion or fresh animal manure. | Buckeye (p. 76), Red Admiral (p. 74), angle-wings (p. 69), and ladies (p. 73) on both; blues (p. 187) especially on manure. |
| Perches (exposed branches, grasses, weeds, wildflowers, fences, etc.). | Buckeye (p. 76), California Sister (p. 67), admirals (p. 63), coppers (p. 180), hairstreaks (p. 155), many skippers (p. 203). |
| Narrow places in canyons (along flyways). | Swallowtails (p. 113), large butterflies in general, whites (p. 124), orange-tips (p. 145), others. |

| Desert waterholes. | Philetas Skipper (p. 256), dusky-wings (p. 248), blues (p. 187), Queen (p. 57), sulfurs (p. 129), many others. |
| --- | --- |
| Flowers in mountain meadows. | Fritillaries (p. 77), checker-spots (p. 99), crescents (p. 94), swallowtails (p. 113), blues (p. 187), coppers (p. 180), alpines (p. 45), many others. |
| Rocky slopes at high elevations. | Arctics (p. 51), alpines (p. 46), swallowtails (p. 113), parnassians (p. 114), many others. |
| Tundra. | Arctics (p. 51), alpines (p. 46), parnassians (p. 114), lesser fritillaries (p. 86), others. |

**Where to watch.** For the most satisfactory butterfly watching, it is best to let the butterflies come to you. Find a sunny location attractive to butterflies (see the chart for some examples) and settle down comfortably in an inconspicuous position. Have your *Field Guide,* a notebook, and binoculars at hand. After a few moments, living things will resume their normal pace and you will be rewarded with a grandstand view of butterfly activities. Watch for feeding, drinking, flight habits, mating, egg-laying, and orientation to the sun. Also note the ways butterflies interact with other species, including predators and parasites.

**Field recognition.** Many butterflies can be identified on sight once you have learned the important field marks (distinctive visual features, such as wing shape, color, and pattern) and behavior patterns. Others can be identified positively only by close examination of anatomical details. After you have gained a little experience, you will be able to place most butterflies by sight in the correct family and many others in the correct genus. With more field experience you will begin to recognize certain species on sight as well.

Satyrs (p. 38), for example, are usually dull in color. Among them, the ringlets (p. 40) are known by their light color and "flipping" or bouncing flight. Alpines (p. 46), usually found in the North, are very dark, blackish brown butterflies. Most have small eyespots and usually fly in the open, nearly in a straight line. Wood nymphs and their relatives (p. 36) are gray — usually dark with conspicuous eyespots — and are found in forest meadows or sagebrush scrub. They fly with a bouncing flight, often near cover. Arctics (p. 51) are lighter in color, and are found either in open woodland or in tundra. They frequently "sit" for long periods of time until flushed.

The Monarch (p. 56) is easily recognized by its large size, tawny color, and conspicuously marked veins. The Queen (p. 57) is similar, but smaller and darker. Both fly mostly in the open and are readily visible. The Viceroy (p. 65), which mimics the Monarch, can be recognized by a prominent, black postmedian line across each hind wing (see front endpapers) that is absent in the Monarch. Also, the male Monarch has a black scent patch or stigma on each hind wing (below vein $Cu_2$) that is not present in the Viceroy.

There are many kinds of brush-footed butterflies; no one characteristic applies to them all. The Red Admiral (p. 74), with its black color and flashing red band across the forewings, is unique. Lorquin's Admiral (p. 66) and the California Sister (p. 67) are also very distinctive. In Lorquin's Admiral the wingtips are brick red; in the California Sister they are pale orange.

Fritillaries of the genus *Speyeria* (p. 77) are usually fairly large, tawny to reddish above, and often have silver spots on the underside of each hind wing. In some species, the spots are not silvered. The small or lesser fritillaries of the genera *Boloria* (p. 86), *Clossiana* (p. 87), and *Proclossiana* (p. 93), are similarly marked, but are smaller and usually more northern.

Checker-spots (p. 99) are small to medium in size and tawny to reddish above, but *banded* below rather than spotted. Crescents (p. 94) are small, and mostly reddish brown to tawny with dark markings on the upperside. They usually fly close to the ground and frequently perch on plants or on the ground with their wings over their backs. In this position the characteristic light-colored crescent present in most species can be seen.

Angle-wings (p. 69) are mostly medium-sized, orange-brown, dark-spotted butterflies with very irregular, ragged-looking wing margins. They are found in forests and along wooded streams. When resting on a tree trunk they are invisible to all but the sharpest eyes, but when they move from one tree to another the bright flash of their wings is highly visible.

Most hairstreaks (p. 155) are small. They usually perch quietly on shrubs or other plants until disturbed, then fly rapidly, sometimes too fast to follow easily. Then they sit again, often near where they were first disturbed. The lines and thecla spot (Fig. 12, p. 156) on the underside of each hind wing may give a clue to their identity. Blues (p. 187) are usually small to very small, and bright to dull blue on the upperside. Coppers (p. 180) are usually a bit larger; they often fly rather conspicuously around vegetation and perch in the open, where their bright colors show up well.

Swallowtails (p. 113) are large. Our species have tails at the lower end of each hind wing. All are yellow with black bands except the Pipe-vine Swallowtail (p. 115), which is dark greenish and spotted below with red. Parnassians (p. 113) are smaller; usually white with small red spots. They are found in the mountains, often in rocky areas, and float with a deceptively slow flight easily seen from some distance.

Whites and sulfurs (p. 124), as the names suggest, are usually recognized easily by their white or yellow color. They are the butterflies most frequently seen from the road when driving.

There are many kinds of skippers, but the dusky-wings and their allies (p. 248) are known by their dark color and by their habit of sitting with the wings spread flat. The checkered skippers (p. 254) are checkered with white and gray; they also usually rest with the wings spread, and are generally found in the open. The tailed skippers (p. 269) are mostly tropical; they can be identified by their conspicuous tails. Branded skippers (subfamily Hesperiinae, p. 213) are mostly small and yellowish, tawny, or rusty in color. They rest with their wings brought together over the back, with the forewings and the hind wings usually held at different angles. There are many similar species of skippers, and they are difficult to identify on sight.

Before going into the field, make up a hypothetical list of the species in each family that you can reasonably expect to find on that trip. Consult the range and habitat sections of the species accounts for this information. Narrowing your list of species to expect will make it easier to identify the butterflies you actually see. Just as in birdwatching, you will find that the more time you spend in the field, the easier it will be to name the butterflies at a glance as they fly quickly by.

At times you may wish to net a specimen in order to compare it more closely with the plates in your guide. After catching the butterfly, grasp it lightly by the thorax with your thumb and forefinger so that its wings are folded up over the body. Examine the pattern on the underside of the wings and then on the upperside as you part the wings gently with your forceps. After identification, carefully release the specimen so that it can fly away.

Since 1975 the Xerces Society (see p. 341) has conducted an annual Fourth of July Butterfly Count, patterned after the highly successful National Audubon Society Christmas Bird Census. After gaining experience in butterfly watching, you may wish to participate in future counts.

For more suggestions on watching instead of collecting butterflies, see Selected References, p. 334.

## *Photographing Butterflies*

Another approach to studying and enjoying butterflies is to photograph them. You may wish to start by photographing in black-and-white or color all the species that visit your backyard. Any camera with a lens that will focus closely enough so that the frame is nearly filled with the butterfly and flower head or similar background will suffice. Telephoto, macro, or zoom lenses and extension rings or bellows are desirable but not necessary. You may stalk your "game" like a hunter, or you may set your camera on a tripod and focus closely on a flower, sap oozing from a tree, or a mud puddle where you have seen butterflies sipping water. Then either stand motionless by the camera until the butterfly returns or devise a remote control method of clicking your shutter from a distance. More sophisticated equipment can include an electronic flash and "magic eye" beams that enable the butterfly to take its own picture.

After you have mastered butterfly photography in your backyard, you may wish to go afield to expand your collection of butterfly portraits.

For more information on equipment and techniques for butterfly photography, see p. 337. For a remarkable collection of 74 color photographs of insects landing, taking off, and in almost unbelievable flight, with information on how the pictures were taken, see *Borne on the Wind: The Extraordinary World of Insects in Flight* by Stephen Dalton, 1975, New York: Reader's Digest Press.

# REARING BUTTERFLIES

A very satisfactory and rewarding way to study butterflies is to rear them from eggs, caterpillars, or pupae collected in the field. This method has several advantages. You may obtain some perfect specimens for your collection if you wish. By releasing most of the freshly emerged adults you may contribute to the conservation and well-being of the species. In nature, a high percentage of the larvae do not survive but are killed by parasites, predators, or insecticides. Most important, you will have the opportunity to observe and record in your notebook and with photographs the details in the life history of the species you rear. You may be able to make a worthwhile contribution to science, since the early stages of some species are still unknown.

**Finding the early stages. Eggs** are most frequently deposited singly on the underside of leaves, but sometimes on the upperside or on stems; one species, the Mourning Cloak (p. 68), deposits its eggs in a mass encircling a twig of the food plant. Diligent searching on the appropriate food plant will reveal the tiny eggs. A surer method is to examine leaves immediately after seeing a female butterfly visit them. If she stops momentarily at the leaves rather than the blossoms, she is probably depositing eggs. You can induce some species to deposit eggs by placing the female in a large cage made of cheesecloth or screen set over the living food plant the butterfly has been visiting. If your female butterfly was not captured at a plant, you must first identify her. Then you can determine the preferred larval food plant for that species by consulting the appropriate section of the species account (see Chapter 6). If the food plant is unknown, try a variety of the plants in the area where you captured the female. Trial and error is often successful.

**Caterpillars** can be found on the food plant, frequently out of sight. They may be diurnal (active during the day) or nocturnal (active at night). Chewed leaves and frass (fecal droppings) on the ground indicate their presence. Some caterpillar species spin a silken web among the leaves and live there in a colony; others pull the edges of a leaf together with silk to form an individual, tent-like shelter. Larvae of other species move about freely.

**Chrysalids** or **pupae** (see Fig. 5, p. 26) may frequently be found attached to the stalk of the food plant; other larvae may wander farther afield when ready to pupate and attach themselves to a nearby tree trunk, shrub, fencepost, barn, or house. A chrysalid must be removed carefully to avoid damaging it. Carefully pry it loose with forceps inserted under the silken pad which attaches the pupa to the surface. Grip only the silken pad with your forceps, not the tissues of the pupa itself.

**Care of eggs and caterpillars.** Eggs require no particular care other than protection from crushing or excess moisture. The eggs will darken shortly before the larvae emerge. At this time they should be placed in a rearing cage with their larval food plant (see **Food** section of species accounts for names of preferred food plants). Vivaria and other glassware useful as rearing cages are available from biological supply houses (see list, p. 340). However, you may wish to make your own.

The simplest rearing cage consists of a wide-mouthed jar (such as a peanut butter or mayonnaise jar) with a strip of cheesecloth or nylon hose fastened around the top with a rubber band. If the leaves of the food plant are simply dropped in, they must be changed daily because they will dry out rapidly. It is better to put a whole branch of the food plant in a vial or tube of water, which will keep it fresh for 3 or 4 days or even a week. Be sure to wrap the stem with cotton or a paper towel to serve as a plug at the top of the vial — this will keep the larvae from crawling down into the water and drowning. You may wish to grow entire plants in clay pots to feed your caterpillars.

A shoe box makes a good, somewhat larger, rearing cage. Cut out all of the lid on the top except for a $\frac{1}{2}$-$\frac{3}{4}$ in. (12.7-19 mm) margin. Glue or tape a sheet of clear plastic or window glass over the opening. Insert a branch of the food plant in a container that will hold a pint or more of water. Make a hole in the container lid for the stem of the plant, but seal the area around it to prevent the larvae from falling into the water. Stand the shoe box on end, insert the food plant and caterpillars, replace the lid, and hold it in place with rubber bands.

Replace the food plants as necessary, when the leaves have been consumed or turn dry. You can transfer small larvae from old plant to new using a fine, camel's-hair watercolor brush to pick them up. Larger larvae can be picked up by hand. Clear the cage of frass (droppings) frequently, or excessive moisture and mold may develop.

# COLLECTING BUTTERFLIES

To make a thorough study of the butterflies in your area, you may wish to make a collection. If you are serious in your intentions, by all means do so. A properly prepared and cared for butterfly collection can be a valuable scientific resource, an excellent teaching aid, and a source of great enjoyment that can last for many years. In fact, butterfly specimens collected in the 1700s are still in good condition and can be seen in European museums. However, don't start a collection unless you are willing to learn and follow accepted rules and procedures. (See also Lepidopterists' Society Statement of the Committee on Collecting Policy, p. 315.)

1. Do not take more butterflies than you need for your collection. Release alive any specimens with damaged wings that you do not wish to keep.
2. Do not take any species on the endangered or threatened list (see p. 22). Use restraint and good judgment in collecting rare or uncommon species.
3. Do not take any specimens if you do not have time to care for them properly.
4. Do not collect any butterflies in areas where it is prohibited. This includes all national parks and monuments and some state, regional, county, or city parks.
5. Do not collect butterflies on private property without permission. If permission is not granted — do not trespass! If it is granted, do not litter, damage fences, or leave gates open. Do not damage crops or growing plants by trampling them or swinging your net carelessly, and do not spook livestock. Respect the privilege you have been granted and you will not spoil it for others.
6. Record data accurately, as described on p. 18.
7. Mount and house your specimens according to the instructions given below.
8. Care for your collection regularly. A neglected collection can turn to dust in a remarkably short time.
9. If you lose interest in collecting or no longer have time to properly care for your collection, consider donating it to a museum or university where it can be well cared for and your efforts will not be lost to science.

## *Equipment and Techniques*

Certain basic items are needed for collecting and mounting butterflies. Some things can be made; others must be purchased. The essentials are a net, killing bottles, forceps, glassine envelopes or paper triangles, insect pins, glass-headed pins, spreading boards or blocks. You will also need glass or paper strips, a relaxer, specimen boxes, a notebook or cards, black India ink, bond paper for labels, and scissors. Other items may be added as needed. Each collector usually develops his or her own techniques, methods, and materials for collecting, handling, and mounting butterflies. The equipment and procedures used by many lepidopterists are described here.

**Net and its use.** A butterfly net can be bought or made at home. The ring should be made of very strong wire with an opening usually 12–15 in. (30–38 cm) in diameter; larger nets may also be used. The handle must also be sturdy, made of wood or metal; it should be 3–4 ft. (about 1 m) long, or even longer if it is to be used for high-flying species. The bag should be made of tough, durable netting $2\frac{1}{4}$ to 3 times as long as the ring diameter, and rounded at the tip since butterflies damage their wings in a pointed net. Good quality silk or nylon bobbinet, marquisette, or bolting cloth make the best nets. The material is sewed to a strip of heavy cloth around the ring, to save wear on the net. It is wise to take along an extra net bag, especially on long trips.

The technique used for netting your specimen depends on the butterfly's location and movement. Try clapping the net over ground-sitting species. If you hold the tip of the net up with your left hand (if right-handed), most butterflies will rise into the net. Then tip the net to the right, and the bag will fold over the ring, trapping the butterfly. Remove the lid from a collecting bottle, insert the bottle into the net, work the specimen into the bottle, and then tighten the netting over the top of the bottle. With the other hand, insert the lid into the net and put it on the bottle. These movements may seem awkward at first, but will become almost automatic with practice. Perched butterflies are easier to catch; they can be swept into the net. A backhand stroke is preferable as it allows a closer approach. "Wing shots" are more difficult — you have to "keep your eye on the ball!" To net a flying insect, follow it with your eye until it is safely in the net. Take care not to snag your net on rigid or thorny plants, or on barbed-wire fences.

Pinching is a useful but tricky technique. Pinch the sides of the thorax lightly with just your thumb and forefinger. This will stun the butterfly so that it then can be easily handled. Pinch only when the wings are folded over the back, and take care not to crush the specimen. The butterfly may now be placed directly in the killing jar or first in a paper triangle (see Fig. 1, p. 15).

**Killing bottles.** The most effective killing bottles or jars contain potassium cyanide, a deadly poison, as the killing agent. They may be purchased (see list of suppliers, p. 340) or you may make your own. Use wide-mouthed bottles with tight-fitting lids, half-pint to quart size. Peanut butter jars are excellent. When you make your killing bottle, *work only in the open air.* Place a ¾-in. (19 mm) layer of granular cyanide in the bottom of the jar, and cover it with an inch of dry sawdust. Cover the sawdust with about a half-inch of medium-thick plaster of Paris. Leave the bottle open outdoors until the plaster has dried thoroughly, then put on the lid. Wrap the bottoms and sides of the bottle as far up as the top of the plaster layer with masking or adhesive tape, to help prevent breakage. This will also hold the glass together if it does break. Finally, label the bottle "POISON — CYANIDE, HANDLE WITH CARE," plainly in large letters.

Cyanide bottles are not dangerous to the user if properly handled. Do not open them indoors, and do not breathe the fumes. Above all, keep cyanide bottles *out of reach of others,* particularly children. The bottles will last a season or more. A collector should have several bottles of various sizes to use for large and small specimens and to prevent damage from overcrowding.

Killing jars with chemicals other than cyanide are easier to make. Liquid chemicals, such as ethyl acetate, carbon tetrachloride, ether, and chloroform, may be used for this purpose. Although the chemicals used in these bottles are much less toxic than cyanide, nevertheless they should be handled with care. They also tend to set the muscles of the butterfly rigidly, and may discolor the specimens if the jar is moist.

Use the same type of jar as for the cyanide bottle. Place cotton in the bottom; cover it with a piece of porous cardboard, cut to fit tightly, and make a hole in the center — about the diameter of a pencil. Use masking tape to hold the cardboard in place. To "charge" the bottle, work in a well-ventilated area and use an eyedropper or pipette to insert the killing fluid into the hole in the cardboard. Moisten the cotton but do not soak it to the point where it runs off. This type of killing jar must be recharged before each field trip, and more often if it is opened frequently while you are collecting.

You also may make this type of killing jar with sawdust covered by a layer of plaster of Paris. To insert the liquid killing agent, place a short length of glass tubing into the sawdust layer before pouring the plaster of Paris.

**Papering.** Butterflies are placed in paper triangles or glassine envelopes until they can be mounted. Duplicate specimens can be stored in such envelopes and exchanged with other collectors. Glassine envelopes can be purchased in various sizes, or you can fold your own paper triangles from soft paper (see Fig. 1). Hard paper and regular mailing envelopes tend to crush fresh specimens.

Many butterflies turn their wings below the body when they die in the killing jar. Before placing these specimens in paper, remove them from the jar and, using forceps, turn the wings so that they fold above the body. If you wait too long the specimens will be too stiff to turn. From time to time, slip your newly caught specimens

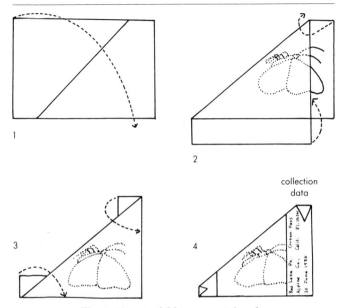

**Fig. 1. How to fold a paper triangle.**

into glassine envelopes or paper triangles and place them in a large killing jar for a time in order to be sure that they do not "come back to life."

It is always best to label your envelopes as you go, but this is not always convenient. Some collectors prefer to enter a code number with the date and locality in a notebook for each collecting stop; this number is placed on each envelope containing a specimen from this stop, and then is used later to prepare complete labels. This data goes on the envelope if the specimen is to be stored, and on the pin if it is to be mounted right away. Specimens without accurate data have little scientific value; see p. 18 for recommended labeling procedures.

**Care of specimens.** Adult butterflies need no preservative; fully dried specimens keep indefinitely if protected from moisture and museum pests such as dermestid or skin beetles. These pests can be killed or discouraged by the placing of napthalene flakes or paradichlorobenzene crystals in your insect boxes, display cases, and storage boxes. Papered butterflies may be stored safely in a cigar box, but only if a generous supply (2–3 tablespoons) of napthalene flakes is scattered among the envelopes and the box is sealed thoroughly with good masking tape or adhesive tape.

**Spreading boards and their use.** The function of spreading boards is to hold the specimen's wings flat until they dry in place. These boards can be bought or made. Spreading boards have grooves to hold the bodies of the specimens (see Fig. 2, p. 17). Three or four sizes are needed: the groove should be about $\frac{1}{8}$ in. (3 mm) across for small butterflies, $\frac{1}{4}$ in. (6 mm) across for most specimens, and $\frac{3}{8}$–$\frac{1}{2}$ in. (9–13 mm) across for the largest. The side pieces must be as wide as the spread specimen, and made of a soft wood such as pine. At the bottom of the groove between the sideboards, affix a pinning surface made of a strip of soft material such as cork, balsa wood, or a foam plastic such as Styrofoam or some other polystyrene plastic. If the sideboards become rough or splintery they can be smoothed with sandpaper. Some collectors prefer to spread each specimen on an individual, handmade grooved block.

**Pins.** Use only special insect pins to mount specimens. These pins are long, slender, strong, and resistant to corrosion by insect body fluids. Ordinary pins are too short, too blunt, and too thick, and are very easily corroded. Insect pins come in a variety of sizes. Size 2 for small butterflies and size 3 for large ones work quite well; smaller sizes usually bend too easily. Sources for insect pins may be found under Supply Houses in the Directory, p. 340. A pinning block will help you gauge the height of the labels on the pins easily. This little gadget is handy and inexpensive, but not essential.

**Butterfly mounting or setting.** Each person will adapt techniques to suit himself. The following is a general procedure for a right-handed person (see also Fig. 2). Hold the specimen in your left hand, with forceps or fingers. Push an insect pin down through the center of the thorax until the body of the specimen is about $\frac{3}{4}$ of the way up the pin. Push the pin into the pinning material in the center groove of the spreading board. Lay the paper strips over the wings and the antennae to hold them open, and pin the strips down lightly. With setting needles, gently move the wings until the hind margins of the forewings make a straight line. Then bring the hind wings into position as shown in Fig. 2. Now pin the paper strips down tightly with glass-headed pins. Support the abdomen with pins to prevent it from sagging. If the antennae do not fit easily under the strips, adjust them separately with pins.

Individual grooved spreading blocks or large cork stoppers with a groove cut in the top may be used with paper strips as described above. Some collectors attach thread to the bottom of the block or cork and then wrap it around and around the specimen and the block or cork to hold the wings in place. Glass strips or wide paper strips are then placed over the wings, particularly the tips and edges, to prevent curling.

Allow several days for drying; the time will vary with the temperature and humidity. The data for each specimen should be recorded either on a temporary or on a permanent pin label and pinned next to the specimen. Caution: butterflies on spreading

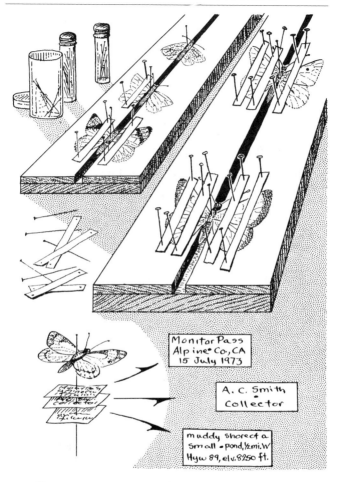

**Fig. 2. Mounting and labeling butterfly specimens.**

boards are vulnerable to attack by ants, wasps, and mice if left
exposed. Protect your specimens!

**Relaxing chamber.** If butterflies are not mounted within a few
hours of killing (the exact time depends on temperature and hu-

midity) they will stiffen and must be relaxed in order to spread them. Any metal can or plastic container with a tight fitting lid can be used as a relaxing chamber. Elaborate and expensive relaxers are sold commercially, but fruitcake tins or plastic food storage containers 6–10 in. (15–26 cm) across are very satisfactory and readily available. Place clean sand, folded clean cloth strips, or cotton on the bottom. Moisten the layer, but not to the point of run-off, with hot water containing a spoonful of a fungicide to prevent mold. Carbolic acid (a phenol derivative) is effective and long-lasting, but is poisonous and must be handled with care. Napthalene flakes, paradichlorobenzene crystals, or Lysol may be substituted. Put your specimens in a tray over the moist material and check them daily. Spread them as soon as they are flexible. Do not let the specimens get wet or they will become stained.

Skippers have a very muscular thorax and are difficult to relax. If necessary, a cut may be made below the base of each wing. Do not cut high enough to damage the wing nor low enough to mar the thorax. It is best to practice on common species first.

**Data.** Specimens without accurate data are nearly worthless. The minimum data to record are the locality where the specimen was collected, the date of capture, and the name of the collector. The elevation should be given if critical. For reared specimens, remember to include the food plant. Use roman numerals for the month and arabic numbers for the day (VII-15-82) or the military form (15 July 1982). For localities, use names found on maps. Give highway numbers and distance in miles or kilometers from town or a landmark such as a highway marker; give county and state. County names can be especially important in large states — localities such as "Deer Creek, Calif." are of little value, as there are many Deer Creeks in California.

Good stiff bond paper is best for your data labels: thin paper will shift on the pin. Use only good quality black India ink; other kinds fade. Printed labels, purchased from dealers (see p. 340), are great time-savers for localities where much collecting is done and for recording the name of the collector. You may type clean "camera-ready" copy for the printer on good $8\frac{1}{2} \times 11$ in. bond paper for any labels you need. Your local "fast-print" shop can then reduce your copy to the size you want and print the number of labels required.

A good collection includes more information than can be recorded on the small labels on the pin beneath the butterfly. A record of detailed observations should be kept for each outing. This should include a more precise description of the collection locality; some indication of the biotic community, with plants and other animals present; interaction of the butterfly species with plant and other animal species; and butterfly behavior and flight characteristics. Your notes might also include the numbers of the butterfly species present, the ratio of males to females, weather conditions at the time of collection or observation, and any other significant activities or conditions seen. As you accumulate data each year, you will acquire a wealth of knowledge on each species you observe or collect. In reviewing your journals over the years you will see population trends, changes in size and condition of habitats, and other year-to-year differences. Since so much is still unknown about butterflies, the information you record may enable you to make important contributions to science.

Some lepidopterists prefer to record their notes in a bound journal with chronological entries. Some prefer a looseleaf notebook so that they may keep additional observations on each species together. Others prefer to use 3 × 5 in. or 4 × 6 in. index cards to be organized in file boxes, or filed electronically, using a personal computer. Regardless of the system you choose, it is essential to record your observations on the spot, if possible, but no later than that evening.

**Preserving the early stages.** You can kill larvae and pupae by dropping them into hot water. The simplest way to preserve them is to place them in 70 percent alcohol for 24 hours, and then change the alcohol. If killed directly in alcohol, larvae turn dark and shrivel. An alternate method preferred by some entomologists is to place them in KAAD first for 24 hours, then transfer them to the 70 percent alcohol solution. (KAAD is 1 part kerosene, 1 part glacial acetic acid, 1 part dioxane, and 10 parts 95 percent ethyl alcohol.)

Preserved larvae and pupae lose their color, so make notes on color before preserving them. Caterpillars and chrysalids also can be freeze-dried quite satisfactorily, if the equipment is available to you. Pupal skins and eggshells may be glued to cards on pins and kept with the adults. Eggs may be preserved in alcohol, as above, or killed with cyanide and glued to cards on pins.

**Where to collect.** Each collector learns mostly by experience, but a few general tips can be provided. You will find that some species visit flowers, while others visit moist spots, honeydew, carrion, sap flows, and even excrement. Some flowers attract many butterflies; others very few. Mixed cover is usually more productive than pure stands of one kind of plant. Deep shady forest is poor habitat for most butterflies, but not all. Meadows, sunny fields, and open woodland trails are usually better. Some butterflies prefer hilltops; others foothill canyons. Take at least a brief look at all sorts of habitats. Some very unpromising-looking places may produce a species that is not found anywhere else. For examples of butterflies that visit some of the habitats mentioned above, see the chart on p. 6.

Learn to avoid poisonous plants such as poison oak and ivy; collect caterpillars from stinging nettles with great care. Use insect repellents against flies, mosquitoes, and chiggers. Keep in mind that not all successful trips need to be to distant places. Many interesting species may be found in and near large population centers, parks, vacant lots, and along waysides.

**Forceps.** Biological supply houses (see list, p. 340) and most college bookstores carry insect forceps with fine points, straight or curved as you prefer. Push the tips into a cork to protect yourself. The forceps may then be carried in your pocket. The price of forceps varies with size and quality.

**Specimen boxes.** These boxes vary in price; the best are expensive. Wooden boxes are better than cardboard. If you have the ability and a shop available, you may wish to make your own. They must be airtight to prevent fumes from escaping, and the lids must be secure to keep museum pests such as dermestid beetles from entering. The inside depth should be 2 in. (5 cm); the pinning bottom should be at least $\frac{3}{8}$ in. (1 cm) thick and soft enough for pins to penetrate easily. Ground cork with glue binder will rust pins. Various cellulose and plastic sheetings work well, but Styrofoam will be destroyed by paradichlorobenzene, which is often used to keep out museum pests. The pinning bottom must be firmly fastened. If it comes loose, specimens may be damaged.

In the field a **collecting bag** is useful for carrying equipment. A shoulder bag that can be dropped quickly to the ground when you are intent on capturing a butterfly works best. Take cans, jars, or ice cream cartons with lids to carry back living materials. A **magnifying glass** or **hand lens** is frequently useful. In the laboratory a **dissecting microscope** is very useful, but may be expensive. For these and many other items used by lepidopterists, you can obtain catalogs from the dealers listed on p. 340.

# 3

## Butterfly Conservation

Fluctuations in butterfly populations have been noted often over the years, but definitive data explaining these phenomena are rarely available. A season of great abundance in the population of the Painted Lady or California Tortoise-shell is usually followed by several seasons of scarcity. Other species may vary in numbers from year to year, with abundance or scarcity influenced by a variety of natural factors. The number of predators, parasites, and disease organisms will influence the number of butterflies each year. Climatic factors such as extreme cold or heat, and rain, snow, or continued excess humidity at critical times in the life cycle also help determine the size of the butterfly population. These are all natural events with which butterfly species have contended over thousands of years.

Natural extinctions have occurred over the years, but at a relatively low rate. In recent years, species extinctions have increased and many lepidopterists report that quite a number of formerly common species are now uncommon, rare, or seldom seen. Many plant and animal species face imminent extermination due to the ever-increasing global population of a single species, *Homo sapiens*. The air, water, and soil pollution that man produces, along with massive alteration of the earth's surface and its virtual destruction of many ecosystems, poses a threat to all life on earth.

Only since the late 1940s and early 1950s have butterflies had to contend with the widespread use of new insecticides and herbicides, both on land and in the air. Many lepidopterists feel that the present reduction in numbers of formerly common butterflies, particularly in areas adjacent to the great agricultural lands of the West, is due primarily to the intensive use of these chemicals. Without confirming data we are left only with opinions, impressions, and incidental observations. With the use of certain pesticides prohibited and much tighter control over others, some entomologists believe that some butterfly species have increased in numbers in recent years. Others are less optimistic in their appraisal.

Virtually all lepidopterists, biologists, ecologists, and environmentalists are agreed that the single most important factor in the decline or extinction of a species, whether plant, mammal, bird, butterfly, or other animal, is habitat destruction.

The first two butterflies to be recorded as extinct in North America were the Sthenele Satyr, in about 1880, and the Xerces Blue, last seen about 1941. Both butterflies inhabited San Francisco. Their habitats, along with their all-important food plants, were destroyed by housing developments and the spread of alien (non-native) plants. In the case of the Xerces Blue, housing development is considered to have been the more important factor. Invasion of its habitat by introduced foreign plants was thought to have been most important in the extinction of the Sthenele Satyr.

For the past 35 years, habitat destruction and alteration have proceeded at an amazing rate, not only in the United States, but throughout much of the world. Worldwide conservation efforts have been underway for many years through the International Union for the Conservation of Nature (IUCN), based in Switzerland. Efforts aimed specifically at conserving butterflies and insects have been carried on by the British Butterfly Conservation Society and the Amateur Entomologists' Society (see p. 341 for addresses). The serious threat of extinction to many plant and animal species in the United States has finally been recognized and steps have now been taken to attempt to preserve species in jeopardy–and to protect their critical habitats.

The Endangered Species Act, first passed by the United States Congress in 1966 and revised and amended in subsequent years, sets forth the official policy of the U.S. Government in regard to the protection of threatened or endangered species and the establishment of critical habitats for those species. Under the terms of this Act an *endangered species* is " . . . any species which is in danger of extinction throughout all or a significant portion of its range other than a species of the Class Insecta determined by the Secretary of the Interior or Commerce to constitute a pest whose protection under the provisions of this Act would present an overwhelming and overriding risk to man." A *threatened species* is " . . . any species which is likely to become an endangered species within the foreseeable future throughout all or a significant portion of its range."

In 1975, 42 butterflies (7 species and 35 subspecies) were proposed for listing as either endangered or threatened. In 1976, 8 butterflies (all subspecies) were given final approval for listing — one as threatened, 7 as endangered. Additional species have been proposed since, and investigations continue for butterflies on which final action has not yet been taken.

## *Roster of Extinct, Threatened, and Endangered Butterflies*

| **Species** | **Locality** | **Status** |
|---|---|---|
| Sthenele Satyr,<br>   *Cercyonis sthenele sthenele* | California | Extinct, 1880 |

*Extinct, Threatened, and Endangered Butterflies, continued*

| Species | Locality | Status |
|---|---|---|
| Xerces Blue, *Glaucopsyche xerces* | California | Extinct, 1943 |
| Strohbeen's Parnassian, *Parnassius clodius strohbeeni* | California | Extinct, 1958 |
| Unsilvered Fritillary *Speyeria adiaste atossa* | California | Extinct, 1960 |
| Hippolyta Fritillary *Speyeria zerene hippolyta* | Oregon | Threatened |
| Lange's Metalmark *Apodemia mormo langei* | California | Endangered |
| San Bruno Elfin, *Incisalia mossii bayensis* | California | Endangered |
| Mission Blue, *Icaricia icarioides missionensis* | California | Endangered |
| Lotis Blue, *Lycaeides argyrognomon lotis* | California | Endangered |
| El Segundo Blue, *Euphilotes battoides allyni* | California | Endangered |
| Smith's Blue, *Euphilotes enoptes smithi* | California | Endangered |
| Palos Verde Blue, *Glaucopsyche lygdamus palosverdesensis* | California | Endangered |

## Some Candidate Species
### (Final Action Not Yet Taken)

| Species | Locality | Proposed Status |
|---|---|---|
| Callippe Fritillary, *Speyeria callippe callippe* | California | Endangered |
| Bay Checker-spot, *Occidryas editha bayensis* | California | Endangered |
| Pawnee Montane Skipper, *Hesperia pawnee montana* | Colorado | Endangered |
| Great Basin Fritillary, *Speyeria nokomis nokomis* | Colorado | Threatened |
| Dakota Skipper, *Hesperia dacotae* | North Dakota, South Dakota, northward and eastward | Threatened |

For current status of proposed or listed threatened and endangered species, write for information to the Endangered Species Program, U.S. Fish & Wildlife Service, or to the Xerces Society (see p. 341 for addresses). See Selected References (p. 334) in the Appendix for additional reading on butterfly conservation and the study of threatened and endangered species.

The Xerces Society was founded in 1971. It is an international non-profit organization based in the United States, and is devoted to habitat protection for rare and endangered butterflies, insects, and other terrestrial arthropods, and to the enhancement of the public's appreciation of insects and their relatives.

# 4

# Life History, Growth, and Structure of Butterflies

Although this book is primarily concerned with identifying adult butterflies, familiarity with the complete life history and growth patterns characteristic of butterflies will help you locate and recognize the early stages, which you may wish to collect and rear to the adult stage. You will also need some knowledge of adult butterfly anatomy to identify all but the most distinctive species.

## Life History and Growth

To become adults, butterflies go through four stages that are collectively called *metamorphosis* — a Greek word that means "change in form." These stages are the egg, the larva or caterpillar, pupa or chrysalis, and the adult.

**Eggs** vary in appearance from family to family (see Fig. 3). They may be laid singly or in masses, usually on the host plant to be eaten by the **larva** (caterpillar) that will hatch from the egg.

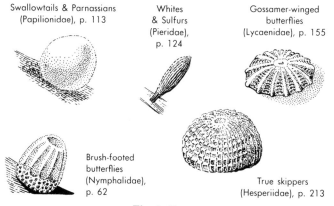

Swallowtails & Parnassians
(Papilionidae), p. 113

Whites
& Sulfurs
(Pieridae),
p. 124

Gossamer-winged
butterflies
(Lycaenidae), p. 155

Brush-footed
butterflies
(Nymphalidae),
p. 62

True skippers
(Hesperiidae), p. 213

**Fig. 3. Eggs.**

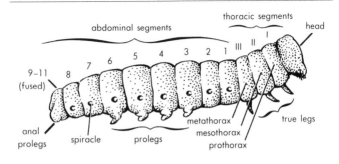

**Fig. 4. Caterpillar anatomy.**

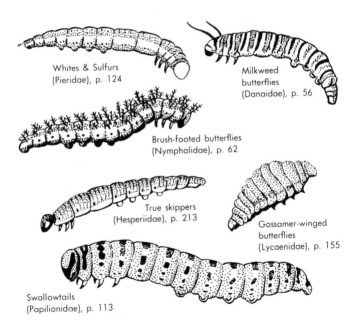

Whites & Sulfurs
(Pieridae), p. 124

Milkweed
butterflies
(Danaidae), p. 56

Brush-footed butterflies
(Nymphalidae), p. 62

True skippers
(Hesperiidae), p. 213

Gossamer-winged
butterflies
(Lycaenidae), p. 155

Swallowtails
(Papilionidae), p. 113

**Fig. 5. Caterpillars.**

The larva may hatch from the egg soon, or may wait a long time before hatching (see **diapause,** p. 28). It has structures as shown in Fig. 4. Note the *prolegs* on the 3rd, 4th, 5th, 6th, and last abdominal segments. The prolegs have small hooks called *crochets.* These are found only on the caterpillars of Lepidoptera, an order of insects that includes the butterflies and moths; other insect larvae with prolegs do not have crochets. The larvae (caterpillars) of each butterfly family differ in appearance (see Fig. 5).

When newly hatched the larva is very small, but it grows rapidly. Insects and their relatives have a protective covering called the *cuticle,* which is the outer layer of the exoskeleton. This layer can stretch only to a very limited degree; it cannot increase in total area or change in its proportions. After the larva has eaten enough to fill out completely, it molts and gets a new cuticle which has formed beneath the old one. This is how the larva grows. Larval growth is not continuous, but is concentrated in short periods of time just after each molt. The period between larval molts is called an *instar.* The larva molts several times before it reaches its full size. Different species of larvae may molt a different number of times.

The **pupa** results from the last larval molt. It is a reorganizational stage between larva and adult. It stays in one place,

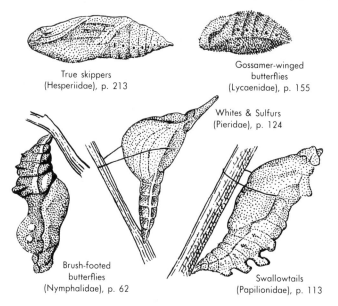

True skippers
(Hesperiidae), p. 213

Gossamer-winged
butterflies
(Lycaenidae), p. 155

Whites & Sulfurs
(Pieridae), p. 124

Brush-footed
butterflies
(Nymphalidae), p. 62

Swallowtails
(Papilionidae), p. 113

**Fig. 6. Chrysalids (pupae).**

usually attached to a twig or some other object, and cannot eat. The adult appendages can be seen through the exoskeleton. The shape of the pupa and the way it is attached differ in each family (Fig. 6). The tiny hooks at the tip of the abdomen, used for suspension, are called the *cremaster*. Many pupae have characteristic colors, such as the green and gold of the Monarch. The amount of time spent in the pupal stage varies among different species — it may be short, or last the whole year or even longer.

The **adult** emerges from the pupa. The adult does not molt, nor does it grow in length or in wingspan once its wings have become inflated and hardened. The adult is the reproductive stage of the butterfly.

**Diapause** is a dormant period that allows an organism to survive a time of unfavorable conditions, such as extreme cold. Butterflies that live in northern and temperate zones usually have a diapause. This dormant period may occur in any of the four stages, but always occurs in the same stage in a given species. Some butterflies of tropical origin have no diapause, and so cannot live in cold areas. Butterflies that migrate, such as the Monarch (p. 56) also have no diapause and cannot live in the north during winter — they must go south or die.

## *Structure of the Adult Butterfly*

Butterflies have three main body parts: the head, thorax, and abdomen. The exoskeleton, the protective outer covering for the body, is formed of plates called *sclerites,* with flexible membranes in between. The sclerites of butterflies are usually obscured by the scales and hairs that cover the body.

**Head.** The head of a butterfly has a pair of *antennae,* long sensory organs that are enlarged (clubbed) at the tip; the antennae of moths are not clubbed. In skippers (p. 203), the tip of each antenna is pointed, forming the *apiculus,* which may be short or long, blunt or slender, or curved back along the shaft of the antenna (see front endpapers). All butterflies have large *compound eyes;* if the inner corner of the eye is notched, it is *emarginate,* as in gossamer-winged butterflies (Lycaenidae, p. 155). The head also has 3-segmented *palpi,* which are clothed with hairs and scales and may be short or long, and smooth or hairy. The palpi may be thrust forward, or be upturned in front of the face. The butterfly uses its *proboscis* or tongue (see front endpapers), a slender coiled tube, to suck up fluids such as water or nectar.

**Thorax.** The thorax has three segments, the *prothorax, mesothorax,* and *metathorax.* Each bears a pair of segmented legs. From base to tip, the parts of the leg are the *coxa, trochanter, femur, tibia,* and a 5-jointed *tarsus.* The enlarged first (basal) tarsal joint is called the *metatarsus*. The last tarsal joint bears the tarsal claws. Between the tarsal claws is a pad, the *pulvillus*. Some butterflies have a flap on the front tibia, the *epiphysis*. The tibia may bear short spines. The hind tibia has long spurs in pairs — 1 pair in true butterflies and giant skippers, 2 pairs in skippers.

**Abdomen.** The abdomen shows little external structure. The genitalia, the reproductive organs, are concealed at the tip of the abdomen. The male genitalia are important in butterfly classification, and are shown in Fig. 8 (p. 31).

**Wings.** Butterflies have 4 wings. The forewings are larger than the hind wings, and overlap them. The shape, venation (vein pattern), male sex scales, color, and pattern of the wings are of great importance in classification. The wings are transparent membranes covered with small overlapping *scales* arranged in fixed rows (see Fig. 7). Most butterflies have completely scaled wings. Some, especially the skippers (p. 203), have spots or areas where scales are lacking (hyaline spots), which are characteristic in size and position for a given species (see Fig. 13, p. 204).

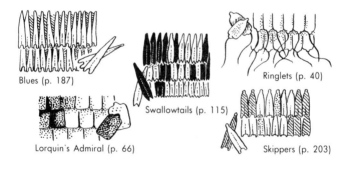

Blues (p. 187)

Ringlets (p. 40)

Swallowtails (p. 115)

Lorquin's Admiral (p. 66)

Skippers (p. 203)

**Fig. 7. Wing scales.**

Terms for the margins and areas of the wing are very useful in descriptions. These are illustrated on the front endpapers, along with the bands of butterfly markings, which are of equal importance for identification. Many butterflies have 1 or 2 crossmarks, called *cell bars,* in the forewing discal cell. Some butterflies, such as many hairstreaks (p. 155) and some blues (p. 187), have an ornate spot in cell $Cu_1$ of the hind wing, often called the *thecla spot.* Many hairstreaks (p. 155) have a prominent postmedian line on the underside, the thecla line, usually across both pairs of wings (Fig. 12, p. 156).

Male butterflies may have sex scales called *androconia*. These may be scattered over the wing surface, as in gossamer-winged butterflies (Lycaenidae, p. 155), or arranged in patches called *stigmata* (sing., *stigma*), as in some hairstreaks (p. 155) and skippers (p. 203), or arranged along certain veins as in the large fritillaries (p. 77). In swallowtails (p. 113), the sex scales are located in a rolled edge of the hind wing called the *anal fold.*

**Wing venation** is very important in identification. The tubular wing veins extend from the base to the edge of the wing, or connect with one another. The veins are usually easier to see from the underside. A few scales may be scraped off in order to follow the course of the veins. When necessary, the wings on one side (usually the right, to match illustrations) may be removed for examination. When bleached in a solution of 10% laundry bleach and 90% water, the position of the veins can be seen. In all butterflies, the base of the media vein (vein M — see front endpapers) is absent, and the 1st and 3rd anal veins (1A and 3A) may be reduced or absent. Some veins branch, others do not.

The areas between the veins are called *cells*. A cell is named from the vein above or just before it — thus, the cell between $R_5$ and $M_1$ is cell $R_5$. However, the large cell in each wing resulting from the absence of the base of vein M is called the *discal cell* or just "the cell." The forewing discal cell is always "closed" at its outer end by crossveins, called *discocellular veins*. The discal cell of the hind wing may be closed as in the forewing, or the crossvein may be missing, so that the cell is described as "open" (see front endpapers).

The names and descriptions of the wing veins and cells are listed below. They are illustrated on the front endpapers.

**Costa (C)** runs from the wing base along the anterior margin (leading edge) of the wing; it is unbranched.

**Subcosta (Sc)** is the second vein from the margin; it is unbranched.

**Radius (R)** may have up to 5 branches ($R_1$, $R_2$, $R_3$, $R_4$, $R_5$), but has only 3–4 branches in some groups of butterflies. Some branches may be *stalked* (2 or more arising from a common stem). The radius forms the anterior margin (upper or forward edge) of the discal cell.

**Media (M)** is absent at the wing base, but beyond the cell it has 3 branches ($M_1$, $M_2$, $M_3$). The base of the media vein is present in many other insects.

**Cubitus (Cu)** has 2 branches ($Cu_1$, $Cu_2$) that arise from the lower outer end of the discal cell. Vein Cu forms the lower boundary of the discal cell.

**First anal vein (1A)** is usually absent in butterflies, but is sometimes indicated by a rudiment at the wing base or by a faint fold.

**Second anal vein (2A)** is present in all butterflies, on both the forewing and hind wing.

**Third anal vein (3A)** is short, rudimentary, or absent in the forewing, but is usually present in the hind wing of butterflies except in swallowtails and parnassians (Papilionidae, p. 113).

The forewing and hind wing do not have the same pattern of veins. The forewing has more vein branches than the hind wing. The radius (R) has fewer branches on the hind wing, and the *humeral area* at the base of the hind wing costa may have a *humeral vein*. The 1st branch of vein R fuses with the subcosta (Sc) to form a single vein called Sc + $R_1$, in the hind wing; the rest of vein R on the hind wing is unbranched, forming a single vein, the *radial sector* (Rs).

**Male genitalia.** The openings of the digestive and reproductive systems are located at the tip of the abdomen. Organs associated with reproduction, the *genitalia,* are usually sclerotized in butterflies. These organs vary consistently from family to family and often even with different species, and so are very useful in classification. In some groups the genitalia are the most reliable means of identification. In butterfly classification the male genitalia have been used more often than those of the female; therefore only male genitalia are discussed here.

For complete examination of these structures, remove them from the abdomen and immerse them in a weak (not over 10 percent) solution of sodium (or potassium) hydroxide overnight; then examine them under a dissecting microscope or hand lens after cleaning off the surrounding tissues. Major differences may often be seen without using this procedure, by simply brushing away the overlying scales and hairs with a small stiff brush. In the few cases where genitalic structures are described in this book, the brushing technique is sufficient to examine them.

Figure 8 is generalized to show the main structures of the male genitalia, seen from the left side. The *uncus* may be single or divided into two prongs. On each side is one of a pair of *valves,* also

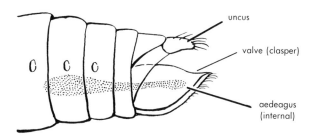

**Fig. 8. Male genitalia (sex organs).**

called harpes or claspers. Each valve has rolled-in edges above and below. The tip of each valve may be toothed, notched, divided, or smooth. The upper edge may bear one or more spines or projections. The valves can move from side to side, and the uncus and valves grasp the female during mating. However, in some genera the valves do not seem to have this function, and in some cases the valves are fused below. Between the valves is the tubular *aedeagus* (also known as the phallus or penis).

**Butterfly colors.** Wing coloration is important in the classification of butterflies, and species often may be identified by color alone. Butterfly colors are of two general types. *Pigments* are specific chemicals that reflect only certain wavelengths of light. *Structural* or *mechanical colors* result when light reflects from the physical structure of scales or hairs, as from a prism or an oil film on water. Both types of colors may occur in the same species. Most structural colors in butterflies are due to one or more of 3 main types of structure: (1) minute ridges or grooves on a flat surface; (2) fine granules in a matrix of a different refractive index; and (3) thin superimposed layers, each of a different refractive index. Structural colors are frequently called *iridescent* colors.

Blue is probably always a structural color. So are most greens, a few reds, and the opalescent (changing) colors, such as the lavender or lilac overlay on the wings of some species. Iridescent colors may cover the entire wing surface as in the Silvery Blue (Pl. 19), or be confined to a few scales as on the underside of the Grand Canyon Brown (Pl. 1), or they may appear as a flush or overlay as on the forewings of the California Dogface (Pl. 22) when seen in certain light. Most non-iridescent colors, such as whites, yellows, rusty reds, browns, grays, tans, and so on, are due to pigments.

# 5

# Butterfly Classification and Key to Families

The order Lepidoptera (Greek: *lepis* — scale, and *pteron* — wing) includes the butterflies and moths. The most evident features of the adults are scaled wings and a tubular sucking tongue, the proboscis. The wings of Lepidoptera are usually broad and flat, although a few moths have very small wings. Butterflies (including skippers) make up the smaller part of the order, but since they fly in the daytime they are more conspicuous and better known than moths.

Color alone will not separate butterflies and moths, since many moths are brightly colored and many butterflies are dull. The day-flying habit is not exclusive, either, since some moths (such as some sphinx moths) fly by day, and in the tropics some butterflies fly early in the morning and late in the evening. A few butterflies will even come to lights at night on occasion.

Butterflies can be recognized by their antennae, which are clubbed at the tip and do not have side processes (pectinations). Moth antennae vary greatly, but if they are enlarged at the tip they also have pectinations.

The term "butterfly" is generally used to include both the true butterflies and the skippers. The main differences are given below.

## *True Butterflies (Superfamily Papilionoidea)*

Body relatively slender. Wings usually broad. Wingbeats often slow. Antennae close together on the small head, and without hair tufts ("eyelashes") at base. Antennal club symmetrical, without slender tip (apiculus). One or more veins of FW stalked (2 or more branches rising from a common vein). Prothorax of larva not narrower than head (see Fig. 4, p. 26). Larva often brightly colored, sometimes with spines, filaments, or tubercles. Pupa usually without cocoon.

## Skippers (*Superfamily Hesperioidea*)

Body usually stout. Wings usually short and strong. Antennae set far apart on the wide head, and with hair tufts ("eyelashes") at the base. Antennal club not symmetrical; slightly curved to completely bent back, and often with a sharp apiculus. All FW veins simple and unbranched. Flight swift and erratic; wingbeats rapid. Prothorax of larva narrower than head or than mesothorax, and therefore often referred to as a "neck." Larva smooth, without spines, filaments, or tubercles. Pupa usually in a slight cocoon.

# KEY TO FAMILIES

The following key is intended to separate those families of butterflies and skippers found in the area covered by this book.

## True Butterflies (*Superfamily Papilionoidea*)

**1a.** Eyes notched at antennal bases; face longer than wide.
**see 8**
**1b.** Eyes not notched at antennal bases; face as wide as long.
**see 2**

**2a.** Front legs of 1 or both sexes greatly reduced; FW radius (vein R) always 5-branched.    **see 3**
**2b.** Front legs not reduced; FW radius (R) with 3 to 5 branches.
**see 9**

**3a.** Front legs of both sexes greatly reduced, the tarsi without knobs or spines.    **see 4**
**3b.** Front tarsi of males reduced; those of females knobbed and spined, or completely developed.    **see 7**

**4a.** 1 or more FW veins swollen at base; antennae weakly clubbed; HW cell usually closed; wings plain-colored.
**Wood Nymphs & Satyrs**
**(Satyridae)    Pls. 1-6**
**4b.** HW veins not swollen at base (except in genus *Mestra,* Pl. 9); HW cell usually open; wings often brightly colored.    **see 5**

**5a.** FW unusually long and narrow.
**Long-wings (Heliconiidae)    Pl. 8**

**5b.** FW not unusually long, though it may be pointed or sickle-shaped.                                                    **see 6**

**6a.** FW usually sickle-shaped; outer margin of FW usually strongly indented, never straight or rounded.
**Leaf-wings & Emperors (Apaturidae)    Pl. 8**
**6b.** FW seldom sickle-shaped; outer margin may be rounded, straight, slightly indented, or irregular.
**Brush-footed Butterflies (Nymphalidae)    Pls. 9-18**

**7a.** Large. Front tarsi of female knobbed and spined; palpi not enlarged; male has sex pouch on HW vein $Cu_2$.
**Milkweed Butterflies (Danaidae)    Pl. 8**
**7b.** Small. Front tarsi of female completely developed; palpi very long, snoutlike.
**Snout Butterflies (Libytheidae)    Pl. 29**

**8a.** HW has humeral and costal veins; antennae more than $\frac{1}{2}$ as long as FW costa; palpi very small.
**Metalmarks (Riodinidae)    Pl. 29**
**8b.** HW lacks humeral and costal veins; antennae $\frac{1}{2}$ or less the length of FW costa; palpi of normal size.
**Gossamer-winged Butterflies**
**(Lycaenidae)    Pls. 19, 29-36**

**9a.** HW has 1 anal vein; antennae long, curved; FW radius vein (R) 5-branched; tarsal claws entire. Large butterflies.
**Parnassians & Swallowtails**
**(Papilionidae)    Pls. 19-21**
**9b.** HW has 2 anal veins; antennae short, straight; FW radius vein with 3 to 5 branches; tarsal claws bilobed.
**Whites, Sulfurs, & Orange-tips**
**(Pieridae)    Pls. 22-28**

## Skippers (*Superfamily Hesperioidea*)

**1a.** Very large and robust. Head narrower than thorax; hind tibia with 1 pair of spurs; palpi small.
**Giant Skippers (Megathymidae)    Pls. 36-40**
**1b.** Small to large. Head as wide as thorax; hind tibia usually has 2 pairs of spurs; palpi moderate to large.
**Skippers (Hesperiidae)    Pls. 41-48**

# 6

## The Western Butterflies: Species Accounts

All species known to the authors at the time of writing that occur in the region covered by this book, even if only rarely, are included. Some found recently or in very remote areas, or known only from one or a few specimens, are not illustrated. The sequence of families and genera is similar in general to that in *A Field Guide to the Butterflies,* by Alexander B. Klots. However, there have been some changes, because our knowledge and understanding of the classification and relationships of butterflies has increased greatly in the more than 30 years since that book was published.

Two recent checklists have reflected many changes from the subspecific level through the family level. In this book the authors have adopted, for the most part, the names presented by Miller and Brown in *A Catalogue/Checklist of the Butterflies of America North of Mexico* (1981), as amended by Miller and Brown in *Checklist of the Lepidoptera of America North of Mexico,* edited by Ronald W. Hodges, *et al.,* and published by E. W. Classey Ltd. (1983). Exceptions have been made only in a few cases, where indicated by more recent field research.

The name of the author (or joint authors) who first formally described each species follows the scientific name. Parentheses around the author's name indicate that subsequent lepidopterists have transferred that species to a genus other than the one in which it was originally described.

## SATYRS and WOOD NYMPHS: Family Satyridae

Small to medium-sized; whitish, tan, gray, brown, or black. Wings often with eyespots. Antennae short, weakly clubbed. Front legs much reduced. 1–3 main FW veins swollen at base in most species (Fig. 9). Flight usually jerky, bouncing; many take refuge in grass or shrubbery if disturbed. This family (Satyridae) is often considered a subfamily of the brush-footed butterflies (Nymphalidae, p. 62).

**Fig. 9. Swelling at bases of FW veins characteristic of most satyrs and wood nymphs.**

**Early stages:** Egg nearly spherical, with a raised network of connecting ridges. Larva spindle-shaped, tapered at each end; rear end often notched. Pupa smooth, usually suspended by cremaster; some species pupate in cells or litter on ground. Life histories of some species unknown.

**Range:** This family is better represented in the Old World and in the New World tropics than in our area. Some satyrs are common and familiar in North America; others are scarce, local, or northern. The arctics *(Oeneis)* and alpines *(Erebia)* are mostly northern or alpine species.

## Pearly Eyes and Eyed Browns: Subfamily Elymniinae

The butterflies in this subfamily all have a well-marked row of submarginal eyespots on both upperside and underside of FW and HW. Two species are found only in the eastern part of our area.

**NORTHERN PEARLY EYE**         **Pl. 1**
*Enodia anthedon* A. H. Clark
**Identification:** 1¾–2¼ in. (33–56 mm). FW pointed; *outer margin of HW scalloped.* **Upperside:** Submarginal eyespots *large, dark.* **Underside:** Spots *light-ringed* and usually *light-centered;* spot row *bordered by whitish areas.*
**Similar species:** Eyed Brown (below) is smaller; FW rounded, outer margin of HW not scalloped.
**Early stages:** Larva yellow-green; anal fork red-tipped. A pair of red-tipped horns on head and on last abdominal segment. One brood. **Food:** Wide-leaved uniola *(Uniola latifolia),* a large grass. **Adults:** Late June–early Aug. They alight on trees.
**Range:** N.D. south to Kans., east to Nova Scotia, south to Va. TL: Lava, Sullivan Co., N.Y. **Habitat:** Grassy woodland.

**EYED BROWN** *Satyrodes eurydice* (Johannson)      **Pl. 1**
**Identification:** 1½–2 in. (38–50 mm). Wings rounded. *Outer margin of HW rounded,* not scalloped. **Upperside:** Light brown; *eyespots black,* conspicuous. **Underside:** *Eyespots small,* all *similar* in size, light-ringed and light-centered. Light brown median

line across HW *irregular, quite close to inner edge of spot row;* area between line and spot row light.
**Similar species:** Northern Pearly Eye (above).
**Early stages:** Larva slender, pale green with narrow dark stripes; a pair of red-tipped horns on head and on last abdominal segment. One brood. **Food:** Sedges *(Carex).* **Adults:** June–July.
**Range:** Manitoba east to Nova Scotia, south to N.D., e. Colo., Neb., Md. Uncommon to scarce in the West. **Habitat:** Marshes, wet meadows.
**Subspecies:** (1) **Eyed Brown,** *S. e. eurydice* (Johannson), Pl. 1, No. 2. Described above. In the West, Saskatchewan, Manitoba, N.D.; very local. TL: Philadelphia. (2) **Smoky Eyed Brown,** *S. e. fumosus* Leussler, Pl. 1, No. 3. *Darker;* eyespots less conspicuous. *Brown median line* on underside of HW *more jagged,* not so close to submarginal spot row. Considered by some to be a separate species. Very scarce and local; some colonies apparently have become extinct. TL: Sarpy Co., Neb.

## Satyrs: Subfamily Satyrinae

Most of our satyrids belong to this subfamily. They vary considerably in appearance, habitat, and behavior.

### Wood Satyrs: Genus *Cyllopsis* R. Felder
### (formerly *Euptychia*)

The next 3 species may all occur in the same general localities and even at the same time.

**PYRACMON BROWN** *Cyllopsis pyracmon* (Butler)          **Pl. 1**
**Identification:** 1½–1¾ in. (38–44 mm). *Upperside:* Brown with a slight tawny flush. Two dark marginal spots on HW. Male has *patch of androconia (sex scales)* in FW discal cell and area below it. *Underside:* A gray patch on outer ⅓ of HW; 2 pairs of marginal spots set with silver spangles. *Raylike projections* (teeth) extend from pm. line toward outer margin of HW, especially on vein $M_1$; upper part of pm. line aligns with corresponding line on FW.
**Similar species:** (1) In Henshaw's Brown (below), pm. line on underside of HW *lacks* raylike projections. (2) In Grand Canyon Brown (p. 39), pm. line on underside of HW points toward *apex of HW,* not toward corresponding line on FW.
**Early stages:** Unknown. Multiple broods. **Adults:** May–Sept.
**Range:** Se. Ariz. and sw. N.M.; Mexico. **Habitat:** Open woodland, streamsides.
**Subspecies:** (1) **Pyracmon Brown,** *C. p. pyracmon* (Butler). Mexico; not in U.S. (2) **Nabokov's Brown,** *C. p. nabokovi* Miller, Pl. 1. Sw. U.S. and n. Mexico. TL: Ramsey Canyon, Huachuca Mts., Cochise Co., Ariz.

## HENSHAW'S BROWN Pl. 1
*Cyllopsis henshawi* (W.H. Edwards)
**Identification:** 1½-1¹³⁄₁₆ in. (38-45 mm). Similar to Pyracmon Brown (above), but usually slightly more reddish. *No outwardly directed rays* or teeth extend from pm. line on underside of HW.
**Early stages:** Little known. Multiple broods. **Food:** Presumed to be grasses. **Adults:** May-Oct.
**Range:** E. Ariz. and w. N.M.; Mexico. TL: Near Camp Lowell, Pima Co., Ariz. **Habitat:** Open woodland, streamsides.

## GRAND CANYON BROWN Pl. 1
*Cyllopsis pertepida* (Dyar)
**Identification:** 1½-1¾ in. (39-44 mm). *Upperside:* Coloration similar to that of Pyracmon Brown and Henshaw's Brown (above). *Underside:* Upper part of pm. line *directed toward apex and outer margin of HW,* not toward corresponding line on FW. Dark spots and spangles similar to those of Pyracmon Brown and Henshaw's Brown.
**Early stages:** Unknown. Multiple broods. **Adults:** May-Sept.
**Range:** S. Colo., s. Ariz., s. N.M., and sw. Tex.; Mexico. **Habitat:** Open forest, streamsides.
**Subspecies:** (1) **Warm Brown,** *C. p. pertepida* (Dyar). Not in U.S. TL: Mexico. (2) **Grand Canyon Brown,** *C. p. dorothea* (Nabokov), Pl. 1, No. 6. Colo., e. Utah, n. and cen. N.M., Ariz. TL: South Rim of Grand Canyon, Coconino Co., Ariz. (3) **Arizona Brown,** *C. p. maniola* (Nabokov). Se. Ariz.; intergrades with Grand Canyon Brown in sw. N.M. TL: Cochise Co., Ariz. (4) **West Texas Brown,** *C. p. avicula* (Nabokov). Jeff Davis and Brewster Cos. south into Mexico. TL: Ft. Davis, Jeff Davis Co., Tex.

## Wood Satyrs: Genus *Megisto* Huebner

## LITTLE WOOD SATYR *Megisto cymela* (Cramer) Pl. 1
**Identification:** 1½-1¾ in. (38-44 mm). *Upperside:* Light brown. Each wing has 2 large, round, dark spots ringed with yellow; the upper spot may be reduced or absent on HW in some individuals. *Underside:* Similar to upperside, but with a pair of narrow darker lines across both FW and HW. *Eyespots a bit larger, with yellow rings* and black centers.
**Early stages:** Larva pale greenish brown, narrowly striped; tubercles small, whitish. One brood, at least in the North. **Food:** Various grasses; also reported to feed on twisted yellow-eyed grass *(Xyris torta),* which is not a true grass.
**Adults:** June-July.
**Range:** Neb. east to Ontario, south to Gulf States, Fla., e. Tex. Barely enters our area. TL: Uncertain. **Habitat:** Woodland openings.

**RED SATYR** *Megisto rubricata* (W. H. Edwards)        **Pls. 1, 2**
**Identification:** 1½–1¾ in. (38–44 mm). *Upperside:* Brown, with
a brick-red patch on FW, and also on HW in some subspecies. *One
eyespot* near FW apex; HW has 1–2 eyespots. *Underside:* Lighter
than upperside; *eyespots repeated.* Extensive rusty patch on FW,
none on HW. Pm. line distinct. Several small, iridescent eyespots
between the large ones with small silver centers.
**Early stages:** Undescribed. Multiple broods. **Food:** Not known
in nature; larva has been reared on Bermuda grass and St. John's
grass in the laboratory. **Adults:** March–Aug.
**Range:** Ariz. east to Okla. and Tex.; Mexico. **Habitat:** Open, often
dry, woodland; oak-covered hills and canyons.
**Subspecies:** (1) **Red Satyr,** *M. r. rubricata* (W. H. Edwards).
Large red patch on upperside of FW; diffuse red patch on underside. Cen. Tex. TL: Waco, Tex. (2) **Arizona Red Satyr,** *M. r.
cheneyorum* (R. Chermock), Pl. 1. Red patches on upperside
smaller, present on both FW and HW. Ariz. TL: Madera Canyon,
Santa Rita Mts., Ariz. (3) **Smiths' Red Satyr,** *M. r. smithorum*
(Wind), Pl. 2. Red patch on underside of FW bright; HW markings distinct. W. Tex. TL: Marfa-Alpine area.

## Wood Satyrs: Genus *Paramacera* Butler

**ALLYN'S SATYR** *Paramacera allyni* Miller        **Pl. 2**
**Identification:** 1⅜–1⅞ in. (34–47 mm). *Upperside:* Warm brown,
with dark borders and *unringed submarginal spots.* Male has
patch of dark sex scales below FW cell. *Underside:* Median and
pm. lines brown, irregular, with a lighter band between them.
Large eyespot at FW apex; 6 small eyespots on HW.
**Early stages:** Unknown. One brood. **Adults:** June–July.
**Range:** Mountains of se. Ariz. south into Mexico. TL: Barfoot
Park, Chiricahua Mts., Cochise Co., Ariz. **Habitat:** Grassy open-
ings in pine forest, at high elevations.
**Remarks:** This species was described in 1972; it was previously
confused with *Paramacera xicaque,* a Mexican species.

## Ringlets: Genus *Coenonympha* Huebner

Small and usually light-colored, ringlets fly with an exaggerated
bouncing motion.
  **Early stages:** Larva slender, tapering, notched at anal end.
Pupa suspended by cremaster. Northern species have 1 brood,
more southern species have 2. **Food:** Grasses.
  **Range:** Temperate and cold parts of the Northern Hemisphere.

**HAYDEN'S RINGLET**        **Pl. 2**
*Coenonympha haydenii* (W. H. Edwards)
**Identification:** 1⅜–1½ in. (34–38 mm). *Upperside:* Male *dark
brown,* unmarked; female much lighter in color. *Underside:* Both

pairs of wings have a narrow marginal row of light metallic scales and a pale terminal line. HW has a marginal row of *5-7 small eyespots* with *white centers* and ringed with buff or yellow. **Early stages:** Unknown. One brood. **Adults:** July–Aug. **Range:** Limited; sw. Mont., se. Idaho, and w. Wyo. south (doubtfully) to Gunnison Co., Colo. TL: Yellowstone Lake, Yellowstone Natl. Park, Wyo. **Habitat:** Mountain meadows, open forest, to 9000 ft. (2956 m).

## KODIAK RINGLET
Pl. 2

*Coenonympha kodiak* W. H. Edwards
**Identification:** 1¼-1⅜ in. (31–34 mm). *Upperside:* FW dull brownish yellow; outer ⅓ gray. HW more grayish. Light markings of underside show through. *Underside: HW base dark;* median band whitish, irregular. Usually no eyespots.
**Similar species:** California Ringlet (p. 42) is much whiter; the ranges do not overlap.
**Early stages:** Unknown. One brood. **Adults:** June–July.
**Range:** Cen. and n. Alaska, Yukon Terr., and Dist. of Mackenzie; Asia. **Habitat:** Meadows, fields, cutover land, tundra.
**Subspecies:** (1) **Kodiak Ringlet,** *C. k. kodiak* W. H. Edwards. Grayer than other subspecies. Kodiak I. and adjacent mainland. TL: "Kodiak." (2) **Arctic Ringlet,** *C. k. mixturata* Alpheraky, Pl. 2. Much of Alaska and Dist. of Mackenzie. TL: Kamchatka, Siberia. (3) **Yukon Arctic Ringlet,** *C. k. yukonensis* Holland. Somewhat lighter. TL: Dawson, Yukon Terr.

## INORNATE RINGLET
Pl. 2

*Coenonympha inornata* W. H. Edwards
**Identification:** 1¼-1⅜ in. (31–34 mm). *Upperside: Darker, more brownish tan* than Ochre Ringlet (below). *Underside:* FW apex and HW *heavily scaled* with gray or greenish. Eyespots few or absent, but very small *eyespot at FW apex* present in some individuals.
**Similar species:** (1) Ochre Ringlet (below). (2) Ringless Ringlet (p. 42).
**Early stages:** Similar to others in genus. One brood. **Adults:** June–early July.
**Range:** British Columbia east to Newfoundland. In the West, south to Mont., N.D., Wyo. **Habitat:** Grasslands.
**Subspecies:** (1) **Inornate Ringlet,** *C. i. inornata* W. H. Edwards, Pl. 2. Underside light greenish gray. Manitoba eastward. TL: Saskatchewan R. between Lake Winnipeg and The Pas. (2) **Prairie Ringlet,** *C. i. benjamini* McDunnough. Underside scaling deep greenish brown; eyespot at FW apex usually well developed. Western part of range. TL: Waterton Lakes, Alberta.

## OCHRE RINGLET
Pl. 2

*Coenonympha ochracea* W. H. Edwards

**Identification:** $1\frac{1}{4}$-$1\frac{1}{2}$ in. (31–38 mm). The *bright tawny color* and *well-developed eyespots* identify it. *Underside:* Eyespot at FW apex *always present* (often lacking or faint in other ringlets). **Similar species:** (1) Ringless Ringlet (p. 42). (2) Inornate Ringlet (above). **Early stages:** Similar to others of the genus. One brood. **Adults:** June–July. **Range:** Dist. of Mackenzie and Northwest Terr. south through the Rocky Mts. to Ariz. and N.M. **Habitat:** Fields, meadows, open woodland, brushland, sagebrush. **Subspecies:** (1) **Ochre Ringlet,** *C. o. ochracea* W. H. Edwards, Pl. 2. Mont., Wyo., w. Neb., w. S.D., Colo., N.M. TL: Turkey Creek, Jefferson Co., Colo. (2) **Davenport's Ringlet,** *C. o. mackenziei* Davenport. Fewer eyespots. TL: Nyarling R., Dist. of Mackenzie. (3) **White Mountains Ringlet,** *C. o. subfusca* Barnes & Benjamin. Small, dark, very different. Local. TL: White Mts., Ariz. (4) **Grand Canyon Ringlet,** *C. o. furcae* Barnes & Benjamin. Clay-colored, very distinctive. Known only from the TL: South Rim, Grand Canyon. (5) **Great Basin Ringlet,** *C. o. brenda* W. H. Edwards. Eyespots on underside very well developed. TL: "Los Angeles" (error); actually found in e. Nev., Utah, and western edge of Colo. (6) **Mono Ringlet,** *C. o. mono* Burdick. Large; very bright tawny color. Mono Basin north to w.-cen. Nev. TL: Bridgeport, Mono Co., Calif.

## RINGLESS RINGLET

Pl. 2

*Coenonympha ampelos* W. H. Edwards
**Identification:** $1\frac{1}{4}$-$1\frac{3}{8}$ in. (31–34 mm). *Upperside:* Yellowish or buffy, unmarked. Light band on underside shows through. *Underside:* FW apex and HW base *shaded with gray.* Median band irregular. *No eyespots,* or 1 small spot at FW apex. **Similar species:** (1) Ochre Ringlet (above). (2) Inornate Ringlet (p. 41). **Early stages:** Similar to others of the genus. Two broods. **Adults:** Spring and late summer. **Range:** W. British Columbia south through Wash. and Ore. to ne. Calif., east to Nev., Idaho and Utah. **Habitat:** Quite widespread at low and middle elevations; very adaptable. **Subspecies:** (1) **Ringless Ringlet,** *C. a. ampelos* W. H. Edwards, Pl. 2. E. Ore., e. Wash., w. Idaho. TL: Oregon. (2) **Dornfeld's Ringlet,** *C. a. eunomia* Dornfeld. Smaller, duller. W. Ore. TL: Wilhoit, Clackamas Co., Ore. (3) **Columbian Ringlet,** *C. a. columbiana* McDunnough. Darker and brighter. S. British Columbia, n. Wash. TL: Aspen Grove, British Columbia. (4) **Vancouver Island Ringlet,** *C. a. insulana* McDunnough. Underside greenish gray. Vancouver I. and adjacent mainland. TL: Victoria, British Columbia. (5) **Nevada Ringlet,** *C. a. elko* W. H. Edwards. Very pale, almost unmarked. Cen. Nev. TL: Elko, Nev.

**CALIFORNIA RINGLET**                                            **Pl. 2**
*Coenonympha california* Westwood
**Identification:** 1¼–1⅜ in. (31–34 mm). The lightest-colored
ringlet, known by its *whitish color*. Spring brood duller, with re-
duced eyespots.
**Early stages:** Egg spherical, with a central "button;" reticulated;
yellow, turning brown before hatching. Larva brown and olive;
median stripe dark, flanked by pale bands. Pupa either brown or
green. At least 2 broods. **Adults:** April–Sept.
**Range:** Calif. west of Sierran Crest, north to s. Ore., south to Baja
California. Characteristic of coast and foothills of Calif. **Habitat:**
Meadows, fields, grassy hills.
**Subspecies:** (1) **California Ringlet,** *C. c. california* Westwood,
Pl. 2. *Eyespots usually present* on underside. N.-cen. Calif. southward. TL: California. (2) **Siskiyou Ringlet,** *C. c. eryngii* H. Ed-
wards. Eyespots often reduced or absent. N. Calif., s. Ore. TL:
Soda Springs, Siskiyou Co., Calif. The summer brood of both sub-
species is often more buffy, and may have better-developed
eyespots than the spring brood.

## Wood Nymphs: Genus *Cercyonis* Scudder

Large to medium; dark. Conspicuous, often common insects.
Upperside of FW has 2 prominent eyespots that are repeated on
underside. May also have smaller eyespots on HW. Much variation, both individually and geographically. Four species: 1 trans-
continental, the other 3 entirely western.
   **Early stages:** Egg barrel-shaped, reticulated. Larva striped,
tapering at each end; anal fork has tapering projections. Larva
overwinters in first instar. The Wood Nymph (below) has 6 instars;
other species have 5. All species have 1 brood, but adults may
emerge over a long period. **Food:** Various grasses.

**WOOD NYMPH** *Cercyonis pegala* (Fabricius)            **Pl. 3**
**Identification:** 1¾–2¾ in. (44–69 mm). The largest species in this
genus. *Upperside:* FW eyespots large, surrounded by a *yellow
area* in some subspecies but not in others. *Underside:* FW
eyespots large; *HW eyespots* range from 6 (in two groups of 3) to
none.
**Early stages:** See genus description (above). One brood. **Food:**
Various grasses. **Adults:** June–Sept., depending on locality.
**Range:** U.S. and s. Canada, except in deserts and alpine regions.
**Habitat:** Moist situations — meadows, glades, marshes.
**Subspecies:** Several subspecies were previously considered full
species. (1) **Texas Wood Nymph,** *C. p. texana* (W. H. Edwards).
Large, with a large brownish yellow FW patch. Kans. and s. Colo.
to Tex. TL: Bastrop, Tex. (2) **Olympian Wood Nymph,** *C. p.
olympus* (W. H. Edwards). Large; eyespots reduced. In our area,

found in Platte R. drainage. TL: Chicago, Ill. (3) **Hall's Wood Nymph,** *C. p. ino* Hall. Small; very dark, eyespots reduced. S. Canada to Wyo. and S.D. TL: Calgary, Alberta. (4) **Ox-eyed Satyr,** *C. p. boöpis* (Behr), Pl. 3, No. 1. The most widespread western subspecies. TL: Contra Costa Co., Calif. (5) **Ariane Satyr,** *C. p. ariane* (Boisduval), Pl. 3, No. 2. Very distinctive. Eyespots on underside of HW large, conspicuous. Female often has large, pale submarginal band on upperside of FW and HW. Alkaline marshes of western Great Basin, in e. Ore., e. Calif., Nev., w. Utah. TL: "California." The very pale form "stephensi" W. G. Wright (Pl. 3, No. 3) is by some considered a subspecies, **Stephens' Satyr.** (6) **Grand Canyon Satyr,** *C. p. damei* (Barnes & Benjamin). *Reddish flush* on FW. Found only in Grand Canyon, below level of the plateau. TL: Grand Canyon, Ariz. (7) **Light Satyr,** *C. p. blanca* Emmel & Matoon. Underside suffused with whitish scaling. Local. TL: Charles Sheldon Antelope Range, Humboldt Co., Nev.
**Remarks:** Four other subspecies occur in the eastern U.S.

**MEAD'S SATYR** *Cercyonis meadii* (W. H. Edwards)          **Pl. 3**
**Identification:** $1\frac{3}{8}$–$1\frac{3}{4}$ in. (34–44 mm). *Upperside:* FW has a reddish brown flush, variable in size, which forms a patch around eyespots. *Upper eyespot usually larger.* Ground color *chocolatebrown. Underside:* Reddish brown flush covers much of FW; a brown line encircles eyespots. HW eyespots few, small. Three brown lines cross HW; outer half often has some whitish scaling.
**Adults:** Late July–early Sept.
**Similar species:** (1) Grand Canyon Satyr (subspecies of Wood Nymph, above), is larger, with both eyespots the same size. Found only in Grand Canyon. (2) Red Satyr (p. 39) has only 1 FW eyespot, not 2; usually red on HW also.
**Range:** Cen. Utah east to w. N.D., e. Wyo., cen. Colo. south to cen. Ariz., se. N.M., w. Tex.; nw. Chihuahua, Mexico. **Habitat:** Dry, open pine forest; juniper-pinyon woodland; 1 subspecies found in saltbush scrub.
**Subspecies:** (1) **Mead's Satyr,** *C. m. meadii* (W. H. Edwards). Reddish brown flush less extensive. Cen. Colo. TL: Bailey, Colo. (2) **Wind's Satyr,** *C. m. melania* (Wind). Larger, darker. W. Tex. TL: Marfa-Alpine, Tex. (3) **Alamosa Satyr,** *C. m. alamosa* T. & J. Emmel. White scaling on underside. Saltbush scrub of s.-cen. Colo. TL: San Luis Valley, Saguache Co., Colo. (4) **Chermock's Satyr,** *C. n. mexicana* (R. L. Chermock), Pl. 3. Large, light. Brown on underside, often heavily mottled. Widespread but very local. Utah to N.D., south to Ariz., N.M., and Mexico. TL: Chihuahua, Mexico.

**WOODLAND SATYR** *Cercyonis sthenele* (Boisduval)          **Pl. 4**
**Identification:** $1\frac{3}{8}$–$1\frac{3}{4}$ in. (34–44 mm). *Upperside:* FW *eyespots*

*small in male;* upper one larger. Eyespots larger in female; light-ringed and of *equal size.* In both sexes, *eyespots equally distant from outer margin. Underside:* Basal half of HW darker; outer edge of the dark area irregular. **Adults:** June–Aug.

**Similar species:** In Least Satyr (below), *lower eyespot* in FW *closer to wing edge;* male usually has only 1 eyespot on upperside of FW.

**Range:** S. British Columbia south to Calif., Baja California; east to Wyo., Colo., Ariz. **Habitat:** Oak woodland, open pine forest, juniper-pinyon woodland, sagebrush.

**Subspecies:** (1) **Sthenele Satyr,** *C. s. sthenele* (Boisduval). Band on underside of HW dark. Formerly San Francisco; extinct since about 1880. (2) **Woodland Satyr,** *C. s. silvestris* (W. H. Edwards), Pl. 4, No. 1. Underside of HW usually nearly devoid of eyespots. S. British Columbia south to Baja California, west of Sierran Crest. TL: California. (3) **Little Satyr,** *C. s. paula* (W. H. Edwards), Pl. 4, No. 2. *Eyespots* on underside of HW *well developed,* white-centered. E. Ore., Nev., w. Utah. TL: Virginia City, Nev. (4) **Mason's Satyr,** *C. s. masoni* (Cross). Underside of HW with usually only the *lower* eyespot well developed. Utah, s. Wyo., Colo., n. Ariz. TL: Black Ridge Breaks, Mesa Co., Colo.

**Remarks:** Behr's Satyr, *Cercyonis behrii* (F. Grinnell), was known only from specimens destroyed in the 1906 San Francisco earthquake and fire. *C. behrii* is now considered a synonym of the Woodland Satyr *(C. sthenele).*

**LEAST SATYR** *Cercyonis oeta* (Boisduval)          **Pl. 3**
**Identification:** $1\frac{1}{4}$–$1\frac{3}{4}$ in. (31–44 mm). *Upperside:* Usually 1 eyespot in male, usually 2 in female. Lower eyespot smaller. *Underside:* In both sexes, lower eyespot on FW smaller, *nearer to wing margin* than upper eyespot. Ground color light (in the west) to very dark (in the north); postbasal and median lines dark and irregular. *Wing fringes checkered.* **Adults:** July–Aug.

**Similar species:** Woodland Satyr (above, Pl. 4).

**Range:** N.-cen. British Columbia east to s. Saskatchewan, south to e. Calif., Nev., cen. Ariz., ne. N.M. Often very common. **Habitat:** Dry (often elevated) grasslands, sagebrush, scrub, meadows, open woodland.

**Subspecies:** (1) **Least Satyr,** *C. o. oeta* (Boisduval), Pl. 3. Wash. east to Idaho, south to Calif. and Nev. TL: California. (2) **Charon Satyr,** *C. o. charon* (W. H. Edwards). Underside markings less distinct. S. Canada south in Rocky Mts. and plains to n. N.M. TL: Twin Lakes, Upper Arkansas Valley, Colo. (3) **Phocus Satyr,** *C. o. phocus* (W. H. Edwards). Underside very dark, smooth. N.-cen. British Columbia. TL: Lac La Hache, British Columbia. (4) **Pale Satyr,** *C. o. pallescens* Emmel & Emmel. Underside very pale, the dark markings distinct. Alkali flats of cen. Nev. TL: Southwest of Austin, Lander Co., Nev.

## Alpines: Genus *Erebia* Dalman

Holarctic; species of northern latitudes and high mountains. Small to medium-sized. Wings broad, rounded. Dark brown or black, usually with brick-red or orange-brown markings; most have conspicuous eyespots.

**Early stages:** Unknown for some species. Larva dull-colored, unmarked or vaguely striped. Pupa forms in cell on surface of ground. One brood. **Food:** Grasses, sedges.

**VIDLER'S ALPINE** *Erebia vidleri* Elwes　　　　**Pl. 4**
**Identification:** $1\frac{5}{8}$–$1\frac{7}{8}$ in. (41–47 mm). *Upperside:* Brownish black. *Orange band encloses 3 eyespots on FW, 1–2 on HW. Underside:* FW eyespots as on upperside; pm. band obscure to distinct and *ashy gray,* at least on costa.
**Similar species:** In Common Alpine (p. 49), eyespots on underside of HW conspicuous.
**Early stages:** Unknown. One brood. **Adults:** July.
**Range:** High mountains of British Columbia south to Olympic Mts. and n. Cascade Mts. of Wash. TL: Above Seton Lake, near Lillooet, British Columbia. **Habitat:** High meadows and ridges in mountain areas.

**ROSS'S ALPINE** *Erebia rossii* (Curtis)　　　　**Pl. 4**
**Identification:** $1\frac{5}{8}$–$1\frac{3}{4}$ in. (41–44 mm). *Upperside:* Male black, with *orange spots reduced to 1 or 2* on FW; often no spots or mere flecks on HW. Female often has an incomplete submarginal row of orange spots; *upper pair on FW larger,* with black centers. *Underside:* In both sexes, markings of FW repeated. HW *median band dark, pm. band light;* boundaries of bands irregular, often projecting out along veins. HW has a line of *dark submarginal chevrons, capped* with *light specks.* **Adults:** June–July.
**Similar species:** (1) Disa Alpine (below) is larger. FW has slight orange flush; 3–5 large, dark-centered orange spots often form a band. (2) In Young's Alpine (p. 49), FW has row of 4 orange spots with black centers.
**Range:** Alaska east to Baffin I., Hudson Bay, south to British Columbia and Manitoba; also cen. and n. Asia. **Habitat:** Tundra; open alpine areas near or above treeline.
**Subspecies:** (1) **Ross's Alpine,** *E. r. rossii* (Curtis), Pl. 4, No. 4. N. and cen. Alaska east across the n. Arctic. TL: Boothia Peninsula. (2) **Kuskokwim Alpine,** *E. r. kuskokwima* Holland. Dark median band on underside of HW prominent; 2 orange spots on upperside of FW slightly larger, separated. Local. TL: Kuskokwim Valley, Alaska. (3) **Gabriel's Alpine,** *E. r. gabrieli* dos Passos. Two orange spots at FW apex on upperside larger, well separated; dark median and light pm. bands on underside of HW well developed. Alaska Range, at about 3500 ft. (1068 m). TL: Mt. McKinley

Natl. Park (now Denali Natl. Park and Preserve). (4) **Ornate Alpine,** *E. r. ornata* Leussler, Pl. 4, No. 5. Upper eyespots on FW *fused.* TL: Churchill, Manitoba.

**DISA ALPINE** *Erebia disa* (Thunberg)          **Pl. 4**
**Identification:** 1⅝-1¾ in. (41-44 mm). *Upperside:* Blackish brown with a *slight orange-brown flush* on FW. An orange band (sometimes separate orange spots) encloses 3-5 (usually 4) *black spots.* HW unmarked. *Underside:* FW markings repeated. HW dark gray marked by dark irregular lines; *1 small light spot at end of cell,* and usually another light spot on costa. **Adults:** June-July. **Similar species:** (1) Ross's Alpine (above). (2) Young's Alpine (p. 49).
**Range:** Circumpolar. Subarctic Alaska and Canada south to British Columbia and Ontario; n. Europe, n. Asia. **Habitat:** Spruce bogs.
**Subspecies:** (1) **Disa Alpine,** *E. d. disa* (Thunberg). N. Europe; not in N. America. TL: Lapland. (2) **Mancina Alpine,** *E. d. mancina* Doubleday, Pl. 4. Alaska, Yukon Terr., Northwest Terr. to British Columbia and Alberta. TL: Rocky Mts. (3) **Stecker's Alpine,** *E. d. steckeri* Holland. Median band on underside of HW very dark. TL: Kuskokwim R., Alaska. (4) **Subarctic Alpine,** *E. d. subarctica* McDunnough. Small, dark; orange spots on upperside of FW small. Northwest Terr. TL: Mackenzie Delta.

**MAGDALENA ALPINE** *Erebia magdalena* Strecker     **Pl. 4**
**Identification:** 1¾-2 in. (44-50 mm). Large. Both upperside and underside of FW and HW black, with no markings.
**Similar species:** Mt. McKinley Alpine (below).
**Early stages:** Egg yellow-brown. Larva pinkish when first hatched, later green. Nothing else known. One brood. **Adults:** Late June-July.
**Range:** High mountains of Colo., w. Wyo. and ne. Utah. TL: Colorado. **Habitat:** Rock slides at or above treeline.

**MT. MCKINLEY ALPINE**                    **Pl. 4**
*Erebia mckinleyensis* Gunder
**Identification:** 1⅝-1⅞ in. (41-47 mm). Very similar to the Magdalena Alpine (above), but with a *reddish flush* on both upperside and underside of FW; flush much more extensive in female. Some individuals have an obscure black band on underside of HW. **Adults:** June-July.
**Range:** High mountains of Alaska, Yukon Terr.; Sayan Mts. in Asia. TL: Sable Pass, Mt. McKinley Natl. Park (now Denali Natl. Park and Preserve). **Habitat:** Rockslides (scree) above treeline.
**Remarks:** Considered by some to be a subspecies of the Magdalena Alpine (above); however, the ranges are widely separated. A rare species.

**BANDED ALPINE** *Erebia fasciata* Butler     **Pl. 5**
**Identification:** $1\frac{3}{4}$-$1\frac{7}{8}$ in. (44–47 mm). *Upperside:* Black. Male has 1–3 suffused, *dull reddish submarginal bars* in FW. Female has extensive *dull reddish flush* on FW. *Underside:* Wide submarginal band on FW, usually with reddish suffusion. HW either dark, with a *light submarginal band,* or base and submarginal band whitish, with the median band dark and contrasting.
**Adults:** June–July.
**Range:** Entirely arctic. W. Alaska to Hudson Bay; n. Asia. **Habitat:** Moist grassy tundra.
**Subspecies:** (1) **Banded Alpine,** *E. f. fasciata* Butler, Pl. 5. Alaska east to Hudson Bay. TL: Arctic America. (2) **Avinoff's Alpine,** *E. f. avinoffi* Holland. More reddish on FW. Extreme western coastal Alaska. TL: Kotzebue Sound and Indian Cape, Alaska.

**RED-DISKED ALPINE** *Erebia discoidalis* (Kirby)   **Pl. 5**
**Identification:** $1\frac{1}{2}$-$1\frac{7}{8}$ in. (38–47 mm). *Upperside:* FW has extensive *dull reddish discal flush;* HW usually unmarked. *Underside:* FW flush repeated, *costa flecked with white.* FW apex and HW with pale irregular overscaling. Basal half of HW darker. Usually 2 pale inconspicuous spots, 1 on HW costa and 1 at cell end. Often common. **Adults:** Late May–early July.
**Range:** W. Alaska to e. Canada, south to s. Canada; also cen. Asia. **Habitat:** Open dry grassy areas; roadsides, cutover land, old fields.
**Subspecies:** (1) **Red-disked Alpine,** *E. d. discoidalis* (Kirby). Eastern part of range. TL: Cumberland House, Saskatchewan. (2) **McDunnough's Red-disked Alpine,** *E. d. mcdunnoughi* dos Passos, Pl. 5. Darker; red area on disc smaller. Cen. Alaska south to British Columbia and Alberta. TL: White Horse, Yukon Terr.

**THEANO ALPINE** *Erebia theano* (Tauscher)     **Pl. 5**
**Identification:** $1\frac{1}{4}$-$1\frac{1}{2}$ in. (31–38 mm). *Upperside:* Dark brown, with a *submarginal row of orange bars* (not eyespots) across both wings. *Underside:* FW markings repeated; HW spots ivory.
**Early stages:** Unknown. One brood. **Adults:** Usually in July; found in scattered local colonies. Some subspecies found in markedly different habitats may be closely related but distinct species.
**Range:** Alaska east to Hudson Bay, south in the West to Colo.; also in Siberia. **Habitat:** Varies for different subspecies (see below).
**Subspecies:** (1) *E. t. theano* (Tauscher). Not in N. America. TL: Altai Mts., Siberia. (2) **Churchill Alpine,** *E. t. sofia* Strecker. Orange bars wide, sometimes merging. Canadian Rocky Mts. and eastward. TL: Churchill, Manitoba. (3) **Holland's Theano Alpine,** *E. t. alaskensis* Holland, Pl. 5. Orange markings smaller. Alaska and Yukon Terr. south to British Columbia. TL: Eagle City and American Creek, Alaska. (4) **Ethel's Alpine,** *E. t. ethela* W. H. Edwards. N.-cen. Colo., nw. Wyo., s. Mont. TL: Trout Creek,

Yellowstone Natl. Park. In Colo., in bogs below treeline; in Wyo., open pine forest. (5) **Demmia Alpine,** *E. t. demmia* Warren. Markings on upperside wider than those on underside. TL: San Juan Mts., La Plata Co., Colo. Local, in moist grassy spots above treeline.

**YOUNG'S ALPINE** *Erebia youngi* Holland                    **Pl. 5**
**Identification:** $1\frac{1}{2}$–$1\frac{3}{4}$ in. (38–44 mm). *Upperside:* Dark brown to blackish. FW has 4–5 *small black spots in a line, each ringed with dull orange.* HW often has 1–3 small orange spots. *Underside:* Markings of upperside repeated; basal half of HW dark, outer half much lighter.
**Similar species:** (1) Ross's Alpine (p. 46). (2) Disa Alpine (p. 46).
**Early stages:** Apparently undescribed. One brood. **Adults:** June–July.
**Range:** Alaska, Yukon Terr., w. Northwest Terr. **Habitat:** Tundra.
**Subspecies:** (1) **Young's Alpine,** *E. y. youngi* Holland, Pl. 5. All of range except as given below. TL: Mountains between Fortymile and Mission Creeks, Alaska. (2) **Herschel Island Alpine,** *E. y. herscheli* Leussler. Larger. TL: Herschel I., Mackenzie Bay, n. Yukon Terr. (3) **Riley's Alpine,** *E. y. rileyi* dos Passos. TL: Mt. McKinley Natl. Park (now Denali Natl. Park and Preserve), Alaska.

**COMMON ALPINE** *Erebia epipsodea* Butler          **Pl. 5**
**Identification:** $1\frac{5}{8}$–$1\frac{3}{4}$ in. (41–44 mm). *Upperside:* Dark brown. A row of black spots on both FW and HW; spots usually have white centers and are surrounded by orange-red rings. Upper 2 spots on FW *always present* and always largest. *Underside:* Spots similar in number and position to those on upperside, but usually reduced on HW. Outer half of HW lighter. **Adults:** June–Aug., depending on latitude and elevation.
**Range:** N.-cen. Alaska east to Manitoba, south to e. Ore., Utah, N.M. **Habitat:** Grassy fields, meadows, open forest.
**Subspecies:** (1) **Common Alpine,** *E. e. epipsodea* Butler. E. British Columbia and w. Alberta south in Rocky Mts. TL: Rocky Mts. (2) **Remington's Alpine,** *E. e. remingtoni* Ehrlich. Eyespots reduced, especially on underside of HW. N.-cen. Alaska, Yukon Terr., n. British Columbia. TL: Dawson, Yukon Terr. (3) **Hopfinger's Alpine,** *E. e. hopfingeri* Ehrlich. Large; eyespots unusually distinct. Ne. Ore. and e. Wash. east to Mont. (4) **Freeman's Alpine,** *E. e. freemani* Ehrlich. Red areas around spots extensive. Manitoba west to British Columbia. TL: Ft. Qu'Appelle, Saskatchewan. (5) **Common Alpine,** *E. e. rhodia* (W. H. Edwards), Pl. 5. Rocky Mts. of the U.S. south to N.M. TL: Fairplay, Park Co., Colo.
**Remarks:** Occurs farther south and in more accessible habitats than most other alpines; the one most commonly found by the average collector.

**MEAD'S ALPINE** *Erebia callias* W. H. Edwards **Pl. 5**
**Identification:** 1⅜-1½ in. (34–38 mm). *Upperside:* Dull grayish brown with a *slight sheen.* FW has *only 2 eyespots near apex,* each with a white center and surrounded by a dull tawny area. *Underside:* HW *soft gray,* with numerous dark flecks; crossed by 1–2 thin, irregular lines. **Adults:** July–early Aug.
**Range:** Wyo., Colo.; also Iran, Mongolia. **Habitat:** Meadows, above treeline.
**Remarks:** In older books on butterflies, Mead's Alpine *(E. callias)* is treated as a synonym or subspecies of a European species, the Swiss Brassy Ringlet *(E. tyndarus)* Esper.

### Tritonia: Genus *Gyrocheilus* Butler
This large, beautiful satyr is the only member of its genus.

**TRITONIA** *Gyrocheilus patrobas* (Hewitson) **Pl. 8**
**Identification:** 2-2⅜ in. (58–59 mm). FW costa strongly curved; fringes checkered. *Upperside:* Dark brown. FW has 3–4 white submarginal dots; *HW has a wide, dull reddish border. Underside:* Markings of upperside repeated.
**Early stages:** Unknown. One brood. **Adults:** Sept. Common in favored years.
**Range:** Cen. Ariz. south to Cen. America. **Habitat:** Streamsides in moist open coniferous forest, on major mountain ranges of cen. and s. Ariz.
**Subspecies:** (1) *G. p. patrobas* (Hewitson). Not found in U.S. TL: Mexico. (2) *G. p. tritonia* (Edwards), Pl. 8. Ariz. TL: White Mts., Ariz.

### Riding's Satyr: Genus *Neominois* Scudder
Confined to the western U.S. One species in the genus.

**RIDING'S SATYR** **Pl. 2**
*Neominois ridingsii* (W. H. Edwards)
**Identification:** 1½-2 in. (38–50 mm). *Upperside:* Grayish brown, with a *row of light bars* (or in some specimens, *chevrons*) across outer part of both FW and HW. FW has *2 black eyespots. Underside:* Very similar to upperside, but usually lighter.
**Early stages:** Egg taller than wide, with vertical ridges. Larva largest near head, tapering to notched anal end. Pupates underground. One brood. **Food:** Grasses. **Adults:** June–July.
**Range:** Found only in w. U.S. E. Calif. (very local) east to N.D. and Neb., south to Ariz. and N.M. **Habitat:** Dry grassland and brushland, usually at moderate or high elevations.
**Subspecies:** (1) **Riding's Satyr,** *N. r. ridingsii* (W. H. Edwards), Pl. 2. E. Calif. east to Neb. TL: Longmont, Boulder Co., Colo. (2) **Stretch's Satyr,** *N. r. stretchii* (W. H. Edwards). Ground color more yellowish. Nye and Eureka Cos., Nev. TL: Mt. Jefferson, Nye Co., Nev. (3) **Dionysus Satyr,** *N. r. dionysus* Scudder. Brown

median band very irregular; overall color lighter. TL: Mt. Trumbull, 60 mi. east of St. George, Utah.

## Arctics: Genus *Oeneis* Huebner

Holarctic; predominantly arctic and alpine. Medium-sized to large; dull-colored. FW narrow, marked with striations in most species. Some species are difficult to identify. Those inhabiting northern and remote areas are scarce in collections and little known. Flight is low and fast; after alighting, the insect leans over on its side.
    **Early stages:** Larva stout, tapering abruptly, with long anal projections; green or brown with dark stripes. Pupates under stones or at roots of grasses. Eggs laid on dried grasses; newly hatched larva overwinters and can withstand freezing. Some species take 2 years to develop. All species have 1 brood. Adults may appear earlier (June) in the far north than on mountain summits in the south. **Food:** Grasses and sedges, as far as is known. The life histories of many species remain unknown.

**GREAT ARCTIC** *Oeneis nevadensis* (C. & R. Felder)    **Pl. 6**
**Identification:** 2¼–2½ in. (56–62 mm). Large, striking. Ranges farther south and at lower elevations than other arctics. *Upperside:* Male has long, dark, *diagonal stigma (sex mark)* on FW. Both sexes brownish tan; FW costa and all wing borders dark brown. Two eyespots on FW; usually 1 small eyespot on HW. *Underside:* In both sexes, FW marks repeated. HW mottled with brown and light gray; 2 irregular dark bars across wing.
**Similar species:** Macoun's Arctic (below) is similar in size, but male *lacks stigma.* Median band on underside of HW distinct (vague in Great Arctic). Ranges widely separated.
**Early stages:** Egg oval, gray-white. Larva brownish buff with a black dorsal stripe; other stripes white and brown. One brood.
**Adults:** May–July, depending on locality. Occurs in a 2-year cycle; adults more common in even years.
**Range:** Vancouver I., British Columbia, south along coast to Sonoma Co., Calif., in Cascade Mts. and Sierra Nevada to Tulare Co., Calif. **Habitat:** Openings in coniferous forest; edges of mountain meadows.
**Subspecies:** (1) **Great Arctic,** *O. n. nevadensis* (C. & R. Felder), Pl. 6. Wash., Ore., w. Nev., and Calif. TL: California. (2) **Giant Arctic,** *O. n. gigas* Butler. Darker; underside heavily marked. Quite local. TL: Vancouver I., British Columbia. (3) **Iduna Arctic,** *O. n. iduna* (W. H. Edwards). Lighter; light mottling on underside. Dark bands on HW usually distinct. Coastal Calif. north of San Francisco Bay. TL: Mendocino Co., Calif.

**MACOUN'S ARCTIC**    **Pl. 6**
*Oeneis macounii* (W. H. Edwards)

**Identification:** 2¼-2½ in. (56-62 mm). Similar in size and coloration to Great Arctic (above), but *male lacks stigma*. Median band on underside of HW distinct in both sexes. The range of Macoun's Arctic does not overlap that of the Great Arctic. **Adults:** Late June-July.
**Range:** British Columbia, s. Northwest Terr. through Alberta, Saskatchewan, and Manitoba east to Ontario and Mich. TL: Nipigon, Ontario. **Habitat:** Moist meadows.

**CHRYXUS ARCTIC** *Oeneis chryxus* (Doubleday)        **Pl. 6**
**Identification:** 1¾-2³⁄₁₆ in. (44-55 mm). *Upperside:* FW and HW tawny; border and costa dark. *FW cell and long stigma dark* in male. Female *lacks dark markings at base* of FW. *Underside:* FW has *thin, dark toothed median line* just beyond cell. HW coarsely striated with dark brown and white, in narrow, irregular, usually incomplete bands. **Adults:** June-July.
**Similar species:** (1) Uhler's Arctic (below). (2) Alberta Arctic (p. 53).
**Range:** S. Alaska and Yukon Terr. south to N.M. at high elevations, east to Ontario, Quebec, n. Mich. Widespread, often common. **Habitat:** In south, rocky summits to 8000 ft. (2440 m) or more; in north, grassy woodland and forest openings at low or moderate elevations.
**Subspecies:** (1) **Chryxus Arctic,** *O. c. chryxus* (Doubleday), Pl. 6. Alberta south to N.M.; e. Nev., w. S.D. TL: Rocky Mts. (2) **Olympic Arctic,** *O. c. valerata* Burdick. Duller; band on underside of HW usually present. Local. TL: Hurricane Hill, Olympic Natl. Park. (3) **Hovanitz's Arctic,** *O. c. stanislaus* Hovanitz. Markings clean-cut; FW narrow. Isolated in cen. Sierra Nevada; range interrupts that of Ivallda Arctic (below). TL: Deadman Creek, Tuolumne-Alpine Cos., Calif. (4) **Cary's Arctic,** *O. c. caryi* Dyar. Band on underside of HW well developed, often white-edged. Alaska, Yukon Terr., s. Northwest Terr., Saskatchewan. TL: Smith Landing, Athabasca, Alberta.

**IVALLDA ARCTIC** *Oeneis ivallda* (Mead)        **Pl. 5**
**Identification:** 1¾-2¼ in. (44-56 mm). Very pale, sandy colored. Pale submarginal bars in FW conspicuous. Resembles Chryxus Arctic (above). Considered a subspecies of Chryxus Arctic by some, but the chemistry of the wing pigments differs. Has the most limited range of any arctic. **Adults:** July-Aug.
**Range:** High Sierra Nevada of Calif. and w. Nev. TL: Summit and Freel Peaks and Mt. Tallac, Lake Tahoe, Calif. Found both north and south of the Chryxus Arctic's range. **Habitat:** Granite summits and rock slides, near or above treeline; less often in open subalpine forest.

**UHLER'S ARCTIC** *Oeneis uhleri* (Reakirt)        **Pl. 6**
**Identification:** 1½-1⅞ in. (38-47 mm). *Upperside:* Tawny; veins

and borders dark. *A submarginal row of eyespots* (often incomplete) *on both FW and HW. **Underside:*** Eyespots repeated; FW costa and cell and all of HW marked with a series of close, dark striations. **Adults:** Late May–early July.

**Similar species:** (1) In Chryxus Arctic (above), underside has dark vertical line at end of cell. (2) Alberta Arctic (below) is smaller, with usually some indication of a median band.

**Range:** S. Alaska, Yukon Terr., and Dist. of Mackenzie south to w. Neb., Colo. **Habitat:** Dry grassy openings in forest or scrub, up to 12,000 ft. (3660 m).

**Subspecies:** (1) **Uhler's Arctic,** *O. u. uhleri* (Reakirt), Pl. 6. Usually no median band on underside of HW. Colo., Wyo., east of Continental Divide. TL: Georgetown, Clear Creek Co., Colo. (2) **Reinthal's Arctic,** *O. u. reinthali* F. M. Brown. Median band on underside of HW usually present. Colo. west of Continental Divide. TL: Gothic, Gunnison Co., Colo. (3) **Varuna Arctic,** *O. u. varuna* (W. H. Edwards). Smaller; median band present. Alberta, Saskatchewan, Manitoba south to Mont., w. Neb. TL: "Plains of Dacotah Territory." (4) **Nahanni Mountains Arctic,** *O. u. nahanni* Dyar. Much darker; no median band on underside of HW. N. Canada. TL: Nahanni Mts., Dist. of Mackenzie. (5) **Cairnes' Arctic,** *O. u. cairnesi* Gibson. Light-colored. Alaska, Northwest Terr., Yukon Terr. TL: White R. Dist., Yukon Terr.

## SENTINEL ARCTIC                    not shown
*Oeneis excubitor* Troubridge

**Identification:** Size and general appearance similar to that of Chryxus Arctic (p. 52), but basal part of wings darker and outer section lighter. The male genitalia are also different, having no basal spine.

**Early stages:** Unknown. One brood. **Adults:** Mid-June to mid-July.

**Range:** Yukon Terr., Alaska, Northwest Terr. **Habitat:** Not stated.

**Remarks:** Described in 1982, this species is not included in current check lists.

## ALBERTA ARCTIC *Oeneis alberta* Elwes          Pl. 5
**Identification:** $1\frac{3}{8}$–$1\frac{3}{4}$ in. (34–44 mm). Small, thin-winged. *Upperside:* Light brown, submarginal marks lighter. Eyespots few, sometimes reduced to 1 at FW apex. Bands on underside show through. *HW spots indistinct.* **Underside:** *Median band* irregular, usually *dark-edged.* **Adults:** May–June; an early species.

**Similar species:** Uhler's Arctic (p. 52). (2) Chryxus Arctic (p. 52).

**Range:** Alberta, Saskatchewan, and Manitoba south to Colo. and Ariz. **Habitat:** Prairies in Canada, mountain parks in Colo., mountain meadows in Ariz.

**Subspecies:** The Alberta Arctic includes 4 subspecies with widely separated ranges, each formerly considered a separate species. (1) **Alberta Arctic,** *O. a. alberta* Elwes, Pl. 5. Alberta to Manitoba. TL: Calgary, Alberta. (2) **Oslar's Arctic,** *O. a. oslari* (Skinner). Band on underside of HW consists of 2 dark lines with a *light space* between. Very limited range: areas with red sedimentary soils south and west of Denver, in Park Co., Colo. TL: Deer Creek Canyon, Colo. (3) **Daura Arctic,** *O. a. daura* (Strecker). Larger, dull tawny. Band on underside of HW consists of 2 dark lines with *ground color* between. White Mts. and San Francisco Peaks, Ariz. TL: Mt. Graham, Ariz.; rare or extinct on Mt. Graham. (4) **Capulin Arctic,** *O. a. capulinensis* F. M. Brown. Appearance varies. Local. TL: Capulin Mt., Union Co., N.M., 8200 ft.

**WHITE-VEINED ARCTIC** *Oeneis taygete* Geyer            **Pl. 5**
**Identification:** $1\frac{1}{2}$–$1\frac{3}{4}$ in. (38–44 mm). *Upperside:* Dull brown, with dark, narrow borders; many have small, light submarginal spots. Dark median band on underside of HW shows through. *Underside:* HW band darker brown, *bordered on each side by white or ashy scaling; veins white* or light-colored. **Adults:** June–Aug.
**Range:** Arctic N. America southward at high elevations to Colo.
**Habitat:** Steep grassy slopes, to 12,000 ft. (3660 m).
**Subspecies:** (1) **White-veined Arctic,** *O. t. taygete* Geyer. Manitoba east to Baffin I., Newfoundland and Quebec; probably not in our area. TL: Hopedale, Labrador. (2) **Edwards' White-veined Arctic,** *O. t. edwardsi* dos Passos, Pl. 5. Mountains of British Columbia, Alberta, Mont., Wyo., Colo. TL: San Juan Mts., Hindale Co., Colo. (3) **Ford's Arctic,** *O. t. fordi* dos Passos. White scaling on underside of HW reduced. Alaska, Dist. of Mackenzie, Yukon Terr. TL: Kuskokwim R., Alaska.
**Remarks:** The taxonomic status and ranges of the butterflies in the White-veined Arctic–Boreal Arctic species complex are not entirely understood, and are still under study.

**BOREAL ARCTIC** *Oeneis bore* (Schneider)            **Pl. 6**
**Identification:** $1\frac{5}{8}$–$1\frac{7}{8}$ in. (41–47 mm). Wings *very thinly scaled,* translucent. *Upperside:* Medium brown, often with *small, round, light spots between HW veins. Underside:* Brown, dark-bordered median band across HW; *much white scaling* on rest of HW. Veins sometimes light, but not truly white. Markings often show through to upperside. **Adults:** June–July. They sometimes sit on fallen logs.
**Similar species:** White-veined Arctic (above).
**Range:** Holarctic. Alaska east to Hudson Bay, south to Yukon Terr.; n. Europe, n. Asia. **Habitat:** Rocky areas in taiga, tundra; rock outcrops.
**Subspecies:** (1) *O. b. bore* (Schneider). N. Europe; not in N. America. TL: Lapland. (2) **Boreal Arctic,** *O. b. hanburyi* Watkins. E.-cen. Alaska to Northwest Terr., east to Hudson Bay. TL: Coronation Gulf, Northwest Terr. (3) **Mt. McKinley Arctic,**

*O. b. mckinleyensis* dos Passos, Pl. 6. Markings on underside of HW clean-cut; white scaling conspicuous. Cen. Alaska. TL: McKinley Natl. Park (now Denali Natl. Park and Preserve).

**JUTTA ARCTIC** *Oeneis jutta* (Huebner)     **Pl. 7**
**Identification:** 1⅞–2¼ in. (47–56 mm). *Upperside:* Dark brown. A light submarginal band or row of spots *encloses round black spots:* 3 spots on FW, 1–2 on HW. Fringes white-checkered. *Underside:* HW densely, finely striated with dark and light brown (dark gray and whitish in some subspecies). Median band of HW obscure or absent. **Adults:** June–July. They often sit on trunks of standing, living trees.
**Range:** Alaska south to Colo., east to Newfoundland and Me.; also n. Europe, Russia, and Siberia. **Habitat:** Acid bogs in east and north; taiga; lodgepole pine forest in Colo.
**Subspecies:** (1) *O. j. jutta* (Huebner). Not in N. America. TL: Lapland. (2) **Riding Mountains Arctic,** *O. j. ridingiana* F. & R. Chermock. Lighter in color. TL: Riding Mts., Manitoba. (3) **Leussler's Jutta Arctic,** *O. j. leussleri* Bryant. Very dark. Northwest Terr., Alberta. TL: Aklavik, Northwest Terr. (4) **Alaskan Jutta Arctic,** *O. j. alaskensis* Holland, Pl. 7, No. 2. Light markings on upperside of male reduced, those of female complete. Striations on underside dark, with much whitish overscaling. Alaska, Yukon Terr. TL: Between Forty-mile and Mission Creeks, Alaska. (5) **Rocky Mountain Jutta Arctic,** *O. j. reducta* McDunnough, Pl. 7, No. 1. Spots and markings reduced. Rocky Mts. from Mont. to Colo. TL: Upper Galatin Canyon, Mont.

**MELISSA ARCTIC** *Oeneis melissa* (Fabricius)     **Pl. 5**
**Identification:** 1⅝–1¾ in. (41–44 mm). Very plain looking. *Upperside:* Dull to dark grayish brown; *no eyespots* (or only a small one near FW apex — see Colorado subspecies on Pl. 5). Fringes light, with black checkering at vein tips. *Underside:* FW costa, apex, and entire HW flecked with light and dark brown; median band variable, often indistinct. **Adults:** June–early Aug.
**Similar species:** Polixenes Arctic (p. 56) is light gray to buffy. Wings thinly scaled, translucent; underside less heavily striated.
**Range:** Alaska east to Newfoundland, south in the West to Colo., N.M.; in East to N.H. **Habitat:** Elevated tundra, alpine fell-fields, above or north of treeline.
**Subspecies:** (1) **Melissa Arctic,** *O. m. melissa* (Fabricius). Labrador and Newfoundland (TL); not in our area. (2) **Northern Melissa Arctic,** *O. m. assimilis* Butler. Very dark, blackish. Far northern Arctic. TL: Repulse Bay, Northwest Terr. (3) **Gibson's Melissa Arctic,** *O. m. gibsoni* Holland. Median band on underside of HW usually distinct. Male lighter. Alaska. TL: Kuskokwim Valley, Alaska. (4) **Colorado Melissa Arctic,** *O. m. lucilla* Barnes & McDunnough, Pl. 5. Small eyespot. High mountains of Colo. and N.M., above treeline. TL: Hall Valley, Colo. (5) **Bean's Me-**

**lissa Arctic,** *O. m. beani* Elwes. Gray; median band obscure. High mountain summits, Alberta to Wyo. TL: Laggan, Alberta.

**POLIXENES ARCTIC** *Oeneis polixenes* (Fabricius)     **Pl. 7**
**Identification:** $1\frac{5}{8}$-$1\frac{3}{4}$ in. (41-44 mm). Wings thinly scaled, *translucent,* especially in male. *Upperside:* Dull gray to buffy, lighter toward margins, with a row of suffused submarginal spots in some subspecies. Male usually grayish, female often buffy. *Underside:* Few markings on FW. HW median band usually brown and well marked (sometimes faint to absent), bordered by white scaling. Vein-ends dark. **Adults:** June–July.
**Similar species:** Melissa Arctic (p. 55).
**Range:** Alaska east to Labrador, south in the West to Colo. and N.M. **Habitat:** Tundra; mountains above or north of treeline.
**Subspecies:** (1) *O. p. polixenes* (Fabricius). Not in our area. TL: Eastern Arctic America. (2) **Subhyaline Polixenes Arctic,** *O. p. subhyalina* (Curtis). Often quite buffy, especially female. Alaska, Northwest Terr. TL: Boothia Peninsula. (3) **Peart's Polixenes Arctic,** *O. p. peartiae* (W. H. Edwards). Dark, small. Far n.-cen. Arctic. TL: Winter Cove, Cambridge Bay, Victoria Land, Northwest Terr. (4) **Bruce's Polixenes Arctic,** *O. p. brucei* (W. H. Edwards), Pl. 7. Colo., N.M., above treeline. TL: Near Bullion and Hayden Mts., Hall Valley, Park Co., Colo. (5) **Yukon Polixenes Arctic,** *O. p. yukonensis* Gibson. Gray, slightly larger; very translucent. Alaska and Yukon Terr. TL: Klutlan Glacier, 8200 ft., Yukon Terr.

# MILKWEED BUTTERFLIES:
## Family Danaidae

Worldwide. Large, usually brightly colored; long-lived. Larvae feed on plants such as milkweed, ingesting poisonous juices that are said to repel birds and other predators. The Viceroy (p. 65) is reported to mimic the bright warning coloration of monarchs and thus gain protection from predators.
     **Early stages:** Larva smooth, with fleshy filaments at each end; whitish or greenish, with narrow dark rings (Fig. 5, p. 26). Pupa stout, cylindrical; suspended by cremaster only (no girdle). Milkweed butterflies as a group are unable to withstand cold weather.

**MONARCH or MILKWEED BUTTERFLY**     **Pl. 8**
*Danaus plexippus* (Linnaeus)
**Identification:** $3\frac{1}{2}$-4 in. (88-100 mm). *Upperside: Orange-brown, with black borders and veins;* many small white spots on borders and on FW apex. Male has *black sex pouch* on HW vein $Cu_2$.

**Similar species:** A mimic, the Viceroy (p. 65), is believed to use the Monarch as its model.
**Food:** Milkweed *(Asclepias)*, dogbane *(Apocynum)*. In Hawaii, crown flower *(Calotropis gigantea)* and other members of the milkweed family (Asclepiadaceae). **Adults:** Long flight season, almost all year in warmer areas; they become active on warm winter days. Monarchs sit or hang in great numbers on trees, especially eucalyptus and Monterey pines.
**Range:** S. Canada to S. America; introduced into Hawaii and now found on all the major islands. Found in many parts of the world where it was not native. **Habitat:** Fields, meadows, roadsides, yards, parks, gardens. In flight, likely to be anywhere.
**Remarks:** The Monarch is famous for its migrations and for gathering together in large, conspicuous groups during the winter. It is protected by city ordinance in Pacific Grove, Calif., where it overwinters.

**QUEEN** *Danaus gilippus* (Cramer)                              **Pl. 8**
**Identification:** 2⅝–3⅜ in. (66–84 mm). *Upperside: Purplish brown* (liver-colored); borders black, narrow. *Many small white spots* on borders and FW apex. Male (not shown) has black sex pouch on HW vein $Cu_2$. *Underside:* Veins outlined in black.
**Similar species:** (1) The Western Viceroy (a dark subspecies of the Viceroy, p. 65) mimics the Queen, but has a dark pm. line across HW that is absent in the Queen. (2) The Monarch (above) often occurs with the Queen, but has a different color pattern.
**Food:** Milkweed *(Asclepias)*, twinevine *(Sarcostemma)*, oleander *(Nerium)*, and others. **Adults:** Long flight season.
**Range:** Southern U.S. and south to S. America. **Habitat:** Very general; sometimes abundant on roadside flowers.
**Subspecies:** (1) *D. g. gilippus* (Cramer). S. America. TL: Rio de Janeiro, Brazil. (2) **Striated Queen**, *D. g. strigosus* (Bates), Pl. 8. Calif. east to Tex. and the Mississippi Valley, south to Cen. America; less common north to Nevada, Utah, cen. Colo., and Kans. TL: Guatemala.

# LONG-WINGS:
## Family Heliconiidae

Neotropical; ranges north to s. U.S. FW long, narrow. Antennae long; body slender. Many species in the tropics.

### Heliconians: Genus *Heliconius* Kluk

**ZEBRA** *Heliconius charitonius* (Linnaeus)                    **Pl. 8**
**Identification:** 3–3⅝ in. (75–91 mm). *Upperside:* Velvet black, banded with *bright yellow.* Unmistakable.

**Early stages:** Larva white with dark spots and 6 rows of branching spines. Pupa angular, with gold-tipped spines and 2 flat projections on head; said to make creaking sounds. Multiple broods. **Food:** Passion vine *(Passiflora).* **Adults:** Long-lived; have long flight season.
**Range:** Tropical America north to s. U.S. In West, s. Tex. north casually to Kans., Colo., Ariz. **Habitat:** Forest trails, parks, gardens, wood lots; usually keeps close to cover.
**Subspecies:** (1) *H. c. charitonius* (Linnaeus). Tropical. Not in U.S. TL: St. Thomas, Virgin Is. (2) **Zebra,** *H. c. vazquezae* W. P. Comstock & F. M. Brown, Pl. 8. Southern U.S., Mexico. TL: Campeche, Mexico.

<h3 style="text-align:center">Gulf Fritillary:<br>Genus Agraulis Boisduval & Le Conte</h3>

**GULF FRITILLARY** *Agraulis vanillae* (Linnaeus)      **Pl. 8**
**Identification:** 2–3 in. (50–75 mm). *Upperside:* Bright brownish orange; veins black. FW has 3 black spots with silver centers. HW border black, enclosing a row of orange spots. *Underside:* Basal ⅔ of FW orange-red; HW and apex of FW chocolate-brown, with numerous *brilliant silver spots.*
**Early stages:** Larva gray with orange stripes. Proleg bases and 6 rows of branching spines black; 1st pair of spines long and slanting forward. Pupa strange; flattened, with bulging wing covers and a humped thorax; it can move slightly to offer less surface to the sun. Multiple broods. **Food:** Passion vine *(Passiflora);* cultivated plantings have greatly expanded the range of this butterfly. **Adults:** Long flight season.
**Range:** North-central U.S. to Argentina. In West, n.-cen. Calif. east to Colo. (not breeding) and Kans. south to Ariz., N.M., and Tex. Wide-ranging; pushes north in summer, retreats south in winter. Introduced in 1977 on Oahu, Hawaii; now well established. **Habitat:** Wood lots, parks, yards, gardens, fencerows, roadsides. **Subspecies:** (1) *A. v. vanillae* (Linnaeus). Tropical America; not in the U.S. (2) **Gulf Fritillary,** *A. v. incarnata* (Riley), Pl. 8. Western U.S.; Mexico. TL: Durango City, Mexico.

<h2 style="text-align:center">LEAF-WINGS and EMPERORS:<br>Family Apaturidae</h2>

Cosmopolitan. Usually large, showy species. Structure very similar to brush-footed butterflies (Nymphalidae, p. 62), with which they previously have been included.

# Charaxines: Subfamily Charaxinae

Worldwide. Usually large, with powerful flight. Only one genus occurs in our area.

## Leaf-wings: Genus *Anaea* Huebner

Large. FW pointed, slightly hooked. Upperside brightly colored; underside resembles a dead leaf. Many tropical species.

**GOATWEED BUTTERFLY or LEAF-WING**  Pl. 8
*Anaea andria* Scudder
**Identification:** $2\frac{1}{4}$–$2\frac{5}{8}$ in. (56–66 mm). ***Upperside:*** Male *bright orange-red with narrow dark border.* Female duller; dark markings more extensive, *pm. band light.* **Underside:** Both sexes dull brown, resembling a dead leaf, with a short tail at end of vein $M_3$ on HW.
**Similar species:** In Tropical Leaf-wing (below), red of upperside darker. HW has 3 short tails.
**Early stages:** Larva green, tapering, covered with small raised points; it makes a shelter by folding a leaf. Pupa stout, with large wing covers that extend part way around sides. Two broods. **Food:** Goatweed *(Croton)*, in spurge family (Euphorbiaceae). **Adults:** April–Nov.; adults of 2nd brood overwinter. Flight very strong and fast. They sit on stems and tree trunks with head down, and visit honeydew and sap flows rather than flowers.
**Range:** E. Colo. and Neb. south to s. Ariz. and Tex.; east to Mich., Ohio, and Gulf States. **Habitat:** Old fields, woodland edges, roadsides.
**Subspecies:** (1) **Goatweed Butterfly,** *A. a. andria* Scudder, Pl. 8. Greater part of range. TL: Not stated. (2) **Arizona Goatweed Butterfly,** *A. a. ops* (Druce). Paler. S. Ariz. to Tex. TL: Texas. Considered a synonym of *A. a. andria* by some lepidopterists.

**TROPICAL LEAF-WING**  Pl. 8
*Anaea aidea* (Guérin-Ménéville)
**Identification:** $2\frac{1}{4}$–$2\frac{3}{8}$ in. (56–59 mm). Short curved tail at end of vein $M_3$; *very short tails at end of vein $Cu_2$ and anal angle.* Female very similar to male. ***Upperside:*** Dark red. FW costa, apex, and outer margin dark reddish brown; cell-end bar black. Narrow, irregular, dark submarginal line on FW. Pm. line dark, wavy. HW apex dark, border narrow, with a marginal row of small red spots; pm. line incomplete..
**Similar species:** Similar in habits and appearance to Goatweed Butterfly (above).
**Early stages:** Undescribed. **Food:** *Croton* (various species). **Adults:** April–Nov.

**Range:** S. Ariz. east to s. Tex., south to s. Mexico; casual in e. Colo. and w. Kans. **Habitat:** Streamsides, bottom lands.
**Subspecies:** (1) **Tropical Leaf-wing,** *A. a. aidea* (Guérin-Ménéville), Pl. 8. S. Tex., Mexico. TL: Taken on shipboard, Campeche Bay, Mexico. (2) **Morrison's Tropical Leaf-wing,** *A. a. morrisoni* (Edwards). Smaller, lighter. S. Ariz., Mexico. TL: Mt. Graham, Ariz.

# Emperors: Subfamily Apaturinae

## Hackberry Butterflies:
## Genus *Asterocampa* Roeber

Medium-sized. Tawny, with numerous small eyespots and 2 dark FW cell bars. All species have rather similar markings. FW pointed in male, rounded in female. Adults visit moisture, honeydew, and sap flows, but seldom flowers. Adults often abundant. May perch on tree trunks, fences, paved roads, cars, and even people!
    **Early stages:** Similar for all our species. Larva tapers to each end; last segment forked; large barbed horns on head. Color green or yellow, and striped. Overwinters as larva; 1 brood in north, 2 or more in south. **Food:** Hackberries (*Celtis,* various species), in the elm family.
    These butterflies were placed in the genus *Chlorippe* in some older books.

**HACKBERRY BUTTERFLY**                                      **Pl. 8**
*Asterocampa celtis* (Boisduval & Le Conte)
**Identification:**    $1\frac{3}{8}$ in.    (34 mm) — small    males — to    $2\frac{1}{2}$ in. (62 mm) — large females. *Upperside: 1st (inner) cell bar divided into 2 spots. Small eyespot* in cell $Cu_1$ of FW and also in cell $M_3$ in some subspecies. Dull brownish tan; FW apex and wing margins darker. Small white spots on FW; HW has submarginal row of black spots. *Underside:* Markings similar to those on upperside; HW spots larger, light-ringed.
**Similar species:** (1) In Empress Leilia (p. 61), FW cell bars on upperside brown, both complete. (2) Tawny Emperor (p. 61) and (3) Pallid Emperor (p. 61) both lack black eyespot in cell $M_3$ of FW.
**Early stages:** Two broods in north, 3 in south. **Food:** Hackberry (*Celtis,* various species). **Adults:** May–Nov.
**Range:** S. Canada, n. plains states, and e. Colo. east to New England, south to Ariz. and Tex.; Mexico. **Habitat:** Open woodland, parks, and wooded roadsides, in association with hackberry.
**Subspecies:** (1) **Hackberry Butterfly,** *A. c. celtis* (Boisduval & Le Conte). One dark eyespot in FW. Found in northeastern part of our area. TL: Georgia. (2) **Antonia's Hackberry Butterfly,** *A. c. antonia* (W. H. Edwards). Two dark eyespots on underside of FW in male; 2 eyespots on upperside and underside of FW in female.

Light tawny. E. Colo. and w. Kans. south to Tex., Mexico. TL:
Norse, Bosque Co., Tex. (3) **Mountain Hackberry Butterfly,**
*A. c. montis* (W. H. Edwards), Pl. 8. Bright tawny; 2 eyespots on
upperside and underside of FW. Ranges east from Ariz. to meet
Antonia's Hackberry Butterfly. TL: Ft. Grant, Graham Mts., Co-
chise Co., Ariz.
**Remarks:** Some lepidopterists consider these subspecies to be dis-
tinct species.

## EMPRESS LEILIA                                          Pl. 8
*Asterocampa leilia* (W. H. Edwards)
**Identification:** $1\frac{1}{2}$-2 in. (38–50 mm). General markings much
like those of other members of the genus. *Upperside:* Rich reddish
brown; markings clear, bright. FW has *2 eyespots; cell bars brown,
both complete.* Often sits on rocks or bare earth.
**Similar species:** (1) Hackberry Butterfly (above). (2) Tawny
Emperor (below). (3) Pallid Emperor (below).
**Early stages:** Two broods. **Adults:** May–Nov.
**Range:** Ariz. to s. Tex.; n. Mexico. **Habitat:** Streamsides, washes,
canyons, thorn forest.
**Subspecies:** (1) **Empress Leilia,** *A. l. leilia* (W. H. Edwards),
Pl. 8. Ariz.; Sonora, Mexico. TL: Camp Lowell and Sonoita Valley,
Ariz. (2) **Cocles' Emperor,** *A. l. cocles* (Lintner). Darker. S. Tex.
and adjacent Mexico. TL: Hidalgo, Tex.

## TAWNY EMPEROR                                           Pl. 8
*Asterocampa clyton* (Boisduval & Le Conte)
**Identification:** $1\frac{5}{8}$-$2\frac{3}{4}$ in. (41–69 mm). *Upperside:* Bright red-
dish brown. *No dark eyespot on FW;* FW *cell bars black, com-
plete.* General pattern much like others of genus. Variable; HW
may be *heavily smudged with blackish brown.* **Underside:**
Ground color light in male, dark markings stand out; spot row on
HW clouded. Female usually larger and lighter, less clearly
marked.
**Similar species:** (1) Hackberry Butterfly (p. 60). (2) Empress
Leilia (above). (3) Pallid Emperor (below).
**Early stages:** Two broods. **Adults:** June–Aug.; to Nov. in s. Tex.
**Range:** N.D. south to Tex., east to New England. **Habitat:** Open
woodland, streamsides, fencerows, parks.
**Subspecies:** (1) **Tawny Emperor,** *A. c. clyton* (Boisduval & Le
Conte). Northern and eastern part of range. TL: "America
Meridionale" — probably Georgia. (2) **Texas Tawny Emperor,**
*A. c. texana* (Skinner), Pl. 8. Lighter; HW much less often dark-
smudged. Cen. and s. Tex. TL: Round Mountain, Tex.

## PALLID EMPEROR                                          Pl. 8
*Asterocampa subpallida* (Barnes & McDunnough)
**Identification:** $1\frac{3}{4}$-$2\frac{1}{2}$ in. (44–62 mm). *Upperside:* Reddish
tawny, dark markings mostly on outer half of wings. *Light mark-*

*ings yellowish,* not white as in Empress Leilia (p. 61) and
Hackberry Butterfly (p. 60). *Dark eyespot on FW absent* (as in
Tawny Emperor). *Underside:* Male very light, dark markings less
distinct. Female pale yellowish brown; dark markings brown, in-
distinct.
**Similar species:** (1) Hackberry Butterfly (p. 60). (2) Empress
Leilia (p. 61). (3) Tawny Emperor (p. 61).
**Early stages:** Little known. Egg less spherical, and horns on head
of larva less branched, than that of Tawny Emperor. Probably 2
broods. **Adults:** At least June–Sept., perhaps longer.
**Range:** Restricted, so far as known, to mountain ranges of s. Ariz.
**Habitat:** Permanent streamsides; frequents sandbars.

# BRUSH-FOOTED BUTTERFLIES:
## Family Nymphalidae

Cosmopolitan; many species. Small to large; bright to dull colored.
Front legs greatly reduced in both sexes. Veins of FW not swollen
at base except in a few genera. HW discal cell usually open. Antennae finely scaled (unscaled in milkweed butterflies — Danaidae,
p. 56).
   **Early stages:** Larva has branching spines (Fig. 5, p. 26). Pupa
often has projections; hangs by cremaster only (Fig. 6, p. 27).

## Dagger-wings: Subfamily Marpesiinae

### Dagger-wings: Genus *Marpesia* Huebner
HW has long tail; shorter tail at anal angle. Tropical.

**MANY-BANDED DAGGER-WING**                                 **Pl. 9**
*Marpesia chiron* (Fabricius)
**Identification:** $2\frac{1}{8}$–$2\frac{3}{8}$ in. (53–59 mm). *Upperside:* Narrow verti-
cal bands of light and dark brown. No similar species in our area; a
straggler, not established.
**Range:** S. Tex. north rarely to Kans. Tropical America. TL:
"India."

**RUDDY DAGGER-WING** *Marpesia petreus* (Cramer)    **Pl. 9**
**Identification:** $2\frac{3}{4}$–3 in. (69–75 mm). FW *pointed, hooked.*
*Upperside:* Bright orange-brown; costa, border, and *3 narrow
bands dark. Underside:* Pale iridescent brown. Two narrow dark
lines and small black spots produce a "dead-leaf" effect.
**Early stages:** Larva red-brown; rear part of abdomen yellow
above and below. Sides have black spots and oblique black lines
edged with white. Abdominal segments have filaments. Head yellow spotted with black, with 2 long, hairy horns. Multiple broods.
**Food:** Fig (*Ficus,* various species). **Adults:** Long flight season.

**Range:** S. Tex., s. Fla.; tropical America. Occasional in Ariz., Colo., and Kans. TL: Surinam.

# Admirals and Relatives:
# Subfamily Limenitidinae

## Hyperia: Genus *Biblis* Fabricius

**HYPERIA** *Biblis hyperia aganisa* Boisduval      **Pl. 9**
**Identification:** 2-2⅜ in. (50–59 mm). Black with a bright red submarginal band across lower HW. Unique.
**Early stages:** Mature larva green with rose and brown spots; large horns on head; moderate body spines grow from red tubercles. Number of broods not stated. **Food:** Noseburn (*Tragia,* various species, in Euphorbiaceae). **Adults:** Occasional in our area.
**Range:** S. Tex. from Big Bend Natl. Park to San Antonio and Brownsville; tropical America. Uncommon to casual in U.S. TL: St. Thomas I. **Habitat:** Thorn forest, parks, gardens, streamsides.

## Bag-wings: Genus *Mestra* Huebner

Wings thin, fragile. Veins at base of FW swollen, as in satyrs and wood nymphs (Satyridae, p. 36).

**AMYMONE or TEXAS BAG-WING**      **Pl. 9**
*Mestra amymone* (Ménétriés)
**Identification:** 1⅜-1¾ in. (34–44 mm). *Slow, floating flight.*
*Upperside:* White; base, costa, and borders dark gray. *Lower half of HW pale orange.* **Underside:** Pale orange marked with white.
**Early stages:** Larva has 2 long spines on head, each ending in a crest of smaller spines. Multiple broods. **Food:** Noseburn (*Tragia,* various species, in family Euphorbiaceae). **Adults:** Long flight season.
**Range:** Cen. Ariz. (uncommon) to s. Tex. (common); tropical America. Strays to Colo., Neb., Kans. TL: Nicaragua. **Habitat:** Open woodland, canopy of thorn forest, forest trails.

## Admirals and Viceroys:
## Genus *Basilarchia* Scudder

Large. Antennae long, gradually clubbed. Some species tend to hybridize.
   **Early stages:** Larva odd-looking; body tapers toward rear, with 2 spiny projections on mesothorax and humps on 2nd, 7th, and 8th abdominal segments. Partially grown larva hibernates in a case made by rolling a leaf. Pupa has strong, rounded dorsal projections. 1–2 broods in north, 2–3 in south.
   Members of this genus have often been placed in the genus *Limenitis.*

**WHITE ADMIRAL** *Basilarchia arthemis* (Drury)     **Pl. 9**
**Identification:** 2¼–3⅛ in. (56–78 mm). *Upperside:* Black; *pm.
band and spots at FW apex white.* Outer ⅓ of HW usually has a
row of *red spots,* and *pale blue shades, spots,* or *crescents.* Variable. *Underside:* Markings similar. Spots in FW and HW dull red.
Light crescents along FW and HW borders.
**Similar species:** (1) In Weidemeyer's Admiral (p. 65), red spots
and blue markings are reduced. (2) In Lorquin's Admiral (p. 66),
tip of FW rusty red. (3) In the Sister (p. 67), tip of FW light orange.
**Early stages:** 1–2 broods. **Food:** Birch *(Betula),* willows *(Salix),*
aspen, poplar, cottonwood *(Populus),* hawthorn *(Crataegus),* and
wild cherry *(Prunus).* Also reported on oak *(Quercus)* and cultivated fruit trees. **Adults:** June–Sept.
**Range:** Alaska south to British Columbia, Mont., east to e. Canada, New England, and mid-Atlantic states. **Habitat:** Forest
edges, openings, open woodland roadsides, trails.
**Subspecies:** (1) **White Admiral,** *B. a. arthemis* (Drury). Red
markings reduced. Eastern U.S. TL: New York. (2) **Northern
White Admiral,** *B. a. rubrofasciata* Barnes & McDunnough,
Pl. 9. Cen. Alaska to British Columbia, Mont., S.D., east to Manitoba. TL: Manitoba, Saskatchewan, Alberta.
**Remarks:** The White Admiral and the Red-spotted Purple
(below) have long been considered two separate species. They are
now treated as a single species because they hybridize extensively
where their ranges meet and overlap. Since they are totally different in appearance throughout their respective ranges (except in or
near the overlap zone where hybrid specimens with a mixture of
characters may be seen), we have described them in separate accounts.

**RED-SPOTTED PURPLE**     **Pl. 9**
*Basilarchia arthemis* (Drury)
**Identification:** 2¼–3⅜ in. (56–84 mm). Somewhat resembles the
Pipe-vine Swallowtail (p. 115, Pl. 19), which it may mimic.
*Upperside:* Blackish; *no broad white pm. band.* FW has a narrow,
broken, submarginal line that appears as a series of whitish spots.
*Median rays* and *submarginal crescents* on HW *bluish green;*
crescents sometimes whitish. *Underside:* Cell bars on FW, 3 spots
near base of HW, and submarginal spots *orange-red.* Crescents at
margin greenish.
**Similar species:** Pipe-vine Swallowtail (p. 115) has tails, is more
glossy green, and has red spots on underside only.
**Early stages:** 1–2 broods. **Food:** Wild cherry *(Prunus,* various
species), poplars and aspens *(Populus,* various species), black oaks
*(Quercus,* various species), hawthorn *(Crataegus),* and deerberry
*(Vaccinium staminium).* **Adults:** May–Sept., depending on locality.
**Range:** More southern than White Admiral (above). S.D. to Ariz.
and w. Tex.; east to New England and cen. Fla. **Habitat:** In the

West, permanent mountain streamsides and wooden canyons.
**Subspecies:** (1) **Red-spotted Purple,** *B. a. astyanax* (Fabricius).
Submarginal spots on upperside of HW crescent-shaped, bluish
green; a series of red spots on FW below apex. S.D., Neb.,
Kans., e. U.S. TL: America. (2) **Arizona Red-spotted Purple,**
*B. a. arizonensis* (W. H. Edwards), Pl. 9. Submarginal spots on
upperside of HW chevron-shaped, whitish; no red spots on FW
below apex. Ariz., N.M., w. Tex. TL: Near Tucson, Ariz.

**VICEROY** *Basilarchia archippus* (Cramer)                **Pl. 9**
**Identification:** 2½–3 in. (62–75 mm). Mimics the Monarch (p. 56).
*Upperside:* Orange-brown; borders and bar below apex black,
enclosing a row of small white spots. HW has narrow *black median
line. Underside:* Markings similar to upperside; ground color
paler.
**Similar species:** (1) Monarch (p. 56) and (2) Queen (p. 57) lack
black median line on HW.
**Early stages:** 1–3 broods. **Food:** Willow *(Salix),* poplar and cot-
tonwood *(Populus),* plum and cherry *(Prunus),* and hawthorn
*(Crateagus).* **Adults:** April–Nov., depending on locality.
**Range:** S. Canada and much of the U.S. In the West, e. Wash. east
to N.D., south to se. Calif. and Tex. Does not occur in the higher
Rocky Mts., nor on the Pacific coast. **Habitat:** Open woodland,
fencerows, willow thickets, streamsides, bottoms.
**Subspecies:** (1) **Viceroy,** *B. a. archippus* (Cramer). Eastern
N. America to Mont., Colo., and s. Canada. TL: Jamaica. (2)
**Watson's Viceroy,** *B. a. watsoni* dos Passos, Pl. 9, No. 5. FW
darker than HW; HW median line *heavy.* La., Tex. TL: Alexandria, La. (3) **Western Viceroy,** *B. a. obsoleta* (W.H. Edwards), Pl. 9,
No. 6. Mimics the Queen (p. 57); formerly considered a separate
species. *Livid brown.* Median line of HW edged with white inwardly. S. Utah, se. Calif., east to w. Tex. (4) **Nevada Viceroy,**
*B. a. lahontani* (Herlan). *Very pale.* E. Wash. south to cen. Nev.,
east to Idaho, Utah, and w. Colo. TL: Fernley, Lyon Co., Nev.

**WEIDEMEYER'S ADMIRAL**                              **Pl. 9**
*Basilarchia weidemeyerii* (W.H. Edwards)
**Identification:** 2¼–3 in. (56–75 mm). *Upperside:* Black, with a
*white median band,* white spots below apex, and submarginal
band of small white dots. Red spots reduced or absent. *Underside:*
FW markings repeated. Cell bars dull red. Dark crosslines be-
tween veins at base of HW. Pm. band with reddish spots or cres-
cents; submarginal and marginal crescents greenish or bluish.
**Similar species:** (1) White Admiral (p. 64). (2) Lorquin's Admiral
(p. 66).
**Early stages:** 1–2 broods. **Food:** Aspen *(Populus tremuloides),*
cottonwood *(Populus,* various species), willow *(Salix).* **Adults:**
June–Aug.
**Range:** S. British Columbia south to e.-cen. Calif., east to N.D.

and N.M. **Habitat:** Deciduous forest in mountain areas; streamsides and edges of coniferous forest.
**Subspecies:** (1) **Weidemeyer's Admiral,** *B. w. weidemeyerii* (W.H. Edwards), Pl. 9. Cen. Rocky Mts. TL: Lakewood, Jefferson Co., Colo. (2) **Narrow-banded Admiral,** *B. w. angustifascia* Barnes & McDunnough. White band narrower. S. Utah, w. Colo., Ariz., w. N.M. TL: White Mts., Ariz. (3) **Oberfoell's Admiral,** *B. w. oberfoelli* (F.M. Brown). Red spots on upperside of HW distinct. Western N.D., w. S.D., w. Neb. TL: Badlands, Slope Co., N.D. (4) **Nevada Admiral,** *B. w. nevadae* Barnes & Benjamin. White band narrow. Underside of HW heavily scaled with bluish gray, the red spots suppressed. Spring Mts., Nev. TL: Clark Co., Nev. (5) **Wide-banded Admiral,** *B. w. latifascia* (E. M. & S. F. Perkins). White band wide. E. Calif., Nev., se. Idaho, Utah, w. Wyo. TL: Mink Creek, Bannock Co., Idaho.
**Remarks:** Weidemeyer's Admiral hybridizes with Lorquin's Admiral (below) where their ranges meet, resulting in Friday's Admiral (below).

## LORQUIN'S ADMIRAL                                    Pl. 9
*Basilarchia lorquini* (Boisduval)
**Identification:** 2–2⅝ in. (50–66 mm). *Upperside:* Black; median band white. FW *apex orange-brown,* without dark border. *Underside:* Ground color reddish brown.
**Similar species:** (1) White Admiral (p. 64). (2) Weidemeyer's Admiral (above). (3) Sister (p. 67). (4) See hybrid (below).
**Early stages:** 1–3 broods, depending on latitude. **Food:** Willow *(Salix),* poplar, cottonwood *(Populus),* wild cherry *(Prunus).* Orchard trees, such as cherry, prune, plum, and apple. **Adults:** March–Oct., depending on locality.
**Range:** British Columbia to s. Calif., east to w. Colo.; Baja California. **Habitat:** Forest edges, wood lots, streamsides, orchards, parks, planted groves and fencerows of poplar and cottonwood.
**Subspecies:** (1) **Lorquin's Admiral,** *B. l. lorquini* (Boisduval), Pl. 9. Southern part of range. TL: California. (2) **Burrison's Admiral,** *B. l. burrisoni* (Maynard). Orange-brown area at FW apex smaller. Northern. TL: British Columbia.

## FRIDAY'S ADMIRAL                                     Pl. 7
*Basilarchia weidemeyerii* × *lorquini*
**Identification:** 2¼–2⅝ in. (56–66 mm). A hybrid between Weidemeyer's Admiral and Lorquin's Admiral (above). General appearance similar to that of Weidemeyer's Admiral, but has a small brown *patch at FW apex,* like Lorquin's Admiral. Originally described as a form of Lorquin's Admiral; quite rare.
**Range:** E. Calif., notably near Mono Lake, where the ranges of these two species meet. TL: Lee Vining Creek, Mono Co., Calif.

## Sisters: Genus *Adelpha* Huebner

Found in the New World tropics. Only 1 species enters our area. Early stages quite similar to those of admirals (*Basilarchia*, p. 63).

**SISTER** *Adelpha bredowii* (Geyer)                    **Pl. 10**
**Identification:** 2¼–3 in. (56–75 mm). *Upperside:* Brownish black; white median band irregular on FW, narrowed and tapering on HW. *Orange patch at FW apex has dark border.* *Underside:* Pattern complex, with prominent *lavender-blue shades.*
**Similar species:** In Lorquin's Admiral (p. 66), patch at FW apex lacks dark border.
**Early stages:** 1–2 broods. **Food:** Oaks (*Quercus,* various species).
**Adults:** June–Sept. in Calif., flight season longer in Tex.
**Range:** Ore. east to Colo., south to s. Calif., Ariz., s. Tex.; Mexico. Absent from great areas in the West where oaks do not grow. **Habitat:** Oak-covered hills, canyons, woodlands.
**Subspecies:** (1) *A. b. bredowii* Geyer. Not in U.S. TL: Mexico. (2) **Arizona Sister,** *A. b. eulalia* (Doubleday), Pl. 10. Larger; more heavily marked. Se. Calif. east to Tex.; Mexico. TL: Mexico. (3) **California Sister,** *A. b. californica* (Butler). Ore., Calif., occasional in s. Wash. TL: Calif.
**Remarks:** The Sister has at times been included in genus *Limenitis,* or in *Heterochroa,* a synonym of *Adelpha.*

# Tortoise-shells, Angle-wings, Red Admirals, Ladies, and Peacocks: Subfamily Nymphalinae

Holarctic. Medium to large in size. The long-lived adults often overwinter. This group includes some of our most common and conspicuous butterflies, as well as some rarities.

## Tortoise-shells: Genus *Nymphalis* Kluk

Outer wing margin wavy, toothed below FW apex and on lower ⅓ of HW. Inner margin of FW *straight* — concave in angle-wings (*Polygonia,* p. 69).
    **Early stages:** Larva has long branching spines. Pupa has short projections on top of each abdominal segment, a single thoracic hump, and projections at side of head. Eggs laid in masses, or in bands around twigs of food plants.

**COMPTON TORTOISE-SHELL**                    **Pl. 10**
*Nymphalis vau-album* (Denis & Schiffermueller)
**Identification:** 2½–2⅞ in. (62–72 mm). *Upperside:* Orange-brown; wing bases darker brown. FW has 3 bars at costa and 4–5 *discal spots,* all black. Spots below apex white, border brown;

submarginal line darker. *HW costal spot large, black,* bordered outwardly with *white.* **Underside** (not shown): Marbled gray and brown, wing bases and borders darker. HW has *small white V at outer end of cell.*
**Similar species:** California Tortoise-shell (below) is smaller, brighter.
**Early stages:** Larva green, spiny. Feeds in groups. One brood.
**Food:** Birch *(Betula),* willow *(Salix),* poplar, cottonwood *(Populus).* **Adults:** June to spring of following year, overwintering. Population fluctuates; common in some years, scarce in others.
**Range:** Alaska and Canada to n. Mont., n. Wyo.; eastern N. America south to Mo. and N.C. **Habitat:** Usually deciduous woodland.
**Subspecies:** (1) *N. v. vau-album* (Denis & Schiffermueller). European. TL: Austria. (2) **Compton Tortoise-shell,** *N. v. j-album* (Boisduval & Le Conte), Pl. 10. Eastern N. America to Colo. TL: N. America. (3) **Watson's Tortoise-shell,** *L. v. watsoni* (Hall). Alaska and British Columbia south to Mont., Wyo. Underside darker. TL: Sicamous, British Columbia.

## CALIFORNIA TORTOISE-SHELL                    Pl. 10
*Nymphalis californica* (Boisduval)
**Identification:** $1\frac{1}{4}$–$2\frac{1}{4}$ in. (44–56 mm). **Upperside:** Bright orange-brown. FW costa, apex, border, costal bars, and *3 small spots black.* Spots near apex small, white. HW border black; discal spot *not edged with white.* **Underside:** Mottled with dark brown; *basal half darker.* Resembles a dead leaf.
**Similar species:** Compton Tortoise-shell (above).
**Early stages:** Larva black, spiny, each spine blue at base; line on back pale. 1–3 broods. **Food:** Buckbrush, wild lilac, snow brush (all *Ceanothus* species); feeds on a wider variety of plants during outbreaks (see Remarks). **Adults:** Emerge in May–June and in fall, and overwinter. They fly in the fall, in winter on warm days, and in early spring.
**Range:** British Columbia south to s. Calif., east to Mont., Wyo., Colo., N.M.; less common easterly. Occasionally occurs much further east. **Habitat:** Brushland, chaparral, open woodland, forest edges, clearings.
**Subspecies:** (1) **California Tortoise-shell,** *N. c. californica* (Boisduval), Pl. 10. Most of range. TL: California. (2) **Herr's Tortoise-shell,** *N. c. herri* Field. Northern part of range. TL: Buckhorn Mts., Wash.
**Remarks:** This species is remarkable for its irregular outbreaks. It is scarce in some years, but in others builds up in vast numbers and attracts considerable public attention.

## MOURNING CLOAK *Nymphalis antiopa* (Linnaeus)     Pl. 10
**Identification:** $2\frac{1}{4}$–3 in. (56–75 mm). **Upperside:** Dark purplish

brown or maroon with *yellow wing borders.* Unique. The Camberwell Beauty of Britain; also called the Yellow-edge.
**Early stages:** Eggs laid in bands around twigs. Larva purplish black; prolegs and dorsal spots orange-red. Pupa wood brown, often attached to tree trunks. Two broods. **Food:** Willow *(Salix),* poplar, cottonwood *(Populus),* elm *(Ulmus);* eats planted elms in the West where elm is not native. Wild rose *(Rosa)* (less often); also reported on hackberry *(Celtis)* and hawthorn *(Crataegus).*
**Adults:** Much of year. Overwintering adults may appear on warm winter days.
**Range:** Alaska and Canada south to Mexico; Europe, n. Asia, Japan. **Habitat:** Woodlands, streamsides, parks, shade trees, yards.
**Subspecies:** (1) **Mourning Cloak,** *N. a. antiopa* (Linnaeus), Pl. 10. Temperate N. America. TL: Sweden. (2) **Northern Mourning Cloak,** *N. a. hyperborea* (Seitz). Arctic N. America. TL: Alaska.

### Tortoise-shells: Genus *Aglais* Dalman

**MILBERT'S TORTOISE-SHELL** Pl. 10
*Aglais milberti* (Godart)
**Identification:** 1⅝-2 in. (41–50 mm). *Upperside:* Blackish brown, with an orange (or partly yellow) *pm. band across FW and HW.* FW cell bars orange; HW borders enclose blue spots. *Underside* (not shown): Wood brown, wing bases darker.
**Early stages:** Larva greenish yellow, spiny; head has 2 whitish bumps. Feeds in colonies. 1–3 broods; overwinters as either pupa or adult. **Food:** Nettle *(Urtica).* **Adults:** May–Sept.; overwintering adults appear early in the spring, badly worn.
**Range:** Alaska east to Newfoundland, south to Calif., Ariz., W. Va. **Habitat:** Fields, moist brushlands, streamsides.
**Subspecies:** (1) **Milbert's Tortoise-shell,** *A. m. milberti* (Godart). Submarginal band entirely orange. Eastern N. America. TL: Philadelphia. (2) **Western Milbert's Tortoise-shell,** *A. m. furcillata* (Say), Pl. 10. Inner half of band yellow. Western N. America. TL: Northwest Terr.
**Remarks:** This butterfly has also been placed in the genus *Nymphalis.*

### Angle-wings: Genus *Polygonia* Huebner

Holarctic. Angle-wing species are separated by minor differences; they are tawny with complex dark markings. Outer margins of wings irregularly toothed, *inner margin of FW concave.* Males are often mottled on underside; females usually more uniform in color. Angle-wings are mainly forest insects. They seldom visit flowers but prefer sap, fruit juices, and honeydew.

**Early stages:** Larva slender, spiny. Pupa resembles bark or a dried leaf. Adults hibernate. Most species have 1 brood in the north, 2 in the south. The 1st (summer) brood is often darker on the upperside of the HW; 2nd (fall) brood is usually lighter.

Angle-wings are placed in the genus *Grapta* in older literature.

## QUESTION MARK                                    Pl. 11
*Polygonia interrogationis* (Fabricius)
**Identification:** $2\frac{3}{8}$–$2\frac{3}{4}$ in. (59–69 mm). Our largest angle-wing. FW apex somewhat *hooked,* HW tail *quite long.* **Upperside:** FW has a dark spot in cell $M_2$. **Underside:** FW costa flecked with white at base, silvery cell spot in HW shaped like a *question mark.*
**Early stages:** Caterpillar reddish brown. Two broods in West and North, more in South. **Food:** Elm *(Ulmus),* hackberry *(Celtis),* false nettle *(Boehmeria),* nettle *(Urtica),* hops *(Humulus).* **Adults:** Fresh adults in June and fall; they overwinter, then fly again in spring.
**Range:** S. Canada and U.S. east of Rocky Mts. In the West, s. Canada south to e. N.M. and Tex.; Mexico. TL: N. America.
**Habitat:** Wooded areas, hackberry woodland, fencerows; also parks, yards.

## HOP MERCHANT or COMMA                             Pl. 11
*Polygonia comma* (Harris)
**Identification:**      $1\frac{3}{4}$–2 in. (44–50 mm). Resembles the Satyr (below); both species are browner on underside than other angle-wings. **Upperside:** Inner spot in cell $Cu_1$ of FW absent or minute. HW border with *wide brown shading* (or entire HW dark); *light submarginal spots* on HW *small.* **Underside:** Mottled and banded with light and dark brown. Silver spot on HW shaped like an *inverted comma.* Underside more evenly brown in female.
**Similar species:** In Satyr Angle-wing (below), inner cell spot in FW cell $Cu_1$ is distinct.
**Early stages:** Larva dark brown to greenish. Two broods. **Food:** Hops *(Humulus),* nettle *(Urtica),* false nettle *(Boehmeria),* elm *(Ulmus).* **Adults:** Long flight season.
**Range:** Cen. Canada, eastern U.S. (east of Rocky Mts.); in the West, s. Canada and N.C. to Kans. and Tex. TL: Massachusetts.
**Habitat:** Woodland edges, trails, openings; hop fields.

## SATYR ANGLE-WING                                  Pl. 11
*Polygonia satyrus* (W. H. Edwards)
**Identification:** $1\frac{3}{4}$–$2\frac{1}{4}$ in. (44–56 mm). **Upperside:** Bright tawny; female often golden. *Two spots in FW cell $Cu_1$,* the inner spot smaller. HW has very little brown shading, a narrow border, and well-marked, light spots near margin. **Underside:** Banded light and dark brown. Silver spot on HW an *inverted comma,* as in Hop Merchant (above).
**Early stages:** One brood. **Food:** Nettle. **Adults:** Emerge June–

early Aug. Long-lived; they overwinter and reappear in early spring.
**Range:** Western and n.-cen. N. America, from Pacific Coast east to Newfoundland and N.Y. **Habitat:** Moist valleys, streamsides, fencerows; where nettle grows.
**Subspecies:** (1) **Satyr Angle-wing,** *P. s. satyrus* (W. H. Edwards). Lighter. Eastern. TL: Empire, Clear Creek Co., Colo. (2) **Western Satyr Angle-wing,** *P. s. neomarsyas* dos Passos, Pl. 11. Pacific Slope. TL: Salmon Meadows, Brewster, Wash.

## GREEN COMMA or FAUN                                    Pl. 11
*Polygonia faunus* (W. H. Edwards)
**Identification:** 1¾–2⅛ in. (44–56 mm). *Upperside:* Deep reddish brown, with heavy dark markings. *Wide dark borders* often cover about half of wing surface. Submarginal spots small but distinct. *Underside:* Dark, heavily mottled; *outer* ⅓ *has many greenish spots.* Silver spot in HW cell L-shaped.
**Similar species:** (1) Colorado Angle-wing (below) is small, with no green spots on underside. (2) Sylvan Angle-wing (below) is lighter; markings on underside have less contrast.
**Early stages:** One brood. **Food:** Black birch *(Betula lenta),* alder *(Alnus),* willow *(Salix),* gooseberry *(Ribes),* and azalea *(Rhododendron).* **Adults:** Emerge June–early Aug. Long flight season; they overwinter and reappear in spring.
**Range:** Most of N. America. In the West, cen. Alaska south to cen. Calif. and n. N.M. **Habitat:** In north, forest; on Pacific Slope, cool streamsides and canyons.
**Subspecies:** (1) **Green Comma,** *P. f. faunus* (W. H. Edwards). Northern and eastern. TL: Hunter, Green Co., N.Y. (2) **Rustic Angle-wing,** *P. f. rustica* (W. H. Edwards), Pl. 11. Western U.S. TL: Big Trees, Calaveras Co., Calif. (3) **Arctic Angle-wing,** *P. f. arctica* Leussler. Alaska, Northwest Terr., Yukon Terr., n. British Columbia. TL: Near Aklavik, Northwest Terr.

## COLORADO ANGLE-WING                                    Pl. 11
*Polygonia hylas* (W. H. Edwards)
**Identification:** 1⅝–1⅞ in. (41–47 mm). *Upperside:* Looks like a small Green Comma (above). *Underside: Silver cell spot on HW L-shaped.* Male heavily mottled with light and dark gray. Female less plainly mottled, coloration more even; may be quite dark.
**Similar species:** (1) Green Comma (above). (2) Sylvan Angle-wing (below).
**Early stages:** Unknown. Apparently 1 brood. **Adults:** July–Sept.
**Range:** Colo., s. Wyo., n. Ariz., n. N.M. TL: Berthoud Pass, Colo.
**Habitat:** Streamside woodland in mountain areas.

## SYLVAN ANGLE-WING                                      Pl. 11
*Polygonia silvius* (W. H. Edwards)
**Identification:** 2–2¼ in. (50–56 mm). Suggests a large, bright

Green Comma (p. 71). *Upperside:* HW borders wide, indefinite. *Light submarginal spots large,* wings edged with lavender-gray. *Underside:* Purplish brown; spots gray; mottling less distinct than on similar species. *Silver cell spot on HW C-shaped,* flattened.
**Similar species:** (1) Green Comma (p. 71). (2) Colorado Anglewing (p. 71).
**Early stages:** Egg pale green. Larva has complex pattern of black, tawny, and white. Pupa tan, marbled with olive and brown. One brood. **Food:** Western azalea *(Rhododendron occidentale).* **Adults:** May–Aug., perhaps longer.
**Range:** North-central counties and Sierra Nevada foothills of Calif. TL: Yosemite Valley, Calif. **Habitat:** Streamsides.
**Remarks:** Previously almost unknown, this species has been much better known since 1975. It is quite rare and local.

### ZEPHYR ANGLE-WING                    Pl. 11
*Polygonia zephyrus* (W. H. Edwards)
**Identification:** 1¾–2⅛ in. (44–53 mm). *Upperside:* Bright tawny. HW border diffuse. Light submarginal spots *shaped like arrowheads,* pointing inward; spots usually have *small dark centers. Underside:* Violet-gray to purplish brown. Area at base dark; outer area *much lighter,* with tiny dark etchings. Silver cell spot on HW thin; curved or L-shaped.
**Similar species:** Oreas Angle-wing (below) is darker on upperside and underside.
**Early stages:** Larva black; spines of front segments reddish buff, those of rear segments white. One brood. **Food:** Squaw currant *(Ribes cereum);* associated with planted elms in Colo. **Adults:** Emerge July–Aug. and overwinter; they reappear April–June.
**Range:** S. Canada east to Riding Mts., Manitoba. Western U.S. east to Great Plains, south to Calif., N.M. TL: Virginia City, Nev. **Habitat:** Forests, brushlands, and streamside woodland in mountain areas. At varied elevations, from foothills to treeline.

### OREAS ANGLE-WING                      Pl. 11
*Polygonia oreas* (W. H. Edwards)
**Identification:** 1⅝–1⅞ in. (41–47 mm). *Upperside: Bright rusty red-brown; wing borders dark,* well defined. Submarginal spots *chevron-shaped. Underside:* Pattern much like that of Zephyr Angle-wing (above), but ground color much darker. Silver cell mark on HW slender, L-*shaped.* A local and uncommon species.
**Early stages:** Little known. Capture dates suggest 2–3 broods. **Food:** Straggly gooseberry *(Ribes divericatus),* perhaps others. **Adults:** Those that overwinter appear in May; others June–Oct.
**Range:** Incompletely known, due to confusion with other species. Pacific Slope, British Columbia to Monterey Co., Calif. **Habitat:**

Coastal canyons and streamsides. In Calif. often associated with redwood forest.
**Subspecies:** (1) **Oreas Angle-wing,** *P. o. oreas* (W. H. Edwards), Pl. 11. Mostly in Calif. TL: California. (2) **Silenus Angle-wing,** *P. o. silenus* (W. H. Edwards). Underside darker. British Columbia south into Ore. TL: Portland, Ore.

### HOARY COMMA                                           Pl. 11
*Polygonia gracilis* (Grote & Robinson)
**Identification:** 1½-1⅞ in. (38-47 mm). *Upperside:* Rusty ground color somewhat dull. Wing bases clouded, borders quite wide, shading into ground color on HW. *Light submarginal spots small, triangular, bright. Underside:* Wing bases dark purplish brown, outer half *frosted with silver-gray.* Silver cell mark L-shaped.
**Similar species:** In Gray Comma (below) underside darker, with less contrast.
**Early stages:** Almost unknown. One brood. **Food:** Unknown.
**Adults:** Emerge July–Aug., overwinter, and fly again in spring.
**Range:** Northern. N.-cen. Alaska and Northwest Terr. south to British Columbia, east to ne. Canada, ne. U.S. Uncommon to scarce. TL: Mt. Washington, N.H. **Habitat:** Forest edges and openings; visits flowers of everlasting *(Gnaphalium).*

### GRAY COMMA *Polygonia progne* (Cramer)          Pl. 11
**Identification:** 1⅝-2 in. (41-50 mm). *Upperside:* Bright orange-brown. *HW border very wide,* sometimes nearly covering entire wing. Submarginal spots on HW *very small,* often partly absent. *Underside:* Wing bases charcoal gray, outer half lighter. Outer border of FW dark, enclosing 3-4 *obscure light chevrons.* Silver cell mark on HW slender, small, L-shaped.
**Similar species:** Hoary Comma (above).
**Early stages:** Larva yellowish brown, blotched and striped with olive; spines black. Two broods. **Food:** Gooseberry *(Ribes).*
**Adults:** Long flight season; they overwinter and reappear in spring.
**Range:** Cen. Canada east to Nova Scotia, southeast of Rocky Mts. to N.D., S.D., and Neb.; scarce in Kans. In eastern U.S. to N.C. TL: New York. **Habitat:** Woodland, forest trails; also yards and gardens.

## Red Admirals and Ladies:
## Genus *Vanessa* Fabricius

Active and fast-flying. The red admirals visit honeydew and sap flows, while ladies usually nectar at flowers.
    **Early stages:** Egg ovoid, vertically ribbed. Larva spiny; it makes a shelter by pulling leaves together with silk. Pupa brown or

gray, with golden or silver spots. 1–2 broods in North, 3 or more in South. In the North, these species hibernate as adults.

**RED ADMIRAL** *Vanessa atalanta* (Linnaeus)          **Pl. 10**
**Identification:** 1¾–2¼ in. (44–56 mm). *Upperside:* Black; *crossband* on FW and *marginal band* on HW *red.* Spots below apex in FW white.
**Similar species:** (1) The Kamehameha (below), found only in Hawaii, is larger, with more orange-red. (2) In hybrid of Red Admiral and West Coast Lady (Pl. 10), wing bases paler; row of black submarginal spots with light centers on HW.
**Food:** Nettle *(Urtica),* false nettle *(Boehmeria),* pellitory *(Parietaria).* In Hawaii, feeds on mamaki *(Pipturus albidus)* and other plants in the nettle family. **Adults:** Long flight season.
**Range:** N. Canada south through U.S. Also in Mexico, West Indies; introduced into Hawaii. Europe, Asia, N. Africa. **Habitat:** Streamsides, wood lots, fencerows, yards, and parks. Inhabits a variety of biotic communities and elevations; adults often wander far from place where they emerged.
**Subspecies:** (1) *V. a. atalanta* (Linnaeus). Europe; not in U.S. TL: Sweden. (2) *V. a. rubria* (Fruhstorfer), Pl. 10. Canada, U.S., Guatemala. TL: Mexico. Introduced into Hawaii and now widely distributed there.

**KAMEHAMEHA** *Vanessa tameamea* (Eschscholtz)          **Pl. 10**
**Identification:** 2¼–2⅝ in. (56–72 mm). A regal species. *Upperside:* Dull red-brown at base, outwardly black. FW has *broad orange-red crossband with 2 black spots;* light spots below apex. HW has *orange-red submarginal spots* with black dots at centers. *Underside:* FW markings repeated. HW mottled gray with a greenish overlay; median and submarginal bands light, very irregular.
**Similar species:** Red Admiral (above).
**Food:** Mamaki *(Pipturus albidus)* and several other plants in the nettle family. **Adults:** Long flight season. They often soar high above the underbrush; flight rapid when alarmed.
**Range:** The only nymphalid native to Hawaii; found only on the major Hawaiian islands. TL: Oahu. **Habitat:** Sunlit trails in mountains.

**PAINTED LADY** *Vanessa cardui* (Linnaeus)          **Pl. 10**
**Identification:** 2–2½ in. (50–62 mm). *Upperside:* Ground color pinkish tawny. Wing bases *heavily clouded with brown.* Cell spot at base of FW *oval, isolated, black.* Bar at FW costa white. Submarginal spots on HW small, *seldom blue-centered. Underside:* Pattern complex, but 2nd and 5th submarginal spots on HW largest.
**Similar species:** (1) In American Painted Lady (p. 75), under-

side of HW has 2 large eyespots. (2) In West Coast Lady (below), bar at FW costa orange; submarginal spots on HW blue-centered. **Early stages:** Larva greenish, head black and hairy; spine tufts yellowish to black. Multiple broods in South, often 1 brood in North. **Food:** Various thistles (*Carduus, Cirsium,* and *Silybum* — in family Asteraceae); nievitas *(Cryptantha),* and yellow fiddleneck *(Amsinckia,* in family Boraginaceae); also mallows *(Malva,* in family Malvaceae) and others. **Adults:** Feb.–Nov. in South; season shorter northward.
**Range:** N. America south of the true Arctic; S. America; introduced in Hawaii. Now established worldwide, except in Australia and New Zealand. TL: Sweden. **Habitat:** General.
**Remarks:** Also called Thistle Butterfly and Cosmopolite. In some years, population buildups in the Southwest culminate in extensive northerly migrations, from which adults do not return.

## AMERICAN PAINTED LADY          Pl. 10
*Vanessa virginiensis* (Drury)
**Identification:** $1\frac{3}{4}-2\frac{1}{4}$ in. (44–56 mm). *Upperside:* Unevenly tawny, lighter near middle of wings. *Small white spot* in cell $Cu_1$ of FW; white bar at costa. 2nd and 5th submarginal spots *large, blue-centered.* *Underside:* Pattern complex; HW has 2 *large eyespots.*
**Similar species:** (1) Painted Lady (above). (2) West Coast Lady (below).
**Early stages:** Larva black, with narrow yellow crossbands and a row of white spots on each side; spines black. Lives in nest near top of food plant. Hibernates as pupa or adult. 2–3 broods. **Food:** Cudweed *(Gnaphalium),* everlasting *(Anaphalis, Antennaria),* and mugwort *(Artemisia heterophylla),* all in the sunflower family (Asteraceae). **Adults:** May–Oct.
**Range:** N. America from Canada south to Cen. America. Introduced into Hawaii, now on all main islands. Also Azores, Madeira, and Canary Is. TL: Virginia. **Habitat:** Forest edges, streamsides, parks, roadsides, fencerows; coastal chaparral (in Calif.).

## WEST COAST LADY *Vanessa annabella* (Field)     Pl. 10
**Identification:** $1\frac{1}{2}-2$ in. (38–50 mm). *Upperside:* Bright orange-brown; *bar* at FW costa *orange* (white in most other *Vanessa* species). 2nd, 3rd, and 4th *submarginal spots* in HW *blue-centered.* *Underside:* Pattern complex; submarginal spots on HW reduced and obscured by other markings.
**Similar species:** (1) Painted Lady (p. 74). (2) American Painted Lady (above).
**Early stages:** Larva varies from tan to black; lined with yellow. Spines black. Lives in nest in rolled leaf. Multiple broods. **Food:** Mallow *(Malva),* tree mallow *(Lavatera),* globe mallow

*(Sphaeralcea)*, bush mallow *(Malvastrum)*, alkali mallow *(Sida)*, checkerbloom *(Sidalcea)*, hollyhock *(Althea)*, and other plants in the mallow family (Malvaceae). **Adults:** Much of year.
**Range:** British Columbia and Alberta south to s. Calif.; in Rocky Mts. to N.D., Mont., Colo., w. Kans (scarce) to w. Tex., south to Guatemala. TL: First valley west of Arroyo Verde Park, Ventura Co., Calif. **Habitat:** Clearings, roadsides, cultivated fields, yards, vacant lots, foothills, chapparal, and disturbed land where mallow grows.
**Remarks:** Previously confused with a South American species, the West Coast Lady will be found as *Vanessa carye* in literature published before 1971.
**Note:** The three Ladies — Painted, American Painted, and West Coast Lady — present a number of variations called aberrations, in which the normal pattern and color are somewhat altered. They have been given names although these names do not have taxonomic status. One of these, the West Coast Lady, *Vanessa annabella* ab. "muelleri," is pictured on Pl. 10 (No. 7). They are all considered rare, but several of these aberrations are seen fairly often in northern California.

## Peacock Butterflies: Genus *Junonia* Huebner

Widely distributed in the tropics of both the Old World and the New World. Outer margin of FW indented just below apex, which is square-cut.

### BUCKEYE or PEACOCK BUTTERFLY Pl. 11
*Junonia coenia* (Huebner)
**Identification:** $1\frac{5}{8}$–$2\frac{3}{8}$ in. (41–59 mm). *Upperside:* Brown. Two eyespots on each wing — upper spot on FW very small, lower one large. *Upper spot on HW largest, with rainbow colors;* lower spot on HW small. FW cell bars orange; bar below apex white. *Underside:* FW markings repeated. HW eyespots obscure or absent. Fall brood may be reddish or purplish on underside of HW.
**Similar species:** Dark Peacock (below) is very dark.
**Early stages:** Larva gray with yellow markings and black spines. One brood in north, 2 or more in south. **Food:** Plantain *(Plantago)*, monkey flower *(Mimulus)*, snapdragon *(Antirrhinum)*, verbena, and others. **Adults:** Have long flight season and may overwinter, appearing on warm days, and on the wing well into late fall. Aggressive; they often chase other butterflies.
**Range:** S. Canada south through the U.S. to tropical America. TL: Cuba. **Habitat:** Clearings, fields, roadsides, fencerows, streamsides, thorn forest, coastal grasslands; very general.

### DARK PEACOCK Pl. 11
*Junonia nigrosuffusa* Barnes & McDunnough
**Identification:** $1\frac{3}{4}$–$2\frac{1}{4}$ in. (44–56 mm). *Upperside: Very dark,*

often blackish. FW cell bars orange; band below apex dull orange when present, but often absent. All eyespots dark, seldom with rainbow colors; *lower eyespot on FW and upper eyespot on HW about the same size. Underside:* FW disc usually has a marked orange flush. Lower eyespot on FW prominent. An obscure pale median band and a slightly darker pm. band often visible.
**Similar species:** Buckeye (above).
**Early stages:** Undescribed. 2–3 broods. **Food:** In Tex., stemodia *(Stemodia tomentosa),* in the figwort family (Scrophulariaceae).
**Adults:** Long flight season. Wary; they usually fly away when disturbed, but may return later.
**Range:** S. Ariz. east to Gulf Coast and offshore islands of Tex., south into Mexico. TL: Palmerlee, Ariz. **Habitat:** Open places; fields, open brushlands in Ariz., sandy islands off Tex.

## Genus *Anartia* Huebner

**WHITE PEACOCK** *Anartia jatrophae* (Johannson)      **Pl. 10**
**Identification:** 2–2⅜ in. (50–59 mm). *Upperside:* White; markings at costa and outer margin light brown. A double row of light chevrons along wing margins. One prominent black eyespot in FW, 2 in HW. *Underside:* Similar to upperside, but eyespots ringed with orange or pink.
**Early stages:** Larva black with silver spots. Head has large branching spines; body has 4 rows of branching spines. Multiple broods. **Food:** Nettlespurge *(Jatropha),* water hyssop *(Bacopa),* fogfruit *(Phyla),* ruellia *(Ruellia).* **Adults:** Long flight season; in s. Tex., most common Sept.–Nov.
**Range:** S. Tex.; tropical America; Fla. Scarce in w. Tex., casual in Kans. **Habitat:** Woodlots, thorn forest, roadsides.
**Subspecies:** (1) *A. j. jatrophae* (Johannson). Tropical. TL: Brazil. (2) *A. j. luteipicta* Fruhstorfer, Pl. 10. S. Tex. to Cen. America. TL: Guatemala.

## Fritillaries: Subfamily Argynninae

Worldwide. A large group of small to large butterflies. Upperside tawny to reddish brown, with many small black markings, usually in rows or bands. Underside ornamented with light or silver spots on HW, and sometimes at apex of FW.

## Greater Fritillaries: Genus *Speyeria* Scudder

Large to medium-sized butterflies found only in N. America. Extremely variable; many subspecies are very dissimilar and were previously considered distinct species. Several species may be found in one locality.
**Early stages:** Eggs laid on or among dead vegetation. Larva dark, spiny; overwinters as a hatchling and develops the following

spring. Feeds at night. One brood. **Food:** Violets. **Adults:** Mid-summer or early fall. Females appear later in season than males.
In older literature, these butterflies are placed in the genus *Argynnis*.

**Terms used to describe species of *Speyeria* (see Fig. 10):**
***Border.*** Dark wing edge; includes fringes, marginal line, and sometimes submarginal chevrons.
***Disc.*** Center of underside of HW, as applied to butterflies in the genus *Speyeria*. In other butterflies, the word *disc* may refer to the center of FW or HW on upperside or underside.
***Postmedian (pm.) band.*** Area between median and submarginal spots, usually light; often called simply "the band."
***Sex scaling.*** Black scales along veins $M_1$–2A of FW; absent in Aphrodite (p. 80) and Mormon Fritillary (p. 85).
***Spangles.*** Silver spots on underside of HW that show through to upperside as light markings.
***Spots.*** Light (often silver) spots forming bands on underside of HW; the submarginal spots are often V-shaped or triangular.
***Submarginal chevrons.*** Triangular or V-shaped marks forming a submarginal line; on underside of HW they form the *shading* of silver submarginal spots.

**GREAT SPANGLED FRITILLARY**                              **Pl. 12**
*Speyeria cybele* (Fabricius)
**Identification:** $2\frac{1}{2}$–$3\frac{1}{2}$ in. (62–88 mm). **Upperside:** Male has *prominent sex scaling* on FW, along veins $M_1$ to 2A (see front endpapers). *Wing bases dark; outer half* of wings *lighter* than basal half. Submarginal markings well developed. Female larger, somewhat darker; female much darker in western subspecies. **Underside:** Disc brown; *band wide, yellowish*. All spots large and well silvered. **Adults:** Late May–Oct., depending on location.
**Similar species:** In Aphrodite (p. 80), male lacks sex scaling on FW. Band on underside of HW often obscure to absent.
**Range:** Alberta to Nova Scotia, south in the West to N.M.; in East to Ga. **Habitat:** Meadows, streamsides, aspen groves, open woodland, prairies, roadsides.
**Subspecies:** (1) **Great Spangled Fritillary,** *S. c. cybele* (Fabricius), Pl. 12, No. 1. N.D. south to Kans., east to New England. TL: New York. (2) **Chermocks' Fritillary,** *S. c. pseudocarpenteri* (F. & R. Chermock). Smaller, slightly darker. Alberta, Saskatchewan, Manitoba. TL: Sand Ridge, Manitoba. (3) **Carpenter's Fritillary,** *S. c. carpenterii* (W. H. Edwards). Small; female dark brown. S. Colo., N.M. TL: Taos Peak, Taos Co., N.M. (4) **Charlott's Fritillary,** *S. c. charlottii* (Barnes). On upperside, basal 2/3 of wings dark brown in male, blackish in female; outer half of wings orange-brown in male, dull yellowish in female. Colo. TL: Colorado Springs. (5) **Leto Fritillary,** *S. c. leto*

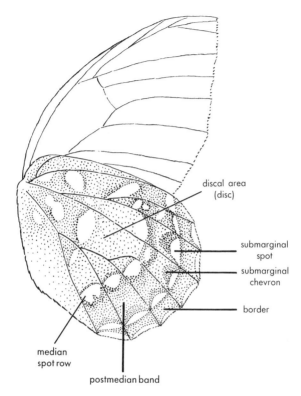

**Fig. 10. Fritillary: pattern on underside of hind wing.**

(Behr), Pl. 12, No. 3. Male bright red-brown on upperside; black markings narrow and irregular. Underside: *HW disc dark*. Female blackish on upperside, the submarginal band *straw-colored* (yellowish). Long considered a separate species. (6) **Letona Fritillary,** *S. c. letona* dos Passos & Grey. Smaller than Leto Fritillary; lighter, markings smaller. Utah. TL: City Creek Canyon, Salt Lake Co., Utah. (7) **Puget Sound Fritillary,** *S. c. pugetensis* F. Chermock & Frechin. Similar to Leto Fritillary but larger and darker. Pacific Northwest. TL: Stimson Creek, near Belfair, Mason Co., Wash.

**APHRODITE**                                                 **Pl. 12**
*Speyeria aphrodite* (Fabricius)
**Identification:** 2½–3 in. (62–75 mm). *Upperside:* Male orange-
brown; dark markings evenly spaced. Wing bases darkened
slightly or not at all; *no sex scaling* on veins $M_1$–2A of FW. Female
similar, but larger and with darker wing bases. *Underside:* HW
disc cinnamon brown to deep red-brown; *pm. band narrow* and
greatly invaded by disc color. Spots large, well silvered. **Adults:**
July–Aug.
**Similar species:** Great Spangled Fritillary (p. 78).
**Range:** British Columbia east to New Brunswick, south in the
West to Ariz. and Neb. In the East to N.C. Absent from Great
Basin and Pacific Slope. **Habitat:** Moist meadows, streamsides,
old fields, mountain slopes, prairies.
**Subspecies:** (1) **Aphrodite,** *S. a. aphrodite* (Fabricius). Eastern
N. America. TL: New York. (2) **Alcestis Fritillary,** *S. a. alcestis*
(W. H. Edwards). Underside of HW deep red-brown; usually no
band. West to Neb. TL: Galena, Jo Davies Co., Ill. (3) **Manitoba
Fritillary,** *S. a. manitoba* (F. & R. Chermock). Smaller, lighter;
reddish flush near HW base on upperside. Manitoba, Saskatche-
wan, N.D. TL: Sand Ridge, Manitoba. (4) **Whitehouse's
Fritillary,** *S. a. whitehousei* (Gunder). Large, heavily marked.
TL: Jaffray, British Columbia. Local. (5) **Columbian Fritillary,**
*S. a. columbia* (Hy. Edwards). Lightly marked on upperside. TL:
Lac La Hache, British Columbia. (6) **Ethne Fritillary,** *S. a. ethne*
(Hemming), Pl. 12. Mont., Wyo., Colo., Utah. TL: Big Horn Mts.,
near Sheridan, Wyo. (7) **Byblis Fritillary,** *S. a. byblis* (Barnes &
Benjamin). Small, lightly marked. Ariz., N.M., sw. Colo. TL:
White Mts., Ariz.

**REGAL FRITILLARY** *Speyeria idalia* (Drury)          **Pl. 7**
**Identification:** 2⅝–3½ in. (66–88 mm). *Upperside:* FW in male
bright orange-brown with black markings. HW black; median
spots white; *submarginal spots orange-brown.* Female similar,
except submarginal spots on HW are white. *Underside:* FW similar to upperside. HW deep olive; *spots large* and brilliantly
silvered.
**Adults:** Mid-June to mid-Sept. May occur in scattered local populations.
**Range:** In the West, Mont. and N.D. south to Colo., Neb., and
n. Okla. In East to Me. and Ga. **Habitat:** Wet meadows,
marshlands.

**NOKOMIS FRITILLARY**                                    **Pl. 12**
*Speyeria nokomis* (W. H. Edwards)
**Identification:** 2½–3⅛ in. (62–78 mm). *Upperside:* Male bright
brownish orange; wing bases lightly to greatly darkened. Dark
markings on outer half of wings small, widely spaced. *Submarginal
dark chevrons do not touch the very even, black marginal line.*

Female similar to female Leto Fritillary (subspecies of Great Spangled Fritillary, p. 78), but *yellowish band paler and wider.* Ground color grayish black to bluish black; outer ⅓ of wings with many cream-colored spots. *Underside:* In both sexes, HW disc yellowish to cinnamon brown, deep olive, or blackish, depending on subspecies. FW mostly orange-brown; *silver spots* on HW have *black edges.*

**Adults:** Late in year, late Aug.–Sept.

**Range:** Colo., Utah, Nev., Calif., Ariz., and N.M. south into Mexico. Known localities are widely separated due to restricted habitat. **Habitat:** Marshlands, boggy streamsides.

**Subspecies:** Subspecies differ mostly in color of HW disc. (1) **Nokomis Fritillary,** *S. n. nokomis* (W. H. Edwards). Disc light brown in male, deep olive in female. Colo., Utah. TL: Mt. Sneffels, Ouray Co., Colo. (2) **Nitocris Fritillary,** *S. n. nitocris* (W. H. Edwards). Disc deep reddish brown in male, black in female. Ariz. TL: White Mts., Ariz. (3) **Apache Fritillary,** *S. n. apacheana* (Skinner), Pl. 12. Disc yellowish buff in male, light olive-green in female. Ruby Lake, White Pine Co., Nev., to w.-cen. Nev. and e.-cen. Calif., east of Sierra Nevada. TL: "Arizona" (in error). (4) **Bluish Fritillary,** *S. n. coerulescens* (Holland). In male, wing bases on upperside dark; disc red-brown. In female, light markings on upperside bluish. The only known U.S. colony is near Sunnyside, Huachuca Mts., Ariz. TL: Rio Piedras Verdes, Chihuahua, Mexico.

## EDWARDS' FRITILLARY                                    Pl. 7
*Speyeria edwardsi* (Reakirt)

**Identification:** 2½–2¾ in. (62–69 mm). *Upperside:* Bright tawny, spangled. Dark markings moderate, evenly spaced; *dark border well marked,* with *chevrons that point inward. Underside:* HW spots large, brilliantly silvered, *oval* or *elongate.* Disc mottled with dull greenish-olive; pm. band poorly defined.

**Adults:** July–Aug.

**Range:** Alberta east to Manitoba, south to Colo. and Neb. **Habitat:** Meadows, fields, glades, roadsides. Seldom found above 10,000 ft. (3050 m) in Colo.

## CROWN FRITILLARY *Speyeria coronis* (Behr)          Pl. 12
**Identification:** 2–2¾ in. (50–69 mm). FW margin nearly straight. *Upperside:* Dull tawny to bright reddish brown (s. Calif.). Wing bases little darkened; wing borders moderately dark. Spangles well developed; median line only moderately wide. *Underside:* Disc mottled brown and buffy. Band narrow, invaded by *brown capping of triangular silver spots* at margin. All spots silvered, *not outlined in black* (but may be outlined in brown or gray). **Adults:** Late May–early Aug., depending on locality and elevation; usually found at low to middle elevations.

**Similar species:** In Zerene Fritillary (*platina-gunderi* pattern,

below), outer margin of FW somewhat concave; median line on upperside of FW quite wide.
**Range:** Wash. east to Wyo. and Neb., south to s. Calif., Nev., Colo.
**Habitat:** Various; meadows, openings, mountain slopes, foothills, sagebrush scrub. From sea level in Calif. to 9000 ft. (2745 m) in Colo.
**Subspecies:** (1) **Crown Fritillary,** *S. c. coronis* (Behr), Pl. 12. Coastal Calif., Lake Co. south to San Luis Obispo Co. TL: Gilroy, Santa Clara Co., Calif. (2) **Henne's Fritillary,** *S. c. hennei* (Gunder). Bright tawny. Tehachapi Mts. of Calif. TL: Mt. Pinos, Ventura Co., Calif. (3) **Semiramis Fritillary,** *S. c. semiramis* (W. H. Edwards). Bright brownish red. Mountains of s. Calif. TL: In vicinity of San Bernardino, Calif. (4) **Simaetha Fritillary,** *S. c. simaetha* dos Passos & Grey. Smaller; disc olive-buff. Cascade Range, Wash., Ore. TL: Black Canyon, near Brewster, Wash. (5) **Snyder's Fritillary,** *S. c. snyderi* (Skinner). Disc yellowish tan. Idaho south to Nev. and e. Calif., east to w. Wyo., n. Ariz. TL: City Creek Canyon, Salt Lake Co., Utah. (6) **Halcyone Fritillary,** *S. c. halcyone* (W. H. Edwards). Darker; disc brown. Colo. and e. Wyo., east of Continental Divide. TL: Estes Park, Larimer Co., Colo.

**ZERENE FRITILLARY** *Speyeria zerene* (Boisduval)       **Pl. 13**
**Identification:** $2\frac{1}{8}$–$2\frac{3}{4}$ in. (53–69 mm). FW margin *slightly concave. Upperside:* Bright red-brown to tawny, depending on subspecies. Median line usually *wide* and *dark* (narrower in Crown Fritillary, above). *Underside:* In HW, the *3 upper spots* in median band are *all separate;* 2nd spot round and larger, 3rd spot narrower, slanted away from 2nd. Color of disc, spot silvering and band differ among various subspecies.
**Adults:** June–Aug.
**Similar species:** (1) Hydaspe Fritillary (p. 85) resembles the *zerene* pattern (see Subspecies) and occurs in the same places, but spots on underside of HW unsilvered and median spot row more conspicuous. (2) Crown Fritillary (p. 81) resembles *platina-gunderi* pattern, but silver spots on underside of HW are not bordered with black.
**Range:** British Columbia east to Mont., south to cen. Calif., Ariz., N.M. TL: Yosemite Valley, Mariposa Co., Calif. Habitat and flight times differ among subspecies.
**Subspecies:** The 16 diverse subspecies may be grouped into 3 major patterns. (1) *zerene* pattern (Pl. 13, No. 1): Upperside red-brown, heavily marked; *spots on underside* of HW unsilvered or silvered. (2) *platina-gunderi* pattern (Pl. 13, No. 2): Upperside tawny. Underside of HW light grayish brown to straw-colored. *Spots silvered.* Great Basin and vicinity. (3) *picta-garreti* pattern (Pl. 13, No. 3): Upperside orange-brown, dark markings heavy, usually spangled. *Disc dull reddish brown* to grayish brown; spots

large, brightly silvered. British Columbia south to e. Ore., Rocky Mts.

## CALLIPPE FRITILLARY                                          Pl. 13
*Speyeria callippe* (Boisduval)
**Identification:** 2–2½ in. (50–62 mm). *Upperside:* Bright red-brown to light tawny, depending on subspecies. Usually spangled. Dark markings evenly spaced, giving a distinctive checkered or "lattice" appearance. *Underside:* Spots large, usually silvered. *Silver submarginal spots triangular, with narrow brown shading.*
**Adults:** May–July.
**Range:** British Columbia to Manitoba, south to s. Calif., Nev., Utah, Colo.; also S.D. TL: San Francisco, San Francisco Co., Calif.
**Habitat:** Varies with subspecies.
**Subspecies:** The 16 subspecies may be grouped into 3 patterns. (1) *callippe* pattern (Pl. 13, No. 4): Upperside light orange-brown to tawny; wing bases very dark. Dark markings heavy, often "sooty"; spangles very distinct. Underside: Disc mottled brown, spots silvered. Low elevations in Calif. (2) *liliana* pattern (Pl. 13, No. 5): Upperside bright red-brown; dark markings moderate to narrow. Underside: *Disc red-brown* to dull brown; band distinct, yellowish. Some populations unsilvered. Mountains of Calif., Ore. (3) *nevadensis* pattern (Pl. 13, No. 6): Upperside light orange-brown to light tawny; dark markings narrow. Underside: *Disc green* to dull greenish brown; spots usually silvered, sometimes dark-edged. Great Basin, Rocky Mts. Often associated with sage-brush habitat.

## LESSER UNSILVERED FRITILLARY                                 Pl. 13
*Speyeria adiaste* (W. H. Edwards)
**Identification:** 2–2⅜ in. (50–59 mm). *Upperside:* Male *bright brick red* (Santa Cruz Co.) to pale, washed-out tawny (s.-cen. Calif.). Female larger and paler than male. Dark markings small, scattered, except for *well-developed pm. line. Underside:* Pale, lavender-gray to dull yellowish; fresh specimens have a bluish gray overlay on underside of HW. *Spots unsilvered, inconspicuous.*
**Adults:** June–July. Very local. Numbers fluctuate from year to year.
**Range:** Restricted to Calif., from San Mateo Co. south to San Luis Obispo Co., east to Kern Co. and n. Los Angeles Co. **Habitat:** Glades in redwood forest, mixed coniferous forest; in south, chaparral and oak woodland.
**Subspecies:** (1) **Lesser Unsilvered Fritillary,** *S. a. adiaste* (W. H. Edwards), Pl. 13. San Mateo and Santa Cruz Cos. TL: Santa Cruz. (2) **Clemence's Fritillary,** *S. a. clemencei* (J. A. Comstock). Lighter, approaching tawny. Monterey Co., San Luis Obispo Co. TL: Atascadero, San Luis Obispo Co. (3) **Unsilvered Fritillary,** *S. a. atossa* (W. H. Edwards). Larger; very pale,

bleached appearance. Tehachapi Mts. TL: Tehachapi, Kern Co., Calif. Now very rare, not seen for years. Considered extinct.

**EGLEIS FRITILLARY** *Speyeria egleis* (Behr)            **Pl. 12**
**Identification:** $1^{3}/_{4}$–$2^{3}/_{8}$ in. (44–59 mm). *Male has sex scaling on FW veins* (absent in male Mormon Fritillary, p. 85). *Upperside:* Light to dull orange-brown. Dark markings moderate, evenly spaced. *Underside:* Spots small, separate, with narrow, dark edges inwardly and heavy dark shading outwardly. Spots usually silvered, but unsilvered in some subspecies. Color of HW disc differs among subspecies.
**Adults:** July–Aug.
**Similar species:** Mormon Fritillary (p. 85) is smaller; dark markings usually narrower. Male lacks sex scaling on FW veins.
**Range:** Ore. east to N.D., south to Calif. and Colo. **Habitat:** Mountain meadows at middle to high elevations.
**Subspecies:** (1) **Egleis Fritillary,** *S. e. egleis* (Behr), Pl. 12. Disc on underside of HW dull brown; band lighter. Sierra Nevada. TL: Gold Lake, Sierra Co., Calif. (2) **Tehachapi Fritillary,** *S. e. tehachapina* (J. A. Comstock). Unsilvered or nearly so. TL (and range): Tehachapi Mts., Kern Co., Calif. (3) **Owen's Fritillary,** *S. e. oweni* (W. H. Edwards). Small, brightly silvered. N. Calif., s. Ore. TL: Mt. Shasta, Siskiyou Co., Calif. (4) **Linda Fritillary,** *S. e. linda* (dos Passos & Gray). Disc brownish yellow. Sawtooth Mts., Idaho. TL: Heyburn Peak, Custer Co., Idaho. (5) **McDunnough's Fritillary,** *S. e. mcdunnoughi* (Gunder). Disc brown; markings heavy. S. Mont., n. Wyo. TL: Elkhorn Ranch Resort, Gallatin Co., Mont. (6) **Albright's Fritillary,** *S. e. albrighti* (Gunder). N.-cen. Mont. TL: Highwood Mts., Mont. (7) **Utah Fritillary,** *S. e. utahensis* (Skinner). Underside of HW buffy; spots unsilvered. Utah. TL: City Creek Canyon, Salt Lake City. (8) **Secret Fritillary,** *S. e. secreta* dos Passos & Gray. Disc reddish brown; spots silvered. Colo. TL: Rocky Mt. Natl. Park. (9) **Toiyabe Fritillary,** *S. e. toiyabe* Howe. Upperside bright orange-brown. Mountains of n.-cen. Nev. TL: Kingston Canyon, Lander Co., Nev.

**ATLANTIS FRITILLARY**                        **Pls. 13, 14**
*Speyeria atlantis* (W. H. Edwards)
**Identification:** $2$–$2^{3}/_{4}$ in. (50–69 mm). Most variable; appearance differs with subspecies. May be large or small, dark or light; spots may or may not be silvered. Most subspecies appear as follows: *Upperside:* Wing bases dark; dark markings heavier on basal half of both wings. *Dark border* usually present. *Underside:* Veins dark where they cross pm. band on HW. Submarginal spots on both wings neatly triangular, capped by narrow dark chevrons. Band usually light, HW disc darker.
**Adults:** June–early Aug.
**Range:** British Columbia east to Labrador, south to Calif., Ariz., N.M. **Habitat:** Varies with subspecies.
**Subspecies:** The 20 subspecies may be grouped into 3 main pat-

terns; there are many intermediate patterns as well. (1) *atlantis* pattern (Pl. 13, No. 8): Disc on underside of HW dark; spots well separated, *brightly silvered. Band light,* crossed by *dark veins.* Eastern N. America; in the West, s. Canada south to Neb., Ariz., N.M. (2) *hesperis* pattern (Pl. 13, No. 9): HW disc brown or maroon; *spots unsilvered.* Veins brown or reddish. S.D., parts of Colo., Idaho., Ore., Calif. (3) *dennisi* pattern (Pl. 14, No. 1): Small. *Light-colored;* dark markings very small. Disc pale; *band light and wide.* Bears little or no resemblance to other patterns. Prairies of Saskatchewan and Manitoba.

## HYDASPE FRITILLARY                                          Pl. 14
*Speyeria hydaspe* (Boisduval)
**Identification:** 2–2½ in. (50–62 mm). **Upperside:** Bright orange-brown; *dark markings heavy.* Wing bases usually very dark. **Underside:** Disc light violet-brown to deep maroon, often mottled light and dark. Band usually only slightly lighter than disc, often narrow. Spots unsilvered in most populations, cream-colored and edged with black. Spots in median band large; *first 3 usually about equal in size,* touching or nearly so (3rd spot sometimes slightly smaller). Submarginal spots large in south, small and narrow in north, sometimes partly silvered.
**Adults:** Late June–Aug.
**Similar species:** Zerene Fritillary (p. 82), *zerene* subspecies pattern.
**Range:** British Columbia to Alberta, south to Calif., Idaho, Mont., and N.M. **Habitat:** Mountain meadows, forest openings.
**Subspecies:** Seven rather similar subspecies, two of which are shown on Pl. 14. (1) **Hydaspe Fritillary,** *S. h. hydaspe* (Boisduval), Pl. 14, No. 2. TL: Yosemite Valley, Mariposa Co., Calif. (2) **Sakuntala Fritillary,** *S. h. sakuntala* (Skinner), Pl. 14, No. 3. TL: Kaslo, British Columbia.

## MORMON FRITILLARY                                           Pl. 14
*Speyeria mormonia* (Boisduval)
**Identification:** 1½–2⅛ in. (38–53 mm). The smallest *Speyeria.* **Upperside:** Male has *no sex scaling* on FW veins. Tawny to bright orange-brown. *Dark markings narrow, well separated.* Borders distinct but not wide or heavy. **Underside:** HW all one color, or disc only slightly darker. Band often not a different color from rest of HW.
**Adults:** July–Aug.
**Similar species:** Egleis Fritillary (p. 84).
**Range:** Alaska, Yukon Terr., Manitoba and British Columbia south to Calif., Nev., Ariz., N.M. Occurs at higher elevations and further north than most other *Speyeria* species. **Habitat:** Alpine meadows and fell-fields; openings in subarctic forest.
**Subspecies:** The 10 subspecies are grouped into 4 patterns. (1) *mormonia* pattern (Pl. 14, No. 4): Underside: HW disc often light brownish. *Silver spots small, bright.* Wash. to Calif., Nev., Utah.

(2) *eurynome* pattern (Pl. 14, No. 5): Markings and borders heavier; spots on underside of HW may or may not be silvered in the same populations. Wing bases on upperside darkened; disc on underside of HW often *dull greenish*. Alaska, Yukon Terr., and British Columbia south to Colo., Ariz., N.M. (3) *artonis* pattern (Pl. 14, No. 6). Very light-colored. Underside dull yellowish to pale buffy, often with a slight bluish gray overlay; HW markings *faintly* indicated in *dull greenish gray*. E. Ore., Nev. (4) *luski* pattern (Pl. 14, No. 7): All spots on underside of HW *large, pale, unsilvered,* with *dark outlines.* Veins reddish brown. White Mts., Ariz.; local.

## Variegated Fritillaries: Genus *Euptoieta* Doubleday

**VARIEGATED FRITILLARY**        Pl. 14
*Euptoieta claudia* (Cramer)
**Identification:** 1³/₄–2¹/₂ in. (44–62 mm). **Upperside:** Tawny; veins and vertical lines dusky; *median band light. Pm. spots small, round, dark.* **Underside:** Markings form a complex pattern.
**Early stages:** Larva has 6 rows of spines, the first pair largest. On each side, 2 dark stripes enclose white spots. Multiple broods.
**Food:** Violet *(Viola),* may apple *(Podophyllum),* beggarticks *(Desmodium),* purslane *(Portulaca),* stonecrop *(Sedum),* passion vine *(Passiflora),* and probably others. **Adults:** Long flight season. Common, widespread. Not resident (they do not overwinter) at northern limits of range, but they move in each year from the south.
**Range:** In the West, N.D. and Wyo. south to e. Calif., Ariz., Tex.; also Baja California and other parts of Mexico. **Habitat:** Usually open land, fields, fencerows, roadsides.

## Lesser Fritillaries: Genera *Boloria* Moore, *Clossiana* Reuss, and *Proclossiana* Reuss

Holarctic; some species found in N. America also occur in Europe and Asia. Small to medium-sized. Many life histories poorly known. Northern or alpine. Many inhabit remote places and are scarce or rare in collections.

In early American literature, and publications through the mid-1940s, the lesser fritillaries were all placed in the genus *Brenthis*. From the late 1940s to 1981 they were placed in the genus *Boloria*. Since publication of the Checklists of 1981 and 1983 (see p. 334), the three genera presented here have been generally recognized.

**NAPAEA FRITILLARY**        Pl. 14
*Boloria napaea* (Hoffmansegg)
**Identification:** 1³/₈–1¹/₂ in. (34–38 mm). Shape of HW unusual — margin slightly angled at end of cell M₃. Female darker than male.

*Upperside:* Male bright orange-brown, *dark markings narrow;* veins and wing bases dark. *Underside:* FW dull orange. HW banded with red-brown and buff, and with a few small silver spots and a *silver mark* at end of cell.
**Early stages:** Not known. One brood. **Food:** Alpine bistort *(Polygonum viviparum)* in Europe; not known for N. America. **Adults:** July–early Aug.
**Range:** Alaska, Northwest Terr., Yukon Terr., and British Columbia to Wyo. **Habitat:** Tundra, high mountain meadows.
**Subspecies:** (1) *B. n. napaea* (Hoffmansegg). Not in N. America. TL: Alps of Tirol. (2) **Alaskan Fritillary,** *B. n. alaskensis* (Holland). Several silver spots on underside. Alaska to British Columbia. TL: Between Forty-mile and Mission Creeks, Alaska. (3) **Nearctic Fritillary,** *B. n. nearctica* Verity. TL: Ne. Alaska. (4) **Hall's Fritillary,** *B. n. halli* (Klots), Pl. 14. Local. Female lighter than male. TL: Green River Pass, Wind River Range, Wyo.
**Remarks:** Formerly misidentified in our fauna as Shepherd's Fritillary, *Boloria pales.*

## SILVER-BORDERED FRITILLARY Pl. 14
*Clossiana selene* (Denis & Schiffermueller)
**Identification:** $1\frac{3}{8}$–$1\frac{7}{8}$ in. (34–47 mm). *Upperside:* Light orange-brown; *dark markings heaviest at base and near border.* Pm. area has 1 row of small black spots. *Underside:* Light spots brightly silvered; *marginal silvered spots complete.* Pm. spots very small, black.
**Early stages:** Larva greenish brown. One brood in West. **Food:** Violets *(Viola).* **Adults:** June–July.
**Range:** Alaska and Yukon Terr. south to N.M.; e. N. America. Europe, Asia. Local in the West. **Habitat:** Meadows, bogs, forest openings, marshes in mountain areas.
**Subspecies:** (1) *C. s. selene* (Denis & Schiffermueller). European. TL: Vienna. (2) **Dark-bordered Fritillary,** *C. s. atrocostalis* (Huard). Borders dark. E. Wash. to N.D., east to northeastern N. America. TL: Chicoutimi, Quebec. (3) **Nebraska Fritillary,** *C. s. nebraskensis* (Holland). Very large. N.D., Neb. TL: Dodge Co., Neb. (4) **Tolland Fritillary,** *C. s. tollandensis* (Barnes & Benjamin), Pl. 14. Wyo. south to N.M. TL: Tolland, Colo. (5) **Whitehorse Fritillary,** *C. s. albequina* (Holland). Smaller, duller; wing bases dark. Alaska south to British Columbia. TL: Whitehorse, Yukon Terr. (6) **Kohler's Fritillary,** *C. s. sabulicollis* (Kohler). On underside, black spots in FW cells $M_3$ and $Cu_1$ are square. W. Neb., w. S.D., w. N.D., and e. Colo. TL: Smith Lake, Sheridan Co., Neb.

## MEADOW FRITILLARY Pl. 14
*Clossiana bellona* (Fabricius)
**Identification:** $1\frac{3}{8}$–$1\frac{7}{8}$ in. (34–47 mm). FW *slightly flattened* below tip. *Upperside:* Dark orange-brown. Wing bases dark, but

*markings not obscured. Dark spots widely spaced* on outer half of wings. **Underside:** HW *purplish brown;* markings obscured but not obliterated; no silvering.

**Similar species:** (1) In Frigga's Fritillary (below), wing bases very dark. (2) In Western Meadow Fritillary (p. 89), upperside bright orange-brown; FW tip rounded.

**Early stages:** Larva dark green; lateral band black, spines yellowish brown. 1–2 broods. **Food:** Violets *(Viola).* **Adults:** June-July in the West.

**Range:** British Columbia east to Maritime Provinces, south to Wash., Mont., Colo., and Neb.; in East to N.C. **Habitat:** Moist meadows, bogs; wet aspen groves in Colo. and Wyo.

**Subspecies:** (1) **Meadow Fritillary,** *C. b. bellona* (Fabricius). Eastern N. America; probably not in our area. TL: N. America. (2) **Todd's Meadow Fritillary,** *C. b. toddi* (Holland). Wing bases dark. Northern U.S., s. Canada; Manitoba, N.D., Neb. TL: St. Margaret's River, Quebec. (3) **Jenista's Meadow Fritillary,** *C. b. jenistai* (Stallings & Turner), P. 14. Northwest Terr., British Columbia, and Saskatchewan south to n. U.S. TL: Lloydminster, Saskatchewan.

## FRIGGA'S FRITILLARY                                     Pl. 14
*Clossiana frigga* (Thunberg)

**Identification:** 1½–1¾ in. (38–44 mm). **Upperside:** Dull tawny. *Wing bases very dark, obscuring the markings;* borders usually wide, dark. **Underside:** Basal half dark, crossed by a band of buffy spots. Outer half lighter, with 2 rows of small dark spots. *Costal bar on HW pearly gray,* enclosing a dark spot; a small light spot at end of cell.

**Similar species:** (1) Meadow Fritillary (above). (2) Western Meadow Fritillary (p. 89).

**Early stages:** Not described. One brood. **Food:** Willow *(Salix);* has laid eggs also on mountain avens *(Dryas integrifolia),* in the rose family. In Europe, cloudberry *(Rubus chamaemorus),* also in rose family. **Adults:** June–July.

**Range:** N. Alaska and n. Canada south in Rocky Mts. to Colo. In East to Labrador, n. Mich.; Europe, Asia. **Habitat:** Willow bogs, tundra. Above 9000 ft. (2745 m) in Colo.

**Subspecies:** (1) *C. f. frigga* (Thunberg). Europe. TL: Lapland. (2) **Saga Fritillary,** *C. f. saga* (Staudinger). Alaska to Labrador, south in Rocky Mts. to British Columbia and Alberta. TL: Labrador. (3) **Frigga's Fritillary,** *C. f. alaskensis* (Lehmann). Large, dark. N. Alaska east to Hudson Bay. TL: Lat. 69° 40′ N., long. 141° W.; NE Alaska. (4) **Sagata Fritillary,** *C. f. sagata* (Barnes & Benjamin), Pl. 14. Wyo., Colo. TL: Hall Valley, Park Co., Colo.

## DINGY NORTHERN FRITILLARY                               Pl. 14
*Clossiana improba* (Butler)

**Identification:** 1⅛–1⅜ in. (28–34 mm). Small, very dull-colored.

*Upperside:* Dingy brown, slightly reddish. Dark bands indistinct; wing bases dark. *Underside:* HW costa ivory white, prominent; ivory band extends from costa to cell. Median band brown.
**Early stages:** Unknown. One brood. **Food:** Unknown for N. America. In Europe, larva feeds on a willow, *Salix herbacea.* **Adults:** July.
**Range:** N. Alaska to Baffin I., south to Yukon Terr. and n. British Columbia. **Habitat:** Tundra, north of or above treeline.
**Subspecies:** (1) **Dingy Northern Fritillary,** *C. i. improba* (Butler). Far north, except Alaska. TL: Winter Cove and Cambridge Bay, Victoria I. (Canada). (2) **Young's Dingy Northern Fritillary,** *C. i. youngi* (Holland), Pl. 14. Brighter, markings clearer. Alaska; Atlin, British Columbia. TL: Between Forty-mile and Mission Creeks, Alaska.

## UNCOMPAGHRE FRITILLARY                    not shown
*Clossiana acrocnema* Gall & Sperling
**Identification:** 1-1¼ in. (25–32 mm). Sexes similar. *Upperside:* Golden brown; pm. line dark, *light markings nearly white. Underside:* Markings similar to upperside, but *margins flushed with reddish brown.*
**Similar species:** Dingy Northern Fritillary (above); the ranges are widely separated.
**Early stages:** Unknown, but eggs laid on snow willow *(Salix nivalis).* One brood. **Adults:** Late July.
**Range:** So far (1985), known only from type locality: Mt. Uncompaghre, Hinsdale Co., Colo. **Habitat:** Above treeline, on summit of Mt. Uncompaghre.
**Remarks:** First described in 1980.

## STRECKER'S SMALL FRITILLARY                    Pl. 14
*Clossiana kriemhild* (Strecker)
**Identification:** 1⅜-1¾ in. (34–44 mm). *Upperside:* Bright orange-brown; *dark markings small, widely spaced.* Wing bases have little dark suffusion. *Underside:* Median band on underside of HW yellow, irregular, the spots outlined in brown. Spots of pm. band small, dark, light-centered. Submarginal line narrow, consisting of *flat brown chevrons pointing outward.*
**Similar species:** Bog Fritillary (p. 93) has white marginal spots. *Brown submarginal chevrons point inward.*
**Early stages:** Undescribed. One brood. **Food:** Violets. **Adults:** June.
**Range:** Rocky Mts. of Mont., Idaho, Wyo., Utah. TL: Rio Florida, La Plata Co., Colo., but not taken there since 1877. **Habitat:** Mountain meadows, streamsides, forest edges and openings.

## WESTERN MEADOW FRITILLARY                    Pl. 15
*Clossiana epithore* (W. H. Edwards)
**Identification:** 1⅜-1¾ in. (34–44 mm). *FW apex rounded.*

*Upperside:* Orange; our brightest *Clossiana.* Markings very evenly spaced on basal half of wings, small and widely spaced on outer half. *Underside: Purplish brown* markings on FW apex and on all of HW. *Pm. spot row formed of small dark rings.* Median band dull yellowish, irregular, the spots dark-bordered.
**Similar species:** In Meadow Fritillary (p. 87), FW apex squared-off.
**Early stages:** Apparently undescribed. One brood. **Food:** Violets.
**Adults:** May–Aug., depending on elevation and latitude.
**Range:** British Columbia east to Alberta and Mont., south coastally to cen. Calif. The only *Clossiana* in Calif. and in much of Ore. **Habitat:** Meadows, streamsides, open woodland.
**Subspecies:** (1) **Western Meadow Fritillary,** *C. e. epithore* (W. H. Edwards), Pl. 15. Santa Cruz Mts., Calif. TL: Saratoga, Calif. (2) **Chermock's Meadow Fritillary,** *C. e. chermocki* (E. & S. Perkins). Duller; wing bases darkened. Pacific Slope, from Marin Co., Calif. north to British Columbia. TL: 2.9 mi. east of Dolph, Yamhill Co., Ore. (3) **Northern Meadow Fritillary,** *C. e. borealis* (E. Perkins). Larger, darker. British Columbia and w. Alberta south to Idaho and Mont. TL: Shingle Creek Rd., Keremos, British Columbia. (4) **Sierra Meadow Fritillary,** *C. e. sierra* (E. Perkins). Small, lightly marked. Sierra Nevada and s. Cascades, Calif. TL: Sentinel Dome, Yosemite Natl. Park.

## PURPLE LESSER FRITILLARY                           Pl. 15
*Clossiana titania* (Esper)
**Identification:** 1$\frac{3}{8}$–1$\frac{7}{8}$ in. (34–47 mm). Variable; several rather dissimilar subspecies. *Upperside:* Tawny to dark orange-brown, depending on subspecies. Wing bases not heavily darkened. Border dark; *submarginal triangles point inward. Underside:* Ground color purplish brown, light markings not silvered. Submarginal triangles as on upperside.
**Similar species:** (1) In Freija's Fritillary (p. 91) median line on underside of HW zigzag. (2) In Polaris Fritillary (p. 91) underside of HW rich brown, with many small silver spots. (3) In Arctic Fritillary (p. 92) spots on underside of HW quite large, usually well silvered.
**Early stages:** Apparently not described. One brood. **Food:** Western bistort *(Polygonum bistortoides).* **Adults:** Late June–Aug.
**Range:** Cen. Alaska east to Labrador. In the West, south to Wash., Utah, N.M. In East to N.H.; Europe, Asia. Holarctic. **Habitat:** Bogs, taiga, alpine meadows.
**Subspecies:** (1) *C. t. titania* (Esper). TL: Sardinia. (2) **Boisduval's Fritillary,** *C. t. boisduvalii* (Duponchel). Lighter. Manitoba eastward. TL: N. Europe. (3) **Rainier Fritillary,** *C. t. rainieri* (Barnes & McDunnough). Very bright. N. Cascades, Olympic Mts. TL: Mt. Rainier, Wash. (4) **Purple Fritillary,** *C. t. grandis* (Barnes & McDunnough), Pl. 15. Borders dark, clearly marked. Alaska, Yukon Terr., British Columbia, east to New

Brunswick. TL: Hymers, Ontario. (5) **Large Purple Fritillary,** *C. t. ingens* (Barnes & McDunnough). Large, bright. Rocky Mts. of nw. Wyo., w. Mont., e. Idaho, s. Canada. TL: Yellowstone Natl. Park. (6) **Colorado Purple Fritillary,** *C. t. helena* (W. H. Edwards). Smaller, lighter. Long considered a separate species. W. Utah east to s. Wyo., Colo., N.M. TL: Mosquito Pass, Lake-Park Cos., Colo.

## POLARIS FRITILLARY                                     Pl. 15
*Clossiana polaris* (Boisduval)
**Identification:** 1¼–1½ in. (31–38 mm). *Upperside:* Light to medium orange-brown. HW bases very dark; wing margins dark, enclosing orange-brown triangles that point out. *Underside:* Many small white markings. Median band rich brown. Pm. spots small, dark, white-capped inwardly. *Marginal markings alternately dark brown and white.*
**Similar species:** (1) Purple Lesser Fritillary (above). (2) Freija's Fritillary (below). (3) Arctic Fritillary (p. 92).
**Early stages:** Unknown. One brood. **Food:** Unknown. May eat avens *(Dryas octopetala)* in Europe, and possibly crowberry *(Empetrum nigrum)* in Alaska. **Adults:** June–early July.
**Range:** Alaska and n. Canada east to Greenland, south to n. Manitoba. Arctic Europe, Asia; circumpolar. TL: Cap Nord, Norway.
**Habitat:** Tundra, north of or above treeline.
**Subspecies:** *C. p. stellata* (Masters), Pl. 15. TL: Churchill, Manitoba.

## FREIJA'S FRITILLARY                                    Pl. 15
*Clossiana freija* (Thunberg)
**Identification:** 1⅜–1½ in. (34–38 mm). Small, broad-winged. *Upperside:* Tawny to orange-brown; wing bases dark. Pm. spots dark, small. *Light marginal spots capped inwardly by dark triangles.* *Underside:* HW has *long, triangular white dash in discal cell.* Median band brown, zigzag. Pm. line white, irregular; marginal spots white, brown-capped.
**Similar species:** (1) Purple Lesser Fritillary (p. 90). (2) Polaris Fritillary (above). (3) Arctic Fritillary (p. 92).
**Early stages:** Not described in detail. One brood. **Food:** Dwarf bilberry *(Vaccinium caespitosum).* In Europe, cloudberry *(Rubus chamaemorus)* and others. **Adults:** Late May–June.
**Range:** N. Alaska east to Ellesmere I. and Labrador, south in the west to Wash. and Colo. In East to Ontario, Quebec. Europe, Asia.
**Habitat:** Bogs, taiga, tundra.
**Subspecies:** (1) **Freija's Fritillary,** *C. f. freija* (Thunberg). Alaska to Labrador; Europe. TL: Lapland. (2) **Tarquinius' Fritillary,** *C. f. tarquinius* (Curtis). Duller, darker. N. Alaska, n. Canada. TL: Not stated. (3) **Mt. Natazhat Fritillary,** *C. f. natazhati* (Gibson). Large, local. TL: 141st Meridian, N. Mt. Natazhat, Northwest Terr. (4) **Nabokov's Fritillary,** *C. f.*

*nabokovi* (D. Stallings & Turner). Little known. TL: Mile 102, Alaska Military Highway, British Columbia. (5) **Brown's Fritillary,** *C. f. browni* (Higgins), Pl. 15. Mont., Wyo., Colo., Utah, N.M. TL: Independence Pass, Pitkin Co., Colo.

## ALBERTA FRITILLARY                                    Pl. 15
*Clossiana alberta* (W. H. Edwards)
**Identification:** 1½–1¾ in. (38–44 mm). Unlike other *Clossiana* species. Very dark and dull. General appearance *sooty* — usual markings present but obscured.
**Early stages:** Unknown. One brood. **Food:** Has laid eggs on avens (a *Dryas* species), which is presumed to be the food. **Adults:** July. Scarce; uncommon in collections.
**Range:** Alberta south to Wash. and Mont.; British Columbia. TL: Laggan, Alberta. **Habitat:** High, barren, windswept ridges.

## ASTARTE FRITILLARY                                    Pl. 15
*Clossiana astarte* (Doubleday & Hewitson)
**Identification:** 1⅝–2 in. (41–50 mm). Our largest *Clossiana*. *Upperside:* Orange-brown, wing bases dark. Dark markings heavier near base, smaller on outer half of wings. *Underside:* Median and pm. *bands whitish* against an orange-brown background. Pm. and submarginal lines consist of *small, round, black spots.*
**Early stages:** Undescribed. One brood. **Food:** Spotted saxifrage *(Saxifraga bronchialis).* **Adults:** July–early Aug. Very scarce; wary.
**Range:** Rocky Mts. of Alberta and Mont.; Lillooet region, British Columbia; Okanogan Co., Wash. **Habitat:** High, barren, windswept ridges, usually above treeline.

## DISTINCT FRITILLARY                                   Pl. 15
*Clossiana distincta* (Gibson)
**Identification:** 1½–1¾ in. (38–44 mm). Large. *Upperside:* Markings small, widely spaced. *Underside:* Median band on HW *wide, extending out along veins.* Specimens from n. Alaska may be dark and suffused.
**Early stages:** Unknown. One brood. **Food:** Unknown. **Adults:** Late June–early July.
**Range:** Alaska, Yukon Terr., Northwest Terr.; Siberia. TL: Harrington Creek, Yukon Terr. **Habitat:** Rock slides (scree) on high ridges.
**Remarks:** Due to the remoteness of its range, this is the rarest N. American *Clossiana* in collections. It has been considered a subspecies of the Astarte Fritillary (above).

## ARCTIC FRITILLARY                                     Pl. 15
*Clossiana chariclea* (Schneider)
**Identification:** 1¼–1½ in. (31–38 mm). Our most northern but-

terfly, found in the true Arctic as far north as the limit of vegetation. Individual wing patterns may vary. *Upperside:* Male bright orange-brown, female usually much darker. Pm. and marginal bands prominent on most specimens; wing bases usually very dark. *Underside:* HW submedian band composed of separate white spots; *discal spot prolonged outward.* Light submarginal spots narrow, parallel to margin. White markings often (but not always) silvered.

**Similar species:** (1) Purple Lesser Fritillary (p. 90). (2) Polaris Fritillary (p. 91). (3) Freija's Fritillary (p. 91).

**Early stages:** Unknown. One brood. **Food:** Unknown. **Adults:** June–July.

**Range:** N. Alaska, n. Canada, Ellesmere I., Greenland, Baffin I., Labrador. Also Europe, Asia; circumpolar. **Habitat:** Tundra.

**Subspecies:** (1) *C. c. chariclea* (Schneider). European. TL: Lapland. (2) **Arctic Fritillary,** *C. c. arctica* (Zetterstedt). White spots on underside of HW usually unsilvered. Yukon Terr. eastward. TL: Greenland. (3) **Butler's Arctic Fritillary,** *C. c. butleri* (W. H. Edwards), Pl. 15. Spots on underside of HW usually silvered. Alaska. TL: Cape Thompson, Kotzebue Sound, w. Alaska.

**BOG FRITILLARY** *Proclossiana eunomia* (Esper)          **Pl. 15**
**Identification:** $1\frac{1}{4}$–$1\frac{5}{8}$ in. (31–41 mm). Appearance varies with subspecies. *Upperside:* Tawny to dark orange-brown; dark markings usually small, widely spaced, occasionally heavy. Dark pm. spots round, well separated from other markings. *Underside:* Light bands on HW distinct, cream to silver. HW has *six small, dark pm. spots with white or silver centers.*

**Early stages:** Undescribed. One brood. **Food:** Snakeweed *(Polygonum viviparum),* in buckwheat family; also violets *(Viola)* and willows *(Salix).* **Adults:** June–Aug., depending on locality.

**Range:** Alaska to Labrador, south in the West to Colo. at high elevations. In East to Me.; Europe, Asia. **Habitat:** Bogs, marshes, moist tundra.

**Subspecies:** (1) *P. e. eunomia* (Esper). European. TL: Not given. (2) **Bog Fritillary,** *P. e. triclaris* (Huebner). Upperside rather dull. Atlin, British Columbia east to Labrador. TL: Not stated. (3) **Celestial Bog Fritillary,** *P. e. caelestis* (Hemming), Pl. 15. TL: Hall Valley, Park Co., Colo. (4) **Nicholl's Bog Fritillary,** *P. e. nichollae* (Barnes & McDunnough). Rocky Mts. of Alberta, British Columbia. TL: Rocky Mts. (5) **Ladd's Bog Fritillary,** *P. e. laddi* (Klots). Small. Spots on underside of HW mostly unsilvered. Very local. TL: Snowy Range, Wyo. (6) **Beartooth Bog Fritillary,** *P. e. ursadentis* (Ferris & Groothuis). Small; pale, very lightly marked. TL: Bear Tooth Pass, Park Co., Wyo. (7) **Denali Bog Fritillary,** *P. e. denali* (Klots). Coloration very bright. Alaska, sw. Yukon Terr. TL: Mt. McKinley Natl. Park (now Denali Natl. Park and Preserve).

# Checker-spots, Patches, and Crescents: Subfamily Melitaeinae

Worldwide. Habitats diverse, ranging from subarctic to tropical. An extremely varied group. Small to medium-sized butterflies. Antennae of medium length; club short and spoon-shaped.

**Early stages:** Eggs globular, ribbed; laid in clusters. Larvae have 9 rows of branching spines. Pupa suspended by cremaster only. **Food:** Many different plant groups.

## Crescents: Genera *Anthanassa* Scudder, *Eresia* Boisduval, and *Phyciodes* Huebner

A New World group of many small, mostly tropical, species. Our species are mostly reddish brown or tawny with complex markings. On the underside, the HW margin has a crescent marking in cell $M_3$.

**TEXAS CRESCENT**                                         **Pl. 15**
*Anthanassa texana* (W. H. Edwards)
**Identification:** $1\frac{1}{4}$–$1\frac{3}{4}$ in. (31–44 mm). Female usually larger than male. *Upperside:* Brownish black; wing bases have rusty spots. Small white spots on FW. HW has *narrow white median band* consisting of *separate spots*. *Underside:* Base of FW orange-brown.
**Similar species:** Tulcis Crescent (below) lacks rusty spots.
**Early stages:** Incompletely known. Multiple broods. **Food:** Various plants in the acanthus family — tubetongue *(Siphonoglossa)*, chuparosa *(Beloperone), Ruellia,* and *Jacobina.* **Adults:** March–Nov. Flight low, fast.
**Range:** Southern U.S. to Guatemala. In the West, s. Ariz. to Tex., north occasionally to Colo. and Kans. TL: New Braunfels, Tex.
**Habitat:** Woodland trails, openings, roadsides, fencerows; in s. Tex., thorn forest.

**TULCIS CRESCENT** *Eresia frisia tulcis* (Bates)          **Pl. 15**
**Identification:** $1\frac{1}{4}$–$1\frac{3}{8}$ in. (31–34 mm). *Upperside:* Our subspecies is black; all light markings *cream-colored.* FW spots large. *HW band wide, its spots connected;* 2 narrow light lines outside this band. *Underside:* Base of FW white, cream, or golden.
**Similar species:** Texas Crescent (above) has some rusty spots.
**Early stages:** Only partly described. Larvae live in groups, feeding at night. Multiple broods. **Food:** *Dicliptera,* in the acanthus family. **Adults:** Long flight period.
**Range:** Ariz. (scarce) to s. Tex.; south to S. America. TL: Central Valley, Guatemala. **Habitat:** Thorn forest trails, openings, subtropical woodland.

**Subspecies:** (1) **Cuban Crescent,** *E. f. frisia* (Poey). Ground color tawny. Cuba, Fla.; not in our area. TL: Cuba. (2) **Tulcis Crescent,** *E. f. tulcis* (Bates). As described above.

## NORTHERN PEARL CRESCENT    Pl. 16
*Phyciodes pascoensis* (W. G. Wright)
**Identification:** 1¼-1¾ in. (31–44 mm). *Upperside:* Orange-brown; border dark, of even width. *Underside:* FW has *extensive orange-brown area* from base to outer ⅓ of wing. HW has brown area surrounding the crescent spot.
**Similar species:** (1) In Tawny Crescent (below), underside is more lightly marked. (2) In Phaon Crescent (p. 96), median line on upperside is lighter than other markings. (3) Field Crescent (p. 96) has few dark markings on underside. (4) In Painted Crescent (p. 96), markings on upperside whitish. Underside of HW cream-colored.
**Early stages:** Larva black, with yellow dots and a lateral band; lives in groups. One brood in north, up to 4–5 broods in south.
**Food:** Asters and crownbeard *(Verbesina),* both in sunflower family. **Adults:** April–Nov., depending on locality. Often very common.
**Range:** Cen. Canada to s. Mexico, except for coastal Ore. and most of Calif. and Nev. **Habitat:** Fields, meadows, fencerows, open woodland.
**Subspecies:** (1) **Northern Pearl Crescent,** *P. p. pascoensis* W. G. Wright, Pl. 16. Light markings more extensive. Wash. and Idaho south to cen. Ariz. TL: Pasco, Wash. (2) **Distinct Crescent,** *P. p. distinctus* Bauer. Fine lines on upperside. Se. Calif. east to w. Tex.; Mexico. TL: Calexico, Calif. (3) **Arctic Pearl Crescent,** *P. p. arcticus* dos Passos. Markings heavier; color of underside darker. Northwest Terr. and British Columbia east to Newfoundland. TL: Newfoundland.
**Remarks:** The Pearl Crescent, *P. tharos,* enters our area, but its western distribution is uncertain and somewhat controversial since the designation of *P. pascoensis* as a separate species in 1980.

## TAWNY CRESCENT *Phyciodes batesii* (Reakirt)    Pl. 16
**Identification:** 1¼-1⅜ in. (31–34 mm). *Upperside:* In FW, *median spot row lighter than pm. spot row. Underside:* Median spot row in FW *black* (some spots small). HW *straw-colored;* pm. spots small, brown. Crescent inconspicuous.
**Similar species:** (1) Northern Pearl Crescent (above). (2) Phaon Crescent (p. 96). (3) Field Crescent (p. 96). (4) Painted Crescent (p. 96).
**Early stages:** Larva gregarious; overwinters. One brood. **Food:** Aster. **Adults:** May–June.
**Range:** Manitoba east to Quebec, south in the West to Colo. (rarely) and Neb.; in East to Va. TL: Gloucester, N.J. **Habitat:** Dry open fields.

**PHAON CRESCENT**                                          **Pl. 16**
*Phyciodes phaon* (W. H. Edwards)
**Identification:** 1–1¼ in. (25–31 mm). A very common, mostly
southern species. *Upperside: Median band whitish;* pm. band a
contrasting orange-brown. *Underside:* FW costa and border
black; spots at center and apex of FW cream-colored. HW light,
with many fine dark lines; crescent flanked by dark area. Dark
patches at base and costa of HW.
**Similar species:** (1) Northern Pearl Crescent (p. 95). (2) Tawny
Crescent (p. 95). (3) Field Crescent (below). (4) Painted Crescent
(below).
**Early stages:** Larva spiny; olive with brown lines and mottled
bands. Head whitish, spotted with brown. Multiple broods. **Food:**
Fogfruit or lippia, in the verbena family. **Adults:** Long flight
season.
**Range:** Southern U.S. to Cen. America. In the West, s. Calif.,
Colo. (scarce) and Kans., south to Tex.; Fla. TL: St. Simon's I.,
Georgia. **Habitat:** Open fields, roadsides, marshes, openings in
thorn forest, yards with lippia lawns.

**FIELD CRESCENT** *Phyciodes campestris* (Behr)        **Pl. 16**
**Identification:** 1–1⅜ in. (25–34 mm). *Upperside:* Ground color
blackish, with many small tawny markings. *Light cell bar* in FW
*separate* from other markings. FW median band interrupted, the
spot in cell $M_3$ small or absent. *Underside:* Yellow-brown with
rusty markings; 2–3 small black patches on inner margin of FW.
**Similar species:** (1) Northern Pearl Crescent (p. 95). (2) Tawny
Crescent (p. 95). (3) Phaon Crescent (above). (4) Painted Crescent
(below).
**Early stages:** Larva black, spiny, with orange spots at bases of
spines. One brood in north, 2–3 broods in south. **Food:** Various
asters. **Adults:** March–Oct. at low elevations and in the south,
June–July at high elevations and in the north.
**Range:** Cen. Alaska and n. Canada to Mexico; west of the
Great Plains. **Habitat:** Fields, meadows, clearings, fencerows,
streamsides.
**Subspecies:** (1) **Field Crescent**, *P. c. campestris* (Behr), Pl. 16,
No. 4. Alaska south to s. Calif., east to w. Wyo., Nev. TL: San
Francisco, Calif. (2) **Mountain Crescent**, *P. c. montanus* (Behr),
Pl. 16, No. 5. Much more rusty; dark markings reduced. Sierra
Nevada; Carson Range, Nev. TL: Headwaters of Tuolumne River,
Yosemite Valley, Calif. (3) **Camillus Crescent**, *P. c. camillus*
W. H. Edwards. Darker; more black markings on underside of HW.
Rocky Mts. from Wyo. south to Ariz. and N.M. TL: Fairplay,
Park Co., Colo.

**PAINTED CRESCENT**                                       **Pl. 16**
*Phyciodes pictus* (W. H. Edwards)
**Identification:** 1–1⅛ in. (24–34 mm). *Upperside:* Ground color

blackish. FW cell bar whitish; median area has 2 well-separated, whitish spots at an angle. Other markings small, dull tawny. *Underside:* FW apex and *all of HW pale yellowish,* the markings absent or reduced. Lower edge of HW may have 1–3 brown spots. **Similar species:** (1) Northern Pearl Crescent (p. 95). (2) Tawny Crescent (p. 95). (3) Phaon Crescent (p. 96). (4) Field Crescent (above).
**Early stages:** Larva yellowish or greenish brown, with short spines. Multiple broods. **Food:** Aster; in Tex., also hairy tubetongue *(Siphonoglossa pilosella).* **Adults:** Long flight season. **Range:** Colo., Neb., and Kans., south to Ariz., N.M., and Tex. **Habitat:** Water courses and washes in grasslands and prairies; fencerows, roadsides.
**Subspecies:** (1) *P. p. pictus* (W. H. Edwards), Pl. 16. Colo. and Neb. to Tex. TL: North Platte, Neb. (2) *P. p. canace* W. H. Edwards. Underside quite yellow. Ariz. TL: Tucson.

**ORSEIS CRESCENT**      **Pl. 16**
*Phyciodes orseis* (W. H. Edwards)
**Identification:** $1\frac{1}{4}$–$1\frac{5}{8}$ in. (31–41 mm). *Upperside:* Bright orange-brown; markings sharp, in distinct bands. *Underside:* Dark markings *reddish brown, thin; scattered over much of surface.*
**Similar species:** (1) Mylitta Crescent (below) has dark markings on an orange-brown background. (2) Pale Crescent (p. 98) is larger and lighter; the ranges do not overlap.
**Early stages:** Unknown. **Food:** Unknown. **Adults:** March–June on the coast, June–Aug. in the Sierra Nevada. Seldom seen. Males perch in the open.
**Range:** Pacific Coast; s. Ore. south to San Francisco; central and northern Sierra Nevada; w. Nev. Local. **Habitat:** Canyons of small streams in the inner Coast Range; mountain meadows inland.
**Subspecies:** (1) **Orseis Crescent,** *P. o. orseis* W. H. Edwards. S. Ore. to San Francisco Bay. TL: Mt. St. Helena, Napa Co., Calif. (2) **Herlan's Crescent,** *P. o. herlani* Bauer, Pl. 16. Lighter; dark markings on upperside narrower. Sierra Nevada, Calif.; w. Nev. TL: Glenbrook Creek, Douglas Co., Nev., 7000 ft. (2135 m).

**MYLITTA CRESCENT**      **Pl. 16**
*Phyciodes mylitta* (W. H. Edwards)
**Identification:** $1\frac{1}{8}$–$1\frac{1}{2}$ in. (28–38 mm). *Upperside:* Bright brownish orange; *dark markings narrow, evenly spaced.* No heavy black spots. *Underside:* No black spot in FW cell $Cu_2$. Rusty brown markings on HW moderate to well developed.
**Similar species:** (1) Orseis Crescent (above). (2) Pale Crescent (below).
**Early stages:** Larva spiny, black, marked with yellow. Two broods in the north and at high elevations, several broods in

the south. **Food:** Native thistle *(Cirsium),* European thistle *(Carduus),* milk thistle *(Silybum marianum).* **Adults:** March–Oct., depending on latitude and elevation.
**Range:** Western N. America, from s. Canada to Mexico. Range in Rocky Mts. not clear due to confusion with the Pale Crescent (below). **Habitat:** Fields, meadows, fencerows, roadsides, roads, parks, vacant lots. From sea level to 8000 ft. (2440 m).
**Subspecies:** (1) **Mylitta Crescent,** *P. m. mylitta* (W. H. Edwards), Pl. 16. All of range except Ariz., N.M., and s. Colo. TL: San Francisco. (2) **Arizona Crescent,** *P. m. arizonensis* Bauer. Markings heavier. Sw. Colo., Ariz., N.M.; Sonora, Mexico. TL: "Arizona, New Mexico, Sonora, s. Colorado."

**PALE CRESCENT**                                                    **Pl. 16**
*Phyciodes pallidus* (W. H. Edwards)
**Identification:** $1\frac{3}{8}$–$1\frac{5}{8}$ in. (34–41 mm). *Black spot* in FW at center of inner margin, *prominent on both upperside and underside.* ***Upperside:*** Pale brownish orange; dark markings reduced. Black wing border narrow. ***Underside:*** Yellowish with reddish brown markings. HW crescent white.
**Similar species:** (1) Orseis Crescent (p. 97). (2) Mylitta Crescent (above).
**Early stages:** Unrecorded. One brood. **Food:** Thistles. **Adults:** Late May to early July.
**Range:** Cen. British Columbia east to Rocky Mts., south to Ore., Utah, Nev., n. Ariz., east to Wyo., Mont., Colo. **Habitat:** Gulches, dry streambeds, dry fields.
**Subspecies:** (1) **Pale Crescent,** *P. p. pallidus* (W. H. Edwards), Pl. 16. E. Colo., n. Ariz. TL: Flagstaff Mt., Boulder Co., Colo. (2) **Barnes' Crescent,** *P. p. barnesi* Skinner. Ground color on underside lighter, brown markings darker. S. British Columbia east to Mont., south to e. Ore., e. Nev., Utah, w. Colo. TL: Glenwood Springs, Garfield Co., Colo. (west of the Continental Divide).

**VESTA CRESCENT**                                                   **Pl. 16**
*Phyciodes vesta* (W. H. Edwards)
**Identification:** $\frac{7}{8}$–$1\frac{1}{4}$ in. (22–31 mm). ***Upperside:*** Brownish black; tawny markings small, separated. ***Underside:*** Pm. and submarginal lines of FW black, connected along veins so that the *pm. band is formed of tawny spots.* Brown markings of HW vary from few to many.
**Early stages:** Multiple broods. **Food:** Hairy tubetongue *(Siphonoglossa pilosella),* in acanthus family. **Adults:** Long flight season.
**Range:** Tex. to Guatemala; strays to Kans., Colo. TL: New Braunfels, Tex. **Habitat:** Fields, roadsides, open woodland.

## Checker-spots: Genus *Charidryas* Scudder

A North American genus of 9 species. Medium-sized; banded or checkered blackish and tawny.

**Early stages:** Eggs laid in masses. Young larva overwinters and develops the following spring. One brood.

These species have previously been placed either in the genus *Phyciodes, Melitaea,* or *Chlosyne.*

### GORGONE CHECKER-SPOT                                Pl. 16
*Charidryas gorgone* (Huebner)
**Identification:** $1\frac{1}{4}$–$1\frac{1}{2}$ in. (31–38 mm). *Upperside:* Ground color blackish; spots and bands orange-brown. Median band complete. Both FW and HW have a small orange chevron in outer edge of cell $M_3$. HW pm. band encloses 5–6 small black spots. *Underside: HW median band irregular,* formed of *silver chevrons.*
**Early stages:** Larva yellow, with black spines and 3 black stripes. One brood in north, 2–3 in south. **Food:** Various members of the sunflower family. **Adults:** May–July, perhaps longer.
**Range:** S. Canada to Mexico. In the West, British Columbia to Manitoba, south to Idaho, Utah, Tex. Not found on Pacific Slope. Sometimes quite local, but often found in numbers. **Habitat:** Plains, foothills, brushlands to 10,000 ft. (3050 m).
**Subspecies:** (1) *C. g. gorgone* (Huebner). S. Georgia; local. TL: Probably coastal Georgia. (2) *C. g. carlota* (Reakirt), Pl. 16. Range as given above. TL: Cedar Hill, Jefferson Co., Mo.

### SILVERY CHECKER-SPOT                                Pl. 16
*Charidryas nycteis* (Doubleday)
**Identification:** $1\frac{3}{8}$–$1\frac{3}{4}$ in. (34–44 mm). *Upperside:* Dark brown areas extensive. Tawny median band wide in eastern subspecies, narrow in western subspecies. *Underside:* Dark areas chocolate brown. *Bands at base and middle of HW silvery white.* A silvery crescent-shaped mark in cell $M_3$, similar to that found in crescents (previous group).
**Early stages:** Larva spiny, black; lateral stripe dull orange. One brood in north, 2 in south. **Food:** Sunflowers *(Helianthus)* and asters *(Aster),* both in sunflower family. **Adults:** May–July.
**Range:** S. Canada south through Wyo. and Colo. to Tex.; east to se. Canada, south to s.-cen. U.S. **Habitat:** Fields in the East, moist valleys in the West.
**Subspecies:** (1) **Silvery Checker-spot,** *C. n. nycteis* (Doubleday). Median band wide. N.D. south to Tex.; eastern states. TL: Middle States. (2) **Dark Silvery Checker-spot,** *C. n. drusius* (W. H. Edwards), Pl. 16. Colo. south to Ariz. TL: Turkey Creek Junction, Colo. (3) **Chermocks' Checker-spot,** *C. n. reversa* (F. & R. Chermock). Light markings extensive. Local. TL: Riding Mts., Manitoba.

**GABB'S CHECKER-SPOT** *Charidryas gabbii* (Behr)    **Pl. 16**
**Identification:** 1¼–1¾ in. (31–44 mm). *Upperside:* Male with narrow, bright orange-brown bands; *median band slightly lighter.* Bands lighter in female (not shown); median band lighter than in male. *Underside:* Light bands in HW have a *pearly luster.*
**Similar species:** (1) In Northern Checker-spot (p. 101), light bands on underside of HW lack pearly luster. (2) In Acastus Checker-spot (below), light bands on upperside slightly wider. (3) Neumoegen's Checker-spot (below) is brighter, the black markings narrow. (4) In Hoffmann's Checker-spot (p. 102), wing bases on upperside very dark.
**Early stages:** Larva black, speckled with white. Dorsal midline velvety black; spines with orange-brown bases. One brood. **Food:** Beach aster *(Corethrogyne filaginifolia),* hazardia *(Haplopappus squarrosus);* both in sunflower family. **Adults:** May–July.
**Range:** Calif. Coast Ranges, Monterey Co. south to Baja California, Sierra Nevada foothills north to Tulare Co., Calif. TL: Mountains near Los Angeles, Calif. **Habitat:** Foothills, coastal gulches and cliffs, canyons.

**ACASTUS CHECKER-SPOT**                          **Pl. 16**
*Charidryas acastus* (W. H. Edwards)
**Identification:** 1½–1⅞ in. (38–47 mm). *Upperside:* Base of HW *darker than base of FW.* Light bands orange-brown. Pm. and submarginal bands on HW wider than those of similar species; median band lighter. *Underside:* Light bands *white to cream-colored, edged with brown.*
**Similar species:** (1) Gabb's Checker-spot (above). (2) Northern Checker-spot (p. 101). (3) Neumoegen's Checker-spot (below). (4) Hoffmann's Checker-spot (p. 102).
**Early stages:** Said to be much like those of Northern Checker-spot (p. 101). 1–2 broods. **Food:** Rabbit brush *(Chrysothamnus viscidiflorus),* in the sunflower family. **Adults:** March (s. Ariz.) to July (Utah).
**Range:** E. Wash., east to Red Deer R., Alberta and e. N.D., south to e. Calif., s. Ariz., and N.M. **Habitat:** Pinyon-juniper woodland, gulches and meadows in sagebrush scrub. Tolerant of elevation.
**Subspecies:** (1) **Acastus Checker-spot,** *C. a. acastus* (W. H. Edwards), Pl. 16. All of range except for that of next subspecies. TL: Provo Canyon, Utah Co., Utah. (2) **Dorothy's Checker-spot,** *C. a. dorothyae* (Bauer). Much darker. Local. TL: Burnt River & Snake River Canyons, Ore.

**NEUMOEGEN'S CHECKER-SPOT**                      **Pl. 17**
*Charidryas neumoegeni* (Skinner)
**Identification:** 1½–1¾ in. (38–44 mm). *Upperside: Very bright, almost orange bands;* median and pm. bands tend to fuse. Black lines narrow. *Underside:* White bands in HW bright, glossy, edged with black. Red bands incomplete.

**Similar species:** (1) Gabb's Checker-spot (p. 100). (2) Northern Checker-spot (below). (3) Acastus Checker-spot (p. 100). (4) Hoffmann's Checker-spot (p. 102).
**Early stages:** Larva black. Usually 1 brood; 2 in favored years.
**Food:** Asters, especially Mojave aster *(Machaeranthera tortifolia).* **Adults:** March–June.
**Range:** S. Nev., s. Utah, se. Calif., Ariz.; Baja California. **Habitat:** Desert scrub, juniper woodland, washes.
**Subspecies:** (1) **Neumoegen's Checker-spot,** *C. n. neumoegeni* (Skinner), Pl. 17. Occurs throughout entire range except in s. Ariz. TL: Utah. (2) **Sabino Canyon Checker-spot,** *C. n. sabina* (Wright). Color less bright; dark lines on upperside heavier. S. Ariz. (east to N.M.?). TL: Sabino Canyon, Pima Co., Ariz.

## NORTHERN CHECKER-SPOT Pl. 17
*Charidryas palla* (Boisduval)
**Identification:** 1⅜-1⅞ in. (34–47 mm). Widespread, common, and variable. *Upperside:* Brownish red. *HW base dark; median band light. Underside:* Light bands creamy, but with no pearly luster. Female may resemble male, or be darker, even black (melanic), with white markings.
**Similar species:** (1) Gabb's Checker-spot (p. 100). (2) Acastus Checker-spot (p. 100). (3) Neumoegen's Checker-spot (above). (4) Hoffmann's Checker-spot (p. 102).
**Early stages:** Larva spiny, black with orange spots. One brood.
**Food:** *C. p. palla* feeds on goldenrod *(Solidago)* and asters. Food plant formerly stated (apparently mistakenly) to be paintbrush *(Castilleja).* **Adults:** April–May in coastal Calif., to June–July in mountains and northern areas.
**Range:** British Columbia and Alberta south to s. Calif., N.M. **Habitat:** Meadows, openings, streamsides, sagebrush.
**Subspecies:** Some subspecies formerly considered distinct species, have different food plants. (1) **Northern Checker-spot,** *C. p. palla* (Boisduval), Pl. 17. Wash. south to Calif. TL: San Francisco, Calif. (2) **Whitney's Checker-spot,** *C. p. whitneyi* (Behr). Very red. Food: Rabbit brush *(Chrysothamnus).* Sierra Nevada of Calif. north into Ore. TL: Sierra Nevada. (3) **Death Valley Checker-spot,** *C. p. vallismortis* (J. W. Johnson). Darker; black blotch on inner margin of FW. Mountains of Death Valley region. TL: Death Valley Natl. Monument, Calif. (4) **Calydon Checker-spot,** *C. p. calydon* (Holland). Darker; wing bases dark. Rocky Mts. TL: Turkey Creek Junction, Jefferson Co., Colo. (5) **Sterope Checker-spot,** *C. p. sterope* (W. H. Edwards). Male dull reddish, female black and white. Food: Rabbit brush. Sagebrush country, e. Ore. and e. Wash. TL: Tygh Valley, Ore. (6) **Flavid Checker-spot,** *C. p. flavula* (Barnes & McDunnough). Small, more tawny. Upper Colorado; Green River drainage. TL: Glenwood Springs, Colo.

**HOFFMANN'S CHECKER-SPOT**                                    **Pl. 17**
*Charidryas hoffmanni* (Behr)
**Identification:** 1⅜–1¾ in. (34–44 mm). *Upperside:* Wing bases
very dark. Median and pm. bands on FW fused into a *wide tawny
band.* HW median and pm. bands not fused, light-colored. *Under-
side:* Bands light yellowish.
**Similar species:** (1) Gabb's Checker-spot (p. 100). (2) Acastus
Checker-spot (p. 100). (3) Northern Checker-spot (p. 101). (4)
Neumoegen's Checker-spot (p. 100).
**Early stages:** Larva black above, brown below. Lateral line
cream-colored. One brood. **Food:** Aster. **Adults:** June–Aug.
**Range:** British Columbia south to Tulare Co., Calif., in the Sierra
Nevada. **Habitat:** Forest edges and openings, mountain terraces.
**Subspecies:** (1) **Hoffmann's Checker-spot,** *C. h. hoffmanni*
(Behr), Pl. 17. Sierra Nevada, w. Nev. TL: Sierra Nevada, Calif.
(2) **Segregated Checker-spot,** *C. h. segregata* (Barnes &
McDunnough). Basal half of wings darkened; tawny bands less
fused. Trinity Mts. of Calif., Siskiyou Mts. of Calif. and Ore.,
w. Ore. TL: Crater Lake, Ore. (3) **Manchada Checker-spot,**
*C. h. manchada* (Bauer). Very dark, median band narrow, whitish.
British Columbia, Wash. TL: Tumwater Canyon, Chelan Co.,
Wash.

**DAMOETAS CHECKER-SPOT**                                      **Pl. 17**
*Charidryas damoetas* (Skinner)
**Identification:** 1¼–1⅝ in. (31–41 mm). Wings shorter and more
rounded than in related species. *Upperside:* Bands dull blackish
and orange-brown; wings have a *slight glossy sheen.*
**Early stages:** Unknown. One brood. **Adults:** July–Aug.
**Range:** British Columbia and Alberta south to Calif., Colo. Un-
common to rare. **Habitat:** Truly alpine; rocky slopes and benches
at or above treeline, 8000–13,000 ft. (2440–3965 m).
**Subspecies:** (1) **Damoetas Checker-spot,** *C. d. damoetas* (Skinner), Pl. 17. British Columbia and Alberta to Colo. TL: Williams
Fork Range, Summit/Grand Cos., Colo. (2) **Malcolm's
Checker-spot,** *C. d. malcolmi* (J. A. Comstock). Coloration
brighter. Alpine Sierra Nevada of Calif. TL: Mammoth, Mono Co.,
Calif. Long considered a separate species.

### Patches: Genus *Chlosyne* Butler

Tropical; a few species occur north of Mexico. Ground color dark,
with brightly colored bands or areas. Sexes similar.

**AARON'S CHECKER-SPOT**                                       **Pl. 17**
*Chlosyne definita* (Aaron)
**Identification:** 1⅛–1½ in. (28–38 mm). Small; FW apex rounded.
*Upperside:* Median band yellowish, pm. band orange-red; these

bands partly fused in some specimens. *A marginal row of small white dots,* sometimes incomplete. *Underside:* Pm. band on HW has reddish orange spots in cells $M_1$, $M_2$, $Cu_1$, and $Cu_2$, but spot $M_3$ is *white,* a unique feature.
**Similar species:** (1) In Theona Checker-spot (p. 105), pm. band on underside of HW consists entirely of reddish orange spots.
**Early stages:** Multiple broods. **Food:** Unknown. **Adults:** Long flight season.
**Range:** S. Ariz. (rare) to s. Tex.; Mexico. Local, uncommon. TL: Near Corpus Christi, Tex. **Habitat:** Openings, edges, and trails in thorn forest.

**BORDERED PATCH** *Chlosyne lacinia* (Geyer)          **Pl. 17**
**Identification:**   Subspecies   *adjutrix*   is   shown.   $1\frac{3}{8}$–2 in.
(34–50 mm). *Upperside:* Blackish, with a *wide orange median band.* Pm spots small, white. *Underside:* Median band yellowish; pm. band of small white spots. Marginal spots cream-colored; the one in cell $M_3$ is the largest spot on FW. Spots on HW larger, all the same size.
**Similar species:** In California Patch (below), marginal spots on upperside orange, not whitish. Spots on upperside of FW all about the same size.
**Early stages:** Larva spiny; may be yellowish, spotted, or striped. Multiple broods. **Food:** Sunflowers *(Helianthus),* cockleburs *(Xanthium),* crownbeard *(Verbesina),* ragweed *(Ambrosia trifida),* and others in sunflower family (Asteraceae). **Adults:** Long flight season.
**Range:** S. Calif. east to Kans. (uncommon), south to Tex.; casual in Colo. and Neb.; south to Argentina. **Habitat:** Fields, brushland, fencerows, roadsides; quite general.
**Subspecies:** *C. l. lacinia* (Geyer). Not found in our area. TL: Mexico. (2) **Bordered Patch,** *C. l. adjutrix* Scudder, Pl. 17, No. 6. Se. N.M., Tex.; Mexico. TL: Texas. (3) **Crocale Patch,** *C. l. crocale* (W. H. Edwards). See below.

**CROCALE PATCH**          **Pl. 17**
*Chlosyne lacinia crocale* (W. H. Edwards)
**Identification:** Subspecies *crocale* is shown. Extremely variable; seldom are two specimens exactly alike. *Upperside:* Median band on HW narrow, white in typical *crocale,* mostly rusty in form "rufescens." In form "nigrescens," median band partly rusty and partly white, or nearly absent.
**Range:** E. Calif., s. Nev., s. Utah, Ariz., n. N.M.; Baja California, Mexico. TL: White Mts., Ariz.

**CALIFORNIA PATCH**          **Pl. 17**
*Chlosyne californica* (W. G. Wright)
**Identification:** $1\frac{1}{4}$–$1\frac{7}{8}$ in. (31–47 mm). *Upperside:* Median band

and submarginal spots *orange*. **Underside:** Submarginal spots on FW all more nearly the same size than in Bordered Patch. **Similar species:** Bordered Patch (p. 103). **Early stages:** Larva spiny, black. Multiple broods. **Food:** Desert sunflower *(Viguiera deltoidea parishii)*. **Adults:** March–Oct. **Range:** S. Nev., se. Calif., sw. Ariz.; Baja California; Sonora, Mexico. **TL:** Colorado Desert, Calif. **Habitat:** Desert washes, barrancas, arroyos. **Remarks:** Population fluctuates greatly, depending on seasonal rains.

## Checker-spots: Genus *Thessalia* Scudder

These checker-spots are southwestern and tropical. Underside of HW white, with black veins and a black or reddish median band. Females usually larger than males.

**LEANIRA CHECKER-SPOT**                          Pls. 17, 18
*Thessalia leanira* (C. & R. Felder)
**Identification:** 1⅜–1¾ in. (34–44 mm). *Upperside:* Extremely variable. Northern populations are black with lines of light yellowish spots. Populations in the extreme south are tawny with black veins. Intermediate populations are black with light spots and tawny borders. *Underside:* Similar in all subspecies: whitish to cream-colored or yellow, with black veins. *Median band black, enclosing a row of light spots.*
**Early stages:** Larva spiny, black, with paired rows of small orange spots. One brood. **Food:** Paintbrush *(Castilleja)*. **Adults:** April–July, depending on latitude and elevation.
**Range:** W. Ore. east to w. Colo., south to Utah, Nev., and s. Calif.; Baja California. Local; occurs in scattered colonies. **Habitat:** Canyons, rocky hills and outcrops, washes, roadcuts.
**Subspecies:** In all subspecies underside is similar to description given above. Upperside varies: (1) **Leanira Checker-spot,** *T. l. leanira* (C. & R. Felder), Pl. 17, No. 9. Coast Ranges of Calif. TL: California. (2) **Oregon Checker-spot,** *T. l. oregonensis* Bauer. Light spots smaller. W. Ore. TL: Siskiyou Mts., Jackson Co., Ore. (3) **Davies' Checker-spot,** *T. l. daviesi* (Wind). Light spots larger. Sierra Nevada foothills. TL: Strawberry Lake, Tuolumne Co., Calif. (4) **Wright's Checker-spot,** *T. l. wrighti* (W. H. Edwards), Pl. 17, No. 10. Borders and some wing spots *rusty.* Mountains of s. Calif. TL: San Bernardino Mts., Calif. (5) **Cerrita Checker-spot,** *T. l. cerrita* (Wright), Pl. 17, No. 11. Upperside tawny, with black veins. Dark bands greatly reduced or even absent. *FW cell tawny.* Desert mountain ranges. Pyramid Lake, Nev., south to Colorado Desert, Calif. TL: S. California. Intergrades with Wright's Checker-spot and Alma Checker-spot where ranges meet. (6) **Alma Checker-spot,** *T. l. alma* (Strecker),

Pl. 17, No. 12. Upperside tawny; wing bases brownish. *FW cell brown;* cell-end bar *light,* with an *irregular brown band* beyond it. Underside of HW has a thin, dark cell bar. Nevada, Utah, w. Colo., n. Ariz. TL: St. George, Washington Co., Utah. Intergrades with Cerrita Checker-spot where ranges meet.

## FULVOUS CHECKER-SPOT                          Pl. 17
*Thessalia fulvia* (W. H. Edwards)
**Identification:** 1¼-1½ in. (31–38 mm). *Upperside:* Male browner than Alma Checker-spot (subspecies of Leanira Checker-spot, above), but *dark veins wider* and bands lighter. Female often larger, much paler, and more tawny. *Underside:* Same pattern as in Alma Checker-spot, but *without dark cell bar* on HW. Veins black, conspicuous. Usually 1–2 black streaks in FW cell, which is otherwise tawny.
**Early stages:** Similar to those of Leanira Checker-spot (above). One brood. **Food:** Paintbrush *(Castilleja).* **Adults:** June–July.
**Range:** S. Colo., Ariz., and N.M. to Tex. TL: Archer Co., Tex.
**Habitat:** Canyons, damp roadsides.

## CYNEAS CHECKER-SPOT                           Pl. 17
*Thessalia cyneas* (Godman & Salvin)
**Identification:** 1⅜-1⅝ in. (34–41 mm). *Upperside:* Dark brown, with *small white spots in neat rows;* marginal spots brownish red. *Underside:* Pattern similar to that of Leanira Checker-spot (p. 104).
**Similar species:** Might be confused with Fulvous Checker-spot (above), but ranges mostly different.
**Early stages:** Unknown. Multiple broods. **Adults:** April–Sept.
**Range:** Se. Ariz. south to s. Mexico. Rare in U.S. TL: Oaxaca, Mexico. **Habitat:** Mountain meadows, forest openings.

## THEONA CHECKER-SPOT                           Pl. 17
*Thessalia theona* (Ménétriés)
**Identification:** 1¼-1¾ in. (31–44 mm). *Upperside:* Dark with light bands; wing bases dark. *Median band pale tawny to white;* pm. band orange-brown. Cell-end bar in FW light; submarginal spots in HW small, light. *Underside:* HW with 5 bands (from base to margin, they are white, reddish, white, reddish, white). Veins black.
**Similar species:** Aaron's Checker-spot (p. 102).
**Early stages:** Larva blackish brown with white dots; middorsal line black. Multiple broods. **Food:** Ceniza *(Leucophyllum frutescens)* in Tex., paintbrush *(Castilleja)* in Ariz.; both in figwort family. **Adults:** Long flight season.
**Range:** Cen. Ariz., s. N.M., and s.-cen. Tex. to Cen. America. **Habitat:** Brushlands in Tex., canyons and streamsides in Ariz.
**Subspecies:** *T. t. theona* (Ménétriés). Not in U.S. TL: Nicaragua.

(2) **Boll's Checker-spot,** *T. t. bollii* (W. H. Edwards), Pl. 17. Median band and pm. band tend to partially fuse on FW. N.M., Tex.; Mexico. TL: San Antonio, Tex. (3) **Thekla Checker-spot,** *T. t. thekla* (W. H. Edwards). Base of FW less darkened, more tawny. Cen. Ariz., n. Mexico. TL: Ft. Lowell, Ariz.

## TINKHAM'S CHECKER-SPOT          Pl. 17
*Thessalia chinatiensis* (Tinkham)
**Identification:** 1¼-1½ in. (31–38 mm). *Upperside:* Bright tawny; wing bases, borders, and veins blackish. Marginal spots small, *white. All markings evenly spaced. Underside:* On HW, *basal, median, and marginal bands whitish.* Postbasal spots and pm. band orange-brown; veins black.
**Similar species:** Theona Checker-spot (p. 105) has many more markings.
**Early stages:** Undescribed. Multiple broods. **Food:** Big Bend silverleaf *(Leucophyllum minus).* **Adults:** Long flight season.
**Range:** W. Tex. TL: Chinati Mts., Presidio Co., Tex. **Habitat:** Brushy gulches and flats.
**Remarks:** Little known. Range limited and mostly remote.

## Checker-spots: Genus *Dymasia* Higgins

These checker-spots are small, southwestern species. Abdomen long; wings long and slender. On underside of HW, *no red line* between black terminal line and white submarginal band. Two species.

## DYMAS CHECKER-SPOT          Pl. 18
*Dymasia dymas* (W. H. Edwards)
**Identification:** ⅞-1⅜ in. (22–34 mm). Female often larger than male, and lighter in color. *Upperside:* Light orange-brown; dark markings narrow, evenly distributed. All spots of median band alike in both size and color. *Underside:* Median band consists of equal-sized spots; *outer edge of white marginal spots flat.*
**Similar species:** In Chara Checker-spot (below), median band irregular, the part near costa much paler. The ranges do not overlap.
**Early stages:** Undescribed. 2–3 broods. **Food:** Hairy tubetongue *(Siphonoglossa pilosella).* **Adults:** April–Nov.
**Range:** Southern N.M., s. Tex.; n. Mexico. TL: San Antonio, Tex. **Habitat:** Streamsides, washes, stony slopes, roadsides.

## CHARA CHECKER-SPOT          Pl. 18
*Dymasia chara* (W. H. Edwards)
**Identification:** ⅞-1¼ in. (22–31 mm). *Upperside:* In both sexes, FW median band irregular; *2–4 whitish costal spots,* set at an angle to rest of median band. Wing borders usually dark. Female

larger, lighter. **Underside:** Outer edge of marginal spots flat, as in Dymas Checker-spot (above).
**Similar species:** Dymas Checker-spot (above).
**Early stages:** Larva gray, mottled with black and white; bases of spines orange. Pupa gray, speckled with black and brown. Multiple broods. **Food:** Chuparosa *(Beloperone californica),* in acanthus family. **Adults:** March–Oct. Flight slow, drifting.
**Range:** S. Calif., cen. Ariz. south to Baja California, Mexico. **Habitat:** Rocky canyons and washes in the desert.
**Subspecies:** (1) **Chara Checker-spot,** *D. c. chara* (W. H. Edwards), Pl. 18. Ariz., Mexico. TL: Tucson, Ariz. (2) **Imperial Checker-spot,** *D. c. imperialis* (Bauer). Border on upperside less dark. S. Calif., Baja California. TL: Palm Springs, Calif.

## Checker-spots: Genus *Texola* Higgins

Abdomen long, as in *Dymasia* (previous genus), but wings more rounded. A *red-brown line* runs between the black terminal line and a white submarginal band on underside of HW (this line absent in *Dymasia*).

**ELADA CHECKER-SPOT** *Texola elada* (Hewitson)     **Pl. 18**
**Identification:** $7/8$–$1\frac{1}{4}$ in. (22–31 mm). **Upperside:** Both sexes dark brown, with orange-brown bands of small spots. Borders unspotted. Fringes have small white spots between veins. In female, colors more intense. **Underside:** White median band on HW double or triple; spots small, black-edged. *2nd spot of pm. band white,* the other spots reddish.
**Similar species:** (1) Dymas Checker-spot (p. 106) and (2) Chara Checker-spot (p. 106) lack red marginal line on outer edge of underside of HW.
**Early stages:** Little known. Multiple broods. **Food:** Hairy tubetongue *(Siphonoglossa pilosella)* in Tex.; not known for Ariz. population. **Adults:** April–Nov. Common; they often fly with Dymas Checker-spot in Tex. and with Chara Checker-spot in Ariz.
**Range:** Ariz. to s. Tex.; Mexico. **Habitat:** Streamsides, washes, desert scrub, roadsides, fencerows.
**Subspecies:** (1) *T. e. elada* (Hewitson). Not in U.S. TL: Mexico. (2) **Callina Checker-spot** (Boisduval), *T. e. callina* (Boisduval), Pl. 18. N.M. to s. Tex.; Mexico. TL: Sonora, Mexico. (3) **Perse Checker-spot,** *T. e. perse* (W. H. Edwards). Paler; light spots larger. Ariz.; Mexico. TL: Vicinity of Ft. Grant, Graham Co., Ariz.

## Elva: Genus *Microtia* Bates

**ELVA** *Microtia elva* Bates                          **Pl. 18**
**Identification:** 1–$1\frac{1}{4}$ in. (25–31 mm). Upperside and underside alike, black with orange patches. Unmistakable.

**Early stages:** Unknown. **Food:** Unknown. **Adults:** Occasional stragglers into the U.S.
**Range:** Cen. America; found occasionally northward to s. Ariz. and s. Tex. TL: Guatemala.

## Checker-spots: Genus *Poladryas* Bauer

N. America, in the U.S. and Mexico. Two species. These checker-spots have no orange-brown in marginal band; black and white only.

**SMALL CHECKER-SPOT**                                          **Pl. 18**
*Poladryas minuta* (W. H. Edwards)
**Identification:** 1¼–1½ in. (31–38 mm). The name is inappropriate; several checker-spots are smaller. *Upperside:* Tawny with black markings. Dark border narrow; pm. band wide. Spots of submarginal band are small crescents. *Underside:* Marginal band edged with black on both outer and inner edges; *white spots at margin deeply crescent-shaped* on outer face.
**Similar species:** Arachne Checker-spot (below).
**Early stages:** Undescribed. Multiple broods. **Food:** Said to be *Penstemon*. **Adults:** Flight season not stated.
**Range:** S.-cen. Tex.; said to occur in Mexico as well. TL: Comfort, Kendall Co., Tex.
**Remarks:** Formerly common, now very scarce. No recent records. Perhaps a victim of overgrazing.

**ARACHNE CHECKER-SPOT**                                        **Pl. 18**
*Poladryas arachne* (W. H. Edwards)
**Identification:** 1¼–1¾ in. (31–44 mm). *Upperside:* Bright orange-brown; dark lines distinct. Median band lighter in some individuals. *Underside:* White marginal spots on HW edged outwardly by a thin black terminal line; black edging on inner margin of these spots very thin. Terminal spots and fringes white, with black points at vein ends.
**Similar species:** Small Checker-spot (above).
**Early stages:** Larva whitish, spines black; 2 subdorsal rows of red spines, Larva overwinters. **Food:** *Penstemon* (various species).
**Adults:** May–Sept.
**Range:** E. Nev., se. Wyo., w. Neb. south through Rocky Mts. to Ariz., N.M., w. Tex.; Mexico. An isolated population in s. Sierra Nevada of Calif. **Habitat:** Mountain fields and meadows; desert grasslands in Ariz.
**Subspecies:** (1) **Arachne Checker-spot,** *P. a. arachne* (W. H. Edwards), Pl. 18. Rocky Mts. TL: Golden, Jefferson Co., Colo. (2) **Arizona Checker-spot,** *P. a. nympha* (W. H. Edwards). Smaller. Median line on upperside of HW pale. Ariz., s. N.M. TL: Ft. Grant, Graham Co., Ariz. (3) **Monache Checker-spot,** *P. a. monache*

(J. A. Comstock). Coloration light, uniform.    S. Sierra Nevada. TL: Monache Meadows, Tulare Co., Calif.

## Checker-spots:
## Genera *Occidryas* Higgins and *Hypodryas* Higgins

Robust; wings black, checkered with red and white or yellowish. Four of our 5 species show great individual and geographical variation. For *Occidryas* species, positive identification is usually possible only by examination of male genitalia (see Fig. 11 and simplified key below); this requires some skill and the use of a binocular microscope or hand lens. Gillette's Checker-spot (p. 113) is the only species in the genus *Hypodryas*. It is easily recognized by its distinctive pattern and conspicuous wide reddish pm. band.

**Early stages:** Eggs laid in masses. Larva spiny, black marked with orange and/or white; overwinters when partly grown. Pupa

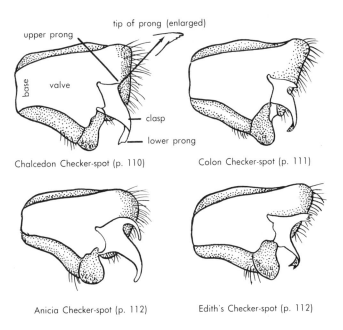

Chalcedon Checker-spot (p. 110)          Colon Checker-spot (p. 111)

Anicia Checker-spot (p. 112)          Edith's Checker-spot (p. 112)

**Fig. 11. Male genitalia (sex organs) of *Occidryas* species.**

light-colored, marked by small dark spots and lines. 1 or 2 broods.
**Food:** Varies for different species and subspecies. **Adults:** Early
(March–May) in mild climates, later (June–Aug.) where weather is
more severe.

Until 1978, these butterflies were placed in the genus
*Euphydryas.*

Key to males of our *Occidryas* species, based on genitalia:

**1a.** Upper prong of clasper short or moderate          **Go to 2**
**1b.** Upper prong of clasper long                       **Go to 3**

**2a.** Upper prong of clasper with very small teeth at tip (Fig. 11).
                              **Chalcedon Checker-spot, below**
**2b.** Upper prong of clasper without teeth, usually slightly turned
down (Fig. 11).             **Colon Checker-spot, p. 111**

**3a.** Upper prong at less than 90° angle to lower prong, long and
usually curved (Fig. 11).     **Anicia Checker-spot, p. 112**
**3b.** Upper and lower prongs separated by more than a 90° angle;
tip of upper prong armed with spines (Fig. 11).
                              **Edith's Checker-spot, p. 112**

## CHALCEDON CHECKER-SPOT                     Pl. 18
*Occidryas chalcedona* (Doubleday)
**Identification:** $1\frac{1}{4}$–$2\frac{1}{4}$ in. (31–56 mm). FW narrow. *Upperside:*
Typically black, with bands of *small yellowish spots. Cell bars
and marginal spots red.* Geographically variable: in the Sierra
Nevada of Calif., e. Calif. and Ariz., the black on the upperside
may be replaced by red-brown, orange-brown, salmon, or tawny,
with dark markings that are greatly reduced. Median band,
submarginal band, and cell spots of such subspecies may be very
light-colored.
**Similar species:** Colon Checker-spot (p. 111).
**Early stages:** Larvae usually either black with white hairs, or
black with white stripes. Both types have orange spots at base of
spine tufts. Pupa typically gray, with small dark speckles. Usually
1 brood. **Food:** Many members of the snapdragon family
(Scrophulariaceae), including California bee plant *(Scrophularia
californica);* many species of monkey flower, especially sticky
monkey flower *(Mimulus aurantiacus);* also paintbrush
*(Castilleja), Penstemon,* and other plants. **Adults:** March–July,
depending on elevation.
**Range:** S. Ore. to Ariz.; Baja California. **Habitat:** General; a
dominant in its range. Coastal to mountain; desert ranges of
s. Calif., s. Nev., Ariz.
**Subspecies:** (1) **Chalcedon Checker-spot,** *O. c. chalcedona*
(Doubleday), Pl. 18, No. 7. Most of cismontane Calif. (west of
Sierra Nevada). TL: Not stated; possibly near San Francisco. (2)

**Dwinelle's Checker-spot,** *O. c. dwinellei* (Hy. Edwards). Considerable red overscaling on upperside. Vicinity of McCloud and Bartle; very local. TL: McCloud Fishing Station, Shasta Co., Calif. (3) **Henne's Checker-spot,** *O. c. hennei* (Scott). Small, with conspicuous yellowish spots. Desert Mts., San Diego-Riverside Cos. TL: Box Canyon, San Diego Co. Called *O. c. quino* in literature prior to Nov., 1981. (4) **McGlashan's Checker-spot,** *O. c. macglashanii* (Rivers). Much like subspecies *chalcedona;* white spots larger. Eastern slope of cen. Sierra Nevada. TL: Truckee, Nevada Co., Calif. (5) **Olancha Checker-spot,** *O. c. olancha* (W. G. Wright). Both red and white spots large; very distinctive. Eastern slope of s. Sierra Nevada. TL: Olancha Peak, Tulare-Inyo Cos., Calif. (6) **Sierra Checker-spot,** *O. c. sierra* (W. G. Wright), Pl. 18, No. 8. Very red. Cen. Sierra Nevada. TL: Sierra Nevadas, Calif. (7) **Klots' Checker-spot,** *O. c. klotsi* (dos Passos). Small. Reddish areas more orange-brown than red. Dry mountains from e. Calif. to cen. Ariz. TL: Roosevelt Dam, Gila Co., Ariz. (8) **Kingston Checker-spot,** *O. c. kingstonensis* (T. & J. Emmel). Salmon-colored, dark markings small. Desert ranges of e. Mojave Desert. TL: Kingston Range, San Bernardino Co., Calif. (9) **Corral Checker-spot,** *O. c. corralensis* (T. & J. Emmel). Spots light red, dark markings narrow. Eastern and northern San Bernardino Mts. TL: Rock Corral, Johnson Valley, San Bernardino Co., Calif.

## COLON CHECKER-SPOT                                    Pl. 18
*Occidryas colon* (W. H. Edwards)
**Identification:** 1⅜-2 in. (34–50 mm). FW relatively broad. *Upperside:* Black; white spots usually small, red spots reduced. Pm. band of *light spots absent or barely visible* as "ghost spots" on HW. (In subspecies *paradoxa,* pm. spots are red.) *Underside:* Red areas brighter and more extensive than in Chalcedon Checker-spot (above).
**Early stages:** Larva spiny, black with white hairs; orange spots at bases of spine tufts. One brood. **Food:** Snowberry *(Symphoricarpos),* in honeysuckle family. In spring, after hibernation, larvae may eat other plants such as *Penstemon* (various species). **Adults:** May–July.
**Range:** British Columbia to n. Calif., east to w. Mont., Idaho. **Habitat:** Meadows, streamsides, forest openings.
**Subspecies:** (1) **Colon Checker-spot,** *O. c. colon* (W. H. Edwards), Pl. 18. N. Calif., w. and cen. Ore., w. Wash. TL: Kalama, Cowlitz Co., Wash. (2) **Perdiccas Checker-spot,** *O. c. perdiccas* (W. H. Edwards). Upperside with more red in discal cell and on wing margins. Mountains of w. Wash. TL: Tenino, Thurston Co., Wash. (3) **Contrary Checker-spot,** *O. c. paradoxa* (McDunnough). Pm. spots on upperside of HW red. British Columbia south to Mont., Idaho. TL: Seton Lake, Lillooet, British Columbia. (4) **Wallace Checker-spot,** *O. c. wallacensis*

(Gunder). Smaller; light spots on upperside small. E. Wash. south to ne. Calif. TL: Wallace, Shoshone Co., Idaho. (5) **Nevada Checker-spot,** *O. c. nevadensis* (Bauer). White areas more extensive. Elko Co., Nev. and adjacent Idaho and Utah. TL: Wildhorse Camp, Elko Co., Nev.

## ANICIA CHECKER-SPOT                                Pl. 18
*Occidryas anicia* (Doubleday)

**Identification:** $1\frac{1}{4}$–2 in. (31–50 mm). General checker-spot pattern — black banded with red and white. An extremely variable species geographically, with many subspecies. Some subspecies are predominantly red-brown or orange-brown, others mostly black with white spots or bands; HW pm. spots, when red, are usually small. Spots of submarginal band may be red or white, depending on subspecies. FW usually narrow and pointed; more rounded in female. No less than 21 subspecies are recognized, some with little resemblance to others.

**Similar species:** In Edith's Checker-spot (below), FW more rounded. Red pm. band on upperside of HW usually wide.

**Early stages:** Larva whitish with black hairs, or dark with whitish stripes. One brood. **Food:** *Penstemon,* for those subspecies whose food is known. **Adults:** June–Aug., depending on location.

**Range:** Alaska (Yukon Valley) south to eastern slope of Cascade Mts., Nev., Ariz., N.M.

**Subspecies:** 21 subspecies; 3 very different ones are described here. (1) **Anicia Checker-spot,** *O. a. anicia* (Doubleday), Pl. 18, No. 10. Black; red bands narrow, median band and cell bars white. Rocky Mts. in British Columbia, Alberta, northern U.S. TL: Banff, Alberta. (2) **Capella Checker-spot,** *O. a. capella* (Barnes), Pl. 18, No. 12. Bright reddish brown; dark markings narrow, white markings few. Eastern slope of Rocky Mts. TL: Manitou and Denver, Colo. (3) **Leussler's Checker-spot,** *O. a. bernadetta* Leussler, Pl. 18, No. 11. Black with white bands; pm. band and marginal spots small, red. Wyo., Mont., Neb. TL: Monroe Canyon, vicinity of Harrison, Sioux Co., Neb.

## EDITH'S CHECKER-SPOT                               Pl. 18
*Occidryas editha* (Boisduval)

**Identification:** $1\frac{1}{4}$–2 in. (31–50 mm). FW usually broad, rounded at tip. Butterfly variable, but the following pattern is usually recognizable. *Upperside:* Black or dark gray, banded with red and white (or pale yellow). Submedian band, pm. band, marginal spots, and 2 cell bars white or yellowish. *Red pm. band wide,* especially on HW, extending from vein to vein. White or yellow submarginal band of small spots.

**Similar species:** Anicia Checker-spot (above).

**Early stages:** Larva dark with light hairs, or blackish banded with white. Prolegs and seta bases usually orange. One brood.

**Food:** Dwarf plantain *(Plantago erecta),* in plantain family, and Indian warrior *(Pedicularis);* also owl's clover *(Orthocarpus)* in coastal Calif., Chinese houses *(Collinsia)* on western slope of Sierra Nevada; elsewhere, penstemons *(Penstemon,* various species) and paintbrush *(Castilleja),* in snapdragon family (Scrophulariaceae). **Adults:** March–May at low elevations, to June–Aug. at high elevations and northward. **Range:** British Columbia and Alberta south to Baja California, Nev., Utah, Colo. TL: Foothills s. edge of San Joaquin Valley, Calif. **Habitat:** Varies with different subspecies, from sea level to treeline. Fields, rocky hills, meadows, alpine terraces, alpine fellfields. **Subspecies:** 21 subspecies and many intergrading populations have been recognized; 3 are illustrated on Pl. 18. (1) **Bay Region Checker-spot,** *O. e. bayensis* (Sternitzky), Pl. 18, No. 14. Ground color grayer than in most subspecies. Formerly ranged from San Francisco to Silver Creek Hills, Santa Clara Co.; now greatly reduced in localities and numbers. TL: Hillsborough, San Mateo Co., Calif. (2) **Ruddy Checker-spot,** *O. e. rubicunda* (Hy. Edwards), Pl. 18, No. 13. Red bands on upperside wide and bright. Foothills of cen. Sierra Nevada. TL: Mariposa Co., Calif. (3) **Cloud-born Checker-spot,** *O. e. nubigena* (Behr), Pl. 18, No. 15. Small, usually very red. Very high elevations in the Sierra Nevada. TL: Headwaters of Tuolumne R., Calif. **Remarks:** Very local. Some subspecies seem restricted to metamorphic soils; found on serpentine in coastal Calif.

### GILLETTE'S CHECKER-SPOT Pl. 18
*Hypodryas gillettii* (Barnes)
**Identification:** $1\frac{1}{2}$–$1\frac{7}{8}$ in. (38–47 mm). Unmistakable. ***Upperside:*** FW cell bars, postbasal spots, and marginal spots orange-red. *Wide, orange-red pm. band on both wings.* Other spots smaller, white. **Early stages:** Larva dark brown; lateral stripe white, middorsal stripe yellow. Spines black. One brood. **Food:** Twin-berry honeysuckle *(Lonicera involucrata).* **Adults:** July. They perch openly on tall flowers and on twigs. Tame. **Range:** Alberta, Mont., e. Idaho, w. Wyo. Very local. TL: Yellowstone Natl. Park, Wyo. **Habitat:** Moist or marshy meadows; streamsides; moist open forest.

# SWALLOWTAILS and PARNASSIANS:
## Family Papilionidae

Worldwide. Large butterflies with the front legs fully developed; tarsal claws simple (not divided). One anal vein in HW. Two subfamilies in our area.

# Parnassians: Subfamily Parnassiinae

Holarctic. HW rounded, with no tail; no cubito-anal crossvein. Antennae short, straight. White or yellow, with dark markings and a set number of red spots. After mating, females develop a *sphragis,* a waxy pouch on the tip of the abdomen that prevents further mating.

**Early stages:** Larva covered with fine, short, dark hair that gives it a velvety appearance (Fig. 5, p. 26). Each body segment has yellow areas. Pupa forms cocoon on ground.

## Parnassians: Genus *Parnassius* Latreille

**EVERSMANN'S PARNASSIAN**                                    **Pl. 19**
*Parnassius eversmanni* Ménétriés
**Identification:** 1¾–2¼ in. (44–56 mm). Male light yellow, female yellowish white; these colors unique among our parnassians. Two red spots on each HW. *Sphragis (pouch) of female white.*
**Early stages:** One brood. **Food:** Corydalis *(Corydalis),* in the bleeding heart family (Fumariaceae). **Adults:** Late June–early Aug. Flight usually low and fast.
**Range:** Interior Alaska, Yukon Terr., n. British Columbia; eastern Asia. **Habitat:** Tundra.
**Subspecies:** (1) *P. e. eversmanni* Ménétriés. Not in U.S. TL: Kansk, Russia. (2) *P. e. thor* Hy. Edwards, Pl. 19. TL: Alaska.

**CLODIUS PARNASSIAN**                                        **Pl. 19**
*Parnassius clodius* Ménétriés
**Identification:** 2–2½ in. (50–62 mm). Antennae black. *Upperside:* Ground color white; FW cell gray or dull black with *3 white bars. No red spots* in FW. HW has 2 red spots; female usually also has a *red anal bar.* Sphragis (pouch) of female large, keeled, white.
**Similar species:** In Phoebus Parnassian (p. 115), FW has 2 red (or yellow) spots beyond cell; cell bars black.
**Early stages:** Larva hides at base of plant, feeds at night. One brood. **Food:** Bleeding heart *(Dicentra),* in the bleeding heart family (Fumariaceae). (Other plants erroneously reported are violets, blueberry, raspberry, stonecrop.) **Adults:** May–early Aug.
**Range:** The only species of parnassian found *only* in N. America. Alaska south to Santa Cruz Mts. and Sierra Nevada, Calif., east to Mont., Idaho, Utah, Wyo. **Habitat:** Meadows, open forest, rock outcrops, alpine fell-fields.
**Subspecies:** 10 rather similar subspecies are recognized, including the **Claudianus Parnassian,** *P. c. claudianus* Stichel, Pl. 19. TL: British Columbia.

**PHOEBUS PARNASSIAN**                                              **Pl. 19**
*Parnassius phoebus* (Fabricius)
**Identification:** $1\frac{3}{4}$-$2\frac{1}{2}$ in. (44–62 mm). Antennal shaft ringed
with black and white. *2 red* (or yellow) *spots on FW beyond cell* in
female and in most males (these spots are black in some males).
FW cell bars black against light ground color. HW has 2 red spots
as in Clodius Parnassian (above). Red anal bar present in some
(but not all) females; sphragis (pouch) small, dark gray.
**Early stages:** See subfamily Parnassiinae (p. 114). One brood.
**Food:** Stonecrop *(Sedum),* including western roseroot *(Sedum
rosea),* in stonecrop family. **Adults:** June–Aug.
**Range:** Alaska, Yukon Terr., British Columbia, and Alberta east
to Wyo. and S.D., south to cen. Calif., Nev., Utah, Colo. **Habitat:**
Always in mountains, usually at high elevations; usually in ex-
posed rocky places.
**Subspecies:** 14 or more N. American subspecies, showing minor
differences in size and markings, are recognized. (1) *P. p. phoebus*
(Fabricius). Does not occur in N. America. TL: Siberia. (2) **Say's
Parnassian,** *P. p. sayii* W. H. Edwards, Pl. 19. TL: Pike's Peak,
Colo. (3) **Smintheus Parnassian,** *P. p. smintheus* Doubleday.
TL: (presumably) vicinity of Banff, Alberta (Canada).
**Remarks:** This butterfly was called *Parnassius smintheus* in
older literature; it is now considered a subspecies of *P. phoebus.*
Called the Small Apollo by Higgins and Riley in *Butterflies of
Britain and Europe,* 1970.

# Swallowtails: Subfamily Papilioninae

Cosmopolitan; most abundant in the tropics. Our species usually
have a "tail" on the HW. Antennae long, curved. Cubito-anal
crossvein present.
   **Early stages:** Larva smooth, or with fleshy filaments. The
osmaterium, an organ on the thorax that produces a strong odor, is
thrust out when the larva is disturbed. Pupa suspended upright,
supported by a silken girdle (Fig. 6, p. 27).
   Swallowtails of some species have great individual and geographic
variation. Some species hybridize in areas where their ranges
meet.

## Aristolochia Swallowtails: Genus *Battus* Scopoli

**PIPE-VINE SWALLOWTAIL**                                           **Pl. 19**
*Battus philenor* (Linnaeus)
**Identification:** $2\frac{3}{4}$-4 in. (69–100 mm). ***Upperside:*** Male black
with bluish green iridescence; female less iridescent. Submarginal
spots white. ***Underside:*** In both sexes, HW has complete pm.
band of orange spots.
**Early stages:** Larva black, with orange spots and fleshy fila-

ments. Multiple broods where climate permits. **Food:** Pipe-vine *(Aristolochia)* and wild ginger *(Asarum),* both in birthwort family. **Adults:** Long flight season.
**Range:** In the West, cen. Calif. east to Neb., south to Ariz., N.M., and Tex. Casual in Colo. East to New England, Fla.; south to Costa Rica. **Habitat:** Open forest, parks, roadsides, fencerows, streamsides, thorn forest.
**Subspecies:** (1) **Pipe-vine Swallowtail,** *B. p. philenor* (Linnaeus), Pl. 19. All of range in U.S., except where next subspecies occurs. TL: America. (2) **Hairy Swallowtail,** *B. p. hirsuta* (Skinner). Smaller; tails shorter, body hairy. Isolated; in Calif. only. Alameda Co. north to Mendocino Co. and Shasta Co. TL: Plumas Co., Calif.
**Remarks:** An unpleasant-tasting species, presumably mimicked by the Spicebush Swallowtail (p. 123), Black Swallowtail (below), dark female Eastern Tiger Swallowtail (p. 121), and Red-spotted Purple (p. 64).

## Fluted Swallowtails: Genus *Papilio* Linnaeus

**BLACK SWALLOWTAIL**                                    **Pl. 19**
*Papilio polyxenes* Fabricius
**Identification:** 2½–3½ in. (62–88 mm). *Tegulae* (scale-like flaps over FW bases) *black,* or only slightly tinged with yellow in far western subspecies. *Upperside:* Both sexes black. Male has pm. and submarginal bands consisting of small yellow spots; HW has blue spots or shades and an *orange anal spot with a round black center.* In female, pm. band often absent, and blue shades more extensive. *Underside:* Light spots usually partly or entirely orange, especially on HW.
**Similar species:** In Baird's Swallowtail (p. 117), *tegulae mostly yellow.*
**Early stages:** Young larva dark, with a light saddle; resembles a bird dropping. Mature larva green; each segmental dark band encloses several yellow spots. Several western swallowtails have somewhat similar larvae. 2–3 broods. **Food:** Many members of the parsley family (Apiaceae), including cultivated as well as native species: carrot, dill, parsley, celery, and others. Also common rue *(Ruta graveolans),* Dutchman's breeches *(Thamnosma texana),* and turpentine broom *(T. montana),* in the rue family (Rutaceae).
**Adults:** May–Nov., depending on locality.
**Range:** S. Canada south across N. America to n. South America; in the West, N.D. and Rocky Mts. south to se. Calif., Baja California, Ariz., N.M., and Tex. Absent from the Great Basin and Pacific Slope. **Habitat:** Quite general in much of its range. In Calif., restricted to the arid southeastern part of the state.
**Subspecies:** (1) *P. p. polyxenes* Fabricius. Neotropical. (2) **Black Swallowtail,** *P. p. asterius* Stoll, Pl. 19, No. 11. E. Ariz. and

Rocky Mts. east to e. U.S. (3) **Wright's Swallowtail,** *P. p. coloro* Wright (formerly *P. rudkini* F. & R. Chermock), Pl. 19, No. 12. Sexes have similar markings (not dimorphic). *Yellow pm. band usually wide.* Has 2 forms: In form "comstocki," yellow band wide; abdomen with yellow stripes on sides. In form "clarki," yellow band narrow; abdomen with yellow spots on sides. Food: Usually turpentine broom. Se. Calif., Baja California, w. Nev., w. Ariz. **Remarks:** The Black Swallowtail and Wright's Swallowtail intergrade in e. Ariz.

## BAIRD'S SWALLOWTAIL                              Pl. 20
*Papilio bairdii* W. H. Edwards
**Identification:** 3-3½ in. (75-88 mm). *Tegulae* (flaps over FW bases) *mostly yellow.* **Upperside:** Black, with a yellow pm. band wider than that in Black Swallowtail (above), and "smudgy" on its inner edge. Black center of orange HW anal spot *touches or nearly touches* inner margin. *P. b. bairdii* has *2 rows of yellow spots* on black abdomen. Female usually darker, often lacks pm. band, and has extensive blue shades.
**Similar species:** (1) Black Swallowtail (above). (2) In Nitra Swallowtail (p. 118) tegulae and abdomen are all black.
**Early stages:** Larva quite similar to that of Black Swallowtail (above). Two broods. **Food:** Dragon sagebrush *(Artemisia dracunculus),* in sunflower family (Asteraceae). **Adults:** May-Aug. Usually uncommon, and often quite shy.
**Range:** S. Canada east to N.D., Neb., south to s. Calif. (San Bernardino Mts.), Ariz., N.M. TL: Fort Whipple, near Prescott, Ariz.
**Habitat:** Mountain areas. Adults wide-ranging.
**Remarks:** Two forms, formerly considered species or subspecies, occur in populations of Baird's Swallowtail. In form "hollandi," yellow pm. band wider than that of subspecies *bairdii,* but narrower than that of the other form ("brucei"). In form "brucei," yellow pm. band wide, reaching HW base; sides of abdomen yellow. These forms occur together in varying percentages.

## OREGON SWALLOWTAIL                              Pl. 20
*Papilio oregonius* W. H. Edwards
**Identification:** 3-3½ in. (75-88 mm). **Upperside:** *Pm. band wide* — nearly reaches base of HW. *Black area at base of FW powdered with yellow scales.* Radial vein yellow near base; tegulae (wing flaps) mostly yellow. *Abdomen yellow,* with black stripes on back and lower sides. Black center of orange anal spot flattened, just touching margin. Sexes similar.
**Similar species:** In Zelicaon Swallowtail (p. 118), abdomen black, with yellow stripe on side.
**Early stages:** Larva grayish green, with black crossbands that are broken by yellow dots. Two broods. **Food:** Dragon sagebrush *(Artemisia dracunculus).* **Adults:** April-June, July-Sept.

**Range:** British Columbia east to Alberta and N.D., south to e. Ore., Idaho, Mont., and Wyo. **Habitat:** Streamsides, sagebrush scrub, roadsides, fencerows.

**Subspecies:** (1) **Oregon Swallowtail,** *P. o. oregonius* W. H. Edwards, Pl. 20. British Columbia, Mont., and Wyo., south into Ore. TL: Near The Dalles, Ore. (2) **Dod's Swallowtail,** *P. o. dodi* McDunnough. FW base not powdered with yellow scales. Alberta, N.D. TL: Red Deer River, Alberta.

**Remarks:** The Oregon Swallowtail has been designated the official State Insect by the Oregon Legislature.

### ZELICAON or ANISE SWALLOWTAIL     Pl. 20

*Papilio zelicaon* Lucas

**Identification:** $2\frac{3}{4}$–$3\frac{3}{8}$ in. (69–84 mm). Also called Western Parsley Swallowtail. Tegulae (wing flaps) mostly yellow; abdomen black with yellow stripe on side. *Upperside:* Spots of yellow pm. band on FW become gradually longer from costa to inner margin; band on HW extends to wing base. Anal cell of HW *mostly yellow;* black center of orange anal spot round, *free from HW margin.* Uppermost light submarginal spot usually yellow, seldom orange. **Similar species:** Oregon Swallowtail (p. 117).

**Early stages:** Larva similar to that of Black Swallowtail (p. 116). Pupa may be either green or brown. Multiple broods. **Food:** Many native and cultivated members of the parsley family (Apiaceae). Prefers anise or fennel *(Foeniculum vulgare)* at low elevations in settled areas. **Adults:** Long flight season at low elevations, shorter season at higher elevations.

**Range:** British Columbia, Alberta, N.D. south to s. Calif., Ariz., N.M.; Baja California; Mexico. Widespread, often common. TL: Calif. **Habitat:** Fields, roadsides, vacant lots, bare hills.

**Subspecies:** Work done in 1977 on the life history and genetics of the Nitra and Gothic Swallowtails has shown that the Nitra Swallowtail is a subspecies of the Zelicaon Swallowtail, and the Gothic Swallowtail is a form of the Nitra Swallowtail. These subspecies are treated in the next account.

### NITRA SWALLOWTAIL     Pl. 20

*Papilio zelicaon nitra* W. H. Edwards

**Identification:** An uncommon insect, described in 1884, and since then usually considered a distinct species. Very unlike Zelicaon Swallowtail (above); general appearance dark. *Upperside:* Yellow pm. band narrow, not extending to wing base on HW; the spots of this band *grade gradually into the black wing bases.* Uppermost submarginal spot often orange. *Underside:* HW pm. spots often tipped with orange.

**Similar species:** Baird's Swallowtail (p. 117).

**Early stages:** Similar to those of Zelicaon Swallowtail. One brood. **Food:** Biscuit roots (*Lomatium,* various species), mountain parsleys *(Harbouria trachypleura, Pseudocymopterus montanus),* cow parsnip *(Heracleum lanatum),* and other members of the carrot or parsley family (Apiaceae). **Adults:** July.

**Range:** Eastern slope of Rocky Mts., Alberta, south to Colo. and rarely N.M. TL: Judith Mts., Mont. Form "gothica" (see Remarks) also occurs on the western slope of the Rocky Mts. **Habitat:** Meadows, forest openings, open woodland.

**Remarks:** Gothic Swallowtail, *P. z. nitra,* form "gothica" Remington was described in 1968 as a distinct species (TL: Gothic, Gunnison Co., Colo.). It is nearly identical to the Zelicaon Swallowtail, and is separated mostly by minor biological differences. It is now considered the yellow form of the Nitra Swallowtail. Both fly in the same localities, the dark Nitra always in smaller numbers.

### KAHL'S SWALLOWTAIL                                  not shown
*Papilio kahli* F. & R. Chermock

**Identification:** A species of restricted range. Measurements not available. *Upperside:* Pm. band narrow; 1 yellow bar at end of FW cell. Submarginal spots larger than those of Zelicaon Swallowtail (p. 118). Orange anal spot has a very small, black center.

**Early stages:** Similar to those of the Black Swallowtail (p. 116). One brood. **Food:** Parsnip *(Pastinaca sativa),* in the parsley family (Apiaceae). **Adults:** July.

**Range:** Manitoba, Saskatchewan. TL: Riding Mts., Manitoba. **Habitat:** Not stated.

### OLD WORLD SWALLOWTAIL                               Pl. 20
*Papilio machaon* Linnaeus

**Identification:** 2½–3 in. (62–75 mm). FW costa and outer margin more than usually convex; tail slender, but usually not long. *Upperside:* Yellow pm. band wide, extending to anal cell on HW; anal cell black. *Orange anal spot* on HW has black margin but *no black center.* Body and edge of HW very hairy.

**Early stages:** Quite similar to those of the Black Swallowtail (p. 116). Overwinters as a pupa. One brood. **Food:** Mountain sagewort *(Artemisia arctica),* in sunflower family (Asteraceae). **Adults:** Late May–July.

**Range:** In N. America, mostly northern: Alaska and Yukon Terr. east to southern end of Hudson Bay, south to British Columbia, Alberta, Manitoba. The most common swallowtail in Europe. **Habitat:** Meadows, tundra; very commonly flies around exposed hilltops.

**Subspecies:** (1) *P. m. machaon* Linnaeus. European. (2) **Alaskan Old World Swallowtail,** *P. m. aliaska* Scudder, Pl. 20. Alaska, n. Canada. TL: Nulato, Alaska. (3) **Hudsonian Swallowtail,**

*P. m. hudsonianus* A. H. Clark. Dark outer areas of HW wider and with more blue. Orange anal spot with conspicuous black lower edge. Manitoba eastward; eastern edge of our area. TL: Kettle Rapids, Nelson R., Manitoba.

**INDRA SWALLOWTAIL** *Papilio indra* Reakirt          **Pl. 20**
**Identification:** $2\frac{1}{2}$-$2\frac{7}{8}$ in. (62-72 mm). *Tail on HW very short* in typical subspecies *(indra,* Pl. 20), *long* in others. **Upperside:** Black; light markings pale yellow. Yellow pm. band narrow in subspecies *indra;* width of band varies among subspecies. Submarginal spots usually small; bar at end of FW cell very narrow to absent.
**Early stages:** Larva banded yellow (or orange) and black. One brood. **Food:** Various plants in the parsley family (Apiaceae) — larvae of different subspecies feed on different plants (see below).
**Adults:** May-Aug., depending on subspecies and locality.
**Range:** Wash. east to S.D., south to s. Calif., Nev., Ariz., N.M.
**Habitat:** Varies with subspecies.
**Subspecies:** There are nine quite different-looking subspecies, with populations that are often isolated or rare, forming a spotty distribution. (1) **Short-tailed Swallowtail,** *P. i. indra* Reakirt, Pl. 20, No. 6. Tail on HW short. Food: Terebrinth pteryxia *(Pteryxia terebrinthina)* and mountain parsley *(Harbouria trachypleura).* Usually in mountain areas. Wash. east to Rocky Mts., south to mountains of Calif. and N.M. TL: Pike's Peak, Colo. (2) **Minor's Swallowtail,** *P. i. minori* Cross. Yellow pm. band narrow; tail long. Food: Eastwood's lomatium *(Lomatium eastwoodae).* Upper Colorado R. drainage. TL: Fruita, Colo. (3) **Edwards' Swallowtail,** *P. i. pergamus* Hy. Edwards, Pl. 20, No. 7. Large. Yellow band narrow but complete; tail long. Food: Parish's tauschia *(Tauschia parishii)* and southern tauschia *(Tauschia arguta).* Mountains of s. Calif. TL: California. (4) **Grand Canyon Swallowtail,** *P. i. kaibabensis* Bauer. Yellow pm. band on FW reduced to separate spots or absent. Food: Rock pteryxia *(Pteryxia petraea).* Grand Canyon region of Ariz. TL: Bright Angel Point, Grand Canyon Natl. Park. (5) **Ford's Swallowtail,** *P. i. fordi* J. A. Comstock & Martin. Small. Yellow pm. band very wide. Food: Panamint Indian parsnip *(Cymopterus panamintensis).* Desert mountains of se. Calif. TL: Granite Mts., San Bernardino Co., Calif. (6) **Martin's Swallowtail,** *P. i. martini* J. & T. Emmel. Yellow pm. band narrow, curved. Food: Parry's lomatium *(Lomatium parryi).* TL: Gilroy Canyon, Providence Mts., San Bernardino Co., Calif. Local. (7) **Nevada Swallowtail,** *P. i. nevadensis* T. & J. Emmel. Yellow band wide; a yellow spot on FW beyond discal cell. Food: Rock pteryxia *(Pteryxia petraea).* Mono Lake area, Calif.; Nev. TL: Jett Canyon, east side of Toyabe Range, Nye Co., Nev. (8) **Phyllis' Swallowtail,** *P. i. phyllisae* J. F. Emmel. Yellow band wide, espe-

cially in female. Food: Parish's tauschia *(Tauschia parishii)*. Eastern side of Sierra Nevada, Kern Co. and Inyo Co. TL: Butterbread Peak, Kern Co., Calif. (9) **Panamint Swallowtail,** *P. i. panamintensis* J. F. Emmel. Upperside: Yellow median band distinct on FW, reduced on HW. Food: Parry's lomatium *(Lomatium parryi)*. TL: Thorndike Campground, Wildrose Canyon, Panamint Range, Inyo Co., Calif.

**XUTHUS SWALLOWTAIL** *Papilio xuthus* Linnaeus     **Pl. 20**
**Identification:** $2\frac{1}{2}$–$3\frac{5}{8}$ in. (62–91 mm). *Upperside:* Black, with narrow cream-colored markings. Wide black borders on both wings, with small light submarginal spots. FW cell black, with 4 very narrow, light, lengthwise lines.
**Early stages:** When small, larva resembles a bird dropping; it becomes more yellowish green in last stage. 4–5 broods in warm climates. **Food:** Citrus. **Adults:** Much of year.
**Range:** A widespread oriental species, introduced into Hawaii. To date, the only swallowtail recorded in Hawaii.

**GIANT SWALLOWTAIL** *Papilio cresphontes* Cramer     **Pl. 21**
**Identification:** $3\frac{3}{4}$–5 in. (94–125 mm). A large swallowtail. *Upperside:* Black; light markings deep yellow. Diagonal band of yellow spots crosses FW from apex to inner margin near base and extends across HW basal area as a solid yellow band. Third spot from FW apex is longer than all other spots; *5th spot is longer* than 4th or 6th spot; *3 spots between diagonal band and FW anal angle.* Anal crescent on HW *red*; tail wide, with a *yellow spot* inside tip.
**Similar species:** Thaos Swallowtail (not shown; see Casual Species, p. 319). On upperside, 5th spot in diagonal band across FW not longer than 6th spot; 4 spots between diagonal band and anal angle of FW.
**Early stages:** Larva (called "Orange Dog") is brown; lateral thoracic stripe, saddle, and tip of abdomen yellow. Multiple broods. **Food:** Prickly ash *(Zanthoxylum),* hoptree *(Ptelea),* common rue *(Ruta graveolans);* all in rue family (Rutaceae). Sometimes a minor pest of cultivated citrus. **Adults:** Long flight season.
**Range:** S.-cen. Calif. east to Colo. and Kans., south to Ariz., N.M., and Tex. Eastern U.S.; south at least to Costa Rica. Usually uncommon in most of the West. **Habitat:** Woodland, orchards, thorn forest, fencerows, streamsides, parks, suburban yards and gardens.

**EASTERN TIGER SWALLOWTAIL**     **Pl. 21**
*Papilio glaucus* Linnaeus
**Identification:** $2\frac{1}{2}$ in. (62 mm) — small northern males — to 5 in. (125 mm) — large southern females. Bright yellow with narrow black bands and black margins. *Upperside: 1st (uppermost) submarginal spot on HW orange.* **Underside:** Submarginal spots

*tinged with orange.* In the southern U.S., some females are dark, resembling the Spicebush Swallowtail (Pl. 21, No. 5); these dark females seldom occur in our area.

**Similar species:** (1) In Western Tiger Swallowtail (below) uppermost submarginal spot on upperside of HW is yellow or absent. (2) Two-tailed Swallowtail (p. 123) has 2 tails on HW. (3) In Pale Swallowtail (p. 123) ground color is cream. (4) In Spicebush Swallowtail (p. 123) submarginal spots on upperside of HW are pale greenish; costal spot orange. Resembles dark female Eastern Tiger Swallowtail.

**Early stages:** Larva smooth, green, with a pair of large, black-centered, orange eyespots in front of an orange and black bar. One brood in north, 2-3 broods in south. **Food:** Wild cherry *(Prunus),* tulip tree *(Liriodendron),* birch *(Betula),* ash *(Fraxinus),* cottonwood, poplar *(Populus),* mountain ash *(Sorbus),* basswood *(Tilia),* willow *(Salix),* and others. **Adults:** Late May to early July in north; long flight season in south.

**Range:** Cen. Alaska, Alberta, Mont., e. Colo. south to Tex. In the East, Canada south to Fla. **Habitat:** Deciduous woodland, parks, suburbs; in north, subarctic woodland, taiga.

**Subspecies:** (1) **Eastern Tiger Swallowtail,** *P. g. glaucus* (Linnaeus), Pl. 21. U.S. TL: America. (2) **Canadian Tiger Swallowtail,** *P. g. canadensis* (Rothschild & Jordan). Canada. TL: Newfoundland. (3) **Arctic Tiger Swallowtail,** *P. g. arcticus* Skinner. Alaska, Yukon. TL: Eagle, Alaska.

## WESTERN TIGER SWALLOWTAIL                              Pl. 21
*Papilio rutulus* Lucas

**Identification:** 3¼-4 in. (81-100 mm). *Outer margin of FW slightly concave.* **Upperside:** Bright yellow; bars and margins black. 1st (uppermost) submarginal spot on HW *yellow or absent.* **Underside:** Dark margins have light blue shading; *submarginal spots yellow,* not orange.

**Similar species:** (1) Eastern Tiger Swallowtail (above). (2) Two-tailed Swallowtail (p. 123). (3) Pale Swallowtail (below).

**Early stages:** Larva smooth, dark green. Eyespots yellow, with black borders and blue centers; behind these spots is a yellow and black bar. One brood in north and at high elevations, 2-3 broods in south and at low elevations. **Food:** Willow *(Salix),* cottonwood, poplar, aspen *(Populus),* alder *(Alnus),* birch *(Betula),* sycamore *(Platanus),* elm *(Ulmus),* and orchard trees such as cherry, apple, and plum. **Adults:** April-Sept., depending on locality.

**Range:** British Columbia east to w. Mont., Colo.; south to s. Calif., N.M.; Baja California; Sonora. **Habitat:** Woodland, streamsides, canyons, parks, roadsides, suburbs, yards, and oases in deserts.

**Subspecies:** (1) **Western Tiger Swallowtail,** *P. r. rutulus* (Lucas). Found in northern, central, and southern parts of range. TL: California. (2) **Arizona Tiger Swallowtail,** *P. r. arizonensis*

(W. H. Edwards), Pl. 21. Black wing borders wider. Ariz. and southern part of range. TL: Old Ft. Grant, Graham Co., Ariz.

**PALE SWALLOWTAIL** *Papilio eurymedon* Lucas **Pl. 21**
**Identification:** $2\frac{3}{4}$–$3\frac{1}{2}$ in. (69–88 mm). FW *narrow, pointed.* HW tail *slender, twisted.* ***Upperside:*** *Creamy white* with black bands. On HW, submarginal spots in cells $M_3$ and $Cu_1$ *orange,* (spot in cell $Cu_1$ sometimes absent).
**Similar species:** (1) Eastern Tiger Swallowtail (p. 121). (2) Western Tiger Swallowtail (p. 122). (3) Two-tailed Swallowtail (below).
**Early stages:** Larva pale green; eyespots on thorax small. Pupa dark brown. 1–2 broods. **Food:** Coffee-berry *(Rhamnus californica),* red-berry *(Rhamnus crocea);* various species of *Ceanothus,* including snow brush *(C. cordulatus);* wild lilac or blueblossom *(C. thyrsiflorus);* and others. Also holly-leaved cherry *(Prunus ilicifolia).* **Adults:** April–July, depending on locality.
**Range:** British Columbia east to Mont., south to s. Calif., Colo., and N.M.; Baja California. TL: California. **Habitat:** Streamsides, chaparral, open woodlands, hilltops.
**Subspecies:** The dark, high-elevation form "albanus" (C. & R. Felder) has at times been considered a subspecies.

**TWO-TAILED SWALLOWTAIL** **Pl. 21**
*Papilio multicaudatus* Kirby
**Identification:** $3\frac{1}{2}$–$4\frac{1}{4}$ in. (88–106 mm). HW with *long tail* at end of vein $M_3$, short tail at end of vein $Cu_1$. Pointed lobe at anal angle. ***Upperside:*** Bright yellow. Black borders quite wide, black bands narrow.
**Similar species:** (1) Eastern Tiger Swallowtail (p. 121). (2) Western Tiger Swallowtail (p. 122). (3) Pale Swallowtail (above).
**Early stages:** Larva apple green, with small, green, black-edged dorsal eyespots, much as in Pale Swallowtail (above). Pupa greenish brown. Two broods; 1 brood in parts of Pacific Slope. **Food:** Ash *(Fraxinus),* wild cherry *(Prunus),* serviceberry *(Amelanchier),* hoptree *(Ptelea),* and probably others. **Adults:** May–June, Aug.–Sept.
**Range:** British Columbia east to N.D., Neb., w. Kans., cen. Tex. South to s. Calif., Ariz.; Mexico. Less common on Pacific Slope. TL: Mexico. **Habitat:** Streamsides, moist valleys in arid areas, woodland, groves, parks, roadsides.

**SPICEBUSH SWALLOWTAIL** **Pl. 21**
*Papilio troilus* Linnaeus
**Identification:** 3–4 in. (75–100 mm). ***Upperside:*** Black. FW unmarked except for ivory submarginal spots. Outer $\frac{2}{3}$ of HW powdered with bluish or greenish; *costal spot orange,* submarginal spots pale green. ***Underside:*** Small pm. and submarginal spots both present in FW. Pm. and submarginal spots orange in HW.

**Similar species:** Dark female of Eastern Tiger Swallowtail (p. 121).
**Early stages:** Larva green, with 2 pairs of thoracic eyespots; front pair larger. Multiple broods. **Food:** Spicebush *(Lindera benzoin),* sweetbay *(Magnolia virginiana),* redbay *(Persea borbonia),* prickly ash *(Zanthoxylum).* **Adults:** Long flight season.
**Range:** S. Manitoba, N.D., w. Colo., w. Kans., Tex.; eastern N. America from s. Canada to Fla. Scarce or casual in the West, common in cen. Tex. and eastward. TL: "India" — not an unusual name for the New World in 1758. **Habitat:** Deciduous forest, groves, parks, roadsides, yards, gardens.

# WHITES and SULFURS:
# Family Pieridae

Worldwide. Large to small butterflies, usually white or yellow, with black markings. HW has 2 anal veins. Front legs well developed in both sexes; tarsal claws divided into two parts (see front endpapers). Antennae short, straight.

   **Early stages:** Egg elongate, upright(Fig. 3, p. 25). Larva slender; skin granulated, often velvety (Fig. 5, p. 26). Pupa suspended upright by girdle, as in swallowtails (Papilionidae, p. 113); head pointed; wing cases large and bulging (Fig. 6, p. 27).

## Whites: Subfamily Pierinae

Worldwide. White with dark markings. In most species, larvae eat members of the mustard family (Brassicaceae). Note: The genera *Pontia* and *Artogeia* were both previously included in the genus *Pieris.*

### Pine Whites: Genus *Neophasia* Behr

**SOUTHERN PINE WHITE** *Neophasia terlootii* Behr    **Pl. 22**
**Identification:** $1^3/_4$–$2^1/_4$ in. (44–56 mm). **Upperside:** Male white; female *orange.* FW cell *entirely black* in both sexes. FW costa and apex black, enclosing white spots near margin and below apex. HW veins black.
**Similar species:** In Pine White (below) FW cell is white.
**Early stages:** Larvae live and pupate communally in a web, feeding at night; they follow one another in "processions." Two broods; 2nd (fall) brood more common. **Food:** Conifers, especially western yellow pine *(Pinus ponderosa).*
**Range:** Higher mountains of Ariz., n., Mexico. TL: Pine forests, Sierra Madre, e. of Mazatlan (Sinaloa), Mexico. **Habitat:** Pine forest.

**PINE WHITE** *Neophasia menapia* (C. & R. Felder) **Pl. 23**
**Identification:** $1\frac{3}{4}$-$2\frac{1}{4}$ in. (45–56 mm). *Upperside:* Male white; female similar but slightly duller. *FW costa and cell bar black;* apex black, enclosing white spots. HW veins often slightly darkened. *Underside:* HW veins black. HW often yellowish in female; margins often trimmed with pink.
**Similar species:** In the male Southern Pine White (above), discal cell on upperside of FW is black.
**Early stages:** Larva green, with white stripes on back and sides. Descends from tree on silk, pupates at tree base. Pupa dark green, with white stripes. One brood. **Food:** Pines (various species), Douglas fir *(Pseudotsuga menziesii),* balsam fir *(Abies balsamea),* and no doubt other conifers. Larva occasionally destructive. **Adults:** June–Sept.
**Range:** British Columbia south to Calif.; Alberta south in Rocky Mts. to Mexico; east to w. S.D. and w. Neb. TL: Utah. **Habitat:** Coniferous forest.
**Subspecies:** (1) **Pine White,** *N. m. menapia* (C. & R. Felder), Pl. 23. All of range except n. Calif. (2) **Coastal Pine White,** *N. m. melanica* Scott. Bar at end of FW discal cell narrow; black patch at FW apex has few white spots. Known at present from outer Coast Ranges in Sonoma and Mendocino Cos. TL: 6 mi. w. of Willits, Mendocino Co., Calif.

## Whites: Genus *Pontia* Fabricius

**BECKER'S WHITE** **Pl. 23**
*Pontia beckerii* (W. H. Edwards)
**Identification:** $1\frac{5}{8}$-2 in. (41–50 mm). *Upperside:* White in both sexes. Spots near FW apex blackish; cell bar black, *squarish, with curved white center.* HW all white in male, has dark markings in female. *Underside:* In both sexes, HW veins *widely* edged with dull green, *interrupted by an incomplete white median band.*
**Similar species:** (1) In Checkered White (p. 126) and (2) Western White (p. 127), veins on underside of HW are narrowly edged with greenish gray; no white band.
**Early stages:** Larva green, with narrow orange bands and small black tubercles. Pupa gray or brown; wing cases lighter; front end blunt. Multiple broods. **Food:** Mustard *(Brassica),* hedge mustard *(Sisymbrium),* and golden prince's plume *(Stanleya pinnata),* all in mustard family (Brassicaceae); also bladder-pod *(Isomeris arborea),* in caper family (Capparaceae). **Adults:** Long flight season.
**Range:** British Columbia and Alberta south to Baja California; mostly east of the Cascades and Sierra Nevada, east to w. Mont., south to N.M. **Habitat:** Arid brushland, fields.
**Subspecies:** (1) *P. b. beckerii* (W. H. Edwards), Pl. 23. Central, southern, and eastern parts of range. TL: Virginia City, Nev. (2)

*P. b. pseudochloridice* (McDunnough). More heavily marked. British Columbia, Wash., n. Idaho, w. Mont. TL: Oliver, British Columbia.

**CALIFORNIA WHITE** *Pontia sisymbrii* (Boisduval)    **Pl. 23**
**Identification:** $1\frac{1}{4}$–$1\frac{3}{4}$ in. (31–44 mm); small for this genus (Pontia). Sexes alike. *Upperside:* White to creamy yellow; FW *cell bar narrow* — twice as long as it is wide. FW costa dark; spots near apex dark. Wing veins *very narrowly darkened* (no broad dark edging). *Underside:* HW veins *edged with olive.* All markings very distinct.
**Early stages:** Larva light yellow, with narrow black bands. Pupa dark brown; its surface granular. One brood — early in the desert, later in the mountains. **Food:** Rock cress *(Arabis), Caulanthus,* jewel flower *(Streptanthus),* hedge mustard *(Sisymbrium),* and others in mustard family. **Adults:** March–July. They fly close to the ground.
**Range:** British Columbia to Baja California, east to w. S.D. and w. Neb. Local. TL: "Californie," probably gold field of Tuolumne River. **Habitat:** Open coniferous forest, outcrops, ledges, rocky canyons, road cuts, desert hills. Withstands wide ranges of elevation and temperature.
**Subspecies:** Four rather similar subspecies are recognized.

**CHECKERED WHITE**                                       **Pl. 23**
*Pontia protodice* (Boisduval & Le Conte)
**Identification:** $1\frac{1}{2}$–2 in. (38–50 mm). *Upperside:* FW cell bar oblong — *less than twice as long as wide.* In male, the dark *spot in FW cell $Cu_2$ is small, indistinct, or absent;* HW all white. In female, spot in FW cell $Cu_2$ is present; all markings of female tend to be *brown* and *diffuse. Underside:* In male, HW markings few or absent. In female, HW veins often have smudgy, yellowish gray edges.
**Similar species:** (1) Becker's White (p. 125). (2) Western White (below).
**Early stages:** Larva bluish or greenish, dotted with black; 4 yellowish stripes along back and sides. Pupa bluish gray, tinted with yellow and speckled with black. Multiple broods. **Food:** Many members of the mustard family (Brassicaceae); also bladder-pod *(Isomeris arborea),* pink bee plant *(Cleome serrulata),* and yellow bee plant *(C. lutea),* all in caper family (Capparaceae). **Adults:** Long flight season.
**Range:** British Columbia east across the continent; south to Baja California, Cen. America. Details of range in parts of the West not clear because of confusion with the Western White (below). TL: Probably Screven Co., Georgia. **Habitat:** Fields, roadsides, cultivated lands, yards, vacant lots. Distribution very general.

**WESTERN WHITE** *Pontia occidentalis* (Reakirt) **Pl. 23**
**Identification:** $1\frac{1}{2}$-2 in. (38–50 mm). *Upperside:* In male, dark markings blackish, distinct. Spot in cell $Cu_2$ of FW *always present.* Cell bar wide. HW not entirely white — has at least some dark markings at margin. Dark markings extensive in female, but general appearance never brownish as in Checkered White (above). *Underside* (both sexes): HW veins greenish gray, *forming chevrons near margin.*
**Similar species:** (1) Becker's White (p. 125). (2) Checkered White (above).
**Early stages:** Much like those of Checkered White. Usually 2 broods. **Food:** Much as for Checkered White, but Western White is found less often on cultivated members of the mustard family and is not known to feed on bladder-pod or bee plant. **Adults:** May–Sept., depending on latitude and elevation.
**Range:** Alaska south to Calif., east to Manitoba, N.D., Colo. **Habitat:** Quite general; less "domestic" than Checkered White. Often frequents hilltops.
**Subspecies:** (1) **Western White,** *P. o. occidentalis* (Reakirt), Pl. 23. Most of range. TL: Empire, Clear Creek Co., Colo. (2) **Nelson's White,** *P. o. nelsoni* (W. H. Edwards). Underside of HW mostly greenish gray, with white rays between the veins. Alaska, Yukon Terr., Northwest Terr. TL: St. Michaels, Alaska.

## Genus *Artogeia* Verity

**MUSTARD WHITE or VEINED WHITE** **Pls. 23, 24**
*Artogeia napi* (Linnaeus)
**Identification:** $1\frac{1}{2}$-$1\frac{7}{8}$ in. (38–47 mm). A very widely distributed species, with great seasonal and geographical variation. *Upperside:* FW has *no cell bar.* Male unmarked, or with some *dark narrow veins;* FW costa usually dark; often a small spot in cell $M_3$ of FW. Female white to pale yellow, usually with dark spots in FW cells $M_3$ and $Cu_2$; wing veins usually *dark.* Cells of both FW and HW sometimes have dark outlines. *Underside:* Varies from nearly pure white to very dark-veined. *HW costa yellow at base.*
**Similar species:** Cabbage Butterfly (p. 128).
**Early stages:** Larva green, with a dark dorsal stripe. Pupa green or white, speckled with black. Pupa overwinters. Two broods at moderate latitudes, 1 in the far north. **Food:** Members of the mustard family (Brassicaceae), especially milkmaids *(Dentaria).*
**Adults:** Emerge in early spring. Feb.–May in coastal Calif., to June–July in Alaska.
**Range:** Very extensive; Alaska and Canada south to cen. Calif.; mountains of Ariz. and N.M. East to N.Y.; also in Europe, N. Africa, Asia, Japan. **Habitat:** Shady woodland, open forest, streamsides, tundra, taiga.

**Subspecies:** (1) **Alaskan Mustard White,** *A. n. pseudobryoniae* (Verity), Pl. 23, No. 6. A pale form with narrow dark veins. Interior of Alaska, Yukon Terr. TL: Finmark, Scandinavia. (2) **Coastal Alaskan White,** *A. n. hulda* (W. H. Edwards). Duller; more gray. Coastal Alaska. TL: Kodiak, Alaska. (3) **Veined White,** *A. n. venosa* (Scudder), Pls. 23, 24. Veins on underside of HW darkly outlined. All FW veins on upperside dark and prominent in female, lighter and narrow in male. Cen. coastal Calif. TL: San Mateo and Mendocino, Calif. (4) **Small-veined White,** *A. n. microstriata* (J. A. Comstock). Veins on underside of HW very narrowly darkened. Inner Coast Ranges and Sierra Nevada foothills of Calif. TL: Eldridge, Sonoma Co., Calif. (5) **Margined White,** *A. n. marginalis* (Scudder), Pl. 24, No. 2. Upperside very lightly marked; both sexes have a narrow dark border, which is lighter in female. Females slightly yellowish. The second brood, form "pallida" Scudder, is nearly unmarked. S. Canada to n. Calif. TL: Gulf of Georgia, Wash. (6) **McDunnough's White,** *A. n. mcdunnoughi* (Remington). Nearly unmarked, except for dark FW tips. High elevations in Mont., Wyo., Colo. TL: Silverton, Colo. (7) **Mogollon White,** *A. n. mogollon* (Burdick). FW tips on upperside dark; veins narrowly outlined in gray on underside. High mountains of Utah, Ariz., N.M. TL: Mogollon Range, Catron Co., N.M.

**CABBAGE BUTTERFLY** *Artogeia rapae* (Linnaeus)    **Pl. 24**
**Identification:** 1⅝-2 in. (41-50 mm). *Upperside:* Chalky white; *small dark spot on HW costa.* FW apex dark; base often has gray overscaling. FW has 1 small spot in male, 2 spots in female. *Underside:* FW spots repeated. HW yellowish gray, unmarked.
**Early stages:** Larva pale green, dotted with black; yellow stripes on sides and back. Pupa green, dotted with black. Multiple broods.
**Food:** Many members of the mustard family; also nasturtium *(Tropaeolum).* Larva a serious pest of cole vegetables such as cabbage, cauliflower, and broccoli. **Adults:** All warm parts of year.
**Range:** Europe, Asia, n. Africa, Japan; introduced in Australia. Widely established in N. America south of the Arctic; introduced from Europe. Also on all major islands of Hawaii. TL: Sweden.
**Habitat:** Nearly everywhere except in densest forest and driest desert.

### Great Whites: Genus *Ascia* Scopoli

**GREAT SOUTHERN WHITE**    **Pl. 24**
*Ascia monuste* (Fabricius)
**Identification:** 2¼-2⅜ in. (56-59 mm). *Upperside:* Male white, with a narrow black edge at FW costa and a *series of black wedges* along FW border; no cell bar. Female yellowish white to brownish gray (seldom brown in Texas), with dark sawtoothed wedges on *both wings* and a faint *FW cell spot.* *Underside:* Male white to

dull yellowish; veins brownish. FW disc whitish in female; FW costa and apex and all of HW yellowish to dull brown; veins and vague chevrons darker.
**Similar species:** Giant White (below).
**Early stages:** Larva lemon yellow, with dark stripes. Pupa whitish, with darker shades. Multiple broods. **Food:** Peppergrass *(Lepidium);* sea rocket *(Cakile);* cultivated cabbage, turnip, and radish; and other plants in mustard family. Also bee plant *(Cleome)* and clammy-weed *(Polanisia),* in the caper family (Capparaceae); nasturtium *(Tropaeolum);* saltwort *(Batis).* **Adults:** Long flight period.
**Range:** Tropical America; Tex. east to Ga., Fla., Gulf Coast. Casual in Colo. and Kans.; vaguely reported from Ariz. **Habitat:** General; usually common where it occurs.
**Subspecies:** (1) *A. m. monuste* (Linnaeus). No longer considered to occur in the U.S. TL: Surinam. (2) *A. m. phileta* (Fabricius), Pl. 24. Our subspecies, as described above. TL: "In America."

## Giant White: Genus *Ganyra* Billberg

**GIANT WHITE** *Ganyra josephina* (Godart) **Pl. 24**
**Identification:** $2\frac{7}{8}$-$3\frac{1}{4}$ in. (72–81 mm). *Upperside:* Male white, with a *round black cell spot* on FW. Female yellowish brown; markings sometimes more extensive. *Underside:* Dull yellowish in both sexes; veins and vague median spots brown.
**Similar species:** Great Southern White (above).
**Early stages:** Apparently unknown. **Adults:** Most records in fall.
**Range:** Cen. America, West Indies. Occasional in s. Tex.; casual in Ariz., Kans. **Habitat:** In Tex., thorn forest. Stragglers may appear most anywhere.
**Subspecies:** (1) *G. j. josephina* (Godart). West Indies. TL: Hispaniola. (2) *G. j. josepha* (Godman & Salvin), Pl. 24. Sw. United States south to Cen. America. TL: Guatemala.
**Remarks:** Rare in the West; few authentic records. Has at times been placed in the genus *Ascia* (above).

# Sulfurs and Yellows: Subfamily Coliadinae

Cosmopolitan. White, yellow, or orange butterflies with dark markings. Larvae of many species feed on plants in the pea family; some feed on blueberry (heath family) and at least 2 on willow. Many are tropical; some arctic and subarctic. Males and females are often quite different in appearance (dimorphic).

## Sulfurs: Genus *Colias* Fabricius

Mostly in the Northern Hemisphere, extending to S. America, n. Africa, and India. Yellow, orange, or greenish; some females white. Borders dark; solid in most males, broken or absent in females. Many species look much alike, and some are puzzlingly similar.

**MEAD'S SULFUR** *Colias meadii* W. H. Edwards          **Pl. 22**
**Identification:** 1½–2 in. (38–50 mm). *Upperside:* Male *deep orange; border wide, dull black.* Orange sex mark on HW costa near base. Female lighter orange; *border broken,* enclosing spots of ground color. *Underside:* Greenish yellow in both sexes. HW discal spot dull white, ringed with red.
**Similar species:** (1) Hecla Sulfur (below) is lighter orange; male lacks sex patch. More northern. (2) Booth's Sulfur (below) is also lighter orange, but dark borders narrow. Male lacks sex patch. Northern.
**Early stages:** Larva green, with small, hair-bearing black tubercles; may have pale stripe on side. Larva overwinters in 3rd instar. Pupa green. One brood. **Food:** Rattleweed *(Astragalus),* clover *(Trifolium),* in pea family (Fabaceae). **Adults:** July–Aug.
**Range:** Rocky Mts., Alberta south to Colo. Local; common in its restricted range. **Habitat:** High mountain areas, at or near treeline.
**Subspecies:** (1) **Mead's Sulfur,** *C. m. meadii* W. H. Edwards, Pl. 22. S. Mont., Wyo., Colo. TL: Mosquito Pass, Park-Lake Cos., Colo. (2) **Elis Sulfur,** *C. m. elis* Strecker. Alberta, e. British Columbia, n. Mont. TL: Kicking Horse Pass, Alberta.

**HECLA SULFUR** *Colias hecla* Lefebre          **Pl. 25**
**Identification:** 1½–1¾ in. (38–44 mm). *Upperside:* Light, somewhat greenish orange. *Dark border* of moderate width. Male *lacks* sex patch on HW costa. Female often heavily clouded above; some individuals have white ground color. *Underside:* Similar to that of Mead's Sulfur (above, Pl. 22).
**Similar species:** (1) Mead's Sulfur (above). (2) Booth's Sulfur (below).
**Early stages:** Much like those of Mead's Sulfur. One brood. **Food:** Alpine milk-vetch *(Astragalus alpinus).* **Adults:** June–July.
**Range:** Circumpolar; north to limit of land, south to Red Deer, Alberta. Alaska to Greenland; Europe; Asia. **Habitat:** Tundra.
**Subspecies:** (1) *C. h. hecla* Lefebre. Dull orange. Eastern N. America. TL: Greenland. (2) *C. h. hela* Strecker, Pl. 25. Brighter orange; *border wider.* Manitoba westward. TL: Churchill, Manitoba.

**BOOTH'S SULFUR** *Colias boothii* Curtis          **Pl. 25**
**Identification:** 1⅜–1⅝ in. (34–41 mm). *Upperside:* Male light orange; HW tinged with *greenish yellow;* FW and HW *border narow;* its width irregular. Female much duller; wide FW and HW border encloses *dull yellowish spots.* Wing base heavily clouded, veins often dark. *Underside:* Greenish yellow in both sexes, with heavy dark overscaling. *HW discal spot white,* with a reddish brown rim that is often *lengthened diagonally* toward outer margin. Outer edge of HW *lighter.*

**Similar species:** (1) Mead's Sulfur (p. 130). (2) Hecla Sulfur (p. 130).
**Early stages:** Little known. One brood. **Adults:** June–Aug.
**Range:** Extreme arctic America, across the continent. TL: Boothia Peninsula, Northwest Terr. **Habitat:** Sheltered hillsides in tundra.
**Remarks:** Booth's Sulfur was formerly thought to be a hybrid between the Hecla Sulfur and the Nastes Sulfur, but it is now considered a separate species.

**ORANGE SULFUR** *Colias eurytheme* Boisduval      **Pl. 22**
**Identification:** First brood smaller — $1\frac{3}{8}$-$1\frac{1}{2}$ in. (34–38 mm); later broods larger — to $1\frac{3}{4}$-$2\frac{1}{4}$ in. (44–56 mm). ***Upperside:*** Male yellow with *heavy orange overlay* that extends to *wing bases.* Black border wide, the veins yellow; FW cell spot *intensely black.* Female either yellow or white; irregular border encloses light spots. ***Underside:*** Submarginal spots prominent in both sexes. HW discal spot silver, with *2 concentric dark rings* and a small *satellite spot* above it. In summer broods, upperside is bright orange with a lavender overlay.
**Similar species:** (1) Clouded Sulfur (below) has no orange tint. (2) In Christina Sulfur (subspecies of Queen Alexandra Sulfur, p. 133), orange overlay does not reach wing bases.
**Early stages:** Larva green, with 2 side stripes; each stripe encloses a red line. Pupa green, marked with yellow and speckled with black. Multiple broods. **Food:** Many native plants in the pea family; larva prefers alfalfa (an introduced legume). **Adults:** Early spring to late fall.
**Range:** N. America from coast to coast; s. Canada south to Mexico. **Habitat:** Fields, meadows, cultivated lands, roadsides.
**Subspecies:** None, although many names have been given to different broods and forms.
**Remarks:** The Orange Sulfur is also called Boisduval's Sulfur and the Alfalfa Butterfly. Abundant; larva often destructive to alfalfa. Very tolerant of conditions.

**CLOUDED SULFUR or COMMON SULFUR**      **Pl. 25**
*Colias philodice* Godart
**Identification:** $1\frac{1}{2}$-$2\frac{1}{8}$ in. (38–53 mm). Markings like those of Orange Sulfur (above), but cell spot usually smaller. Wings *bright lemon yellow.* HW discal spot *orange.*
**Similar species:** (1) Orange Sulfur (above). (2) All of our yellow (not orange-colored) sulfurs are similar, separated by small differences (*Colias* species, pp. 129–137).
**Early stages:** Larva dark green, with a dark dorsal stripe and a pink stripe on lower side. Multiple broods. **Food:** Various members of the pea family; larva said to prefer white clover *(Trifolium repens).* **Adults:** Long flight period.
**Range:** Subarctic N. America, south to southern U.S.; Alaska east

to Newfoundland. In the West, south to s. Calif., Tex. Absent from the Pacific Coast and deserts of the Southwest. An isolated population in Guatemala. **Habitat:** Meadows, fields, cultivated land, roadsides, cutover land, brushland.

**Subspecies:** (1) **Clouded Sulfur,** *C. p. philodice* Godart. Veins of border usually not yellow. Eastern N. America west to Great Plains and Tex. TL: Virginia. (2) **Western Clouded Sulfur,** *C. p. eriphyle* W. H. Edwards, Pl. 25. Border crossed by yellow veins. British Columbia to Calif. east of Cascades and Sierra Nevada, east to Rocky Mts. TL: Lac La Hache, British Columbia. (3) **Lively Clouded Sulfur,** *C. p. vitabunda* Hovanitz. Dark border narrower. Alaska, Yukon Terr. TL: Mt. McKinley Natl. Park (now Denali Natl. Park and Preserve).

**HARFORD'S SULFUR** Pl. 25

*Colias harfordii* Hy. Edwards

**Identification:** $1^3/_4$-2 in. (44–50 mm). Usually the only yellow (not orange) *Colias* in its range. *Upperside:* Male a *warm, rich yellow* with no lemon tint. FW cell spot medium-sized, black, often *white-centered. Wing bases not darkened.* FW border wide, HW border more narrow. HW discal spot *inconspicuous.* Female colored like male, but border less distinct and sometimes reduced or even nearly absent. *Underside:* Submarginal spots present or absent. HW discal spot with single ring; satellite spot usually present.

**Early stages:** Larva green; lateral line red, bordered above and below by white. Many short-haired tubercles. Pupa yellow-green; lateral stripe red, edged with yellow. Two broods. **Food:** Rattleweed *(Astragalus).* **Adults:** Feb.–May and June–Aug.

**Range:** Mountains of s. Calif., San Diego Co. to Kern Co. TL: Havilah, Kern Co. **Habitat:** Openings in brushland and forest.

**WESTERN or GOLDEN SULFUR** Pl. 26

*Colias occidentalis* Scudder

**Identification:** $1^3/_4$-$2^1/_4$ in. (44–56 mm). *Upperside:* FW cell spot small. Male bright yellow; female light yellow to greenish white. *Border wide,* intensely *black* in male; *cloudy, incomplete,* or nearly absent in female. *Underside:* All wing edges pink in both sexes. FW nearly unmarked. *HW deep golden yellow,* powdered with dark scales. Pm. spots often present. Discal spot ringed with brown or reddish.

**Early stages:** Not described in detail. One brood. **Food:** In Washington, reported to be vetch *(Vicia angustifolia)* and white sweet clover *(Melilotus albus);* suspected to eat lupine *(Lupinus)* and rattleweed *(Astragalus),* all in pea family (Fabaceae). **Adults:** Late May to July.

**Range:** Pacific Coast, from British Columbia south to cen. Calif. **Habitat:** Forest glades and clearings; forest openings and mead-

ows, especially in Douglas fir forest. Seldom found in cultivated areas.
**Subspecies:** (1) **Western Sulfur,** *C. o. occidentalis* Scudder, Pl. 26. British Columbia south into Ore. TL: Gulf of Georgia, Wash. (2) **Gold and Black Sulfur,** *C. o. chrysomelas* Hy. Edwards. Larger. Black borders wider in male. Female seldom white. N. and cen. Calif., in both Coast Ranges and Sierra Nevada. TL: Napa Co., Calif.

### PINK-EDGED SULFUR *Colias interior* Scudder          Pl. 26
**Identification:** $1\frac{1}{2}$–$1\frac{7}{8}$ in. (38–47 mm). All wing edges *bright pink.* **Upperside:** *FW cell spot small,* sometimes nearly absent. Male bright yellow; wing bases not dark-scaled. Black border on FW wide at apex, narrower on outer margin; inner edge of border often sawtoothed. Dark border on HW narrow. Female may be yellow or white; border narrow or incomplete, often *reduced to FW apex.* **Underside:** Dark scaling slight in both sexes. Discal spot red-ringed.
**Similar species:** (1) Pelidne Sulfur (p. 135) is lighter yellow. Wing bases heavily dark-scaled; much dark overscaling on underside of HW. (2) In Palaeno Sulfur (p. 136), FW cell spot usually absent. Cell spot on underside of HW has no ring; dark overscaling heavy.
**Early stages:** Larva yellow-green, with a dark dorsal stripe; the lateral stripe encloses a red line. One brood. **Food:** Blueberry (*Vaccinium,* various species). **Adults:** June–Aug.; long flight season.
**Range:** British Columbia east to Newfoundland, south in the West to Ore., Idaho, Mont. In East to Mich., New England, mountains of Va. TL: N. shore of Lake Superior. **Habitat:** Brushlands; often in burned-over areas where blueberry grows.
**Subspecies:** Western populations are considered to be *C. i. interior.* Two eastern subspecies are not found in our area.

### QUEEN ALEXANDRA SULFUR                          Pls. 22, 26
*Colias alexandra* W. H. Edwards
The subspecies of this extremely variable species can be divided into two groups — one with yellow coloration, the other with orange. These would be more easily understood if considered separate species. The yellow and orange populations blend where their ranges meet. For convenience, the yellow group is treated first in the description below.
**Identification:** Yellow subspecies $1\frac{5}{8}$–$2\frac{1}{4}$ in. (41–56 mm); orange subspecies $1\frac{3}{4}$–$2\frac{1}{8}$ in. **Upperside (yellow subspecies)**: Bright yellow in male, paler near wing bases. Black border narrow, crossed by yellow veins. *FW cell spot usually small.* HW discal spot inconspicuous but present. Female yellow (occasionally white); *FW border poorly developed or absent.* **Underside:** HW greenish gray

in both sexes. Discal spot *white, with no ring;* wing edge yellow, seldom pink. ***Upperside (orange subspecies):*** Male distinctively two-toned — *orange, with yellow* at wing bases and costa. Female duller orange, usually heavily marked with wide dark borders and dark veins. ***Underside:*** Dull orange to greenish gray in both sexes; often much dark overscaling. HW discal spot usually ringed.

**Similar species:** Orange Sulfur (p. 131) is similar to orange group of subspecies, but the orange extends to wing bases on upperside. **Early stages:** Larva yellow-green, with a white lateral stripe that encloses orange dashes. One brood. **Food:** Locoweed, rattleweed *(Astragalus),* false lupine *(Thermopsis),* wild pea *(Lathyrus),* sweet vetch *(Hedysarum),* all in pea family (Fabaceae). **Adults:** June–Aug.

**Range** (of entire species): Western N. America; cen. Alaska, western Northwest Terr. east to Manitoba, south to e. Calif., Ariz., N.M., Neb. Orange subspecies occupy the northern part of this range. **Habitat:** Meadows, fields, brushland, roadsides, cut-over land. Orange subspecies seem to prefer cut-over land and clearings. **Subspecies:** *Yellow subspecies* — (1) **Queen Alexandra Sulfur,** *C. a. alexandra* W. H. Edwards, Pl. 22. Mont. and N.D. south to N.M., Ariz., Neb. TL: Foothills west of Denver, Colo. (2) **Edwards' Sulfur,** *C. a. edwardsii* W. H. Edwards. Larger and brighter yellow than *C. a. alexandra.* Wash. and Ore. west of Cascades; e. Calif., Nev., Utah. TL: Virginia City, Nev. (3) **Columbian Sulfur,** *C. a. columbiensis* Ferris. FW more blunt; dark wing borders narrow. HW discal spot orange. S. British Columbia. TL: Anderson Lake, D'Arcy, British Columbia. *Orange subspecies* — (4) **Christina Sulfur,** *C. a. christina* W. H. Edwards, Pl. 26. Alaska, nw. Canada. TL: Portage of Slave R., Northwest Terr. (5) **Astraea Sulfur,** *C. a. astraea* W. H. Edwards. Usually a blend of orange-yellow. Found in a large area in s. Canada and northern U.S., between the ranges of the Christina Sulfur and the Alexandra Sulfur. TL: Yellowstone Lake, Wyo. (6) **Krauth's Sulfur,** *C. a. krauthii* Klots. Large; less yellow on base of FW. Black Hills of S.D. north to Manitoba. TL: 12 mi. west of Custer, Custer Co., S.D. (7) **Kluane Sulfur,** *C. a. kluanensis* Ferris. Upperside more evenly orange; underside more evenly green. Found in northern Yukon and se. Alaska. TL: Lake Kluane, Yukon Terr., Canada.

**SCUDDER'S SULFUR** *Colias scudderii* Reakirt          **Pl. 26**
**Identification:** $1\frac{1}{2}$–$1\frac{7}{8}$ in. (38–47 mm). This species lacks definite field marks and is hard to "pin down." ***Upperside:*** Lemon yellow in male, with a *wide dark border that is crossed by yellow veins.* FW cell spot small or absent. HW discal spot small, pale, inconspicuous. Female usually white, with a *small black FW cell spot;* border vague, very incomplete to absent. ***Underside:*** Dull greenish in both sexes, heavily dusted with dark scales. HW discal spot pearly, ringed with pale red. Wing fringes pale or pinkish.

**Similar species:** (1) Pelidne Sulfur (below). (2) Palaeno Sulfur (p. 136).
**Early stages:** Not well known. One brood. **Food:** Willow *(Salix),* in the willow family (Salicaceae). **Adults:** Late June–Aug.
**Range:** Rocky Mts.; se. Wyo., ne. Utah, Colo., n. N.M. **Habitat:** Mountain meadows, open woodland.
**Subspecies:** (1) **Scudder's Sulfur,** *C. s. scudderii* Reakirt, Pl. 26. Wyo., Utah. TL: Vicinity of Empire, Clear Creek Co., Colo. (2) **Ruckes' Sulfur,** *C. s. ruckesi* Klots. Dark border wider in male. Female often yellow. Local. TL: Windsor Creek Canyon, west of Cowles, San Miguel Co., N.M.

**GIANT SULFUR** *Colias gigantea* Strecker                    **Pl. 28**
**Identification:** $1\frac{3}{4}$–$2\frac{1}{4}$ in. (44–56 mm). A large, bright species; one of the largest sulfurs of the genus *Colias* in our area. *Upperside: FW cell spot distinct.* Male lemon yellow, with very little dark scaling at wing base. Dark border narrow, crossed by yellow veins. Wings yellow or white in female; border reduced or absent. *Underside:* Wings yellow in both sexes, with very little dark overscaling. FW cell spot present. *HW discal spot pearly,* with a *brown ring* that sometimes looks smeared. Fringes pink.
**Similar species:** Might be confused with Clouded Sulfur (p. 131), but dark overscaling at wing base is more extensive in Clouded Sulfur.
**Early stages:** Little known. **Food:** Willow *(Salix),* in willow family (Salicaceae). **Adults:** June–July.
**Range:** Alaska and Canada south to British Columbia, east to Manitoba; south in Rocky Mts. to Wyo. **Habitat:** Willow bogs.
**Subspecies:** (1) **Giant Sulfur,** *C. g. gigantea* Strecker, Pl. 28. Most of range. TL: West coast Hudson Bay, above Fort York. (2) **Harrower's Sulfur,** *C. g. harroweri* Klots. In male, dark border wider and underside more greenish. Idaho, Mont., Wyo. TL: Green River Lake, Sublette Co., Wyo.

**PELIDNE SULFUR**                                        **Pl. 28**
*Colias pelidne* Boisduval & Le Conte
**Identification:** $1\frac{3}{8}$–$1\frac{3}{4}$ in. (34–44 mm). *Upperside:* Wing bases dark scaled in both sexes. FW discal spot *small,* HW discal spot faint. Male pale yellow, with a medium to narrow dark border. Female white or yellow, with a *dark broken border* that is often *incomplete. Underside:* Heavily dark-scaled in both sexes. Discal spot on HW *red-ringed* or all-red. Wing edges pink.
**Similar species:** (1) Scudder's Sulfur (p. 134). (2) Palaeno Sulfur (p. 136).
**Early stages:** Little known. **Food:** Blueberry *(Vaccinium),* alpine wintergreen *(Gaultheria hemifusa),* both in heath family (Ericaceae). **Adults:** June–July.

**Range:** W. British Columbia east to Baffin I., Labrador, south to Idaho, Mont., Wyo. Absent from arctic and subarctic Northwest. **Habitat:** Tundra, fell-fields, subalpine meadows, and subalpine forest openings.
**Subspecies:** (1) **Pelidne Sulfur,** *C. p. pelidne* Boisduval & Le Conte, Pl. 28. Dark border quite wide in male. Arctic regions. TL: Labrador. (2) **Bean's Sulfur,** *C. p. minisni* Bean. Small. Dark border narrow in male. Canadian Rockies. TL: Laggan, Alberta. (3) **Skinner's Sulfur,** *C. p. skinneri* Barnes. Male warmer yellow; female often yellow. Underside of HW heavily dark-scaled. Mont., Idaho, Wyo. TL: Yellowstone National Park.

**PALAENO SULFUR** *Colias palaeno* (Linnaeus)        **Pl. 28**
**Identification:** $1\frac{3}{8}$–$1\frac{5}{8}$ in. (34–41 mm). Wing edge and costa bright pink. *Upperside:* Pale yellow in male, often paler on HW; wing bases dark-scaled. *Wide dark border* on FW and HW. FW cell spot minute or absent; HW cell spot inconspicuous. Female usually white, sometimes yellow; apex black on both FW and HW. *Underside* (both sexes): Dark scaling dense. *HW discal spot small and white, not ringed.*
**Similar species:** (1) Scudder's Sulfur (p. 134). (2) Pelidne Sulfur (above).
**Early stages:** Not recorded in detail. One brood. **Food:** Bog blueberry *(Vaccinium uliginosum),* heath family (Ericaceae). **Adults:** June–July.
**Range:** Europe, n. Asia, N. America. Alaska to Baffin I., south to British Columbia, Alberta, Manitoba. **Habitat:** Tundra, taiga; bogs and moist hillsides in southern parts of its range.
**Subspecies:** (1) *C. p. palaeno* (Linnaeus). Much larger, brighter. Europe. TL: Sweden. (2) *C. p. chippewa* W. H. Edwards, Pl. 28. Entire N. American range except Baffin I. TL: W. end Great Slave Lake, Northwest Territories.

**BEHR'S SULFUR** *Colias behrii* W. H. Edwards        **Pl. 22**
**Identification:** $1\frac{3}{8}$–$1\frac{5}{8}$ in. (34–41 mm). Costa pink, wing edges pale. *Upperside: Dull greenish* in male; border dark. *HW discal spot pale.* Female yellowish or whitish; wing veins and diffuse border darker. *Underside:* Greenish in both sexes. HW cell spot white, not ringed.
**Early stages:** Larva green, with a pink, dark-edged line on back and a salmon, light-edged line on side; segmental spots dark. One brood. **Food:** Dwarf bilberry *(Vaccinium nivictum),* in heath family, and gentian *(Gentiana newberryi).* **Adults:** July–Aug.
**Range:** Sierra Nevada, Tulare Co. north to Tuolumne Co., Calif. Common within its isolated range. TL: Vicinity of Tioga Pass, Tuolumne-Mono Cos., Calif. **Habitat:** Alpine meadows, mostly above 8000 ft. (2438 m).

**NASTES SULFUR** *Colias nastes* Boisduval **Pl. 28**
**Identification:** 1⅜-1¾ in. (34-44 mm). *Upperside:* Greenish yellow or greenish white in both sexes; heavily dusted with dark scales. Veins dark; *wing borders dark, enclosing light spots* in male as well as female. *Underside:* Greenish, with heavy dark dusting. Submarginal spots usually well developed. HW discal spot dark-ringed, extending along vein; wing edges pink.
**Early stages:** Larva moss green; light lines on upper side and spiracular lines edged with red. Overwinters as mature larva. One brood. **Food:** Plants (legumes) in the pea family, especially alpine milk vetch *(Astragalus alpinus)* and white clover *(Trifolium repens).* **Adults:** June–July.
**Range:** Europe, Siberia, and N. America; Alaska to Baffin I., Labrador, south in high mountains to British Columbia and Alberta. TL: Above Fort Churchill, Manitoba. **Habitat:** Tundra; high mountains of the Arctic and subarctic, at or above treeline.
**Subspecies:** Six subspecies occur in N. America, 4 in our area. They differ in depth of ground color and extent of markings. The Moina Sulfur, *C. nastes moina,* is shown on Pl. 28.

**THULA SULFUR** *Colias thula* Hovanitz **not shown**
**Identification:** Originally described as a subspecies of the Nastes Sulfur (above), the Thula Sulfur is probably a distinct species. It resembles the Nastes Sulfur, but the dark border on the male's wings is more solid, and the light spots tend to form a submarginal band inside the dark border. Both sexes are less heavily clouded on wings.
**Similar species:** Nastes Sulfur (above).
**Early stages:** Unknown. One brood. **Food:** Unknown. **Adults:** July.
**Range:** Extreme northern Alaska. TL: "Near the Meade River, Alaska Territory, N 70° 45′ × 156°-30′ W."

### Dogfaces: Genus *Zerene* Huebner

Apex of HW sickle-shaped. Waxy sex-brand in male at base of HW. Often considered a subgenus of *Colias* (pp. 129–137).

**CALIFORNIA DOGFACE** *Zerene eurydice* (Boisduval) **Pl. 22**
**Identification:** 2-2⅜ in. (50–59 mm). *Upperside:* In male, outer half of FW black, enclosing a *yellow "dog's head" with lavender iridescence;* veins and "eye" (FW cell spot) black; the "eye" near or touching the black border. HW all yellow, or with a narrow black border in form "bernardino." Female usually *all yellow except for black FW cell spot;* female occasionally has some brown banding on FW in form "amorphae."
**Similar species:** Southern Dogface (p. 138).
**Early stages:** Larva dull green, with an orange-edged, whitish

line along side; one dark spot or bar on the side of each segment. Two broods. **Food:** False indigo *(Amorpha californica),* in pea family (Fabaceae). **Adults:** April–May, July–Aug.
**Range:** N.-cen. Calif. south to Baja Calif., west of the main north-south divides and deserts. TL: Mountains of Calif. **Habitat:** Foothills; lower mountain slopes.
**Remarks:** The California Dogface has been designated the official State Insect by the California Legislature.

**SOUTHERN DOGFACE** *Zerene cesonia* (Stoll)          **Pl. 28**
**Identification:** $2\frac{1}{8}$–$2\frac{5}{8}$ in. (53–66 mm). *Upperside:* "Dog's face" on male FW *lacks lavender iridescence;* "eye" does not touch black border. *Black border* on HW always present in male. Female similar, but markings more *dull and diffuse;* "snout" of "dog's face" *shorter or flattened.*
**Similar species:** California Dogface (above).
**Early stages:** Larva green, variably banded or striped with yellow and black. Three or more broods. **Food:** False indigo *(Amorpha),* clover *(Trifolium);* also soybean *(Glycine)* and alfalfa *(Medicago),* all in the pea family (Fabaceae). **Adults:** Much of year.
**Range:** In the West, N.D. south to se. Calif., Ariz., N.M., and Rocky Mts. south to Tex., Cen. America. In East to N.Y., Fla. TL: Georgia. **Habitat:** General; fields, meadows, roadsides, washes, thorn forest, pastures.

## Angled Sulfurs: Genus *Anteos* Huebner

Our largest pierids. FW arched; apex sickle-shaped, outer margin concave. HW has projection at end of vein $M_3$. Males have long sex patch above vein Rs in HW.

**CLORINDE** *Anteos clorinde* (Godart)          **Pl. 26**
**Identification:** $3$–$3\frac{1}{2}$ in. (75–88 mm). *Upperside:* Male *white,* with a *yellow patch* on FW from costa through cell. Cell spots on both FW and HW black, ringed with orange. *White sex patch* on HW. Female similar, but duller; yellow FW patch more diffuse.
*Underside:* Pale green in both sexes; cell spots dull brown. *Several veins* enlarged and silvered.
**Similar species:** Maerula (p. 139).
**Early stages:** Little known. **Food:** Senna *(Cassia),* in pea family (Fabaceae). **Adults:** Occur irregularly in the U.S., as migrants or strays.
**Range:** Tropical America north to cen. Tex., w. Kans. (several records), w. Ariz. (irregular). **Habitat:** Thorn forest, scrub, cut-over land.
**Subspecies:** (1) *A. c. clorinde* (Godart). S. America. TL: Brasil. (2) *A. c. nivifera* Fruhstorfer (Pl. 26). Southwestern U.S. to Cen. America. TL: Honduras.

**MAERULA** *Anteos maerula* (Fabricius)                    **Pl. 26**
**Identification:** 3–3½ in. (75–88 mm). *Upperside:* Male *uniform greenish yellow;* FW discal spot *black*. HW discal spot *bright yellow,* small; sex patch on HW *bright yellow*. Female *dull white;* FW cell spot black, HW cell spot orange. *Underside:* Pale green in both sexes; vein Rs of HW silvered.
**Similar species:** Clorinde (p. 138).
**Early stages:** Apparently not recorded. **Adults:** Occur irregularly in the U.S., as migrants or strays.
**Range:** Tropical America north to Dallas, Tex., and s. Ariz. (irregular). Accidental in Neb.; casual in Fla.
**Subspecies:** (1) *A. m. maerula* (Fabricius). TL: Tropical America. (2) *A. m. lacordairei* (Boisduval), Pl. 26. Southern U.S. south to Cen. America. TL: Mexico.

## Giant Sulfurs: Genus *Phoebis* Huebner

Large butterflies; strong fliers. Largely tropical, but 3 species reach our area. Sexually dimorphic — males quite unlike females in appearance. Females may be yellow or white. Giant sulfurs often migrate in large numbers.

**CLOUDLESS SULFUR** *Phoebis sennae* (Linnaeus)     **Pl. 26**
**Identification:** 2¼–2⅝ in. (56–66 mm). *Upperside:* Male *light yellow, unmarked*. Female may be (1) light yellow, with *dark FW cell spot* and *dotted brown border,* (2) *dull yellow* or *orange,* with broken dark border and heavy FW cell spot, or (3) *white,* with broken dark border and heavy FW cell spot.
**Similar species:** (1) Female of Orange-barred Sulfur (below). (2) Female of Large Orange Sulfur (p. 140).
**Early stages:** Larva a variable pale yellow-green, with small black hairs; yellow stripes on each side, blue dots along upper edge of each stripe. Pupa curves upward, head pointed; wing cases large and bulging. Two or more broods. **Food:** Various species of senna *(Cassia),* in pea family. **Adults:** Long flight season. Attracted to mud puddles and flowers.
**Range:** Cen. Calif. east to Neb. and New England, south to Ariz., N.M., Tex., Fla. Mexico. Cen. and S. America, to Patagonia. **Habitat:** Open woodland, forest edges, trails, roadsides, parks, yards, gardens.
**Subspecies:** (1) *P. s. sennae* (Linnaeus). West Indies. TL: Jamaica. (2) *P. s. eubele* (Linnaeus). Eastern U.S. to Tex., Fla. TL: Carolina. (3) *P. s. marcellina* (Cramer), Pl. 26. Female more heavily marked. Calif. east to s. Tex., south to tropical America. TL: Surinam.

**ORANGE-BARRED SULFUR**                              **Pl. 27**
*Phoebis philea* (Johannson)
**Identification:** 2¾–3¼ in. (69–81 mm). *Upperside:* Male bright

yellow; *FW discal patch and border of HW orange.* FW costa and
vein tips black. Sex patch at base of HW. Female dull whitish; FW
cell spot, apex, *zigzag pm. band* and *border spots* on both wings
*brown.*
**Similar species:** (1) White form of female Cloudless Sulfur (p.
139). (2) White form of female Large Orange Sulfur (below).
**Early stages:** Larva yellow-green, tapering to each end. Stripe on
side dark; stripe on lower side yellow, enclosing dark spots. Multiple broods. **Food:** Senna *(Cassia bicapsularis).* **Adults:** Long
flight season.
**Range:** Southern U.S. to Argentina. In the West, Tex. north spo-
radically to Neb., Kans., Colo., and rarely to Ariz. Infrequent in
our area. TL: Probably Surinam. **Habitat:** Most often found in
parks, yards, and gardens; also open woodland, scrub, roadsides.

**LARGE ORANGE SULFUR**                                    **Pl. 27**
*Phoebis agarithe* (Boisduval)
**Identification:** 2¼-2¾ in. (56–69 mm). ***Upperside:*** Male *uniform
light orange,* unmarked except for minute black vein tips. Vein Rs
of HW has a *hair pencil* (rounded hair tuft). Female deep orange,
darker on HW, or dull white. *Brown FW cell spot,* spotted border,
and diagonal pm. band. ***Underside:*** Both sexes have numerous
small brown spots and speckling. A *straight, diagonal pm. band*
on FW.
**Similar species:** (1) Female Cloudless Sulfur (p. 139). (2) Female
Orange-barred Sulfur (above). (3) In Argante Sulfur (Casual species, p. 322), pm. line on underside of FW zigzag.
**Early stages:** Larva reddish. Multiple broods. **Food:** Lindheimer
senna *(Cassia lindheimeriana)* and perhaps other members of the
pea family (Fabaceae). **Adults:** Long flight season.
**Range:** Tex. south to Cen. America. Scarce or casual in s. Calif.,
s. Ariz., Colo., Neb., Kans. TL: Mexico. **Habitat:** Thorn forest,
roadsides, parks, trails, yards, waste places. Attracted to wet places
and mud puddles, also flowers.
**Subspecies:** All individuals found in our area are currently considered to be the nominate subspecies, *agarithe.* A second subspecies occurs in Florida and the Gulf states.

## Statira: Genus *Aphrissa* Butler

**STATIRA** *Aphrissa statira* (Cramer)                    **Pl. 27**
**Identification:** 2⅜-2⅝ in. (59–66 mm). ***Upperside:*** In male,
inner ⅔ of FW and HW is cream to yellow; outer ⅓ is a wide,
"mealy" border of fluffy scales, lighter in color. FW costa and narrow border of apex black. Two sex scale patches, at base of HW on
upperside and underside. Female yellow; *FW costa and border
narrowly black; cell spot black.*
**Early stages:** Little known. Multiple broods. **Food:** In Fla.,
calliandra *(Calliandra)* and rosewood *(Dalbergia ecastophyllum),*

in pea family (Fabaceae). **Adults:** May occur almost any time of year. A straggler in our area.
**Range:** S. Tex., Fla., tropical America straying north to w. Kans. and Colo. **Habitat:** In Tex., openings in thorn forest.
**Subspecies:** (1) *A. s. statira* (Cramer). TL: Coast of Coromandel and Tranquebar (in error, 1777). Probably Surinam. (2) *A. s. jada* (Butler), Pl. 27. Southwestern U.S. and southward. TL: Guatemala.

## Lyside: Genus *Kricogonia* Reakirt

**LYSIDE** *Kricogonia lyside* (Godart)                    **Pl. 27**
**Identification:** $1\frac{1}{2}$–$1\frac{3}{4}$ in. (38–44 mm). FW apex *sickle-shaped.* **Upperside:** Male white; wing bases yellow. HW has *black bar on costa,* which is often reduced or absent. Female like male, all white, or all pale yellow; unmarked. **Underside:** Greenish white to pale yellowish in both sexes, often with a *raised line of white scales* from base of HW through cell to outer margin.
**Early stages:** Multiple broods. **Food:** Guayacan *(Porlieria angustifolia),* in the caltrop family (Zygophyllaceae). **Adults:** Long flight season, March–Nov. Flight rapid. They often seek shade in hot weather.
**Range:** S. Ariz. to Tex. and Fla., south to tropical America. Common; occasional or casual in w. Kans., Neb., Colo. TL: By designation, Haiti. **Habitat:** Thorn forest, woodland, scrub, roadsides, fencerows.

## Small Sulfurs: Genus *Eurema* Huebner

Many species. Small to medium-sized, delicate sulfurs; sexually and sometimes seasonally dimorphic. Largely tropical.

**BOISDUVAL'S SULFUR**                    **Pl. 28**
*Eurema boisduvaliana* (C. & R. Felder)
**Identification:** $1\frac{3}{8}$–$1\frac{5}{8}$ in. (34–41 mm). *HW lobed between veins* $M_3$ and $Cu_1$. **Upperside:** Male *bright yellow,* with a small, pale orange area below HW costa just inside black border. Black border wide, invaded by yellow on FW, forming a fanciful *"dog's head" without an "eye."* HW border deeply invaded by yellow *opposite the discal cell.* Female yellow; FW apex black. **Underside:** Both sexes light yellow. FW apex and lower outer edge of HW rusty.
**Similar species:** (1) Mexican Sulfur (p. 142). (2) Salome Sulfur (p. 142).
**Early stages:** Little known. Multiple broods. **Food:** Apparently unknown. In Texas, associated with a shrubby species of senna *(Cassia).* **Adults:** Long flight season.
**Range:** S. Ariz., s. Tex. south to Cen. America. Scarce or casual in the U.S. except in extreme s. Tex. TL: Mexico. **Habitat:** Edges of thick thorn forest, usually near water.

**MEXICAN SULFUR or MEXICAN YELLOW**          **Pl. 27**
*Eurema mexicana* (Boisduval)
**Identification:** $1\frac{1}{2}$–2 in. (38–50 mm). HW has pointed lobe between veins $M_3$ and $Cu_1$. **Upperside:** Male cream-white; wide band along HW costa *deep yellow*. Cream-white on FW invades the wide black border, forming a *long-nosed "dog's head."* HW border suddenly narrows below cell. Female similar, but HW border *broken into 3–5 dashes.* **Underside:** Creamy yellow in both sexes, flecked with rusty. Rust-colored crossband on HW.
**Similar species:** (1) Boisduval's Sulfur (p. 141). (2) Salome Sulfur (below).
**Early stages:** Incompletely known. Multiple broods. **Food:** Senna (*Cassia,* various species). **Adults:** May–Nov.
**Range:** S. Calif. to Tex., to S. America; occasionally to N.D., Wyo., Colo. TL: Mexico. **Habitat:** Pine forest, desert scrub, oak woodland, meadows, roadsides, waste lands.

**SALOME SULFUR** *Eurema salome* (C. & R. Felder)          **Pl. 28**
**Identification:** $1\frac{3}{4}$–$1\frac{7}{8}$ in. (44–47 mm). HW has short, pointed lobe at end of vein $Cu_1$. **Upperside:** Male *bright yellow, deeper yellow along HW costa.* Black border on FW wide at apex, *narrower and turned-in along tornus;* HW border narrow. Female much paler; border present on FW, absent on HW. **Underside:** Both sexes yellowish; FW apex and HW border pale rusty. 3–5 small, rusty spots in HW disc.
**Similar species:** (1) Boisduval's Sulfur (p. 141). (2) Mexican Sulfur (above).
**Early stages:** Little known. **Adults:** Taken late in the year in our area, in the fall.
**Range:** Colombia and Venezuela, northward through Mexico. Rarely to s. Ariz., s. Tex. **Habitat:** Not known for our area.
**Subspecies:** (1) *E. s. salome* (C. & R. Felder). TL: Ecuador. (2) *E. s. limoneus* (C. & R. Felder), Pl. 28. From extreme southern U.S. southward to S. America. TL: Venezuela.

**PROTERPIA ORANGE**          **Pls. 28, 38**
*Eurema proterpia* (Fabricius)
**Identification:** $1\frac{3}{8}$–$1\frac{3}{4}$ in. (34–44 mm). HW *angled* between veins $M_3$ and $Cu_1$; winter brood (Pl. 28) has a *short, sharp tail* between these veins. **Upperside:** Male bright orange. *FW costa and veins black,* at least at ends (apex also black in winter brood; *vein ends black* in *some* individuals). Female dull yellowish orange; narrow HW border and vein ends dull black. FW apex black, extending halfway along costa and nearly all the way down outer margin. **Underside:** FW orange in both sexes, with yellow at costa. HW yellow, unmarked or with small brown markings. Both sexes of winter brood yellow, with a network of rusty brown markings.
**Early stages:** Undescribed. Multiple broods. **Adults:** March–Nov.

**Range:** S. Ariz. to Tex., south to S. America. TL: Jamaica. **Habitat:** Moist woodland, streamsides.
**Remarks:** The winter brood (Pl. 28) was long considered a separate species, **Gundlach's Orange,** *E. gundlachia* (Poey). TL: Cuba.

**LITTLE SULFUR** *Eurema lisa* (Boisduval & Le Conte)   **Pl. 27**
**Identification:** $1^{3}/_{16}$–$1^{1}/_{2}$ in. (31–38 mm). *Upperside:* Male *butter yellow.* Border coal black, *wider on FW.* FW cell spot small but present; *FW costa broadly obscured by dark gray scales.* Female light yellow, cream, or white; FW apex and broken HW border black. Costa gray-scaled as in male. *Underside:* Pale yellow; veins black-tipped. *FW cell spot small and dark,* but visible. Terminal line and small spot at end of vein $M_1$ on HW rusty brown. HW often flecked with rusty.
**Similar species:** Nise Sulfur (below).
**Early stages:** Larva downy; bright green, with white lines along sides. Multiple broods. **Food:** Legumes, including senna *(Cassia),* clover *(Trifolium),* hog-peanut *(Amphicarpa),* sensitive plant *(Mimosa),* and others. **Adults:** Long season; in south, March–Nov.
**Range:** Colo. and Neb. east to New England, south to Ariz., Tex., Fla. Common in south, scarce to rare northward. TL: United States. **Habitat:** Fields, open woodland, thorn forest, roadsides.

**NISE SULFUR** *Eurema nise* (Cramer)   **Pl. 28**
**Identification:** $1^{3}/_{16}$–$1^{3}/_{8}$ in. (31–34 mm). *Upperside:* Male bright lemon yellow; female lighter, duller. FW costa *narrowly* black; *FW apex and HW vein tips black.* No gray overscaling on costa. *Underside:* Light yellow in both sexes. HW may have a few small gray spots or flecks. *No red-brown markings* as in Proterpia Orange (p. 142) or Little Sulfur (above).
**Early stages:** Little known. Multiple broods. **Food:** Sensitive plant *(Mimosa),* in pea family (Fabaceae). **Adults:** Long flight season; most common in the fall.
**Range:** S. Ariz. to s. Tex. and south to Brazil. **Habitat:** Streamsides and under canopy of thorn forest; seldom found in the open.
**Subspecies:** (1) *E. n. nise* (Cramer). Tropical America. TL: Jamaica. (2) *E. n. nelphe* (R. Felder), Pl. 28. S. Ariz. (uncommon) to s. Tex. and south into Mexico. TL: Vicinity of Nogales, Sonora, Mexico.

**DINA SULFUR** *Eurema dina* (Poey)   **Pl. 28**
**Identification:** $1^{5}/_{8}$–2 in. (41–50 mm). *Upperside:* Male brilliant yellow, with a faint orange tint around outer edge of both FW and HW. FW has a *narrow black costa and border;* HW has a black terminal line. Female very different — light yellow, with a *dull orange tint around HW edge;* FW apex and cell ends black. *Un-*

*derside:* Male *entirely yellow,* except for a very small black cell spot. In female, *both FW and HW red-brown at apex.*
**Early stages:** Little known. A straggler in the U.S. **Food:** Bitterbush (*Picramnia pentandra,* quassia or ailanthus family) in Cuba; larval food not known for the U.S. **Adults:** Taken mostly in Oct.–Nov.
**Range:** Rare or casual from s. Ariz. to s. Tex.; common in the tropics. **Habitat:** Not known for our area; taken as a stray.
**Subspecies:** (1) *E. d. dina* (Poey). TL: Cuba. (2) *E. d. westwoodi* (Boisduval), Pl. 28. Extreme southern U.S., southward into the tropics. TL: Mexico.

**SLEEPY ORANGE** *Eurema nicippe* (Cramer)           **Pl. 28**
**Identification:** 1½–1⅞ in. (30–47 mm). *Upperside:* Male *deep orange. Wide black border projects inward* at HW discal cell. FW *cell bar distinct.* Fringes pink or whitish. Female somewhat similar, but duller; dark borders less complete. *Underside* (both sexes): HW yellow, often with a network of red-brown markings. Rectangular spot between radial sector (vein Rs) and HW costa, bar across HW disc, and sometimes other markings are all a darker brown.
**Early stages:** Larva slender; covered with short hairs. Body green; yellow stripe on side bordered with black. 2–3 broods. **Food:** Prefers senna *(Cassia),* especially shrubby species; may occur in yards on ornamental senna. Also found on clover *(Trifolium).* **Adults:** April–Nov.
**Range:** Much of U.S.; south to Brazil. In the West, Colo., Neb., and e. and s. Calif. south to s. Ariz. and s. Tex. TL: Virginia. **Habitat:** Fields, meadows, fencerows, desert scrub, washes, gardens, yards, parks, and vacant lots; at low elevations.

## Dainty Sulfur: Genus *Nathalis* Boisduval

**DAINTY SULFUR** *Nathalis iole* Boisduval           **Pl. 28**
**Identification:** ¾–1⅛ in. (19–28 mm). Our smallest pierid. *Upperside:* Male pale yellow; FW apex and inner margin black. *HW costa and vein tips black.* Female similar, but black markings more extensive and HW deep dull yellow or buffy. *Underside:* Greenish yellow to gray in both sexes. FW cell orange, disc yellow. Inner margin of FW and 2–3 pm. spots black. HW costa and pm. band dull gray.
**Early stages:** Larva dark green, with a purple stripe on back and a yellow and black stripe on side. Multiple broods where conditions permit. **Food:** Many plants, including dogweed *(Dyssodia),* marigold *(Tagetes),* and beggarticks *(Bidens),* all in sunflower family (Asteraceae); also chickweed *(Stellaria),* in pink family (Caryophyllaceae); storksbill *(Erodium),* in geranium family (Geraniaceae); and others. **Adults:** March–Nov., depending on locality and elevation.

**Range:** E. Calif. and N.D. south to Ariz., N.M., and Tex. In East, from Great Lakes region to Fla.; south to S. America. Absent from Pacific Slope. TL: Mexico. **Habitat:** Meadows, grassland, roadsides, and open places in brushland. To treeline in summer in mountains of the West, but does not overwinter there.

## Orange-tips and Marbles: Subfamily Euchloeinae

Holarctic. Medium-sized. White, with dark markings on upperside of FW and characteristic *marbling* on underside of HW.

### Orange-tips: Genus *Anthocharis* Boisduval, Rambur, & Graslin

Known by the bright *reddish orange tips* on FW. Marbling on underside of HW usually fine and "mossy."

**FELDER'S ORANGE-TIP**                      **Pl. 38**
*Anthocharis cethura* (C. & R. Felder)
**Identification:** $1\frac{1}{4}$-$1\frac{1}{3}$ in. (32–38 mm). *Upperside:* In male, orange patch near tip of FW separated from apex by a double row of *black and white spots along margin.* Orange tip smaller in female. *Underside:* Heavy green marbling on HW. Two forms occur: in form "caliente," upperside ground color yellowish; in form "deserti," orange tips reduced or even absent in both sexes.
**Similar species:** (1) Pima Orange-tip (below) is bright yellow. (2) In Sara Orange-tip (p. 146), the orange tip is larger. Marbling on underside of HW dark and mossy-looking.
**Early stages:** Larva green, with light stripes on side. Pupa brown; the slender front end is straight. One brood. **Food:** Hedge mustard *(Sisymbrium),* tansy-mustard *(Descurainia),* longbeak *(Streptanthella longirostris),* and desert candle *(Caulanthus),* all in mustard family (Brassicaceae). **Adults:** March–April.
**Range:** Southern and eastern Calif., cen. Nev., w. Ariz., Baja California. **Habitat:** Juniper woodland, desert.
**Subspecies:** (1) **Felder's Orange-tip,** *A. c. cethura* (D & R. Felder), Pl. 38. Most of range. TL: California. (2) **Catalina Orange-tip,** *A. c. catalina* Meadows. Range and TL: Catalina I. (3) **Morrison's Orange-tip,** *A. c. morrisoni* W. H. Edwards. Larger. Marbling on underside darker. Female lacks orange on wing tips. Lower San Joaquin Valley of Calif. TL: Kern River, Kern Co., Calif.

**PIMA ORANGE-TIP** *Anthocharis pima* Edwards      **Pl. 38**
**Identification:** $1\frac{3}{8}$-$1\frac{5}{8}$ in. (34–41 mm). *Upperside:* Bright yellow, with a large orange patch on FW. Wide black bar across end of FW cell. Large *blackish area* at FW apex. *Underside:* Marbling *very distinct.*
**Similar species:** Felder's Orange-tip (above).

**Early stages:** Unknown. One brood. **Adults:** Feb–April.
**Range:** S. Nev., Ariz. **Habitat:** Desert hills.

**SARA ORANGE-TIP** *Anthocharis sara* Lucas          **Pl. 38**
**Identification:** 1⅜–1⅞ in. (34–47 mm). *Upperside:* In male, orange *FW spot large, orange-red;* dark border at apex *narrow.* In female, orange spot smaller; black apex has white wedges along vein ends. Some individuals are partly yellow. *Underside:* Marbling on HW olive-green, scattered, "mossy." Marbling heavier in spring brood ("Reakirt's Orange-tip," form "reakirtii").
**Similar species:** Felder's Orange-tip (p. 145).
**Early stages:** Larva dull green. Pupa silvery gray; wing cases marked with white. Front end of pupa gradually upturned. Nominate subspecies *sara* has 2 broods; other subspecies have 1. **Food:** Various plants in the mustard family: hedge mustard *(Sisymbrium),* rock cress *(Arabis),* winter cress *(Barbarea),* fringe pod *(Thysanocarpus),* jewel flower *(Streptanthus),* tansy-mustard *(Descurainia),* and others. **Adults:** March–June where 2-brooded, May–July where 1-brooded, varying with latitude and elevation. **Range:** Coastal Alaska south to Baja California, east to Wyo., Colo., N.M. TL: Calif. **Habitat:** Meadows, fields, fencerows, roadsides, orchards, vacant lots.
**Subspecies:** There are nine similar subspecies, including the **Stella Orange-tip,** *A. s. stella* W. H. Edwards, Pl. 38. Ground color yellowish in both sexes. TL: Marlette Peak, Carson Range, Washoe Co., Nev.

## Genus *Falcapica* Klots

**BOISDUVAL'S MARBLE**                                 **Pl. 25**
*Falcapica lanceolata* (Lucas)
**Identification:** 1½–1⅞ in. (38–47 mm). FW *sickle-shaped; outer margin concave. Upperside:* White, except for dark FW apex and cell spot. *Underside:* FW markings repeated. HW has dark veins and fine, dense marbling, dull brown or gray. Conspicuous *white dash* below HW costa.
**Similar species:** In marbles of the genus *Euchloe* (Creusa, Edwards', Large, and Olympia Marbles, below), FW not sickle-shaped. Marbling on underside of HW greenish, thicker.
**Early stages:** Larva green, with a thin yellow line through spiracles, and below this a wider white line. Pupa light brown, the front end much upcurved. One brood. **Food:** Rock cress *(Arabis).*
**Adults:** March–April in s. Calif., April–June northward.
**Range:** Sw. Ore. to s. Calif., Baja California Norte, and Carson Range of Nev. **Habitat:** Rocky canyons, roadcuts.
**Subspecies:** (1) **Boisduval's Marble,** *F. l. lanceolata* (Lucas), Pl. 25. Marbling on underside of HW brownish. Northern part of range. TL: California. (2) **Grinnell's Marble,** *F. l. australis*

(F. Grinnell). Marbling on underside gray rather than brown. S. Calif. TL: Arroyo Seco and Millard Canyons, Los Angeles Co., Calif.

**Remarks:** Previously placed in the genus *Anthocharis.*

## Marbles: Genus *Euchloe* Huebner

Holarctic. Marbling on underside of HW forms a pattern of greenish spots.

**CREUSA MARBLE** *Euchloe creusa* (Doubleday)     **Pl. 25**
**Identification:** 1⅜-1⅝ in. (34–41 mm). *Upperside:* Dark markings at FW apex slight; *FW cell bar narrow.* Bases of FW and HW much darkened. *Underside:* HW marbling *dark* and *extensive,* the white interspaces few and small.
**Similar species:** (1) In Edwards' Marble (below), ground color on underside of HW has a pearly luster. (2) In Large Marble (p. 148), HW marbling on underside coarse, yellowish green. (3) In Olympia Marble (p. 148), HW marbling on underside consists of a few wide bars.
**Early stages:** Unknown. One brood. **Food:** Unknown. **Adults:** Late May to early June.
**Range:** N. Alaska, Yukon Terr., Northwest Terr. south to British Columbia, Alberta, Saskatchewan. TL: Near Banff, Alberta. **Habitat:** Mountain areas; rocky banks and outcrops; trails, roadsides.

**EDWARDS' MARBLE**                                       **Pl. 25**
*Euchloe hyantis* (W. H. Edwards)
**Identification:** 1⅜-1⅝ in. (34–41 mm). Smaller and more delicate than the Large Marble (p. 148); markings clean-cut. *Upperside: FW cell bar* comes *very close* to black-speckled costa; ground color seldom tinged with yellow. *Underside:* White ground color has *pearly luster.* HW marbling green; white interspaces of moderate size.
**Similar species:** (1) Creusa Marble (above). (2) Large Marble (p. 148). (3) Olympia Marble (p. 148).
**Early stages:** Larva green, dotted with black; lateral line white. Pupa brown; front end straight. One brood. **Food:** Rock cress *(Arabis),* jewel flower *(Streptanthus),* tansy-mustard *(Descurainia),* desert candle *(Caulanthus),* and peppergrass *(Lepidium),* all in mustard family (Brassicaceae). **Adults:** March–May.
**Range:** British Columbia south to n. Baja California, east to Idaho, Colo., N.M. **Habitat:** Rocky canyons, ridges, cutbanks. In s. Calif., hills and washes.
**Subspecies:** (1) **Edwards' Marble,** *E. h. hyantis* (W. H. Edwards), Pl. 25. Cell bar on upperside of FW *narrow.* Calif. Coast Ranges, Sierra Nevada. TL: Vicinity of Ukiah, Mendocino Co.,

Calif. (2) **Andrew's Marble,** *E. h. andrewsi* Martin. FW cell bar
*very narrow;* wing-tip markings darker. Quite local. TL: Crest
Line Hwy., near Lake Arrowhead, San Bernardino Co., Calif. (3)
**Lotta Marble,** *E. h. lotta* (Beutenmueller). FW cell bar *wide,*
nearly square. Rest of range. TL: Colorado, Arizona, Utah, Southern California.

**LARGE MARBLE** *Euchloe ausonides* (Lucas)          **Pl. 25**
**Identification:** 1½–2 in. (38–50 mm). Our largest marble.
*Upperside:* FW cell bar usually a *short distance from costa.*
Ground color often tinged with yellow, at least on HW. *Underside:* White ground color *lacks* pearly luster. HW marbling *often
partly yellow;* white interspaces in marbling moderate to large in
size.
**Similar species:** (1) Creusa Marble (p. 147). (2) Edwards' Marble
(above). (3) Olympia Marble (below).
**Early stages:** Larva dark green; dorsal and lateral stripes yel-
low-green. Pupa light brown; wing covers and 5 lines on abdomen
darker. One brood in north, 2 broods in cen. Calif. **Food:** Rock
cress *(Arabis),* winter cress *(Barbarea),* tansy-mustard
*(Descurainia),* hedge mustard *(Sisymbrium),* wall flower
*(Erysimum),* and other plants in the mustard family
(Brassicaceae). **Adults:** June–July in north, March–June in cen.
Calif.
**Range:** Alaska east to Manitoba, south to s.-cen. Calif., Neb.,
N.M. **Habitat:** Pacific coastal plain, open forest in mountain
areas; fields, meadows, taiga. In cen. Calif., often partly "domes-
tic" — occurs in orchards, along roadsides, and in vacant lots.
Ranges to treeline in Rocky Mts.
**Subspecies:** Four quite similar subspecies are recognized.

**OLYMPIA MARBLE**                                      **Pl. 25**
*Euchloe olympia* (W. H. Edwards)
**Identification:** 1⁵⁄₁₆–1⁵⁄₈ in. (33–42 mm). *Upperside:* Dark mark-
ings few — often reduced to FW cell bar, dash near FW apex, and
gray-black bar not quite halfway down outer margin of FW. *Un-
derside:* Marbling forms a network of 3 irregular *bands across
HW, leaving extensive white areas.*
**Similar species:** Creusa Marble (p. 147). (2) Edwards' Marble
(p. 147). (3) Large Marble (above).
**Early stages:** Larva green, striped with slate and yellow. One
brood. **Food:** Rock cress *(Arabis),* hedge mustard *(Sisymbrium).*
**Adults:** April–June.
**Range:** Mont. south to cen. Tex., east to N.D., Pa., W. Va. **Habitat:** Open woodland, meadows, river banks, open hills.
**Subspecies:** (1) **Olympia Marble,** *E. o. olympia* (W. H. Ed-
wards). Eastern part of range. TL: Coalburgh, W. Va. (2) **Rosy
Marble,** *E. o. rosa* (W. H. Edwards), Pl. 25. Underside often
flushed with pink. Western. TL: Texas.

# SNOUT BUTTERFLIES:
## Family Libytheidae

Worldwide. Very few species. Labial palpi *very long,* forming a protruding "snout." FW apex square. Front legs reduced in male, well developed in female.

### American Snout Butterflies:
### Genus *Libytheana* Michener

**SNOUT BUTTERFLY**                                     **Pl. 29**
*Libytheana bachmanii* (Kirtland)
**Identification:** $1\frac{3}{8}$-$1\frac{7}{8}$ in. (34–47 mm). Note *"snout" (labial palpi). Upperside:* Dark brown. Much of FW cell and markings beyond cell on both FW and HW orange-brown. Outer spots on FW white, the spots at costa and cell-end spots *in line or overlapping. Underside:* FW — underside similar to upperside. HW may be uniform gray to dark brown, or mottled with a lighter crossband.
**Similar species:** In Mexican Snout Butterfly (a casual species — see p. 320), cell-end spots nearer to wing apex than costal spots.
**Early stages:** Larva green to blackish, with yellow stripes; head small, turned down; thorax humped over head. Pupa green, triangular in side view. Multiple broods. **Food:** Various hackberries, especially spiny hackberry *(Celtis pallida),* in the elm family. Larvae often strip food plants. **Adults:** Long flight season. They sometimes migrate in enormous numbers.
**Range:** Rocky Mts. east to New England, south to Fla. **Habitat:** Very general; adults wander widely and may occur almost anywhere within the range.
**Subspecies:** (1) *L. b. bachmanii* (Kirtland). Colo. to eastern U.S. TL: N. Ohio. (2) *L. b. larvata* (Strecker), Pl. 29. Larger; wing outlines less angular. Se. Calif. to Tex. TL: San Antonio, Tex.

# METALMARKS:
## Family Riodinidae

Small, mostly tropical butterflies. Some have spots or lines of small, metallic scales. Front legs reduced in male, normal in female. In male, prothoracic coxa extends spinelike beyond articulation of trochanter (see front endpapers). Head small, eyes notched at base of antennae; labial palpi small. Antennae long, straight. Humeral vein on HW has 2 spur veins.
   **Early stages:** Larva either cylindrical, or broad and flattened,

often with very long hairs. Pupa covered with short hairs; stout and rounded, suspended by a cremaster and often also by a girdle.

## Metalmarks: Genus *Apodemia* C. & R. Felder

General appearance spotted or checkered, either with white or with orange-brown. No metallic scales. Flight rapid.

**MORMON METALMARK**                                      Pl. 29
*Apodemia mormo* (C. & R. Felder)
**Identification:** $\frac{7}{8}$-$1\frac{1}{4}$ in. (22-31 mm). **Upperside:** Black to orange-brown, with white and black spots. FW discal area tawny to brick red; area beyond discal cell in HW also that color in some subspecies (see below). **Underside:** Gray spotted with white; FW discal area brick-red.
**Early stages:** Larva cylindrical; covered with short hairs. One brood in north, 2 or more in south. **Food:** Various species of wild buckwheat *(Eriogonum)*. **Adults:** July–Sept. in north; flight season longer in south.
**Range:** E. Wash. to N.D. (scarce), south to s. Calif., Ariz., N.M., and w. Tex.; also in Baja California and other parts of Mexico.
**Habitat:** Arid land — dry rocky hills, dry sandy soils.
**Subspecies:** There are 9 subspecies, showing 3 different patterns: (1) *mormo* pattern — reddish markings on FW only; see *A. m. mormo* (C. & R. Felder), Pl. 29, no. 2. TL: Near Pyramid Lake, Washoe Co., Nev. (2) *virgulti* pattern — reddish markings on both FW and HW; see **Behr's Metalmark,** *A. m. virgulti* (Behr), Pl. 29, no. 3. TL: Near Los Angeles, Calif. (3) *mejanicus* pattern (not shown) — ground color on upperside orange-brown instead of black. Subspecies that live near each other may have different patterns.

**PALMER'S METALMARK**                                    Pl. 29
*Apodemia palmerii* (W. H. Edwards)
**Identification:** $\frac{3}{4}$-$1\frac{1}{8}$ in. (19-28 mm). **Upperside:** Dark gray or brown, with some coppery suffusion. *Many small white spots,* including a *submarginal row* along FW and HW margins. **Underside:** Orange-brown to coppery, with white spots and black submarginal dots.
**Early stages:** Larva green, with short hairs. It makes a nest in leaves of its food plant. Multiple broods. **Food:** Honey mesquite *(Prosopis glandulosa* var. *torreyana)* and screwbean mesquite *(P. pubescens),* both in the pea family. **Adults:** Long flight season.
**Range:** S. Calif., s. Nev., s. Utah, Ariz., N.M., w. Tex. **Habitat:** Streamsides, mesquite thickets, thorn scrub, fencerows.
**Subspecies:** (1) **Palmer's Metalmark,** *A. p. palmerii* (W. H. Edwards), Pl. 29. Nev. to Tex. TL: St. George, Utah. (2) **Margined Metalmark,** *A. p. marginalis* (Skinner). Browner; FW and HW margins coppery. S. Calif., Baja California. TL: Acme, Calif.

**HEPBURN'S METALMARK**                          not shown
*Apodemia hepburni* Godman & Salvin
**Identification:** $\frac{3}{4}$-$1\frac{1}{8}$ in. (19–28 mm). *Upperside:* Dark gray,
with some coppery suffusion. Many small white spots, but *no
submarginal row* as in Palmer's Metalmark (above).
**Similar species:** Closely resembles Palmer's Metalmark (above).
**Early stages:** Unknown. **Food:** Unknown. **Adults:** July in Tex.
**Range:** Mexico. Has been collected a few times near Patagonia,
Ariz. and in the Chisos Mts. of Tex. **Habitat:** Unknown.
**Remarks:** Hepburn's Metalmark has usually been considered a
subspecies of Palmer's Metalmark (above), but the two are now
known to occur together as separate species in many places in
Mexico.

**CHIRICAHUA METALMARK**                         not shown
*Apodemia phyciodoides* Barnes & Benjamin
**Identification:** This rare metalmark looks like a small crescent
(*Phyciodes* species, pp. 95–98). *Upperside:* Checkered with or-
ange-brown and dark brown. *Underside:* HW dull gray, with 2
whitish bands.
**Range:** Chiricahua Mts., Ariz. south to Sonora and Chihuahua,
Mexico. TL: Chiricahua Mts., Cochise Co., Ariz.
**Remarks:** Exceedingly rare; known primarily from the 1 male
and 1 female (type specimens) taken many years ago. In 1982, the
species was rediscovered in the Sierra Madre of Sonora and Chihuahua, Mexico.

**NAIS METALMARK** *Apodemia nais*              Pl. 29
(W. H. Edwards)
**Identification:** $1\frac{1}{4}$-$1\frac{3}{8}$ in. (31–34 mm). FW apex pointed in male,
more rounded in female. *Upperside:* Checkered with blackish
brown and orange-brown; *white spot near FW apex.* Fringes
checkered with white and gray. *Underside:* FW orange, dotted
with black. HW ash-gray with many black dots; those forming the
median line irregular. Spots in discal area and near margin orange.
**Similar species:** Chisos Metalmark (below).
**Early stages:** Larva pale green, with tufts of short hairs. One
brood. **Food:** Probably Fendler's snowbrush *(Ceanothus fendleri).*
**Adults:** June–July.
**Range:** Cen. Colo. south in Rocky Mts. to Ariz., N.M.; Mexico.
TL: Prescott, Ariz. **Habitat:** Open forest where food plant grows;
streamsides.

**CHISOS METALMARK**                             not shown
*Apodemia chisosensis* H. A. Freeman
**Identification:** $1\frac{1}{8}$-$1\frac{1}{4}$ in. (28–31 mm). Male FW less pointed
than in Nais Metalmark (above). *Upperside:* Resembles that of
Nais Metalmark, but the orange is brighter and the black spots are
smaller. *Underside:* FW apex and all of HW *almost white;* little

or no orange on HW. Black dots very clear. Fringes on each wing have *3 white dots.*
**Early stages:** Unknown. One brood. **Food:** Unknown. **Adults:** Early Aug.
**Range:** Big Bend Natl. Park, in the vicinity of the TL: Chisos Mts., 5400 ft. (1646 m), Brewster Co., Tex.
**Remarks:** Rare and local; known only from a few specimens.

## Little Metalmarks:
## Genus *Calephelis* Grote & Robinson

A large group of small, dark brown species, all very similar. They have lines of small metallic spots ("metal marks") across both front and hind wings. FW usually narrow and pointed in male, wider and more blunt in female. The primary classification is based on examination of the male genitalia; identification by color and markings is often less reliable. These butterflies are found in both North and South America.

**FATAL METALMARK**                                    **Pl. 29**
*Calephelis nemesis* (W. H. Edwards)
**Identification:** $3/4$–1 in. (19–25 mm). FW pointed in male; outer margin indented. *Upperside:* Dull brown, with a median band that is slightly darker than ground color; *outer edge of band projects slightly opposite discal cell and vein $Cu_2$ in FW.* Metallic spots ("metal marks") have silver-green iridescence. *Underside:* Dull yellowish brown, with many dark dots that are close together. Metallic spots silvery.
**Early stages:** Larvae covered with rather short hairs that lie flat. Two broods in s. Calif.; multiple broods in Tex. **Food:** Varies with subspecies (see below). **Adults:** May–June and Aug.–Oct. in Calif.; all year in s. Tex.
**Range:** Calif. to s. Tex.; Mexico. **Habitat:** Streamsides, ditch banks, roadsides, understory of thorn forest, washes.
**Subspecies:** (1) **Fatal Metalmark,** *C. n. nemesis* (W. H. Edwards), Pl. 29. Food unknown; extent of range uncertain. TL: Arizona. (2) **Southern Metalmark,** *C. n. australis* (W. H. Edwards). Spots on underside larger than in *C. n. nemesis.* Food: Virgin's bower *(Clematis drummondi, C. henryi).* N.M., Tex.; Mexico. TL: San Antonio, Tex. (3) **Dammer's Metalmark,** *C. n. dammersi* McAlpine. Lighter brown. Food believed to be seepwillow *(Baccharis glutinosa).* Occurs locally near the TL: Blythe, Calif. (4) **Dusky Metalmark,** *C. n. californica* McAlpine. Smaller, darker. Food: Seepwillow. TL: Riverside, Riverside Co., Calif.

**LOST METALMARK**                                     **Pl. 29**
*Calephelis perditalis* Barnes & McDunnough
**Identification:** $5/8$–$7/8$ in. (16–22 mm). *Upperside:* Deep warm brown; median band vaguely darker. Pm. band just perceptibly

lighter than ground color; metallic spots distinct. *Underside:* Dull orange-yellow, with tiny black dots. Metallic pm. and submarginal spots bright and clear.
**Early stages:** Multiple broods. **Food:** Christmas-bush *(Eupatorium odoratum),* in the sunflower family. **Adults:** All year in s. Tex.
**Range:** Reported from Ariz.; s. Tex.; Mexico. Common where found. TL: San Benito, Tex. **Habitat:** Thorn forest, woodlots, fencerows, roadsides.

## WRIGHT'S METALMARK                                Pl. 29
*Calephelis wrighti* Holland
**Identification:** 1-1⅛ in. (25-28 mm). FW long and pointed in male, its outer margin indented; FW more rounded in female. *Upperside: Light dull reddish brown,* with rows of dark spots; looks checkered. *Median band usually not evident. Underside: Brownish yellow;* black dots very small. Metallic spots not conspicuous.
**Early stages:** Larva covered with long white hairs. Three broods. **Food:** Sweet-bush *(Bebbia juncea,* Asteraceae); larva feeds on bark of stems. **Adults:** Feb.–March, June–July, and Sept.–Oct.
**Range:** S. Calif.; w. Ariz.; Baja California. Local. **Habitat:** Oases, canyons, and washes — usually near water or moisture.

## RAWSON'S METALMARK                                Pl. 29
*Calephelis rawsoni* McAlpine
**Identification:** ⅞-1⅛ in. (22-28 mm). *Upperside:* Dark reddish brown. Dark markings numerous but obscure. Median band just perceptibly darker than ground color; *band does not project outward opposite discal cell* on either FW or HW (as in Fatal Metalmark, p. 152). Metallic spots small. *Underside: Light brownish orange;* the minute black spots and metallic spots are bright and distinct.
**Early stages:** Undescribed. Probably 2 or more broods. **Food:** Shrubby boneset *(Eupatorium havanense),* palmleaf eupatorium *(E. greggii),* in sunflower family (Asteraceae). **Adults:** May–Oct.
**Range:** W. Tex. to s.-cen. Tex. Local; not usually very common. TL: Kerrville. **Habitat:** Usually moist localities; streamsides, gulches, woodland.

## FREEMAN'S METALMARK                          not shown
*Calephelis freemani* McAlpine
**Identification:** ⅞-1 in. (22–25 mm). Coloration lighter and somewhat browner than most metalmarks in genus *Calephelis.* This species differs mainly in the form of the male genitalia.
**Early stages:** Unknown. **Food:** Unknown. **Adults:** Have been collected in June.
**Range:** So far, found only at the TL: 12 mi. northwest of Alpine,

Tex., along State Highway 18. **Habitat:** Along a small stream in Tex.
**Remarks:** Described in 1971 from specimens taken at the type locality; only 18 specimens known as of 1982.

## ARIZONA METALMARK                                      Pl. 29
*Calephelis arizonensis* McAlpine
**Identification:** 1–1⅛ in. (25–28 mm). *Fringes white in several spaces between veins,* but not truly checkered. *Upperside:* Cinnamon brown, with a vague, narrow median band. FW has an indefinite pale patch below apex, best seen in daylight. *Underside:* Dull orange, with small, distinct markings. Metallic spots bright.
**Early stages:** Unknown. **Food:** Unknown; may be seepwillow *(Baccharis glutinosa).* **Adults:** Feb.–April, Aug.–Sept.
**Range:** S. Ariz. TL: Brown Canyon, Baboquivari Mts. **Habitat:** Near permanent streams.
**Remarks:** First described in 1971.

## DREISBACH'S METALMARK                               not shown
*Calephelis dreisbachi* McAlpine
**Identification:** ⅞–1 in. (22–25 mm). *Upperside:* Uniform reddish-brown; markings not well defined — median band indefinite. *Underside:* Light yellowish brown; markings well defined.
**Early stages:** Unknown. **Food:** Unknown. **Adults:** July–Sept.
**Range:** Santa Cruz Co., Ariz. south to San Blas, Nayarit, Mexico. **Habitat:** Unknown.
**Remarks:** Described in 1971 from a few specimens, one of which was found 6 mi. (9.7 km) north of Nogales, Ariz.

## Metalmarks: Genus *Emesis* Fabricius

A large, tropical genus; two species occur in our area. They are large, for metalmarks. Wings narrow in male; FW pointed. Wings more ample in female; FW rounded.

## ARES METALMARK *Emesis ares* (Edwards)           Pl. 29
**Identification:** 1¼–1⅜ in. (31–34 mm). A *short projection* on edge of HW at anal angle. *Fringes mostly white. Upperside:* Dark brown, with many narrow dark markings. *Orange-brown patch on HW,* more extensive in female. *Underside:* Brownish orange, with lines of small black dots.
**Similar species:** Zela Metalmark (below).
**Early stages:** Unknown. One brood. **Food:** Unknown. **Adults:** Aug.–Sept.
**Range:** S. Ariz., Mexico. TL: Ft. Grant, Graham Co., Ariz. **Habitat:** Streamsides and washes, usually in oak woodland.

## ZELA METALMARK *Emesis zela* Butler               Pl. 29
**Identification:** 1⅛–1¼ in. (28–31 mm). Resembles Ares Metal-

mark (above), but smaller. FW *slightly indented below apex.* Fringes mostly white in male; in female, fringes dark on FW, pale on HW. *Upperside:* Dull, slightly reddish brown. Median band irregular, dark, more noticeable on HW. Outer $\frac{1}{3}$ of FW has few markings. Orange-brown patch on HW extensive. *Underside:* Pinkish brown. *Dark dots small, scattered.*

**Early stages:** Unknown. Two broods. **Food:** Unknown. **Adults:** March–April and June–Aug.

**Range:** S. Ariz. south to Cen. America. **Habitat:** Canyons, streamsides, oak woodland.

**Subspecies:** (1) *E. z. zela* Butler. Not in U.S. (2) **Cleis Metalmark,** *E. z. cleis* (W. H. Edwards), Pl. 29. TL: Ft. Grant, Ariz.

# GOSSAMER-WINGED BUTTERFLIES:
## Family Lycaenidae

Worldwide; many species. Small butterflies, with notched eyes at base of antennae. Sexes often very different on the upperside; they look alike on the underside. Adults of many species *rub their hind wings together;* this is thought to be a defense, drawing the attention of predators away from the head.

**Early stages:** Egg flattened (Fig. 3, p. 25). Larva broad, the head small and retractable; body often covered with velvety hairs (Fig. 5, p. 26). Larva secretes fluids that are attractive to ants. Pupa short; underside flat; may have cremaster and girdle (Fig. 6, p. 27). Pupa attached to plants or concealed in leaf litter or under bark.

## Hairstreaks: Subfamilies Theclinae and Eumaeinae

FW triangular, at least in male. Male may have a sex patch (stigma) on upperside of FW. In both sexes, HW may have 1–2 short tails (often broken off) or an elongated lobe or tab at anal angle, or both; in some species, the HW is rounded. Usually a visible pm. line (thecla line) on underside of HW, and often a dark spot or colored patch called the thecla spot near anal angle in cell $Cu_1$ (see Fig. 12, p. 156). The thecla spot may be visible on the upperside as well as the underside of the HW.

## Hairstreaks: Subfamily Theclinae

### Boisduval's Hairstreak: Genus *Habrodais* Scudder

**BOISDUVAL'S HAIRSTREAK**                                    **Pl. 29**
*Habrodais grunus* (Boisduval)
**Identification:** 1–1¼ in. (25–31 mm). Very plain-colored. Both sexes have short tail on HW. *Upperside:* Male dark brown, with a *yellowish brown flush* in discal area of FW; no stigma. Female lighter. *Underside:* Pale yellowish brown, with a narrow, darker

thecla (pm.) line. HW has *thin crescents near margin — last 2 iridescent.*
**Early stages:** Larva bluish green. 1-2 broods. **Food:** Oaks, especially canyon oak *(Quercus chrysolepis)* and huckleberry oak *(Q. vaccinifolia).* **Adults:** June–Aug. They visit moisture, not flowers. Adults fly in morning and evening and rest on banks and tree trunks in heat of day. They may aggregate in large numbers. **Range:** Ore. and Calif. east to Idaho, Colo., Ariz.; rare or local eastward. **Habitat:** Mountain ridges, canyons.
**Subspecies:** (1) **Boisduval's Hairstreak,** *H. g. grunus* (Boisduval), Pl. 29. Sierra Nevada to San Diego Co. TL: California. (2) **Lorquin's Hairstreak,** *H. g. lorquini* Field. Darker. Coastal Calif. TL: Mt. Diablo, Calif. (3) **Herr's Hairstreak,** *H. g. herri* Field. Underside very light. N. Calif., Ore. TL: McKenzie Pass, Ore.

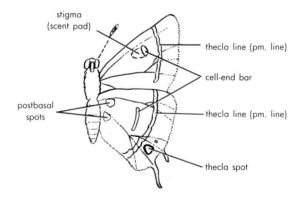

**Fig. 12. Hairstreak: wing pattern (composite figure).** The stigma is present on the upperside of the forewing in the male only. All other pattern elements occur in both sexes on the underside, except for the thecla spot, which may be visible on both upperside and underside of the hind wing.

## Colorado Hairstreak: Genus *Hypaurotis* Scudder

### COLORADO HAIRSTREAK                                      Pl. 30
*Hypaurotis crysalus* (W. H. Edwards)
**Identification:** 1¼-1½ in. (31–38 mm). In both sexes, HW has small projection at vein Cu$_1$, slender tail at vein Cu$_2$. **Upperside:**

Violet, with a wide dusky border. Coral red spots at anal angle of both FW and HW. Male has no stigma on FW.
**Early stages:** Undescribed. One brood. **Food:** Oaks, especially gambel oak. **Adults:** June–Aug., depending on locality. Not attracted to flowers. They often rest high in trees, out of reach.
**Range:** Colo., Utah, Ariz., N.M. **Habitat:** Oak woodland, oak scrub, canyons.
**Subspecies:** (1) **Colorado Hairstreak,** *H. c. crysalus* (W. H. Edwards), Pl. 30. Colo., s. Utah, Ariz., N.M. TL: Palmer Lake, El Paso Co., Colo. (2) **Citima Hairstreak,** *H. c. citima* (Hy. Edwards). Underside light gray with dark bands. W. Colo., Utah. TL: Mt. Nebo, Utah.

# Hairstreaks: Subfamily Eumaeinae

### GREAT PURPLE HAIRSTREAK                     Pl. 32
*Atlides halesus* (Cramer)
**Identification:** $1\frac{1}{4}$–$1\frac{5}{8}$ in. (31–41 mm). Though traditionally called the Great Purple Hairstreak, this butterfly is really blue. HW has 1 short and 1 long tail in the nominate subspecies, *A. h. halesus;* in the other subspecies, the upper tail is reduced to a short stub. *Upperside:* Male a *brilliant, iridescent blue,* with a wide black border; has dark FW stigma. Female slightly duller. *Underside:* Brown to blackish. Dash at base of FW blue; spots at base of FW and HW red. Inner spots at anal angle of HW blue; outer spots golden green; inner spots sometimes separated by red bar.
**Early stages:** Larva velvet green; overwinters as a pupa. Multiple broods. **Food:** Greenleaf mistletoe *(Phoradendron tomentosum),* which grows on broad-leaved trees; also mesquite mistletoe *(P. californica),* on mesquite. **Adults:** March–Nov.
**Range:** S. Ore. east to N.J., south to s. Calif., Tex., Fla.; Mexico. **Habitat:** Woodland, parks, yards, fencerows, roadsides, city shade trees.
**Subspecies:** (1) *A. h. halesus* (Cramer). Red bar at tornus (anal angle) separates golden green spots on underside of HW, as described above. Eastern; west to N.M. TL: Se. United States. (2) *A. h. estesi* Clench, Pl. 32. Usually only 1 tail. Markings at HW tornus on underside all green; no red bar. Western. Widely distributed; usually uncommon. TL: Riverside, Calif.

### Genus *Chlorostrymon* Clench

### SIMAETHIS HAIRSTREAK                        Pl. 32
*Chlorostrymon simaethis* (Drury)
**Identification:** $\frac{7}{8}$–1 in. (22–25 mm). HW has 1 very slender tail (broken off in specimen shown on Pl. 32) and a pointed lobe at tornus (anal angle). *Upperside:* Male dull purplish, lacks FW stigma. Female slightly lighter. *Underside:* Both sexes bright

green. Outer edge of HW brownish; *thecla (pm.) line a shining silvery white.*
**Early stages:** Not described. Multiple broods. **Food:** Developing seeds of balloon vine *(Cardiospermum halicacabum),* in soapberry family (Sapindaceae). **Adults:** Long flight season.
**Range:** San Diego Co., Calif. (occasional); Ariz. (casual); s. Tex.; Mexico. **Habitat:** Vine-covered scrub, fencerows, thorn-forest edges and trails.
**Subspecies:** (1) **Simaethis Hairstreak,** *C. s. simaethis* (Drury). TL: St. Kitts, Lesser Antilles. (2) **Sarita Hairstreak,** *C. s. sarita* (Skinner), Pl. 32. Southern U.S., Mexico. TL: New Braunfels, Tex.
**Remarks:** Prior to 1961, the Simaethis Hairstreak was placed in the genus *Strymon.*

## Alcestis Hairstreak: Genus *Phaeostrymon* Clench

**ALCESTIS HAIRSTREAK**                                         **Pl. 29**
*Phaeostrymon alcestis* (W. H. Edwards)
**Identification:** 1-1¼ in. (25–31 mm). In both sexes, HW has 1 short tail and 1 long, slender tail. *Upperside:* Deep brown; fringes white-tipped. Male stigma very small. *Underside:* Cell-end dashes white. *Thecla (pm.) line inwardly black,* outwardly white. Submarginal line black, white-edged inwardly. Orange submarginal band on HW encloses a black thecla spot; HW also has a blue-gray patch and a small black spot at tornus.
**Early stages:** Not described. One brood. **Food:** Soapberry, also called chinaberry *(Sapindus drummondi),* a native shrub. Erroneously reported as *Melia azedarach,* an introduced ornamental tree also known as chinaberry. **Adults:** April–July.
**Range:** Ariz. (uncommon), Tex., Kans., Okla. **Habitat:** Woodland, fencerows, roadsides; always close to food plant.
**Subspecies:** (1) **Alcestis Hairstreak,** *P. a. alcestis* (W. H. Edwards), Pl. 29. Kans., Okla., Tex. TL: Dallas, Tex. (2) **Oslar's Hairstreak,** *P. a. oslari* (Dyar). More olive-green. Ariz. to w. Tex. TL: Tucson, Ariz.
**Remarks:** This butterfly was placed in the genus *Strymon* prior to 1961.

## Coral Hairstreak: Genus *Harkenclenus* dos Passos

**CORAL HAIRSTREAK**                                         **Pl. 29**
*Harkenclenus titus* (Fabricius)
**Identification:** 1-1¼ in. (25–31 mm). FW pointed in male, rounded in female. In both sexes, HW elongate, with no tails. *Upperside:* Uniform dark brown. Male has *well-developed stigma on FW. Underside:* Light brown, usually with many small black spots. Spots near HW margin coral red.
**Early stages:** Larva green, marked with pink. One brood. **Food:**

Wild cherry, wild plum (*Prunus* species). **Adults:** Usually in July.
**Range:** S. Canada south to e. Calif., Tex.; in East to Ga. Widely
distributed; local and uncommon in the West. **Habitat:** Woodland
openings, mountainous brushland, streamsides.
**Subspecies:** There are four rather similar subspecies, including
the **Immaculate Hairstreak,** *H. t. immaculosus* (W. P. Com-
stock), Pl. 29. Dark spots greatly reduced or absent. TL: Provo,
Utah.
**Remarks:** The Coral Hairstreak *(H. titus)* was placed in the genus
*Strymon* before 1970.

## Hairstreaks: Genus *Satyrium* Scudder

Plain-colored species, rather similar in appearance. The male has a
FW stigma. HW tailed in some species, but not in others. These
hairstreaks overwinter as eggs on food plants, which are often
shrubs or trees.

**SOOTY GOSSAMER-WING**                                     **Pl. 29**
*Satyrium fuliginosum* (W. H. Edwards)
**Identification:** 1-1¼ in. (25-31 mm). Very plain and drab. HW
rounded, neither pointed nor tailed. Fringes pale-tipped.
*Upperside:* Dark gray, fading in old specimens. *Underside:* Ash
gray to dull grayish brown. *Thecla (pm.) line on FW a series of
dark spots with whitish rings,* but line is variable and sometimes
nearly absent.
**Early stages:** Undescribed. One brood. **Food:** Lupine *(Lupinus),*
in the pea family (Fabaceae). **Adults:** July-Aug.
**Range:** S. British Columbia east to Wyo., south to Calif., n. Colo.
Distribution spotty and discontinuous. **Habitat:** Fields, roadsides,
meadows, brushland.
**Subspecies:** (1) **Sooty Gossamer-wing,** *S. f. fuliginosum* (W. H.
Edwards), Pl. 29. British Columbia to Calif. TL: Norden, Eldorado
Co., Calif. (2) **Half Moon Hairstreak,** *S. f. semiluna* Klots. Spots
on underside of HW better developed. Alberta to nw. Colo. TL:
Half Moon Ranch, Jackson Hole, Wyo.

**BEHR'S HAIRSTREAK**                                      **Pl. 29**
*Satyrium behrii* (W. H. Edwards)
**Identification:** 1-1¼ in. (25-31 mm). HW rounded; no tails.
*Upperside:* Dark brown, with a *large yellowish brown patch* on
each wing. *Underside:* Brownish gray, with an *irregular thecla
line* and a *submarginal line* formed of *small dark spots, bordered
by white* on the outer edge. Thecla spot on HW black, with a
tawny cap.
**Early stages:** Larva green, with a white line down the back and
dark green and yellow markings on sides. One brood. **Food:** Antelope brush *(Purshia),* in the rose family. Reports of various le-

gumes (lupine, bird's-foot trefoil, rattleweed) for larva of this hairstreak are in error; these are the food plants of a subspecies of the Silvery Blue, *Glaucopsyche lygdamus incognitus* (*G. l. behrii* of authors) — see p. 202.
**Range:** British Columbia east to Wyo., south to s. Calif., Ariz., N.M., w. Tex. Local; absent or unreported from large areas within range. **Habitat:** Mixed brushland, juniper-pinyon woodland, juniper-sagebrush association.
**Subspecies:** (1) **Behr's Hairstreak,** *S. b. behrii* (W. H. Edwards), Pl. 29. Pacific Slope. TL: Mono Lake, Calif. (2) **Cross's Hairstreak,** *S. b. crossi* (Field). Spots on underside larger. Rocky Mts. TL: Nederland, Colo. (3) **Columbian Hairstreak,** *S. b. columbia* (McDunnough). Darker. Northern. TL: Fairview, B.C.
**Remarks:** Prior to 1960, Behr's Hairstreak *(Satyrium behrii)* was placed in the genus *Callipsyche.*

## ACADIAN HAIRSTREAK                                    Pl. 30
*Satyrium acadicum* (W. H. Edwards)
**Identification:** 1⅛-1¼ in. (28–31 mm). One long, slender tail on HW. *Upperside:* Dark olive-brown, with a *small orange spot* near base of tail. Another orange spot towards HW inner margin that is smaller and indistinct. *Underside:* Quite similar to that of California Hairstreak (below), but much darker.
**Early stages:** Larva green, with 2 yellowish lines along each side and oblique yellowish markings. One brood. **Food:** Willow (*Salix,* various species). **Adults:** Late June to July.
**Range:** In the West, British Columbia to Manitoba, south to e. Ore., ne. Calif., Colo. In the East to Nova Scotia, south to N.J. TL: London, Ontario. **Habitat:** Willow thickets, edges of moist woodland, streamsides.
**Subspecies:** Four subspecies are recognized, all visually similar. **Coolin Hairstreak,** *S. a. coolinensis,* Pl. 30. TL: Coolin, Idaho.
**Remarks:** This and the next 8 species were all placed in the genus *Strymon* prior to 1960.

## CALIFORNIA HAIRSTREAK                                 Pl. 30
*Satyrium californicum* (W. H. Edwards)
**Identification:** 1-1¼ in. (25–31 mm). HW has 1 long tail, 1 short tail. *Upperside:* Olive-brown, with a dull orange spot at HW tornus. A row of *orange-brown markings usually present along outer edge of FW. Underside:* Brownish gray. Thecla (pm.) line composed of small black spots; submarginal line of small black dashes on FW and HW. Thecla spot on HW, and usually some small adjacent spots are red.
**Similar species:** Acadian Hairstreak (above) is darker, with no orange or yellow markings on outer edge of FW.
**Early stages:** Larva gray, with light chevrons on sides. One brood. **Food:** Buck brush, wild lilacs (*Ceanothus,* various species),

mountain mahogany *(Cercocarpus)*. Larva first reared on oak, but found in many places where no oaks grow. **Adults:** May–July. **Range:** British Columbia east to Colo., south to s. Calif. TL: Capell Creek, Napa Co., Calif. **Habitat:** Open woodland, chaparral, brushland, forest edges.

## SYLVAN HAIRSTREAK                                          Pl. 30
*Satyrium sylvinum* (Boisduval)
**Identification:** 1-1⅜ in. (25–34 mm). HW has *1 long tail and 1 very short tail.* **Upperside:** Light grayish brown. HW has small orange patch at base of tails. Female usually has yellowish brown discal flush. **Underside:** Pale gray. Thecla (pm.) line of small black spots; thecla spot yellow to red, black-centered. Bluish patch at anal angle of HW. Some individuals have red submarginal spots on underside of HW.
**Similar species:** Dryope Hairstreak (below) has no tails.
**Early stages:** Larva pale green. One brood. **Food:** Willows *(Salix,* various species). **Adults:** May–July.
**Range:** Ore. east to Colo., south to Calif., Ariz., N.M.; Baja California. **Habitat:** Willow thickets, streamsides, open woodland, oases in arid places.
**Subspecies:** (1) **Sylvan Hairstreak,** *S. s. sylvinum* (Boisduval), Pl. 30. Calif. west of the Sierran Crest south to Baja California. TL: California. (2) **Desert Hairstreak,** *S. s. desertorum* (F. Grinnell). Large, paler. Eastern slope of the Sierra Nevada. TL: Oak Creek, Kern Co., Calif. (3) **Itys Hairstreak,** *S. s. itys* (W. H. Edwards). Underside browner; dark spots larger. Ariz., N.M. TL: Prescott, Ariz. (4) **Putnam's Hairstreak,** *S. s. putnami* (Hy. Edwards). Very light-colored; whitish on underside. Great Basin, w. Colo. TL: Mt. Nebo, Utah.

## DRYOPE HAIRSTREAK                                          Pl. 30
*Satyrium dryope* (W. H. Edwards)
**Identification:** 1-1¼ in. (25–31 mm). Resembles Sylvan Hairstreak (above), but *HW rounded,* with *no tails.* **Underside:** Nearly white, with only a few small dark spots. Thecla spot on HW small — may be yellow, orange, or red.
**Early stages:** Larva dull green. One brood. **Food:** Willow *(Salix);* wrongly reported as oak. **Adults:** Late May–June, July–Aug. east of the Sierra Nevada.
**Range:** Inner ranges of Calif., Alameda Co. to Los Angeles Co., at low elevations; also Mono Co., east of the Sierra Nevada. TL: Santa Clara Co., Calif. **Habitat:** Streamsides.
**Remarks:** Some lepidopterists consider this a subspecies of the Sylvan Hairstreak (above).

## BANDED HAIRSTREAK                                          Pl. 30
*Satyrium calanus* (Huebner)
**Identification:** 1-1¼ in. (25–31 mm). HW has 2 tails — 1 very

short, 1 longer. *Upperside:* Both sexes blackish brown. Male has a *large oval stigma* on FW. *Underside:* Dark brown. Thecla (pm.) line and submarginal line irregular — a series of oblong spots edged with white. Thecla spot red, edged above and below with black. Patch at tornus bluish.
**Similar species:** Striped Hairstreak (below).
**Early stages:** Larva either green or brown, with light and dark lengthwise lines. One brood. **Food:** Oak *(Quercus),* hickory *(Carya),* and butternut *(Juglans cinerea);* in Tex., little walnut *(Juglans microcarpa).* **Adults:** June–July.
**Range:** S. Canada to Gulf States. In the West, south to N.M. and cen. Tex. **Habitat:** Deciduous forest, mixed woodland.
**Subspecies:** (1) **Banded Hairstreak,** *S. c. calanus* (Huebner). Mostly in Fla.; not found in the West. TL: Not stated. (2) **Banded Hairstreak,** *S. c. falacer* (Godart), Pl. 30. Series of dark spots in thecla line on underside of FW and HW more connected. More eastern; s. Canada to Tex. TL: Philadelphia, Pa. (3) **Godart's Hairstreak,** *S. c. godarti* (Field). Rocky Mts. TL: Rosemont, Teller Co., Colo.

**STRIPED HAIRSTREAK**                                    **Pl. 30**
*Satyrium liparops* (Le Conte)
**Identification:** 1–1¼ in. (25–31 mm). *Upperside:* Dark brown; male has a *long oval stigma along FW veins.* Specimens from northern and western parts of range often have an orange-brown patch in discal area (see Subspecies, below). *Underside:* Violet-brown, crossed by thin white lines. Thecla spot red, edged with black above and below. Spot at anal angle bluish, edged with red.
**Similar species:** Banded Hairstreak (above).
**Early stages:** Larva green, with oblique yellow-green lines along sides. One brood. **Food:** Many plants in the East. Hawthorn *(Crataegus)* and box elder *(Acer negundo)* in Colo. Larva eats buds and fruit as well as leaves. **Adults:** July in the West.
**Range:** S. Canada south in Rocky Mts. to Colo., east to New England, south to Fla. Widely distributed, but local. Usually uncommon. **Habitat:** Thickets, fields.
**Subspecies:** (1) **Striped Hairstreak,** *S. l. liparops* (Le Conte). Southeastern. TL: Screven Co., Ga. (2) **Fletcher's Hairstreak,** *S. l. fletcheri* (Michener & dos Passos). Large orange-brown patch in discal area of FW. Northern. TL: Manitoba. (3) **Striped Hairstreak,** *S. l. aliparops* (Michener & dos Passos), Pl. 30. Rocky Mts. TL: Glenwood Springs, Colo.

**GOLD-HUNTER'S HAIRSTREAK**                              **Pl. 29**
*Satyrium auretorum* (Boisduval)
**Identification:** 1–1¼ in. (25–31 mm). FW pointed in male. HW has 1 short tail, often broken off. *Upperside:* Male sepia brown. Female usually has yellowish brown flush in discal area. *Underside:* Thecla (pm.) line faint on both FW and HW; crescents near

HW outer margin dark. *Thecla spot on HW dull orange, with a black center;* blue-gray patch at tornus.
**Similar species:** Gray Hairstreak (below).
**Early stages:** Larva dull orange to green, covered with white dots that are tufted with short rusty hairs. Pupa reddish brown, mottled with black. One brood. **Food:** Oaks (*Quercus,* several species).
**Adults:** Late May–July.
**Range:** Calif., from Mendocino and Shasta Cos. to San Diego Co. west of Sierran Crest and deserts; also Baja California. Formerly considered rare; common but very local. **Habitat:** Oak-covered hills, oak chaparral, lone oak trees in fields.
**Subspecies:** (1) **Gold-hunter's Hairstreak,** *S. a. auretorum* (Boisduval), Pl. 29. Northern to s.-cen. Calif. TL: California. (2) **Nut-brown Hairstreak,** *S. a. spadix* (Hy. Edwards). Lighter; markings more obscure. S. Calif. TL: Tehachapi, Calif.

## GRAY HAIRSTREAK                                    Pl. 29
*Satyrium tetra* (W. H. Edwards)
**Identification:** 1–1¼ in. (25–31 mm). *Fringes white-tipped.* FW pointed in male. HW tail short, sometimes missing. *Upperside:* Brownish gray. *Underside:* Olive-gray, with ashy powdering. *Thecla (pm.) line whitish;* often faint, occasionally absent. Spot at anal angle of HW bluish gray.
**Similar species:** Gold-hunter's Hairstreak (above).
**Early stages:** Larva silvery green; has rows of golden hairs. One brood. **Food:** Mountain mahogany *(Cercocarpus).* **Adults:** June–July.
**Range:** S. Ore., Calif., west of deserts to San Diego Co.; w. Nev.; Baja California. TL: Arroyo Bayo, Santa Clara Co., Calif. **Habitat:** Chaparral, mixed woodland.
**Remarks:** Formerly called *S. adenostomatis.*

## HEDGEROW HAIRSTREAK                              Pl. 30
*Satyrium saepium* (Boisduval)
**Identification:** 1–1¼ in. (25–31 mm). A common, widespread hairstreak. *Upperside: Bright coppery brown;* distinctive. FW stigma in male *usually black* (sometimes faint, as in specimen shown on Pl. 30). *Underside:* Brown. Thecla (pm.) and submarginal lines present on FW and HW, but inconspicuous. Bluish patch at HW tornus.
**Early stages:** Larva green, with diagonal yellowish chevrons on sides. Pupa brown, speckled with black. One brood. **Food:** Buckbrush *(Ceanothus cuneatus)* and other species of *Ceanothus.* **Adults:** April–Aug., depending on elevation and latitude.
**Range:** British Columbia east to Mont., south to s. Calif. and Colo.; Baja California. TL: Tuolumne Co., Calif. **Habitat:** Diverse: chaparral, brushy woodland, open forest.
**Subspecies:** There are six similar-looking subspecies. The nominate subspecies *saepium* is shown on Pl. 30.

## Little Hairstreaks: Genus *Ministrymon* Clench

**LEDA HAIRSTREAK**                                    **Pl. 30**
*Ministrymon leda* (W. H. Edwards)
**Identification:** $\frac{3}{4}$–$\frac{7}{8}$ in. (19–22 mm). Very small. Quite tame.
Male has small stigma on FW. This species has two well-marked
forms (see Pl. 30), long considered separate species. Breeding ex-
periments have shown that the Ines Hairstreak is actually a fall
form of the Leda Hairstreak. *Upperside:* In form "leda," FW dark
brown, with a *pale blue base; most of HW pale blue.* Blue areas
more extensive in form "ines." *Underside:* Thecla (pm.) *line* irregular; *red* in form "leda," *bordered by white;* thecla spot also red,
with a black center. In form "ines," *thecla line blackish,* with little
or no red. Discal area of HW often darker than rest of wing surface.
Thecla and tornal spots on HW small and dark, with little or no
red.
**Early stages:** Larva green, with short reddish brown hairs and
yellowish chevrons on back. Multiple broods. **Food:** Mesquite
*(Prosopis glandulosa* var. *torreyana).* **Adults:** Form "leda"
May–Aug.; form "ines" Oct.–Nov.
**Range:** S. Calif., s. Ariz.; Baja California, Mexico. TL: Prescott,
Ariz. **Habitat:** Thorn scrub, mixed woodland.
**Remarks:** Placed in the genus *Strymon* before 1961.

## Hairstreaks: Genus *Tmolus* Huebner

HW tailed in both sexes. Male has large stigma on FW, filling outer
half of cell (stigma same color as surrounding wing).

**ECHION HAIRSTREAK** *Tmolus echion* (Linnaeus)    **Pl. 30**
**Identification:** 1–1$\frac{1}{4}$ in. (25–31 mm). *Upperside:* Male *iridescent
blue.* Female dull bluish gray, with pale rays between HW veins.
*Underside:* White to silver-gray; veins darker. *HW spots that
form thecla line oblong, coppery.* HW thecla spot orange, with a
black center.
**Early stages:** Not described. Multiple broods. **Food:** Lantana
*(Lantana camara),* in verbena family. **Adults:** Long flight season.
**Range:** Neotropical. In 1902, this butterfly was intentionally in-
troduced into Hawaii to control the spread of *Lantana camara,* a
non-native plant pest. Butterfly now established on all major is-
lands; recently becoming scarce in Hawaii. TL: In America.
**Subspecies: Larger Lantana Butterfly,** *T. e. echiolus* (Draudt),
Pl. 30. This is the subspecies now found in Hawaii. Has been taken
in extreme southern Tex. TL: Mexico.
**Remarks:** Previously placed in the genus *Strymon.*

**AZIA HAIRSTREAK** *Tmolus azia* (Hewitson)        **Pl. 30**
**Identification:** Very small; $\frac{5}{8}$–$\frac{13}{16}$ in. (16–20 mm). *Upperside:*

Male dull grayish brown; *FW stigma large, dark.* Female lighter, especially on HW. *Underside:* Pale gray. *Thecla (pm.) line on both FW and HW red, with a white border;* thecla spot on HW coppery, with a black center.
**Early stages:** Unknown. Multiple broods. **Adults:** Long flight season.
**Range:** Ariz. (rare), s. Tex.; casual in Kans., Colo.; south to S. America. TL: Mexico.
**Remarks:** An obscure species; may be more common than the few widely scattered records in the U.S. indicate. Formerly placed in the genus *Strymon.*

## Green Hairstreaks: Genus *Callophrys* Billberg

Holarctic; most species occur in the western U.S. All species look much alike. No tails; HW margin slightly scalloped; lobe at tornus (anal angle) turned down. Underside green. Eggs laid on flower heads of food plant.

### GREEN-WINGED HAIRSTEAK                    Pl. 31
*Callophrys affinis* (W. H. Edwards)
**Identification:** 1-1⅛ in. (25-28 mm). Terminal line dark; fringes white, not checkered. *Upperside:* Bright reddish brown (subspecies *affinis*) or gray with tawny shadings (subspecies *washingtonia*). *Underside:* Bright green. Thecla line *absent* or merely indicated by *3-4 very small spots.* Lower ⅓ of FW brownish gray.
**Early stages:** Larva either green or dark red, with a light line along upper side. One brood. **Food:** Sulfur flower *(Eriogonum umbellatum).* **Adults:** June.
**Range:** S. British Columbia, Wash., Utah, Wyo., Colo. **Habitat:** Meadows, scattered brushland.
**Subspecies:** (1) **Green-winged Hairstreak,** *C. a. affinis* (W. H. Edwards), Pl. 31. Rocky Mts. TL: Ft. Bridger, Wyo. (2) **Washington Hairstreak,** *C. a. washingtonia* Clench. Darker, much grayer. Wash.; British Columbia. TL: Alta Lake, Wash.

### SHERIDAN'S HAIRSTREAK                     Pl. 31
*Callophrys sheridanii* (W. H. Edwards)
**Identification:** ⅞-1⅛ in. (22-28 mm). Fringes white. *Upperside:* Dark grayish brown; costa and stigma darker. *Underside: Dark green;* no tawny markings. Lower ⅓ of FW gray. *Thecla (pm.) line white, straight, complete.*
**Early stages:** Larva green to pink. One brood. **Food:** Wild buckwheats *(Eriogonum,* various species). **Adults:** April–early May.
**Range:** S. British Columbia, e. Wash., e. Ore., s. Alberta south in Rocky Mts. to N.M. **Habitat:** Sagebrush scrub.

**Subspecies:** (1) **Sheridan's Hairstreak,** *C. s. sheridanii* (W. H. Edwards), Pl. 31. Wyo. south to Ariz., N.M. TL: W. of Sheridan, Wyo. (2) *C. s. neoperplexa* Barnes & Benjamin. Thecla line on underside reduced. Mont. to Utah. TL: Eureka, Utah. (3) **Newcomer's Hairstreak,** *C. s. newcomeri* Clench. Thecla line on underside narrow; line may be absent on FW. British Columbia, Wash., e. Ore. TL: Mill Creek, Yakima Co., Wash.

## BRAMBLE HAIRSTREAK                                   Pl. 31
*Callophrys dumetorum* (Boisduval)

**Identification:** 1-1¼ in. (25-31 mm). **Upperside:** Fringes pale-tipped, not pure white. Male brownish gray. Female tawny, at least on discs of both FW and HW. **Underside:** FW green at base, costa and apex; rest of FW gray or brown. HW *grass green.* Thecla (pm.) line *white, black inwardly,* either complete or reduced to a few spots. Fringes and terminal line with *brown scales* mixed in. **Early stages:** Larva dark green with 2 light lines along upper sides. One brood. **Food:** Deerweed *(Lotus scoparius),* naked eriogonum *(Eriogonum nudum),* and others. **Adults:** March–May. **Range:** Wash. and w. Idaho south to s. Calif., w. Nev.; Baja California. TL: Calif. **Habitat:** Chaparral, brushland, burns, cutover land.

**Subspecies:** (1) **Bramble Hairstreak,** *C. d. dumetorum* (Boisduval), Pl. 31. Ore. south to s.-cen. Calif. (2) **Perplexing Hairstreak,** *C. d. perplexa* Barnes & Benjamin. Underside of HW often entirely unmarked. S. Calif., Baja California. (3) **Oregon Hairstreak,** *C. d. oregonensis* Gorelick. Smaller, grayer. Wash., Idaho, n. Ore. TL: Kusshi Creek, Yakima Co., Wash.

## APAMA HAIRSTREAK                                     Pl. 31
*Callophrys apama* (W. H. Edwards)

**Identification:** 1-1¼ in. (25-31 mm). **Upperside:** Fringes pale-tipped. Male dark grayish brown. Female coppery brown, border dusky. **Underside:** FW coppery brown; base, costa, and apex green. HW green, with coppery scales mixed in. Thecla (pm.) line *inwardly brown, outwardly white;* very irregular. Thecla line reduced or even absent in northern populations.

**Early stages:** Not recorded. One brood. **Food:** Has laid eggs on deer brier *(Ceanothus fendleri);* however, the larval food in Mexico is known to be wild buckwheat *(Eriogonum).* **Adults:** March to July or Aug., depending on locality.

**Range:** Wyo., Colo., s. Utah, Ariz., N.M.; also n. Mexico. **Habitat:** Open coniferous forest.

**Subspecies:** (1) **Apama Hairstreak,** *C. a. apama* (W. H. Edwards), Pl. 31. Thecla line irregular, well developed. Southern and western part of range. TL: Ft. Grant, Ariz. (2) *C. a. homoperplexa* Barnes & Benjamin. Thecla line often absent. E. Wyo. to e. N.M. TL: Golden, Colo.

**COMSTOCK'S HAIRSTREAK**                                  **Pl. 31**
*Callophrys comstocki* Henne
**Identification:** $\frac{7}{8}$-1 in. (22–25 mm). Usually smaller than other green hairstreaks (*Callophrys species*). *Fringes white. Upperside:* Gray; terminal line black. *Underside:* Apple green, with slightly darker veins. Lower half of FW gray. Thecla (pm.) line narrow, irregular, usually complete; it is *white, edged inwardly with black.* **Early stages:** Not described. 1–3 broods, depending on rainfall. **Food:** Probably sulfur flower *(Eriogonum umbellatum).* **Adults:** March, June–July, Aug.–Sept.
**Range:** Desert ranges of s. Calif. TL: Providence Mts. **Habitat:** Brush-covered desert mountains.

**LEMBERT'S HAIRSTREAK**                                   **Pl. 32**
*Callophrys lemberti* Tilden
**Identification:** $\frac{7}{8}$-1$\frac{1}{4}$ in. (22–31 mm). Fringes white. *Upperside:* Male light brownish gray. Female slightly more buff-colored. *Underside: Yellowish green. Very thinly scaled* — the gray or brown ground color often shows through. Thecla (pm.) line narrow, sometimes incomplete; composed of separate, short white lines, bordered inwardly by dark brown.
**Early stages:** Not described. One brood. **Food:** Eggs laid on flowers of frosty eriogonum *(E. incanum).* **Adults:** Late June–Aug.
**Range:** Cen. Ore. south to w. Nev., Sierra Nevada of Calif. TL: W. above Tioga Pass, Yosemite Natl. Park, Calif. **Habitat:** Alpine fell-fields, rocky slopes, forest openings.

**GREEN HAIRSTREAK**                                       **Pl. 32**
*Callophrys viridis* (W. H. Edwards)
**Identification:** 1–1$\frac{1}{4}$ in. (25–31 mm). *Antennae white.* FW pointed; outer margin straight or slightly concave. *Fringes white. Upperside:* Male dark gray (may be brownish in old, faded specimens). Female usually gray, less often somewhat buffy. *Underside:* Vivid *bluish green* in fresh specimens; lower edge of FW gray. Thecla (pm.) line narrow, white, occasionally incomplete.
**Early stages:** Larva green. One brood. **Food:** Coast eriogonum *(Eriogonum latifolium).* **Adults:** March–May.
**Range:** Narrowly coastal: s. Ore. south to Monterey Co., Calif. TL: San Francisco. **Habitat:** Bare coastal hills, terraces, sea cliffs.

### Juniper Hairstreaks: Genus *Mitoura* Scudder

About a dozen species, all found in the U.S. All are tailed; most are green on the underside. Males have a stigma. Most species feed on junipers or cedars.

**THICKET HAIRSTREAK**                                     **Pl. 31**
*Mitoura spinetorum* (Hewitson)
**Identification:** 1–1$\frac{1}{4}$ in. (25–31 mm). Fringes white, not check-

ered. *Upperside:* Male *steel blue,* female slightly duller. *Underside:* Sepia brown. Thecla (pm.) line white, *forming a W on HW.* Spots near HW margin dark; marginal area bluish gray. Thecla spot red-brown with a black center.

**Similar species:** In Johnson's Hairstreak (below), upperside brown.

**Early stages:** Larva yellowish olive, with light bars along upper sides. One brood; emergence irregular. **Food:** Dwarf mistletoe (*Arceuthobium,* various species), which grows on pine, fir, and juniper trees. **Adults:** May–Aug. They often sit on warm paved roads, at some distance from food plants.

**Range:** British Columbia east to Rocky Mts., south to s. Calif., Ariz., N.M.; Baja California, Mexico. Very local and uncommon. TL: Calif. **Habitat:** Coniferous forest, mixed woodland, pinyon-juniper woodland, in both moist and dry mountain ranges.

### JOHNSON'S HAIRSTREAK                                    Pl. 31
*Mitoura johnsoni* (Skinner)
**Identification:** $1\frac{1}{4}$-$1\frac{3}{8}$ in. (31–34 mm). Usually larger than related species. *Upperside:* Male *dull rusty brown,* female more reddish. Veins, stigma, and narrow border darker. *Underside:* Dull grayish brown; wing bases darker. *Thecla (pm.) line white, edged with black inwardly.*

**Similar species:** Thicket Hairstreak (above).

**Early stages:** Larva much like that of Thicket Hairstreak. One brood. **Food:** Pine dwarf mistletoe *(Arceuthobium campylopodum),* growing on conifers. **Adults:** Late May to July, depending on locality. Attracted to flowers.

**Range:** Mountains of Pacific Slope, British Columbia, Wash., Ore. to cen. Calif. Very local; scarce to rare. TL: British Columbia. **Habitat:** Openings and clearings in coniferous forest; may visit nearby fields and meadows.

### BARRY'S HAIRSTREAK                                      Pl. 36
*Mitoura barryi* K. Johnson
**Identification:** $\frac{7}{8}$-$1\frac{1}{8}$ in. (22–28 mm). *Upperside:* Male grayish brown, FW costa and HW thecla spot rusty. Stigma gray, inconspicuous. Female rusty; FW costa and all wing borders darker. *Underside:* Markings much like those of Siva Hairstreak (p. 170), but *brownish,* not green.

**Similar species:** (1) Rosner's Hairstreak (p. 169). (2) Byrne's Hairstreak (p. 169).

**Early stages:** Unknown. One brood. **Food:** Probably western juniper *(Juniperus occidentalis),* since adults are closely associated with it. **Adults:** Early June.

**Range:** S. Canada south to ne. Calif. **Habitat:** Juniper woodland.

**Subspecies:** (1) **Barry's Hairstreak,** *M. b. barryi* K. Johnson, Pl. 36. N.-cen. and e. Ore. TL: Union Co., Ore. (2) **Acuminate Hairstreak,** *M. b. acuminata* K. Johnson. Darker, browner. Vancouver I. south to Jackson Co., Ore. TL: Butte Falls, Jackson Co., Ore.

**Remarks:** Very little is known about Barry's Hairstreak and the next two species, Rosner's Hairstreak and Byrne's Hairstreak. All were first described in 1976, and are distinguished mainly by differences in male genitalia.

### ROSNER'S HAIRSTREAK                                      not shown
*Mitoura rosneri* K. Johnson

**Identification:** 1-1⅛ in. (25-28 mm). **Upperside:** Very similar to Barry's Hairstreak (above). **Underside:** Area at base of HW darker than area beyond thecla line.

**Early stages:** Unknown. One brood. **Food:** Giant cedar *(Thuja plicata)*. **Adults:** May–July.

**Range:** N. Wash., north in Canada to 52° latitude. **Habitat:** Openings in coniferous forest.

**Subspecies:** (1) **Rosner's Hairstreak,** *M. r. rosneri* K. Johnson. Underside darker, more russet. Eastern part of range. TL: 2 mi. (3.2 km) south of Kaslo, British Columbia. (2) **Pleated Hairstreak,** *M. r. plicataria* K. Johnson. Underside more brownish. Puget Sound, north into Canada. TL: Cameron L., S. Vancouver I.

### BYRNE'S HAIRSTREAK                                       not shown
*Mitoura byrnei* K. Johnson

**Identification:** 1 in. (25 mm). **Upperside:** Similar to Barry's Hairstreak (p. 168), but ground color darker. **Underside:** Ground color darker than Barry's and Rosner's Hairstreaks (above).

**Early stages:** Unknown. One brood. **Food:** Probably giant cedar *(Thuja plicata)*. **Adults:** Late April to early June.

**Range:** So far, known only from a few specimens taken in Watah, Benewah, and Wallace Cos., Idaho. TL: 5.6 mi. s. Emida, Benewah Co., Idaho. **Habitat:** Not stated.

### NELSON'S HAIRSTREAK                                        Pl. 31
*Mitoura nelsoni* (Boisduval)

**Identification:** 1-1⅛ in. (25-28 mm). **Upperside:** Male dark brown; *rusty shades* in outer lower corners of wings. Female mostly tawny, margins darker. **Underside:** *Lilac brown.* Thecla (pm.) line irregular, dark, usually outlined in white; line may be reduced or even almost absent. Spots near margin small, dark; area at margin bluish gray. Thecla spot indistinct.

**Similar species:** Muir's Hairstreak (p. 170).

**Early stages:** Larva green, with yellow crescents on sides. One brood. **Food:** Incense cedar *(Calocedrus decurrens)*. **Adults:** May–July, depending on locality.

**Range:** S. British Columbia south to s. Calif., east to Idaho and Nev. The exact extent of the range is not clear, because some populations have not been studied well enough to determine whether they belong to a different species. TL: California. **Habitat:** Openings and clearings in coniferous forest and woodland.

## MUIR'S HAIRSTREAK                                    Pl. 36
*Mitoura muiri* (Hy. Edwards)
**Identification:** $7/8$-1 in. (22-25 mm). *Upperside:* Very similar to that of Nelson's Hairstreak (p. 169). *Underside:* Dark purplish brown. Thecla (pm.) line *very irregular; inwardly dark, outwardly white.* 3-4 small black spots near HW margin; also 3-4 reddish spots separated by blue-gray.
**Early stages:** Not described. One brood. **Food:** Cypress *(Cupressus)*, especially sargent cypress *(C. sargentii).* **Adults:** May. They visit flowers of wild lilac *(Ceanothus).*
**Range:** Inner Coast Ranges of Calif. from Mt. Diablo, Contra Costa Co., to Mendocino Co. TL: Mendocino Co., Calif. **Habitat:** Hilly, usually rocky places near food plant.

## SIVA HAIRSTREAK *Mitoura siva* (W. H. Edwards)    Pl. 31
**Identification:** 1-1$1/4$ in. (25-31 mm). *Upperside:* Costa and wing borders dark brown. Much of wing surface dull reddish brown in male. In female, most of wings, except borders, tawny. *Underside:* FW largely rusty. HW dull to bright green. Thecla line *irregular, white, shaded with brown inwardly.* Submarginal spots dark when present; submarginal area bluish gray. Thecla spot small, dull red, with a black center. Submarginal markings reduced in some specimens.
**Similar species:** (1) Skinner's Hairstreak (below). (2) Olive Hairstreak (p. 171).
**Early stages:** Larva green, with darker green raised areas and lemon-yellow bars along sides. Two broods. **Food:** California juniper *(Juniperus californica),* Utah juniper *(J. osteosperma),* perhaps others. **Adults:** March–May and June–Aug.
**Range:** Mont. to N.D., Neb., south to s. Calif., Ariz., N.M.; Baja California, Mexico. **Habitat:** Juniper woodland, pinyon-juniper woodland.
**Subspecies:** (1) **Siva Hairstreak,** *M. s. siva* (W. H. Edwards), Pl. 31. Rocky Mts. TL: Ft. Wingate, N.M. (2) **Juniper Hairstreak,** *M. s. juniperaria* J. A. Comstock. Smaller, underside lighter. S. Calif. TL: Mint Canyon, Los Angeles Co., Calif. (3) **Mansfield's Hairstreak,** *M. s. mansfieldi* Tilden. Underside dark green. TL: Seven miles west of Simmler, San Luis Obispo Co., Calif. (4) **Clench's Hairstreak,** *M. s. chalcosiva* Clench. Underside greenish brown. Desert ranges of the Great Basin. TL: Stansbury Mts., Tooele Co., Utah.

## SKINNER'S HAIRSTREAK *Mitoura loki* (Skinner)    Pl. 31
**Identification:** $7/8$-1 in. (22-25 mm). Male stigma dark.

*Upperside:* Male grayish brown, with a tawny flush on outer part of both FW and HW. Female tawny, with a dark brownish border. *Underside:* Grayish green. Median band on HW *dark reddish brown, irregular,* bordered outwardly by the *irregular white thecla (pm.) line.* Submarginal spots numerous and dark; band at margin pale greenish.
**Similar species:** Siva Hairstreak (above).
**Early stages:** Larva similar to that of Siva Hairstreak. Two broods. **Food:** California juniper *(Juniperus californica).* **Adults:** March–April, June–July.
**Range:** S. Calif. west of deserts; Riverside Co., San Diego Co.; Baja California. Local, usually uncommon; range quite restricted. TL: Mt. Springs, San Diego Co., Calif. **Habitat:** Juniper woodland.

### THORNE'S HAIRSTREAK                                    Pl. 36
*Mitoura thornei* J. W. Brown
**Identification:** 1–1⅛ in. (25–29 mm). General appearance very similar to Skinner's Hairstreak (above). *Underside: Brown median band on HW indented near wing base* (this indentation much shallower in Skinner's Hairstreak). Outer edge of HW widely shaded with shiny greenish gray.
**Early stages:** Undescribed. **Food:** Tecate cypress *(Cupressus forbesii).* **Adults:** Two broods.
**Range:** So far, only the TL: Little Cedar Canyon, Otah Mt., San Isidro Mts., San Diego Co., Calif. **Habitat:** Where tecate cypress grows.
**Remarks:** First described in 1983.

### OLIVE HAIRSTREAK *Mitoura gryneus* (Huebner)    Pl. 31
**Identification:** 1–1⅛ in. (25–28 mm). *Upperside:* Male dark brown, with a yellowish olive suffusion; FW stigma lighter. Female blackish brown. *Underside:* FW green; disc tawny. HW green. Thecla (pm.) line *white, very irregular,* brown-edged inwardly. *Postbasal spots white.* Area near margin blue-gray; *line at margin white.* Thecla spot small, dull red, black-centered.
**Similar species:** Siva Hairstreak (p. 170) has no postbasal spots.
**Early stages:** Larva dark green, with very light green, slanting bars along sides. In Tex., 1–3 overlapping broods. **Food:** Red cedar *(Juniperus virginiana),* western red cedar *(J. scopulorum).* **Adults:** March–Nov.
**Range:** Neb. east to Ontario and New England, south to Tex. and Fla. **Habitat:** Juniper woodland (called "cedar breaks" in the South).
**Subspecies:** (1) **Olive Hairstreak,** *M. g. gryneus* (Huebner). Neb., Kans., and eastward. TL: Virginia. (2) **Castalis Hairstreak,** *M. g. castalis* (W. H. Edwards), Pl. 31. Duller; female very dark. Tex. west to Davis Mts. TL: Waco, Tex.

## Genus *Xamia* Clench

This species, the only one in its genus, resembles species of the previous genus, *Mitoura*. The Xami Hairstreak was formerly placed in *Mitoura*.

**XAMI HAIRSTREAK** *Xamia xami* (Reakirt)              **Pl. 31**
**Identification:** 1-1⅛ in. (25–28 mm). HW has 2 tails — 1 short, 1 long. *Upperside:* Male buffy olive; FW stigma dark. Female reddish brown. Both sexes have wide, dusky borders. *Underside:* Golden green. Thecla (pm.) line shiny white, extending out as teeth along veins Cu₁ and Cu₂. Thecla spot small, dark.
**Similar species:** In Siva Hairstreak (p. 170) thecla line is bordered by brown. The two species have different habitats, and their ranges seldom overlap.
**Early stages:** Larva yellow green, with rose-colored markings. Multiple broods. **Food:** Live-for-ever *(Echeveria gibbiflora),* stonecrop *(Sedum allanoides)*. **Adults:** April–Dec.
**Range:** Ariz. (scarce) to s. Tex.; Mexico. A single record from Calif. TL: Mexico. **Habitat:** In Tex., sandy hills, banks, and levees.

## Genus *Sandia* Clench & Ehrlich

HW rounded; no tails, but a lobe at anal angle. Underside green.

**McFARLAND'S HAIRSTREAK**              **Pl. 31**
*Sandia mcfarlandi* Ehrlich & Clench
**Identification:**  1⅛-1¼ in.  (28–31 mm). *Upperside: Fringes white.* Male buffy brown. Female rusty brown, with a *narrow black border. Underside:* Golden green. *Thecla (pm.) line white, inwardly black-bordered.* Area near margin mint green. Subterminal line white, terminal line black.
**Early stages:** Larva variable, pink to maroon. Two broods. **Food:** Flowers and young seedpods of beargrass *(Nolina microcarpa),* in the agave family. **Adults:** May–June.
**Range:** N.M., w. Tex. (Chisos Mts., Davis Mts.). Very local. TL: Sandia Mts., N.M. **Habitat:** Yucca-agave desert.
**Remarks:** Not discovered until 1960.

## Elfins: Genus *Incisalia* Scudder

Brown. HW has lobe at tornus. Edges of HW scalloped. Male has FW stigma. One brood. Elfins overwinter as pupae, and adults emerge early in the year.

**HOARY ELFIN** *Incisalia polia* Cook & Watson              **Pl. 30**
**Identification:** 1-1⅛ in. (25–28 mm). HW evenly scalloped; lobe at tornus small. Fringes dark at vein ends. *Upperside:* Smooth

grayish brown. *Underside:* Outer margin of FW narrowly *frosty gray;* thecla (pm.) line narrow; black inwardly, white outwardly. HW dark at base, *outer half usually frosty gray.*

**Similar species:** In Henry's Elfin (below), male lacks stigma. No frosty gray edge on underside.

**Early stages:** Larva dull green. One brood. **Food:** Bearberry *(Arctostaphylos uva-ursi),* in the heath family. **Adults:** April–May.

**Range:** E. Alaska, Mackenzie R. drainage south to Wash., in Rocky Mts. to N.M. In East, Nova Scotia to N.J. **Habitat:** Dry rocky or barren open areas, undergrowth of open woodland; closely associated with food plant.

**Subspecies:** (1) **Hoary Elfin,** *I. p. polia* Cook & Watson. Northern and eastern. TL: Lakewood, N.J. (2) **Obscure Elfin,** *I. p. obscura* Ferris & Fisher, Pl. 30. Grayer. Rocky Mts. TL: Lookout Mt., Jefferson Co., Colo.

**HENRY'S ELFIN**                                                    **Pl. 31**
*Incisalia henrici* (Grote & Robinson)
**Identification:** 1–1⅛ in. (25–28 mm). Fringes light-checkered. HW scallops long, forming short tails; lobe at tornus long. Male has no FW stigma. *Upperside:* Dark brown. Outer part of FW and area near HW tornus often have a *dull orange-brown flush. Underside:* HW dark at base, outer half lighter. Pm. spots and outer margin dark brown.

**Similar species:** Hoary Elfin (above).

**Early stages:** Larva green or reddish brown, with lighter markings. **Food:** Blueberry *(Vaccinium),* wild plum *(Prunus),* redbud *(Cercis).* **Adults:** March to early May.

**Range:** Ill. to Nova Scotia, south to Tex. and Fla. Widely distributed but local. **Habitat:** Mixed and deciduous woodland.

**Subspecies:** (1) *I. h. henrici* (Grote & Robinson), Pl. 31. Eastern. TL: Philadelphia. (2) *I. h. solata* Cook & Watson. Larva feeds on Texas persimmon *(Diospyros texana).* Tex. west to Guadeloupe Natl. Park. TL: Blanco Co., Tex. There are 2 other subspecies that do not occur in our area.

**STRECKER'S ELFIN** *Incisalia fotis* (Strecker)          **Pl. 31**
**Identification:** ¾–1⅛ in. (19–28 mm). HW scallops small. Fringes pale, but dark at vein tips. *Upperside:* Male gray, female slightly browner. *Underside:* Brownish gray. Base of HW darker; *outer half pale gray to ashy.*

**Early stages:** Not described. One brood. **Food:** Cliff rose *(Cowania mexicana* var. *stansburiana).* **Adults:** March–May.

**Range:** Se. Calif., w. Ariz., e. Nev., Utah. TL: Arizona. **Habitat:** Rocky hills and canyons, often in the desert.

**MOSS'S ELFIN** *Incisalia mossii* (Hy. Edwards)          **Pl. 31**
**Identification:** ⅞–1⅛ in. (22–28 mm). HW scallops and tornal

lobe well developed. Fringes white, dark at vein tips. *Upperside:* Male grayish brown with a small buffy patch at HW tornus. Female light brown to buffy, with dark borders. *Underside:* Purplish brown to coppery brown. Inner half of HW much darker — dark color projects out along veins $M_3$ to $Cu_2$; *outer half of HW much lighter.* A white or pale line usually separates HW base and outer band.

**Early stages:** Larva either yellowish or reddish; it feeds in the open on flowers of food plant. One brood. **Food:** Stonecrop (*Sedum,* various species). **Adults:** March–May, depending on locality. Inconspicuous. "Sits tight"; easily overlooked.

**Range:** Vancouver I. south to s.-cen. Calif., east to Colo. Distribution spotty — the populations are isolated from one another. **Habitat:** Rocky outcrops and cliffs where stonecrop grows.

**Subspecies:** (1) **Moss's Elfin,** *I. m. mossii* (Hy. Edwards). Underside mahogany red; dark area at base edged with white. TL: Esquimalt, Vancouver I. (2) **Schryver's Elfin,** *I. m. schryveri* Cross. White line on underside of HW distinct; spots near margin and marginal area dark. TL: Chimney Gulch, Colo. (3) **San Bruno Elfin,** *I. m. bayensis* (R. M. Brown). On underside, outer half of wings reddish brown. Local; endangered. TL: San Bruno Mts., San Mateo Co., Calif. (4) **Doudoroff's Elfin,** *I. m. doudoroffi* dos Passos, Pl. 31. Coastal, quite local. TL: Big Sur, Monterey Co., Calif. (5) **Wind's Elfin,** *I. m. windi* Clench. Underside light reddish brown; markings reduced. S. Cascades south to western slope of the Sierra Nevada. TL: Placer Co., Calif.

**BROWN ELFIN** *Incisalia augusta* (W. Kirby)     **Pl. 31**
**Identification:** $7/8$–$1\frac{1}{8}$ in. (22–28 mm). Very plain and inconspicuous. Scallops at edge of HW *nearly absent,* but tornal lobe large. *Upperside:* Male grayish brown, female reddish brown. *Underside:* Reddish brown to dull brown; wing bases and pm. spots darker.

**Early stages:** Larva brown or green, with lighter bars. One brood. **Food:** Many plants: blueberry *(Vaccinium),* buck brush, snow brush, wild lilac *(Ceanothus),* madrone *(Arbutus),* manzanita *(Arctostaphylos),* salal *(Gaultheria),* dodder *(Cuscuta),* and others. Larvae often eat the fruit of these plants. **Adults:** Feb.–April in south, May–June in north.

**Range:** Much of Canada and the U.S. In the West, Alaska to Saskatchewan, south to Calif., Ariz., N.M. **Habitat:** Woodland, openings, brushland, chaparral.

**Subspecies:** (1) **Brown Elfin,** *I. a. augusta* (W. Kirby). Small and dark. Northern. TL: Cumberland House, Saskatchewan. (2) **Western Brown Elfin,** *I. a. iroides* (Boisduval), Pl. 31. Much of western N. America. TL: California. (3) **Annette's Elfin,** *I. a. annettae* dos Passos. Lighter, more rusty. Markings on underside reduced. Sw. U.S. TL: New Mexico. There are 2 other eastern and southern subspecies.

**EASTERN BANDED ELFIN**                              **Pl. 31**
*Incisalia niphon* (Huebner)
**Identification:** 1-1⅛ in. (25–28 mm). HW scalloped; fringes checkered. ***Upperside:*** Male dark brown, with a reddish brown tornal spot. Female extensively buffy or tawny, with dark border. ***Underside:*** Banded with dark brown; general appearance grayish brown to reddish brown. FW cell has 2 dark bars. Dark submarginal line *very irregular, closer to outer margin* in cells $M_3$ and $Cu_1$ than in Western Banded Elfin (below).
**Early stages:** Larva green, with whitish stripes. One brood.
**Food:** Pines (*Pinus,* various species). **Adults:** March–April in south, April–June in north.
**Range:** Manitoba to Nova Scotia, south to Fla., Tex. In the West, has been reported from Colo., perhaps in error. TL: Florida. **Habitat:** Openings in pine forest.

**WESTERN BANDED ELFIN**                              **Pl. 31**
*Incisalia eryphon* (Boisduval)
**Identification:** 1-1⅛ in. (25–28 mm). HW scalloped; fringes checkered. ***Upperside:*** Male grayish brown, with orange-brown tornal spot. Female tawny or buffy, with dark borders. ***Underside:*** Dark-banded as in Eastern Banded Elfin (above), but *FW cell has only 1 bar* (sometimes none). Submarginal line on HW dark brown, *evenly sawtoothed, not closer to margin* opposite cells $M_3$ and $Cu_1$.
**Similar species:** Eastern Banded Elfin (above).
**Early stages:** Larva olive or green, with yellowish bars. One brood. **Food:** Pines (*Pinus,* various species). **Adults:** April–May at low elevations, May–July at high elevations.
**Range:** British Columbia to Manitoba, south to s. Calif., Ariz., N.M., Neb. **Habitat:** In the vicinity of pines; also visits flowers. Usually mountainous areas, to sea level on the Pacific Coast.
**Subspecies:** (1) **Western Banded Elfin,** *I. e. eryphon* (Boisduval), Pl. 31. Ore., Calif., Rocky Mts. TL: California. (2) **Shelton Elfin,** *I. e. sheltonensis* F. Chermock & Frechin. Underside more reddish brown. Pacific Northwest. TL: Shelton, Wash.

### Genus *Eurystrymon* Clench

This genus was proposed in 1961. Its members were previously placed in the genus *Strymon* (p. 176).

**POLING'S HAIRSTREAK**                              **Pl. 32**
*Eurystrymon polingi* (Barnes & Benjamin)
**Identification:** 1-1¼ in. (25–31 mm). Fringes pale-tipped. Male FW stigma *same color as rest of wing.* HW has 1 long tail. ***Upperside:*** FW dark olive-brown, its base and all of HW *slightly lighter. Terminal line white at HW tornus; tail white-tipped.* ***Underside:*** Brown. Thecla (pm.) line white, inwardly black-edged,

narrow; line forms a W in cubital area of HW. Thecla spot reddish, black-centered; tornal shade bluish. Terminal line black, inwardly edged with white.
**Early stages:** Unknown. One brood. **Food:** Mountain white oak *(Quercus grisea)*. **Adults:** Late May to June.
**Range:** W. Tex. Very local, usually scarce. TL: Sunny Glen Ranch, near Alpine, Brewster Co., Tex. **Habitat:** Oak woodland.

### NORTHERN HAIRSTREAK    Pl. 32
*Eurystrymon ontario* (W. H. Edwards)
**Identification:** $\frac{7}{8}$-$1\frac{1}{4}$ in. (22–31 mm). Male FW stigma large, oval. HW has 1 long tail and 3 short projections. *Upperside:* In our area both sexes are brown, with prominent orange-brown patches (patches may be absent in specimens from the Northeast). *Underside:* Markings much like those of Poling's Hairstreak (above), but *submarginal line present*.
**Early stages:** Poorly known. Apparently 1 brood, perhaps 2 in Ariz. **Food:** Hawthorn *(Crataegus)* in East; in Ariz., scrub oak *(Quercus turbinella)*. **Adults:** April–June; Aug. in s. Ariz.
**Range:** In the West, Ariz., N.M., and Kans. south to Tex. In the East, Ontario and Mass. south to Ga. **Habitat:** Oak woodland, mixed woodland, chaparral.
**Subspecies:** (1) **Northern Hairstreak,** *E. o. ontario* (W. H. Edwards), Pl. 32, No. 6. Eastern U.S. west to Kans. TL: Port Stanley, Ontario. (2) **Autolycus Hairstreak,** *E. o. autolycus* (W. H. Edwards). Discal patches on upperside large; underside markings clear. Okla., Tex. TL: Dallas, Tex. (3) **Viola's Hairstreak,** *E. o. violae* (Stallings & Turner). Discal patches on upperside smaller. N.M. TL: Folsom, N.M. (4) **Ilavia Hairstreak,** *E. o. ilavia* (Beutenmueller), Pl. 32, No. 7. Orange discal patches on upperside *large;* underside markings reduced. Ariz. TL: Tex. (error?).

## Genus *Strymon* Huebner

HW tailed in some species, but not in others. FW stigma present or absent.

### COMMON HAIRSTREAK *Strymon melinus* Huebner    Pl. 32
**Identification:** $\frac{7}{8}$-$1\frac{1}{4}$ in. (22–31 mm). Two tails on HW — 1 short, 1 long. Tip of abdomen either gray or pink. Male lacks stigma. *Upperside:* Blue-gray. *Thecla spot red — outer end black. Underside:* Dark gray to nearly white, depending on the subspecies. Thecla line either black or red; white-edged. Thecla spot and tornal spot red, both with black centers.
**Early stages:** Larva reddish brown to green. Multiple broods. **Food:** Larva eats buds, flowers, and fruit of many plants, including hops, beans, mallow, knotweed, yucca, and many others. **Adults:** Long flight season; most of the year.

*(Text continues on p. 179)*

# PLATES

Instructions on how to use the plates for identifying butterflies are given in Chapter 1, pp. 1-2. Keep in mind that the butterfly pictured is just one specimen, representing a species which may take several forms and may consist of many populations of thousands or hundreds of thousands of butterflies. Within that species, individuals may vary considerably in size (see measurements in species accounts), but are quite uniform in wing shape. Although some species are quite consistent in markings and pattern, others may show variations in placement, shape, and size of markings. The most obvious characteristic, color, is probably the least reliable. Freshly emerged specimens have a brilliance and intensity of color that does not survive long after emergence. Chemical or pigment colors tend to fade in daylight. Structural or mechanical colors do not fade, but are altered by wear and tear, and loss of scales. Also, pinned or papered specimens will generally appear duller than living butterflies. As a result, the specimens you seek to identify may be either brighter, or duller, or a slightly different color than shown in the plates or described in the species accounts. The markings may be similar but not a precise match. Keep these variables in mind as you compare your specimen with those figured in the plates.

## PLATE INDEX AT A GLANCE

PLATE 1

# EYED BROWNS AND WOOD SATYRS:
## Satyridae (all × 1)

1. **NORTHERN PEARLY EYE** *Enodia anthedon*  p. 37
   Elbow Lake, Becker Co., Minn. 6 July 1976
   *Upperside:* 5 dark submarginal spots on HW, upper 2 largest.
   *Underside:* Dark submarginal spots light-ringed, usually light-centered.

2. **EYED BROWN** *Satyrodes eurydice eurydice*  p. 37
   Lakehurst, Ocean Co., N.J. 5 July 1960
   *Upperside:* Spots in submarginal row relatively small, but conspicuous. *Underside:* Submarginal spots pale-ringed, light-centered.

3. **SMOKY EYED BROWN** *S. e. fumosus*  p. 38
   Crescent Lake Refuge, Garden Co., Neb. 13 July 1970
   *Upperside:* Darker than in Eyed Brown (above).

4. **HENSHAW'S BROWN** *Cyllopsis henshawi*  p. 39
   ♂, Madera Canyon, Santa Rita Mts., Ariz. 25 Aug. 1953
   *Upperside:* ♂ has patch of sex scales on FW. *Underside:* Dark pm. line on HW not toothed — angled toward costa.

5. **NABOKOV'S BROWN**  p. 38
   *Cyllopsis pyracmon nabokovi*
   ♂, Ramsey Canyon, Huachuca Mts., Ariz. 31 Aug. 1952
   *Upperside:* ♂ has dark sex scales on FW, as do all *Cyllopsis* males; scales mostly below discal cell. *Underside:* Dark pm. line on HW has outward-pointing tooth near costa.

6. **GRAND CANYON BROWN**  p. 39
   *Cyllopsis pertepida dorothea*
   ♂, 25 mi. (40 km) n. of Lordsburg, N.M., Rte. 189. 19 June 1963
   *Upperside:* ♂ has sex scales on FW. *Underside:* Upper end of submarginal line on HW angled toward apex of outer margin.

7. **LITTLE WOOD SATYR** *Megisto cymela*  p. 39
   Prairie Village, Johnson Co., Kans. 1 June 1960
   *Upperside:* 2 dark eyespots on FW, 1–2 on HW. *Underside:* 2 large buff-ringed eyespots on FW and 2 large ones on HW.

8. **ARIZONA RED SATYR**  p. 40
   *Megisto rubricata cheneyorum*
   Southwestern Research Station, Chiricahua Mts., Ariz. 25 June 1967
   *Upperside:* Wing discs rusty; 1 eyespot at FW apex, another at anal angle of HW. *Underside:* 1 eyespot on FW, 2 on HW, all 3 with small silver centers.

1                UN

2                UN

3

4 ♂            UN

5 ♂            UN

6 ♂            UN

7                UN

8                UN

PLATE 2

# WOOD SATYRS AND RINGLETS:
## Satyridae (all × 1)

1. **SMITHS' RED SATYR** p. 40
   *Megisto rubricata smithorum*
   ♂, ♀, Marfa-Alpine, 10 mi. (16 km) w. of Alpine, Tex. 17 July 1941
   Slightly larger and general appearance lighter than other subspecies (see Pl. 1 and p. 178). Rusty markings more extensive.

2. **ALLYN'S SATYR** *Paramacera allyni* p. 40
   ♂, Chiricahua Mts., Ariz. 24 June 1936
   *Upperside:* ♂ has extensive sex scaling in FW; eyespots not ringed. *Underside:* Complicated, ornate markings are distinctive.

3. **HAYDEN'S RINGLET** *Coenonympha haydenii* p. 40
   ♂, Targhee Pass, Fremont Co., Idaho. 29 June 1958
   *Upperside:* ♂ entirely dark brown; ♀ lighter. *Underside:* A row of buff-ringed eyespots on HW margin.

4. **ARCTIC RINGLET** *C. kodiak mixturata* p. 41
   Mile 1135, Alaska Hwy., Yukon Terr. 16 July 1970
   *Upperside:* Eyespots reduced, usually absent. HW grayer than FW. *Underside:* Wing bases dark; margins light. Median band white.

5. **INORNATE RINGLET** *C. inornata inornata* p. 41
   Roosevelt Natl. Park, N.D. 4 June 1966
   *Upperside:* Ground color darker brownish yellow than in other ringlets. *Underside:* Eyespots reduced; light overscaling extensive.

6. **OCHRE RINGLET** *C. ochracea ochracea* p. 41
   Woods Landing, Wyo. 30 May 1954
   *Upperside:* Bright brownish yellow; eyespot at FW apex. *Underside:* Eyespot at FW apex. HW often has light markings.

7. **RINGLESS RINGLET** *C. ampelos ampelos* p. 42
   Dooly Summit, Baker Co., Ore. 13 July 1965
   *Upperside:* Pale brownish yellow; no markings. *Underside:* HW basal area slightly darker than outer area.

8. **CALIFORNIA RINGLET** *C. california california* p. 43
   Brisbane, San Mateo Co., Calif. 21 April 1962
   *Upperside:* White; eyespot at FW apex present or absent. *Underside:* Median line light; eyespots at FW apex and on HW.

9. **RIDING'S SATYR** *Neominois ridingsii ridingsii* p. 50
   Mother Cabrini Shrine, Jefferson Co., Colo. 6 July 1957
   *Upperside and underside:* Markings distinctive, unique.

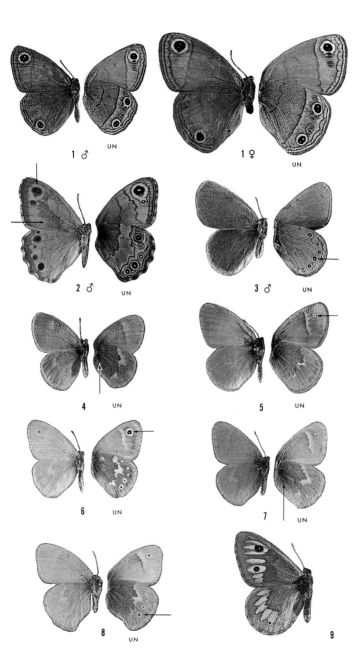

1 ♂    UN

1 ♀    UN

2 ♂    UN

3 ♂    UN

4    UN

5    UN

6    UN

7    UN

8    UN

9

PLATE 3
# WOOD NYMPHS: Satyridae (all × 1)

1. **OX-EYED SATYR** *Cercyonis pegala boöpis*      p. 43
   ♂, Santa Cruz, Calif. 11 July 1934; ♀, Pt. Richmond, Contra
   Costa Co., Calif. 4 June 1966
   *Upperside:* ♂ dark; ♀ with vague light area around FW
   eyespots. *Underside:* Usually some spots in HW of ♂; often no
   HW spots in ♀.

2. **ARIANE SATYR** *C. p. ariane*      p. 43
   ♂, 3 mi. (4.8 km) s. of Carson City, Nev. 20 July 1973
   *Upperside:* Dark; FW eyespots have light ring. 1 HW eyespot.
   *Underside:* HW has 6 eyespots, the central spot in each group of
   3 largest.

3. **STEPHENS' SATYR** *C. p. ariane* form "stephensi"      p. 44
   ♀, 3 mi. (4.8 km) s. of Carson City, Nev. 26 July 1973
   *Upperside:* Light, with a wide, straw-colored submarginal band.
   *Underside:* Markings as in Ariane Satyr (above), but much
   lighter.

4. **MEAD'S SATYR** *Cercyonis meadii mexicana*      p. 44
   Mingus Mt., Yavapai Co., Ariz. 31 Aug. 1955
   *Upperside:* Reddish brown flush surrounds FW eyespots. *Underside:* FW flush extensive. Outer margin of HW banded.

5. **LEAST SATYR** *Cercyonis oeta oeta*      p. 45
   ♂, ♀, Monitor Pass, Alpine Co., Calif.
   On upperside and underside, lower eyespot in FW nearer to wing
   margin than other spot. *Upperside:* FW sex scaling prominent
   in ♂. *Underside:* HW mottled with dark color. Eyespots reduced; lower eyespot smaller. (Compare with Woodland Satyr,
   Pl. 4.)

1 ♂    1 ♀    UN

1 ♀    2 ♂
UN        UN

3 ♀    4
UN

4    5 ♂    5 ♀
UN        UN

PLATE 4

# WOOD NYMPHS AND ALPINES:
## Satyridae (all × 1)

1. **WOODLAND SATYR** *Cercyonis sthenele silvestris*    p. 44
   Silver Creek, Santa Clara Co., Calif. 17 June 1949
   *Upperside:* Both eyespots equally distant from FW margin. *Underside:* Usually no eyespots on HW.

2. **LITTLE SATYR** *C. s. paula*    p. 45
   Whitney Portal, Inyo Co., Calif. 29 June 1950
   *Underside:* Light submarginal band on HW; eyespots present.

3. **VIDLER'S ALPINE** *Erebia vidleri*    p. 46
   Tiffany Lake, Okanogan Co., Wash. 15 July 1956
   *Upperside:* FW eyespots surrounded by orange band. *Underside:* HW has silvery gray pm. band.

4. **ROSS'S ALPINE** *Erebia rossii rossii*    p. 46
   ♀, Eagle Summit, Steese Hwy., Alaska. 27 July 1975
   Anterior spots twinned on upperside and underside of FW. *Underside:* HW has a line of dark submarginal chevrons, each capped inwardly by a light speck.

5. **ORNATE ALPINE** *E. r. ornata*    p. 46
   Ft. Churchill, Manitoba, Canada. 6 July 1933
   *Upperside:* Anterior FW spots fused. *Underside:* Banding less distinct than in Ross's Alpine (above).

6. **DISA ALPINE** *Erebia disa mancina*    p. 47
   Baldy Mt. Trail, Mordega, Alberta, Canada. 5 July 1960
   *Upperside:* 3–4 small black spots in FW, ringed with orange. *Underside:* Small white spot at end of HW cell.

7. **MAGDALENA ALPINE** *Erebia magdalena*    p. 47
   Mt. Audubon, Boulder Co., Colo. 5 July 1955
   All black on upperside and underside.

8. **MT. McKINLEY ALPINE** *Erebia mckinleyensis*    p. 47
   Eagle Summit, Steese Hwy., Alaska. 28 June 1975
   *Upperside:* Black. Reddish flush on FW small in ♂, much more extensive in ♀.

1     UN            2     UN

3     UN            4 ♀     UN

5     UN            6     UN

7            8 ♂            8 ♀

PLATE 5

# ALPINES AND ARCTICS: Satyridae *(all × 1)*

1. **YOUNG'S ALPINE** *Erebia youngi youngi* p. 49
   Eagle Summit, Steese Hwy., Alaska. 1 July 1975
   *Upperside:* FW has 4 black spots with orange rings. *Underside:* HW has small orange spots in a broad pale band.

2. **THEANO ALPINE** *Erebia theano alaskensis* p. 48
   Mile 90.2, Steese Hwy., Alaska. 28 June 1975
   *Upperside:* FW has several short orange bars (not eyespots).
   *Underside:* HW has several small ivory spots in a narrow band.

3. **BANDED ALPINE** *Erebia fasciata fasciata* p. 48
   ♂, Murphy Dome, near Fairbanks, Alaska. 12 June 1975
   *Upperside:* Reddish FW flush. *Underside:* Broad white HW band.

4. **RED-DISKED ALPINE** p. 48
   *Erebia discoidalis mcdunnoughi*
   Calgary, Alberta, Canada. 20 May 1959
   *Upperside:* Reddish discal flush on FW. *Underside:* White flecks along FW costa.

5. **COMMON ALPINE** *Erebia epipsodea rhodia* p. 49
   Selkirk Camp, Park Co., Colo. 15 June 1977
   *Upperside:* 4 eyespots below FW apex; top 2 spots white-centered. *Underside:* Quite similar to upperside.

6. **MEAD'S ALPINE** *Erebia callias* p. 50
   Cottonwood Pass, Gunnison Co., Colo. 8 Aug. 1961
   *Upperside:* Reddish FW flush; 2 prominent eyespots below apex. *Underside:* HW silvery gray, with minute dark markings.

7. **IVALLDA ARCTIC** *Oeneis ivallda* p. 52
   ♂, Tioga Pass, Tuolumne Co., Calif. 16 Aug. 1962
   *Upperside:* FW has pale submarginal bars. *Underside:* Ground color light; dark, narrow, irregular bands.

8. **WHITE-VEINED ARCTIC** p. 54
   *Oeneis taygete edwardsi*
   Cottonwood Pass, Chaffee Co., Colo. 12 July 1964
   *Upperside:* Dark HW median band on underside shows through. *Underside:* HW veins whitish (dark in most other arctics).

9. **ALBERTA ARCTIC** *Oeneis alberta alberta* p. 53
   Miniota, Manitoba, Canada. 24 May 1921
   *Upperside:* Median band with faint, dark edges. HW spots indistinct. *Underside:* Narrow dark cell bar on FW. HW median band dark-edged.

10. **COLORADO MELISSA ARCTIC** p. 55
    *Oeneis melissa lucilla*
    Mt. Evans, Clear Lake Co., Colo. 12 July 1955
    *Upperside:* Plain; usually no eyespots. Wings thinly scaled; markings on underside of HW show through. *Underside:* Markings quite even; HW band often indistinct.

1               UN             2          UN

3 ♂         UN         4          UN

5          UN          6          UN

7 ♂         UN         8          UN

9          UN          10         UN

PLATE 6

## ARCTICS: Satyridae (all × 1)

1. **CHRYXUS ARCTIC** *Oeneis chryxus chryxus*            p. 52
   ♂, Nederland, Colo. 6 July 1938; ♀, Marble Canyon, British Columbia, Canada. 15 July 1968
   *Upperside:* FW in ♂ has long dark sex stigma. FW in ♀ has narrow, dark, vertical median line between eyespots and wing base, repeated on underside. *Underside:* In both sexes, dark median line in FW toothed at cell end. HW median band often indistinct.

2. **GREAT ARCTIC** *Oeneis nevadensis nevadensis*            p. 51
   Bear Spring Camp, State Hwy. 52, Ore. 14 July 1954
   *Upperside:* ♂ stigma dark, prominent (absent in ♀). *Underside:* HW neatly marbled; median band often indistinct.

3. **UHLER'S ARCTIC** *Oeneis uhleri uhleri*            p. 52
   Lefthand Canyon, Boulder Co., Colo. 24 May 1953
   *Upperside:* Eyespots in both wings, number variable. *Underside:* Ground color light, narrow bands dark. Eyespots vary from several to almost none.

4. **MACOUN'S ARCTIC** *Oeneis macounii*            p. 51
   Riding Mts., Manitoba, Canada. 23 June 1961
   *Upperside:* Similar to Great Arctic (No. 2, above), but ♂ lacks sex mark. *Underside:* HW median band distinct (vague in Great Arctic).

5. **BOREAL ARCTIC** *Oeneis bore mckinleyensis*            p. 54
   Mile 14, Denali Hwy., Alaska. 11 July 1975
   *Upperside:* Outer $\frac{1}{3}$ of HW lighter, with round light spots between veins; wing scaling thin. *Underside:* HW median band dark; outer $\frac{1}{3}$ of wing very pale.

1 ♂    UN

1 ♀    UN

2 ♂    UN

2 ♂    UN

3    UN

4

5    UN

4 UN

PLATE 7

# ARCTICS, ADMIRAL, FRITILLARIES:
## Satyridae, Nymphalidae
(Nos. 1–3 × 1, the rest × ¾)

1. **ROCKY MOUNTAIN JUTTA ARCTIC**       p. 55
*Oeneis jutta reducta*
Near Kabell Hollow, 8400 ft. (2560 m), Uintah Co., Utah.
15 July 1966
*Upperside:* FW eyespots surrounded by pale band. *Underside:* FW as on upperside; HW evenly mottled with brown.

2. **ALASKAN JUTTA ARCTIC** *O. j. alaskensis*       p. 55
♂, Goldstream, near Fairbanks, Alaska. 15 June 1975
*Upperside:* FW eyespots buff-ringed; buffy chevrons on HW.
*Underside* (not shown): Median band edged with whitish.
Submarginal area of HW may have a row of small white dots.

3. **POLIXENES ARCTIC** *Oeneis polixenes brucei*       p. 56
♂, Mt. Evans, Clear Creek Co., Colo. 10 July 1955
*Upperside:* Overscaling very thin; band on underside of HW shows through. *Underside:* HW band dark. Overscaling thin, wings partly translucent.

4. **FRIDAY'S ADMIRAL**       p. 66
*Basilarchia weidemeyerii × lorquini* (hybrid)
Mono Lake, Mono Co., Calif. 6 July 1968
*Upperside:* FW apex has small reddish brown tip. White median band wider than in Lorquin's Admiral (Pl. 9, No. 7). *Underside:* Broad white band, as in Weidemeyer's Admiral (p. 65), not Lorquin's. (Lorquin's has narrower white band.)

5. **REGAL FRITILLARY** *Speyeria idalia*       p. 80
♂, Webster, N.H. No date given.
*Upperside:* HW marginal spots rusty in ♂, white in ♀. *Underside:* Large silver spots cover HW; no bands evident.

6. **EDWARDS' FRITILLARY** *Speyeria edwardsi*       p. 81
Pole Mt., Laramie Range, Wyo. 1 Aug. 1953
*Upperside:* Wing border dark, the chevrons pointing in. *Underside:* Silver median spots elongate. Disc and pm. band greenish olive.

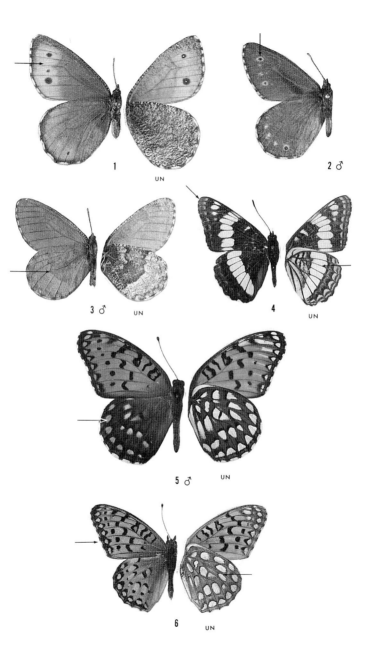

1

2 ♂

3 ♂    UN

4    UN

5 ♂    UN

6    UN

UN

PLATE 8

# SATYR, MONARCHS, LONGWING, LEAF-WINGS, HACKBERRY BUTTERFLIES:
## Satyridae, Danaidae, Heliconiidae and Apaturidae
(Nos. 2, 4, & 5 × $\frac{2}{3}$, the rest × $\frac{3}{4}$)

1. **TRITONIA** *Gyrocheilus patrobas tritonia*  p. 50
Madera Canyon, Santa Rita Mts., Ariz. 15 Sept. 1960

2. **MONARCH** *Danaus plexippus*  p. 56
♀, San Jose, Santa Clara Co., Calif. 8 Aug. 1949
*Upperside:* Note black wing veins. ♂ (not shown) has sex pouch on HW vein $Cu_2$.

3. **STRIATED QUEEN** *Danaus gilippus strigosus*  p. 57
♀, Jerome, Yavapai Co., Ariz. 5 July 1958
Many small white spots on borders and FW apex. *Upperside:* Brownish. ♂ (not shown) has sex pouch on HW vein $Cu_2$.

4. **ZEBRA** *Heliconius charitonius vazquezae*  p. 57
Medina R., 7 mi. (11.3 km) s. of San Antonio, Bexar Co., Tex. 12 Dec. 1968

5. **GULF FRITILLARY** *Agraulis vanillae incarnata*  p. 58
♂, Hidalgo, Hidalgo Co., Tex. 28 Aug. 1955

6. **TROPICAL LEAF-WING** *Anaea aidea aidea*  p. 59
♂, Brownsville, Cameron Co., Tex. 24 Oct. 1963
Short curved tail at end of vein $M_3$; very short tails at end of vein $Cu_2$ and anal angle.

7. **GOATWEED BUTTERFLY** *Anaea andria andria*  p. 59
Welder Wildlife Refuge, San Patricio Co., Tex. 6 Nov. 1963
*Upperside:* ♂ bright orange-red, with dark border; ♀ has complex pattern.

8. **HACKBERRY BUTTERFLY**  p. 60
*Asterocampa celtis montis*
Brown Canyon, Baboquiviri Mts., Ariz. 27 Aug. 1955
*Upperside:* 1st (inner) cell bar on FW divided into 2 parts. Small eyespot in FW cell $Cu_1$.

9. **EMPRESS LEILIA** *Asterocampa leilia leilia*  p. 61
Madera Canyon, Santa Rita Mts., Ariz. 25 Aug. 1953
*Upperside:* Both FW cell bars complete, *brown.* Dark eyespots in cells $M_3$ and $Cu_1$.

10. **TAWNY EMPEROR** *Asterocampa clyton texana*  p. 61
Bexar Co., Tex. ♂ emerged 28 April 1961, ♀ emerged 22 May 1961; reared from larvae.
*Upperside:* FW cell bars complete, *black.* ♀ usually larger, lighter; often looks quite different from ♂.

11. **PALLID EMPEROR** *Asterocampa subpallida*  p. 61
Elkhorn Ranch, Baboquiviri Mts., Ariz. 13 Sept. 1959
*Upperside:* Note pale color. HW has 2 light spots below costa.

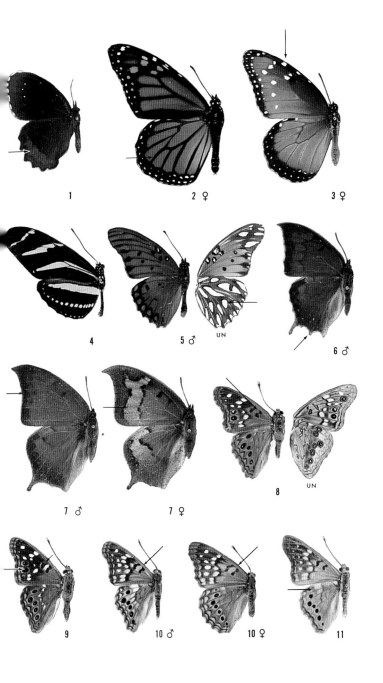

1

2 ♀

3 ♀

4

5 ♂

UN

6 ♂

7 ♂

7 ♀

8

UN

9

10 ♂

10 ♀

11

PLATE 9

# DAGGER-WINGS, VICEROYS, ADMIRALS, AND OTHERS: Nymphalidae
## (No. 4 × 1, the rest × ¾)

1. **MANY-BANDED DAGGER-WING**  p. 62
   *Marpesia chiron*
   Chiltepec, Oaxaca, Mexico. 26 July 1962

2. **RUDDY DAGGER-WING** *Marpesia petreus*  p. 62
   Sayula, Vera Cruz, Mexico. 19 July 1948

3. **HYPERIA** *Biblis hyperia aganisa*  p. 63
   Comaltapec, Oaxaca, Mexico. 14 Oct. 1962

4. **AMYMONE** *Mestra amymone*  p. 63
   Welder Wildlife Refuge, San Patricio Co., Tex. 3 Nov. 1963

5. **WATSON'S VICEROY**  p. 65
   *Basilarchia archippus watsoni*
   Lake Corpus Christi, Live Oak Co., Tex. 7 Nov. 1963
   *Upperside:* Narrow black median band on HW.

6. **WESTERN VICEROY** *B. a. obsoleta*  p. 65
   Patagonia, Santa Cruz Co., Ariz. 12 Aug. 1953

7. **LORQUIN'S ADMIRAL**  p. 66
   *Basilarchia lorquini lorquini*
   Sierra City, Sierra Co., Calif. 28 June 1960
   *Upperside:* FW apex orange-brown; white band on HW narrow. (See Weidemeyer's, below, and hybrid, Pl. 7.)

8. **NORTHERN WHITE ADMIRAL**  p. 64
   *Basilarchia arthemis rubrofasciata*
   Lac La Hache, British Columbia, Canada. 13 July 1968
   *Upperside:* Small red submarginal spots on HW. *Underside:* Note extensive red shades.

9. **WEIDEMEYER'S ADMIRAL**  p. 65
   *Basilarchia weidemeyerii weidemeyerii*
   Lefthand Canyon, Boulder Co., Colo. 28 June 1952
   *Upperside:* The only white-banded admiral with little or no reddish brown markings; basically black and white.

10. **ARIZONA RED-SPOTTED PURPLE**  p. 65
    *Basilarchia arthemis arizonensis*
    Patagonia, Santa Cruz Co., Ariz. 8 Sept. 1949
    *Upperside:* HW median rays and marginal crescents bluish green. *Underside:* Submarginal spots orange-red. This subspecies and subspecies *astyanax* of the Red-spotted Purple are the only admirals in this genus without prominent white pm. bands.

1

2

3

4

5

6

7    UN

8    UN

9

10    UN

PLATE 10
## TORTOISE-SHELLS, LADIES, AND OTHERS:
### Nymphalidae (all $\times \frac{3}{4}$)

1. **SISTER** *Adelpha bredowii eulalia*  p. 67
   Ramsey Canyon, Huachuca Mts., Ariz. 9 Sept. 1949
   *Upperside:* Patch at FW apex orange; white band narrow on HW. *Underside:* Extensive bluish shades.
2. **MILBERT'S TORTOISE-SHELL**  p. 69
   *Aglais milberti furcillata*
   Clear Lake Oaks, Lake Co., Calif. 24 May 1941
   *Upperside:* Orange and yellow pm. band on both wings.
3. **KAMEHAMEHA** *Vanessa tameamea*  p. 74
   Tantalus, Oahu, Hawaii. 1 Aug. 1963
4. **PAINTED LADY** *Vanessa cardui*  p. 74
   Reared from pupa, Danby, San Bernardino Co., Calif., 24 March 1958; emerged San Jose, Calif., 7 April 1958
   *Upperside:* Isolated black oval spot at base of FW cell. Base of HW heavily clouded with brown.
5. **AMERICAN PAINTED LADY** *V. virginiensis*  p. 75
   Santa Cruz, Santa Cruz Co., Calif. 22 July 1939
   *Upperside:* Small white spot in cell $Cu_1$ of FW. *Underside:* 2 large eyespots on HW.
6. **WEST COAST LADY** *Vanessa annabella*  p. 75
   San Francisco, Calif. 16 March 1957
   *Upperside:* Bar at FW costa orange, not white. HW submarginal spots blue-centered.
7. **WEST COAST LADY** *V. annabella* ab. "muelleri"  p. 76
   San Jose, Santa Clara Co., Calif. 23 Sept. 1950
   *Upperside:* Light spots on FW merged. HW eyespots white. (not blue with black rings).
8. **WEST COAST LADY $\times$ RED ADMIRAL**  p. 74
   *V. annabella $\times$ V. atalanta* (hybrid)
   San Lorenzo, Alameda Co., Calif. 2 Aug. 1976
   *Upperside:* This hybrid has most of the characteristics of the Red Admiral (below), but the HW has the black-ringed, blue eyespots of the West Coast Lady.
9. **RED ADMIRAL** *Vanessa atalanta rubria*  p. 74
   Leigh's Ferry, Stanislaus Co., Calif. 14 May 1961
10. **MOURNING CLOAK** *Nymphalis antiopa antiopa*  p. 68
    Arroyo Bayo, Santa Clara Co., Calif. 8 June 1957
11. **COMPTON TORTOISE-SHELL**  p. 67
    *Nymphalis vau-album j-album*
    Pocono Mts., Pa. 3 July 1934
    *Upperside:* HW has dark costal spot with white border.
12. **CALIFORNIA TORTOISE-SHELL**  p. 68
    *Nymphalis californica californica*
    Jerseydale, Mariposa Co., Calif. 30 May 1959
    *Upperside:* Note dark wing borders.
13. **WHITE PEACOCK** *Anartia jatrophae luteipicta*  p. 77
    Villa Nueva, Cameron Co., Tex. 25 Oct. 1963

1

3

4

5      UN      6      7

8      9      10

11      12      UN      13

PLATE 11

# BUCKEYES AND ANGLE-WINGS:
## Nymphalidae (all × ³⁄₄)

1. **BUCKEYE** *Junonia coenia*                          p. 76
   Long Valley, Lake Co., Calif. 19 May 1963
   *Upperside:* Upper spot on HW largest.

2. **DARK PEACOCK** *Junonia nigrosuffusa*               p. 76
   Patagonia, Santa Cruz Co., Ariz. 8 Oct. 1949
   *Upperside:* Dark. Upper spot on HW smaller than in Buckeye,
   dark.

3. **QUESTION MARK** *Polygonia interrogationis*         p. 70
   Santa Ana Wildlife Refuge, Hidalgo Co., Tex. 11 Nov. 1963
   Note wing shape. *Upperside:* FW cell $M_2$ has black oval spot.

4. **SATYR ANGLE-WING**                                  p. 70
   *Polygonia satyrus neomarsyas*
   Santa Cruz, Santa Cruz Co., Calif. 1 June 1935
   *Upperside:* FW cell $Cu_1$ has small, dark 2nd (inner) spot. *Un-
   derside:* Small silver spot on HW, shaped like a comma.

5. **HOP MERCHANT** *Polygonia comma*                    p. 70
   Overland, Mo. 1 Sept. 1935
   *Upperside:* Wing borders dark; HW submarginal spots dis-
   tinct.

6. **GREEN COMMA** *Polygonia faunus rustica*            p. 71
   Mt. Hood, Ore. 11 Aug. 1934
   *Upperside:* Wide dark borders. *Underside:* Some of spots usu-
   ally greenish.

7. **COLORADO ANGLE-WING** *Polygonia hylas*             p. 71
   ♂, Mammoth, Yellowstone Natl. Park, Wyo. 21 July
   *Underside:* Silver spot on HW ∟-shaped.

8. **SYLVAN ANGLE-WING** *Polygonia silvius*             p. 71
   Echo Summit, El Dorado Co., Calif. 7 Sept. 1933
   *Upperside:* Wings edged with lavender-gray; light submarginal spots large. *Underside:* Silvery, flattened, C-shaped
   spot on HW disc; submarginal spots gray (not greenish).

9. **ZEPHYR ANGLE-WING** *Polygonia zephyrus*            p. 72
   Echo Summit, El Dorado Co., Calif. 7 July 1938
   *Upperside:* HW submarginal spots have dark centers.

10. **OREAS ANGLE-WING** *Polygonia oreas oreas*         p. 72
    Santa Cruz, Santa Cruz Co., Calif. 17 Sept. 1931
    *Underside:* Ground color very dark. HW silver spot ∟-shaped.

11. **HOARY COMMA** *Polygonia gracilis*                 p. 73
    Carr Pond, Maine. 31 July 1937
    *Underside:* Outer half of both wings frosted with silver-gray.

12. **GRAY COMMA** *Polygonia progne*                    p. 73
    Birmingham, Jackson Co., Mo. 14 Sept. 1963
    *Upperside:* HW border wide; submarginal spots very small.
    *Underside:* FW has small, pale submarginal chevrons.

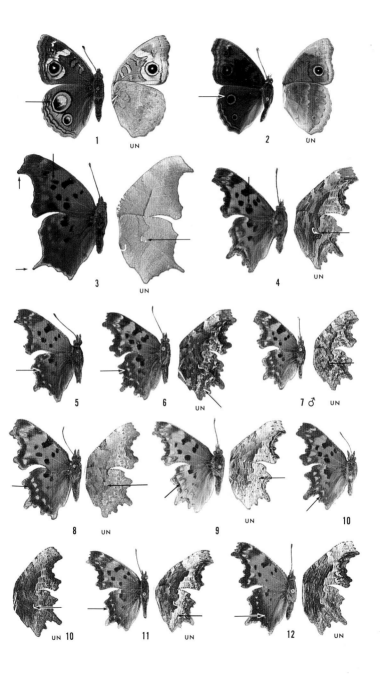

1                    UN

2                    UN

3                    UN

4                    UN

5          6          UN          7 ♂          UN

8          UN          9          UN          10

UN 10          11          UN          12          UN

PLATE 12

# FRITILLARIES: Nymphalidae
## (No. 5 × 1; all others × ¾)

1. **GREAT SPANGLED FRITILLARY**                                    p. 78
*Speyeria cybele cybele*
♂, Slippery Rock, Pa. 25 Aug. 1940
*Upperside:* Outer ⅓ of HW has small dark markings on broad
orange submarginal band. Base of FW and HW dark. ♂ has sex
scaling along FW veins $M_1$ to 2A. *Underside:* Light submarginal
band on HW wide; marginal spots silver, large.

2. **APHRODITE** *Speyeria aphrodite ethne*                        p. 80
♂, Boulder, Colo. 27 June 1951
*Upperside:* No sex scaling on longitudinal veins of ♂. *Under-
side:* Pm. band on HW narrow, invaded by disc color.

3. **LETO FRITILLARY** *Speyeria cybele leto*                      p. 78
♂, Pine Creek, Baker Co., Ore., 4100 ft. (1253 m). 10 July 1957;
♀, McDonald Forest, Benton Co., Ore. 23 July 1961
*Upperside:* ♂ bright red-brown with black markings. In ♀,
discal and basal areas and outer margins suffused with blackish;
submarginal band yellowish. *Underside:* ♂ HW disc dark; marginal spots small. In ♀, discal and basal areas dark chocolate
brown.

4. **EGLEIS FRITILLARY** *Speyeria egleis egleis*                  p. 84
♂, Gin Flat, Yosemite Natl. Park, Calif. 14 July 1957
*Upperside:* Longitudinal FW veins have dark sex scaling in ♂.

5. **CROWN FRITILLARY** *Speyeria coronis coronis*                 p. 81
♂, Alma, Santa Clara Co., Calif. 1 June 1935
*Underside:* Silver spots in HW discal area large and bright;
marginal spots broadly bordered inwardly with dark brown.

6. **NOKOMIS FRITILLARY**                                          p. 80
*Speyeria nokomis apacheana*
♂, Mono Lake, Mono Co., Calif. 13 Aug. 1950; ♀, Gull Lake,
Mono Co., Calif. 2 Sept. 1958
*Upperside:* ♂ has very distinct marginal line on both FW and
HW. ♀ similar to ♀ Leto Fritillary (No. 3, above), but blackish
areas lighter; yellowish band paler and wider. *Underside:* Both
sexes have silver spots with black margins. In ♀, areas at HW
base and disc yellowish green; submarginal band pale yellow.
Other subspecies differ in the color of the HW disc.

1 ♂    UN

2 ♂    UN

3 ♂    UN

4 ♂    UN

5 ♂    UN

3 ♀

6 ♂    UN

6 ♀

PLATE 13

# FRITILLARIES: Nymphalidae (all × ³⁄₄)

1. **ZERENE FRITILLARY** *Speyeria zerene zerene* p. 82
Strawberry, El Dorado Co., Calif. 10 July 1938
*zerene* pattern. *Upperside:* Median line strong, wider than usual. *Underside:* Discal spots unsilvered (marginal spots may be silvered). 3 upper spots in median band on HW all separated — central spot largest, lower spot smallest.

2. **ZERENE FRITILLARY** *S. z. platina* p. 82
Timpanogos Cave Natl. Monument, Utah. 7 July 1962
*platina-gunderi* pattern. *Upperside:* Markings much as in *zerene* pattern (above); ground color lighter. *Underside:* HW spots silvered, especially those in marginal band.

3. **ZERENE FRITILLARY** *S. z. picta* p. 82
Pine Creek, Baker Co., Ore. 10 July 1957
*picta-garretti* pattern. *Underside:* HW disc reddish in *picta* pattern, more brownish in *garretti* pattern.

4. **CALLIPPE FRITILLARY** p. 83
*Speyeria callippe callippe*
San Bruno Mts., San Mateo Co., Calif. 6 June 1963
*callippe* pattern. *Upperside:* Dark; brownish. *Underside:* HW disc brown; spots silver. Marginal markings triangular.

5. **CALLIPPE FRITILLARY** *S. c. liliana* p. 83
Butte River Canyon, Mendocino Co., Calif. 15 June 1958
*liliana* pattern. *Upperside:* Bright reddish. *Underside:* HW disc reddish brown.

6. **CALLIPPE FRITILLARY** *S. c. nevadensis* p. 83
Mono Lake, Mono Co., Calif. 23 June 1962
*nevadensis* pattern. *Underside:* HW disc green.

7. **LESSER UNSILVERED FRITILLARY** p. 83
*Speyeria adiaste adiaste*
*Upperside:* Bright red; FW median line prominent. *Underside:* Pale; HW spots mere "ghosts," unsilvered.

8. **ATLANTIS FRITILLARY** *S. atlantis hollandi* p. 84
Hudson Bay Jct., Manitoba, Canada. 2 July 1962
*atlantis* pattern. *Upperside:* Wing borders and bases dark; veins dark. *Underside:* Spots silvered. HW disc and border dark. Band light, crossed by dark veins. Median row of silver marks bordered by small dark outer spots. (See also Pl. 14.)

9. **ATLANTIS FRITILLARY** *S. a. hesperis* p. 84
Boulder Canyon, Boulder Co., Colo. 8 July 1952
*hesperis* pattern. *Upperside:* Dark. *Underside:* HW spots entirely unsilvered. (See also Pl. 14, No. 1.)

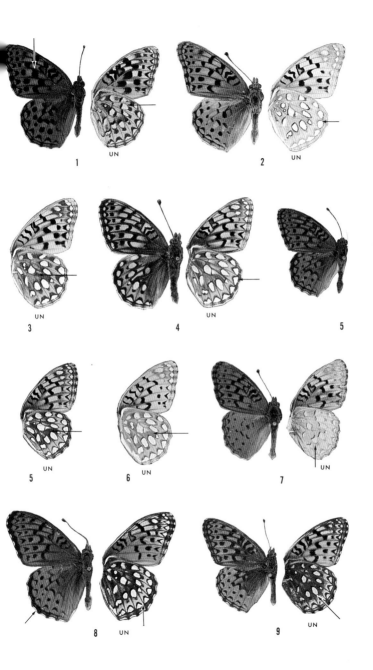

1

UN

2

UN

UN

3

UN

4

5

UN

5

UN

6

UN

7

UN

8

UN

UN

9

PLATE 14

# FRITILLARIES AND LESSER FRITILLARIES:
## Nymphalidae (Nos. 1–8 × ³⁄₄, 9–14 × 1)

1. **ATLANTIS FRITILLARY** *Speyeria atlantis dennisi*   p. 84
   Whirlpool R., Riding Mts. Natl. Park, Manitoba. 26 July 1961
   Pm. band light and wide. See also Pl. 13.
2. **HYDASPE FRITILLARY** *S. hydaspe hydaspe*   p. 85
   Crane Flat, Yosemite Natl. Park, Calif. 3 July 1954
   *Underside:* Unsilvered; upper 3 HW spots about same size.
3. **SAKUNTALA FRITILLARY** *S. h. sakuntala*   p. 85
   Marias Pass, Glacier Co., Mont. 21 July 1968
   Smaller than *hydaspe* (above); very dark.
4. **MORMON FRITILLARY** *S. mormonia mormonia*   p. 85
   Little Cottonwood Canyon, Salt Lake Co., Utah. 24 July 1943
   *Upperside:* No sex scaling on FW veins in ♂ (not shown); wing
   border dark. *Underside:* Silver spots small and bright.
5. **MORMON FRITILLARY** *S. m. eurynome*   p. 85
   Marias Pass, Glacier Co., Mont. 21 July 1968
   *Underside:* Spots silvered or unsilvered; HW disc greenish.
6. **MORMON FRITILLARY** *S. m. artonis*   p. 85
   Ruby Mts., Elko Co., Nev. 27 July 1959
   *Underside:* Pale yellow-buff. HW spots and markings faint.
7. **MORMON FRITILLARY** *S. m. luski*   p. 85
   Horseshoe Ciénaga, Apache Co., Ariz. 18 July 1955
   *Underside:* HW spots large, pale, unsilvered, dark-outlined.
8. **VARIEGATED FRITILLARY** *Euptoieta claudia*   p. 86
   Madera Canyon, Santa Rita Mts., Ariz. 28 Aug. 1955
9. **HALL'S FRITILLARY** *Boloria napaea halli*   p. 87
   ♂, near Palmer Lake, Wind River Range, Wyo. 1 Aug. 1970
   *Upperside:* Outer edge of HW angled slightly; markings small.
   *Underside:* HW submedian band complete; cell mark often
   silver.
10. **SILVER-BORDERED FRITILLARY**   p. 87
    *Clossiana selene tollandensis*
    Roger's Park, Boulder Canyon, Boulder Co., Colo. 3 July 1958
11. **MEADOW FRITILLARY** *Clossiana bellona jenistai*   p. 87
    Cypress Hills Provincial Park, Saskatchewan. 25 June 1968
    *Upperside:* FW apex slightly flattened below tip. Heavy dark
    markings near wing base.
12. **FRIGGA'S FRITILLARY** *Clossiana frigga sagata*   p. 88
    Caribou, Boulder Co., Colo. 1 July 1974
13. **DINGY NORTHERN FRITILLARY**   p. 88
    *Clossiana improba youngi*
    Eagle Summit, Steese Hwy., Alaska. 1 July 1974
14. **STRECKER'S SMALL FRITILLARY**   p. 89
    *Clossiana kriemhild*
    Shingle Creek Camp, Uintah Co., Utah. 13 June 1960
    *Underside:* Dark submarginal chevrons on FW flat, point-
    ing outward.

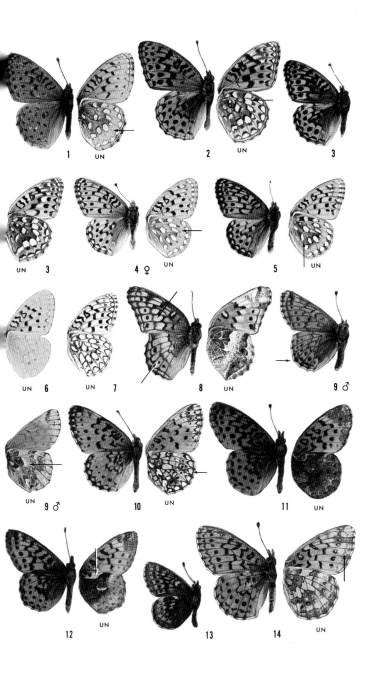

UN 1  UN 2  3

UN 3  4 ♀ UN  5 UN

UN 6  UN 7  8 UN  9 ♂

UN 9 ♂  10 UN  11 UN

12 UN  13  14 UN

PLATE 15

# LESSER FRITILLARIES AND CRESCENTS:
## Nymphalidae (all × 1)

1. **PURPLE LESSER FRITILLARY** p. 90
   *Clossiana titania grandis*
   Riding Mts., Manitoba, Canada. 26 July 1933
   *Upperside and underside:* Dark submarginal triangles on HW.
2. **WESTERN MEADOW FRITILLARY** p. 89
   *Clossiana epithore epithore*
   Empire Grade, Santa Cruz Co., Calif. 16 May 1969
   FW apex rounded. *Upperside:* Dark markings small, separate.
   *Underside:* Pm. spot row of small dark rings.
3. **POLARIS FRITILLARY** p. 91
   *Clossiana polaris stellata*
   Churchill, Manitoba, Canada. 2 July 1951
   *Underside:* Border has complete row of small white triangles.
   Alternating brown and white (or silver) spot rows across HW.
4. **FREIJA'S FRITILLARY** p. 91
   *Clossiana freija browni*
   Caribou, Boulder Co., Colo. 19 July 1955
   *Upperside:* Light border spots capped by dark triangles. *Underside:* HW pm. markings very irregular.
5. **ALBERTA FRITILLARY** *Clossiana alberta* p. 92
   Mt. St. Bride, near Banff, Alberta, Canada. 29 July 1964
   Large. *Upperside:* Dark, smoky coloration.
6. **ASTARTE FRITILLARY** *Clossiana astarte* p. 92
   Slate Peak, Okanogan Co., Wash. 24 July 1968
   Our largest *Clossiana. Underside:* HW median band whitish, distinct.
7. **DISTINCT FRITILLARY** *Clossiana distincta* p. 92
   Eagle Summit, Alaska. 10 July 1972
   Large. *Underside:* Median band wide.
8. **ARCTIC FRITILLARY** p. 92
   *Clossiana chariclea butleri*
   Mile 90.2, Steese Hwy., Alaska. 25 June 1974
   *Upperside:* Wing bases dark; dark spots small, round, separate.
   *Underside:* Light submedian band usually well developed.
9. **BOG FRITILLARY** p. 93
   *Proclossiana eunomia caelestis*
   Tolland, Gilpin Co., Colo. 30 June 1963
   *Upperside:* Pm. spots small, dark, round, well spaced. *Underside:* Pm. spots are small, light-centered rings.
10. **TEXAS CRESCENT** *Anthanassa texana* p. 94
    Comal Co., Tex. Emerged 5 Sept. 1959; reared from egg.
    *Upperside:* HW median band formed of small white spots. *Underside:* Base of FW orange-brown.
11. **TULCIS CRESCENT** *Eresia frisia tulcis* p. 94
    Santa Ana Wildlife Refuge, Hidalgo Co., Tex. 26 Oct. 1970
    *Upperside:* White band on HW, not separate spots. *Underside:* FW base white, cream, or brownish yellow, not orange-brown.

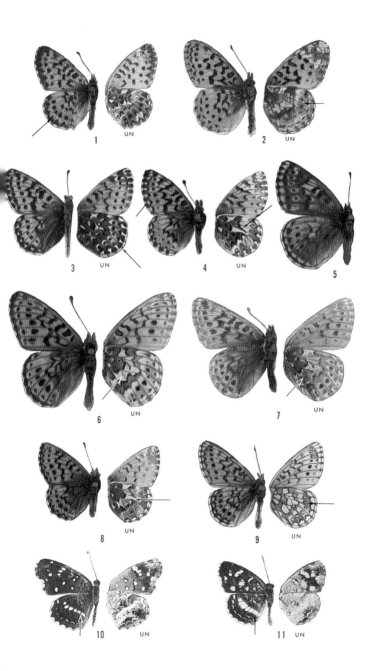

UN 1

UN 2

3 UN UN 4 5

6 UN 7 UN

8 UN 9 UN

10 UN 11 UN

PLATE 16

# CRESCENTS AND CHECKER-SPOTS:
## Nymphalidae (all × 1)

1. **NORTHERN PEARL CRESCENT** p. 95
   *Phyciodes pascoensis pascoensis*
   Poudre Canyon, Larimer Co., Colo. 7 July 1953
   *Underside:* Median area of FW orange-brown, plain.
2. **TAWNY CRESCENT** *Phyciodes batesii* p. 95
   Ottawa, Ontario, Canada. 22 June 1958
   *Underside:* Median spot row on FW black; some spots small.
3. **PHAON CRESCENT** *Phyciodes phaon* p. 96
   Santa Ana Wildlife Refuge, Hidalgo Co., Tex. 31 Oct. 1963
   *Upperside and underside:* Light median band whitish.
4. **FIELD CRESCENT** p. 96
   *Phyciodes campestris campestris*
   Santa Cruz, Santa Cruz Co., Calif. 21 March 1932
   *Upperside and underside:* Median band formed of separate spots.
5. **MOUNTAIN CRESCENT** *P. c. montanus* p. 96
   Echo Summit, El Dorado Co., Calif. 13 July 1933
   *Upperside:* Much of HW bright tawny.
6. **PAINTED CRESCENT** *Phyciodes pictus pictus* p. 96
   2 mi. (3.2 km) w. of Alpine, Brewster Co., Tex. 24 June 1963
7. **ORSEIS CRESCENT** *Phyciodes orseis* p. 97
   Echo Lake, Shasta Co., Calif. 12 July 1907
   *Upperside:* Wing bases darkened; light bands reddish yellow.
8. **VESTA CRESCENT** *Phyciodes vesta* p. 98
   Presidio Co., Tex. 11 June 1960
9. **PALE CRESCENT** *Phyciodes pallidus pallidus* p. 98
   Flagstaff Mt., Boulder Co., Colo. 18 June 1966
   *Upperside and underside:* Black spot in FW at center of inner margin.
10. **MYLITTA CRESCENT** *Phyciodes mylitta mylitta* p. 97
    Payette, Payette Co., Idaho. 1 July 1936
11. **SILVERY CHECKER-SPOT** p. 99
    *Charidryas nycteis drusius*
    Pennsylvania Gulch, near Sunset, Colo. 1 July 1953
    *Underside:* Basal and median bands on HW silvery white.
12. **GORGONE CHECKER-SPOT** p. 99
    *Charidryas gorgone carlota*
    Independence, Jackson Co., Mo. 6 June 1962
13. **GABB'S CHECKER-SPOT** *Charidryas gabbii* p. 100
    ♂, Gavilan Hills, Riverside Co., Calif. 19 April 1957
    *Upperside:* Bright orange-brown bands; median band lighter.
    *Underside:* Light bands on HW have a pearly luster.
14. **ACASTUS CHECKER-SPOT** p. 100
    *Charidryas acastus acastus*
    Mill Creek, Salt Lake Co., Utah. 7 June 1942
    *Upperside:* Base of HW darker than base of FW. *Underside:* Light bands edged with brown.

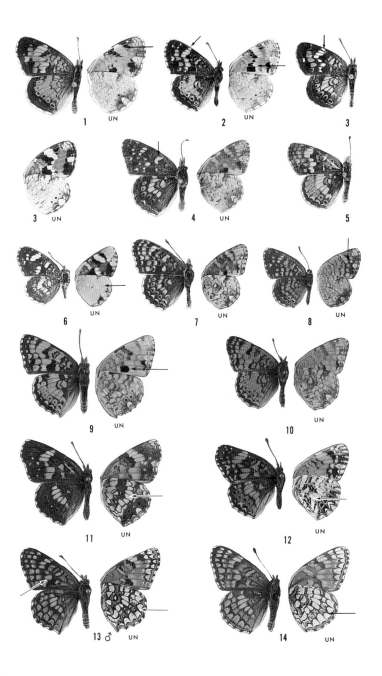

1

UN

2

UN

3

3 UN

4 UN

5

6 UN

7 UN

8 UN

9 UN

10 UN

11 UN

12 UN

13 ♂ UN

14 UN

PLATE 17

# CHECKER-SPOTS AND PATCHES:
## Nymphalidae (all × 1)

1. **NEUMOEGEN'S CHECKER-SPOT** p. 100
*Charidryas neumoegeni neumoegeni*
Providence Mts., San Bernardino Co., Calif. 22 March 1952
2. **NORTHERN CHECKER-SPOT** p. 101
*Charidryas palla palla*
♂, El Portal, Mariposa Co., Calif. 16 April 1961; ♀(melanic), Sonoma, Sonoma Co., Calif. 1 June 1938
*Upperside:* Base of HW dark; median band light.
3. **HOFFMANN'S CHECKER-SPOT** p. 102
*Charidryas hoffmanni hoffmanni*
Echo Summit, El Dorado Co., Calif. 23 July 1935
4. **DAMOETAS CHECKER-SPOT** p. 102
*Charidryas damoetas damoetas*
Corona Pass, Boulder Co., Colo. 5 July 1966
5. **AARON'S CHECKER-SPOT** *Chlosyne definita* p. 102
McKelligan's Park, Franklin Mts., Tex. 2 April 1969
6. **BORDERED PATCH** *Chlosyne lacinia adjutrix* p. 103
Santa Ana Wildlife Refuge, Hidalgo Co., Tex. 17 Nov. 1970
7. **CROCALE PATCH** *C. l. crocale,* form "rufescens" p. 103
Sabino Canyon, Pima Co., Ariz. 30 March 1938
8. **CALIFORNIA PATCH** *Chlosyne californica* p. 103
Yarnell Hill, Yavapai Co., Ariz. 1 Sept. 1955
9. **LEANIRA CHECKER-SPOT** p. 104
*Thessalia leanira leanira*
Santa Cruz, Santa Cruz Co., Calif. 10 April 1938
10. **WRIGHT'S CHECKER-SPOT** *T. l. wrightii* p. 104
Glendora Mt., Los Angeles Co., Calif. 17 June 1959
11. **CERRITA CHECKER-SPOT** *T. l. cerrita* p. 104
Little Rock, Los Angeles Co., Calif. 10 April 1952
12. **ALMA CHECKER-SPOT** *T. l. alma* p. 104
♂, Trail of the Serpent, Colo. Natl. Mon., Colo. 11 May 1963
*Underside:* FW cell brown, cell-end bar light; brown bar beyond.
13. **CYNEAS CHECKER-SPOT** *Thessalia cyneas* p. 105
Chiricahua Mts., Cochise Co., Ariz. 25 June 1908
14. **THEONA CHECKER-SPOT** p. 105
*Thessalia theona bollii*
4 mi. (6.5 km) w. of Boca Chica, Cameron Co., Tex. 26 Oct. 1963
15. **TINKHAM'S CHECKER-SPOT** p. 106
*Thessalia chinatiensis*
12 mi. (19 km) n. of Van Horn, Culberson Co., Tex. 9 Sept. 1969
16. **FULVOUS CHECKER-SPOT** *Thessalia fulvia* p. 105
♂, 3.5 mi. (5.5 km) nw. of Flagstaff, Coconino Co., Ariz. 5 Nov. 1959
*Underside:* No dark cell bar in HW.

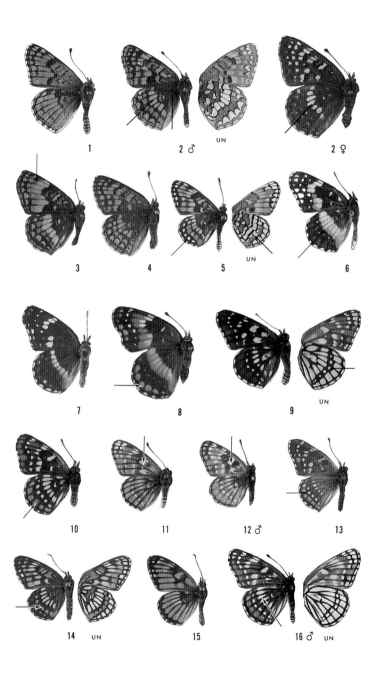

1

2 ♂    UN

2 ♀

3

4

5    UN

6

7

8

9    UN

10

11

12 ♂

13

14    UN

15

16 ♂    UN

PLATE 18

# CHECKER-SPOTS AND ELVA:
## Nymphalidae (all × 1)

1. **DYMAS CHECKER-SPOT** *Dymasia dymas*          p. 106
   ♂, Big Aguja Canyon, Jeff Davis Co., Tex. 6 Sept. 1965; ♀, Jeff
   Davis Co., Tex. Emerged 14 June 1969; reared from egg.

2. **CHARA CHECKER-SPOT** *Dymasia chara chara*          p. 106
   ♂, Sabino Canyon, Pima Co., Ariz. 6 Sept. 1949; ♀, Madera
   Canyon, Santa Rita Mts., Ariz. 29 Aug. 1955

3. **ELADA CHECKER-SPOT** *Texola elada callina*          p. 107
   ♂, Bexar Co., Tex. Emerged 7 Aug. 1960, reared from egg; ♀,
   Santa Ana Wildlife Refuge, Hidalgo Co., Tex. 31 Oct. 1963

4. **SMALL CHECKER-SPOT** *Poladryas minuta*          p. 108
   Kerrville, Tex. A very old specimen, no date given.

5. **ARACHNE CHECKER-SPOT**          p. 108
   *Poladryas arachne arachne*
   Neal's Spring, N. Rim of Grand Canyon, Ariz. 9 July 1953

6. **GILLETTE'S CHECKER-SPOT**          p. 113
   *Hypodryas gillettii*
   Granite Creek, Gros Ventre Mts., Teton Co., Wyo. 9 July 1967

7. **CHALCEDON CHECKER-SPOT**          p. 110
   *Occidryas chalcedona chalcedona*
   Santa Cruz, Santa Cruz Co., Calif. 30 April 1931

8. **SIERRA CHECKER-SPOT** *O. c. sierra*          p. 111
   Bishop Pass, Inyo Co., Calif. 23 July 1933

9. **COLON CHECKER-SPOT** *O. colon colon*          p. 111
   Roseburg, Douglas Co., Ore. 5 June 1936

10. **ANICIA CHECKER-SPOT** *O. anicia anicia*          p. 112
    Glacier National Park, Mont. 6 July 1949

11. **LEUSSLER'S CHECKER-SPOT** *O. a. bernadetta*          p. 112
    Ft. Robinson, Sioux Co., Neb. 18 May 1951

12. **CAPELLA CHECKER-SPOT** *O. a. capella*          p. 112
    Nederland, Boulder Co., Colo. 4 July 1938

13. **RUDDY CHECKER-SPOT**          p. 113
    *Occidryas editha rubicunda*
    Indian Flat, Mariposa Co., Calif. 27 May 1960

14. **BAY REGION CHECKER-SPOT** *O. e. bayensis*          p. 113
    San Bruno Mts., San Mateo Co., Calif. 31 March 1962

15. **CLOUD-BORN CHECKER-SPOT** *O. e. nubigena*          p. 113
    Tioga Pass, Yosemite Natl. Park, Calif. 18 July 1957

16. **ELVA** *Microtia elva*          p. 107
    Puente Nacional, Vera Cruz, Mexico. 11 Aug. 1949

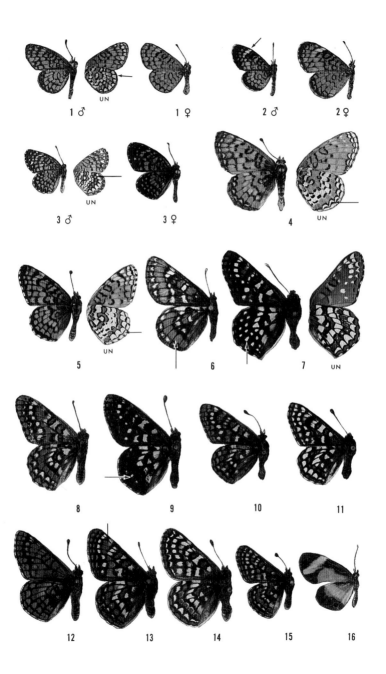

1 ♂    UN    1 ♀    2 ♂    2 ♀

3 ♂    UN    3 ♀    4    UN

5    UN    6    7    UN

8    9    10    11

12    13    14    15    16

PLATE 19

# BLUES, PARNASSIANS, AND SWALLOWTAILS:
## Lycaenidae and Papilionidae
(Nos. 1–6 × 1, 7–11 × $\frac{2}{3}$, 12 × $\frac{3}{4}$)

1. **SPALDING'S BLUE** *Euphilotes spaldingi*      p. 200
   ♂, Neal's Spring, N. Rim of Grand Canyon, Ariz. 9 July 1953
   *Underside:* Note aurora on both FW and HW.

2. **SMALL BLUE** *Philotiella speciosa speciosa*      p. 201
   ♂, near Randsburg, Kern Co., Calif. 26 April 1936
   Small. *Upperside:* Pale blue. *Underside:* Black dots on HW.

3. **ARROWHEAD BLUE** *Glaucopsyche piasus piasus*      p. 201
   ♂, Satus Creek, Yakima Co., Wash. 27 May 1951
   Our only large blue with checkered fringes. *Underside:* HW
   has white submarginal chevrons (arrowheads).

4. **SILVERY BLUE** *Glaucopsyche lygdamus incognita*      p. 202
   ♂, Alum Rock Park, Santa Clara Co., Calif. 18 March 1955
   *Underside:* Pm. spots on FW and HW black, ringed with white.

5. **XERCES BLUE** *Glaucopsyche xerces*      p. 202
   ♂, San Francisco, Calif. 20 March 1932
   *Upperside:* Lavender blue. *Underside:* White spots on HW.

6. **SPRING AZURE** *Celastrina ladon echo*      p. 203
   ♂, Stevens Creek, Santa Clara Co., Calif. 27 March 1953; ♀,
   Ukiah, Mendocino Co., Calif. 31 May 1952
   *Upperside:* ♂ sky blue; fringes checkered. ♀ has dark border on
   FW, and often light submarginal rings on HW.

7. **EVERSMANN'S PARNASSIAN**      p. 114
   *Parnassius eversmanni thor*
   ♂, Mile 14, Denali Hwy., Alaska. 11 July 1975; ♀, Keno Hill,
   Yukon. 5 July 1971

8. **CLODIUS PARNASSIAN** *P. clodius claudianus*      p. 114
   ♂, Alta Lake, Mt. Garibaldi Park, British Columbia. 7 July
   1968; ♀, Forbidden Plateau, Vancouver I., Canada. 9 July 1968
   Antennae black. *Upperside* (both sexes): No red spots on FW.

9. **PHOEBUS PARNASSIAN** *P. phoebus sayii*      p. 115
   ♂, ♀, Tin Cup, Gunnison Co., Colo. 5 Aug. 1961
   Antennae ringed. *Upperside:* In ♂, FW spots may be red, yel-
   low, or black. ♀ has 2 red (or yellow) FW spots.

10. **PIPE-VINE SWALLOWTAIL**      p. 115
    *Battus philenor philenor*
    ♂, Independence, Jackson Co., Mo. 13 July 1962
    *Upperside:* Iridescent green. Light submarginal spots on HW.

11. **BLACK SWALLOWTAIL**      p. 116
    *Papilio polyxenes asterius*
    ♂, Independence, Jackson Co., Mo. 3 May 1960; reared from
    pupa.
    *Upperside:* Black center of orange anal spot on HW does not
    touch edge (inner margin) of wing.

12. **WRIGHT'S SWALLOWTAIL** *P. p. coloro*      p. 117
    ♂, Providence Mts., San Bernardino Co., 22 March 1952
    *Upperside:* Yellow more extensive than in Black Swallowtail.

1 ♂ UN

2 ♂ UN

3 ♂ UN

4 ♂ UN

5 ♂ UN

6 ♂ UN

6 ♀

7 ♂

7 ♀

8 ♂

8 ♀

9 ♂

9 ♀

10 ♂

11 ♂

12 ♂

PLATE 20

## SWALLOWTAILS: Papilionidae
(No. 8 × $\frac{2}{3}$, all others × $\frac{3}{4}$)

1. **BAIRD'S SWALLOWTAIL** *Papilio bairdii*          p. 117
   1 mi. (1.6 km) se. of Salida, Chaffee Co., Colo. 1 Aug. 1965
   *Upperside:* Tegulae (wing flaps) yellow. Black center of orange
   HW anal spot usually touches inner margin.

2. **OREGON SWALLOWTAIL**          p. 117
   *Papilio oregonius oregonius*
   Priest Rapids, Yakima Co., Ore. 23 Aug. 1961
   *Upperside:* Black area at FW base powdered with yellow scales.
   Abdomen yellow with black stripes on back and lower sides.

3. **OLD WORLD SWALLOWTAIL**          p. 119
   *Papilio machaon aliaska*
   Keno Hill, Yukon Terr., Canada. 19 June 1969
   FW costa and outer margin convex. HW tail slender. *Upperside:*
   Orange anal spot on HW has no black center.

4. **ZELICAON SWALLOWTAIL**          p. 118
   *Papilio zelicaon zelicaon*
   San Jose, Santa Clara Co., Calif. Emerged 28 Aug. 1956; reared
   from pupa.
   *Upperside:* Black center of orange anal spot does not touch
   inner margin of HW.

5. **NITRA SWALLOWTAIL** *P. z. nitra*          p. 118
   Teton Natl. Forest, Rt. 89, Teton Co., Wyo. 23 July 1970
   *Upperside:* Pm. spots similar in size and shape; spots broader at
   outer edge and dusted with dark scales.

6. **INDRA or SHORT-TAILED SWALLOWTAIL**          p. 120
   *Papilio indra indra*
   Pine Creek, Baker Co., Ore. 7 July 1957
   HW tail very short. *Upperside:* Yellow band narrow.

7. **EDWARDS' SWALLOWTAIL** *P. i. pergamus*          p. 120
   Tecate Peak, San Diego Co., Calif. 7 May 1960
   HW tail longer than in Indra Swallowtail. *Upperside:* Yellow
   band very narrow.

8. **XUTHUS SWALLOWTAIL** *Papilio xuthus*          p. 121
   Heta Izo, Shizuoka, Japan. 17 July 1954
   *Upperside:* Cream-colored markings narrow, numerous.

PLATE 21

# SWALLOWTAILS: Papilionidae
(all × ⅔)

1. **GIANT SWALLOWTAIL** *Papilio cresphontes*    p. 121
   ♂, Pleasant Hill, Cass Co., Mo. 17 July 1960
   *Upperside:* Prominent band of yellow spots from FW apex to inner margin, continuing across HW basal area as a solid band. Note yellow spot in tail and red anal crescent in HW.

2. **EASTERN TIGER SWALLOWTAIL**    p. 121
   *Papilio glaucus glaucus*
   ♂, Shawnee Mission Park, Johnson, Kans. 13 July 1960; ♀ (dark form), w. of Lost Brush Mt., Montgomery Co., Va. 14 July 1961
   *Upperside:* 1st submarginal spot in HW orange in both sexes. Dark ♀ similar to Spicebush Swallowtail (No. 5, below), but FW submarginal spots smaller; large orange spot located farther out from base of HW. *Underside:* In ♂, edge of light area on HW tinged with orange, also inside spots.

3. **WESTERN TIGER SWALLOWTAIL**    p. 122
   *Papilio rutulus arizonensis*
   ♂, Tucson, Ariz. 8 June 1948
   Outer margin of FW slightly concave. *Upperside:* 1st marginal spot on HW yellow or absent. *Underside:* Pale yellowish areas lack orange tint, except for 2 spots near end of HW inner margin.

4. **PALE SWALLOWTAIL** *Papilio eurymedon*    p. 123
   ♂, Wawona, Mariposa Co., Calif. 26 June 1962
   The pale, creamy white markings are distinctive.

5. **SPICEBUSH SWALLOWTAIL** *Papilio troilus*    p. 123
   ♂, Warsaw, Benton Co., Mo. 1 May 1963
   *Upperside:* HW has pale green submarginal spots, an orange spot at costa, and a dusting of greenish or bluish scales on outer part of wing.

6. **TWO-TAILED SWALLOWTAIL**    p. 123
   *Papilio multicaudatus*
   ♀, Durkee, Baker Co., Ore. 8 July 1957
   Two narrow tails on each HW: a long one at end of vein $M_3$ and a short one at end of vein $Cu_1$. *Upperside:* Ground color bright yellow. Black bands on FW narrower than in subspecies *arizonensis* of Western Tiger Swallowtail (No. 3, above).

1 ♂

2 ♂

UN

2 ♀

3 ♂

UN

4 ♂

5 ♂

6 ♀

PLATE 22

# WHITES AND SULFURS: Pieridae
## (all × 1)

1. **SOUTHERN PINE WHITE** *Neophasia terlootii*        p. 124
   Madera Canyon, Santa Rita Mts., Ariz. ♂, 24 Oct. 1959; ♀, 18
   Oct. 1954
   *Upperside:* White in ♂, orange in ♀. FW cell black in both sexes.

2. **MEAD'S SULFUR** *Colias meadii meadii*        p. 130
   ♂, Arapahoe Pass Trail, Boulder Co., Colo. 23 July 1952; ♀,
   Kingston, Gilpin Co., Colo. 26 July 1952
   *Upperside:* Orange; black borders very wide in ♂, interrupted
   by light spots in ♀.

3. **BEHR'S SULFUR** *Colias behrii*        p. 136
   Tioga Pass, Yosemite Natl. Park, Calif. 13 Aug. 1950
   *Upperside:* Greenish; border dark. HW discal spot light.

4. **ORANGE SULFUR** *Colias eurytheme*        p. 131
   ♂, Sherman I., Sacramento Co., Calif. 12 Sept. 1962; ♀ (yellow
   form), Hidalgo, Hidalgo Co., Tex. 31 Oct. 1963; ♀ (white form),
   Hidalgo, Hidalgo Co., Tex., 31 Oct. 1963
   ♂ *Upperside:* Yellow washed with orange; black border wide.
   FW cell spot large. Wing bases heavily dusted with dark scales.
   ♂ *Underside:* HW discal spot double-ringed, with a satellite
   spot above it.

5. **QUEEN ALEXANDRA SULFUR**        p. 133
   *Colias alexandra alexandra*
   ♂, Lefthand Canyon, Boulder Co., Colo. 28 June 1952; ♀, Pole
   Mountain, Albany Co., Wyo. 7 July 1950
   *Upperside:* Lemon yellow in ♂, paler near wing bases. ♀ yellow
   (seldom white); dark borders reduced. FW cell spot small in
   both sexes. (See also orange subspecies — Christina Sulfur — on
   Pl. 26.)
   *Underside* (both sexes): Greenish gray; HW discal spot pearly,
   not ringed. Wing margins whitish, not pink.

6. **CALIFORNIA DOGFACE** *Zerene eurydice*        p. 137
   ♂, Austin Creek, Cazadero, Sonoma Co., Calif. 5 July 1963; ♀,
   Mt. Tamalpais, Marin Co., Calif. 10 Aug. 1903
   ♂ *Upperside:* "Head" of dog's-face marking iridescent; "eye"
   close to dark border. ♀ *Upperside:* Usually all yellow; FW has
   dark cell spot.

1 ♂     1 ♀     2 ♂

2 ♀     3 ♂     4 ♂     UN

4 ♀
yellow form

4 ♀
white form

5 ♂

5 ♀     6 ♂     6 ♀

PLATE 23

# WHITES: Pieridae
## (all × 1)

1. **PINE WHITE** *Neophasia menapia menapia*    p. 125
   Buffalo Creek, Jefferson Co., Colo. 8 Aug. 1959
   *Upperside:* FW costa and cell bar black; cell white.

2. **BECKER'S WHITE** *Pontia beckerii beckerii*    p. 125
   ♂, Rte. 33, 20 mi. (32 km) sw. of Duchesne, Duchesne Co., Utah
   1 Aug. 1961
   *Upperside:* FW cell bar black, squarish; white-centered. *Under-side:* Markings on HW heavy, greenish; ground color white.

3. **CALIFORNIA WHITE**    p. 126
   *Pontia sisymbrii sisymbrii*
   ♂, Alum Rock Park, Santa Clara Co., Calif. 9 April 1933
   *Upperside:* Veins dark; markings narrow. *Underside:* Olive vein
   edgings in HW nearly complete.

4. **CHECKERED WHITE** *Pontia protodice*    p. 126
   Arroyo Bayo, Mt. Hamilton, Santa Clara Co., Calif. 12 Sept.
   1954
   *Upperside:* In ♂, dark spot in FW cell $Cu_2$ vague or absent; HW
   all white. In ♀, markings extensive, brown and smudgy.

5. **WESTERN WHITE**    p. 127
   *Pontia occidentalis occidentalis*
   ♂, Lake Tahoe, El Dorado Co., Calif. 23 June 1935
   *Upperside:* FW markings heavy; dark spot always present in
   cell $Cu_2$. HW usually has at least vague borders. *Underside:*
   HW veins and chevrons near margin greenish.

6. **ALASKAN MUSTARD WHITE**    p. 128
   *Artogeia napi pseudobryoniae*
   Anchor R., Alaska. ♂, 12 June 1959; ♀, 13 June 1961
   *Upperside:* FW costa and all veins dark but narrow in ♂. All
   veins with wide, dark edges in ♀. No dark FW cell bar. *Under-side:* In ♂, FW veins dark but narrow; HW veins with broader
   dark edges. All veins moderately dark-edged in ♀.

7. **VEINED WHITE** *A. n. venosa*    p. 127
   ♂, Alum Rock Canyon, Santa Clara Co., Calif. 4 March 1946
   *Upperside:* Wing bases, spot in FW cell $M_3$, and markings at
   FW apex blackish; no dark cell bar on FW. HW veins show
   through from below. *Underside:* Veins with heavy, dark out-lines, especially on HW. (See also Pl. 24 for other subspecies of
   the Mustard or Veined White, *A. napi.*)

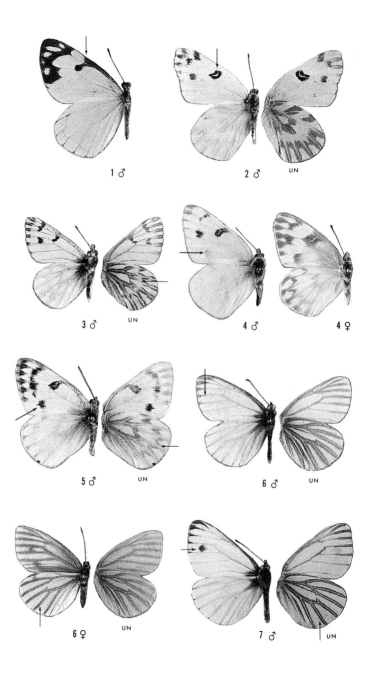

1 ♂

2 ♂    UN

3 ♂    UN

4 ♂    4 ♀

5 ♂    UN

6 ♂    UN

6 ♀    UN

7 ♂    UN

PLATE 24

# WHITES: Pieridae
## (all × 1)

1. **VEINED WHITE** *Artogeia napi venosa*                    p. 127
   ♀, Stevens Creek, Santa Clara Co., Calif. 27 March 1953
   *Upperside:* All markings dark and heavy. No cell bar on FW.
   *Underside:* All veins dark-bordered. See also Pl. 23 (♂).

2. **MARGINED WHITE** *A. n. marginalis*                    p. 128
   ♂, Lake Casidy, Snohomish Co., Wash. 22 April 1956; ♀,
   Chuchanut Dr., Skagit Co., Wash. 21 April 1958
   A subspecies of the Mustard White. *Upperside:* Both sexes have
   narrow dark FW border, lighter in ♀. FW costa and veins
   dark — veins narrow in ♂, wide in ♀. ♀ has faint spots on FW.
   *Underside:* All veins narrowly outlined in both sexes. ♀ a bit
   more yellowish.

3. **CABBAGE BUTTERFLY** *Artogeia rapae*                    p. 128
   ♂, Alum Rock Park, Santa Clara Co., Calif. 17 May 1961; ♀,
   San Francisco, Calif. 14 March 1959
   *Upperside:* FW apex dark. Dark spot in cell $M_3$; ♀ also has dark
   spot in cell $Cu_2$. Dark spot at HW costa. No spot in discal cell.
   *Underside:* HW unmarked in both sexes. FW spots repeated.

4. **GREAT SOUTHERN WHITE**                    p. 128
   *Ascia monuste phileta*
   ♂, 4 mi. (6.5 km) w. of Boca Chica, Cameron Co., Tex. 26 Oct.
   1963; ♀, Southmost, Cameron Co., Tex. 12 Oct. 1963
   *Upperside:* ♂ has black wedges along FW border, but no markings on HW. ♀ has wedges along borders of both wings, and a
   faint cell bar on FW. *Underside:* Unmarked in ♂. HW yellowish
   in ♀ (sometimes brown), with dusky borders, veins, and light
   HW band.

5. **GIANT WHITE** *Ganyra josephina josepha*                    p. 129
   ♂, Santa Ana Wildlife Refuge, Hidalgo Co., Tex. 3 Oct. 1974
   *Upperside:* All white, except for black FW cell spot. ♀ (not
   shown) has several dark spots on FW and narrow dark wedges
   along border, more prominent on FW than on HW.

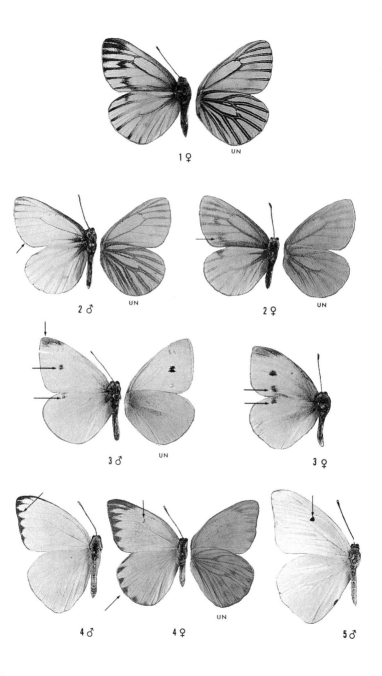

1 ♀
UN

2 ♂
UN

2 ♀
UN

3 ♂
UN

3 ♀

4 ♂

4 ♀
UN

5 ♂

PLATE 25

# MARBLES AND SULFURS: Pieridae
## (all × 1)

1. **CREUSA MARBLE** *Euchloe creusa*      p. 147
   ♂, Mile 90.2, Steese Hwy., Alaska. 25 June 1974
   *Upperside:* Dark markings at FW apex slight; cell bar narrow.
   Wing bases much darkened. *Underside:* HW marbling dark and
   extensive; white interspaces reduced.

2. **EDWARDS' MARBLE** *Euchloe hyantis hyantis*      p. 147
   ♂, Geysers, Sonoma Co., Calif. 8 April 1961
   *Upperside:* Upper end of wide FW cell bar close to costa. *Underside:* Ground color has pearly luster. Marbling on HW
   green-gray; white interspaces moderate in size.

3. **LARGE MARBLE** *Euchloe ausonides ausonides*      p. 148
   Santa Cruz, Calif. 7 April 1938
   *Upperside:* FW cell bar does not touch costa. *Underside:* No
   pearly luster. HW marbling green, veins yellow.

4. **OLYMPIA MARBLE** *Euchloe olympia rosa*      p. 148
   Shawnee Mission Park, Johnson Co., Kans. 24 April 1960
   *Upperside:* Dark markings few. *Underside:* Network of irregular greenish bands on HW.

5. **BOISDUVAL'S MARBLE**      p. 146
   *Falcapica lanceolata lanceolata*
   The Geysers, Mendocino Co., Calif. 22 April 1959
   *Upperside:* FW cell bar, apex, and terminal line dark. *Underside:* HW veins dark; marbling fine; white dash below costa.

6. **HECLA SULFUR** *Colias hecla hela*      p. 130
   ♂, Coppermine, N.W. Terr., Canada. 10 June 1966
   *Upperside:* FW and HW greenish orange, with wide borders and
   darkened bases.

7. **BOOTH'S SULFUR** *Colias boothii*      p. 130
   ♂, Coppermine, N.W. Terr., Canada. 3 July 1966; ♀, Repulse
   Bay, N.W. Terr., Canada. 3 Aug. 1951
   *Upperside:* FW light orange in ♂, HW yellowish or greenish;
   black border narrow, especially on HW. ♀ dull; FW and HW
   borders spotted, HW darkened. *Underside:* HW dull greenish
   (outer edge lighter); discal spot white with red-brown rim.

8. **CLOUDED SULFUR** *Colias philodice eriphyle*      p. 131
   ♂, Durkee, Baker Co., Ore. 8 July 1957
   *Upperside:* FW and HW bright canary yellow; black wing borders crossed by yellow veins. HW discal spot orange.

9. **HARFORD'S SULFUR** *Colias harfordii*      p. 132
   ♂, Glendora Mt., Los Angeles Co., Calif. 3 Aug. 1956; ♀, Laguna
   Lakes, San Diego Co., Calif., 7 June 1962
   *Upperside:* Warm yellow in ♂; HW discal spot inconspicuous;
   borders moderate; wing bases not dark-scaled. In ♀, FW border
   usually broken and HW border greatly reduced.

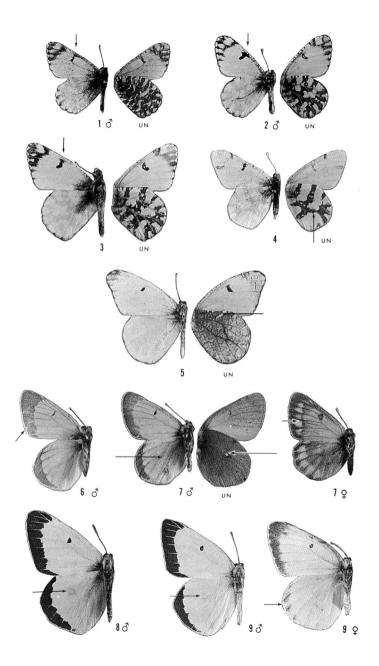

1 ♂    UN      2 ♂    UN

3    UN      4    UN

5    UN

6 ♂      7 ♂    UN      7 ♀

8 ♂      9 ♂      9 ♀

PLATE 26

# SULFURS, ANGLED SULFURS, AND GIANT SULFURS: Pieridae
(Nos. 5, 6, and 7 × ¾, all others × 1)

1. **WESTERN SULFUR** p. 132
*Colias occidentalis occidentalis*
♂, near Plain, Chelan Co., Wash. 30 May 1956; ♀, Hurricane Ridge, Olympic Natl. Park, Wash. 31 July 1962
*Upperside:* Bright yellow. FW cell spot small, HW spot pale. Borders black in ♂, reduced to absent in ♀.

2. **PINK-EDGED SULFUR** *Colias interior interior* p. 133
Riding Mts., Manitoba, Canada. ♂, 8 July 1938; ♀, 27 July 1938
Wing edges pink. *Upperside:* Dark border on HW narrow in ♂; borders in ♀ often reduced to FW apex. Cell spot in FW inconspicuous or absent, pale in HW.

3. **SCUDDER'S SULFUR** *Colias scudderii scudderii* p. 134
♂, Rocky Mt. Natl. Park, Colo. 15 July 1937; ♀, Marble Canyon, British Columbia, Canada. 15 July 1968
*Upperside:* ♂ HW heavily dusted with blackish scales; FW discal spot small, HW spot pale. Dark border crossed by yellow veins. ♀ white; apex and FW cell spot dark.

4. **CHRISTINA SULFUR** *Colias alexandra christina* p. 134
An orange subspecies of the Queen Alexandra Sulfur, Pl. 22. ♂, Sunwapta Pass, Alberta, Canada. 19 July 1940
*Upperside:* Orange; costa and outer base of FW yellow; lower base and inner marginal area of HW yellow.

5. **MAERULA** *Anteos maerula lacordairei* p. 139
♂, Yolox, Oaxaca, Mexico. 15 Dec. 1962
*Upperside:* Yellow; FW cell spot black. ♂ has large yellow sex patch just below costal margin of HW. HW discal spot faint.

6. **CLORINDE** *Anteos clorinde nivifera* p. 138
♂, Chiltapec, Oaxaca, Mexico. 17 Sept. 1962
*Upperside:* White; yellow patch below FW costa. ♂ has long, narrow, white sex patch below HW costal margin. Cell spots on FW and HW black, ringed with orange.

7. **CLOUDLESS SULFUR** *Phoebis sennae marcellina* p. 139
♂, Sycamore Canyon, Santa Cruz Co., Ariz. 16 Sept. 1960; ♀ (yellow form), R.R. tracks n. of mouth of Little Blue R., Atherton, Mo. 20 July 1956; ♀ (white form), Sycamore Canyon, Santa Cruz Co., Ariz. 16 Sept. 1960
*Upperside:* ♂ unmarked yellow. ♀ may be yellow, orange, or white, the wing edges and FW cell spot brown. Some specimens have more extensive brown markings.

1 ♂     1 ♀     2 ♂   UN

2 ♀     3 ♂     3 ♀   UN

4 ♂     5 ♂     6 ♂

1 ♂     yellow form 1 ♂     white form 1 ♀

PLATE 27

# GIANT SULFURS, SMALL SULFURS AND OTHERS: Pieridae
### (Nos. 1–3 × ¾, 4–6 × 1)

1. **ORANGE-BARRED SULFUR** *Phoebis philea*      p. 139
   Chiltapec, Oaxaca, Mexico. ♂, 19 Sept. 1962; ♀, 18 Sept. 1962
   *Upperside:* ♂ yellow, with orange FW patch and HW border. ♀ dull white; FW apex, cell spot, border spots, and zigzag pm. band brown.

2. **LARGE ORANGE SULFUR** *Phoebis agarithe*      p. 140
   ♂, Eagle Pass, Maverick Co., Tex. 8 Oct. 1963; ♀, Quemada, Maverick Co., Tex. 8 Oct. 1963
   *Upperside:* ♂ entirely light orange with a hair tuft near HW costal margin. ♀ either yellowish orange or white; FW cell spot, apex, spotted margin, and diagonal pm. band brown. *Underside:* Diagonal pm. band on FW.

3. **STATIRA** *Aphrissa statira jada*      p. 140
   ♂, X-Can, Quintano Roo, Mexico. 7 Sept. 1961; ♀, Temosique, Tabasco, Mexico. 14 Aug. 1962
   *Upperside:* Pale yellow. ♂ has wide, whitish, "mealy" border on outer ⅓ of FW and HW. In ♀, FW costa, border, and cell spot black.

4. **LYSIDE** *Kricogonia lyside*      p. 141
   ♂, Stanfield, Pinal Co., Ariz. 19 July 1959; ♀, Brownsville, Cameron Co., Tex. 30 Oct. 1963
   *Upperside:* ♂ white; wing bases yellow. Dark bar just below HW costa present or absent. ♀ all pale yellow, all white, or white with yellow wing bases. *Underside:* Yellowish to greenish white, often with a line of raised scales from HW base through cell to outer margin.

5. **MEXICAN SULFUR** *Eurema mexicana*      p. 142
   ♂, Ramsey Canyon, Huachuca Mts., Ariz. 27 Sept. 1961
   *Upperside:* FW has long-nosed, fanciful "dog's head." Wide yellow band along HW costa.

6. **LITTLE SULFUR** *Eurema lisa*      p. 143
   ♂, Matheson Hammock, Fla. 27 Feb. 1944
   *Upperside:* FW border wider than HW border. Wide, dark gray overscaling along FW costa. *Underside:* Dark cell spot on FW small but visible.

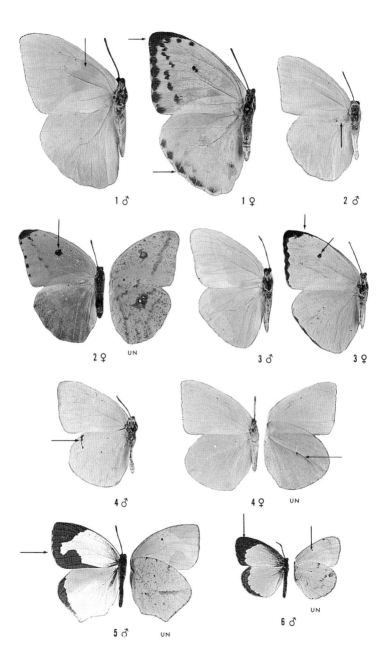

1 ♂        1 ♀        2 ♂

2 ♀        UN        3 ♂        3 ♀

4 ♂        4 ♀        UN

5 ♂        UN        6 ♂        UN

PLATE 28 **SULFURS: Pieridne (all × 1)**

1. **GIANT SULFUR** *Colias gigantea gigantea*      p. 135
   ♂, Buck Pass, Okanogan Co., Wash. 4 July 1957
   Large. *Upperside:* Bright yellow; FW cell spot distinct. *Under-side:* HW discal spot brown-ringed.

2. **PELIDNE SULFUR** *Colias pelidne pelidne*      p. 135
   Ne. Belle Isle, Newfoundland, Canada. ♀, 17 July 1937; ♂, 30 July 1939
   *Upperside:* FW discal spot small; HW discal spot faint. ♂ yellow, ♀ white or yellow. *Underside:* Discal spot red-ringed in both sexes.

3. **PALAENO SULFUR** *Colias palaeno chippewa*      p. 136
   ♂, Ft. Churchill, Manitoba, Canada. 26 July 1939
   *Upperside:* FW cell spot usually absent; HW cell spot incon-spicuous. *Underside:* HW cell spot not ringed.

4. **NASTES SULFUR** *Colias nastes moina*      p. 137
   ♂, Ft. Churchill, Manitoba, Canada. 20 July 1939
   Sexes similar. *Upperside:* Veins dark; borders enclose pale spots.

5. **SOUTHERN DOGFACE** *Zerene cesonia*      p. 138
   ♂, Ft. Lauderdale, Fla. 21 April 1955; ♀, Huntersville, Madison Co., Tenn.
   No iridescence in ♂. (Compare with ♂ California Dogface, Pl. 22.) *Underside:* Black borders more diffuse in ♀.

6. **BOISDUVAL'S SULFUR** *Eurema boisduvaliana*      p. 141
   X-Can, Quintano Roo, Mexico. 4 Oct. 1961
   Both sexes yellow with black markings. FW in ♂ marked with a vague "dog's head." FW in ♀ has black apex; HW margins lack black borders or markings.

7. **SALOME SULFUR** *Eurema salome limoneus*      p. 142
   ♂, Vista Hermosa, Comaltepec, Oaxaca, Mexico. 3 Oct. 1962
   *Upperside:* Black border on FW turns in sharply at tornus.

8. **GUNDLACH'S ORANGE**      p. 143
   *Eurema proterpia* (winter form)
   ♂, Santa Ana Refuge, Hidalgo Co., Tex. 17 Nov. 1970
   Outer angle of HW forms a short, sharp-pointed "tail."

9. **DINA SULFUR** *Eurema dina westwoodi*      p. 143
   X-Can, Quintano Roo, Mexico. ♂, 6 May 1962; ♀, 4 May 1961
   *Upperside:* ♂ bright yellow; FW costa and borders of FW and HW narrow, black. ♀ pale yellow; FW apex black. HW mar-gins orange.

10. **NISE SULFUR** *Eurema nise nelphe*      p. 143
    ♂, Santa Ana Refuge, Hidalgo Co., Tex. 11 Nov. 1963
    *Upperside:* Lemon yellow. FW costa and apex black. HW vein tips black.

11. **SLEEPY ORANGE** *Eurema nicippe*      p. 144
    ♂, Shafter, Presidio Co., Tex. 7 Oct. 1963
    *Upperside:* Bright orange, with wide, black borders.

12. **DAINTY SULFUR** *Nathalis iole*      p. 144
    ♂, Strayhorse, Greenlee Co., Ariz. 7 July 1950
    Very small. *Upperside:* HW costa and vein tips black.

1 ♂    UN     2 ♀    UN

2 ♂     3 ♂    UN     4 ♂

5 ♂     5 ♀     6 ♂     6 ♀

7 ♂     8 ♂     9 ♂     9 ♀

10 ♂     11 ♂     12 ♂

PLATE 29

# SNOUT BUTTERFLY, METALMARKS, AND HAIRSTREAKS:
## Libytheidae, Riodinidae, and Lycaenidae
### (all × 1)

1 ♂    2    3    4    5 ♂

6    7    8 ♂    9

10    ♂ 11    ♂ 12    13 ♂    UN

14 ♂    UN    15 ♂    UN    16 ♂    UN

17    UN    18 ♂    UN    19 ♂    UN

PLATE 30

# HAIRSTREAKS: Lycaenidae (all × 1)

1. **COLORADO HAIRSTREAK** p. 156
   *Hypaurotis crysalus crysalus*
   Bear Creek Park, Jefferson Co., Colo. 15 July 1957
2. **HEDGEROW HAIRSTREAK** p. 163
   *Satyrium saepium saepium*
   ♂, Putah Canyon, Yolo Co., Calif. 7 June 1952
   *Upperside:* Bright chestnut. ♂ stigma usually black (sometimes faint, as in this specimen).
3. **STRIPED HAIRSTREAK** p. 162
   *Satyrium liparops aliparops*
   ♂, Bluebell Canyon, Boulder Co., Colo. 12 July 1965
   *Upperside:* ♂ has long stigma on FW. *Underside:* Fine lines.
4. **BANDED HAIRSTREAK** *Satyrium calanus falacer* p. 161
   ♂, Forest Hills, Allegheny Co., Pa. 4 July 1954
   *Upperside:* ♂ has oval stigma on FW. *Underside:* Short, oblong markings.
5. **SYLVAN HAIRSTREAK** p. 161
   *Satyrium sylvinum sylvinum*
   Bear Creek, Mendocino Natl. Forest, Calif. 18 June 1957
   Tailed. Wings only slightly rounded. *Upperside:* Light brown.
6. **DRYOPE HAIRSTREAK** *Satyrium dryope* p. 161
   Arroyo Bayo, Santa Clara Co., Calif. 12 June 1952
   No tail. Wings more rounded. *Upperside:* Light-colored.
7. **CALIFORNIA HAIRSTREAK** p. 160
   *Satyrium californicum*
   Mono Lake, Mono Co., Calif. 30 June 1950 *Upperside:* Orange-brown markings on outer edge of lower FW.
8. **ACADIAN HAIRSTREAK** p. 160
   *Satyrium acadicum coolinensis*
   Durkee, Baker Co., Ore. 8 July 1957
   *Upperside and underside:* Dark. HW thecla spot small.
9. **LEDA HAIRSTREAK** p. 164
   *Ministrymon leda,* form "leda"
   ♂, Ramsey Canyon, Huachuca Mts., Ariz. 24 Aug. 1953
   *Upperside:* Wings blue near base. *Underside:* Thecla line red.
10. **INES HAIRSTREAK** *M. leda,* form "ines" p. 164
    ♂, Box Canyon, Santa Rita Mts., Ariz. 14 Sept. 1960
    *Upperside:* Blue extensive. *Underside:* Thecla line black.
11. **LARGER LANTANA BUTTERFLY** p. 164
    *Tmolus echion echiolus*
    ♂, Niihau, Hawaii. 1 Oct. 1919 *Upperside:* Blue. *Underside:* Series of oblong, coppery gray spots form thecla line.
12. **AZIA HAIRSTREAK** *Tmolus azia* p. 164
    ♂, Pharr, Hidalgo Co., Tex. 29 Sept. 1945 Small. *Upperside:* ♂ stigma large. *Underside:* Red thecla line.
13. **HOARY ELFIN** *Incisalia polia obscura* p. 172
    Offut, Thurston Co., Wash. 17 May 1954 *Upperside:* No tornal spot on HW. *Underside:* Wide hoary (frosted) edge on HW.

1

2 ♂

3 ♂ UN

4 ♂ UN

5 UN

6 UN

7 UN

8 UN

9 ♂ UN

10 ♂ UN

11 ♂ UN

12 ♂ UN

13 UN

PLATE 31

# HAIRSTREAKS: Lycaenidae (all × 1)

1. **HENRY'S ELFIN** *Incisalia henrici henrici*     p. 173
   Marine Corps Reservation, Quantico, Va. 11 May 1953
2. **STRECKER'S ELFIN** *Incisalia fotis*     p. 173
   Lookout Pass (no other data). 19 April 1931
3. **MOSS'S ELFIN** *Incisalia mossii doudoroffi*     p. 173
   Partington Canyon, Monterey Co., Calif. 26 May 1957
4. **BROWN ELFIN** *Incisalia augusta iroides*     p. 174
   Tanbark Flat, Los Angeles Co., Calif. 13 May 1957
5. **EASTERN BANDED ELFIN** *Incisalia niphon*     p. 175
   Lakehurst, N.J. 14 May 1961
6. **WESTERN BANDED ELFIN**     p. 175
   *Incisalia eryphon eryphon*
   Mono Lake, Mono Co., Calif. 5 July 1938
7. **McFARLAND'S HAIRSTREAK**     p. 172
   *Sandia mcfarlandi*
   West Slope, Sandia Mts., N.M. 20 June 1965
8. **XAMI HAIRSTREAK** *Xamia xami*     p. 172
   5 mi. w. of Boca Chica, Cameron Co., Tex. 20 Oct. 1970
9. **SKINNER'S HAIRSTREAK** *Mitoura loki*     p. 170
   Gavilan Hills, Riverside Co., Calif. Emerged 9 Oct. 1946; reared
   from pupa.
10. **OLIVE HAIRSTREAK** *Mitoura gryneus castalis*     p. 171
    ♂, ♀, Bexar Co., Tex. Emerged 22–30 May 1959; reared from
    egg.
11. **SIVA HAIRSTREAK** *Mitoura siva siva*     p. 170
    Pine, Gila Co., Ariz. 10 July 1948
12. **THICKET HAIRSTREAK** *Mitoura spinetorum*     p. 167
    Satus Pass, Klickitat Co., Wash. 12 July 1962
13. **JOHNSON'S HAIRSTREAK** *Mitoura johnsoni*     p. 168
    ♂, Wilson Lake, Tehama Co., Calif. 26 June 1960
14. **NELSON'S HAIRSTREAK** *Mitoura nelsoni*     p. 169
    Jerseydale, Mariposa Co., Calif. 30 May 1959
15. **GREEN-WINGED HAIRSTREAK**     p. 165
    *Callophrys affinis affinis*
    Aspen (0–3 mi. W), Pitkin Co., Colo. 12–15 June 1959
16. **SHERIDAN'S HAIRSTREAK**     p. 165
    *Callophrys sheridanii sheridanii*
    Red Rocks Park, Colo. 24 May 1957
17. **BRAMBLE HAIRSTREAK**     p. 166
    *Callophrys dumetorum dumetorum*
    El Portal, Mariposa Co., Calif. 16 May 1961
18. **APAMA HAIRSTREAK**     p. 166
    *Callophrys apama apama*
    Strayhorse, Greenlee Co., Ariz. 7 July 1958
19. **COMSTOCK'S HAIRSTREAK**     p. 167
    *Callophrys comstocki*
    Providence Mts., San Bernardino Co., Calif. 20 April 1938

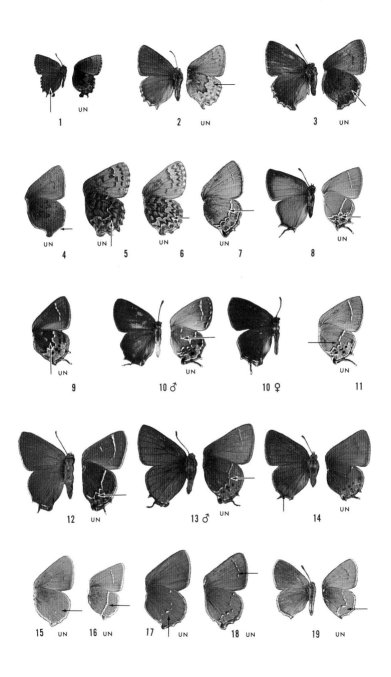

1      UN      2    UN      3    UN

4   UN    5   UN    6   UN    7   UN    8   UN

9   UN    10 ♂   UN    10 ♀    11   UN

12   UN    13 ♂   UN    14   UN

15   UN    16   UN    17   UN    18   UN    19   UN

PLATE 32

# HAIRSTREAKS AND OTHERS: Lycaenidae
## (all × 1)

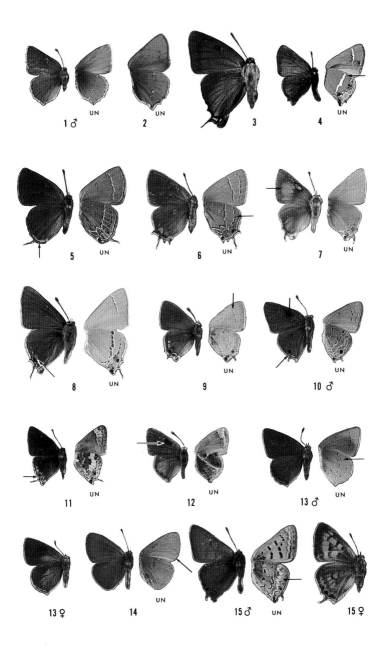

1 ♂    UN    2 UN

3    4 UN

5 UN    6 UN    7 UN

8 UN    9 UN    10 ♂ UN

11 UN    12 UN    13 ♂ UN

13 ♀    14 UN    15 ♂ UN    15 ♀

PLATE 33

# COPPERS: Lycaenidae (all × 1)

1. **HERMES COPPER** *Hermelycaena hermes*          p. 187
   ♂, San Diego Co., Calif. 29 May 1936
   HW tailed. *Underside:* HW bright yellow.

2. **VARIED BLUE** *Chalceria heteronea*          p. 184
   ♂, Sonora Pass, Stanislaus Co., Calif. 7 Aug. 1953
   *Upperside:* ♂ blue. ♀ (see Pl. 36) brown, with dark spots. *Underside:* FW spotted. HW usually white or with a few dark spots.

3. **RUDDY COPPER** *Chalceria rubida rubida*          p. 184
   ♂, Cottonwood Creek, Yakima Co., Wash. 15 July 1959; ♀, Payette, Payette Co., Idaho. 1 July 1931

4. **GORGON COPPER** *Gaeides gorgon*          p. 183
   ♂, Alum Rock Park, Santa Clara Co., Calif. 12 May 1953
   *Underside:* HW has submarginal row of dull red spots.

5. **GREAT COPPER** *Gaeides xanthoides xanthoides*          p. 182
   ♂, Oak Creek Pass, Kern Co., Calif. 21 June 1962
   *Underside:* Small white submarginal chevrons.

6. **EDITH'S COPPER** *Gaeides editha editha*          p. 182
   ♂, Pilot Peak, Mono Co., Calif. 31 Aug. 1958
   *Underside:* Note "raindrop" spots on HW.

7. **BRONZE COPPER** *Hyllolycaena hyllus*          p. 183
   ♂, George Reserve, Pinckney, Mich. 5 Aug. 1934; ♀, Louisville, Ky. 30 Sept. 1962
   *Upperside:* Orange marginal band on HW.

8. **MARIPOSA COPPER**          p. 186
   *Epidemia mariposa mariposa*
   ♂, Mt. Shasta, Siskiyou Co., Calif. 15 Aug. 1965
   *Upperside:* Dark; small orange marks on outer edge of HW.
   *Underside:* Pale submarginal chevrons on HW.

9. **NIVALIS COPPER** *Epidemia nivalis nivalis*          p. 186
   ♂, Tioga Pass, Yosemite Natl. Park, Calif. 15 Aug. 1951
   *Upperside:* Ground color light. Submarginal orange line on HW.

10. **PURPLISH COPPER** *Epidemia helloides*          p. 185
    ♂, Jersey I., Contra Costa Co., Calif. 19 Sept. 1956; ♀, Mono Lake, Mono Co., Calif. 5 July 1938
    *Upperside:* Purple reflections in ♂. ♀ spotted, dark-bordered.

11. **DORCAS COPPER** *Epidemia dorcas claytoni*          p. 185
    ♂, Springfield, Me. 24 Aug. 1959
    Small. *Underside:* Submarginal row of dull orange crescents.

12. **AMERICAN COPPER**          p. 181
    *Lycaena phlaeas americana*
    ♂, Pittsburgh, Pa. 15 May 1936
    *Upperside:* FW bright copper. *Underside:* Most of FW orange.

1 ♂   UN

2 ♂   UN

3 ♂   UN

3 ♀

4 ♂   UN

5 ♂   UN

6 ♂   UN

7 ♂   UN

7 ♀

8 ♂   UN

9 ♂   UN

10 ♀

10 ♂   UN

11 ♂   UN

12 ♂   UN

PLATE 34

# COPPERS AND BLUES: Lycaenidae (all × 1)

1. **LUSTROUS COPPER** *Lycaena cuprea cuprea*　　　p. 182
   ♂, Tioga Pass, Yosemite Natl. Park, Calif. 1 Aug. 1965

2. **LONG-TAILED BLUE** *Lampides boeticus*　　　p. 188
   ♂, originally from the collection of Vazquez de Madrid; later
   acquired by the Oberthur Collection. Date and locality not
   recorded. *Upperside:* HW thecla and tornal spots black.

3. **MARINE BLUE** *Leptotes marina*　　　p. 189
   ♂, San Antonio Wash, Los Angeles Co., Calif. 2 July 1952; ♀,
   Oak Creek Canyon, Yavapai Co., Ariz. 12 July 1953

4. **PYGMY BLUE** *Brephidium exile*　　　p. 187
   ♂, Brownsville, Cameron Co., Tex. 22 Oct. 1963
   Very small. *Upperside:* Small white patch at outer end of FW.

5. **CYNA BLUE** *Zizula cyna*　　　p. 188
   ♂, Alpine, Brewster Co., Tex. 10 July 1949

6. **CERAUNUS BLUE** *Hemiargus ceraunus gyas*　　　p. 189
   ♂, Madera Canyon, Santa Rita Mts., Ariz. 2 Sept. 1952
   *Underside:* 1 (seldom 2) dark marginal spots on HW.

7. **REAKIRT'S BLUE** *Hemiargus isola alce*　　　p. 190
   ♂, Madera Canyon, Santa Rita Mts., Ariz. 2 Sept. 1952

8. **NORTHERN BLUE** *Lycaeides idas anna*　　　p. 190
   ♂, Gin Flat, Yosemite Natl. Park, Calif. 19 July 1957; ♀, Crane
   Flat, Yosemite Natl. Park, Calif. 19 July 1957

9. **MELISSA BLUE** *Lycaeides melissa melissa*　　　p. 191
   ♂, Poudre Canyon, Colo. 9 July 1934

10. **GREENISH BLUE** *Plebejus saepiolus saepiolus*　　　p. 191
    Crane Flat, Yosemite Natl. Park, Calif. ♂, 3 July 1954; ♀, 28
    July 1931
    *Upperside:* FW with dark wide borders in ♂ and a dark cell bar
    in ♂ and ♀; ♀ darker.

11. **SAN EMIGDIO BLUE** *Plebulina emigdionis*　　　p. 192
    ♂, ♀, Victorville, San Bernardino Co., Calif. 15 June 1957
    *Underside:* Pm. spot in FW cell $Cu_1$ displaced inward.

12. **BOISDUVAL'S BLUE**　　　p. 192
    *Icaricia icarioides icarioides*
    ♂, ♀, Jerseydale, Mariposa Co., Calif. 30 May 1959

13. **SHASTA BLUE** *Icaricia shasta shasta*　　　p. 193
    ♂, Sonora Pass, Stanislaus Co., Calif. 16 July 1957
    *Upperside:* Dark cell bar on FW and HW. HW has weak au-
    rora.

14. **ACMON BLUE** *Icaricia acmon acmon*　　　p. 193
    ♂, Arroyo Bayo, Santa Clara Co., Calif. 8 June 1957; ♀, Santa
    Cruz, Santa Cruz Co., Calif. 1 June 1935
    *Upperside:* Aurora pink in ♂, orange in ♀. Iridescent spots on
    HW.

1 ♂ UN  2 ♂  3 ♂ UN  3 ♀

4 ♂ UN  5 ♂  6 ♂ UN  7 ♂ UN

8 ♂ UN  8 ♀  9 ♂ UN

10 ♂ UN  10 ♀  11 ♂ UN

11 ♀  12 ♂ UN  12 ♀

13 ♂ UN  14 ♂ UN  14 ♀

PLATE 35

# BLUES: Lycaenidae (all × 1)

1 ♂    1 ♀    2 ♂ UN    2 ♀

3 ♂    4 ♂    5 ♂ UN

6 ♂ UN    7 ♂ UN    7 ♀

8 ♂ UN    8 ♀    9 ♂    9 ♀

10 ♂    10 ♀    11 ♂ UN    12 ♂ UN

13 ♂    13 ♀    14 ♂ UN    14 ♀

PLATE 36

# HAIRSTREAKS, COPPERS, BLUES AND GIANT SKIPPERS:
## Lycaenidae and Megathymidae
(Nos. 12–14 × ¾, all others × 1)

1. **BARRY'S HAIRSTREAK** *Mitoura barryi barryi*  p. 168
   Rte. 97 at Crooked R., Jefferson Co., Ore. 10 June 1979

2. **MUIR'S HAIRSTREAK** *Mitoura muiri*  p. 170
   St. Helena Creek, Lake Co., Calif. 23 May 1972

3. **THORNE'S HAIRSTREAK** *Mitoura thornei*  p. 171
   Little Cedar Canyon, San Diego Co., Calif. 28 Oct. 1979

4. **GORGON COPPER** *Gaeides gorgon*  p. 183
   ♀, San Antonio Wash, Los Angeles Co., Calif. 2 July 1952

5. **GREAT COPPER** *Gaeides xanthoides*  p. 182
   ♀, Silver Creek Hills, Santa Clara Co., Calif. 11 June 1962

6. **EDITH'S COPPER** *Gaeides editha*  p. 182
   ♀, Pilot Peak, Mono Co., Calif. 31 Aug. 1958

7. **MARIPOSA COPPER** *Epidemia mariposa*  p. 186
   ♀, Tioga Pass, Tuolumne Co., Calif. 6 Aug. 1953

8. **NIVALIS COPPER** *Epidemia nivalis*  p. 186
   ♀, Echo Summit, El Dorado Co., Calif. 6 Aug. 1937

9. **VARIED BLUE** *Chalceria heteronea heteronea*  p. 184
   ♀, Spring Creek, Baker Co., Ore. 10 July 1959

10. **FERRIS'S COPPER** *Chalceria ferrisi*  p. 184
    ♂, Horseshoe Ciénaga, Apache Co., Ariz. 18 July 1959
    *Underside:* HW duller, more grayish, than that of Ruddy Copper (Pl. 33, p. 184).

11. **PALLID BLUE** *Euphilotes pallescens pallescens*  p. 200
    ♂, Dugway Proving Ground, Tooele Co., Utah. 16 July 1953; ♀, Little Granite Mt., Dugway Proving Ground, Tooele Co., Utah. 20 Aug. 1953

12. **MANFREDA BORER** *Stallingsia maculosa*  p. 205
    ♂, Sinton, San Patricio Co., Tex. 19 Aug. 1952, reared from larva.

13. **COLORADO YUCCA BORER**  p. 205
    *Megathymus coloradensis martini*
    ♂, Little Rock, Los Angeles Co., Calif. 7 Feb. 1938; ♀, Valyermo, Los Angeles Co., Calif. 16 Feb. 1936

14. **VIOLA'S YUCCA BORER** *Megathymus violae*  p. 207
    Carlsbad Caverns Natl. Park, Eddy Co., N.M. ♂, 23 June 1960; ♀, 28 June 1960

1

2

3

UN

UN

UN

4 ♀

5 ♀

6 ♀

7 ♀

UN

8 ♀

9 ♀

10 ♂

UN

11 ♂

UN

11 ♀

12 ♂

13 ♂

UN

13 ♀

14 ♂

UN

14 ♀

PLATE 37

# GIANT SKIPPERS: Megathymidae
(No. 1 × ¾, all others × 1)

1. **TEXAS YUCCA BORER** *Megathymus texanus*     p. 206
   ♂, White Deer, Carson Co., Tex. 27 May 1943; ♀, Hwy. 70, 18 mi.
   sw. of Portales, Roosevelt Co., N.M.
   ♀ larger than ♂. *Upperside:* FW spots small in ♂, large and
   yellow in ♀. No HW spots in ♂; HW spots large and numerous
   in ♀ (repeated on underside). *Underside:* FW spots repeated;
   HW spots few and small in ♂.

2. **MARIE'S AGAVE BORER** *Agathymus mariae*     p. 211
   ♂, ♀, Franklin Mts., 5 mi. ne. of Winton, El Paso Co., Tex. 5 Oct.
   1961
   *Upperside:* ♂ dull-colored, overscaling olive; spots small but
   complete. Spot bands wider in ♀; spots often fused.

3. **ARYXNA AGAVE BORER** *Agathymus aryxna*     p. 209
   ♀, 1 mi. w. of Peña Blanca Canyon, Ruby Rd., Santa Cruz Co.,
   Ariz. 25 Sept. 1960
   Fringes white, dark at vein tips. *Upperside:* Dark-colored; spots
   yellowish. Spots 7-8-9 about equal in size (see Fig. 13, p. 204).

4. **CHINATI MTS. AGAVE BORER**     p. 211
   *Agathymus chinatiensis*
   ♂, Hwy. 67, 2.7 mi. s. of Shafter, 4000 ft., Presidio Co., Tex. 21
   Oct. 1965; reared from pupa.

5. **RINDGE'S AGAVE BORER** *Agathymus rindgei*     p. 211
   ♂, 14 mi. n. of Bracketville on Hwy. 674, 1500 ft., Kinney Co.,
   Tex. 21 Oct. 1965; reared from pupa.
   ♀, 28 mi. n. of Del Rio, Tex. on Hwy. 277. 22 Oct. 1965; reared
   from pupa.
   *Upperside:* All 14 light spots present (see Fig. 13, p. 204), small
   and separate. Spots 7-8-9 progressively larger. HW spot band
   curved, complete. ♀ similar to ♂, but spots larger.

6. **GILBERT'S AGAVE BORER** *Agathymus gilberti*     p. 212
   ♂, ♀, 14 mi. n. of Bracketville on Hwy. 674, 1500 ft., Kinney Co.,
   Tex. 24 Oct. 1965; reared from pupa.
   *Upperside:* In ♂, all spots greatly reduced; spots 1-6 absent or
   nearly so; HW spot row of 2-3 spots in a straight line. In ♀, spots
   present but smaller than those of others in the Marie's Agave
   Borer group (see p. 210).

1 ♂

UN

1 ♀

UN

2 ♂

2 ♀

UN

3 ♀

4 ♂

5 ♂

5 ♀

6 ♂

6 ♀

PLATE 38

# SULFUR, ORANGE-TIPS, AND GIANT SKIPPERS:
## Pieridae and Megathymidae
(Nos. 1-5 × 1, all others × ¾)

1. **PROTERPIA ORANGE** *Eurema proterpia*     p. 142
   ♂, Sycamore Canyon, Santa Cruz Co., Ariz. 20 Sept. 1959
   *Upperside:* FW costa black; all veins black, at least in part.

2. **SARA ORANGE-TIP** *Anthocharis sara sara*     p. 146
   ♂, Partington Creek, Monterey Co., Calif. 19 May 1962
   *Upperside:* Orange FW tip large; apex black. *Underside:* HW marbling dense and "mossy."

3. **STELLA ORANGE-TIP** *Anthocharis sara stella*     p. 146
   ♀, Fallen Leaf Lake, El Dorado Co., Calif. 3 July 1971
   *Upperside:* Ground color yellowish in both sexes.

4. **PIMA ORANGE-TIP** *Anthocharis pima*     p. 145
   ♂, Sabino Canyon, Pima Co., Ariz. 30 July 1938
   *Upperside:* Ground color yellow; large blackish area at FW apex. *Underside:* Marbling very distinct.

5. **FELDER'S ORANGE-TIP** *Anthocharis cethura*     p. 145
   ♂, Little Rock, Los Angeles Co., Calif. 29 March 1931
   *Upperside:* FW apex has white spots along margin. *Underside:* Heavy marbling on HW.

6. **STRECKER'S YUCCA BORER**     p. 205
   *Megathymus streckeri*
   Petrified Forest, Apache Co., Ariz. ♂, 15 April 1966; ♀, 11 April 1966
   *Upperside:* Dull brownish black. FW spots larger on ♀ than on ♂. No spots on HW. *Underside:* Pm. spots large and white, forming irregular band on HW.

7. **URSUS YUCCA BORER**     p. 206
   *Megathymus ursus ursus*
   ♂, Miller Canyon, Huachuca Mts., Ariz. Emerged 3 Oct. 1965; reared from pupa. ♀, Peppersauce Canyon, Santa Catalina Mts., Pinal Co., Ariz. Emerged 1 July 1968; reared from pupa.
   Very large. Antennal club white. *Upperside:* Spots at FW apex white. FW band dark yellow, wider in ♀. No HW spots. *Underside:* Wing veins black in both sexes. HW dark gray.

8. **NEUMOEGEN'S AGAVE BORER**     p. 207
   *Agathymus neumoegeni*
   Rt. 89, 11 mi. sw. of Prescott, Yavapai Co., Ariz. ♂ emerged 3 Oct. 1965; ♀ emerged 30 Sept. 1966; both reared from pupa.
   *Upperside:* In ♂, spot 8 slightly larger than spot 9; outer end of spot 7 overlaps end of spot 6. FW costa dark in ♀; inner end of FW spot 9 pointed. *Underside:* HW dark gray in both sexes; light band indistinct.

1 ♂

2 ♂    UN

3 ♀

4 ♂    UN

5 ♂    UN

6 ♀

6 ♂    UN

1 ♂

7 ♀    UN

7 ♂    UN

8 ♂    UN

8 ♀

PLATE 39

# GIANT SKIPPERS AND SKIPPERS:
## Megathymidae and Hesperiidae
### (Nos. 1–4 × ¾, all others × 1)

1. **FREEMAN'S AGAVE BORER**          p. 210
   *Agathymus freemani*
   ♂, ♀, 1 mi. s. of Hillside, Yavapai Co., Ariz.; reared from pupa.
   *Upperside:* Overscaling orange; spots light yellowish. FW
   spots separate in ♂. *Underside:* Blackish in both sexes, with
   dull orange bands on HW.

2. **BAUER'S AGAVE BORER** *Agathymus baueri*     p. 209
   ♂, ♀, Verde Hot Springs, Yavapai Co., Ariz. Oct. 1963
   *Upperside:* Spots small. Fringes yellowish; vein tips dark.

3. **EVANS' AGAVE BORER** *Agathymus evansi*      p. 210
   ♂, Ramsey Canyon, Huachuca Mts., Cochise Co., Ariz.; ♀,
   Miller Park Trail, Huachuca Mts., Ariz. Reared from
   pupa. *Upperside:* Spots separated by dark veins; orange cell spot on
   FW. *Underside:* HW mottled gray; light bands indistinct.

4. **ALLIE'S AGAVE BORER** *Agathymus alliae*      p. 213
   ♂, ♀, Hwy. 64, 15 mi. w. of Cameron, Coconino Co., Ariz.
   Reared from pupa.
   *Upperside:* Spots orange, separated by dark veins.

5. **EUFALA SKIPPER** *Lerodea eufala*          p. 215
   Antioch, Contra Costa Co., Calif. 9 Sept. 1954
   *Upperside:* Subapical spots very small. *Underside:* Very gray.

6. **BRONZE ROADSIDE SKIPPER**         p. 217
   *Amblyscirtes aenus*
   Sierra Ancha Mts., Gila Co., Ariz. 16 July 1959
   *Upperside:* Greenish olive. *Underside:* FW cell dark.

7. **DEVA SKIPPER** *Atrytonopsis deva*        p. 221
   Chiricahua Mts., Cochise Co., Ariz. 23 May 1934
   *Upperside:* No FW cell spot; HW fringes white.

8. **DUN SKIPPER** *Euphyes ruricola ruricola*     p. 223
   Mendocino, Mendocino Co., Calif. 17 June 1962

9. **TAXILES SKIPPER** *Poanes taxiles*        p. 226
   ♂, Timpanogos Cave Natl. Monument, Utah. 27 June 1963; ♀,
   Boulder, Colo. 29 June 1954
   *Upperside and underside:* ♂ and ♀ very different.

10. **UMBER SKIPPER** *Paratrytone melane melane*    p. 225
    Santa Cruz, Santa Cruz Co., Calif. 1 Oct. 1934
    *Upperside:* Rich brown; FW spots light. ♂ lacks stigma.

11. **WOODLAND SKIPPER**           p. 227
    *Ochlodes sylvanoides sylvanoides*
    ♂, Riverton, El Dorado Co., Calif. 10 July 1938; ♀, Swanton,
    Santa Cruz Co., Calif. 10 Sept. 1953

12. **SANDHILL SKIPPER** *Polites sabuleti sabuleti*    p. 230
    Sherman I., Sacramento Co., Calif. 27 Aug. 1960
    *Upperside:* Border toothed. ♂ stigma ends in tawny ground
    color. *Underside:* Veins yellow. Irregular yellow band on HW.

1 ♂    UN      1 ♀      2 ♂

2 ♀      3 ♂   UN      3 ♀

4 ♂   UN      4 ♀   UN

5    UN      6    UN      7   UN

8   UN      9 ♂      9 ♀

10      11 ♂   UN      11 ♀      12 ♂   UN

PLATE 40

# GIANT SKIPPERS AND SKIPPERS:
## Megathymidae and Hesperiidae
(Nos. 1–3, 6 × ¾; all others × 1)

1. **VAL VERDE AGAVE BORER**      p. 212
   *Agathymus valverdiensis*
   ♂, 28 mi. n. of Del Rio, Val Verde Co., Tex. 23 Sept. 1965;
   reared from pupa.
   *Upperside:* Dark; FW spots small, complete. HW has 4 small
   spots in a line.

2. **STEPHENS' AGAVE BORER** *A. stephensi*      p. 212
   ♂, La Puerta Valley, San Diego Co., Calif. 18 Oct. 1965; ♀, ½
   mi. n. of Scissors Crossing, San Diego Co., Calif. 9 Oct. 1964
   *Upperside:* Buffy overscaling at wing bases. Straw-colored
   spots small but even; spots larger in ♀.

3. **POLING'S AGAVE BORER** *Agathymus polingi*      p. 212
   Molina Basin, Santa Catalina Mts., Pima Co., Ariz. ♂, 22 Oct.
   1961; ♀, 11 Oct. 1961
   Our smallest agave borer. Markings resemble those of the
   Neumoegen's Agave Borer group (pp. 207–209).

4. **WANDERING SKIPPER** *Panoquina errans*      p. 213
   Balboa, Orange Co., Calif. 21 Aug. 1934

5. **SYLVAN SKIPPER** *Panoquina sylvicola*      p. 214
   Santa Ana Wildlife Refuge, Hidalgo Co., Tex. 11 Nov. 1963
   *Upperside:* Light dash in FW cell. *Underside:* Pm. band of
   small powdery spots on HW.

6. **BRAZILIAN SKIPPER** *Calpodes ethlius*      p. 215
   Huntersville, Madison Co., Tenn. 22 Sept. 1951

7. **ARABUS SKIPPER** *Lerodia arabus*      p. 215
   Sabino Canyon, Pima Co., Ariz. 30 March 1938
   *Underside:* Brown patch in center of HW.

8. **LARGE ROADSIDE SKIPPER**      p. 216
   *Amblyscirtes exoteria*
   Madera Canyon, Santa Rita Mts., Ariz. 9 July 1960
   Large. *Underside:* Small white spots on HW.

9. **SIMIUS ROADSIDE SKIPPER** *A. simius*      p. 216
   Ft. Davis, Jeff Davis Co., Tex. 30 July 1953
   *Underside:* HW ashy gray. Row of small spots across FW and
   HW.

10. **CASSUS ROADSIDE SKIPPER** *A. cassus*      p. 216
    Rustler Park, Chiricahua Mts., Ariz. 13 July 1916
    *Upperside:* Tawny. *Underside:* FW cell tawny.

11. **OSLAR'S ROADSIDE SKIPPER** *A. oslari*      p. 217
    Red Rocks Park, Colo. 11 May 1956
    Color uniform. ♂ stigma black. *Underside:* HW gray; pm. spot
    row pale.

12. **ERNA'S ROADSIDE SKIPPER** *A. erna*      p. 217
    Palo Duro Canyon, Randall Co., Tex. 11 May 1966
    *Underside:* HW unmarked or nearly so.

1 ♂    UN

2 ♂

2 ♀    3 ♂    3 ♀

4    UN

5    UN

6

7    UN

8    UN

9    UN    10    UN    11    UN    12    UN

PLATE 41

# SKIPPERS: Hesperiidae (all × 1)

UN 1

UN 2

UN 3

UN 4

5 UN

6 UN

7

8

9 ♂ UN

10 ♂ UN

11 ♂ UN

12 ♂

13 ♂ UN

14 ♂ UN

15 ♂ UN

16 ♂ UN

17 ♀

18 ♂ UN

19 ♂ UN

PLATE 42

# SKIPPERS: Hesperiidae (all × 1)

1 ♂    UN

2 ♂    UN

3 ♂    UN

4 ♂    UN

4 ♀

5 ♂    UN

6 ♂    UN

7 ♂    UN

8 ♂    UN

9 ♂    UN

10 ♂    UN

11 ♂    UN

12 ♂    UN

13 ♂

14 ♂    UN

15 ♂    UN

16 ♂    UN

16 ♀    UN

17 ♂    UN

17 ♀

PLATE 43

# SKIPPERS: Hesperiidae (all × 1)

**Note:** The first 11 skippers are part of the Comma Skipper species complex (see p. 234).

1. **TILDEN'S SKIPPER** *Hesperia comma tildeni*     p. 236
   Arroyo Bayo, Mt. Hamilton, Calif. 7 Aug. 1954
2. **MANITOBA SKIPPER** *H. c. manitoba*     p. 234
   Alkali Lake, s. of Williams Lake, B.C. 14 Aug. 1968
3. **ASSINIBOIA SKIPPER** *H. c. assiniboia*     p. 235
   Miniota, Manitoba. 24 July 1931
4. **LEUSSLER'S SKIPPER** *H. c. leussleri*     p. 236
   San Ignacio, San Diego Co., Calif. 9 June 1956
5. **YOSEMITE SKIPPER** *H. c. yosemite*     p. 236
   Sherwin Hill, Calif. No date.
6. **DODGE'S SKIPPER** *H. c. dodgei*     p. 236
   Santa Cruz, Santa Cruz Co., Calif. 2 Aug. 1934
7. **OREGON SKIPPER** *H. c. oregonia*     p. 237
   Mt. Shasta, Siskiyou Co., Calif. 15 Aug. 1965
8. **HULBIRT'S SKIPPER** *H. c. hulbirti*     p. 237
   Hurricane Ridge, Olympic Natl. Park, Wash. 31 July 1962
9. **OCHRACEOUS SKIPPER** *H. c. ochracea*     p. 237
   Buffalo Creek, Colo. 29 July 1958
10. **COLORADO SKIPPER** *H. c. colorado*     p. 237
    Chicago Basin Trail, La Plata Co., Colo. 18 July 1934
11. **SUSAN'S SKIPPER** *H. c. susanae*     p. 237
    Graham Mts., Ariz. 27 July 1934
12. **YUBA SKIPPER** *Hesperia juba*     p. 238
    ♂, Coon Canyon, Oywanh Mts., Salt Lake Co., Utah. 25 May 1962
13. **WOODGATE'S SKIPPER** *Hesperia woodgatei*     p. 238
    1 mi. ne. of Turkey Creek, below Onion Saddle, Chiricahua Mts., Ariz. 28 Sept. 1969
14. **OTTOE SKIPPER** *Hesperia ottoe*     p. 238
    ♂, Higgins (Kansas?). 13 June. ♀, Barber Co., Kans. No date.
15. **PAWNEE SKIPPER** *Hesperia pawnee*     p. 239
    ♂, Rocky Flats, Boulder Co., Colo. 25 Aug. 1952
16. **PAHASKA SKIPPER** *Hesperia pahaska pahaska*     p. 239
    Lookout Mt., Clear Creek Co., Colo. 30 June 1977
17. **COLUMBIAN SKIPPER** *Hesperia columbia*     p. 240
    Mt. Hamilton, Santa Clara Co., Calif. 1 May 1954
18. **GREEN SKIPPER** *Hesperia viridis*     p. 239
    Lookout Mt., Clear Creek Co., Colo. 20 June, 1937
19. **DAKOTA SKIPPER** *Hesperia dacotae*     p. 240
    3 mi. se. of Felton, Clay Co., Minn. 4 July 1966
20. **LINDSEY'S SKIPPER** *Hesperia lindseyi*     p. 240
    Ukiah, Mendocino Co., Calif. 31 May 1952
21. **MIRIAM'S SKIPPER** *Hesperia miriamae*     p. 241
    Mt. Star, e. of Mono Pass, 12,500 ft., Inyo Co., Calif. 3 Aug. 1968
22. **NEVADA SKIPPER** *Hesperia nevada*     p. 241
    Golden, Colo. 4 June 1939

UN 1

UN 2

UN 3

UN 4

UN 5

UN 6

UN 7

UN 8

UN 9

UN 10

UN 11

12 ♂

13 UN

14 ♂ UN

14 ♀

15 ♂ UN

16 UN

17 UN

18 UN

19

20 UN

21 UN

22 UN

PLATE 44

# SKIPPERS: Hesperiidae
## (No. 24 × ⅔, all others × 1)

1

2 ♂

3 ♂

4

5

6

7 UN

8

9

10

11

12

13 UN

14 UN

15 UN

16

17 UN

18 UN

19 UN

20 UN

21 UN

22

23

24

PLATE 45

# SKIPPERS: Hesperiidae (all × 1)

1

2 UN

3 ♂   3 ♀

4   5   6   7   8 UN

9   10   11   12

13   14   15 UN   16

17   18   19 UN

20   21   22 ♂

PLATE 46

# SKIPPERS: Hesperiidae (all × 1)

1. **ASYCHIS SKIPPER** *Chiomara asychis georgina*     p. 263
   4 mi. w. of Boca Chica, Cameron Co., Tex. 20 Oct. 1963
   *Upperside:* Chalky white design on FW and HW.
2. **POWDERED SKIPPER** *Systasea pulverulenta*     p. 263
   Bexar Co., Tex. Emerged 10 June 1957; reared from larva.
   *Upperside:* Spots of FW hyaline band all in a line.
3. **EDWARDS' POWDERED SKIPPER** *S. zampa*     p. 263
   Madera Canyon, Santa Rita Mts., Ariz. 25 Aug. 1953
   *Upperside:* FW hyaline band displaced inward below cell
   (forms a "stair step").
4. **CEOS SOOTY-WING** *Staphylus ceos*     p. 264
   Cherry Lodge, Greenlee Co., Ariz. 8 July 1958
   *Upperside:* White spots near FW apex very small, translucent.
5. **SOUTHERN SOOTY-WING** *Staphylus hayhursti*     p. 264
   Des Moines, Iowa. 22 Aug. 1923
   *Upperside:* Wings crossed by two obscure darker bands.
6. **HIPPALUS SKIPPER** *Cogia hippalus*     p. 264
   Patagonia, Santa Cruz Co., Ariz. 1 Aug. 1940
7. **OUTIS SKIPPER** *Cogia outis*     p. 265
   San Antonio, Bexar Co., Tex. 2 June 1963; reared from larva.
   Smaller than the Hippalus Skipper (above). Fringes pale but
   not white.
8. **CAICUS SKIPPER** *Phoedinus caicus moschus*     p. 265
   Pinery Canyon, Chiricahua Mts., Ariz. 27 July 1967
   FW long. *Upperside:* FW spots small. *Underside:* Outer edge
   of HW frosted with white scales.
9. **MYSIE SKIPPER** *Phoedinus mysie*     p. 266
   Patagonia, Santa Cruz Co., Ariz. 1 Aug. 1940
   *Upperside:* Curved row of spots on FW. *Underside:* HW bands
   black on inner edges.
10. **NORTHERN CLOUDY-WING**     p. 266
    *Thorybes pylades albosuffusa*
    Ft. Davis, Jeff Davis Co., Tex. 9 June 1949
11. **DIVERSE CLOUDY-WING** *Thorybes diversus*     p. 266
    Mather, Tuolumne Co., Calif. 10 June 1961
12. **MEXICAN CLOUDY-WING**     p. 267
    *Thorybes mexicana nevada*
    W. slope of Mt. Dana, Yosemite Natl. Park, Calif. 20 July 1958
    *Upperside:* FW hyaline spots large, dark-edged.
13. **DRUSIUS CLOUDY-WING** *Thorybes drusius*     p. 267
    Washington Camp, Patagonia Mts., Ariz. 24 July 1960
14. **CASICA SKIPPER** *Achalarus casica*     p. 268
    Alpine, Brewster Co., Tex. 10 June 1944
    HW lobed; white fringes dark-scaled at bases.

PLATE 47

## SKIPPERS: Hesperiidae (all × 1)

1. **GOLDEN-BANDED SKIPPER** *Autochton cellus*       p. 268
   Atlanta, Fulton Co., Ga. 18 May 1958
   *Upperside:* Wide yellow FW band unique, except for next species.

2. **ARIZONA BANDED SKIPPER**                       p. 268
   *Autochton pseudocellus*
   Ramsey Canyon, Huachuca Mts., Ariz. 28 June 1936
   Antennal club has yellow ring at base.

3. **ARIZONA SKIPPER** *Codatractus arizonensis*       p. 269
   Box Canyon, Santa Rita Mts., Ariz. 2 Aug. 1959
   HW lobed. *Upperside:* Overscaling olive-brown; FW spots white. *Underside:* HW dark-banded, with a white edge.

4. **ARIZONA ARAXES SKIPPER**                       p. 272
   *Pyrrhopyge araxes arizonae*
   Madera Canyon, Santa Rita Mts., Ariz. 27 Aug. 1952
   Very large. HW outer margin scalloped. Fringes white, checkered. *Upperside:* FW spots white.

5. **SHORT-TAILED SKIPPER** *Zestusa dorus*       p. 270
   Madera Canyon, Santa Rita Mts., Ariz. 30 July 1960
   HW tail short. *Upperside:* Large angular FW spots. HW spots hyaline (clear).

6. **ARIZONA HAMMOCK SKIPPER**                       p. 271
   *Polygonus leo arizonensis*
   Box Canyon, Santa Rita Mts., Ariz. 30 July 1952
   FW long, square-ended; HW has short tail. *Upperside:* 3 large FW spots. *Underside:* Black spot at HW base, below costa.

7. **WHITE-STRIPED LONGTAIL**                       p. 270
   *Chioides catillus albofasciatus*
   Brownsville, Cameron Co., Tex. 30 Oct. 1963
   *Underside:* Conspicuous white stripe on HW.

1

2

3   UN

4   UN

5   UN

6   UN

7   UN

PLATE 48

# SKIPPERS: Hesperiidae (all × 1)

1. **HARPALUS SKIPPER** *Hesperia comma harpalus*    p. 235
   ♂, Leavitt Meadows, Mono Co., Calif. 14 Aug. 1950; ♀, Bridge-port, Mono Co., Calif. 14 Aug. 1950
   *Upperside:* ♂ tawny; border distinct; no dark marks near stigma. ♀ paler. *Underside:* Irregular macular band on HW white, complete.

2. **FIERY SKIPPER** *Hylephila phyleus*    p. 229
   ♂, Comaltepec, Oaxaca, Mexico. 8 Oct. 1961; ♀, Swanton, Santa Cruz Co., Calif. 20 Sept. 1957
   *Upperside:* ♂ bright; light anal vein crosses HW border at anal angle. ♀ dark, with small pale spots; anal vein as in ♂. *Under-side:* Small dark spots on HW; anal area black.

3. **LARGE WHITE SKIPPER** *Heliopetes ericetorum*    p. 253
   ♂, Padua Hills, Los Angeles Co., Calif. 12 Sept. 1949; ♀, San Antonio Valley, Santa Clara Co., Calif. 25 Aug. 1956
   *Upperside:* ♂ white, with a "lacy" border. ♀ slate gray, with a white median band and submarginal chevrons.

4. **COMMON CHECKERED SKIPPER**    p. 255
   *Pyrgus communis communis*
   Hanagan Meadows, Greenlee Co., Ariz. 8 June 1963
   *Upperside:* White spots narrow, crowded; 6 marginal dots on FW. *Underside:* White bars on HW distinct; white crescent at HW margin.

5. **PROPERTIUS DUSKY-WING** *Erynnis propertius*    p. 261
   Mt. Hamilton, Santa Clara Co., Calif. 31 March 1950
   *Upperside:* FW scales erect; gray scaling abundant.

6. **ARCTIC SKIPPER**    p. 248
   *Carterocephalus palaemon mandan*
   Brewster, Okanogan Co., Wash. 7 July 1960
   *Upperside:* Ground color dark; many orange spots. Unique.

7. **DORANTES SKIPPER** *Urbanus dorantes*    p. 269
   Brown Canyon, Baboquiviri Mts., Ariz. 7 Sept. 1949
   Wings broad; flaring tail on HW. *Upperside:* Brown. *Under-side:* Brown bands on HW broken into spots.

8. **LONG-TAILED SKIPPER** *Urbanus proteus*    p. 269
   Welder Wildlife Refuge, San Patricio Co., Tex. 5 Nov. 1963
   Long tails. *Upperside:* Wing bases green. *Underside:* Outer (submarginal) brown band on HW complete.

9. **NORTHERN CLOUDY-WING**    p. 266
   *Thorybes pylades pylades*
   Clear Lake Oaks, Lake Co., Calif. 24 May 1941
   *Upperside:* Dark brown (not black). *Underside:* Dark HW bands complete but irregular.

10. **SILVER-SPOTTED SKIPPER**    p. 271
    *Epargyreus clarus huachuca*
    Ramsey Canyon, Huachuca Mts., Ariz. 1 July 1936
    *Upperside:* Yellow FW spots unique in western U.S. *Under-side:* Large silver spot on HW.

1 ♂  UN

1 ♀

2 ♂  UN

2 ♀

3 ♂

3 ♀

4  UN

5

6  UN

7  UN

8  UN

9  UN

10  UN

**Range:** N. America, from British Columbia and Nova Scotia to Mexico; Cen. America; Venezuela. Common, widespread. **Habitat:** Very diverse; sea level to 10,000 ft. (3050 m).
**Subspecies:** Six similar subspecies are recognized. The **Modest Hairstreak,** *S. m. pudicus,* is shown on Pl. 32. TL: Contra Costa Co., Calif.

**AVALON HAIRSTREAK** *Strymon avalona* (Wright)      **Pl. 32**
**Identification:** ³/₄–1 in. (19–25 mm). Small, tailed. Male lacks stigma. *Upperside:* Mouse gray. HW may have small, whitish spots or rays near margin. Thecla spot small, yellow or red with a black base. *Underside:* Ash gray; inner half slightly darker. *Thecla (pm.) line and submarginal line faint.*
**Early stages:** Larva pale green to pink, covered with short white hairs. Three broods. **Food:** Silverleaf lotus *(Lotus argophyllus* var. *ornithopus).* **Adults:** Feb.–Oct.
**Range:** Catalina I., Calif. TL: Avalon. **Habitat:** Not stated.

**COLUMELLA HAIRSTREAK**                              **Pl. 32**
*Strymon columella* (Fabricius)
**Identification:** 1–1⅛ in. (25–28 mm). FW pointed in male, rounded in female. 1 HW tail. *Thecla spot black.* Male FW stigma large. *Upperside:* Male dark gray; in female, lower half of HW blue-gray, with 2–3 dark spots near margin. *Underside:* In both sexes, HW has many small dark crescent-shaped markings. Thecla spot black, ringed with dull orange-yellow; 2 small distinct black spots at HW costa.
**Early stages:** Larva dark green. Multiple broods. **Food:** Larva eats buds and green seeds of alkali mallow *(Sida hederacea).* **Adults:** Most of year in Tex.; Aug–Nov. in se. Calif.
**Range:** Southern U.S. to Cen. America and the West Indies. **Habitat:** Weedy fields, fencerows, roadsides, woodland trails.
**Subspecies:** (1) *S. c. columella* (Fabricius). TL: Hispaniola, West Indies. (2) *S. c. istapa* (Reakirt), Pl. 32. S. Calif. to Tex.; Mexico, Cen. America. TL: Vera Cruz, Mexico.

**LACEY'S HAIRSTREAK**                                **Pl. 32**
*Strymon alea* (Godman & Salvin)
**Identification:** 1–1⅛ in. (25–28 mm). *Upperside:* Gray; thecla spot and tornal spot *black, edged with white. Underside:* Median band dark in some specimens. Thecla (pm.) line dark, white-bordered. Submarginal markings well developed on HW, enclosing a more or less complete row of small dark spots, including the black thecla spot.
**Early stages:** Undescribed. Multiple broods. **Food:** Myrtle croton *(Bernardia myricifolia),* in the spurge family (Euphorbiaceae). **Adults:** Long flight season.
**Range:** S. Tex. to cen. Mexico; limits unknown, since so few speci-

mens have been collected. TL: Tres Marias Is., Nayarit, Mexico.
**Habitat:** Streamsides, small gulches.
**Remarks:** Very rare and local. Formerly known as *S. laceyi*
(Barnes & McDunnough). TL: Del Rio, Texas.

**BAZOCHII HAIRSTREAK**                                    **Pl. 32**
*Strymon bazochii* (Godart)
**Identification:** $\frac{7}{8}$-$1\frac{1}{8}$ in. (22-28 mm). No tails on HW. Male has
*large black FW stigma.* **Upperside:** FW dark grayish brown. HW
dull blue; border dusky; 2-3 dark marginal spots. **Underside:** FW
brown; narrow, inverted *pale triangle* at apex. HW mottled dark
brown, with a dark, white-ringed spot at costa and a pale diagonal
ray across entire wing. Female usually paler. Markings less complete in some individuals.
**Early stages:** Larva dark green, with light and dark bristles. Multiple broods. **Food:** In Tex., usually lippia (*Lippia,* various species). In Hawaii, usually lantana *(Lantana camara).* **Adults:**
Long flight season.
**Range:** S. Tex. to tropical America. Intentionally introduced into
Hawaii to control unwanted growth of lantana; now found on all
of the islands. TL: Brazil. **Habitat:** Brushy land and forest edges,
near food plant.
**Remarks:** Called the Smaller Lantana Butterfly in Hawaii.

### Genus *Erora* Scudder

**QUADERNA HAIRSTREAK**                                   **Pl. 32**
*Erora quaderna* (Hewitson)
**Identification:** $\frac{7}{8}$-$1\frac{1}{8}$ in. (22-28 mm). No tails. FW pointed. Male
has no stigma. **Upperside:** Male glossy dark brown; fringes *pale-
tipped.* Terminal line on HW *blue at anal angle.* Female has an
*iridescent blue area* on each wing; *fringes orange.* **Underside:**
Pale apple green. Submarginal and terminal lines on HW and the
thecla line across both wings broken into many *short coppery
dashes.*
**Early stages:** Unknown. Apparently one brood. **Food:** Unknown. **Adults:** June–July.
**Range:** S. Utah, Ariz., N.M., Mexico. Local, usually scarce, occasionally common. **Habitat:** Forest openings, trails and roadsides
in mountainous areas.
**Subspecies:** (1) **Quaderna Hairstreak,** *E. q. quaderna*
(Hewitson). TL: Mexico. (2) **Sanford's Hairstreak,**
*E. q. sanfordi* dos Passos, Pl. 32. Southwestern U.S. TL: Santa
Catalina Mts., Ariz.

## Coppers: Subfamily Lycaeninae

Small to medium-sized butterflies, best represented in N. America.
On upperside, males coppery, purplish, gray, or blue; females
much duller, often spotted. Sexes similar in appearance on under-

side. Most coppers live in temperate to cool mountainous localities. Some species are quite local.

## Tailed Copper: Genus *Tharsalea* Scudder

**TAILED COPPER** *Tharsalea arota* (Boisduval)  **Pl. 32**
**Identification:** 1⅛-1⅜ in. (28–34 mm). FW pointed; HW tailed. Looks like a hairstreak (pp. 155–180). *Upperside:* Male coppery brown; female spotted with orange-brown. *Underside:* In both sexes, FW gray, with a tawny flush in discal area. Spots black; submarginal band whitish. HW gray, scrawled with black; submarginal band composed of *whitish crescents*. Thecla spot black; tornal line red.
**Early stages:** Egg overwinters on bare twigs of food plant. Larva bright green. One brood. **Food:** Currant, gooseberry (*Ribes* species). **Adults:** May–July.
**Range:** Ore. east to Colo., south to s. Calif., Ariz., N.M., Baja California. **Habitat:** Mixed woodland, chaparral, sagebrush, forest edges.
**Subspecies:** (1) **Tailed Copper,** *T. a. arota* (Boisduval), Pl. 32. Ore., Nev., Calif. (TL). (2) **California Cloudy Copper,** *T. a. nubila* Comstock. Duller. Local. TL: Los Angeles, Calif. (3) **Virginia City Copper,** *T. a. virginiensis* (W. H. Edwards). Underside lighter. Nev. TL: Virginia City, Nev. (4) **Schellbach's Copper,** *T. a. schellbachi* Tilden. Much darker. Rocky Mts. TL: North Rim, Grand Canyon, Colo.

## Typical Coppers: Genus *Lycaena* Fabricius

**AMERICAN COPPER** *Lycaena phlaeas* (Linnaeus)  **Pl. 33**
**Identification:** ⅞-1¼ in. (22–31 mm). *Upperside:* FW bright copper; border dark grayish brown. 2 cell spots and pm. spots black — these spots vary in size and shape. HW dark grayish brown; marginal band copper. *Underside:* FW orange, with black spots and a gray border. HW light grayish brown, with small black spots and a *narrow reddish orange line* along margin.
**Early stages:** Larva rosy red, yellowish on sides, or green with a reddish stripe on back. Multiple broods in East, 1 brood in North and West. **Food:** Dock, sorrel *(Rumex),* knotweed *(Polygonum)* in East; not known for northern and western subspecies. **Adults:** July–Aug.
**Range:** Unusual; several isolated populations: (1) Far north, (2) Cen. and s. Canada, (3) near Miles City, Mont., (4) Yellowstone Natl. Park, (5) Sierra Nevada, Calif., (6) Carbon Co., Mont., and (7) Wallowa Co., Ore. In East, Nova Scotia to Georgia in the mountains. Common in parts of the East, uncommon to rare elsewhere. **Habitat:** In the West, mostly high mountain areas.
**Subspecies:** At least six subspecies are recognized, all quite similar. *L. p. americana* is shown on Pl. 33. TL: Massachusetts.

**LUSTROUS COPPER**                                           **Pl. 34**
*Lycaena cuprea* (W. H. Edwards)
**Identification:** 1⅛–1¼ in. (28–31 mm). Our brightest copper.
*Upperside:* Male *brilliant coppery red;* border and small spots
black. Black spots larger in female. *Underside:* Light gray, with
many small black spots. FW has an extensive copper flush.
Submarginal line black on FW, red on HW.
**Early stages:** Undescribed. One brood. **Food:** Dock, including
alpine sorrel *(Rumex pauciflorus)*. **Adults:** Late June–Aug.
**Range:** British Columbia south in Rocky Mts. to N.M., at high
elevations. On Pacific Slope, at moderate to high elevations; in cen.
Ore. to Sierra Nevada of Calif.; w. Nev. **Habitat:** Mountain mead-
ows, alpine fell-fields.
**Subspecies:** (1) **Lustrous Copper,** *L. c. cuprea* (W. H. Edwards),
Pl. 34. Ore., Calif., w. Nev. TL: Oregon. (2) **Snow's Copper,**
*L. c. snowi* (W. H. Edwards). Brassy copper; underside heavily
spotted. Rocky Mts. TL: Gray's Peak, Summit and Clear Creek
Cos., Colo. (3) **Henry's Copper,** *L. c. henryae* (Cadbury). Little
known. TL: Caribou Pass, British Columbia.

## Coppers: Genus *Gaeides* Scudder

**GREAT COPPER** *Gaeides xanthoides* (Boisduval)     **Pl. 33**
**Identification:** 1¼–1¾ in. (31–44 mm). *Upperside:* Male *brownish gray;* terminal line black, fringes pale. HW marginal spot
small, black, enclosed by dull orange. Female more heavily spotted, with a marginal orange band on HW and lower corner of FW.
*Underside:* Buffy to light gray, with many small dark spots.
*Submarginal chevrons often present on HW,* sometimes faint or
absent. Crescents at anal angle yellow, orange, or red.
**Similar species:** Edith's Copper (below) is smaller; underside
more heavily spotted. The two species do not occur together.
**Early stages:** Larva may be green, or dark orange barred with
magenta. Pupa pink or buff, marked with black. One brood. **Food:**
Dock *(Rumex,* various species). **Adults:** May–July, depending on
locality.
**Range:** The two subspecies are widely separated; see below. **Habitat:** Moist meadows, weedy fields, streamsides, marsh borders;
where dock grows.
**Subspecies:** (1) **Great Copper,** *G. x. xanthoides* (Boisduval), Pl.
33. Ore. and Nev. south to Baja California. TL: California. (2)
**Dione Copper,** *G. x. dione* (Scudder). Very large and dark; underside heavily spotted. Grasslands and prairies of the Plains states,
from Alberta south to Okla. TL: Denison & New Jefferson, Iowa.

**EDITH'S COPPER** *Gaeides editha* (Mead)           **Pl. 33**
**Identification:** 1⅛–1¼ in. (28–31 mm). *Upperside:* Male dark
brownish gray. Terminal line dark, fringes nearly white. 1–3 dark

spots at anal angle of HW. Dark markings on underside sometimes show through. Female spotted, with pale orange rays between veins, especially on FW. Some females from northern part of range may be very dark. *Underside:* Ground color dull gray in both sexes. FW spots black; those on HW show a "raindrop" effect — *flat, dull, more or less open, each enclosing a pale spot.* HW submarginal chevrons white; those at anal angle enclose 1–3 small orange spots.
**Similar species:** Great Copper (above).
**Early stages:** Undescribed. One brood. **Food:** Cinquefoil *(Potentilla),* horkelia *(Horkelia).* **Adults:** Late June–Aug.
**Range:** Wash. east to Mont., south to e.-cen. Calif., Nev., Utah, Colo. **Habitat:** Mountain meadows, forest openings, alpine fell-fields.
**Subspecies:** (1) **Edith's Copper,** *G. e. editha* (Mead), Pl. 33. Pacific Slope, Great Basin. TL: Near Carnelian Bay, Lake Tahoe, Calif. (2) **Montana Copper,** *G. e. montana* (Field). More heavily marked. Rocky Mts. region. TL: Broadwater Co., Mont.

**GORGON COPPER** *Gaeides gorgon* (Boisduval)        **Pl. 33**
**Identification:** 1¼–1½ in. (31–44 mm). *Upperside:* Male coppery brown with *bright reddish purple reflections;* dusky border narrow, fringes white. Female dark brown, checkered with tawny, spotted with black; HW border has a row of *small black spots* capped by *orange crescents.* *Underside:* Both sexes gray, with many small black spots. HW has a submarginal row of *small red spots* between two rows of smaller black spots.
**Early stages:** Larva pale green, with many white hairs. Pupa pale blue-green. One brood. **Food:** Long-stemmed eriogonum *(E. elongatum)* in s. Calif.; naked eriogonum *(E. nudum)* in cen. Calif. and Ore. **Adults:** May–June.
**Range:** S. Ore. to s. Calif.; Baja California. TL: Mountains of Calif. **Habitat:** Coastal sage scrub, rocky outcrops, rocky hills, cut banks.

## Bronze Copper: Genus *Hyllolycaena* Miller & Brown

**BRONZE COPPER** *Hyllolycaena hyllus* (Cramer)        **Pl. 33**
**Identification:** 1¼–1½ in. (31–38 mm). *Upperside:* Male copper brown, with dark wing borders and pale fringes; *HW has marginal orange band.* In female, FW orange, with dark border and many small dark spots; HW as in male. *Underside:* FW pale orange in both sexes; outer edge gray. HW ashy gray, with an orange marginal band as on upperside. Wings covered with many small black spots.
**Early stages:** Larva yellowish green, with a dark stripe down the back. Two broods. **Food:** Curly dock *(Rumex crispus),* and perhaps other species of dock. **Adults:** May–June and in Aug.
**Range:** Ft. Simpson, Northwest Terr. south to e. Colo., N.D., S.D.,

Neb., Kans., east to Me., N.J. TL: "Smyrna," in error. **Habitat:** Wet meadows, edges of marshes, lakes, and ponds. **Remarks:** Called *Lycaena thoe* in older literature.

## Genus *Chalceria* Scudder

**RUDDY COPPER** *Chalceria rubida* (Behr)               **Pl. 33**
**Identification:** $1\frac{1}{8}$–$1\frac{3}{8}$ in. (28–34 mm). *Upperside:* Male *bright reddish copper,* with a black terminal line and white fringes. Base of HW has dusky overscaling. Marginal line or crescents lighter. Female heavily spotted, with dark borders; fringes usually white or light-colored. Ground color either orange or brown. *Underside:* Whitish to dull yellow-gray. FW has well-developed black spots; HW may or may not have small dark spots, depending on subspecies.
**Early stages:** Little known. One brood. **Food:** Dock (*Rumex,* various species). **Adults:** Late June–Aug., depending on locality. **Range:** British Columbia, Alberta, N.D. south to cen. Calif., e. Ariz., Colo. TL: Ore. **Habitat:** Dry fields, meadows, sagebrush, shadscale scrub, streamsides in arid areas.
**Subspecies:** Work published in 1977 recognizes six rather similar subspecies. *C. r. rubida* is shown on Pl. 33.

**FERRIS'S COPPER**                                      **Pl. 36**
*Chalceria ferrisi* (Johnson & Balogh)
**Identification:** $1\frac{1}{8}$–$1\frac{1}{4}$ in. (28–31 mm). *Wings shorter and more rounded* than those of Ruddy Copper (above). *Upperside:* In both sexes, markings like those of Ruddy Copper, but ground color deeper and more reddish. *Underside:* Both sexes light gray to buffy gray; disc of FW dull orange. Spots near base of FW present. *Pm. spots* on FW and HW form a complete row; *the spots are small and black.*
**Similar species:** In Ruddy Copper (above), underside brighter, less grayish.
**Early stages:** Unknown. One brood. **Food:** Desert rhubarb, canaigre *(Rumex hymenosepalus).* **Adults:** July–Aug.
**Range:** White Mts., Apache Co., Ariz. TL: Apache Ditch Camp, 13 mi. east of McNary, Ariz. **Habitat:** Meadows, ciénagas.
**Remarks:** First distinguished from the Ruddy Copper and described in 1977.

**VARIED BLUE or BLUE COPPER**                          **Pls. 33, 36**
*Chalceria heteronea* (Boisduval)
**Identification:** $1\frac{1}{8}$–$1\frac{3}{8}$ in. (28–34 mm). *Upperside:* Male (shown on Pl. 33) is *brilliant blue,* with slightly darker veins. Terminal line black, fringes white. Female (Pl. 36) is dull bluish to dark gray or dark brown, with *many small dark spots.* Fringes whitish, terminal line indistinct. *Underside:* Shiny white to cream in both sexes.

FW always has several small black dots. *HW varies from unspotted* to rather heavily spotted depending on local variants or populations.
**Early stages:** Larva greenish gray, covered with short white hairs. Pupa green, suspended by a girdle. **Food:** Various species of wild buckwheat *(Eriogonum)*.
**Range:** S. British Columbia and s. Alberta south to s.-cen. Calif., Ariz., n. N.M. **Habitat:** Mixed brushland, sagebrush, mountain meadows, open forest; usually at high elevations, but at low elevations in cen. coastal Calif.
**Subspecies:** (1) **Varied Blue,** *C. h. heteronea* (Boisduval), Pl. 36. All of range, except where the following subspecies occurs. TL: Mountains of Calif. (2) **Bright Blue Copper,** *C. h. clara* (Hy. Edwards). Female bluish. Tehachapi Mts. of s.-cen. Calif. TL: Tehachapi, Kern Co., Calif.

## Genus *Epidemia* Scudder

**DORCAS COPPER** *Epidemia dorcas* (W. Kirby)          **Pl. 33**
**Identification:** $7/8$–$1\frac{1}{8}$ in. (22–28 mm). Small. *Upperside:* Male dark brown, with violet reflections visible in certain lights. Dusky borders *wide;* several small black spots on each wing. Orange markings at HW margin *reduced,* often to only a spot at anal angle. Female duller, with or without lighter, dull orange or brownish yellow areas. *Underside:* FW brownish yellow in both sexes, with many black spots. FW apex and all of HW light violet-brown. Spots on HW few and small; a row of *dull orange crescents near margin.*
**Similar species:** Purplish Copper (below).
**Early stages:** Undescribed. One brood. **Food:** Shrubby cinquefoil *(Potentilla fruticosa).* **Adults:** Late June to Aug.
**Range:** Alaska east to Labrador, Newfoundland, south in Rocky Mts. to Utah, N.M. In East to Mich., Me. TL: The Pas, Manitoba. **Habitat:** Fields, openings, bogs, tundra, taiga.
**Subspecies:** Seven subspecies have been placed under the Dorcas Copper. They are reasonably similar. Subspecies *claytoni* is shown on Pl. 33.
**Remarks:** Some lepidopterists consider at least some of the seven subspecies to belong under the Purplish Copper (below). The matter remains unresolved.

**PURPLISH COPPER** *Epidemia helloides* (Boisduval)     **Pl. 33**
**Identification:** 1–$1\frac{3}{8}$ in. (25–34 mm). *Upperside:* Male coppery brown with brilliant purple reflections and numerous small black spots. Dusky border *narrow.* HW submarginal line formed of *connected orange crescents.* Female usually orange-brown, with *dark* wing bases and *wide, dark margins;* many black spots. Occasional females are very dark. *Underside:* In both sexes, HW dull yellow-

ish-brown with a few small black spots; submarginal orange crescents distinct to faint.
**Similar species:** (1) Dorcas Copper (p. 185). (2) Nivalis Copper
(below).
**Early stages:** Larva green, with a double line along back; also has
a stripe and a series of oblique yellow dashes along side. Multiple
broods. **Food:** Yard knotweed *(Polygonum aviculare),* willow
smartweed *(P. lapathifolium),* sheep sorrel *(Rumex acetosella),*
and others. **Adults:** March–Oct. at low elevations, June–Aug. at
high elevations.
**Range:** S. Canada south through western N. America, east to Ontario, Mich.; Baja California. Often very common. TL: San Francisco, Calif. **Habitat:** General; mountain meadows, desert oases,
marshes, yards, vacant lots, roadsides.

## NIVALIS COPPER                                     Pl. 33, 36
*Epidemia nivalis* (Boisduval)
**Identification:** 1–1⅜ in. (25–34 mm). *Upperside:* Male (Pl. 33)
coppery brown, with lilac reflections; dusky border moderate.
Submarginal line on HW *orange, irregular.* 2–4 small, dark spots
at margin. Female (Pl. 36) usually dull orange, *the borders and
spots black; FW spots larger. Underside:* Variable in both sexes.
FW yellowish white to brownish yellow, heavily spotted. HW
pinkish gray, the overscaling at base greenish gray, discal area usu-
ally unspotted, but heavily spotted in some Oregon populations.
**Similar species:** Purplish Copper (above).
**Early stages:** One brood. **Food:** Douglas's knotweed *(Polygonum
douglasii);* perhaps others. **Adults:** Late June–Aug.
**Range:** British Columbia south in mountains to cen. Calif. (Sierra
Nevada), Nev., Utah, Colo. **Habitat:** Mountain meadows, forest
openings, streamsides, sagebrush flats, alpine fell-fields.
**Subspecies:** (1) **Nivalis Copper,** *E. n. nivalis* (Boisduval), Pls.
33, 36. Calif., Nev., s. Ore. TL: Calif. (2) **Brown's Copper,** *E. n.
browni* (dos Passos). In male, outer ⅓ of HW pink on underside.
Female often dark, and spotted on underside of HW. Northern;
Rocky Mts. TL: Snowslide, Idaho.

## MARIPOSA COPPER                                    Pls. 33, 36
*Epidemia mariposa* (Reakirt)
**Identification:** 1⅛–1¼ in. (28–31 mm). *Upperside:* Male (Pl. 33)
copper brown; dusky border moderate to wide. Orange spot or line
at anal angle present or absent. Female (Pl. 36) heavily spotted
with black; *broken orange-brown bands* on FW and HW. *Underside:* FW yellowish in both sexes, with black spots and gray
overscaling. HW light to dark gray, with *narrow black crescents.*
Submarginal line composed of *inward-facing light chevrons* that
partially enclose dark marginal spots.
**Early stages:** Unknown. One brood. **Food:** Douglas's knotweed
*(Polygonum douglasii);* perhaps others. **Adults:** July–Aug.

**Range:** Yukon Terr. to Alberta, south to cen. Calif., Colo. **Habitat:** Forest openings, edges of mountain meadows.
**Subspecies:** (1) **Mariposa Copper,** *E. m. mariposa* (Reakirt), Pls. 33, 36. W. Ore., W. Nev., Calif. TL: Calif. (2) **Penrose's Copper,** *E. m. penrosae* (Field). Pacific Northwest, Rocky Mts. Much darker. TL: Lake Eleanor, Yellowstone Natl. Park, Wyo. (3) **Northern Copper,** *E. m. charlottensis* (Holland). Small, dark; underside heavily spotted. Northern. TL: Queen Charlotte Is., British Columbia.

## Genus *Hermelycaena* Miller & Brown

**HERMES COPPER**                                                    **Pl. 33**
*Hermelycaena hermes* (W. H. Edwards)
**Identification:** 1-1¼ in. (25-31 mm). HW has 1 tail. *Upperside:* Brown. FW has a yellow or orange area enclosing several black spots. HW marginal spots or band orange; terminal line black. *Underside:* FW yellow, with 4-6 black spots; *HW bright yellow,* with 3-6 black dots.
**Early stages:** One brood. **Food:** Redberry *(Rhamnus crocea),* in the buckthorn family. **Adults:** May–July. They visit flowers of wild buckwheat *(Eriogonum).*
**Range:** Very local. S. San Diego Co. south into Baja California. TL: California. **Habitat:** Chaparral, mixed woodland.

# Blues: Subfamily Polyommatinae

Small butterflies. Males are usually blue; females are brown or spotted. Both sexes look similar on underside. Wings more rounded, less triangular, than those of other butterflies in the family (Lycaenidae). Blues are found worldwide; there are many species in our region.

## Pygmy Blues: Genus *Brephidium* Scudder

**PYGMY BLUE** *Brephidium exile* (Boisduval)                      **Pl. 34**
**Identification:** ½-¾ in. (12-19 mm). *Very small;* usually considered our smallest butterfly. *Upperside:* Coppery brown; wing bases dull blue. *Outer angle of FW has a small white spot.* Outer margin of HW has a row of small dark spots (sometimes indistinct). Fringes white. *Underside:* Coppery brown, dappled with white. HW has 3 small black postbasal spots; outer margin has a row of 4-6 black iridescent spots.
**Early stages:** Larva has tubercles with white projections; it resembles the scurfy surface of its food plants. Multiple broods. **Food:** Saltbush *(Atriplex,* various species), lamb's-quarters *(Chenopodium album),* and many other plants in the saltbush family (Chenopodiaceae). **Adults:** Long flight season. Weak fliers; they hover over food plants.

**Range:** E. Ore. east to Neb., south to Calif., Ariz., N.M., Tex.; south to Venezuela. Common. Found on Oahu, Hawaii, in 1978. TL: California. **Habitat:** Shadscale scrub, alkali flats, salt marshes, vacant lots, weedy fields, roadsides, farm yards.

## Grass Blues: Genus *Zizula* Chapman

**CYNA BLUE** *Zizula cyna* (W. H. Edwards)          **Pl. 34**
**Identification:** Very small; $\frac{5}{8}$–$\frac{7}{8}$ in. (16–22 mm). Wings long and narrow. *Upperside:* Dull blue with *wide dusky borders. Underside:* Dull white or pale gray with many small black dots.
**Early stages:** Unknown. Multiple broods. **Food:** Unknown. **Adults:** March–Sept. Flight low and weak.
**Range:** S. Ariz., N.M., Tex., south to Colombia. TL: San Antonio, Bexar Co., Tex. **Habitat:** Not stated.
**Remarks:** Very local. Once thought to be introduced from Africa, but now believed to be native. Uncommon. Easily overlooked.

## Long-tailed Blue: Genus *Lampides* Huebner

**LONG-TAILED BLUE** *Lampides boeticus* (Linnaeus)     **Pl. 34**
**Identification:** 1–1$\frac{3}{8}$ in. (25–34 mm). HW tailed. *Upperside:* Light brownish, with strong lavender-blue reflections. Border narrow, dusky. *Thecla spot and tornal spot on HW black. Underside:* FW and HW pale brown, with many wavy white lines. Submarginal band white; HW anal area dull orange. Thecla spot and tornal spot black with green iridescence.
**Early stages:** Larva yellowish green, with a dark stripe down the back. Multiple broods. **Food:** Various legumes, including cultivated beans. **Adults:** Long flight period. Strong fliers.
**Range:** Widely distributed; Europe, Africa, Asia, Australia. Accidentally introduced into the Hawaiian Islands about 100 years ago, and now found on all the islands; not in continental U.S. TL: Algeria. **Habitat:** Yards, parks, gardens, fields, roadsides, brushlands.

## Genus *Vaga* Zimmerman

**BLACKBURN'S BLUE** *Vaga blackburni* (Tuely)          **Pl. 32**
**Identification:** $\frac{7}{8}$–1$\frac{1}{8}$ in. (22–28 mm). The only native blue in Hawaii. *Upperside:* Deep iridescent violet (looks gray in dim light). *Underside: Iridescent green; lower half of FW gray.*
**Early stages:** Multiple broods. **Food:** Originally koa *(Acacia koa),* but now feeds on a number of introduced legumes. **Adults:** Long flight season.
**Range:** Restricted to the Hawaiian Is. TL: Upper Nuuanu Valley, Oahu. **Habitat:** Hills, mountains, usually above coastal plain. Common on the slopes of Mt. Tantalus, Oahu.

## Tropical Blues: Genus *Leptotes* Scudder

**MARINE BLUE** *Leptotes marina* (Reakirt)          **Pl. 34**
**Identification:** $7/8$–$1\frac{1}{8}$ in. (22–28 mm). *Upperside:* Fringes white.
Male pale, iridescent lavender-blue, with a narrow dark border.
Vague dark spots at anal angle of HW. Female has light streaks
and vague dark spots; dark border wide. *Underside:* Pale brown,
with *many narrow, irregular, light bands.* Two small black iridescent spots at HW anal angle.
**Similar species:** (1) Ceraunus Blue (below) has small black
postbasal spots on underside of HW. (2) Reakirt's Blue (p. 190) has
pm. band of black spots on underside of FW.
**Early stages:** Larva variable, green to brown. Multiple broods.
**Food:** Various legumes; wisteria, alfalfa, rattleweed *(Astragalus),*
pea *(Lathyrus),* and many others; also leadwort. Larva eats buds,
blossoms and seedpods. **Adults:** During warm part of year.
**Range:** N.-cen. Calif. east to Neb. and Kans., south to s. Calif.,
Ariz., N.M., Tex. South to Cen. America. TL: Orizaba and near
Vera Cruz, Mexico. **Habitat:** Thorn scrub, desert, yards, parks,
roadsides, fencerows. Follows cultivated legumes into urban areas.

## Eyed Blues: Genus *Hemiargus* Huebner

**CERAUNUS BLUE** *Hemiargus ceraunus* (Fabricius)          **Pl. 34**
**Identification:** $3/4$–1 in. (19–25 mm). *Upperside:* Fringes white.
Male light blue, with a narrow dark border; often a small dark spot
on outer margin of HW. Female dark brown; wing bases often
blue; dark spots usually present at HW margin. *Underside:* Both
sexes dull gray, with narrow whitish lines and small dusky spots.
HW has 3 small dark postbasal spots and *1–2 yellow-ringed, black,
iridescent spots* at margin.
**Similar species:** (1) Marine Blue (above). (2) Reakirt's Blue (p.
190).
**Early stages:** Larva red or green with a red stripe on back. Multiple broods. **Food:** Buds and seedpods of legumes, including
mesquite *(Prosopis glandulosa* var. *torreyana),* screwbean
*(P. pubescens),* whiteball acacia *(Acacia angustissima* var. *hirta),*
snoutbean *(Rhynchosia minima),* and others. **Adults:** March–
Nov.
**Range:** S. Calif., s. Nev., s. Utah south to Ariz., east to Tex. Also
Fla., Ala.; Mexico; Antilles. **Habitat:** Deserts, mesquite land,
scrub brush, roadsides, fencerows.
**Subspecies:** (1) **Ceraunus Blue,** *H. c. ceraunus* (Fabricius). Antilles; not in our area. (2) **Zachaeina Blue,** *H. c. zachaeina* (But-
ler & Druce). Larger, darker. Tex. southward. TL: Cartago, Costa
Rica. (3) **Gyas Blue,** *H. c. gyas* (W. H. Edwards), Pl. 34. Much
lighter. Calif., Ariz. TL: Tucson, Pima Co., Ariz.

**REAKIRT'S BLUE** *Hemiargus isola* (Reakirt)                    **Pl. 34**
**Identification:** ³/₄–1 in. (19–25 mm). Fringes white. *Upperside:*
Male light blue with slightly darker wing veins; dusky border
blends into blue of wing. HW has 1–3 dark marginal spots. Female
similar, but much darker. *Underside:* Light gray with narrow pale
lines. *Pm. spots on FW black, ringed with white.* HW has 3–5
small, dark postbasal spots and 1–3 iridescent marginal spots.
**Similar species:** (1) Marine Blue (p. 189). (2) Ceraunus Blue
(p. 189).
**Early stages:** Undescribed. Multiple broods in south, 1 in north,
where it reinvades each year after overwintering in the south.
**Food:** Many legumes, including mesquite, screwbean, indigo
*(Indigofera),* rattleweed *(Astragalus),* and many others. **Adults:**
April–Oct.
**Range:** N.-cen. Calif. east to Neb., south to s. Calif., Ariz., N.M.,
Tex., east to Minn., La.; south to Costa Rica. Scarce or rare at
northern limits of range; has been reported from British Columbia.
**Habitat:** General, but most common at low elevations southward.
**Subspecies:** (1) *H. i. isola* (Reakirt). TL: Veracruz, Mexico. (2)
*H. i. alce* (W. H. Edwards), Pl. 34. United States. TL: Turkey
Creek, Jefferson Co., Colo.

### Orange-margined Blues: Genus *Lycaeides* Huebner

**NORTHERN BLUE** *Lycaeides idas* (Linnaeus)              **Pl. 34**
**Identification:** ⁷/₈–1¹/₄ in. (22–31 mm). *Upperside:* Male iridescent violet-blue, with a narrow black border and white fringes. HW
may have small, indistinct dark marginal spots. Female brown,
often glossed with blue, or blue only at wing bases; a *submarginal
band of orange chevrons* crosses both FW and HW. *Underside:*
Both sexes have submarginal orange spots, capped with black and
each enclosing an iridescent green spot; these spots *cross both FW
and HW* but are usually better developed on HW. FW terminal
line very narrow. *Each HW vein tip has a small black end.*
**Similar species:** Melissa Blue (p. 191).
**Early stages:** Little known. One brood. **Food:** Not known for
most subspecies. Legumes, including lupine, lotus, pea *(Lathyrus).*
In Nova Scotia, female lays eggs on crowberry *(Empetrum ni-
grum).* In Europe, larva feeds on axseed *(Coronilla varia),* in the
pea family. **Adults:** June–Aug.
**Range:** Holarctic. Alaska, n. Canada south to cen. Calif., Colo.
Europe; n. Asia. **Habitat:** Mountain meadows, forest clearings,
trails, openings, and bogs; always in cool climates.
**Subspecies:** *L. i. idas.* Not found in N. America. TL: Sweden.
Nine other subspecies occur in the West, including the **Anna Blue,**
*L. i. anna,* Pl. 34. TL: "California"; near Truckee, Nevada Co.,
Calif.
**Remarks:** *Lycaeides idas* was formerly called *L. argyrognomon.*

**MELISSA BLUE** *Lycaeides melissa* (W. H. Edwards)    **Pl. 34**
**Identification:** $\frac{7}{8}$-1$\frac{1}{4}$ in. (22-31 mm). *Upperside:* Male lilac blue, with a narrow black border and white fringes. Dark marginal spots on HW very faint. Female similar to that of Northern Blue (p. 190), but orange submarginal band usually *wider* and more solid. *Underside:* In both sexes, submarginal band usually wider and brighter than that of Northern Blue. *Terminal line* usually well developed, *connecting the dark spots* at the ends of the veins.
**Similar species:** Northern Blue (p. 190).
**Early stages:** Larva green, darker above, yellowish on sides. 2-3 broods. **Food:** Lotus, lupine, alfalfa, rattleweed *(Astragalus),* American licorice *(Glycyrrhiza lepidota),* all in the pea family.
**Adults:** May-Sept.
**Range:** Cen. Canada south through the West except in Tex.; east to N.H., N.C.; Mexico. **Habitat:** Varied. Mountain meadows, openings, alkali sinks, marshes, oases, farms, unused fields, roadsides.
**Subspecies:** (1) **Melissa Blue,** *L. m. melissa* (W. H. Edwards), Pl. 34. Widely distributed. TL: La Plata Peak, Lake Co., Colo. (2) **Annetta Blue,** *L. m. annetta* (W. H. Edwards). Very pale. Great Basin. TL: Near Salt Lake City. (3) **Friday's Blue,** *L. m. fridayi* (F. H. Chermock). Eastern slope of Sierra Nevada. TL: Mammoth, Calif. (4) **Orange-margined Blue,** *L. m. paradoxa* (F. H. Chermock). Large, bright; female often blue at wing bases on upperside. S. Sierra Nevada, Owens Valley, e. Calif., w. Nev. TL: Tehachapi Mts., Calif.

## Genus *Plebejus* Kluk

**GREENISH BLUE** *Plebejus saepiolus* (Boisduval)    **Pl. 34**
**Identification:** 1-1$\frac{1}{4}$ in. (25-31 mm). *Upperside:* Male iridescent blue, usually with greenish reflections; *border wide,* fringes white. Female may be dark brown, gray with blue wing bases, blackish shot with blue, or bluish, but is always darker than the male. Both sexes have a *FW cell bar. Underside:* Male whitish; female pale brown or gray. Both sexes have many small black spots. Spots of pm. line the *same size on both FW and HW.* Marginal spots in cells $Cu_1$ to 2A of HW usually tipped with dull orange.
**Similar species:** Boisduval's Blue (p. 192).
**Early stages:** Not described. 1-2 broods. **Food:** Clover *(Trifolium),* bird's-foot trefoil *(Lotus).* **Adults:** May-Aug.
**Range:** Cen. Alaska, cen. and s. Canada, western U.S. south to s. Calif., N.M.; Baja California. In East to Me. and Mich. **Habitat:** Open forest, meadows, bogs, roadsides, fields, pastures.
**Subspecies:** Six rather similar subspecies are recognized, including *P. s. saepiolus,* shown on Pl. 34. TL: Mountains of California.

## Genus *Plebulina* Nabokov

**SAN EMIGDIO BLUE**                                          **Pl. 34**
*Plebulina emigdionis* (F. Grinnell)
**Identification:** $7/8$-$1\frac{1}{8}$ in. (22-28 mm). *Upperside:* Male pale
powdery blue with *wide dusky borders;* HW has faint orange aurora and 2-4 dark marginal spots. Female brown, wing bases bluish; FW has orange-brown rays between ends of wing veins. Aurora
as in male but wider. *Underside:* Dull white, with many black
spots. *Pm. spot in cell Cu$_1$ of FW displaced inward.* Marginal spots
iridescent green with black centers that are capped with orange or
yellow.
**Similar species:** (1) Acmon Blue (p. 193) and (2) Lupine Blue
(p. 194) have a conspicuous orange or pink aurora on upperside of
HW. (3) Dotted blues (genus *Euphilotes,* p. 197) do not have irides-
cent green spots on underside of HW.
**Early stages:** Larva variable: green, blue-green, gray, or brown.
Multiple broods; the early brood is always successful. **Food:**
Shadscale *(Atriplex canescens).* **Adults:** April–Sept., depending
on rainfall.
**Range:** Inyo Co., Calif. south through Mojave Desert, lower San
Joaquin Valley, Bouquet and Mint Canyons, Los Angeles Co.
Local; lives in colonies. TL: San Emigdio Canyon, Kern Co., Calif.
**Habitat:** Shadscale scrub, often near streambeds or washes.
**Remarks:** The San Emigdio Blue has usually been placed in the
genus *Plebejus.*

## Genus *Icaricia* Nabokov

**BOISDUVAL'S BLUE**                                          **Pl. 34**
*Icaricia icarioides* (Boisduval)
**Identification:** $1\frac{1}{8}$-$1\frac{3}{8}$ in. (28-34 mm). A large species, without
aurora or iridescent spots. In both sexes, cell bars usually visible on
both FW and HW. *Upperside:* Male light blue with lilac reflections; wing veins slightly darker. Border dark, moderately wide on
FW, narrow on HW. HW usually has 2-4 indistinct dark marginal
spots. Female variable — may be dark blue with wide dark border,
or brown. *Underside:* In both sexes, *pm. spots much larger on FW
than on HW;* all black spots more or less *white-ringed.* In some
subspecies these spots are white, with or without dark centers.
**Similar species:** Greenish Blue (p. 191).
**Early stages:** Larva green, with 3 indistinct oblique bars on the
side of each segment. One brood. **Food:** Lupine, especially perennial species. **Adults:** April–Aug., depending on locality.
**Range:** British Columbia east to Manitoba and western edge of
the Great Plains, south to mountains of s. Calif., Ariz., N.M.; Baja
California. Widely distributed, often common. **Habitat:** Open
woodland, chaparral, forest edges, coastal dunes and hills, uncultivated fields.

**Subspecies:** Sixteen are currently recognized, differing in the shade of blue and in the underside markings, but recognizably similar. *I. i. icarioides* is shown on Pl. 34. TL: Mountains of California.
**Remarks:** Although the genus *Icaricia* was proposed in 1945, the species placed in it have been retained in the genus *Plebejus* by some authors.

**SHASTA BLUE** *Icaricia shasta* (W. H. Edwards)          **Pl. 34**
**Identification:** $^7/_8$-1$^1/_8$ in. (22-28 mm). *Upperside:* Male lilac blue, with a wide brownish border. Cell bars dark, *well marked on both FW and HW.* HW marginal spots dark, sometimes missing; fringes white. Female similar but darker; HW may have a weak orange aurora, enclosing the dark marginal spots. *Underside:* Light to dull gray in both sexes. Pm. spots black; other spots dark gray; all spots usually white-ringed. HW aurora yellow or buffy, enclosing 4-6 iridescent green spots *edged inwardly by an indefinite light band.*
**Early stages:** Little known. One brood. **Food:** Lyall's lupine *(Lupinus lyalli)* in Calif.; King's locoweed *(Astragalus calycosus)* in Nev.; also clover *(Trifolium,* various species). **Adults:** June–Aug.
**Range:** Wash. east to Alberta, Mont., Neb., south to cen. Calif., Colo.; at high elevations. **Habitat:** Alpine fell-fields; forest openings (Ore.), cold prairies (Wyo., Neb., N.D.).
**Subspecies:** (1) **Shasta Blue,** *I. s. shasta* (W. H. Edwards), Pl. 34. (2) **Minnehaha Blue,** *I. s. minnehaha* (Scudder). Markings on underside reduced. Uncommon. Found on cold prairies. TL: Heart River Crossing, N.D. (3) **Brown's Blue,** *I. s. pitkinensis* (Ferris). Small, dull. Colo., at very high elevations. TL: Snowmass Lake, Pitkin Co., Colo.

**ACMON BLUE**                                              **Pl. 34**
*Icaricia acmon* (Westwood & Hewitson)
**Identification:** $^3/_4$-1 in. (19-25 mm). *Upperside:* Fringes white. Male pale lilac blue, dark border narrow; no cell bars. HW marginal spots black, separate; *aurora pink.* Female brown, with or without blue gloss; FW cell bar present. Aurora orange. *Underside:* Both sexes whitish with small black spots. Aurora orange, its spots elongate; marginal spots *iridescent green.*
**Similar species:** Lupine Blue (p. 194).
**Early stages:** Larva dull yellow, with dark spots and a green stripe on back. Multiple broods. **Food:** Clover *(Trifolium),* rattleweed *(Astragalus),* deerweed *(Lotus scoparius),* alfalfa *(Medicago sativa),* lupine, sweet clover *(Melilotus),* and other legumes; also wild buckwheat *(Eriogonum).* **Adults:** March–Oct.
**Range:** S. British Columbia east to N.D., south to s. Calfornia, w. Tex.; Baja California. **Habitat:** Very general.
**Subspecies:** (1) **Acmon Blue,** *I. a. acmon* (Westwood & Hewitson), Pl. 34. Western part of range. TL: California. (2)

**Lutz's Blue,** *I. a. lutzi* (dos Passos). Spots on underside larger. Rocky Mts. TL: Snowslide Canyon, Bear Lake Co., Idaho. (3) **Texas Blue,** *I. a. texana* Goodpasture. Small; aurora very bright. Southwest. TL: 1 mi. s. of Hillside, Yavapai Co., Ariz. (4) **Spangled Blue,** *I. a. spangelatus* (Burdick). Small, dull. Alpine. TL: Olympic Mts., Wash.

**LUPINE BLUE** *Icaricia lupini* (Boisduval)                **Pl. 35**
**Identification:** $\frac{7}{8}$-$1\frac{1}{8}$ in. (22–28 mm). FW cell bar usually present. *Upperside:* Male lavender blue with sky blue reflections; wing veins slightly darker; dark wing border wide. HW marginal spots black. *Aurora orange-red,* often broken into *separate chevrons.* Female much darker, brown, often with a brilliant blue gloss. HW aurora usually wide, orange. *Underside:* Similar to that of Acmon Blue (p. 193).
**Early stages:** Undescribed. One brood. **Food:** Sulfur flower *(Eriogonum umbellatum),* flat top *(E. fasciculatum),* and other species of perennial wild buckwheat. Despite its name, this species does not feed on lupine. **Adults:** April–Aug., depending on latitude and elevation.
**Range:** S. British Columbia to s. Calif. Extent of range not clear, due to confusion with Acmon Blue (p. 193). May also occur in the Rocky Mts. **Habitat:** Sagebrush, chaparral, rocky outcrops, mountain meadows, usually at intermediate elevations.
**Subspecies:** (1) **Lupine Blue,** *I. l. lupini* (Boisduval), Pl. 35, No. 1. British Columbia to s. Calif. TL: Southern Calif. (2) **Clemence's Blue,** *I. l. monticola* (Clemence), Pl. 35, No. 2. Male sky blue, female dark blue; both have a distinctive *pale area* just inside dark FW border, better developed in female. Mountains of s. Calif. TL: Pasadena, Calif. (3) **Green Blue,** *I. l. chlorina* (Skinner), Pl. 35, No. 3. Male greenish blue. Female usually brown on upperside, with blue overscaling; aurora may extend onto FW. Tehachapi Mts., Calif. TL: Tehachapi, Calif.
**Remarks:** Clemence's Blue and the Green Blue were formerly considered distinct species.

**VEINED BLUE** *Icaricia neurona* (Skinner)                **Pl. 35**
**Identification:** $\frac{3}{4}$-$\frac{7}{8}$ in. (19–22 mm). Structurally a blue, but has *no blue color.* Unmistakable. *Upperside: Dark brown,* with *orange* veins and marginal markings. *Underside:* Like that of Acmon Blue (Pl. 34 and p. 193).
**Early stages:** Larva green, with diagonal white bars on sides and a faint dark stripe on back; covered with white hairs. Two broods. **Food:** Wright's eriogonum *(Eriogonum wrightii).* **Adults:** May–Aug.
**Range:** Limited to a few localities in s. Calif.: Walker Pass, Kern Co.; Tehachapi Mts. in Kern, Los Angeles and Ventura Cos.; mountains of San Bernardino Co. TL: Doble, San Bernardino Co.,

Calif. **Habitat:** Rocky hills, rocky shoulders and outcrops in mountains.

## Cranberry Blue: Genus *Vacciniina* Tutt

**CRANBERRY BLUE** *Vacciniina optilete* (Knoch)       **Pl. 35**
**Identification:** $7/8$–1 in. (22–25 mm). *Upperside:* Male deep violet blue, with no border. Female duller, may have small dark marginal spots on HW. In both sexes, terminal line narrow and black, fringes white. *Underside:* Light gray, the black spots white-bordered. Pm. spots black, those on HW oval. Submarginal spots small, gray; those on HW larger, blacker. HW aurora of *3 orange spots — spot in cell $Cu_1$ largest.*
**Early stages:** Not described. One brood. **Food:** Buds and flowers of cranberry and blueberry *(Vaccinium).* **Adults:** June–July. They usually stay near larval food plants.
**Range:** Holarctic. In N. America, Alaska east to Manitoba, south to Yukon Terr., n. British Columbia. **Habitat:** Tundra, taiga, blueberry bogs.
**Subspecies:** (1) **Cranberry Blue,** *V. o. optilete* (Knoch). European. TL: Braunschweig, Germany. (2) **Yukon Blue,** *V. o. yukona* (Holland), Pl. 35. N. America. TL: Mountains between Mission and Twenty-mile Creeks, Alaska.
**Remarks:** In U.S. literature, the Cranberry Blue has usually been kept in the genus *Plebejus.*

## Arctic Blues: Genus *Agriades* Huebner

**ARCTIC BLUE** *Agriades franklinii* (Curtis)       **Pl. 35**
**Identification:** $7/8$–$1\frac{1}{8}$ in. (22–28 mm). *Upperside:* Male *grayish blue.* Both FW and HW have dark cell bars. HW often has 2–5 light-ringed, dark spots along outer edge. Female dark brown or gray; markings similar to those of male. *Underside:* Both sexes either have *dark spots* with light rings or *light spots* with or without dark centers.
**Early stages:** Undescribed. One brood. **Food:** Has laid eggs on diapensia *(Diapensia lapponica)* in the Arctic, on shooting star *(Dodecatheon)* in Calif., and on rock-jasmine *(Androsace septentionalis)* in Colo. **Adults:** June–Aug.
**Range:** Alaska east to Labrador, south to British Columbia, Manitoba. In mountains of the West to cen. Calif., n. Ariz., n. N.M., S.D. **Habitat:** Tundra, bogs, wet subalpine meadows, alpine fellfields.
**Subspecies:** (1) **Arctic Blue,** *A. f. franklinii* (Curtis). Very small. Dark spots on underside of HW. Far north. TL: Arctic America. (2) **Lake-side Blue,** *A. f. lacustris* (T. N. Freeman). Small, very light; few dark markings. N.-cen. Canada. TL: Norway House, Manitoba. (3) **Bryant's Blue,** *A. f. bryanti* (Leussler). Small, dull;

spots on underside of HW white. Cen. and w. Arctic. TL: Black
Mt., 30 mi. sw. of Aklavik, Northwest Terr. (4) **Large-spotted
Blue,** *A. f. megalo* (McDunnough), Pl. 35, No. 7. Larger. Bor-
ders on upperside dark. *Light spots* on underside of HW *large*.
British Columbia, Alberta, Wash. TL: Mt. McLean, British Columbia. (5) **Rustic Blue,** *A. f. rustica* (W. H. Edwards), Pl. 35, No. 6.
Male light blue, female dark brown. Markings on underside of HW
*light*. Rocky Mts. TL: Vicinity of Empire, Clear Creek Co.,
Colo. (6) **Gray Blue,** *A. f. podarce* (C. & R. Felder). Ore. south to
cen. Calif. TL: California.
**Remarks:** In literature published before 1981, this species was
listed either as *Agriades glandon* or *A. aquilo.* These species are
now considered to be entirely European, not found in the U.S. The
subspecies of the Arctic Blue, *A. franklinii,* will appear in the
genus *Plebejus* in much of the literature.

## Tailed Blues: Genus *Everes* Huebner

**EASTERN TAILED BLUE** *Everes comyntas* (Godart)   **Pl. 35**
**Identification:** $7/8$-$1\frac{1}{8}$ in. (22–28 mm). Short, slender tail at HW
vein $Cu_2$. **Upperside:** Male iridescent lavender-blue. Female dull
blue to blackish brown. Both sexes have narrow dusky border and
pale fringes. 1 or more small, dark submarginal spots on HW, the
spot in cell $Cu_2$ *capped by pink or orange.* **Underside:** Dark spots
small but distinct. HW has 1–2 pink or orange submarginal spots.
**Similar species:** Western Tailed Blue (below).
**Early stages:** Larva green, with brown back and side stripes.
Multiple broods. **Food:** Various legumes; bush clover *(Lespedeza),*
tick-trefoil *(Desmodium),* milk pea *(Galactia),* wild pea *(Lathyrus),* rattleweed *(Astragalus),* vetch *(Vicia),* clover *(Trifolium),*
and others. **Adults:** March–Sept.
**Range:** N. America from s. Canada to Fla., Tex., south to Cen.
America. Very common in East, much less common in West. Re-
corded from Dakotas, Neb., Kans., and the Pacific Coast, in Calif.,
Ore., Wash. **Habitat:** Meadows, marshes, fields, clearings, fence-
rows, yards.
**Subspecies:** (1) **Eastern Tailed Blue,** *E. c. comyntas* (Godart),
Pl. 35. TL: North America. (2) **Texas Tailed Blue,** *E. c. texanus*
F. Chermock. Small, light-colored. Ranges from Tex. south into
Mexico. TL: San Antonio, Tex. Reportedly becoming scarce in
type locality.

**WESTERN TAILED BLUE**                              **Pl. 35**
*Everes amyntula* (Boisduval)
**Identification:** $7/8$-$1\frac{1}{4}$ in. (22–31 mm). General appearance like
that of Eastern Tailed Blue (above), but usually *larger;* male geni-
talia distinct. *Much commoner* in the West than the Eastern
Tailed Blue. **Upperside:** In male, marginal spot in HW cell $Cu_2$

usually *lacks pink cap.* In female, dusky borders wider, wing bases brighter blue; 2–3 *pink crescents* cap dark marginal spots on HW. *Underside:* Ground color usually *white,* the dark spots usually *smaller* and sometimes nearly absent.
**Similar species:** Eastern Tailed Blue (p. 196).
**Early stages:** Larva straw-colored to yellowish green, with pink to maroon markings. One brood in colder elevated areas, 2–3 broods southward and at low elevations. **Food:** Wild pea *(Lathyrus),* rattleweed *(Astragalus),* vetch *(Vicia).* Partial to giant vetch *(V. gigantea)* on Pacific Coast. **Adults:** April–Sept.
**Range:** Cen. Alaska, Yukon Terr., Dist. of Mackenzie south to s. Calif., Ariz., N.M.; Baja California. **Habitat:** Open woodland, chaparral, coastal plain, roadsides, meadows.
**Subspecies:** (1) **Western Tailed Blue,** *E. a. amyntula* (Boisduval), Pl. 35. Pacific Slope. TL: California. (2) **Valerie's Tailed Blue,** *E. a. valeriae* Clench. Spots on underside reduced. Cen. Rocky Mts., Black Hills. TL: Lead, S.D. (3) **Albright's Tailed Blue,** *E. a. albrighti* Clench. Border on upperside very narrow; underside light gray. Alaska to Mont. TL: Kings Hill, Mont. (4) **Herr's Tailed Blue,** *E. a. herri* F. Grinnell. Lighter blue. Ariz. TL: Cochise Co.

### Sonoran Blue: Genus *Philotes* Scudder

**SONORAN BLUE**                                              **Pl. 35**
*Philotes sonorensis* (C. & R. Felder)
**Identification:** $7/8$–1 in. (22–25 mm). Our only blue with *red spots on FW. Fringes checkered.* **Upperside:** Silvery blue; FW apex and pm. spots black. Terminal line black. Red spots in cells $M_3$–$Cu_1$ of FW. HW unmarked in male; female has red spots in cells $M_3$–$Cu_1$.
**Early stages:** Larva pale green to mottled rose. It bores into the fleshy leaves of food plants and pupates under stones. One brood. **Food:** Rock lettuce *(Dudleya cymosa)* and related species in the stonecrop family. **Adults:** Feb.–May.
**Range:** Calif. north along coast to Santa Clara Co., inland to Placer Co.; s. Calif.; Baja California. Very local. TL: Sonora, Mexico. **Habitat:** Cliffs, rocky outcrops and washes, cutbanks.

### Dotted Blues: Genus *Euphilotes* Mattoni

Dotted blues resemble members of the genus *Icaricia* (pp. 192–194), but the marginal spots on the underside of the HW lack iridescent spangles, and the wing fringes are checkered. The members of genus *Euphilotes* resemble one another quite closely; all are found only in the immediate vicinity of their food plants, various species of wild buckwheat *(Eriogonum).*
Before 1974, dotted blues were included in the genus *Philotes.*

## SQUARE-SPOTTED BLUE                                Pl. 35
*Euphilotes battoides* (Behr)
**Identification:** $\frac{3}{4}$-$1\frac{1}{4}$ in. (19-22 mm). The following describes the Square-spotted Blue *(E. b. battoides)*, from the Sierra Nevada, Calif.; other subspecies differ considerably. Some resemble the Dotted Blue (p. 199) very closely. *Upperside:* Male bright blue, with a narrow dark border; HW marginal spots usually present. Female brown, with black marginal spots and an orange aurora. *Underside:* All spots *black and heavy in both sexes; pm. spots square.* The corners of the spots tend to touch one another. Submarginal and terminal lines black; submarginal spots round and separate. Aurora orange.
**Similar species:** In the Dotted Blue (p. 199), spots of underside usually small; aurora usually reduced. Positive identification is by examination of the male genitalia — the valve of the Dotted Blue is not divided; the valve of the Square-spotted Blue is split into an upper and a lower part. At high elevations both species may emerge at the same time, but at low elevations the Square-spotted Blue appears earlier in the year (March–June), the Dotted Blue later (Aug.-Oct.).
**Early stages:** Larva variable: pink, or green to yellow with chocolate markings. One brood. **Food:** Flowers of wild buckwheat, especially flat top *(Eriogonum fasciculatum)* and sulfur flower *(E. umbellatum).* **Adults:** March–May at low elevations, July-Aug. at high elevations.
**Range:** S. British Columbia and the western U.S. Distribution spotty. **Habitat:** Varies among subspecies, but usually hilly or rocky terrain.
**Subspecies:** (1) **Square-spotted Blue,** *E. b. battoides* (Behr), Pl. 35. Sierra Nevada. TL: Headwaters of the San Joaquin River, at 11,000 ft. elevation. (2) **Oregon Blue,** *E. b. oregonensis* (Barnes & McDunnough). Dark borders wide on upperside. British Columbia to s.-cen. Ore. TL: Crater Lake, Ore. (3) **Intermediate Blue,** *E. b. intermedia* (Barnes & McDunnough). Spots on underside small, aurora narrow. N. Calif. TL: Castella, Shasta Co. (4) **Glaucous Blue,** *E. b. glaucon* (W. H. Edwards). Dark marginal spots on upperside of HW. E. Ore., Nev., e. Calif. TL: Storey Co., Nev. (5) **Bernardino Blue,** *E. b. bernardino* (Barnes & McDunnough). Small; markings on underside bright and clear. S. Calif. north to Monterey Co. TL: Camp Baldy, San Bernardino Co., Calif. (6) **Martin's Blue,** *E. b. martini* (Mattoni). Aurora on underside of HW wide, red. Se. Calif., w. Ariz. TL: Oatman, Ariz. (7) **Central Blue,** *E. b. centralis* (Barnes & McDunnough). Male often has small pink aurora on upperside of HW. Utah, Colo., Ariz., N.M. TL: Salida, Chaffee Co., Colo. (8) **El Segundo Blue,** *E. b. allyni* (Shields). Small; male has small HW aurora on upperside; markings of underside very distinct. Coastal s. Calif. TL: El Segundo, Los Angeles Co., Calif. Range greatly reduced;

endangered. (9) **Comstock's Blue,** *E. b. comstocki* (Shields). Small; spots on underside small. Extent of range not known. TL: Tehachapi, Kern Co., Calif. (10) **Ellis's Blue,** *E. b. ellisii* (Shields). Range not known. TL: W. Creek, Unaweep Canyon, 6 mi. east of Gateway, Mesa Co., Colo. (11) **Bauer's Blue,** *E. b. baueri* (Shields). Range not known. TL: W. side Gilbert Pass, 6200 ft., Inyo Co., Calif.

**DOTTED BLUE** *Euphilotes enoptes* Boisduval          **Pl. 35**
**Identification:** 3/4-1 1/8 in. (19–28 mm). The description below is of the Dotted Blue *(E. e. enoptes),* from the Cascades and Sierra Nevada of Calif. and w. Nev. Other subspecies differ, some of them greatly. *Upperside:* Male lilac blue, the dusky borders wide (narrow in other subspecies). Female brown, with or without an orange aurora. *Underside:* In both sexes, *dark spots small;* aurora weak.
**Similar species:** Square-spotted Blue (p. 198).
**Early stages:** Larva whitish, with pink shades; brownish bars on sides, pink line down middle of back. One brood. **Food:** Flower heads of *Eriogonum,* as with other butterflies of this genus. **Adults:** Late June–July at high elevations, Aug.–Oct. at low elevations, where they emerge long after the Square-spotted Blue's flight season is over.
**Range:** Western N. America; similar to that of Square-spotted Blue. **Habitat:** Mountain slopes; rocky, often arid, localities.
**Subspecies:** (1) **Dotted Blue,** *E. e. enoptes* (Boisduval). Pl. 35. Calif., Siskiyou Co. to Kern Co., w. Nev. TL: California. (2) **Columbian Blue,** *E. e. columbiae* (Mattoni). Large. Male has marginal spots on upperside of HW. Cascades of Wash. and Ore. TL: Near Brewster, Wash. (3) **Dammers's Blue,** *E. e. dammersi* (J. A. Comstock & Henne). Underside of FW smudged. S. Calif. east to w. Ariz. TL: Snow Creek, Riverside Co., Calif. (4) **Smith's Blue,** *E. e. smithi* (Mattoni). Male vivid blue; in both sexes, aurora on underside of HW bright. Cen. coast of Calif. TL: Burns Creek, Monterey Co. An endangered population. (5) **Ancilla Blue,** *E. e. ancilla* (Barnes & McDunnough). Underside of HW gray, aurora bright. Rocky Mts. TL: Eureka, Utah. (6) **Tilden's Blue,** *E. e. tildeni* (Langston). Small, pale, lightly marked. Dry Inner Coast Ranges. TL: Del Puerto Canyon, Stanislaus Co., Calif. (7) **Bay Region Blue,** *E. e. bayensis* (Langston). Male bright blue. Underside dull and dark in both sexes. Points and shores of San Francisco Bay. TL: China Camp, Marin Co., Calif. (8) **Langston's Blue,** *E. e. langstoni* (Shields). Little known. TL: Mono Co., 1.6 mi. n. of Mono-Inyo Co. line, Hwy. 395.

**RITA BLUE** *Euphilotes rita* (Barnes & McDunnough)     **Pl. 35**
**Identification:** 3/4-1 1/8 in. (19–28 mm). Wings short, wide, and rounded. *Upperside:* Male brilliant lilac-blue, with moderately wide dusky borders; HW has dark marginal spots and a *small pink*

*aurora.* Female brown, with gray overscaling on wing bases; marginal spots on HW clear and distinct; *aurora wide, orange.* **Underside:** White, with clear and distinct dark spots. *HW aurora wide, bright red.*
**Early stages:** Undescribed. One brood. **Food:** Wright's eriogonum *(E. wrightii)* in Ariz.; yellow eriogonum *(E. flavum)* in Wyo.; effuse eriogonum *(E. effusum)* in Colo. **Adults:** Late in year, Aug.–Sept. Stays close to food plants. Often overlooked.
**Range:** Arid areas in Wyo., Colo., Ariz., N.M. **Habitat:** Desert scrub, rocky outcrops in arid grasslands, prairie grasslands. Found in dry waste places.
**Subspecies:** (1) **Rita Blue,** *E. r. rita* (Barnes & McDunnough), Pl. 35. Ariz. TL: Ramsey Canyon, Huachuca Mts., Ariz. (2) **Colorado Blue,** *E. r. coloradensis* (Mattoni). Smaller, darker. E. Wyo., e. Colo. TL: Kendrick, Lincoln Co., Colo. (3) **Emmel's Blue,** *E. r. emmeli* (Shields). TL: ca. 11–12 mi. se. of Utah Hwy. 14, Emery Co., Utah. (4) **Mattoni's Blue,** *E. r. mattonii* (Shields). TL: West of Charleston Reservoir, Elko Co., Nev.
**Remarks:** Subspecies *emmeli* and *mattonii,* described in 1975, may be subspecies of the Pallid Blue *(E. pallescens),* below.

**PALLID BLUE**                                             **Pl. 36**
*Euphilotes pallescens* (Tilden & Downey)
**Identification:** $\frac{5}{8}$–$\frac{7}{8}$ in. (16–22 mm). Very pale. **Upperside:** Male *very pale blue,* with moderately wide, dark borders; *3–5 small HW marginal dots.* Female light brownish gray, the basal $\frac{1}{3}$ to $\frac{1}{2}$ washed with bluish gray. *FW cell-end bar dark;* HW marginal dots dark, aurora pale pinkish orange. **Underside:** Ash gray in both sexes. All dark spots on FW small and black, those on HW reduced to tiny dots. Aurora pale orange, greatly reduced.
**Early stages:** Unknown. One brood. **Food:** Known only for subspecies *elvirae,* which feeds on a wild buckwheat, plumatella eriogonum *(E. plumatella).* **Adults:** Aug.–early Sept.
**Range:** Arid areas of se. Calif., s. Nev., w. Utah. **Habitat:** Low desert scrub, along washes and flats.
**Subspecies:** (1) **Pallid Blue,** *E. p. pallescens* (Tilden & Downey), Pl. 36. W. Utah. TL: Little Granite Mts., Tooele Co., Utah. (2) **Elvira's Blue,** *E. p. elvirae* (Mattoni). Very small. Markings on underside of HW heavy. Deserts of e. Calif. and w. Nev. TL: 3.5 mi. sw. of Pearblossom, Los Angeles Co., Calif.

**SPALDING'S BLUE**                                         **Pl. 19**
*Euphilotes spaldingi* (Barnes & McDunnough)
**Identification:** 1–1$\frac{1}{8}$ in. (25–28 mm). **Upperside:** Male lilac blue, with a wide dusky border; dark spots at margin and pink aurora reduced. Female brown; dark marginal spots on HW distinct; prominent orange aurora on both FW and HW. **Underside:** Aurora on both FW and HW in both sexes.

**Early stages:** Not described. One brood. **Food:** Racemose eriogonum *(E. racemosum).* **Adults:** Late June–July.
**Range:** Utah, sw. Colo., n. Ariz., ne. N.M. TL: Provo, Utah. **Habitat:** Rocky outcrops on elevated plateaus.

**MOJAVE BLUE**                                    **Pl. 35**
*Euphilotes mojave* (Watson & W. R. Comstock)
**Identification:** $^3/_4$-1 in. (19-25 mm). *Upperside:* The male's pale color and the female's blue gloss are distinctive. Male *pale silvery blue;* border dusky — inner edge somewhat irregular. Female brown with *blue iridescence;* aurora orange. *Underside:* Black spots and aurora as in other dotted blues (pp. 197-201). Inner margin of FW gray, rest of wing whitish.
**Early stages:** Larva yellow, with red lines. One brood. **Food:** Puny eriogonum *(E. pusillum).* **Adults:** Late March to early June.
**Range:** Mojave and Colorado Deserts of Calif. and Nev. Best known from eastern edge of San Gabriel Mts. TL: Mojave Desert. **Habitat:** Desert hills, especially along washes.

### Small Blue: Genus *Philotiella* Mattoni

The one species was previously placed in the genus *Philotes.*

**SMALL BLUE** *Philotiella speciosa* (Hy. Edwards)      **Pl. 19**
**Identification:** $^5/_8$-$^7/_8$ in. (16-22 mm). A tiny, plain species; easily overlooked. FW fringes strongly checkered, those of HW less so. *Upperside:* Male pale lavender-blue, with a *narrow dusky border.* Female *uniform brown.* *Underside:* Dull white. FW spots large, HW spots small; *no aurora.*
**Early stages:** Larva green, with a rose-colored median band; covered with short white hairs. One brood. **Food:** Round-leaf spineflower *(Oxytheca perfoliata),* three-lobed spineflower *(O. trilobata),* kidney-leaf eriogonum *(E. reniforme).* Larvae eat the small fleshy points on the stem near the places where the leaves attach. **Adults:** April–May.
**Range:** E. and se. Calif., w. Nev.; in arid places, deserts. Very local; usually uncommon to scarce. **Habitat:** Margins of desert playas (dry lakes); stream edges in Sierra Nevada.
**Subspecies:** (1) **Little Blue,** *P. s. speciosa* (Hy. Edwards), Pl. 19. E. Calif., w. Nev. TL: Havilah, Kern Co. (2) **Boharts' Blue,** *P. s. bohartorum* (Tilden). Dull blue; wide dusky border. Dark spots on underside of HW very small. S. Sierra Nevada foothills. TL: Briceburg, Mariposa Co., Calif.

### Silvery Blues: Genus *Glaucopsyche* Scudder

**ARROWHEAD BLUE**                                **Pl. 19**
*Glaucopsyche piasus* (Boisduval)
**Identification:** $1^1/_8$-$1^3/_8$ in. (28-34 mm). *Fringes checkered* (our

only *large* blue with checkered fringes). **Upperside:** Male violet-blue to glossy blue; border wide, shading gradually into ground color. Female duller. **Underside:** Gray, with many small black spots. HW pm. band composed of *white "arrowheads"* (chevrons); the points face inward.

**Similar species:** Silvery Blue (below) has no arrowheads on underside of HW.

**Early stages:** Larva dull white, with dark red, broken bands along back. One brood. **Food:** Lupine (*Lupinus,* various species). **Adults:** March–June, depending on locality.

**Range:** Mountains of western N. America; British Columbia, s. Alberta south to s. Calif., n. Ariz., w. Neb. Local, usually uncommon. Formerly common in s. Calif., now greatly reduced due to human settlement. **Habitat:** Lowland in s. Calif., usually in mountains elsewhere. Forest openings, trails, roadsides, grassy meadows, sagebrush scrub, clearings, streamsides.

**Subspecies:** Five subspecies are recognized, all similar. *G. p. piasus* (Boisduval) is shown on Pl. 19. TL: California.

**Remarks:** Before 1971, the Arrowhead Blue was placed either in genus *Phaedrotes* or *Scolitantides.*

**SILVERY BLUE** *Glaucopsyche lygdamus* (Doubleday)     **Pl. 19**
**Identification:** 1-1¼ in. (25-31 mm). A common, widely distributed species. Fringes white. **Upperside:** Male sky blue; FW veins silvery, border dark and narrow. Female dark brown, often glossed with blue. **Underside:** Light gray. Pm. spots on FW and HW *round, well separated, black, ringed with white* — the only conspicuous markings on underside.

**Similar species:** Arrowhead Blue (above).

**Early stages:** Larva light green, with dark line along back. Hibernates as pupa. One brood. **Food:** Wild pea *(Lathyrus),* vetch *(Vicia),* deerweed *(Lotus scoparius),* rattleweed *(Astragalus),* lupine *(Lupinus).* **Adults:** March–June at low elevations, June–Aug. at high elevations.

**Range:** In West, cen. Alaska and Dist. of Mackenzie south to s. Calif., Ariz., N.M., w. Kans.; Baja California. In East to Nova Scotia, south to Ga. **Habitat:** Uncultivated fields, open brushlands, forest edges, meadows, roadsides. Found in a variety of elevations and cover.

**Subspecies:** Nine rather similar subspecies are recognized, including **Behr's Blue,** *G. l. incognita* Tilden, Pl. 19. TL: Alum Rock Park, Santa Clara Co., Calif.

**XERCES BLUE** *Glaucopsyche xerces* (Boisduval)       **Pl. 19**
**Identification:** 1-1¼ in. (25-31 mm). A variable species, once quite common in its limited range. Now extinct, a victim of urban expansion; it was last seen in San Francisco Presidio in 1941. Specimens still exist in collections. Fringes white. **Upperside:** Male

soft purplish blue, with a narrow black border; veins slightly silvered. Female dusky brown, with or without blue gloss at wing bases. *Underside:* Light gray or brown. Nominate *xerces* had *large white spots without dark centers;* the more common form *polyphemus,* called the Eyed Blue, had large dark centers in the white spots.
**Early stages:** One brood. **Food:** Deerweed *(Lotus scoparius),* Nuttall's rattleweed *(Astragalus nuttallii),* small-flowered lupine *(Lupinus micranthus),* tree lupine *(L. arboreus).* **Adults:** March–April.
**Range:** San Francisco Peninsula. TL: California. **Habitat:** Coastal sand dunes.

### Spring Azure: Genus *Celastrina* Tutt

**SPRING AZURE** *Celastrina ladon* (Cramer)           **Pl. 19**
**Identification:** $7/8$–$1\frac{1}{4}$ in. (22–31 mm). Widespread and variable. *Fringes faintly checkered.* **Upperside:** Male sky blue to violet-blue, with a *black terminal line.* Female duller blue, FW costa and wide border dusky; FW cell-end spot present; HW costa and border lighter dusky, the outer margin with *3-5 light-ringed dark dots.* **Underside:** Dull white. Pm. spots usually complete, but often small and faint. Often a complete row of marginal crescents, each enclosing a small dusky spot; this row may be faint in some individuals.
**Early stages:** Eggs laid on buds. Larva pale green or pinkish; back stripe and slanting side stripes dull green. Attended by ants. Overwinters as pupa. One brood in north, 2–3 in south. **Food:** Wild lilac, buckbrush *(Ceanothus);* oak *(Quercus);* buckeye *(Aesculus);* Spirea; dogwood *(Cornus);* manzanita *(Arctostaphylos);* blueberry *(Vaccinium);* deerweed *(Lotus scoparius),* and many others. Larvae feed on buds, flowers, young fruit. **Adults:** Feb.–May in coastal Calif., April–June in north and east, April–Oct. in s. Ariz.
**Range:** N. America from Alaska and Canada south through the U.S., south to Cen. America. Confined to mountains in southern part of range. **Habitat:** Forest, brushland, groves, parks, shade trees.
**Subspecies:** Six similar subspecies, including the **Echo Blue,** *C. l. echo* (W. H. Edwards), Pl. 19. TL: San Francisco, Calif.
**Remarks:** In most previous literature, the Spring Azure will appear in the genus *Lycaenopsis,* with the species name either *pseudargiolus* or *argiolus.*

# Skippers: Superfamily *Hesperioidea*

Worldwide; most numerous in the neotropics. Body stout; thorax muscular; wings strong-veined and powerful. Flight fast, erratic.

Veins simple, unbranched, all arising from discal cell. Antennae far apart, divergent. The base of each antenna has a hair tuft ("eyelashes"). Antennal club usually curved, usually with a slender, pointed tip, the *apiculus,* which may be curved back against the club in some genera.

**Early stages:** Larva smooth, the head large, the prothorax slender, forming a neck. Pupa usually has a thin cocoon.

Many skippers are similar in color and markings, and the distinctions are not always immediately evident. In some genera, identification of every specimen is not possible by markings alone; some require dissection of the male genitalia.

# GIANT SKIPPERS:
## Family Megathymidae

Very large skippers, with robust bodies. Head narrower than thorax. Midtibia has one pair of spurs. Palpi small. Larva bores in stems or fleshy leaves of *Yucca, Agave,* and *Manfreda.*

The arrangement of genera and species is that of Freeman in 1969 (see Bibliography, p. 336).

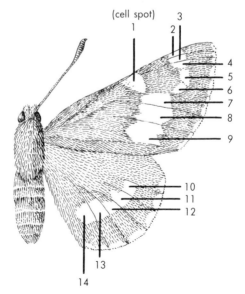

**Fig. 13. Giant skipper: spots used in identification.**

## Manfreda Borer: Genus *Stallingsia* H. A. Freeman

Antennal club has short apiculus. Coloration dull brown.

### MANFREDA BORER                                    Pl. 36
*Stallingsia maculosa* (H. A. Freeman)
**Identification:** $1\frac{3}{4}$–2 in. (44–50 mm). **Upperside:** Male has *hair tuft* on HW. Both sexes *dull brown,* with *dull yellowish FW spots* in cell, *at apex,* and in *pm. area. Fringes dull yellowish,* dark at vein tips. No spots on HW in male; female may have a row of small inconspicuous spots.
**Similar species:** The smaller species of agave borers (pp. 207–213) have spots that are larger, more numerous, and usually yellower. Their males lack the hair tuft on upperside of HW.
**Early stages:** Two broods. **Food:** Larva bores in woody base (caudex) of Texas tuberose *(Manfreda maculosa)*. **Adults:** May, and Sept.–Oct.
**Range:** S. Tex., n. Mexico. TL: Kingsville, Tex. **Habitat:** Closely associated with food plant.

## Yucca Borers: Genus *Megathymus* Scudder

Male black; FW spots and HW border whitish, yellow, or orange. Female larger, with broader wings; spots larger on upperside of FW. Some species have spots on upperside of HW. Some of the larger species have a hair tuft on upperside of HW; the smaller species do not.
    **Early stages:** Larva bores in woody base (caudex) of small yucca plants. **Adults:** Early fliers; Feb.–June.

### COLORADO YUCCA BORER                             Pl. 36
*Megathymus coloradensis* Riley
**Identification:** $2\frac{1}{8}$–$2\frac{5}{8}$ in. (53–66 mm). FW narrow. Outer $\frac{2}{3}$ of antennal club black. **Upperside:** Male black; FW spots and *outer margin of HW whitish to lemon yellow.* Female similar, usually with 3–4 *small submarginal light spots on HW.* **Underside:** Gray; veins same color as rest of wing. HW costa pale, with 2 white subcostal spots.
**Early stages:** One brood. **Food:** Larva bores in caudex of yucca, the species of yucca varying with the subspecies of butterfly.
**Adults:** Late Jan. to late June, depending on locality.
**Range:** Nev., Utah east to Colo., Kans., south to s. Calif., Ariz., N.M., Tex.; Mexico. TL: Colorado.
**Subspecies:** 11 similar subspecies occur in our area, including *M. c. martini,* Pl. 36. TL: Little Rock, Los Angeles Co., Calif.

### STRECKER'S YUCCA BORER                           Pl. 38
*Megathymus streckeri* (Skinner)
**Identification:** $2\frac{1}{4}$–$2\frac{3}{4}$ in. (56–69 mm). FW *wide.* Outer half of

antennal club *black*. Male has *hair tuft* on underside of FW and on upperside of HW. ***Upperside:*** Male dull black; FW spots and HW margin white to dull pale yellow. Female larger, with larger FW spots; *pm. spots yellow*. ***Underside:*** FW black in both sexes, the spots on upperside repeated. HW gray mottled with black, the spots *large, white,* and forming an *irregular band*.
**Similar species:** Texas Yucca Borer (below).
**Early stages:** One brood. **Food:** Bailey's yucca *(Yucca baileyi)* and fineleaf yucca *(Y. angustissima)*. **Adults:** April–June.
**Range:** N. Ariz., ne. N.M., s. Colo. TL: Petrified Forest, Ariz.

## TEXAS YUCCA BORER                                    Pl. 37
*Megathymus texanus* Barnes & McDunnough
**Identification:** 2¼–2¾ in. (56–69 mm). FW *wide*. Outer half of antennal club *black*. Female larger than male. Male has *large hair tuft* on underside of FW and upperside of HW. ***Upperside:*** Male grayish black; FW spots and HW margin *cream to yellow;* no spots on HW. In female, black markings on FW reduced; orangish overscaling extends to discal area. FW spots large, yellow; pm. spots and marginal spots yellow. ***Underside:*** FW black in both sexes; spots of upperside repeated. HW gray, *not mottled;* spots *few and small* in male, *larger* in female.
**Similar species:** Strecker's Yucca Borer (above).
**Early stages:** One brood. **Food:** Small soapweed *(Yucca glauca),* Buckley yucca *(Y. constricta)*. **Adults:** April–early July.
**Range:** E. Mont. and western N.D. south through plains to cen. Tex.
**Subspecies:** (1) **Texas Yucca Borer,** *M. t. texanus* Barnes & McDunnough, Pl. 37. Colo., N.M., Tex. TL: Kerrville, Tex. (2) **Leussler's Yucca Borer,** *M. t. leussleri* Holland. Male usually has 1 small spot on upperside of HW. Mont., N.D., w. Neb., w. S.D. TL: Valentine, Neb.

## URSUS YUCCA BORER *Megathymus ursus* Poling      Pl. 38
**Identification:** 2½–3 in. (62–75 mm). A scarce and local species. Very large. FW narrow. *Antennal club white*. ***Upperside:*** Male black; spots at apex white. *FW spot band deep yellow;* no spots on HW. Female very similar, but FW spot band somewhat wider. ***Underside:*** HW overscaling pale, rather rough. *Veins black*. Two white spots near HW costa.
**Similar species:** Viola's Yucca Borer (p. 207).
**Early stages:** One brood. **Food:** Mountain yucca *(Yucca schottii),* Arizona yucca *(Y. arizonica),* and fleshy fruited yucca *(Y. baccata)*. **Adults:** June–Aug.
**Range:** Mountains of s. Ariz.; Santa Catalina Mts., Santa Rita Mts., Huachuca Mts., and perhaps others.
**Subspecies:** (1) **Ursus Yucca Borer,** *M. u. ursus* Poling, Pl. 38. Se. Ariz. TL: Pinal Co., Ariz. (2) **Desert Yucca Borer,** *M. u. deserti* R., J., & D. Wielgus. Broad gray band on underside of

HW. Cen. Ariz., in Maricopa and Yavapai Cos. Described in 1972. TL: $\frac{1}{2}$ to $1\frac{1}{2}$ mi. n. of Camp Creek, Maricopa Co., Ariz.

## VIOLA'S YUCCA BORER Pl. 36
*Megathymus violae* D. Stallings & Turner
**Identification:** $2\frac{3}{8}$–$2\frac{7}{8}$ in. (59–72 mm). *Antennae white.* Female much like male, but larger. **Upperside: FW band wide, orange.** No spots on HW. **Underside:** HW overscaling *smooth;* veins black.
**Similar species:** Ursus Yucca Borer (p. 206).
**Early stages:** One brood. **Food:** Faxon yucca *(Yucca faxoniana),* Trecul yucca *(Y. treculiana)* and Torrey yucca *(Y. torreyi).*
**Adults:** May–June.
**Range:** Southern N.M., sw. Tex. Very local; found in very few places. TL: Carlsbad Caverns Natl. Park, Eddy Co., N.M.

## Agave Borers: Genus *Agathymus* Freeman

Antennal club has no apiculus. Light spots on upperside of both FW and HW. Larva bores in agave. Adults appear in late summer and fall. Some of the species look very much alike.

## Neumoegen's Agave Borer
## *(Agathymus neumoegeni)* Group

Some authorities consider the next seven species to be subspecies of Neumoegen's Agave Borer. They are all very similar, but each has a separate range that helps in identification. Large butterflies; upperside orange and black. Underside dark gray, a light band on HW present or not. See Fig. 13 (p. 204) for numbering of spots used in the following descriptions.

## NEUMOEGEN'S AGAVE BORER Pl. 38
*Agathymus neumoegeni* (W. H. Edwards)
**Identification:** 2–$2\frac{3}{8}$ in. (50–59 mm). **Upperside:** In male, spots orange, forming a band on both FW and HW; wing bases rather dark; *outer end of spot 7 overlaps inner end of spot 6 on FW.* Orange band wider in female, the inner end of *spot 9 on FW pointed.* **Underside:** HW dark gray, with little pattern; pale band faint.
**Early stages:** One brood. **Food:** Parry's agave *(Agave parryi).*
**Adults:** Oct.
**Range:** Cen. Ariz., w.-cen. N.M. TL: 9 mi. south of Prescott, Ariz.

## CARLSBAD AGAVE BORER not shown
*Agathymus carlsbadensis* (D. Stallings & Turner)
**Identification:** $2\frac{1}{8}$–$2\frac{3}{8}$ in. (53–59 mm). **Upperside:** FW spot 8 wider than spots 7 or 9. In male, wing bases heavily overscaled with

tawny. Orange band on HW narrow in male, wider in female. *Underside:* Medium to light brownish gray. Light band faint to distinct.
**Similar species:** Other members of the Neumoegen's Agave Borer group (pp. 207–209).
**Early stages:** One brood. **Food:** Parry's agave *(Agave parryi).*
**Adults:** Sept.
**Range:** Guadalupe Mts., N.M. and n. Tex. TL: Carlsbad Caverns Natl. Park, N.M.

**FLORENCE'S AGAVE BORER**                    **not shown**
*Agathymus florenceae* (D. Stallings & Turner)
**Identification:** 2¼–2⅜ in. (56–59 mm). *Upperside:* FW spot 8 wider than spots 7 and 9. Male has *small orange spot* in black area just below FW cell. *Black markings on FW reduced* in female, but dark median band on HW *well developed.* **Underside:** Dark gray, the HW median area slightly darker. Light band indistinct.
**Similar species:** Other members of the Neumoegen's Agave Borer group (pp. 207–209).
**Early stages:** One brood. **Food:** Young plants of an unidentified species of *Agave.* **Adults:** Sept.–Oct.
**Range:** W. Tex. TL: Davis Mts., 6200 ft. (1891 m).

**JUDITH'S AGAVE BORER**                    **not shown**
*Agathymus judithae* (D. Stallings & Turner)
**Identification:** 2⅛–2⅜ in. (53–59 mm). *Upperside:* In male, wing bases have extensive orange overscaling; spots 7-8-9 about equal in size; *orange band on HW narrow.* Orange very extensive in female; FW spots 7-8-9 separated from wing bases by small black spots only. *Underside:* Light gray. Dark median band on HW evident, *light band complete.*
**Similar species:** Other members of the Neumoegen's Agave Borer group (pp. 207–209).
**Early stages:** One brood. **Food:** Medium-sized or large plants of Parry's agave *(Agave parryi).* **Adults:** Sept.–Oct.
**Range:** Extreme w. Tex. TL: 8 mi. east of Hueco, in Hueco Mts., Hudspeth Co., Tex.

**DIABLO MTS. AGAVE BORER**                    **not shown**
*Agathymus diabloensis* H. A. Freeman
**Identification:** 2–2⅛ in. (50–53 mm). *Upperside:* In male, FW cell mostly black; *spot below cell is large and touches cell spot.* In female, orange on FW very extensive; *black cell spot small,* entirely surrounded by orange. *Underside:* Medium gray; both dark and light bands usually well developed on HW.
**Similar species:** Other members of the Neumoegen's Agave Borer group (pp. 207–209).
**Early stages:** One brood. **Food:** Larva bores in medium-sized to large plants of Parry's agave *(Agave parryi).* **Adults:** Sept.

**Range:** W. Tex. TL: 5 mi. w. Victoria Cyn., Diablo Mts., Hudspeth Co., Tex.

## McALPINE'S AGAVE BORER                          not shown
*Agathymus mcalpinei* (H. A. Freeman)
**Identification:** $2\frac{1}{4}$-$2\frac{1}{2}$ in. (56–62 mm). *Upperside:* Black cell spot small in male; orange band on HW narrow. FW spots reduced in female. *Underside:* Dark median band and light pm. band not distinct.
**Similar species:** Other members of the Neumoegen's Agave Borer group (pp. 207–209).
**Early stages:** One brood. **Food:** Medium-sized to large plants of *Agave*. **Adults:** Sept.–Oct.
**Range:** Glass Mts., north and east of Marathon, w. Tex. TL: 5 mi. n. of Marathon, Brewster Co., Tex.

## CHISOS AGAVE BORER                          not shown
*Agathymus chisosensis* (H. A. Freeman)
**Identification:** $1\frac{3}{4}$-$2\frac{1}{4}$ in. (44–56 mm). *Upperside:* Male blackish brown, *the orange band narrow;* wing bases dark; FW has a small orange spot at end of cell and another spot in base of cell $Cu_2$. In female, FW mostly orange, the *costa dark;* black cell spot small; *HW median band dark. Underside:* Dark gray; light band poorly developed.
**Similar species:** Other members of the Neumoegen's Agave Borer group (pp. 207–209).
**Early stages:** One brood. **Food:** Medium-sized to large plants of rough agave *(Agave scabra).* **Adults:** Sept.–Oct.
**Range:** In vicinity of the TL: Chisos Mts., Brewster Co., Tex.

## ARYXNA AGAVE BORER                          Pl. 37
*Agathymus aryxna* (Dyar)
**Identification:** 2–$2\frac{1}{2}$ in. (50–62 mm). *Fringes white,* the vein tips dark. *Upperside:* Male blackish brown, with sparse orange overscaling at base of FW and HW. Spots small, orange-yellow (not bright orange as in members of the Neumoegen's Agave Borer group, pp. 207–209); spots separated by black veins. FW spot 7 does not overlap 6; spots 7-8-9 nearly equal in size. *HW spot band unusually narrow.* Female similar, but *spot band wide; spots 7-8 of FW wider than spot 9. Underside:* Gray with ashy overscaling; light bands indistinct.
**Similar species:** (1) Bauer's Agave Borer (below). (2) Freeman's Agave Borer (p. 210). (3) Evans' Agave Borer (p. 210).
**Early stages:** One brood. **Food:** Larva bores in medium-sized to large plants of Palmer's agave *(A. palmeri).* **Adults:** Sept.–Oct.
**Range:** S. Ariz., n. Mexico. TL: Se. of Nogales, Sonora, Mexico.

## BAUER'S AGAVE BORER                          Pl. 39
*Agathymus baueri* (D. Stallings & Turner)
**Identification:** $2\frac{1}{8}$-$2\frac{1}{4}$ in. (53–56 mm). Fringes *yellow* (worn in

female specimen shown), vein tips black. In male, spot band narrow; individual spots usually separate, not fused together. *Spot 7 closer to wing base than spot 6, and entirely separate from it.* Female similar, but spots 7-8-9 larger.
**Similar species:** (1) Aryxna Agave Borer (p. 209). (2) Freeman's Agave Borer (below). (3) Evans' Agave Borer (below).
**Early stages:** One brood. **Food:** Parry's agave *(Agave parryi).* **Adults:** Oct.
**Range:** W.-cen. Ariz. (Sycamore Creek, Mayer, Cactus Mts.). TL: Verde Hot Springs, Yavapai Co., Ariz.

### FREEMAN'S AGAVE BORER                         Pl. 39
*Agathymus freemani* D. Stallings, Turner, & J. Stallings
**Identification:** 2¼-2⅜ in. (56–59 mm). **Upperside:** Brownish black; FW costa and wing bases heavily overscaled with orange. *Spots orange in male, small and separate;* spot band narrow on both FW and HW. Female similar, but band slightly wider; FW spots 7-8 wider than spot 9. **Underside:** HW dark gray, with coarse light overscaling; *crossed by 2 dull orange bands.*
**Similar species:** (1) Aryxna Agave Borer (p. 209). (2) Bauer's Agave Borer (above). (3) Evans' Agave Borer (below).
**Early stages:** One brood. **Food:** Desert agave *(A. deserti).* **Adults:** Sept.
**Range:** W.-cen. Ariz. (Bagdad, Kirkland, Hillside, Date Creek). TL: Bagdad, Yavapai Co., Ariz.

### EVANS' AGAVE BORER                            Pl. 39
*Agathymus evansi* (H. A. Freeman)
**Identification:** 1¾-2⅜ in. (44–59 mm). **Upperside:** Male *very dark,* blackish. Spot band *narrow, yellow, the spots separated by black veins.* FW base dark; small orange spot in cell Cu$_2$. Tawny overscaling on FW slight. HW band narrow and isolated by the dark ground color. Female similar, but spots larger, orange-yellow. **Underside:** HW gray, with dark mottling and pale overscaling. Pale band vague or incomplete.
**Similar species:** (1) Aryxna Agave Borer (p. 209). (2) Bauer's Agave Borer (p. 209). (3) Freeman's Agave Borer (above).
**Early stages:** One brood. **Food:** Larva bores in both Parry's agave *(A. parryi)* and Palmer's agave *(A. palmeri).* **Adults:** Sept.–Oct.
**Range:** Se. Ariz. (Huachuca Mts., Chiricahua Mts.). TL: Ramsey Canyon, Huachuca Mts., Ariz.

## Marie's Agave Borer *(Agathymus mariae)* Group

The next five species form a distinctive group. All are very similar, small and dark. The light bands are narrow in the male, wider in the female; the spots that form the bands are yellowish, buffy, or whitish, and often small and well separated. The HW underside is gray, usually mottled with dark color; light bands indistinct to complete. All five species feed on lechuguilla *(Agave lecheguilla)*.

## MARIE'S AGAVE BORER                                    Pl. 37
*Agathymus mariae* (Barnes & Benjamin)
**Identification:** 1⅝–1⅞ in. (41–47 mm). *Upperside:* Male blackish brown; wing bases overscaled with olive. Cell spot (spot 1) moderate in size; spots 2–6 small; spots 7-8-9 separate. *Spot 9 larger than spot 8.* HW band narrow, its spots small and separated by dark veins. In female, FW spots as in ♂, but *spot band wider,* the spots yellow and connected. *Underside:* HW gray, with vague dark markings; light band present, but sometimes indistinct.
**Similar species:** Other members of the Marie's Agave Borer group (pp. 210–212).
**Early stages:** One brood. **Adults:** Sept.–Nov.
**Range:** W. Tex., s. N.M., n. Mexico. TL: Franklin Mts., El Paso Co., Tex.

## CHINATI MTS. AGAVE BORER                               Pl. 37
*Agathymus chinatiensis* H. A. Freeman
**Identification:** 1¾–1⅞ in. (44–47 mm). *Upperside:* Male blackish brown; wing bases overscaled with olive. *Cell spot* (spot 1) *small;* spots 2–6 *greatly reduced;* spots 7-8-9 moderate, about equal in size. Female similar, but spots larger and overall color slightly lighter. *Underside:* Light band on HW usually visible in both sexes.
**Similar species:** Other members of the Marie's Agave Borer group (pp. 210–212).
**Early stages:** One brood. **Adults:** Sept.–Oct.
**Range:** Sw. Texas. TL: 2.7 mi. south of Shafter, Presidio Co., Tex.

## LAJITAS AGAVE BORER                                    not shown
*Agathymus lajitaensis* H. A. Freeman
**Identification:** 1⅝–1¾ in. (41–44 mm). Not readily distinguishable from Marie's Agave Borer (above). *Upperside:* Male dull black, with sparse pale overscaling. Female similar, but spot band wider. Light spots small, separate. *Underside:* Overscaling on HW pale gray in both sexes; light bands present.
**Early stages:** One brood. **Adults:** Sept.–Oct.
**Range:** Sw. Texas. TL: 10 mi. west of Lajitas, Presidio Co., Tex.

## RINDGE'S AGAVE BORER                                   Pl. 37
*Agathymus rindgei* H. A. Freeman
**Identification:** 1¾–1⅞ in. (44–47 mm). *Upperside:* Male brownish black; wing bases overscaled with olive. FW cell spot (spot 1) narrow; spots 2–6 very small. *Spots 7-8-9 small, separate; spot 9 largest.* HW spot band narrow, *evenly curved;* the spots small, separated by black veins. All spots larger in female. *Underside:* HW dark gray, slightly mottled; light bands distinct.

**Similar species:** Other members of the Marie's Agave Borer group (pp. 210–212).
**Early stages:** One brood. **Adults:** Sept.–Nov.
**Range:** Sw. Texas. TL: 14 mi. north of Brackettville, Kinney Co., Tex.

### GILBERT'S AGAVE BORER                                    Pl. 37
*Agathymus gilberti* H. A. Freeman
**Identification:** $1^{3}/_{4}$–$1^{7}/_{8}$ in. (44–47 mm). Fringes whitish, vein ends dark. *Upperside:* Male very dark, brownish black; light markings small. FW cell spot (spot 1) and spots 2–6 very small or entirely absent; *spots 7-8-9 small, conspicuous against dark ground color.* HW spots 2–4 small. Female similar, but spots larger. *Underside:* Dull gray in both sexes; light bands present, but indistinct.
**Similar species:** Other members of the Marie's Agave Borer group (pp. 210–212).
**Early stages:** One brood. **Adults:** Oct.–Nov.
**Range:** Sw. Tex. Shares part of the range of Rindge's Agave Borer (above), but is more widely distributed. TL: 14 mi. north of Brackettville, Kinney Co., Tex.

### VAL VERDE AGAVE BORER                                    Pl. 40
*Agathymus valverdiensis* H. A. Freeman
**Identification:** $1^{5}/_{8}$–$1^{7}/_{8}$ in. (41–47 mm). *Upperside:* Male deep *brownish black.* Spots yellowish white, small, separate. HW band composed of *4 very small spots in a straight line.* Female similar, but spots larger; spots separate as in male. *Underside:* Dark, with ash gray overscaling; mottled with black. HW spot band of 4 small, *elongate, white spots in a line.*
**Early stages:** One brood. **Food:** Lechuguilla. **Adults:** Aug.–Nov.
**Range:** Sw. Tex. (Del Rio area) in Val Verde and Kinney Cos. TL: 28 mi. n. of Del Rio, Val Verde Co., Tex.

### STEPHENS' AGAVE BORER                                    Pl. 40
*Agathymus stephensi* (Skinner)
**Identification:** 2–$2^{1}/_{4}$ in. (50–56 mm). *Upperside:* Brownish black. Spots complete, straw-colored; small to moderate in male, larger in female. Wing bases with *buffy or yellowish overscaling.* *HW cell spot* usually present; spot band curved, formed of 5–7 small, nearly equal spots; band wider and *cell spot larger* in female. *Underside:* Gray with dark mottling. Spot bands irregular, formed of angular yellowish spots.
**Early stages:** One brood. **Food:** Desert agave *(Agave deserti).* **Adults:** Sept.–Oct.
**Range:** Colorado Desert, in Riverside and San Diego Cos., Calif. TL: Mason Valley (La Puerta), San Diego Co.

### POLING'S AGAVE BORER                                    Pl. 40
*Agathymus polingi* (Skinner)
**Identification:** $1^{5}/_{8}$–$1^{3}/_{4}$ in. (41–44 mm). Our *smallest* agave borer.

*Upperside:* Brownish black; wing bases and FW costa dull tawny. Spots dull orange-yellow, fused into bands. In male, *FW spots 7-8 much wider than spot 9;* HW band narrow, complete. In female, *spots much larger, forming a wide band. Underside:* Mottled light and dark gray. Pale band on HW usually complete; wider in female.
**Early stages:** One brood. **Food:** Larva feeds in caudex (woody base) of Schott's agave *(Agave schottii).* **Adults:** Sept.–Nov.
**Range:** S. Ariz., se. N.M., n. Mexico. TL: Baboquiviri Mts., Pima Co., Ariz.

**ALLIE'S AGAVE BORER**                 **Pl. 39**
*Agathymus alliae* (D. Stallings & Turner)
**Identification:** $2\frac{1}{4}$–$2\frac{1}{2}$ in. (56–62 mm). Large, broad-winged; heavily built. *Upperside:* Blackish, wing bases and costa dull tawny. Fringes orange-yellow, dark at vein tips. In male, FW cell spot entirely surrounded by black; *spots 7-8-9 wedge-shaped.* Spots larger in female, FW spots 7-8 wider than spot 9. *Underside:* HW mottled gray, the bands composed of *large, separate, buffy orange spots.*
**Early stages:** One brood. **Food:** Utah agave *(Agave utahensis).* **Adults:** Aug.–Oct.
**Range:** Nw. Ariz., s. Utah, s. Nev., e.-cen. Calif. (n. San Bernardino Co., s. Inyo Co.). TL: 15 mi. west of Cameron, Coconino Co., Ariz., along the canyon of the Little Colorado R.

# TRUE SKIPPERS:
## Family Hesperiidae

Head as wide as thorax. Hind tibia usually has 2 pairs of spurs. Palpi well developed. Larva (Fig. 5, p. 26) feeds on leaves; it lives in a rolled or folded leaf, or in a nest formed of several leaves.

### Branded Skippers: Subfamily Hesperiinae

Usually tawny, less often dark brown or blackish. Many species are quite similar in appearance. Vein $M_2$ of FW curved, usually arising nearer to $M_3$ than $M_1$. Midtibia usually spined. Males usually have FW sex brand (stigma), shown in Fig. 14 (p. 214). Larva feeds on grasses, sedges, and related plants. Adults usually rest with their wings brought together over the back.

#### Genus *Panoquina* Hemming

**WANDERING SKIPPER**                **Pl. 40**
*Panoquina errans* (Skinner)
**Identification:** 1–$1\frac{1}{4}$ in. (25–31 mm). FW cell $\frac{2}{3}$ wing length. *FW*

*pointed,* HW lobed at anal angle. Fringes pale. ***Upperside:*** Olive-brown. All FW spots *hyaline (clear); spots small, forming a diagonal median row.* HW unmarked. ***Underside:*** FW spots of upperside repeated. HW veins light; HW has *a short curved pm. row of 3–5 pale spots.*
**Early stages:** Larva green, with 4 whitish stripes on back and a yellowish stripe on side. Two broods. **Food:** Salt grass *(Distichlis spicata).* **Adults:** July–Sept.
**Range:** Coastal s. Calif., coastal Baja California. TL: California.
**Habitat:** Salt marsh.
**Remarks:** Placed in the genus *Prenes* in older literature.

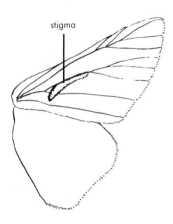

stigma

**Fig. 14. Branded skipper: upperside of forewing in male.**

**SYLVAN SKIPPER**                                    **Pl. 40**
*Panoquina sylvicola* (Herrich-Schaeffer)
**Identification:** 1⅑–1¾ in. (28–44 mm). Like the Wandering Skipper (above), but larger; FW longer, outer margin concave. ***Upperside:*** Dark brown, with a *long light dash in FW cell.* FW light spots in a diagonal row; the $M_3$ spot largest, shaped like an *arrowhead.* ***Underside:*** FW as on upperside, but duller. HW dark brown, washed with blue in female. Both sexes have a pm. band of *small bluish white spots* on HW.
**Early stages:** First 2 segments of larva blue-green, the others gray-green; a dark stripe on back and greenish white stripes on sides. Multiple broods. **Food:** Wild grasses, also sugar cane.
**Adults:** Long flight season. Probably March–Nov.

**Range:** S. Ariz. (casual), to s. Tex.; tropical America. TL: Cuba. **Habitat:** Usually found at flowers under canopy of thorn forest; fencerows, parks, gardens.

## Brazilian Skipper: Genus *Calpodes* Huebner

**BRAZILIAN SKIPPER** *Calpodes ethlius* (Stoll)          **Pl. 40**
**Identification:** $1\frac{3}{4}$–$2\frac{1}{4}$ in. (44–56 mm). Large; a powerful flyer. FW long and narrow; HW lobed. *Upperside:* Dark brown; wing bases olive. Fringes pale. All light spots hyaline. FW has small spots at apex and a small cell spot; 3 discal spots in a line — center one largest. *HW has a row of 3–4 equal-sized spots.*
**Early stages:** Larva gray-green, translucent; head dark orange. Lives in rolled-up leaves of canna. Multiple broods. **Food:** Cultivated canna. **Adults:** Long flight season.
**Range:** S. Ariz. east to Tex.; casual in s. Calif., Kans.; east to N.Y. South to Fla.; tropical America to Argentina. TL: Surinam. **Habitat:** Largely domestic in western U.S.; found on cultivated canna.

## Genus *Lerodea* Scudder

**EUFALA SKIPPER** *Lerodea eufala* (W. H. Edwards)          **Pl. 39**
**Identification:** 1–$1\frac{1}{4}$ in. (25–31 mm). FW narrow, pointed. Overall color grayer than similar species. *Upperside:* Grayish brown. *FW spots small, hyaline;* spots near apex tiny; no spot in cell $Cu_2$. HW unmarked. *Underside:* FW spots of upperside repeated. *HW ashy gray,* all markings vague or absent.
**Similar species:** (1) Arabus Skipper (below) has brown band on underside of HW. (2) In Julia's Skipper (p. 246), underside of HW slightly reddish brown; anal area darker.
**Early stages:** Larva grass green; stripes dark green, bordered by yellow blotches. Multiple broods. **Food:** St. Augustine grass *(Stenotaphrum secundatum),* Bermuda grass *(Cynodon dactylon),* Johnson grass *(Sorghum halpense),* and others. **Adults:** Long flight season.
**Range:** N.-cen. Calif. east to Neb., south to Ariz., Tex. In East, Minn. south to Fla. Tropical America. TL: Apalachicola, Florida. **Habitat:** Grassy flats, uncultivated fields, marshes, roadsides.

**ARABUS SKIPPER**          **Pl. 40**
*Lerodea arabus* (W. H. Edwards)
**Identification:** 1–$1\frac{1}{4}$ in. (25–31 mm). Structure and general appearance much like Eufala Skipper (above). *Upperside:* Brownish; spots *near FW apex larger* than in Eufala Skipper. HW may have *light spots,* especially in female. *Underside:* Light gray, with a *dark brown patch* in center of HW.
**Similar species:** (1) Eufala Skipper (above). (2) Julia's Skipper (p. 246).

**Early stages:** Unknown. One brood in Ariz. **Adults:** April.
**Range:** S. Ariz.; Baja California; Mexico. **TL:** S. Arizona. **Habitat:** Grassy flats along permanent lowland streams.
**Remarks:** Rare in collections; apparently also rare in nature.

## Roadside Skippers: Genus *Amblyscirtes* Scudder

An extensive genus of similar-looking, small, dark skippers. FW usually pointed. Apiculus on antenna slender, as long as the thickness of the club. Male has FW stigma; genitalia peculiar, the aedeagus very long (see Fig. 8, p. 31). Some species live in arid rocky places. Early stages of most species are unknown.

### SIMIUS ROADSIDE SKIPPER Pl. 40
*Amblyscirtes simius* W. H. Edwards
**Identification:** $\frac{7}{8}$-$1\frac{1}{4}$ in. (22-31 mm). *Upperside:* Male has small FW stigma. Both sexes dull bronzy brown with conspicuous pale fringes. *FW pm. band complete,* composed of *small pale spots;* band *angled outward* opposite cell. HW has indistinct pale spots at end of cell. *Underside:* FW apex and all of HW ashy gray; FW cell rusty. Pm. spot row *complete across both FW and HW.*
**Early stages:** Unknown. One brood. **Food:** Blue grama grass *(Bouteloua gracilis).* **Adults:** June–July.
**Range:** Saskatchewan, Neb., Wyo. south to Ariz., N.M., Tex.; n. Mexico. **TL:** Oak Creek Canyon, Custer Co., Colo. **Habitat:** High shortgrass prairie.

### LARGE ROADSIDE SKIPPER Pl. 40
*Amblyscirtes exoteria* (Herrich-Schaeffer)
**Identification:** $1\frac{1}{4}$-$1\frac{1}{2}$ in. (31-38 mm). Our largest roadside skipper. Fringes checkered. *Upperside:* Olive-brown; spots small and white. FW has 3 spots near apex, a small cell spot, tiny dots in cells $M_1$ and $M_2$, and a *small round spot in cell* $M_3$; sometimes also a spot in cell $Cu_1$. HW unspotted. Male has narrow, dark FW stigma. *Underside:* Dark brown, powdered with white scales. Pattern distinctive. FW spots of upperside repeated, but larger. HW has *numerous, clearly marked, small white spots.*
**Early stages:** Undescribed. One brood. **Adults:** June–July.
**Range:** Se. Ariz. south into Mexico. Sometimes fairly common. **TL:** Not stated. **Habitat:** Open woodland, streamsides.

### CASSUS ROADSIDE SKIPPER Pl. 40
*Amblyscirtes cassus* W. H. Edwards
**Identification:** 1-$1\frac{1}{4}$ in. (25-31 mm). Our only roadside skipper with a tawny tint. Fringes checkered. *Upperside:* Tawny brown; FW cell and *pm. spot row tawny.* HW unspotted. Male has small

dark FW stigma. *Underside: FW cell rusty;* pm. spots as on upperside. HW dark gray with pale flecks; postbasal and pm. spot rows pale, visible but faint.
**Similar species:** Bronze Roadside Skipper (below) is darker, not tawny.
**Early stages:** Unknown. One brood. **Adults:** June–July.
**Range:** Colo. south to Ariz., N.M., w. Tex.; n. Mexico. TL: Mt. Graham, Ariz. **Habitat:** Mostly in oak woodland; trails, rocky washes. Often suns itself on rocks.

## BRONZE ROADSIDE SKIPPER                          Pl. 39
*Amblyscirtes aenus* W. H. Edwards
**Identification:** $1\frac{1}{8}$–$1\frac{1}{4}$ in. (28–31 mm). Fringes checkered. *Upperside:* Olive-brown to greenish brown, lighter on HW. Spots near FW apex and spot in cell $M_3$ white; spots in cells $Cu_1$ and $Cu_2$ dull yellowish brown, inconspicuous. HW unspotted. Male FW stigma small, inconspicuous. *Underside: FW dark brown, including cell;* pm. spot row whitish. HW dark with light powdering; postbasal and pm. spot rows whitish.
**Similar species:** Cassus Roadside Skipper (above).
**Early stages:** Unknown. One brood. **Adults:** May–July in Tex., June–Sept. in Ariz.
**Range:** Colo., w. Kans. south to Ariz., w. Tex., Okla. TL: Hardscrabble Rd., Pueblo Co., Colo. **Habitat:** Sparse open oak woodland, washes, dry streambeds, roadsides, rock outcrops. Usually sits on open rocks.

## OSLAR'S ROADSIDE SKIPPER                          Pl. 40
*Amblyscirtes oslari* (Skinner)
**Identification:** 1–$1\frac{1}{8}$ in. (25–31 mm). FW pointed. Fringes obscurely checkered, *same color as wings.* Head and palpi brown. *Upperside:* Uniform dull brown, without markings. Male FW stigma *small, black. Underside:* Gray, with light powdering; FW cell brown. *Pm. spot row pale gray, usually complete* across both FW and HW.
**Similar species:** (1) Phylace Roadside Skipper (p. 219) has pale fringes. (2) Bellus Roadside Skipper (p. 220) has orange fringes. (3) Dun Skipper (p. 223) is larger and darker. Male stigma conspicuous.
**Early stages:** Unknown. One brood. **Adults:** May–July.
**Range:** Saskatchewan and N.D. south to Ariz., w. Tex. Usually uncommon. TL: Chimney Gulch, Colo. **Habitat:** Dry streambeds, foothills; draws, ravines, on prairie.

## ERNA'S ROADSIDE SKIPPER                          Pl. 40
*Amblyscirtes erna* H. A. Freeman
**Identification:** 1–$1\frac{1}{8}$ in. (25–28 mm). Fringes faintly checkered.

*Upperside:* Brown, with tawny overscaling, unmarked except for tawny spots near FW apex. Male stigma well developed. *Underside: Light brown;* FW darker at base and apex. HW overscaled with light gray; *markings usually absent.*
**Early stages:** Unknown. **Adults:** April–Aug.
**Range:** W. Kans., w. Okla., w. Tex.; n. Mexico. TL: Palo Duro Canyon, Armstrong Co., Tex. **Habitat:** Rocky streambeds.
**Remarks:** Little known, local; scarce in collections.

### TEXAS ROADSIDE SKIPPER                    Pl. 41
*Amblyscirtes texanae* Bell
**Identification:**    1-1¼ in.    (25–31 mm).    Fringes    checkered.
*Upperside:* FW dark brown; HW slightly lighter. FW has spots near apex, a *small cell spot,* and *spots in cells* $M_3$ *and* $Cu_1$. All spots yellowish or off-white, not pure white. Usually a small dash in FW cell $Cu_2$. HW either without spots, or with faint pm. spots.
*Underside:* FW dark brown; spots of upperside repeated. HW overscaled with gray; *light spots faint and powdery.*
**Early stages:** Unknown. **Adults:** April–Sept.
**Range:** Southern N.M., w. Tex.; Palo Duro Canyon south to Presidio and Brewster Cos., Tex. TL: Alpine, Brewster Co. **Habitat:** Rocky washes and streambeds. Sits on rocks and soil.

### PRENDA ROADSIDE SKIPPER                   Pl. 41
*Amblyscirtes prenda* Evans
**Identification:** 1-1¼ in. (25–31 mm). Our only roadside skipper with many small *white spots on both FW and HW on both upperside and underside.* *Upperside:* Dark brown. Male FW stigma well developed, same color as rest of wing. *Underside:* Lighter brown.
**Early stages:** Unknown. **Adults:** April–Aug.
**Range:** Se. Ariz., n. Mexico. TL: Tucson, Ariz. **Habitat:** Openings and trails in oak woodland.

### NEREUS ROADSIDE SKIPPER                   Pl. 41
*Amblyscirtes nereus* (W. H. Edwards)
**Identification:** 1-1⅛ in. (25–31 mm). Fringes *not checkered.*
*Upperside:* Blackish brown, with white spots. *FW spot row complete.* HW spot row complete, reduced, or absent. Male FW stigma inconspicuous. *Underside:* FW dark brown; spots as on upperside. FW costa and apex, and HW *powdered grayish green; HW anal area dark brown.* HW spots pale, visible but not sharply contrasting.
**Early stages:** Unknown. **Adults:** May–June in Tex., June–Aug. in Ariz.
**Range:** Ariz. to w. Tex.; Mexico. Uncommon. TL: South Apache, Ariz. **Habitat:** Rocky gulches in oak woodland; washes, rock outcrops.

**EOS ROADSIDE SKIPPER**                              Pl. 41
*Amblyscirtes eos* (W. H. Edwards)
**Identification:** $\frac{7}{8}$–$1\frac{1}{8}$ in. (22–28 mm). Fringes white, checkered dark at vein ends. *Upperside:* Dark brown; spots near FW apex small, white. *2–4 tiny white spots in central part of FW.* HW usually unmarked. *Underside:* Brown; FW costa and apex gray. HW powdered pale gray; *spots white, ringed with dark brown;* pattern distinctive.
**Early stages:** Unknown. **Adults:** April–July in Tex., Aug–Sept. in Ariz.
**Range:** Ariz., N.M., Tex.; n. Mexico. TL: Dallas, Tex. **Habitat:** Woodland trails and roadsides, canyons.

**NYSA ROADSIDE SKIPPER**                            Pl. 41
*Amblyscirtes nysa* W. H. Edwards
**Identification:** $\frac{3}{4}$–1 in. (19–25 mm). Small; FW short. *Upperside:* Dark brown, unmarked except for small spots near FW apex and checkered fringes. Male stigma obscure. *Underside:* HW has *dark brown patches* separated by lighter areas.
**Early stages:** Larva pale green, with a dark line on back; head white with vertical orange-brown stripes. 2–3 broods. **Food:** St. Augustine grass *(Stenotaphrum secundatum),* crabgrass *(Digitaria sanguinalis),* barnyard grass *(Echinochloa pungens),* bristlegrass *(Setaria glauca).* **Adults:** March–Oct. They sit on rocks and soil, even in the heat of the day. Common at times, but easily overlooked.
**Range:** Mo. and Kans., south to Ariz., Tex.; Mexico. TL: Texas. **Habitat:** Usually dry rocky places, but also thorn forest, brushland, yards, gardens, parks.

**ROADSIDE SKIPPER**                                 Pl. 41
*Amblyscirtes vialis* (W. H. Edwards)
**Identification:** $\frac{7}{8}$–$1\frac{1}{4}$ in. (22–31 mm). Fringes buffy, checkered with dark brown. *Upperside:* Entirely *deep coffee brown;* spots near apex white. *Underside:* FW dark except for subapical spots. *FW apex and outer half of HW clouded with violet gray.*
**Early stages:** Larva pale green, with short hairs; head dull white with vertical red stripes. Overwinters as pupa. Two broods in south, one in north. **Food:** Bluegrass *(Poa pratensis),* oats *(Avena striata);* has been reared on Bermuda grass *(Cynodon dactylon).*
**Adults:** April–Sept., depending on locality.
**Range:** S. Canada south to Calif., cen. Tex., east to se. Canada, New England. Widespread. TL: Rock Island, Ill. **Habitat:** In the West, grassy streamsides, forest edges, mountain meadows.

**PHYLACE ROADSIDE SKIPPER**                         Pl. 41
*Amblyscirtes phylace* (W. H. Edwards)
**Identification:** $\frac{7}{8}$–$1\frac{1}{8}$ in. (22–28 mm). FW pointed. Fringes pale, not checkered. Head and palpi have dull yellow scaling.

*Upperside: Dull brown, unmarked.* Male FW stigma *small, black.* *Underside: Dark brown;* no markings.
**Similar species:** (1) Oslar's Roadside Skipper (p. 217). (2) Bellus Roadside Skipper (below). (3) Dun Skipper (p. 223).
**Early stages:** Unknown. One brood. **Adults:** June–Aug.
**Range:** Southern Rocky Mts., Colo., N.M., Ariz., w. Tex. TL: Southern Colorado. **Habitat:** Elevated grasslands.

## BELLUS ROADSIDE SKIPPER                          Pl. 41
*Amblyscirtes fimbriata* (Ploetz)
**Identification:** $1\frac{1}{8}$–$1\frac{1}{4}$ in. (28–31 mm). Appearance simple but distinctive. *Head, palpi, and fringes orange-yellow.* *Upperside:* Dark bronzy brown, unmarked. Male FW stigma very narrow, slightly lighter than wing. *Underside:* Similar to upperside, but has a *slight gloss;* HW veins slightly darker.
**Early stages:** Mature larva grass-green, with a black head. One brood. **Food:** An undetermined grass. **Adults:** June in Ariz.
**Range:** High mountains of se. Ariz. Common in its restricted range. TL: Mexico. **Habitat:** Open pine forest at high elevations.
**Remarks:** Better known by its former scientific name, *A. bellus* (W. H. Edwards).

## Genus *Atrytonopsis* Godman

Moderate to large butterflies. Male has slender, obscure stigma. FW pointed in male, more rounded in female. Antennal apiculus slender, as long as diameter of club. Most spots hyaline (clear). Some species are most active during the morning hours. Life histories largely unknown.

## DUSTED SKIPPER *Atrytonopsis hianna* (Scudder)      Pl. 41
**Identification:** $1\frac{1}{4}$–$1\frac{3}{8}$ in. (31–34 mm). Markings more reduced than in other members of this genus (*Atrytonopsis* species, pp. 221–223). *Upperside:* Wing bases dark brown, outer $\frac{1}{3}$ lighter. Spots near apex and 2–3 pm. spots *very small, hyaline.* Fringes pale, not checkered. Male stigma absent. *Underside:* Both FW and HW dark at base, *outer $\frac{1}{3}$ heavily powdered with light gray.* FW spots as on upperside. HW has 1–2 very small white postbasal spots; pm. band dark brown, narrow.
**Early stages:** Undescribed. One brood. **Food:** Thought to be little bluestem *(Andropogon scoparius).* **Adults:** April–June.
**Range:** Manitoba, Neb., Colo., Wyo. south to Okla., east to New England, Ga. Quite local. **Habitat:** In East, dry open fields; in West, narrow valleys and gulches with permanent streams.
**Subspecies:** (1) **Dusted Skipper,** *A. h. hianna* (Scudder). Eastern. TL: Quincy and Dorchester, Mass. (2) **Turner's Skipper,** *A. h. turneri* H. A. Freeman, Pl. 41. Smaller, grayer; spots reduced. Western. TL: Barber Co., Kans.

**DEVA SKIPPER** *Atrytonopsis deva* (W. H. Edwards)    **Pl. 39**
**Identification:** $1\frac{1}{4}$-$1\frac{3}{4}$ in. (31-44 mm). *Upperside:* Medium brown; spots near apex, small spot in cell $M_3$, and narrow vein-to-vein spot in cell $Cu_1$ all hyaline. No FW cell spot; fringe same color as wing. HW unmarked, with *whitish fringe;* fringe *not checkered.* Wings more rounded in female; spots larger. *Underside:* FW as on upperside. HW powdered gray, with an obscure dark pm. bar across middle of wing.
**Similar species:** (1) In Viereck's Skipper (below), FW has double hyaline spot in cell. (2) Python Skipper (p. 222) has checkered fringes and a double spot in FW cell. (3) Lunus Skipper (below) is larger. All spots larger; HW fringes white on upper part of outer margin.
**Early stages:** Unknown. One brood. **Adults:** Late May–June.
**Range:** S. Colo., Utah, Ariz., w. N.M.; Mexico. Locally common. TL: Prescott, Ariz. **Habitat:** Open woodland, small side canyons opening onto fields or plains.

**LUNUS SKIPPER**                                    **Pl. 41**
*Atrytonopsis lunus* (W. H. Edwards)
**Identification:** $1\frac{5}{8}$-2 in. (41-50 mm). Large, robust. *Upperside:* Brown. FW fringes brown, HW fringes *yellowish white* at upper outer margin, brown near anal angle. FW spots large, hyaline. HW unmarked. *Underside:* Brown, with bluish gray overscaling on outer $\frac{1}{3}$ of HW. FW spots as on upperside. HW has a *narrow, dark pm. bar that encloses 2-3 small light spots.*
**Similar species:** (1) Viereck's Skipper (below). (2) Deva Skipper (above). (3) Python Skipper (p. 222).
**Early stages:** Unknown. One brood. **Adults:** June–early Aug.
**Range:** Se. Ariz., n. Mexico. Local, uncommon. TL: Arizona. **Habitat:** Seems to favor rocky canyons and slopes.

**VIERECK'S SKIPPER**                                **Pl. 41**
*Atrytonopsis vierecki* (Skinner)
**Identification:** $1\frac{1}{4}$-$1\frac{5}{8}$ in. (31-41 mm). *Upperside:* Light grayish brown; fringes same color as wing. Hyaline spots as in Deva Skipper (above), except for *double FW cell spot.* HW unmarked. Male has well-developed stigma on FW. *Underside:* Pale grayish brown, dusted with light scales. FW spots dull. HW has 1-2 small white spots below costa, and *short dark postbasal and pm. bars.*
**Similar species:** (1) Deva Skipper (above). (2) Lunus Skipper (above). (3) Python Skipper (p. 222).
**Early stages:** Unknown. One brood. **Adults:** May–June.
**Range:** Wyo., Colo., Ariz., N.M., w. Tex. TL: Dry Canyon, Almagordo Co., N.M. **Habitat:** Canyons and streams in prairie and elevated plains.

**PITTACUS SKIPPER**                                    **Pl. 41**
*Atrytonopsis pittacus* (W. H. Edwards)
**Identification:** 1¼-1½ in. (31–38 mm). *Upperside:* Brown with
greenish gray overscaling; fringes pale, not checkered. FW spots
well developed. HW has short row of 4 *square hyaline spots in a
straight line. Underside:* Similar to upperside, but overscaling
dense, purplish gray.
**Similar species:** (1) In Cestus Skipper (p. 223), fringes checkered;
hyaline spots on HW not in a line. (2) In Ovinia Skipper (below),
fringes checkered; HW hyaline spots small, irregular.
**Early stages:** Unknown. One brood. **Adults:** March–May in
Tex., April–June in Ariz.
**Range:** S. Ariz., N.M., w. Tex.; n. Mexico. TL: Fort Grant, Ariz.
**Habitat:** Small permanent streams in the mountains.

**OVINIA SKIPPER** *Atrytonopsis ovinia* (Hewitson)       **Pl. 41**
**Identification:** 1¼-1½ in. (31–38 mm). FW fringes checkered.
*Upperside:* Dark brown; spots on FW much as in Cestus Skipper
(p. 223). HW postbasal spot small; *pm. spots small, separate, not
in a line. Underside:* Spots as on upperside. FW brown. HW heav-
ily and uniformly overscaled with gray.
**Similar species:** (1) Pittacus Skipper (above). (2) Cestus Skipper
(p. 223).
**Early stages:** Not described. Broods unknown. **Adults:** March–
Sept. in Ariz., April–Nov. in Tex.
**Range:** S. Ariz. to w. Tex., south to Nicaragua. Fairly common.
**Habitat:** Washes, streamsides; often rests on sides of banks.
**Subspecies:** (1) *A. o. ovinia* (Hewitson). Spot in cell $Cu_1$ overlaps
FW double cell spot. TL: Nicaragua. (2) *A. o. edwardsi* Barnes &
McDunnough, Pl. 41. FW cell spot $Cu_1$ entirely separate from cell
spot. Ariz., Tex. TL: Redington and Baboquiviri Mts., Ariz.

**PYTHON SKIPPER**                                     **Pl. 41**
*Atrytonopsis python* (W. H. Edwards)
**Identification:** 1⅜-1⅝ in. (34–41 mm). Fringes checkered. FW
long, pointed. *Upperside:* Brown; FW spots translucent, slightly
yellowish. HW usually has *1–4 very small light spots at end of cell.
Underside:* FW marked as on upperside. HW mottled light and
dark brown; postbasal and pm. spots small.
**Similar species:** (1) Deva Skipper (p. 221). (2) Viereck's Skipper
(p. 221). (3) Lunus Skipper (p. 221).
**Early stages:** Larva pinkish, the abdomen bluish green; head
pale brown; covered with short light hair. Number of broods unknown. **Food:** Not known. **Adults:** March–Aug. Avid flower visitors.
**Range:** Se. Ariz., s. N.M., w. Tex. **Habitat:** In Ariz., forest openings.
**Subspecies:** (1) **Python Skipper,** *A. p. python* (W. H. Edwards),

Pl. 41. Larger; spots yellowish. Ariz. TL: Ft. Grant, Graham Co.
(2) **Margarita's Skipper,** *A. p. margarita* (Skinner). Smaller,
spots whiter. N.M., Tex. TL: Jemez Springs, N.M.

**CESTUS SKIPPER**                                                **Pl. 41**
*Atrytonopsis cestus* (W. H. Edwards)
**Identification:** 1⅜–1½ in. (34–38 mm). *Upperside:* Dark brown;
FW spots large, hyaline; HW has 1 postbasal spot and a short row
of *4 pm. spots, not in a line. Underside:* Spots dull, glassy. Markings of FW like those on upperside. HW has 2 spots at costa, 2 large
postbasal spots, and the 4 out-of-line pm. spots, all ringed with
dark brown. Upper 2 spots may appear to be 1 because of fold in
wing.
**Similar species:** (1) Pittacus Skipper (p. 222). (2) Ovinia Skipper
(p. 222).
**Early stages:** Unknown. **Adults:** April, Aug.
**Range:** S.-cen. Arizona. The few known records seem to be mostly
from the Baboquiviri Mts., Pima Co., Ariz. TL: S. Arizona. **Habitat:** Unknown. A rare and local species.

### Genus *Euphyes* Scudder

Midtibia not spined (see front endpapers). Male has FW stigma.
Male and female somewhat to very unlike in appearance. This
genus includes about 20 species, only 2 found in our area.
    The members of *Euphyes* have frequently been included in the
genus *Atrytone* (p. 224).

**DUN SKIPPER** *Euphyes ruricola* (Boisduval)          **Pl. 39**
**Identification:**   1⅛–1⅜ in.   (28–34 mm).   Very   plain-looking.
*Upperside:* Male dark glossy brown; FW stigma long, black,
*edged with rusty scales.* Top of head has dull yellow scaling. Female similar, but lacks stigma; FW has 2–3 pale powdery spots.
*Underside:* Both sexes somewhat lighter than on upperside. Dash
at base of FW dark. HW usually has a very faint pm. band.
**Similar species:** (1) Oslar's Roadside Skipper (p. 217). (2)
Phylace Roadside Skipper (p. 219). (3) Bellus Roadside Skipper
(p. 220).
**Early stages:** Larva green, with many small white dashes; head
brown, with 2 vertical cream lines and a central black spot. One
brood in Calif. and much of the West; apparently 2 or more broods
in Tex. **Food:** Umbrella sedge (a *Cyperus* species) and grasses, especially purpletop *(Tridens flavus). Adults:* May–July; to Aug.–
Oct. in Tex.
**Range:** Most of the U.S. and s. Canada. Very local in Pacific
States, less so eastward. **Habitat:** Moist meadows, streamsides, at
low and moderate elevations.
**Subspecies:** (1) *E. r. ruricola* (Boisduval), Pl. 39. Pacific Slope.

TL: California. (2) *E. r. metacomet* (Harris). Very dark; rusty scaling reduced. Most of the U.S. and s. Canada. TL: Massachusetts.

**TWO-SPOTTED SKIPPER**　　　　　　　　　　　**Pl. 41**
*Euphyes bimacula* (Grote & Robinson)
**Identification:** 1¼-1⅜ in. (31–34 mm). Fringes pale to white, not checkered. *Upperside:* Male dark olive-brown; *stigma long and narrow, black, narrowly edged with tawny on both sides.* Female dark brown; FW has *2-3 small, powdery, light spots* beyond cell. *Underside: Cinnamon brown* in both sexes; FW base darker. Light spots as on upperside. HW uniform cinnamon brown, except for *very narrow, white line along anal margin.*
**Similar species:** (1) In Tawny-edged Skipper (p. 231), FW costa tawny. (2) In Cross-line Skipper (p. 232), base of FW tawny on upperside in male.
**Early stages:** Little known. One brood. **Adults:** July.
**Range:** Colo. east to Ontario, New England, south to Va. TL: Philadelphia, Pa. **Habitat:** Boggy, marshy meadows; pond edges (Neb.).

### Genus *Atrytone* Scudder

Midtibia without spines (see front endpapers). Male has no FW stigma. Sexes unlike in appearance.

**AROGOS SKIPPER**　　　　　　　　　　　**Pl. 41**
*Atrytone arogos* (Boisduval & Le Conte)
**Identification:** 1⅛-1¼ in. (28–31 mm). *Upperside:* Male dull yellow with *wide dusky borders.* Female much less yellow, often nearly all dusky. *Underside:* Both sexes bright yellow; *FW anal edge and HW veins dusky.*
**Early stages:** Larva yellowish green; head white, striped with orange-brown. One brood in north, 2 broods in south. **Food:** Big bluestem *(Andropogon gerardi).* **Adults:** June–July in north; March–May and Aug.–Sept. in south.
**Range:** Colo., Neb. south to Tex., east to Minn., N.J., Fla. **Habitat:** Undisturbed grasslands.
**Subspecies:** (1) **Arogos Skipper,** *A. a. arogos* (Boisduval & Le Conte). Dark borders wide. Eastern. TL: North America. (2) **Iowa Skipper,** *A. a. iowa* (Scudder), Pl. 41. Dark borders narrow. Western. TL: Denison and New Jefferson, Iowa.

**DELAWARE SKIPPER**　　　　　　　　　　　**Pl. 41**
*Atrytone logan* (W. H. Edwards)
**Identification:** 1¼-1½ in. (31–38 mm). *Upperside:* Male *bright orange-yellow;* veins dark. FW cell bar, wing border, and anal edge dark. Fringes orange-yellow. In female, dark border wide; veins darker; FW base dark. *Underside:* Unmarked bright orange-yellow in both sexes. *FW base and anal edge black.*

**Early stages:** Larva bluish white, with many small black tubercles and a black band on the next-to-last segment; head white with black bands. One brood in north, two broods in south.
**Food:** Woolly beardgrass *(Erianthus divaricatus)*, bluestem *(Andropogon)*, switchgrass *(Panicum virgatum)*. **Adults:** June–July in north, March–June and Aug.–Sept. in south.
**Range:** Saskatchewan south to Ariz., Tex.; east to Conn., south to Fla. **Habitat:** Open woodland, dry fields.
**Subspecies:** (1) **Delaware Skipper,** *A. l. logan* (W. H. Edwards). Dark borders moderate. Eastern U.S., west to Great Plains. TL: Philadelphia. (2) **Lagus Skipper,** *A. l. lagus* (W. H. Edwards), Pl. 41. Dark borders narrow. Western part of range. TL: Oak Creek Canyon, Colo.

### Genus *Paratrytone* Godman

Similar in structure to *Poanes* species (below). Antennal club very short and thick, less than $\frac{1}{4}$ as long as shaft. Nine species, only 1 in our area.

**UMBER SKIPPER**            **Pl. 39**
*Paratrytone melane* (W. H. Edwards)
**Identification:** $1\frac{1}{4}$–$1\frac{3}{8}$ in. (31–34 mm). *Upperside:* Male rich umber brown; FW disc darker. *Spots at FW apex* and spots in cells $M_3$, $Cu_1$, and $Cu_2$ are *pale brownish yellow.* HW pm. band light yellowish brown. Female similar, but spots somewhat larger and lighter. *Underside:* Markings similar to upperside but larger and lighter; FW base black.
**Early stages:** Larva yellowish green with a dark line on back and yellowish side stripes. Two broods. **Food:** Not stated. **Adults:** March–May and Sept.–Oct.
**Range:** Calif. west of Sierran Crest, s. Ariz. (occasional); Baja California, Mexico. Locally common. **Habitat:** Open oak woodland, streamsides, trails, roadsides, parks.
**Subspecies:** (1) **Umber Skipper,** *P. m. melane* (W. H. Edwards), Pl. 39. TL: California. (2) **Vitelline Skipper,** *P. m. vitellina* (Herrich-Schaeffer). Darker. Ariz., s. Tex., Mexico. TL: Tropical America.
**Remarks:** Formerly placed in the genus *Poanes*.

### Genus *Poanes* Scudder

Palpi shaggy; tibia spined. Male lacks FW stigma. Antennal club long, $\frac{1}{3}$ length of shaft. Sexes unlike in appearance. 11 species, only 2 in our area.

**HOBOMOK SKIPPER** *Poanes hobomok* (Harris)     **Pl. 42**
**Identification:** 1–$1\frac{1}{4}$ in. (25–31 mm). *Upperside:* Male tawny, with a *wide, dark irregular border.* The light spaces between the

veins end in squarish "stair steps" against the dark border. FW cell-end bar black. Female may be similar to male, or deep brown with whitish FW spots and indistinct HW rays. *Underside:* Much like upperside in male. In female, FW as on upperside; HW purplish brown, outer edge slightly lighter.

**Early stages:** Larva dark green to brown, with many small black tubercles bearing black spines; head black with white hairs. One brood. **Food:** Grasses, the species not stated. **Adults:** May–early July.

**Range:** Saskatchewan south through eastern plains to Okla.; east to Nova Scotia, south to Ga. Enters our area only on the eastern edge. TL: Massachusetts. **Habitat:** Open woodland.

**TAXILES SKIPPER** *Poanes taxiles* (W. H. Edwards)    **Pl. 39**
**Identification:**  1¼-1⅝ in. (31–41 mm). Sexes *very different.*
*Upperside:* Male *brassy yellow; border dark, narrow, and slightly irregular;* a very narrow diagonal dark dash at end of FW cell. Female dark brown; FW spots and HW median patch dull orange-yellow. *Underside:* Male orange-yellow, FW base and border dark; HW border and 2 postbasal patches dark. In female, HW dull violet-brown; light median band obscure; anal area dull orange-brown.

**Early stages:** Unknown. One brood. **Adults:** June–July.

**Range:** Nev. east to Colo., Neb., south to Ariz., N.M., w. Tex. Reports from Georgia, Iowa, Ohio and Calif. are apparently in error. TL: Arizona, s. Colorado, Nevada. **Habitat:** Forest meadows, open woodland.

## Genus *Wallengrenia* Berg

**BROKEN DASH** *Wallengrenia otho* (J. E. Smith)        **Pl. 42**
**Identification:**  1⅛-1¼ in. (28–31 mm). *Upperside: Male FW stigma unique — black,* with a small lower section that is separate from the larger upper section, forming a "*broken dash.*" Warm brown with tawny overscaling. FW costa, spots at apex and *small spot at end of cell tawny.* HW unmarked. *Underside:* Deep reddish brown. HW pm. band pale, faint.

**Early stages:** Larval descriptions in the literature probably refer to the Northern Broken Dash, *W. egemeret.* The Broken Dash has been reared in Tex. by Kendall. Larvae are case-bearers, cutting a piece of leaf to make a protective case. Multiple broods. **Food:** Reared on St. Augustine grass. **Adults:** Long flight season.

**Range:** Southern U.S. to Cen. America. Enters our area only in Tex. TL: Georgia. **Habitat:** Quite general; common at flowers.

**Remarks:** The Broken Dash was formerly placed in the genus *Catia.* The Northern Broken Dash *(W. egemeret),* now considered a separate species, was previously considered to be the northern subspecies of the Broken Dash *(W. otho).*

## Genus *Ochlodes* Scudder

Six New World species, 5 of them in N. America. Twelve Old World species, mostly in Cen. Asia. Male genitalia peculiar, with projections at the outer end of the aedeagus. All N. American species occur in the West.

WOODLAND SKIPPER                              Pl. 39
*Ochlodes sylvanoides* (Boisduval)
**Identification:** 1-1¼ in. (25-31 mm). Flies in *late summer* and in the *fall;* very common. ***Upperside:*** Male FW bright tawny, the ground color meeting the dusky border as pointed rays along veins. Stigma black, its center also black. An *oblong dusky patch between end of stigma and FW apex.* Large tawny patch in HW. Female similar, with a diagonal band in place of stigma. ***Underside:*** *Extremely variable* — dull yellow, tawny, or brown. HW median band yellow to tawny or brown, obscure to very distinct. **Similar species:** (1) In Meadow Skipper (below) FW pointed. Small, pale; *flies in June.* (2) Farmer (p. 228) is much darker and smaller; center of stigma gray (outer edge black). Flies May–June. **Early stages:** Larva dull green; full grown in May, has summer diapause, emerges in fall. One brood. **Food:** Many kinds of grasses, including those that grow in lawns. **Adults:** Late July–Oct. **Range:** British Columbia south to s. Calif., east to Mont., Colo., Ariz. **Habitat:** Very general; found "everywhere." **Subspecies:** (1) **Woodland Skipper,** *O. s. sylvanoides* (Boisduval), Pl. 39. Most of the range given above. TL: California. (2) **Napa Skipper,** *O. s. napa* (W. H. Edwards). Larger; less variable. Mostly in Colo. TL: Empire City, Colo. (3) **Bonneville Skipper,** *O. s. bonnevilla* Scott. Very pale. Great Basin of Idaho, Nev. TL: Thomas Canyon, Ruby Mts., Elko Co., Nev. (4) **Santa Cruz Island Skipper,** *O. s. santacruza* Scott. Very dark; spot band on underside of HW very well developed. Coastal cen. Calif., Santa Cruz I. (TL). (5) **Oregon Coast Skipper,** *O. s. orecoasta* Scott. Very dark. Coastal and w. Ore. TL: Cullaby, Clatsop Co., Ore.

MEADOW SKIPPER                                Pl. 42
*Ochlodes pratincola* (Boisduval)
**Identification:** ⅞-1 in. (22-25 mm). A scarce, inconspicuous species of limited range. ***Upperside:*** Closely resembles Woodland Skipper (above), but *much smaller and paler.* Male FW stigma black, conspicuous against light ground color, its center *dark gray.* ***Underside:*** Orange-brown, with a pale pm. band on HW. **Similar species:** (1) Woodland Skipper (above) appears later, in late summer and fall. (2) Farmer (p. 228). **Early stages:** Unknown. One brood. **Adults:** June. **Range:** S.-cen. Calif.; known mostly from the Tehachapi Mts. TL: California. **Habitat:** Streamsides in foothills, low mountains.

**FARMER or RURAL SKIPPER**       **Pl. 42**
*Ochlodes agricola* (Boisduval)
**Identification:** $\frac{7}{8}$-$1\frac{1}{8}$ in. (22–28 mm). **Upperside:** Male dark brown; spots near FW apex, costa, and small spots bordering stigma tawny, *translucent when held up to light.* Stigma not surrounded by tawny area; center of stigma gray. Tawny area on HW irregular, the veins dark. Female similar, but lacks stigma; FW spots lighter, more translucent. **Underside:** Reddish brown. HW median band indistinct to absent.
**Similar species:** (1) Woodland Skipper (p. 227). (2) Meadow Skipper (p. 227).
**Early stages:** Undescribed. One brood. **Adults:** May–June.
**Range:** Calif. west of Sierran Crest; Baja California. Usually common. **Habitat:** Forest openings and trails, cutover land, old fields, fencerows, streamsides.
**Subspecies:** (1) **Farmer,** *O. a. agricola* (Boisduval), Pl. 42. N., cen., and s. Calif. TL: California. (2) **Verus Skipper,** *O. a. verus* (W. H. Edwards). Much paler. Tehachapi Mts. TL: Havilah, Kern Co., Calif.

**YUMA SKIPPER** *Ochlodes yuma* (W. H. Edwards)     **Pl. 42**
**Identification:** $1\frac{1}{8}$-$1\frac{3}{8}$ in. (28–34 mm). **Upperside:** Male bright tawny; wing veins dark. Spots near FW apex and cell spot small, pale, indistinct. *Stigma long, narrow, black.* Wing border narrow, dusky, grading gradually into ground color. Female larger, duller, more suffused with dusky; FW spots more distinct. **Underside:** FW dull orange, wing base black. HW *yellow, unmarked.*
**Early stages:** Larva pale greenish; head cream-colored with brown stripes. Lives in a shelter formed of a rolled-up leaf. Two broods. **Food:** Common reed *(Phragmites australis),* a very large marsh grass. **Adults:** June–July, late Aug.–Sept.
**Range:** Calif., Nev., Utah, Colo., Ariz. TL: Darwin Falls, Inyo Co., Calif. **Habitat:** Freshwater marshes, slow stream courses, reedy ponds, desert oases.
**Remarks:** Formerly considered rare, now known to be common in its peculiar and limited habitat.

**SNOW'S SKIPPER** *Ochlodes snowi* (W. H. Edwards)     **Pl. 42**
**Identification:** $1\frac{1}{8}$-$1\frac{3}{8}$ in. (28–34 mm). Dark colored, unlike other *Ochlodes* species (pp. 227–228). FW narrow, pointed. **Upperside:** Umber brown. *All FW spots hyaline (clear):* spots near apex, small cell spot, small spot in cell $M_3$, *larger spot in cell* $Cu_1$, and small dash in cell $Cu_2$. HW has median row of small tawny spots. Male FW stigma narrow, black. **Underside:** Reddish brown. FW base black; spots as on upperside on both FW and HW.
**Early stages:** Unknown. One brood. **Adults:** Late June–Aug.
**Range:** Colo., Ariz., N.M., at high elevations. TL: Ute Pass, Colo. **Habitat:** Forest openings, mountain meadows.

## Genus *Atalopedes* Scudder

**SACHEM or FIELD SKIPPER**                                    **Pl. 42**
*Atalopedes campestris* (Boisduval)
**Identification:** $1\frac{1}{4}$-$1\frac{3}{8}$ in. (31–34 mm). ***Upperside:*** Male *FW stigma unique in our area: very large, oval, black.* Inner $\frac{2}{3}$ of FW dull tawny, extending along veins into wide dusky border. Small spots near FW apex and in cells $M_1$ and $M_2$. Female darker; most FW spots as in male, but a round hyaline spot in cell $Cu_1$. ***Underside:*** HW pm. band narrow, dull white to yellowish. Anal area unmarked, yellow to dusky.
**Similar species:** Female somewhat resembles members of the genus *Hesperia* (true skippers, p. 234) in color and markings.
**Early stages:** Larva pale green, clouded with dark green; brown stripe along back; black papillae (projections) bear short hairs. Head black. Lives in a "tent" made from a leaf, to which it brings bits of food. Multiple broods in south, 2 broods over much of range; 1 brood in north. **Food:** Various grasses. **Adults:** March–Oct., depending on locality.
**Range:** Most of the U.S. south to Brazil. Very common in south, scarce northward. TL: California. **Habitat:** Fields, meadows, fencerows, yards, parks, lawns.

## Genus *Hylephila* Billberg

HW lobed. Antennae short; antennal club short, stout, its apiculus formed of 1 pointed segment. Eleven species; only 1 in our area.

**FIERY SKIPPER** *Hylephila phyleus* (Drury)         **Pl. 48**
**Identification:** $1\frac{1}{8}$-$1\frac{3}{8}$ in. (28–34 mm). Male and female differ in appearance. ***Upperside:*** Orange-yellow in male, with a dark serrate border and a black FW stigma; black dash between stigma and apex. HW anal area dark, *2nd anal vein (2A) orange, crossing the dark border in both sexes.* Female dark brown, with a complex arrangement of small orange-brown spots and streaks; vaguely similar to male. ***Underside:*** Reddish tan. Dash at FW base, submarginal spots, HW discal spots and anal area dark. Female more buffy, with larger and darker spots.
**Early stages:** Larva pale green, head dark; line on back brown, line on side light. Lives in a silken tube in sod. Multiple broods, at least in south. **Food:** Bermuda grass *(Cynodon dactylon),* St. Augustine grass *(Stenotaphrum secundatum),* bluegrass *(Poa,* various species), and others. **Adults:** Long flight period.
**Range:** Temperate N. America south to Argentina. Very common in south, scarcer northward. Recently found in Hawaii (1970). TL: Antigua. **Habitat:** Moist grassland, marshes, uncultivated fields, lawns, yards, gardens.

## Genus *Polites* Scudder

Closely related to both *Ochlodes* (p. 227) and *Hesperia* (p. 234). A New World genus of 10 species, 9 of which occur in our area. Wings short. Third (terminal) joint of palpi rather long, cylindrical. Male FW stigma complex, with several different areas, not all dark in color. Males and females often differ in appearance.

**PECK'S SKIPPER** *Polites coras* (Cramer)                    **Pl. 42**
**Identification:** 1-1⅛ in. (25-28 mm). *Upperside:* Male dark brown with tawny markings: spots near FW apex, FW from costa to stigma, narrow dash beyond cell, and HW discal rays. Female similar but darker and with more conspicuous spots; lacks stigma. *Underside:* Both sexes have *irregular area of fused, oblong yellow spots* at center of HW.
**Early stages:** Larva maroon, mottled with light brown; head black, streaked with white. Two broods in North, 3 in South; perhaps 1 brood at high elevations in West. **Food:** Various grasses — species not reported. **Adults:** May-Sept.
**Range:** British Columbia south to Ore., east to Saskatchewan, Mont., Colo., Ariz. In East to Maritime Provinces, south to Georgia. A mountain species in the West. TL: Surinam (must be in error). **Habitat:** Forest meadows, fields in the mountains.

**SANDHILL SKIPPER** *Polites sabuleti* (Boisduval)       **Pl. 39**
**Identification:** ⅞-1¼ in. (22-31 mm). Very common; extremely variable. *Upperside:* Male tawny; *dusky border toothed.* Outer end of stigma does not border. In female, dark markings heavier; light spots less tawny, nearly hyaline (translucent). *Underside:* HW buffy in both sexes; veins yellow. Median band *yellowish, irregular, projecting outward opposite cell.* Dark submarginal chevrons between veins; dark points at vein ends.
**Similar species:** Draco Skipper (p. 231) has long dash in HW cell on underside.
**Early stages:** Larva dull green, mottled with chocolate markings (Calif.) or gray with brown patches (Wash.). 1-2 broods in south at low elevations, 1 brood at high elevations. **Food:** Bermuda grass *(Cynodon dactylon);* also various native grasses and lawn grasses. **Adults:** March-Nov. in south and at low elevations, June-Aug. at high elevations.
**Range:** E. Wash., east to Colo., south to s. Calif., Ariz.; Baja California. **Habitat:** Varied; found from salt marshes and alkali sinks to sand dunes and subalpine meadows, alpine fell-fields, sagebrush flats.
**Subspecies:** (1) **Sandhill Skipper,** *P. s. sabuleti* (Boisduval), Pl. 39. Widely distributed. TL: California. (2) **Chusca Skipper,** *P. s. chusca* (W. H. Edwards). Very pale. Moist spots in sw. deserts. TL: Arizona. (3) **Tecumseh Skipper,** *P. s. tecumseh* (F. Grinnell).

Very small, dark. Sierra Nevada; alpine. TL: Little Crabtree Meadows, near Mt. Whitney, Calif.

**MARDON SKIPPER**                                    **Pl. 42**
*Polites mardon* (W. H. Edwards)
**Identification:** ⅞–1 in. (22–25 mm). Nondescript, yet quite unlike any other species. FW short, rounded. *Upperside:* Male *dark brown;* FW stigma *short,* black. Spots near FW apex, costa, pm. spots and HW median band tawny. Female darker, the spots lighter and more conspicuous. *Underside:* Markings much like those of upperside in both sexes.
**Early stages:** Larva gray with dark brown dots and a black line along back. One brood. **Food:** Grasses. **Adults:** May–June.
**Range:** W. Wash., w. Ore. Local, uncommon; scarce in collections. TL: Small prairies of Washington, near Puget Sound. **Habitat:** Grasslands.

**DRACO SKIPPER** *Polites draco* (W. H. Edwards)    **Pl. 42**
**Identification:** 1–1¼ in. (25–31 mm). *Upperside:* Male dark brown; FW costa, spots near apex, and pm. spots tawny. HW median band tawny; *the bar opposite the cell by far the longest.* Female similar, but lacks stigma; FW spots much lighter, more conspicuous. *Underside:* Both sexes mottled light and dark brown; *veins same color as wing.* Markings of upperside repeated. HW median band irregular, white to ivory; dash in HW cell long as on upperside. Dark dots at vein ends.
**Similar species:** (1) In Sandhill Skipper (p. 230), veins on underside of HW yellow. (2) Morrison's Skipper (p. 241) has silky white spots on underside of HW. Long dash in HW above cell, not through it.
**Early stages:** Unknown. One brood. **Adults:** Late June–Aug.
**Range:** Yukon Terr., British Columbia, Alberta, Saskatchewan south through Idaho, Mont., Wyo., Utah, Colo., Ariz. One record for Nev. TL: Colorado. **Habitat:** Grassy meadows at high elevations.

**TAWNY-EDGED SKIPPER**                               **Pl. 42**
*Polites themistocles* (Latreille)
**Identification:** 1–1¼ in. (25–31 mm). *Upperside:* Male olive-brown; *FW tawny from costa to black stigma.* Spots near FW apex and pm. spots a bit lighter, small. Light band on HW much reduced or absent; HW looks all dark. Female may be similar or much darker, deep brown with only 2–3 small light pm. spots. *Underside:* HW uniform greenish tan to dull brown in both sexes; *median band faint or absent.*
**Similar species:** Cross-line Skipper (p. 232).
**Early stages:** Larva yellowish to chocolate, faintly lined, covered with short black hairs; head black with white stripes. Two broods

in East, 1 in West. **Food:** Grasses, especially members of the genus *Panicum.* **Adults:** May–Aug. in West.
**Range:** British Columbia east to Nova Scotia, south to Calif. and Ariz. In East to Fla. Very common in the East; less common, mostly in mountains in the West. TL: "Middle America." **Habitat:** In West, forest glades, streamsides, small mountain meadows.

## CROSS-LINE SKIPPER                                 Pl. 42
*Polites origenes* (Fabricius)
**Identification:** 1⅛–1⅜ in. (28–34 mm). *Upperside:* Pattern in male like that of Tawny-edged Skipper (above). Cross-line Skipper larger; light markings more yellowish; ground color more olive-green. Stigma long. *HW median band usually distinct.* Female variable, usually quite dark; spots near FW apex, pm. spots, and HW median band whitish. *Underside:* HW dull brown; median band may be present as a row of small spots.
**Similar species:** Tawny-edged Skipper (above) is more common.
**Early stages:** Larva like that of Tawny-edged Skipper, but head all black. One brood. **Food:** In East, purpletop *(Tridens flavus).*
**Adults:** Late June–Aug.
**Range:** In West, Wyo., S.D., Colo., Neb., N.M.; east to New England, south to Ga. **Habitat:** In West, gulches, small watercourses, canyons opening onto plains.
**Subspecies:** (1) **Cross-line Skipper,** *P. o. origines* (Fabricius). Much darker. S.D., Neb. and eastward. TL: "in Indiis," probably New York. (2) **Rhena Skipper,** *P. o. rhena* (W. H. Edwards), Pl. 42. Much lighter. Western. TL: Southern Colorado.

## LONG DASH *Polites mystic* (W. H. Edwards)          Pl. 42
**Identification:** 1⅛–1⅜ in. (28–34 mm). *Upperside:* Male tawny with wide dusky border. Upper end of dark FW stigma connected to dark dash below apex, making a *long diagonal streak* (the "long dash"). Tawny band on HW *separated into rays by dark veins.* Female similar, but darker; markings broader in some specimens. *Underside:* Light brown, with a wide, curved, yellowish median band on HW, but HW nearly unmarked in some specimens.
**Similar species:** In Sonora Skipper (p. 233), terminal line on upperside of wings darker than the border; light spots smaller.
**Early stages:** Larva chocolate, mottled with dull white; many short-spined projections; head rough, black. One brood in West.
**Food:** Grasses, especially bluegrass *(Poa).* **Adults:** June–July.
**Range:** In West, British Columbia, Wash., Saskatchewan south to Colo., Neb., N.M. In East, s. Canada south to Virginia. **Habitat:** Grasslands, moist meadows.
**Subspecies:** (1) **Long Dash,** *P. m. mystic* (W. H. Edwards). Darker. Eastern. TL: White Mts., N.H. (2) **Dacotah Long Dash,** *P. m. dacotah* (W. H. Edwards), Pl. 42. Lighter, western. TL: Near Georgetown, Colo.

**SONORA SKIPPER** *Polites sonora* (Scudder) **Pl. 42**
**Identification:** 1-1¼ in. (25-31 mm). *Upperside:* Male tawny; border wide, light brown. FW stigma wide, black, conspicuous. Terminal line dark. Light band on HW formed of rays between the veins. Light markings more diffuse in female. *Underside:* Both sexes have spot at base of HW. *Median band on HW dull yellowish white, narrow, often broken into separate spots.*
**Similar species:** Long Dash (above).
**Early stages:** Larva grayish green; head black. One brood. **Food:** Not known; possibly Idaho fescue *(Festuca idahoensis).*
**Adults:** May-June at low elevations, July-Aug. in high mountains.
**Range:** British Columbia south to s. Calif., east to Idaho, Wyo., Colo. **Habitat:** Moist grasslands, mountain meadows, coastal plains, streamsides, wet bottom lands in high arid country. From sea level in Pacific States to 11,000 ft. (3355 m) in Rocky Mts.
**Subspecies:** (1) **Sonora Skipper,** *P. s. sonora* (Scudder), Pl. 42, No. 14. British Columbia, w. Great Basin, Sierra Nevada south to Baja California. TL: Sierra Nevada. (2) **Utah Skipper,** *P. s. utahensis* (Skinner). Olive-green; underside of HW greenish gray, band whitish. Idaho, Utah, Wyo., Colo. TL: Park City, Utah. (3) **Dog-star Skipper,** *P. s. siris* (W. H. Edwards), Pl. 42, No. 15. *Very dark reddish brown.* Band on underside of HW *creamy white,* very striking. Coastal region and Cascade Mts., British Columbia to Sonoma Co., Calif. TL: Small prairies near Puget Sound, Wash.

**WHIRLABOUT** *Polites vibex* (Geyer) **Pl. 42**
**Identification:** 1-1⅜ in. (25-34 mm). Sexes *very different.* *Upperside:* Male tawny; border dusky. Stigma *wide, black,* a dark bar between its upper end and FW apex. HW border even; veins dark. Female *dark olive-brown;* spots near FW apex and in cells $M_3$ and $Cu_1$ *hyaline (clear).* *Underside:* Male tawny; base of FW dark. HW has *a few widely separated dark spots.* Female greenish gray; spots vague.
**Early stages:** Larva pale green, with obscure dark lines; head black with white lines. Multiple broods. **Food:** Various grasses, including fringeleaf grass *(Paspalum ciliatifolium),* St. Augustine grass *(Stenotaphrum secundatum),* Bermuda grass *(Cynodon dactylon).* **Adults:** Long flight season.
**Range:** Southern U.S., tropical America. In West, Ariz. (rare) to Tex. (common). **Habitat:** Grassy fields, golf links, roadsides, openings in thorn forest, yards, gardens, parks.
**Subspecies:** (1) *P. v. vibex* (Geyer). Spots on underside of HW large, dark. Southeastern U.S. and south to Argentina. TL: West Indies. (2) *P. v. praeceps* (Scudder), Pl. 42. S. Tex. and southward. TL: Tehuantepec, Mexico. (3) *P. v. brettoides* (W. H. Edwards). Male pale, with narrow border. Ariz. (rare) to n.-cen. Tex. TL: W. Texas, in vicinity of Archer Co.

## True Skippers: Genus *Hesperia* Fabricius

An extensive holarctic genus, best represented in temperate N. America. FW pointed; HW has small anal lobe. Apiculus on antenna short. Male FW stigma long, narrow, curved, black. A median band formed of light spots (macular band) on underside of HW shows against a darker background. Specific differences in the macular band are of great importance in identifying species and subspecies.

*Hesperia* is a complex genus. Some species are quite similar to one another; others are extremely variable, both individually and geographically. Females are usually similar to males in general appearance, but are larger and lack the stigma.

**UNCAS SKIPPER** *Hesperia uncas* W. H. Edwards          **Pl. 42**
**Identification:** $1\frac{1}{8}$-$1\frac{5}{8}$ in. (28–41 mm). Female larger, less tawny than male. *Underside:* Both sexes recognized by the *white veins* and *dark mottling* on HW.
**Early stages:** Little known; 1–3 broods, depending on locality.
**Food:** Varies with subspecies. **Adults:** Long flight season.
**Range:** Alberta to Manitoba, south to e. Calif., Ariz., w. Tex. Sometimes common. Usually quite local, as are many species of *Hesperia*. **Habitat:** Dry grassland, sagebrush.
**Subspecies:** (1) **Uncas Skipper,** *H. u. uncas* W. H. Edwards (Pl. 42). Food: In Colo., blue grama grass *(Bouteloua gracilis).* Canada south to w. Tex. TL: Denver, Colo. (2) **Lasus Skipper,** *H. u. lasus* (W. H. Edwards). Larger, more tawny. Great Basin, Ariz. TL: Southern Ariz. (3) **MacSwain's Skipper,** *H. u. macswaini* MacNeill. Food: Needlegrass *(Stipa nevadensis).* Sierra Nevada, White Mts. of Calif. and Nev., at high elevations. TL: Blancos Corral, White Mts., Mono Co., Calif.

## The Comma Skipper Complex

The next 13 skippers are currently regarded as subspecies of the Comma Skipper (called the Silver-spotted Skipper by Higgins and Riley in *Butterflies of Britain and Europe*). Many of these skippers were once regarded as distinct species. Each differs considerably from the others, and each of the currently recognized western subspecies is given a brief separate treatment. Differences in the macular band (spot band) on the underside of the HW are the main field marks that identify the various subspecies.

The nominate subspecies, *Hesperia comma comma* (Linnaeus), is European; it does not occur in N. America.

**MANITOBA SKIPPER**                                        **Pl. 43**
*Hesperia comma manitoba* (Scudder)
**Identification:** $1\frac{1}{8}$-$1\frac{1}{4}$ in. (28–31 mm). *Upperside:* Male tawny, wing border wide and dark. Dark border wider in female, dark

markings heavier. *Underside:* Both sexes golden-brown to medium brown. Macular band complete, glossy white; its spots extend as *small teeth* along HW veins.
**Similar subspecies:** Boreal Skipper (below) is darker, especially on underside of HW.
**Early stages:** Not recorded. One brood. **Adults:** June–July.
**Range:** British Columbia and Alberta south to n. Wash. and n. Wyo. TL: "Colorado; Canada." **Habitat:** Meadows, openings, trails and roadsides in coniferous forest.

### BOREAL SKIPPER                                        not shown
*Hesperia comma borealis* Lindsey
**Identification:** $1\frac{1}{8}$–$1\frac{1}{4}$ in. (28–31 mm). *Upperside:* Both sexes very dark; the tawny markings often reduced to separate spots. *Underside:* Ground color dark brown. Spots reduced, often separate, sometimes dark-outlined.
**Similar subspecies:** Manitoba Skipper (above) is not so dark.
**Early stages:** Unknown. One brood. **Adults:** June–July.
**Range:** Northern N. America and Alaska to Labrador. TL: Nain, Labrador. **Habitat:** Meadows, openings, trails, roadsides, in boreal coniferous forest.

### ASSINIBOIA SKIPPER                                        Pl. 43
*Hesperia comma assiniboia* (Lyman)
**Identification:** $1\frac{1}{8}$–$1\frac{3}{8}$ in. (28–34 mm). *Upperside:* Male tawny; dusky border wide on FW, narrow on HW. Female brownish; FW costa and HW band usually tawny; pm. spots nearly white. *Underside:* Both sexes greenish yellow to greenish gray. *Macular band on HW dull white to yellowish; its spots small, few, or faint.*
**Early stages:** Undescribed. One brood. **Adults:** July–Aug.
**Range:** Alberta to Manitoba and N.D. TL: Regina, Saskatchewan. **Habitat:** Grasslands.

### HARPALUS SKIPPER                                        Pl. 48
*Hesperia comma harpalus* (W. H. Edwards)
**Identification:** $1\frac{1}{8}$–$1\frac{1}{4}$ in. (28–31 mm). *Upperside:* Male bright tawny. Female duller, paler. *Underside:* In both sexes, *HW macular band white, complete.*
**Early stages:** Larva dark brown, the head marked with tan or buff. Pupa brown, with no grayish bloom as in Yosemite Skipper (below). 1–2 broods. **Food:** Thurber needlegrass *(Stipa thurberiana).* **Adults:** June–Sept.
**Range:** Great Basin, British Columbia to e. Calif., s. Nev., Mont., Wyo., Colo. TL: Vicinity of Carson City, Ormsby Co., Nev. **Habitat:** Sagebrush, rabbitbrush scrub, dry grassland, juniper woodland, shadscale scrub.
**Remarks:** Formerly known as the Idaho Skipper, *Hesperia idaho.*

**YOSEMITE SKIPPER**                                          **Pl. 43**
*Hesperia comma yosemite* Leussler
**Identification:** $1\frac{1}{8}$-$1\frac{1}{4}$ in. (28–31 mm). *Upperside:* Dull tawny;
border moderately wide and darker. *Underside:* Light tawny;
spots of macular band *small, separate,* whitish to yellowish.
**Early stages:** Like those of Harpalus Skipper (p. 235), but pupa
covered with a *bluish gray bloom.* One brood.
**Adults:** June–July.
**Range:** Western slope of Sierra Nevada, Calif. TL: Near Yosemite, Calif. **Habitat:** Grassy openings in mixed forest; undisturbed
fields.

**LEUSSLER'S SKIPPER**                                       **Pl. 43**
*Hesperia comma leussleri* Lindsey
**Identification:** $1\frac{1}{8}$-$1\frac{1}{4}$ in. (28–31 mm). FW pointed. Club on an-
tenna very small. *Upperside:* Bright tawny, with wide borders.
*Underside:* HW yellowish brown; *anal area bright tawny.* Macu-
lar band on HW complete, *dull whitish.*
**Early stages:** Undescribed. One brood. **Adults:** June–July.
**Range:** Mountains of s. Calif.; Baja California. TL: Warner Hot
Springs, San Diego Co., Calif. **Habitat:** Canyons, grassy slopes.

**TILDEN'S SKIPPER**                                         **Pl. 43**
*Hesperia comma tildeni* H. A. Freeman
**Identification:** 1-$1\frac{1}{8}$ in. (25–28 mm). Small. Female usually
larger, darker. *Upperside:* Male bright tawny; dusky borders variable, narrow to moderately wide. *Underside:* Both sexes yellowish
brown to dull brown. *Macular band on HW variable:* dull white
to dull yellowish; usually narrow; sometimes indistinct, or absent
from back part of wing.
**Early stages:** Similar to those of Yosemite Skipper (above). One
brood. **Food:** Pine bluegrass *(Poa scabrella).* **Adults:** Late Aug. to
early Oct., during the driest season.
**Range:** Dry Inner Coast Ranges of Calif., from Lake Co. to San
Luis Obispo Co. TL: Cherry Flat Reservoir, Santa Clara Co., Calif.
**Habitat:** Dry grassy openings and clearings in oak woodland.

**DODGE'S SKIPPER** *Hesperia comma dodgei* (Bell)      **Pl. 43**
**Identification:** $1\frac{1}{8}$-$1\frac{1}{4}$ in. (28–31 mm). *Upperside:* Dark reddish
brown; dark border wide. *Underside:* Chocolate; macular band
dull white to cream, *strongly contrasting;* spots of band reduced in
occasional specimens.
**Early stages:** Similar to those of Yosemite Skipper (above), but
pupa lacks bluish gray bloom. One brood. **Food:** Red fescue
*(Festuca rubra).* **Adults:** July–Sept.
**Range:** Humid coast strip of Calif., from Sonoma Co. to Santa
Cruz Co. Very local. TL: Santa Cruz. **Habitat:** Grassy flats and
slopes, old ungrazed fields.

## OREGON SKIPPER Pl. 43

*Hesperia comma oregonia* (W. H. Edwards)
**Identification:** 1⅛-1¼ in. (28–32 mm). *Upperside:* Tawny areas bright, but reduced by dark wing bases and wide borders. *Underside:* Golden brown, often with a slight greenish tint. Macular band dull white to yellowish; its spots *slightly edged with black.*
**Early stages:** One brood. **Food:** Rye grass *(Lolium);* brome grass *(Bromus).* **Adults:** July–Aug.
**Range:** Pacific Slope from British Columbia to n. Calif. TL: Trinity Co., Calif. **Habitat:** Openings in forest and brushland; forest edges.

## HULBIRT'S SKIPPER Pl. 43

*Hesperia comma hulbirti* Lindsey
**Identification:** 1–1¼ in. (25–31 mm). *Upperside: Very dark;* grayish brown. Area around stigma, small FW spots, and HW band bright tawny. *Underside:* Yellowish brown. HW *anal area dark;* macular band dull white to dull yellowish.
**Early stages:** Unknown. One brood. **Adults:** July–Aug.
**Range:** High ridges of Olympic Natl. Park, Wash. TL: Hurricane Hill. **Habitat:** Alpine meadows, open forest.

## OCHRACEOUS SKIPPER Pl. 43

*Hesperia comma ochracea* Lindsey
**Identification:** 1¼-1⅜ in. (31–34 mm); large, for a Comma Skipper. *Upperside:* Very bright tawny; dark border neat and even. *Underside:* Golden brown. *Macular band white, its spots sometimes separate.*
**Early stages:** Not described. One brood. **Adults:** July–Aug.
**Range:** Eastern slope of Rocky Mts. in Wyo., Colo., N.M. TL: Platte Canyon, Jefferson Co., Colo. **Habitat:** Mountain grassland.

## COLORADO SKIPPER Pl. 43

*Hesperia comma colorado* (Scudder)
**Identification:** 1–1⅛ in. (25–28 mm). Small, dark. *Upperside:* Tawny areas reduced. *Underside:* Dark brown. Postbasal spots and macular band form *white chevrons* on HW; the points face the outer margin.
**Early stages:** Undescribed. One brood. **Adults:** July–Aug.
**Range:** High elevations in cen. Colo. TL: Colorado. **Habitat:** Alpine fell-fields.

## SUSAN'S SKIPPER Pl. 43

*Hesperia comma susanae* L. Miller
**Identification:** 1⅛-1¼ in. (28–31 mm). Very dark. *Upperside:* Very dark brown; rusty areas greatly reduced. *Underside:* Deep golden greenish brown. *Macular band slender, sometimes incomplete,* dull white to yellowish.

**Early stages:** Little known. One brood. **Adults:** Late June–Sept., depending on locality.
**Range:** High mountains of Ariz., N.M., w. Tex. TL: Horseshoe Ciénaga, White Mts., Ariz. **Habitat:** Grassy openings in coniferous forest.

**YUBA SKIPPER** *Hesperia juba* (Scudder)                    **Pl. 43**
**Identification:** $1\frac{1}{4}$–$1\frac{5}{8}$ in. (31–41 mm). Female larger than male.
*Upperside:* Male bright tawny; *dark border heavy, toothed inwardly; border clean-cut* — does not grade into tawny ground color. Light markings bright and extensive in female. *Underside:* In both sexes, HW golden brown, greenish brown, or dark brown; anal area tawny. Macular band *silky white,* well developed; each of its spots *projects slightly along the veins.*
**Early stages:** Larva cream-colored; head dark with pale bars. Emergence season long; no definite broods. **Adults:** May–Oct.
**Range:** British Columbia south to s. Calif., east to Mont., Wyo., Colo. Wide-ranging, usually uncommon. TL: California. **Habitat:** Usually uncultivated, ungrazed hilly grasslands, but may occur anywhere.

**WOODGATE'S SKIPPER**                                          **Pl. 43**
*Hesperia woodgatei* (R. C. Williams)
**Identification:** $1\frac{1}{4}$–$1\frac{3}{8}$ in. (31–34 mm). A distinctive-looking species, scarce in collections. Large, dark. Shaft of antenna very long, club very short; white ring at base of club. *Upperside:* Dark reddish brown. Border wide, dark, somewhat smudgy. Light spots small, indistinct. *Underside:* FW apex and all of HW dark brown. *HW spots small, rounded, white.*
**Early stages:** Little known. One brood. **Adults:** Late in year, Sept.–Oct.
**Range:** Cen. and s. Ariz. east to N.M. and Tex. (Edwards Plateau). TL: Jemez Mts., N.M. **Habitat:** Mountain meadows and forest openings.

**OTTOE SKIPPER** *Hesperia ottoe* W. H. Edwards         **Pl. 43**
**Identification:** $1\frac{1}{4}$–$1\frac{1}{2}$ in. (31–38 mm). A large, strong-flying, *early summer* species. *Upperside:* Male tawny; dusky border narrow, *not touching tip of stigma.* Center of stigma *black.* In female, dark markings diffuse; FW has 1–2 *translucent spots* beyond disc. *Underside:* Yellow to light brown, unspotted or with a few indistinct spots.
**Similar species:** (1) In male Pawnee Skipper (below), center of stigma is yellow and dark border on FW touches tip of stigma. (2) Dakota Skipper (p. 240) is smaller, with an indistinct macular band on underside of HW.
**Early stages:** Larva dark greenish brown; head dark. One brood.
**Food:** In Mich., fall witchgrass *(Leptoloma cognatum);* no doubt other plants elsewhere. **Adults:** June–early July.

**Range:** W. Colo. and Tex. east to Mich. TL: Kansas. **Habitat:** Undisturbed prairie.
**Remarks:** As with other prairie-dwelling species, the number of Ottoe Skippers has been greatly reduced by extensive grazing and farming.

**PAWNEE SKIPPER** *Hesperia pawnee* Dodge **Pl. 43**
**Identification:** $1\frac{1}{4}$-$1\frac{1}{2}$ in. (31–38 mm). A fast, strong flier; wary. *Upperside:* Male dusky; light tawny above and below stigma and in center of HW. Variable, may be quite dark. *Dark border of FW touches tip of stigma;* center of stigma *light yellow.* Female dark; tawny markings reduced. FW light spots translucent, *clean-cut, often whitish.* **Underside:** Usually unspotted in both sexes, but may have a few indistinct spots.
**Similar species:** (1) Ottoe Skipper (above) emerges sooner, flies in early summer. (2) Dakota Skipper (p. 240).
**Early stages:** Undescribed. One brood. **Adults:** Aug.–Sept.
**Range:** Great Plains, s. Canada south to Colo., Kans., east to Iowa. TL: Glencoe, Neb. **Habitat:** Sparsely wooded grasslands, open pine forest.

**PAHASKA SKIPPER** *Hesperia pahaska* Leussler **Pl. 43**
**Identification:** $1\frac{1}{4}$-$1\frac{1}{2}$ in. (31–38 mm). Male has a FW stigma with a *yellow center* (use a pin to tease out color if necessary). *Upperside:* Male light tawny; dark border wide, light areas reduced. In female, dark areas extensive, light areas small; looks somewhat smudgy. **Underside:** HW brown; anal area tawny. Macular band complete; *last spot in line with the others.*
**Similar species:** In Green Skipper (below), center of male stigma black. Last spot of macular band on underside of HW displaced outward.
**Early stages:** Larva pale brown (Calif.). Two broods. **Food:** Fluff grass *(Erioneuron pulchellum)* in Calif.; blue grama grass *(Bouteloua gracilis)* in Colo. **Adults:** March–May, Aug.–Oct.
**Range:** S. Canada south to e. Calif., Ariz., w. Tex.; Mexico. **Habitat:** Grassland; grassy areas among oak or juniper.
**Subspecies:** (1) **Pahaska Skipper,** *H. p. pahaska* Leussler, Pl. 43. Eastern part of range. TL: Harrison, Sioux Co., Neb. (2) **William's Skipper,** *H. p. williamsi* Lindsey. Spots on underside of HW small, rounded, separate. S. Ariz. east to s. Tex. TL: Baboquiviri Mts., Ariz. (3) **Martin's Skipper,** *H. p. martini* MacNeill. Large, bright. Spots on underside of HW large, white. Se. Calif., s. Neb., s. Utah to ne. Ariz. TL: Ivanpah, San Bernardino Co., Calif.

**GREEN SKIPPER** *Hesperia viridis* (W. H. Edwards) **Pl. 43**
**Identification:** $1\frac{1}{4}$-$1\frac{1}{2}$ in. (31–38 mm). In spite of its name, the Green Skipper cannot be identified by its color — it is not really green. *Upperside:* Center of male FW stigma *black.* Male tawny;

dark border usually wide, but individually variable. Female duller; light spots on FW may be whitish and translucent. *Underside:* Golden brown to greenish brown. Whitish spots of HW macular band usually dark-edged; *last spot displaced outward.*
**Similar species:** In Pahaska Skipper (p. 239), last spot in HW macular band is in line with other spots. **Early stages:** Undescribed. Two broods, at least in Tex. **Food:** Female seen to lay eggs on blue grama grass *(Bouteloua gracilis).* **Adults:** April–June, Aug.–Oct.
**Range:** Colo., Kans., Okla. south to Ariz., N.M., Tex.; Mexico. TL: Las Vegas, N.M. **Habitat:** Mountain grassland, prairie, grassy woodland.

## COLUMBIAN SKIPPER                                      Pl. 43
*Hesperia columbia* (Scudder)
**Identification:** 1⅛–1⅜ in. (28–34 mm). *Upperside:* Male bright tawny; border and wing bases dark, quite wide. Female similar, but lacks stigma. *Underside:* FW apex and HW *golden brown.* FW disc and HW anal area orange-brown. The *fused postbasal spots* and the *short, curved macular band* are *silvery white* — quite striking.
**Early stages:** Larva light yellow. Two broods. **Adults:** April–June, late Aug.–Oct. **Food:** June grass *(Koeleria cristata).*
**Range:** Pacific Slope, from Ore. to Baja California. TL: California. **Habitat:** Chaparral, oak woodland.

## LINDSEY'S SKIPPER                                      Pl. 43
*Hesperia lindseyi* (Holland)
**Identification:** 1⅛–1¼ in. (28–31 mm). *Upperside:* Male bright tawny; dark border narrow. FW spots reduced to those at apex and 2 upper pm. spots. Female duller; light spots more extensive, those on FW translucent. *Underside:* Both sexes light brown to greenish brown; HW veins pale. Spots of macular band *large, irregular, extending along veins.* Terminal line and vein ends dark.
**Early stages:** Eggs are laid on a lichen *(Usnea florida)* that grows on trees and fenceposts; eggs overwinter. Larva emerges in the spring. Larva brown, with pale bars on back and upper sides. One brood. **Food:** Idaho fescue *(Festuca idahoensis),* California oat grass *(Danthonia californica).* **Adults:** May–July.
**Range:** Pacific Slope, Ore. south to Riverside Co., Calif. TL: Nellie and Ukiah, Calif. **Habitat:** Usually foothill grasslands; less often found at higher elevations.

## DAKOTA SKIPPER *Hesperia dacotae* (Skinner)           Pl. 43
**Identification:** 1–1¼ in. (25–31 mm). Our rarest true skipper *(Hesperia);* variable and somewhat nondescript. Smaller than the Ottoe Skipper (p. 238), FW more pointed; antennal club unusually long. *Upperside:* Male — FW stigma black, slightly curved. Wings dull tawny. *Outer ends of FW veins tawny against the wide*

*dusky border.* HW border narrow. Female duller; border wide and indefinite. FW pm. spots whitish, translucent. **Underside:** Dull yellow to yellowish gray; HW macular band faint to barely visible. **Similar species:** (1) Pawnee Skipper (p. 239). (2) Ottoe Skipper (p. 238).
**Early stages:** Under study (1980). One brood. **Adults:** June–July.
**Range:** S. Manitoba, N.D., w. Minn., cen. Iowa; perhaps Ill. TL: Volga, N.D. and Grinnell, Iowa. **Habitat:** Wet prairie.

**MIRIAM'S SKIPPER** *Hesperia miriamae* MacNeill **Pl. 43**
**Identification:** 1⅛–1¼ in. (28–31 mm). A scarce, truly alpine species of very restricted range. **Upperside:** Male pale tawny, with a slight sheen. Dusky FW border wide; *spots near apex unusually large.* HW border narrow, veins dark; anal area dark. Female usually lighter, looks more "washed out." **Underside:** Gray in both sexes, with a slight sheen; light areas pale, somewhat tawny on FW cell. Spots of HW macular band *dull white, crossed by dark veins, and extending along veins.*
**Early stages:** Little known. One brood. **Adults:** July–early Sept.
**Range:** Sierra Nevada, Tuolumne Co. to Inyo Co., Calif.; White Mts. of e. Calif. and w. Nev. TL: Near Mono Pass, nw. Inyo Co., 12,000 ft., Calif. **Habitat:** Alpine fell-fields and summits, at 11,000–14,000 ft. (3355–4270 m).

**NEVADA SKIPPER** *Hesperia nevada* (Scudder) **Pl. 43**
**Identification:** 1⅛–1⅜ in. (28–34 mm). **Upperside:** Male tawny; dusky border grades gradually into ground color. Markings more diffuse in female. White spots on underside show through as lighter markings in both sexes. **Underside:** Light brown to greenish brown. HW macular band *very irregular,* spots often separated; *last spot displaced far inward.*
**Early stages:** Larva brownish; several brown and white markings on face. One brood. **Food:** Western needlegrass *(Stipa occidentalis)* in Calif.; squirrel-tail grass *(Sitanion hystrix)* also reported. **Adults:** June–Aug. They often sun themselves on exposed rocks, a habit shared by other alpine species.
**Range:** British Columbia south through higher mountains of the West to Calif., Nev., Ariz., N.M. TL: "Colorado, Oregon." **Habitat:** High mountains to alpine areas, high sagebrush to fell-fields, summits; 7000–12,000 ft. (2135–3660 m).

## Genus *Stinga* Evans

**MORRISON'S SKIPPER** **Pl. 44**
*Stinga morrisoni* (W. H. Edwards)
**Identification:** 1–1⅛ in. (25–28 mm). Unique. **Upperside:** Male orange-brown, FW stigma black; border brown and very wide. Female similar, with a dark bar on FW in place of stigma. **Under-**

*side:* HW dark brown in both sexes; anal area *orange-brown.* Pm. band and *long bar at upper edge of cell silky white.*
**Similar species:** Draco Skipper (p. 231).
**Early stages:** Unknown. One brood. **Adults:** April (Tex.) to May–early June (Colo.) They fly early in the year for a mountain-dwelling species. Said to be fast and wary.
**Range:** Colo., Ariz., N.M., w. Tex.; n. Mexico. Very local. TL: S. Colorado, Hardscrabble Canyon, Custer Co. **Habitat:** Grassy mountain meadows, 7000–9000 ft. (2135–2745 m).
**Remarks:** Scarce in collections.

## Genus *Pseudocopaeodes* Skinner & Williams

**EUNUS SKIPPER** Pl. 44
*Pseudocopaeodes eunus* (W. H. Edwards)
**Identification:** 1-1¼ in. (25–31 mm). *Upperside:* Bright orange-brown to yellowish orange. Vein ends usually dark (absent in very light individuals). Border dark, narrow. Male stigma black, slender, diagonal. *Underside:* Dull yellow; FW disc tawny. FW apex and HW have dark veins (in light individuals veins may not be dark). Usually *2 light lengthwise rays on HW.*
**Early stages:** Little known. 2–3 broods. **Food:** Desert salt grass *(Distichlis spicata* var. *stricta)*. **Adults:** March–Sept.
**Range:** E. Calif. (Mono Basin) and s. San Joaquin Valley (Kings Co.), south to San Diego Co. and s. Nev.; Baja California. TL: Bottoms of Kern River near Bakersfield. **Habitat:** Streamsides and moist places in arid wastelands.

## Genus *Yvretta* Hemming

Members of this genus resemble true skippers (*Hesperia* species, p. 234), but are darker, not tawny. Club on antenna blunt; almost no apiculus. Two species, occurring from the southwestern U.S. to Panama.

**RHESUS SKIPPER** *Yvretta rhesus* (W. H. Edwards) Pl. 44
**Identification:** 1-1¼ in. (25–31 mm). *Fringes white. Upperside:* Male blackish brown; FW stigma obscured by ground color. Spots near FW apex and pm. spots white. HW often has a light central chevron. Female similar, but FW spots much larger; HW markings also larger. *Underside:* HW greenish buff to light brown in both sexes, with *irregular dark spots.* Veins white. Pm. band white, forming a part of the general pattern.
**Similar species:** Carus Skipper (below) is lighter; fringes not white.
**Early stages:** Unknown. One brood. **Adults:** May.
**Range:** E. Wyo., e. Colo., w. Kans., w. Ariz., N.M.; n. Mexico. Uncommon. TL: Hardscrabble Canyon west of Pueblo, Colo. **Habitat:** Prairie.

**CARUS SKIPPER** *Yvretta carus* (W. H. Edwards)  **Pl. 44**
**Identification:** 1-1¼ in. (25-31 mm). Fringes *pale* but not white.
*Upperside:* Male grayish brown; spots near FW apex and pm.
spots white. *Stigma dark, easily seen.* HW pm. band present or
absent. Female similar, but spots much larger. *Underside:* Green-
ish buff to yellowish gray; FW markings repeated. HW veins whit-
ish, with *dark dots at tips.* Pm. band complete, narrow, dull
whitish.
**Similar species:** In Rhesus Skipper (above), fringes white.
**Early stages:** Unknown. Multiple broods. **Adults:** April–Sept.
**Range:** S. Ariz. to sw. Tex.; Mexico. Has been recorded from
s. Calif., along Colorado R. Uncommon. TL: Archer Co., Tex.
**Habitat:** Grassy patches along small streams and washes.
**Subspecies:** (1) **Carus Skipper,** *Y. c. carus* (W. H. Edwards),
Pl. 44. Range as given above. (2) **Subreticulate Skipper,**
*Y. c. subreticulata* (Ploetz). More heavily marked on underside.
Extreme sw. Tex. to Panama. TL: Not stated.

## Genus *Adopaeoides* Godman

**PRITTWITZ'S SKIPPER**  **Pl. 44**
*Adopaeoides prittwitzi* (Ploetz)
**Identification:** ⅞-1 in. (22-25 mm). *Upperside:* Dull yellowish
orange; *narrow border and veins dark. Underside:* Yellowish.
HW has *light stripe through cell from base to outer margin.*
**Early stages:** Unknown. Multiple broods. **Adults:** May–Sept.
**Range:** S. Ariz., sw. Tex.; Mexico. TL: Mexico. **Habitat:** Has been
found along small permanent streams.

## Genus *Copaeodes* Speyer

Antennae short, without apiculus. FW triangular; outer margin
slightly concave. Abdomen extends beyond HW. Male has straight
black stigma on FW. Three species; 2 in the U.S.

**ORANGE SKIPPERLING**  **Pl. 44**
*Copaeodes aurantiacus* (Hewitson)
**Identification:** ¾-1 in. (19-25 mm). *Upperside:* Male bright
orange-yellow; *FW stigma straight, black, located below cell.* Terminal line black; fringes pale-tipped. Female slightly duller. *Underside:* Similar to upperside; anal margin of FW marked with
black.
**Similar species:** Southern Skipperling (p. 244) is smaller; light
stripe from HW base to outer margin on underside.
**Early stages:** Larva green, with purple lengthwise stripes; head is
banded with pink and has 2 projecting points; cheek patches purple. Multiple broods. **Food:** Bermuda grass *(Cynodon dactylon).*
**Adults:** Long flight season.

**Range:** S. Calif., s. Nev., sw. Utah, w. Kans., Ariz., N.M., Tex.; south to Panama. TL: Not stated. **Habitat:** Grassy streamsides, washes, fields.

## SOUTHERN SKIPPERLING Pl. 44
*Copaeodes minimus* (W. H. Edwards)
**Identification:** $\frac{5}{8}$-$\frac{7}{8}$ in. (16–22 mm). *Upperside:* A small "replica" of the Orange Skipperling (above). *Underside:* HW has a *pale stripe or ray* through cell from base to outer margin.
**Early stages:** Undescribed. Multiple broods. **Food:** Bermuda grass *(Cynodon dactylon)*. **Adults:** Feb.–Nov.
**Range:** Arkansas, Texas, and southeastern U.S. south to Cen. America. TL: Waco, Tex. **Habitat:** Grassy fields.

### Genus *Oarisma* Scudder

Antennae short; club lacks apiculus. Both FW and HW triangular. Abdomen extends beyond HW. Male lacks stigma in our species.

## POWESHEIK SKIPPER Pl. 44
*Oarisma powesheik* (Parker)
**Identification:** 1–1$\frac{1}{4}$ in. (25–31 mm). *Upperside:* Dark brown; FW tawny from costa to cell. *Underside:* Blackish. *Veins silvery white* on FW costa and apex and on *HW, except in anal area.*
**Similar species:** (1) Garita Skipperling (below) is brown; veins on underside of HW pale. (2) Edwards' Skipperling (below) is tawny; underside of HW yellowish.
**Early stages:** Unknown. One brood. **Adults:** June–July.
**Range:** N.D. south to Neb., east to Wisc., Mich. TL: Grinnell, Iowa. **Habitat:** Prairie.

## GARITA SKIPPERLING *Oarisma garita* (Reakirt) Pl. 44
**Identification:** $\frac{3}{4}$–1 in. (19–25 mm). *Upperside:* Warm brown; FW costa tawny. Fringes same color as wings. *Underside:* FW dull tawny; veins slightly darker. HW yellowish gray; *veins lighter but not white;* anal area tawny.
**Similar species:** (1) Powesheik Skipper (above). (2) Edwards' Skipperling (below).
**Early stages:** Larva green, striped with white. One brood. **Food:** Bluegrass *(Poa pratensis)* and other grasses. **Adults:** June–Aug. Weak flyers.
**Range:** British Columbia east to Manitoba, south to Wash., Idaho, Ariz., Neb. Common. TL: Colorado Territory. **Habitat:** Grassland, open forest, mountain meadows, to 10,000 ft. (3050 m).

## EDWARDS' SKIPPERLING Pl. 44
*Oarisma edwardsii* (Barnes)
**Identification:** $\frac{7}{8}$–1$\frac{1}{8}$ in. (22–28 mm). Fringes white-tipped. Sexes

similar. ***Upperside:*** Brownish tawny; *FW cell brighter.* Terminal line and HW costa black. ***Underside:*** Upper $\frac{2}{3}$ of FW tawny, lower $\frac{1}{3}$ black. HW grayish yellow; anal area tawny.
**Similar species:** (1) Powesheik Skipper (p. 244). (2) Garita Skipperling (above).
**Early stages:** Unknown. One brood in Rocky Mts.; apparently multiple broods in w. Tex. **Adults:** June–Aug. in Rocky Mts., Apr.–Sept. in w. Tex.
**Range:** Colo., Utah, Ariz., N.M., w. Tex.; Mexico. TL: Denver, Colo. **Habitat:** Mountain grassland, meadows, open forest and woodland.

## Genus *Ancyloxypha* C. Felder

Antennae short; club pointed. FW long, narrow. Abdomen long; extends beyond HW. Male lacks FW stigma.

**TROPICAL LEAST SKIPPERLING**      Pl. 44
*Ancyloxypha arene* (W. H. Edwards)
**Identification:** $\frac{3}{4}$–1 in. (19–25 mm). Female slightly duller than male. ***Upperside:*** Dull orange. *Border and FW cell bar blackish.* ***Underside:*** Entirely dull orange, but FW black at base.
**Early stages:** Unknown. Multiple broods. **Food:** Water bentgrass *(Polypogon simiverticillata).* **Adults:** April–Oct.
**Range:** S. Ariz. east to s. Tex., south to Cen. America. TL: Near Tucson, Pima Co., Ariz. **Habitat:** Edges of fresh water; small streams, ditches, ponds, marshes.

## Genus *Lerema* Scudder

**CLOUDED SKIPPER** *Lerema accius* (J. E. Smith)     Pl. 44
**Identification:** $1\frac{1}{4}$–$1\frac{1}{2}$ in. (31–38 mm). ***Upperside:*** Male deep glossy violet-brown. *FW spots very small, white, hyaline (clear);* no spots on HW. FW stigma well developed but inconspicuous against ground color. Female similar, but FW spots larger. ***Underside:*** Markings of upperside repeated on FW in both sexes. HW base, costa, and incomplete median band brown; postbasal and marginal areas overscaled with violet-gray, extending along anal area.
**Early stages:** Larva whitish, with small dark lines; head white, with dark markings. Multiple broods. **Food:** Plumegrass *(Erianthus alopecuroides),* corn *(Zea mays),* St. Augustine grass *(Stenotaphrum secundatum),* and other grasses. **Adults:** Feb.–Nov. They take refuge in grass and brush when disturbed.
**Range:** W. Tex. east to Ill., Mass. south to Fla. Rare northward, common southward. TL: Georgia. **Habitat:** Open woodland, streamsides, roadsides.

## Genus *Nastra* Evans

**NEAMATHLA SKIPPER** **Pl. 44**
*Nastra neamathla* (Skinner & R. C. Williams)
**Identification:** $7/8$-$1\frac{1}{8}$ in. (22–29 mm). Very dull-colored and inconspicuous. Sexes alike. *Upperside:* Grayish brown. Light spots on FW very small or nearly absent; HW unmarked. *Underside:* FW markings repeated. *HW nearly uniform dull grayish brown.* **Similar species:** (1) In Julia's Skipper (below), underside more reddish brown. (2) Eufala Skipper (p. 215). (3) Arabus Skipper (p. 215).
**Early stages:** Undescribed. Multiple broods. **Food:** Unknown.
**Adults:** March–Sept.
**Range:** Has been recorded from s. Ariz. and Tex. More common in the Gulf States. TL: Central Florida. **Habitat:** Moist, usually open areas; marsh edges.
**Remarks:** This species was originally placed in the genus *Lerodea.*

**JULIA'S SKIPPER** *Nastra julia* (H. A. Freeman) **Pl. 44**
**Identification:** 1-$1\frac{1}{8}$ in. (24–28 mm). Coloration dull but quite distinctive. *Upperside:* Brown, with a slight gloss. FW spots small, powdery, not hyaline. HW unmarked. *Underside:* Warm, slightly reddish, brown; *lower half of FW and anal area of HW blackish brown.*
**Similar species:**(1) Neamathla Skipper (above) is much grayer. (2) Eufala Skipper (p. 215). (3) Arabus Skipper (p. 215).
**Early stages:** Undescribed. Multiple broods. **Food:** Reared on St. Augustine grass; food in nature not known. **Adults:** All year in s. Tex.
**Range:** Lower Colorado R., Calif., s. Ariz., to s. Tex. TL: Pharr, Tex. **Habitat:** Fields, streamsides, river bottoms, lawns.
**Remarks:** Originally described in the genus *Lerodea,* Julia's Skipper was placed in genus *Nastra* in 1955.

## Genus *Erionota* Mabille

**BANANA SKIPPER** *Erionota thrax* (Linnaeus) **Pl. 44**
**Identification:** $2\frac{3}{8}$-$2\frac{1}{2}$ in. (60–64 mm). *Very large. Upperside:* Medium brown; fringes light but not white. Two *large median spots* and 1 small *pm. spot,* all *dull yellow* and hyaline. HW unmarked. *Underside:* FW spots repeated; wing surface mottled with yellowish gray. HW slightly lighter; inconspicuous postbasal spot and incomplete median band just slightly darker.
**Early stages:** Apparently not described in detail. Multiple broods. **Food:** Banana trees; larva can be destructive to plantations. **Adults:** Long flight season. Said to fly mostly in early morning and in the evening.

**Range:** Southern and southeast Asia. Introduced into Hawaii in 1973; now found on all the islands. TL: Java. **Habitat:** Said to stay quite close to food plant, banana.

## Subfamily Heteropterinae

### Genus *Piruna* Evans

Small, dark species with hyaline (clear) spots. Wings broad; outer margin rounded. Abdomen extends beyond wings. Club on antennae flattened, curved; point triangular. Palpi long and hairy.

Prior to 1955, the species now in genus *Piruna* were placed in *Butleria.*

**PIRUS SKIPPERLING**                                    **Pl. 44**
*Piruna pirus* (W. H. Edwards)
**Identification:** 1-1⅛ in. (25-28 mm). Our commonest *Piruna. Upperside:* Dark brown. *White hyaline spots on FW minute,* sometimes reduced to apex only. HW unmarked. *Underside:* Warm reddish brown. FW cell darker; spots as on upperside. HW unmarked.
**Similar species:**(1) In Small-spotted Skipperling (below), many minute spots on underside of HW. (2) In Poling's Skipperling (below), spots on underside of HW large, white. (3) In Hafernik's Skipperling (p. 248), discal area on underside of HW darker than rest of wing.
**Early stages:** Unknown. One brood. **Adults:** June–July.
**Range:** Wyo., Colo., Utah, N.M., Ariz. TL: Southern Colorado.
**Habitat:** Open forest, dry meadows.

**SMALL-SPOTTED SKIPPERLING**                            **Pl. 44**
*Piruna microsticta* (Godman)
**Identification:** ⅞-1 in. (22-25 mm). *Upperside:* Very dark brown; FW spots mere dots. *Two spots at FW apex, far apart —* similar species have 3 spots at FW apex. Cell spot narrow, extending vertically across entire cell. HW has 3-4 minute spots. *Underside: Many minute spots on HW.*
**Similar species:** (1) Pirus Skipperling (above). (2) Poling's Skipperling (below). (3) Hafernik's Skipperling (p. 248).
**Early stages:** Unknown. One brood. **Adults:** July.
**Range:** S. Ariz., w. Tex.; Mexico. TL: Mexico. **Habitat:** Not known.
**Remarks:** Very rare. Few records known, some of them doubtful.

**POLING'S SKIPPERLING**                                 **Pl. 44**
*Piruna polingii* (Barnes)
**Identification:** 1-1⅛ in. (25-28 mm). *Upperside:* Dark glossy brown. *Small white spots on FW conspicuous;* 3 spots at FW apex.

HW has 2–3 white spots. *Underside:* FW spots repeated. HW has 1 small postbasal spot and 3 silvery median spots.
**Similar species:** (1) Pirus Skipperling (p. 247). (2) Small-spotted Skipperling (p. 247). (3) Hafernik's Skipperling (below).
**Early stages:** Unknown. One brood. **Adults:** June–July.
**Range:** Ariz., N.M.; Mexico. TL: Huachuca Mts., Ariz. **Habitat:** Moist places with lush vegetation.

## HAFERNIK'S SKIPPERLING                    not shown
*Piruna haferniki* H. A. Freeman
**Identification:** 1 in. (25 mm). *Upperside:* Blackish brown. *3 spots at FW apex all about the same size;* pm. spots distinct, oval. HW unmarked. *Underside:* FW spots repeated. HW *purplish gray;* central brown area *darker than rest of wing.*
**Similar species:** (1) Pirus Skipperling (p. 247). (2) Small-spotted Skipperling (p. 247). (3) Poling's Skipperling (above).
**Early stages:** Unknown. One brood. **Adults:** Late July–early Aug.
**Range:** Known only from the TL: Green Gulch, Big Bend Natl. Park, Brewster Co., Tex., 5700 ft. (1739 m).

## Genus *Carterocephalus* Lederer

## ARCTIC SKIPPER                    Pl. 48
*Carterocephalus palaemon* (Pallas)
**Identification:** 1–1¼ in. (25–31 mm). Unique. *Upperside: Black, with orange spots. Underside:* FW dull orange, with black spots. HW orange-brown; spots creamy white, narrowly outlined in black.
**Early stages:** Larva cream-colored, with a faint dark stripe down back. Sides dark-spotted, with yellowish stripes. Head green. One brood. **Food:** Various grasses. In Calif., purple reedgrass *(Calamagrostis purpurascens).* **Adults:** May–July. Flight low and weak for a skipper. Tame: They often sit with head down.
**Range:** Not truly arctic. Alaska south to Sonoma and Sierra Cos., Calif. In Rocky Mts. to Wyo., east to e. Canada, New England. **Habitat:** Woodland meadows, forest openings, usually in moist areas; trails, roadsides. In Alaska, taiga.
**Subspecies:** (1) *C. p. palaemon* (Pallas). Does not occur in N. America. TL: Russia. (2) *C. p. mandan* (W. H. Edwards), Pl. 48. N. America. TL: Pine Ridge, Manitoba, Canada.

# Dusky-wings, Checkered Skippers, and Allies: Subfamily Pyrginae

Small to large species; may be blackish, white, dark brown, or checkered. Many adults rest with the wings horizontal (open); some bring their wings together over the back. Vein $M_2$ of FW arises halfway between veins $M_1$ and $M_3$, and is not curved at base. Midtibia not spined. Tip (apiculus) of antennal club blunt in some genera, sharply pointed in others. Male may have FW costal fold (Fig. 15), hair tuft on hind tibia (Fig. 16), both, or neither. Males of a few genera have a hair tuft at base of HW.

**Early stages:** Larvae feed on dicotyledonous plants (flowering plants with two seed leaves).

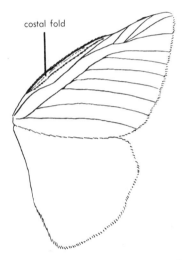

**Fig. 15. Dusky-wing: leading edge of forewing in male.**

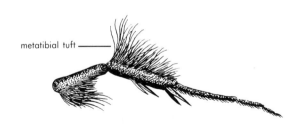

**Fig. 16. Skipper: hind leg of male.**

## Sooty-wings: Genus *Pholisora* Scudder

Small; black or dusky. Wings rounded. Antennae short; club curved; apiculus flat and blunt. Palpi long, slender, drooping, white on underside. Five species; all occur in the western U.S.

### COMMON SOOTY-WING                                 Pl. 44
*Pholisora catullus* (Fabricius)
**Identification:** 1-1⅛ in. (25-28 mm). **Upperside:** Sooty black. *Small white spots on outer* ⅓ *of FW;* cell spot sometimes present. HW all black, or with a submarginal row of small white dots. **Underside:** FW as on upperside. HW entirely black.
**Similar species:** In Mexican Sooty-wing (below), underside bluish gray, with black veins.
**Early stages:** Larva olive, granulated with yellow; head rough, black. One black stripe and 2 green stripes on first thoracic segment. 2-3 broods. **Food:** Lamb's quarters *(Chenopodium album),* tumbleweed *(Amaranthus graecizans).* **Adults:** March–Sept.
**Range:** S. Canada south through U.S. into Mexico; found throughout the West. Uncommon to scarce in some localities. TL: "in India," probably Georgia in the U.S. **Habitat:** Weedy fields, pastures, waste land, roadsides.

### MEXICAN SOOTY-WING                                 Pl. 44
*Pholisora mejicana* (Reakirt)
**Identification:** 1-1⅛ in. (25-28 mm). **Upperside:** Similar to the Common Sooty-wing (above). **Underside:** *HW bluish brown; veins black.*
**Early stages:** Unknown. **Adults:** May–Aug.
**Range:** Colo., Ariz., N.M., Tex.; Mexico. Very scarce in the U.S. TL: Near Veracruz, Mexico.

### MOJAVE SOOTY-WING *Pholisora libya* (Scudder)     Pl. 44
**Identification:** ⅞-1¼ in. (22-31 mm). Terminal line and tips of fringes *white.* **Upperside:** Small white spots on FW, varying in number and size; some individuals have spots on HW as well. **Underside:** FW black; apex, submarginal spots, and wing edge whitish. HW light to dark brown with pale gray overscaling; *postbasal, median, and pm. spots white,* often quite *large.*
**Early stages:** Larva blue-green with many small, white, raised points; black dots on the body segments. Head black, covered with short orange hairs. 2-3 broods. **Food:** Shadscale *(Atriplex canescens),* and perhaps other plants in the saltbush family (Chenopodiaceae). **Adults:** March–Oct.
**Range:** E. Ore. to Mont., south to s. Calif., Ariz. Usually common where found. **Habitat:** Shadscale scrub, alkali flats, desert streamsides.
**Subspecies:** (1) **Mojave Sooty-wing,** *P. l. libya* (Scudder), Pl. 44.

Southern part of range. TL: Beaver Dam, Ariz. (2) **Lena Sooty-wing,** *P. l. lena* (W. H. Edwards). Northern part of range. Fewer white spots on underside of HW. TL: Miles City, Mont.

## ALPHEUS SOOTY-WING                    Pl. 44
*Pholisora alpheus* (W. H. Edwards)
**Identification:** $7/8$-1 in. (22–25 mm). *Upperside:* Blackish; spots at FW apex and pm. spots white. FW has pm. row of *short dark bars,* more or less outlined with gray or white. HW black, or with faint light spots. *Underside:* Quite similar to upperside.
**Similar species:** In MacNeill's Sooty-wing (below), FW markings smaller.
**Early stages:** Undescribed; previous descriptions under this name apply to MacNeill's Sooty-wing. One brood northward, 2–3 broods southward. **Food:** Shadscale *(Atriplex canescens).* **Adults:** Flight season varies with subspecies (see below). Inconspicuous; flight low.
**Range:** E. Ore. east to Colo., south to Mexico. **Habitat:** Shadscale scrub, desert, arid waste land; salt flats in Tex.
**Subspecies:** (1) **Alpheus Sooty-wing,** *P. a. alpheus* (W. H. Edwards). Dark dashes on FW more conspicuous. Flies March–Sept. Ariz., N.M., Colo. TL: Colfax Co., N.M. (2) **Texas Sooty-wing,** *P. a. texana* Scott, Pl. 44. Flies March–Nov. Texas. TL: Boca Chica, Cameron Co., Tex. (3) **Oricus Sooty-wing,** *P. a. oricus* (W. H. Edwards). Larger, with more white overscaling. Flies April–June. E. Ore., Nev., e. Calif. TL: Buffalo Canyon, Churchill Co., Nev.

## MACNEILL'S SOOTY-WING                    Pl. 44
*Pholisora gracielae* MacNeill
**Identification:** $3/4$-1 in. (19–25 mm). Similar to Alpheus Sooty-wing (above), but smaller. *Palpi longer, more thickly scaled.* All markings smaller; fringes plainly checkered. *Upperside:* Blackish, fading to dusky in old specimens. *Underside:* Pale overscaling conspicuous. HW spots small, complete.
**Early stages:** Larva dull green, covered with small whitish nodules; head brownish black, clothed with yellowish pile. Two broods. **Food:** Quail brush *(Atriplex lentiformis),* in the saltbush family (Chenopodiaceae). **Adults:** April–May, July–Oct.
**Range:** Lower Colorado R., in Nev., Calif., Ariz. TL: Bennett Wash, near Parker Dam, San Bernardino Co., Calif. **Habitat:** In the vicinity of quail brush; seldom ventures into the open.

### Genus *Celotes* Godman & Salvin

HW scalloped. Male has both FW costal fold and metatibial tuft on hind leg (Figs. 15 and 16, p. 249). Two very similar species, both in our area.

**STREAKY SKIPPER** *Celotes nessus* (W. H. Edwards)   **Pl. 44**
**Identification:** $7/8$–$1\frac{1}{8}$ in. (22–28 mm). Very odd-looking, but inconspicuous. Fringes checkered. *Upperside:* Yellowish brown, with *many dark brown streaks between the veins.* Each wing has several *very narrow hyaline streaks.*
**Similar species:** Burns' Skipper (below).
**Early stages:** Undescribed. Multiple broods. **Food:** Indian mallow *(Abutilon incanum),* violet sida *(Sida filipes),* globe mallow *(Sphaeralcea lobata),* and other mallows. **Adults:** March–Nov.
**Range:** Ariz., N.M., Tex.; Mexico. TL: San Antonio, Tex. **Habitat:** Open woodland, thorn forest, desert washes.

**BURNS' SKIPPER** *Celotes limpia* Burns            **not shown**
**Identification:** 1–$1\frac{1}{4}$ in. (25–31 mm). Very similar to Streaky Skipper (above), but slightly larger. Male genitalia distinctly different. *Underside:* Somewhat more lightly marked than in Streaky Skipper.
**Early stages:** Undescribed. Multiple broods. **Food:** Same plants as for Streaky Skipper. **Adults:** March–Sept.
**Range:** Trans-Pecos section of Tex. and south into Mexico. TL: Limpia Canyon, 5000 ft., Davis Mountains, 4 miles nw. of Fort Davis, Jeff Davis Co., Tex. **Habitat:** As described by Burns: ". . . alluvial fans, foothills, lower canyon reaches. . ."
**Remarks:** First described in 1974.

## White Skippers: Genus *Heliopetes* Billberg

Moderate to large, with extensive white markings. Structure similar to that of checkered skippers (*Pyrgus* species, pp. 254–256). Males have both FW costal fold and metatibial tuft on hind leg (Figs. 15 and 16, p. 249). Fourteen or 15 species, 4 in our area.

**ERICHSON'S SKIPPER**                              **Pl. 45**
*Heliopetes domicella* (Erichson)
**Identification:** $1\frac{1}{8}$–$1\frac{3}{8}$ in. (28–34 mm). Fringes checkered. *Upperside:* Slaty gray, with a *wide white median band* on both wings. Wing bases unmarked, clothed with bluish gray hair. Many small white spots on outer $1/3$ of wings. *Underside:* Basal and median bands whitish. Postbasal band, FW apex, and wide HW margin dull yellowish brown. Blackish pm. band on FW encloses 5–6 small white spots.
**Early stages:** Undescribed. Two or more broods. **Food:** Unknown. **Adults:** April–Oct.
**Range:** Se. Calif. (Parker Dam, San Bernardino Co.), s. Ariz. to s. Tex.; south to Argentina. Local and uncommon. TL: British Guiana. **Habitat:** Open thorn forest, desert washes, streamside flats.

**LARGE WHITE SKIPPER** Pl. 48
*Heliopetes ericetorum* (Boisduval)
**Identification:** $1\frac{1}{4}$–$1\frac{1}{2}$ in. (31–38 mm). *Upperside:* Male white, with a *border of dark chevrons along outer margin.* Female very different, slate-gray, with an irregular white median band and *submarginal chevrons.* *Underside:* Both sexes whitish, the basal and submarginal shading reddish brown to dull gray.
**Similar species:** (1) In Laviana Skipper (below), underside markings darker. (2) In Macaira Skipper (below), dark markings on underside form a definite pattern. (3) Common Checkered Skipper (p. 255) is smaller and darker on underside.
**Early stages:** Larva greenish yellow, with short white hair and greenish lines on back and sides. 2–3 broods. **Food:** Globe mallow *(Sphaeralcea)* and other mallows. **Adults:** April–Oct.
**Range:** E. Wash. east to w. Colo. (scarce), south to s. Calif., Ariz.; Baja California, Mexico. TL: California. **Habitat:** Foothills, uncultivated arid land. Desert mountains in s. Calif.; open coniferous forest in Sierra Nevada of Calif. (less common).

**LAVIANA SKIPPER** *Heliopetes laviana* (Hewitson) Pl. 45
**Identification:** $1\frac{3}{8}$–$1\frac{5}{8}$ in. (34–41 mm). *Upperside:* Male white; *FW outer margin and apex blackish.* The narrow black HW border encloses small white spots; border absent from HW apex. Female similar, but dark borders wider; wing bases gray. *Underside:* Dark markings olive-gray in both sexes. A *straight light line* runs from HW apex to tornus.
**Similar species:** (1) Large White Skipper (above). (2) Macaira Skipper (below).
**Early stages:** Undescribed. Multiple broods. **Food:** Indian mallow *(Abutilon),* globe mallow *(Sphaeralcea),* alkali mallow *(Sida),* and other mallows. **Adults:** Long flight season.
**Range:** S. Calif. (1 record from Riverside Co.), s. Ariz. (scarce), s. Tex. (common), to S. America. TL: Nicaragua. **Habitat:** Open woodland, streamsides, and thorn forest, often in partial shade.

**MACAIRA SKIPPER** *Heliopetes macaira* (Reakirt) Pl. 45
**Identification:** $1\frac{1}{4}$–$1\frac{3}{8}$ in. (31–34 mm). *Upperside:* Male white; FW apex and border dark; a *white dash opposite cell end.* HW border dark, narrow. Both FW and HW borders enclose small white spots. Female similar, but borders much wider; *wing bases gray. Underside:* FW markings repeated. HW has a dark submedian band and a rounded, dark olive marginal band.
**Similar species:** (1) Large White Skipper (above). (2) Laviana Skipper (above).
**Early stages:** Undescribed. Multiple broods. **Food:** Turk's cap *(Malvaviscus drummondii).* **Adults:** Long flight season.
**Range:** S. Tex. south to S. America. There are unverified reports of its occurrence in s. Ariz. TL: Mexico. **Habitat:** Mixed forest edges and openings, thorn forest.

## Checkered Skippers: Genus *Pyrgus* Huebner

An extensive genus, found in Europe, Asia, and the Americas. All
species rather similar in appearance: small and dark, with many
small white spots or dashes. Fringes checkered. Antennal club
blunt, evenly curved. FW costal fold and metatibial tuft present in
males of some species (Figs. 15 and 16, p. 249).

**GRIZZLED SKIPPER** *Pyrgus centaureae* (Rambur)       **Pl. 45**
**Identification:** 1–1¼ in. (25–31 mm). Male has both FW costal
fold and metatibial tuft. *Upperside:* Slate gray. Body and wing
bases covered with bluish gray hair. White spots on FW squarish,
well spaced; *2 spots near center of inner margin.* *Underside:*
Checkered white and brownish gray; veins whitish.
**Similar species:** (1) In Two-banded Skipper (below), 3 spots
near center of FW inner margin. Markings on underside of HW
brownish.
**Early stages:** Not known for N. America. One brood. **Food:** In
Europe, cloudberry *(Rubus chamaemorus),* in the rose family.
Larval food not known for N. America. **Adults:** June–Aug.
**Range:** In West, n.-cen. Alaska south to Colo. In East, Labrador
south to N.C. Northern and alpine; usually uncommon. **Habitat:**
In Colo., high mountains at or above treeline. In Alaska, mossy
openings in taiga. (Has also been taken flying over marshes and
bogs.)
**Subspecies:** (1) *P. c. centaureae* (Rambur). European. TL: Lap-
land. (2) **Freija's Grizzled Skipper,** *P. c. freija* (Warren). Alaska,
Yukon Terr., and eastward. Underside white and gray, not brown-
ish. TL: Labrador. (3) **Loki's Grizzled Skipper,** *P. c. loki* Evans,
Pl. 45. Rocky Mts., from British Columbia and Alberta to Colo.
TL: Long's Peak, Colo.

**TWO-BANDED SKIPPER** *Pyrgus ruralis* (Boisduval)    **Pl. 45**
**Identification:** 1–1⅛ in. (25–28 mm). Male has both FW costal
fold and metatibial tuft. *Upperside:* Blackish, with well-spaced
white spots of medium size. *3 spots near center of FW inner margin.* HW usually has 2 rows of white spots. *Underside:* Brown or
gray; light spots often indistinct — seldom white, usually dull.
**Similar species:** Grizzled Skipper (above).
**Early stages:** Mostly undescribed. One brood. **Food:** Santa Rosa
horkelia *(Horkelia tenuiloba),* dusky horkelia *(Horkelia fusca),*
Cleveland's horkelia *(Horkelia bolanderi clevelandii),* and no
doubt others. **Adults:** April–July, depending on locality.
**Range:** British Columbia and Alberta south in mountains to s.
Calif., Ariz., N.M. Widespread. Usually uncommon and local; inconspicuous. TL: California. **Habitat:** Meadows, pastures, forest
openings, stream terraces. From sea level in coastal Calif. to
10,000 ft. (3050 m) in Colo.

## XANTHUS SKIPPER Pl. 45
*Pyrgus xanthus* W. H. Edwards
**Identification:** ³/₄-1 in. (19–25 mm). Uncommon; often confused with other species. Male lacks FW costal fold, but has metatibial tuft. *Upperside:* Dark gray; spots white, medium-sized, well separated. *Spots at FW apex and cell bar usually larger and more conspicuous* than in other checkered skippers (*Pyrgus* species, pp. 254–256). Pm. band complete, the spots separate. *Underside:* Markings as on upperside, but somewhat duller.
**Early stages:** Unknown. One brood. **Food:** Cinquefoil *(Potentilla ambigens),* silverweed *(Potentilla anserina),* and perhaps others. **Adults:** Late May to early July.
**Range:** S. Colo. to s. N.M. and cen. Ariz. TL: Colorado. **Habitat:** High mountain areas, from 8000 to 10,500 ft. (2440–3100 m).

## SMALL CHECKERED SKIPPER Pl. 45
*Pyrgus scriptura* (Boisduval)
**Identification:** ³/₄-1 in. (19–25 mm). Easily overlooked due to its small size and low flight. Male lacks FW costal fold, but has metatibial tuft. *Upperside:* Blackish brown; *FW spots very small,* well separated. HW spots reduced in number, the submarginal row usually mere dots and occasionally absent. *Underside:* FW dark, apex pale; white spots as on upperside. HW pale, usually light brown; markings often scarcely contrasting.
**Early stages:** Undescribed. Multiple broods. **Food:** Alkali mallow *(Sida hederacea).* **Adults:** March–Nov.
**Range:** Calif. east and north to Wyo., Colo., south to s. Calif., Ariz., N.M., Tex.; Baja California. TL: California. **Habitat:** Alkaline fields and marshes in Calif., open grasslands in Colo.

## COMMON CHECKERED SKIPPER Pl. 48
*Pyrgus communis* (Grote)
**Identification:** 1-1¼ in. (25–31 mm). Male has costal fold, but lacks metatibial tuft. *Upperside:* Male slate gray, the wing bases clothed with blue-gray hair. White spots form a median band on both wings; submarginal spots and marginal dots also present. FW has 6–7 marginal dots, but *none at FW apex.* FW spots tend to be crowded, not well separated. Female similar but darker. *Underside:* HW dull white, the postbasal and pm. bands yellowish brown to dark gray. A white crescent on outer margin of HW, between veins $M_1$ and $M_3$.
**Similar species:** Philetas Skipper (p. 256).
**Early stages:** Larva greenish gray with white-knobbed hairs; lives concealed in leaf nest. Multiple broods. **Food:** Many members of the mallow family (Malvaceae); especially common on introduced mallows in yards, gardens, along roadsides, fencerows, and in vacant lots. **Adults:** Most of year in warm climates.
**Range:** N. America from cen. Canada south; south to S. America. **Habitat:** Very general; may be found almost anywhere. Common and conspicuous, often in yards and gardens.

**Subspecies:** (1) **Common Checkered Skipper,** *P. c. communis* (Grote), Pl. 48. Canada and most of U.S. TL: Cen. Alabama. (2) **Southern Checkered Skipper,** *P. c. albescens* Ploetz. Lighter; male genitalia slightly different. S. Calif. to s. Tex. TL: Mexico. Status remains unsettled; some experts consider it a separate species.

## PHILETAS SKIPPER                                    Pl. 45
*Pyrgus philetas* W. H. Edwards
**Identification:** 1–1⅛ in. (25–28 mm). Male has both FW costal fold and metatibial tuft. *Upperside:* White spots very much as in Common Checkered Skipper (above), but *FW has 8 marginal white dots — dot at apex present. Underside:* HW light gray or light brownish, with a few small, indistinct dark spots. No white crescent on outer margin of HW.
**Early stages:** Unknown. 2–3 broods. **Food:** Not known. **Adults:** Long flight season.
**Range:** Ariz., N.M., Tex.; Mexico. TL: Western Texas. **Habitat:** Washes, openings in desert scrub or thorn forest.

## Dusky-wings: Genus *Erynnis* Schrank

Holarctic; best represented in N. America. Moderate to large, dark brown or black, usually with small hyaline (clear) spots on wings. Antennal club blunt and curved. Palpi of medium length, thrust forward. Females usually have larger hyaline spots and more light markings. Males all have the FW costal fold (Fig. 15, p. 249), and in some species males also have a metatibial tuft (Fig. 16, p. 249). Male genitalia offer the most positive means of identification; the right and left valves differ in shape.

A most complex genus, with many similar species. Appearance is not always a trustworthy means of identification; use habitat and food plants as aids.

## DREAMY DUSKY-WING                                    Pl. 45
*Erynnis icelus* (Scudder & Burgess)
**Identification:** 1⅛–1¼ in. (28–31 mm). Male has costal fold and metatibial tuft. FW short, wide. *Upperside:* No hyaline spots. FW has 2 indefinite dark bands; *median band dusted with pale scales* and usually slightly paler than rest of wing.
**Similar species:** In Sleepy Dusky-wing (p. 257), dark bands on upperside of FW more definite.
**Early stages:** Larva green, with a yellow prothorax; dark line on back, pale line on side. One brood. **Food:** Willow (*Salix,* various species), quaking aspen *(Populus tremuloides),* and other species of *Populus.* **Adults:** May–June.
**Range:** S. Canada, south in West to Calif., Ariz., and N.M.; in East to n. Georgia. Mostly mountains in the West. TL: New England. **Habitat:** Woodland openings, clearings, trails.

## SLEEPY DUSKY-WING Pl. 45
*Erynnis brizo* (Boisduval & Le Conte)
**Identification:** 1¼–1⅝ in. (31–41 mm). FW long, narrow. Male has costal fold but lacks metatibial tuft. *Upperside:* No hyaline spots. FW dusted with pale scales; *2 distinct bands of dusky spots edged by short black lines.*
**Similar species:** Dreamy Dusky-wing (p. 256).
**Early stages:** Larva pale green, with light and dark green stripes. One brood. **Food:** Oaks. **Adults:** Early spring; the month varies with locality and thus with subspecies (see below).
**Range:** Calif. east to Colo., south to Baja California, Ariz., N.M., Tex. **Habitat:** Oak woodland, chaparral.
**Subspecies:** (1) **Sleepy Dusky-wing,** *E. b. brizo* (Boisduval & Le Conte). Flies in June. Manitoba, eastern U.S. TL: N. America. (2) **Burgess's Dusky-wing,** *E. b. burgessi* (Skinner), Pl. 45. Larger; markings distinct. Flies March–April. Colo. south to Ariz., Tex. TL: Mt. Graham, Ariz. (3) **Lacustra Dusky-wing,** *E. b. lacustra* (Wright). Smaller; very dark. Flies March–May. Lake Co. to San Diego Co., Calif.; Baja California. TL: Blue Lakes, Calif.

## AFRANIUS DUSKY-WING Pl. 45
*Erynnis afranius* (Lintner)
**Identification:** 1¼–1⅜ in. (31–34 mm). This species and all the following dusky-wings (*Erynnis* species, pp. 257–262) have 4 hyaline spots near FW apex. Male has costal fold and metatibial tuft. *Fringes pale-tipped. Upperside:* Male has several hyaline pm. spots on FW and considerable pale overscaling; FW scales *flat to surface.* In female, hyaline spots usually larger, more prominent.
**Similar species:** Persius Dusky-wing (below).
**Early stages:** Little known. Multiple broods. **Food:** Lupine (*Lupinus,* various species), deerweed *(Lotus scoparius).* **Adults:** Most common May–Aug.
**Range:** Western. Mont. and N.D. south to s. Calif., Ariz., N.M.; Mexico. Absent on Pacific Slope from cen. Calif. northward. TL: Colorado. **Habitat:** Open coniferous forest; forest openings and edges.

## PERSIUS DUSKY-WING *Erynnis persius* (Scudder) Pl. 45
**Identification:** 1⅛–1⅜ in. (28–34 mm). Male has costal fold and metatibial tuft. *Upperside:* Brownish black. FW hyaline spots few, reduced to tiny dots. Markings more than usually obscure. FW has *erect hairs* among flat scales. *Fringes dark,* not pale-tipped. In female, pale scaling is more extensive and hyaline spots are a bit larger.
**Similar species:** Afranius Dusky-wing (above).
**Early stages:** Not described. One brood over much of range; multiple broods in parts of Calif. and Ore. **Food:** Willow *(Salix),* cottonwood, poplar *(Populus)* over much of range. False lupine

*(Thermopsis pinetorum)* in Ariz. Closely associated with poplar in Alaska. **Adults:** May–July over much of range; March–Sept. in parts of Calif. and Ore.
**Range:** Alaska and Canada south in the West to cen. Calif., Ariz., N.M. In East to Ky., N.J. **Habitat:** Mountain areas. Forest openings, wooded streamsides.
**Subspecies:** (1) **Persius Dusky-wing,** *E. p. persius* (Scudder), Pl. 45. Widely distributed. TL: New England. (2) **Frederick's Dusky-wing,** *E. p. fredericki* H. A. Freeman. Dark markings of FW more evident. N. Rocky Mts., N.D., S.D. TL: Spearfish Canyon, S.D. (3) **Boreal Dusky-wing,** *E. p. borealis* (Cary). Smaller; very dark. Alaska, n. Canada. TL: North Nahanni R., Mackenzie Dist., Canada.

## FUNEREAL DUSKY-WING                           Pl. 45
*Erynnis funeralis* (Scudder & Burgess)
**Identification:** 1⅜–1¾ in. (34–44 mm). Male has metatibial tuft — the only white-fringed dusky-wing that does — and costal fold. FW narrow. ***Upperside:*** Black. Spots near FW apex, spot in cell, and 2–4 pm. spots small, hyaline. FW has dull brown patch at end of cell. *HW fringes pure white,* with few or no dark scales at their bases.
**Similar species:** (1) Pacuvius Dusky-wing (p. 259). (2) Scudder's Dusky-wing (p. 262). (3) Mournful Dusky-wing (p. 259). (4) Clitus Dusky-wing (p. 261). All 4 have white HW fringes, but none has the narrow FW nor the male metatibial tuft of the Funereal Dusky-wing.
**Early stages:** Larva pale green, covered with minute yellow hairs; green stripe on back, yellow stripe on side; underside blue. Multiple broods. **Food:** Various legumes; deerweed *(Lotus scoparius),* alfalfa *(Medicago sativa),* bur clover *(Medicago hispida),* New Mexican locust *(Robinia neomexicana),* desert ironwood *(Olneya tesota),* vetch *(Vicia,* various species), and others. **Adults:** Feb.–Oct. in s. Calif.
**Range:** Calif., Ariz., N.M., Tex.; casual in Utah, Colo., Neb., and Kans. Occurs southward to Argentina. TL: Texas. **Habitat:** Warm, often arid, lowlands; deserts.

## MOTTLED DUSKY-WING                            Pl. 45
*Erynnis martialis* (Scudder)
**Identification:** 1⅛–1⅜ in. (28–34 mm). Male has costal fold but lacks metatibial tuft. Wings short and broad. ***Upperside:*** Irregular dark bands against a brownish background give a *mottled appearance on both FW and HW,* the only dusky-wing so marked.
**Early stages:** Undescribed. Two broods, at least in some areas. **Food:** Jersey tea *(Ceanothus americanus).* Old reports of pigweed and various legumes are apparently in error. **Adults:** Recorded April–Sept., depending on locality.
**Range:** In West, e. Wyo., e. Colo., and western S.D., south to Tex.

In East, s. Canada to Ala. TL: New Jefferson, Dallas Co., Iowa. **Habitat:** Open woodland, shrubby foothills.

## PACUVIUS DUSKY-WING                                    Pl. 45
*Erynnis pacuvius* (Lintner)
**Identification:** 1¼-1⅜ in. (31–34 mm). Male has costal fold but lacks metatibial tuft. *Upperside:* Brown, with irregular dark bands on FW. The submarginal spots are small and dull, but complete. *HW fringes white, with tufts of dark scales at their bases* in nominate subspecies; fringes *brown* in all other subspecies.
**Similar species:** (1) Funereal Dusky-wing (p. 258). (2) Scudder's Dusky-wing (p. 262). (3) Mournful Dusky-wing (below). (4) Clitus Dusky-wing (p. 261).
**Early stages:** Undescribed. One brood in north; 2 broods in s. Calif., Ariz., N.M. **Food:** Given under each subspecies. **Adults:** June–July in north, May–Sept. in south.
**Range:** Mountains of western N. America. British Columbia to Mont., south to s. Calif., Ariz., N.M.; Baja California, Mexico.
**Habitat:** Open coniferous forest, cutover land.
**Subspecies:** Four, quite different. (1) **Pacuvius Dusky-wing,** *E. p. pacuvius* (Lintner), Pl. 45, No. 15. More than the usual contrast on upperside. HW fringes white. Food: Deer brier *(Ceanothus fendleri)*. Colo., Utah, Ariz., N.M. TL: New Mexico. (2) **Dyar's Dusky-wing,** *E. p. lilius* (Dyar). Smaller; markings obscure. HW fringes brown. Food: Mountain whitethorn *(Ceanothus cordulatus)*. British Columbia, Idaho, Mont. south to cen. Calif. TL: Kaslo, British Columbia. (3) **Artful Dusky-wing,** *E. p. callidus* (F. Grinnell). Browner; hyaline spots more distinct. HW fringes brown. Food: Hairy ceanothus *(Ceanothus oliganthus)*. Monterey Co., Calif. south to Baja California. TL: Mt. Wilson, Calif. (4) **Grinnell's Dusky-wing,** *E. p. pernigra* (F. Grinnell), Pl. 45, No. 16. *Very black.* HW fringes brown. Food: *Ceanothus,* various species. Outer Coast Ranges, Calif., Sonoma Co. to Santa Cruz Co. TL: Mill Valley, Calif.

## MOURNFUL DUSKY-WING                                   Pl. 45
*Erynnis tristis* (Boisduval)
**Identification:** 1¼-1⅝ in. (31–41 mm). Male has costal fold but lacks metatibial tuft. *Upperside:* Brown. FW scales lie flat; few white scales. Cell spot, spots near apex, and *postdiscal spots usually prominent, hyaline (clear).* Median and pm. lines formed of blackish spots. HW uniformly dark; fringes white, with *no dark scales at their bases.* Female similar, but hyaline spots on FW much larger.
**Similar species:** (1) Funereal Dusky-wing (p. 258). (2) Pacuvius Dusky-wing (above). (3) Scudder's Dusky-wing (p. 262). (4) Clitus Dusky-wing (p. 261).
**Early stages:** Undescribed. Three broods. **Food:** Oaks, including

coast live oak *(Quercus agrifolia),* valley oak *(Q. lobata),* blue oak *(Q. douglasii),* and others. **Adults:** March–Nov.
**Range:** Cen. Calif. south to Ariz., s. Utah, s. N.M., w. Tex.; Mexico. **Habitat:** Oak woodland, forest edges.
**Subspecies:** (1) **Mournful Dusky-wing,** *E. t. tristis* (Boisduval), Pl. 45. TL: California. (2) **Tatius Dusky-wing,** *E. t. tatius* (W. H. Edwards). White submarginal marking just inside fringes on underside of HW. S. Utah, Ariz., N.M., w. Tex.; Mexico. TL: Mt. Graham, Ariz.

## HORACE'S DUSKY-WING                               Pl. 45
*Erynnis horatius* (Scudder & Burgess)
**Identification:** $1\frac{1}{2}$–$1\frac{3}{4}$ in. (38–44 mm). Fringes brown in both sexes. Male has costal fold but lacks metatibial tuft. *Upperside:* Male brown, with brown overscaling; very few white hairs. Hyaline spots, dark spots, and *light dots near apex usually distinct.* Female has much more contrast; the hyaline spots are larger and the dark markings stand out against the brown ground color.
**Early stages:** Not described in detail. Two broods in the West, 3 in the Southeast. **Food:** Oaks of several species. Old reports of legumes seem to be in error. **Adults:** May–Aug. in the West.
**Range:** In West, Colo., N.M., and Tex. Found in much of the East and South. TL: New England. **Habitat:** Open woodland, clearings, fencerows, roadsides.

## Juvenal's Dusky-wing *(Erynnis juvenalis)* Group

Four similar species, difficult to separate by appearance. All females have *spots below apex* (spots 6 and 7, Fig. 13, p. 204) on underside of HW; most males also have these spots. Males all have FW costal fold (Fig. 15, p. 249) but *lack the metatibial tuft* on hind leg (Fig. 16, p. 249); male genitalia distinctive for each species.

## JUVENAL'S DUSKY-WING                               Pl. 45
*Erynnis juvenalis* (Fabricius)
**Identification:** $1\frac{1}{4}$–$1\frac{3}{4}$ in. (31–44 mm). *Upperside:* Brownish; dark markings vague. Distinct hyaline spots at FW apex, in disc and beyond disc. Light spots at FW margin, and at and near HW margin present but inconspicuous. Female has much more contrast; dark markings and translucent spots larger. *Underside: Spots below HW apex* plainly visible, as are the *light submarginal and marginal spots.*
**Similar species:** Other members of the Juvenal's Dusky-wing group (pp. 260–261).
**Early stages:** Larva green, with many small yellow papillae; line on side lemon yellow. One brood. **Food:** Oaks of several species. **Adults:** March–June, depending on locality.
**Range:** In West, N.D., e. Wyo., w. S.D., Tex. In East, s. Canada to Fla. The Clitus Dusky-wing, a white-fringed subspecies, occurs in Ariz. **Habitat:** Oak woodland.

**Subspecies:** (1) **Juvenal's Dusky-wing,** *E. j. juvenalis* (Fabricius), Pl. 45, No. 19. TL: America, probably Georgia. (2) **Clitus Dusky-wing,** *E. j. clitus* (W. H. Edwards), Pl. 45, No. 20. Formerly considered a distinct species. Smaller; HW fringes *white.* Uncommon. Ariz., Mexico. TL: Graham Mts., Ariz.

## TELEMACHUS DUSKY-WING                          Pl. 45
*Erynnis telemachus* Burns

**Identification:** 1⅜-1¾ in. (34–44 mm). Looks quite similar to Propertius Dusky-wing (below), but the ranges do not overlap. *Upperside:* Gray scaling on FW erect, dense. Hyaline spots distinct. *Dark markings barely visible against dark ground color.* Female much like male, but hyaline spots larger. *Underside:* Spots below HW apex small but visible. Light submarginal and marginal spots on HW obscure in male, distinct in female.
**Similar species:** Other members of the Juvenal's Dusky-wing group (pp. 260–261).
**Early stages:** Undescribed. One brood. **Food:** Gambel oak *(Quercus gambeli).* **Adults:** April–July, depending on locality.
**Range:** S. Wyo., Utah, se. Nev., Colo., Ariz., N.M., w. Tex. TL: Hualapai Mts., 10 mi. se. of Kingman, Ariz. **Habitat:** Oak woodland, openings in mixed forest.

## PROPERTIUS DUSKY-WING                          Pl. 48
*Erynnis propertius* (Scudder & Burgess)

**Identification:** 1⅜-1¾ in. (34–44 mm). A dominant species in the Pacific States, the most common and conspicuous dusky-wing. Looks like Telemachus Dusky-wing (above), but the ranges do not overlap. *Upperside: FW scaling erect, gray, abundant;* hyaline spots and dark markings usually clear and distinct. Light spotting on HW usually visible, especially in female. *Underside:* Spots below HW apex usually well marked.
**Similar species:** Other members of the Juvenal's Dusky-wing group (pp. 260–261).
**Early stages:** Incompletely described. One brood. **Food:** Coast live oak *(Quercus agrifolia),* Garry oak *(Q. garryana),* perhaps others. **Adults:** May–June.
**Range:** Pacific Slope, s. British Columbia, Vancouver I., south to n. Baja California. TL: California. **Habitat:** Meadows, fields, near oaks; oak woodland, forest edges and openings, sea level to middle elevations. Absent from deserts and hot central valleys.

## MERIDIAN DUSKY-WING                          Pl. 45
*Erynnis meridianus* Bell

**Identification:** 1⅜-1¾ in. (34–44 mm). HW fringes *pale-tipped,* but not white. May occur in the same localities as the much grayer but otherwise similar Telemachus Dusky-wing (above). *Upperside:* Dark. FW scaling flat and smooth; few gray scales. (FW costal fold of male clearly visible in specimen shown.) HW

dark in both sexes, the *pale submarginal spots barely visible.* In female, FW markings more distinct; hyaline spots much larger. *Underside:* HW dark, *uniform in color;* spots below apex greatly reduced or absent.
**Similar species:** Other members of the Juvenal's Dusky-wing group (pp. 260–261).
**Early stages:** Undescribed. Two broods. **Food:** Arizona oak *(Quercus arizonica),* plateau oak *(Q. fusiformis).* **Adults:** April–Sept.
**Range:** S. Nev., Ariz., N.M., w. Tex. TL: Arizona. **Habitat:** Oak woodland, canyons, open or cutover forest, oak thickets.

### SCUDDER'S DUSKY-WING                              not shown
*Erynnis scudderi* (Skinner)
**Identification:** $1\frac{1}{4}$–$1\frac{3}{8}$ in. (31–34 mm). *Upperside:* Males much like males of Mournful Dusky-wing (p. 259); females more plainly marked. HW *fringes white,* with tufts of dark scales at bases as in Pacuvius Dusky-wing (p. 259). Identification is certain by dissection of male genitalia: the left valve is broader and its outer process shorter than in other white-fringed dusky-wings. A rare species, quite local in our area.
**Similar species:** (1) Pacuvius Dusky-wing (p. 259). (2) Funereal Dusky-wing (p. 258). (3) Mournful Dusky-wing (p. 259). (4) Clitus Dusky-wing (p. 261).
**Early stages:** Unknown. Capture dates suggest 2 broods. **Food:** Not known; possibly oak. **Adults:** May–Aug.
**Range:** S. Ariz.; Mexico. TL: Fort Grant, Ariz. **Habitat:** Not stated.

## Dusky-wings: Genus *Gesta* Evans

### GESTA DUSKY-WING                                  Pl. 45
*Gesta gesta* (Herrich-Schaeffer)
**Identification:** $1\frac{1}{8}$–$1\frac{3}{9}$ in. (28–34 mm). Male lacks costal fold but has metatibial tuft. FW narrow. Basal $\frac{2}{3}$ of FW costa *arched,* outer $\frac{1}{3}$ slightly *concave. Upperside:* Dark median band formed of 2–3 black spots; *pm. band dull brown.* Submarginal band powdered with gray scales. HW has 2 barely visible light spot bands; fringes pale-tipped.
**Early stages:** Larva yellow-green, paler toward rear, with a green stripe on rear $\frac{2}{3}$ of back and bright yellow spots on sides. Multiple broods. **Food:** Wild indigo *(Indigofera suffruticosa, I. lindheimeriana).* **Adults:** March–Nov.
**Range:** S. Tex., West Indies, south to Argentina. **Habitat:** Hilly grasslands where food plants grow. Stays near plants.
**Subspecies:** (1) *G. g. gesta* (Herrich-Schaeffer). TL: Cuba. (2) *G. g. invisus* (Butler & Druce), Pl. 45. S. Tex. to tropical America. Has been reported from Ariz.; present but scarce in w. Tex. TL: Costa Rica.

**Remarks:** Prior to 1953, the Gesta Dusky-wing was included in the genus *Erynnis.*

## Genus *Chiomara* Godman & Salvin

**ASYCHIS SKIPPER** *Chiomara asychis* (Stoll)          **Pl. 46**
**Identification:** $1\frac{1}{4}$–$1\frac{1}{2}$ in. (31–38 mm). *Upperside:* Dark, with a *complex but distinctive chalky white design.*
**Early stages:** Larva and pupa pale green (as described from S. America). Multiple broods. **Food:** Mexican myrtle *(Malpighia glabra),* in Malpighiaceae. **Adults:** March–Nov., depending on locality.
**Range:** S. Ariz. (scarce), s. Tex. (frequent); Mexico, S. America, West Indies. **Habitat:** Thorn forest, brushlands, woodland openings, roadsides, fencerows, streamsides.
**Subspecies:** (1) *C. a. asychis* (Stoll). TL: Surinam. (2) *C. a. georgina* (Reakirt), Pl. 46. Ariz., Tex., Mexico. TL: Vera Cruz, Mexico.

## Powdered Skippers: Genus *Systasea*
## W. H. Edwards

**POWDERED SKIPPER**                              **Pl. 46**
*Systasea pulverulenta* (R. Felder)
**Identification:** 1–$1\frac{3}{8}$ in. (25–34 mm). Two *deep scallops* in outer margin of HW. *Upperside:* Greenish tawny. Spots form a *narrow hyaline band* on FW; *spots all in a line.* HW has a pale median line.
**Similar species:** In Edwards' Powdered Skipper (below), hyaline spot band on FW offset just below cell.
**Early stages:** Undescribed. Multiple broods. **Food:** Indian mallow *(Abutilon),* globe mallow *(Sphaeralcea),* and *Wissadula.*
**Adults:** Feb.–Nov. in s. Tex.
**Range:** Tex. south to Guatemala. TL: Orizaba, Mexico. **Habitat:** Openings and trails in thorn forest and scrub.

**EDWARDS' POWDERED SKIPPER**                    **Pl. 46**
*Systasea zampa* (W. H. Edwards)
**Identification:** 1–$1\frac{1}{2}$ in. (25–38 mm). Two *deep scallops* in outer margin of HW. Same pattern as Powdered Skipper (above), but slightly larger, paler, and smoother-looking. *Upperside:* Hyaline band on FW *offset inward just below cell,* so that the inner edge of the band forms a "stair step."
**Similar species:** In Powdered Skipper (above), spots of FW hyaline band all in a line. The ranges of these two species overlap, so they cannot be identified by locality alone.
**Early stages:** Undescribed. Multiple broods. **Food:** Not known; probably various plants in the mallow family (Malvaceae), similar to food plants for Powdered Skipper. **Adults:** April–Oct.

**Range:** S. Calif., Ariz., N.M., w. Tex. TL: South Apache, Ariz. **Habitat:** Washes, canyons, and other openings onto the desert; thorn forest, brushland.

## Sooty-wings: Genus *Staphylus* Godman & Salvin

Appearance very similar to butterflies in genus *Pholisora* (pp. 250–251); our species were formerly included in that genus. Antennal apiculus pointed; club bent before the middle. Abdomen does not extend beyond HW. HW usually slightly scalloped. Light spots on FW few, small, translucent.

**CEOS SOOTY-WING** *Staphylus ceos* (W.H. Edwards)   **Pl. 46**
**Identification:** 1–1⅛ in. (25–28 mm). *Upperside:* Sooty black. White spots near FW apex *very small, translucent.* Upperside of head and palpi *golden.* *Underside:* Uniformly sooty black; chest and underside of palpi *white.*
**Early stages:** Unknown. Multiple broods. **Adults:** April–Sept. They fly low to ground and may seek shelter in shrubbery when disturbed.
**Range:** S. Ariz., N.M., western and southern Tex.; n. Mexico. TL: Ft. Grant, Graham Mts., Ariz. **Habitat:** Desert washes, streamside banks.

**SOUTHERN SOOTY-WING** **Pl. 46**
*Staphylus hayhursti* (W. H. Edwards)
**Identification:** 1–1⅛ in. (25–28 mm). Fringes faintly checkered. HW scalloped. *Upperside:* Grayish black to brownish black. Spots near FW apex and 1–2 postdiscal spots minute, white, translucent. *Wings crossed by 2 obscure darker bands.*
**Early stages:** Larva dark green, with short white hairs; head dark purple. Three broods. **Food:** Goosefoot *(Chenopodium),* chaffflower *(Alternanthera).* **Adults:**   March–Nov. Alights on leaves; takes shelter in shrubbery if disturbed.
**Range:** In the West, Colo., Neb., Kans. In the East, Pa. south to Fla. TL: Sedalia, Missouri. **Habitat:** Woodland roads, trails.

## Genus *Cogia* Butler

Antennal apiculus sharply pointed, bent at a right angle to the club. Palpi shorter than head as seen from above. Lower (4th) spot near FW apex displaced outward, towards apex. Male has a *short dense hair tuft* at base of HW.

**HIPPALUS SKIPPER** **Pl. 46**
*Cogia hippalus* (W.H. Edwards)
**Identification:** 1⅝–1⅞ in. (41–47 mm). Fringes white, those of FW checkered. *Upperside:* Sepia brown, outer halves of wings darker.

Spots at disc and in cell Cu$_1$ *large, shaped like dumb-bells, and lined up next to each other,* forming a conspicuous white band across center of FW. Smaller pm. spots in cells M$_2$ and M$_3$. HW unmarked. ***Underside:*** Lavender gray; FW spots repeated. Two irregular gray crossbands on HW.
**Similar species:** (1) Outis Skipper (below) is smaller and duller. (2) In Caicus Skipper (below), FW long and narrow; male hair tuft small. (3) See also cloudy-wings of the genus *Thorybes* (pp. 266–267).
**Early stages:** Unknown. Multiple broods. **Adults:** April–Sept.
**Range:** S. Ariz. to w. Tex.; Mexico. TL: Tucson, Pima Co., Ariz.
**Habitat:** Canyons, washes, above open desert.

**OUTIS SKIPPER** *Cogia outis* (Skinner)                **Pl. 46**
**Identification:** 1$\frac{3}{8}$–1$\frac{5}{8}$ in. (34–41 mm). Resembles the Hippalus Skipper (above), but much smaller and duller. FW spots small; *fringes pale, not pure white.*
**Similar species:** (1) Hippalus Skipper (above). (2) Caicus Skipper (below). (3) Cloudy-wings of the genus *Thorybes* (pp. 266–267).
**Early stages:** Little known. Multiple broods. **Food:** Whiteball acacia *(A. angustissima* var. *hirta).* **Adults:** April–Oct.
**Range:** Texas; found in w. Tex. TL: Round Mountain, Blanco Co.
**Habitat:** Local; closely associated with its food plant.
**Remarks:** Some consider the Outis Skipper to be a subspecies of the Hippalus Skipper, but they occur together in w. Texas.

## Genus *Phoedinus* Godman & Salvin

Apiculus on antenna bent at a right angle to club, and lower (4th) spot at FW apex out of line, as in *Cogia* species (above), but palpi longer than head as seen from above. Males lack HW hair tuft. Some consider this genus a synonym of *Cogia.*

**CAICUS SKIPPER**                                       **Pl. 46**
*Phoedinus caicus* (Herrich-Schaeffer)
**Identification:** 1$\frac{5}{8}$–1$\frac{3}{4}$ in. (41–44 mm). FW long and narrow. FW fringes brown; HW fringes white between veins M$_1$ and Cu$_2$, brown at wing apex and tornus. ***Upperside:*** Glossy dark brown. Hyaline spots on FW small. ***Underside:*** Dark brown; FW markings repeated. HW has 2 blackish brown crossbands; *outer edge of wing frosted with white scales.*
**Similar species:** (1) Hippalus Skipper (p. 264). (2) Outis Skipper (above). (3) Drusius Cloudy-wing (p. 267).
**Early stages:** Unknown. Multiple broods. **Adults:** March–Aug.
**Range:** Ariz. south to Guatemala. Local, usually quite scarce.
**Habitat:** Forest edges and openings; trails, roadsides.
**Subspecies:** (1) *P. c. caicus* (Herrich-Schaeffer). Mexico to Guatemala. TL: Not stated. (2) *P. c. moschus* (W.H. Edwards), Pl. 46. Ariz., n. Mexico. TL: Ft. Grant and Graham Mts., Ariz.

**MYSIE SKIPPER** *Phoedinus mysie* (Dyar)  **Pl. 46**
**Identification:** $1\frac{5}{8}$–$1\frac{3}{4}$ in. (41–44 mm). Very rare; few specimens known. Fringes pale brown, *evenly checkered.* **Upperside:** Brown. Spots at apex and postdiscal spots *arranged in a curve around end of FW cell.* HW unmarked. **Underside:** Two irregular dark bands on HW; *inner edges of bands blackish.*
**Early stages:** Unknown. One brood. **Food:** Not known. **Adults:** Aug.
**Range:** Ariz.; Mexico. TL: Patagonia Mts., Santa Cruz Co., Ariz.
**Habitat:** Has been taken in open oak woodland.
**Remarks:** The Mysie Skipper has at times been (erroneously?) listed as a synonym of the Valeriana Cloudy-wing, *Thorybes valeriana,* which is found in Mexico.

### Cloudy-wings: Genus *Thorybes* Scudder

HW rounded or slightly lobed. Antennal apiculus strongly recurved, often bent back along the shaft. FW always has a small white spot in outer upper edge of cell $Cu_2$. Spots near FW apex all in a line.

### NORTHERN CLOUDY-WING  **Pls. 46, 48**
*Thorybes pylades* (Scudder)
**Identification:** $1\frac{1}{4}$–$1\frac{7}{8}$ in. (31–47 mm). HW evenly rounded. Fringes brown, obscurely checkered. Male has *costal fold* on FW (Fig. 15, p. 249). **Upperside:** Dark brown; hyaline spots on FW small. **Underside:** Overscaling light brown to dusky gray. *Two dark bands on HW.*
**Similar species:** In Diverse Cloudy-wing (below), male lacks FW costal fold.
**Early stages:** Larva green, with a black head; line on back dusky, lines on sides salmon. Lives in leaf nest. Two broods in South, 1 in North and far West. **Food:** Legumes. Clover *(Trifolium),* bush clover *(Lespedeza),* tick clover *(Desmodium),* rattleweed *(Astragalus),* snoutbean *(Rhynchosia),* and others. **Adults:** May–June in North and West, March–Dec. in southern part of range.
**Range:** Cen. Canada to Mexico; throughout West in proper habitats. **Habitat:** Undisturbed hills and mountains at low or moderate elevations; forest edges, chaparral, woodland openings.
**Subspecies:** (1) **Northern Cloudy-wing,** *T. p. pylades* (Scudder), Pl. 48. All of range except w. Tex. TL: Massachusetts. (2) **Suffused Cloudy-wing,** *T. p. albosuffusa* H.A. Freeman, Pl. 46. Outer edge of HW has pale suffusion on underside. W. Texas. TL: Fort Davis, Tex.

### DIVERSE CLOUDY-WING  *Thorybes diversus* Bell  **Pl. 46**
**Identification:** $1\frac{1}{4}$–$1\frac{1}{2}$ in. (31–38 mm). Smaller and duller than Northern Cloudy-wing (above); larger and darker than Mexican

Cloudy-wing (below). Male lacks FW costal fold. HW evenly rounded. *Upperside:* Smooth dull brown, with small pale spots. *Underside:* Pale overscaling plentiful; *dark crossbands of HW poorly developed.*
**Early stages:** Larva olive-brown, with many short hairs arising from pale dots; line on back dark olive; 2 pale side stripes. One brood. **Food:** Cow clover *(Trifolium wormskjoldii).* **Adults:** June–July.
**Range:** Mountains of Ore. (s. Cascades) and Calif. (Sierra Nevada). Local, scarce; poorly known. TL: Plumas Co., Calif. **Habitat:** Openings in coniferous forest, at median elevations.

## MEXICAN CLOUDY-WING                    Pl. 46
*Thorybes mexicanus* (Herrich-Schaeffer)
**Identification:** 1⅛–1⅜ in. (28–34 mm). Our smallest cloudy-wing. Fringes slightly lighter than wing, obscurely checkered. Male lacks FW costal fold. *Upperside: Hyaline spots usually large,* each spot *dark-edged. Underside:* Pale brownish, flecked with dark scales. Two broken, dark crossbands on HW.
**Early stages:** Undescribed. One brood. **Food:** Has laid eggs on clover *(Trifolium)* in Calif. and on wild pea *(Lathyrus)* in Colo. **Adults:** June–Aug.
**Range:** Mountains of western U.S. south into Mexico, at high elevations. **Habitat:** Alpine and subalpine meadows, slopes.
**Subspecies:** (1) **Mexican Cloudy-wing,** *T. m. mexicanus* (Herrich-Schaeffer). TL: Not stated, presumably Mexico. (2) **Dobra Cloudy-wing,** *T. m. dobra* Evans. Hyaline spots smaller. Ariz., ne. N.M., se. Utah, sw. Colo. TL: Fort Grant, Apache Co., Ariz. (3) **Nevada Cloudy-wing,** *T. m. nevada* Scudder, Pl. 46. Ore. and Calif. east to Colo. TL: Sierra Nevada, Calif. (4) **Aemilea's Cloudy-wing,** *T. m. aemilea* (Skinner). Underside brighter; FW spots larger. S. Ore., nw. Calif. TL: Ft. Klamath, Ore. (5) **Scott's Cloudy-wing,** *T. m. blanco* Scott. Light markings on underside of HW more extensive. High elevations in White Mts. of Calif. and Nev. TL: Crooked Creek Lab., Mono Co., Calif., 3 airline miles n. of Inyo Co. line.

## DRUSIUS CLOUDY-WING                    Pl. 46
*Thorybes drusius* (W.H. Edwards)
**Identification:** 1½–1¾ in. (38–44 mm). Large. HW lobed, FW pointed. *Lower half of HW fringes white.* Male has FW costal fold. *Upperside:* Blackish brown; hyaline spots on FW very small. *Underside:* Dark brown. Crossbands on HW are dark outlines, not solid bands.
**Similar species:** (1) Caicus Skipper (p. 265). (2) Casica Skipper (p. 268).
**Early stages:** Unknown. Probably 1 brood. **Food:** Unknown. **Adults:** June–Aug. in Ariz., April–June in w. Tex.

**Range:** Ariz. to w. Tex.; Mexico. Local and uncommon. TL: Southern Arizona. **Habitat:** Canyons, streamsides.

## Genus *Achalarus* Scudder

Larger than *Thorybes* species (above). HW longer than it is wide; anal angle lobed.

### CASICA SKIPPER                                          Pl. 46
*Achalarus casica* (Herrich-Schaeffer)
**Identification:** $1\frac{3}{4}$-2 in. (44–50 mm). Larger than similar species. Fringes on outer margin of HW *pure white, with clumps of dark scales at vein ends.* **Upperside:** Dark brown. Hyaline spots small, arranged in an S-curve on outer $\frac{1}{3}$ of FW. **Underside:** HW crossbands black against very dark ground color; outer edge of HW *widely frosted with white scales.*
**Similar species:** Drusius Cloudy-wing (p. 267) is smaller; HW more rounded. Outer margin of HW not white-scaled on underside.
**Early stages:** Not known. Multiple broods. **Adults:** May–Oct.
**Range:** Se. Ariz. to Tex.; Mexico. TL: Not stated. **Habitat:** Canyons, streamsides, washes, river bottoms.

## Banded Skippers: Genus *Autochton* Huebner

HW long, lobed as in *Achalarus* species (above). FW has a wide yellow band.

### GOLDEN-BANDED SKIPPER                                   Pl. 47
*Autochton cellus* (Boisduval & Le Conte)
**Identification:** $1\frac{3}{8}$-$1\frac{7}{8}$ in. (34–47 mm). Antennae brown, with *no pale band* at base of club. Fringes checkered. **Upperside:** Dark brown; FW has a *wide yellow band.* Spots at FW apex white. **Underside:** Dark brown, with 2–3 darker crossbands. HW edge often overscaled with gray.
**Similar species:** Arizona Banded Skipper (below) has pale band at base of antennal club.
**Early stages:** Larva yellowish green, with many small yellow spots; line on side yellow; head brown, with 2 yellow spots. 2–3 broods. **Food:** Hog-peanut *(Amphicarpa pitcheri).* **Adults:** April–Sept.
**Range:** In the West, se. Ariz., w. Tex. In East, N.Y. to Fla.; south to S. America. TL: North America. **Habitat:** Wooded streamsides and pond edges.

### ARIZONA BANDED SKIPPER                                  Pl. 47
*Autochton pseudocellus* (Coolidge & Clemence)
**Identification:** $1\frac{1}{2}$-$1\frac{7}{8}$ in. (38–47 mm). Similar to the Golden-banded Skipper (above), but usually slightly smaller; *pale band at base of antennal club.* Male genitalia differ. **Underside:** HW duller, with *no gray edge.*

**Early stages:** Unknown. Probably 2 broods. **Adults:** June–Sept.
**Range:** Se. Ariz., n. Mexico. Occurs with the Golden-banded Skipper in Ariz., but usually in smaller numbers. Rare and local; range restricted. Few known localities. **Habitat:** Permanent streams in wooded canyons.

## Tailed Skippers: Genus *Urbanus* Huebner

**LONG-TAILED SKIPPER**                                       **Pl. 48**
*Urbanus proteus* (Linnaeus)
**Identification:** 1³/₄–1⁷/₈ in. (44–47 mm). Our only long-tailed skipper with a *green gloss* on body and wing bases. FW has conspicuous hyaline spots. *Upperside:* Dark brown (not black). *Underside: Dark outer band on HW complete.*
**Similar species:** (1) Dorantes Skipper (below) has shorter tails and no green gloss. (2) White-striped Longtail (p. 270) has a white stripe on underside of HW.
**Early stages:** Larva, called the Bean-leaf Roller, is green, with a dark line on back; yellow line on side above 2 green lines. Rear segments may be tinged red. It lives in a nest of rolled leaves. Multiple broods. **Food:** Tick-trefoil *(Desmodium),* pigeon-wings *(Clitoria),* wisteria, and other legumes. Larva sometimes a pest of cultivated beans *(Phaseolus).* **Adults:** Much of year.
**Range:** Southern U.S. south to Argentina. In the West, s. Calif. to Tex. TL: America. **Habitat:** River bottoms, thorn forest, roadsides, fencerows, cultivated bean patches.

**DORANTES SKIPPER** *Urbanus dorantes* (Stoll)     **Pl. 48**
**Identification:** 1¹/₂–2 in. (38–50 mm). Long HW tails shorter than those of Long-tailed Skipper (above), the tips far apart. *Upperside:* Dark brown; no green gloss. Hyaline (clear) spots on FW conspicuous. Fringes pale, checkered. *Underside:* Light grayish brown. HW has *2 dark bands* that are *broken into spots.*
**Similar species:** (1) Long-tailed Skipper (above). (2) White-striped Longtail (p. 270).
**Early stages:** Larva yellowish green with pale spots; head black, with rough surface. Multiple broods. **Food:** Various legumes. **Adults:** April–Oct.
**Range:** S. Calif. (scarce), s. Ariz., s. Tex. south to Argentina. Widely distributed. Sometimes quite common. TL: Surinam. **Habitat:** Thorn forest, streamsides, fencerows, roadsides; yards and gardens in Tex.

## Genus *Codatractus* Lindsey

**ARIZONA SKIPPER**                                           **Pl. 47**
*Codatractus arizonensis* (Skinner)
**Identification:** 1³/₄–2 in. (44–50 mm). Unusual-looking; uncommon. Fringes pale, checkered. *Upperside:* Dark brown. FW base

and much of HW overlaid with olive-brown. Hyaline spots on FW *large, shining white,* forming a conspicuous median band of *4 spots in a line.* **Underside:** Dark brown; FW spots repeated. HW has 2 blackish brown crossbands. Grayish white scaling on outer ⅓ of HW.
**Early stages:** Unknown. Probably multiple broods. **Adults:** June–Oct.
**Range:** S. Ariz., w. Tex.; Mexico. TL: Baboquiviri Mts., Ariz.
**Habitat:** Rocky canyons and washes, usually near water.

## Short-tailed Skippers: Genus *Zestusa* Lindsey

**SHORT-TAILED SKIPPER**                                   **Pl. 47**
*Zestusa dorus* (W. H. Edwards)
**Identification:** 1⅜–1⅝ in. (34–41 mm). HW tail short. **Upperside:** Our only large skipper with *conspicuous hyaline spots on both FW and HW.* **Underside:** Mottled gray and brown; hyaline spots much less conspicuous.
**Early stages:** Larva greenish; light yellow band on back, with a darker green line down its center. Lines on sides yellow. Probably 2 broods. **Food:** Emory oak *(Quercus emoryi),* Arizona oak *(Q. arizonica).* **Adults:** April–July.
**Range:** Sw. Colo., Ariz., N.M., w. Tex.; Mexico. TL: Ft. Grant, Ariz. **Habitat:** Oak-juniper woodland.

## Longtails: Genus *Chioides* Lindsey

**WHITE-STRIPED LONGTAIL**                              **Pl. 47**
*Chioides catillus albofasciatus* (Hewitson)
**Identification:** 1¾–2⅛ in. (44–53 mm). A very showy species in flight. HW tail very long. **Upperside:** Dark brown. Hyaline spots on FW large, forming a triangle. **Underside:** A *long, silky white stripe* runs from HW costa to base of tail.
**Early stages:** Larva pinkish or purplish; side stripe yellow. Head red with black facial marks. Multiple broods. **Food:** Lindheimer tephrosia *(T. lindheimeri),* least snoutbean *(Rhynchosia minima),* purple bean *(Phaseolus atropurpureus),* and other legumes. **Adults:** Long flight season.
**Range:** S. Ariz. to se. Tex., south to Columbia. Common in s. Tex.; less common in Ariz. TL: Guatemala. **Habitat:** Moist areas with considerable vegetation.
**Remarks:** The Catillus Longtail, *C. c. catillus* (Cramer), found in S. America, lacks the shining white band on underside of HW.

## Genus *Polygonus* Huebner

**HAMMOCK SKIPPER** *Polygonus leo* (Gmelin)      **Pl. 47**
**Identification:** 1¾–2⅛ in. (44–53 mm). FW long, narrow, *square*

*at apex;* outer margin concave. HW strongly lobed, forming a short tail. **Upperside:** Dark brown, with a *bluish sheen* near wing bases. FW has 3 large, white hyaline spots. HW has 2 indistinct light bands. **Underside:** HW iridescent violet-gray, with 2 distinct dark bands and a *single black spot near base, below costa.*
**Early stages:** Larva yellow-green, with a yellow line on side above a series of yellow blotches. Multiple broods. **Food:** Jamaica dogwood *(Ichthyomethia piscipula)* in Fla.; food in Ariz. not known. **Adults:** May–Sept. in Ariz.
**Range:** S. Calif. (scarce), Ariz., w. Tex., and Fla. south to Argentina. **Habitat:** In Fla., shaded hardwood hammocks. In Ariz., in the vicinity of small, permanent streams.
**Subspecies:** (1) **Hammock Skipper,** *P. l. leo* (Gmelin). Dark. S. Fla. TL: America. (2) **Arizona Hammock Skipper,** *P. l. arizonensis* (Skinner), Pl. 47. Much paler. Calif., Ariz., w. Tex. TL: Florence, Ariz.

## Genus *Epargyreus* Huebner

**SILVER-SPOTTED SKIPPER**                                    **Pl. 48**
*Epargyreus clarus* (Cramer)
**Identification:** $1\frac{3}{4}$–$2\frac{1}{2}$ in. (44–62 mm). FW long; HW strongly lobed. Fringes checkered. **Upperside:** Dark brown. Hyaline spots on FW large, yellow. **Underside:** Dark brown. *Large silver median spot* on HW.
**Early stages:** Larva yellow; head brownish, with 2 eyelike orange-red spots. Multiple broods over most of range; 1 brood on Pacific Slope. **Food:** Black locust *(Robinia pseudo-acacia),* New Mexican locust *(R. neomexicana),* honey locust *(Gleditsia triacanthos),* false indigo *(Amorpha),* and many other legumes. **Adults:** Long flight season in Ariz.; May–July in Calif.
**Range:** S. Canada south through the U.S.; n. Mexico, Baja California. Probably occurs in all western states. Common in the East and in s. Rocky Mts.; much less common on Pacific Slope. **Habitat:** Open woodland, gardens, parks, roadsides, at low to moderate elevations.
**Subspecies:** (1) **Silver-spotted Skipper,** *E. c. clarus* (Cramer). Spot in FW cell $Cu_2$ large, touching large spot in cell $Cu_1$. Eastern. (2) **Arizona Silver-spotted Skipper,** *E. c. huachuca* Dixon, Pl. 48. Spot in FW cell $Cu_2$ small, not touching large spot in cell $Cu_1$. Western. TL: Huachuca Mts., Ariz.

# Subfamily Pyrrhopyginae
## Genus *Pyrrhopyge* Huebner

Antennal club long, entirely bent back along the shaft to form a hook. Numerous tropical species; a single species reaches our area.

**ARAXES SKIPPER** *Pyrrhopyge araxes* (Hewitson)     **Pl. 47**
**Identification:** 1¾–2¼ in. (44–56 mm). Large and very broad-winged; *HW outer margin scalloped.* Very bright and clean-looking. Fringes white, checkered. *Upperside:* Smooth dark brown. FW has conspicuous white hyaline spots. HW uniformly dark. *Underside:* FW base and inner half of HW orange-yellow, with obscure dark spots.
**Early stages:** Larva stout, red-brown, with yellow bars. Multiple broods. **Food:** Arizona oak *(Quercus arizonica)*. **Adults:** May–Nov. Flight strong and rapid. They usually sit with wings spread open. Sometimes quite tame when at flowers.
**Range:** S. Ariz. to w. Tex.; Mexico. **Habitat:** Open woodland, streamsides, roadsides, forest edges and trails.
**Subspecies:** (1) **Araxes Skipper,** *P. a. araxes* (Hewitson). Less orange-yellow on underside of HW. TL: Mexico. (2) **Arizona Araxes Skipper,** *P. a. arizonae* (Godman & Salvin), Pl. 47. Ariz., w. Tex. TL: Ft. Grant, Ariz.

# Appendixes

*Checklist/Life List
of Western Butterflies*

*Lepidopterists' Society
Statement of the Committee on
Collecting Policy*

*Casual and Stray Species*

*Hawaiian Butterflies*

*Alaskan Butterflies*

# Glossary

# Bibliography

*Directory of Equipment, Materials,
Publications, and Services*

# Indexes

# Butterflies of Western North America

Species and subspecies known to have been recorded within the area covered by this guide are listed below. Dubious records and stray or casual species wrongly attributed to our area are omitted here; they appear in a separate section starting on p. 319. Subspecific names are prefixed by "a," "b," etc., and indented under species. Certain well-marked forms have been noted in the species accounts, but are not listed here. An asterisk (*) before a subspecific name indicates that the nominate subspecies — the one first described and considered the "type" for the species — does not occur in the area covered by this book. No real synonymy has been included, but some recently changed names that were widely used are noted here in italics to avoid confusion.

## *Superfamily Papilionoidea — the True Butterflies*

### Family Satyridae — Satyrs and Wood Nymphs

#### Subfamily Elymniinae

*Enodia* Huebner
_____ 1. anthedon A. H. Clark — Northern Pearly Eye
*Satyrodes* Scudder
    1. eurydice (Johannson) — Eyed Brown
_____     a. eurydice (Johannson) — Eyed Brown
_____     b. fumosus Leussler — Smoky Eyed Brown

#### Subfamily Satyrinae

*Cyllopsis* R. Felder
    1. pyracmon (Butler) — Pyracmon Brown
    *a. pyracmon (Butler) — Pyracmon Brown (Mexico)
_____     b. nabokovi Miller — Nabokov's Brown

275

_____   2. henshawi (W. H. Edwards) — Henshaw's Brown
       3. pertepida (Dyar) — Warm Brown
        *a. pertepida (Dyar) — Warm Brown (Mexico)
_____     b. dorothea (Nabokov) — Grand Canyon Brown
_____     c. maniola (Nabokov) — Arizona Brown
_____     d. avicula (Nabokov) — West Texas Brown

**_Megisto_ Huebner**
_____   1. cymela (Cramer) — Little Wood Satyr
       2. rubricata (W. H. Edwards) — Red Satyr
_____     a. rubricata (W. H. Edwards) — Red Satyr
_____     b. smithorum (Wind) — Smiths' Red Satyr
_____     c. cheneyorum (R. Chermock) — Arizona Red Satyr

**_Paramacera_ Butler**
_____   1. allyni Miller — Allyn's Satyr

**_Coenonympha_ Huebner**
_____   1. haydenii (W. H. Edwards) — Hayden's Ringlet
       2. kodiak W. H. Edwards — Kodiak Ringlet
_____     a. kodiak W. H. Edwards — Kodiak Ringlet
_____     b. mixturata Alpheraky — Arctic Ringlet
_____     c. yukonensis Holland — Yukon Arctic Ringlet
       3. inornata W. H. Edwards — Inornate Ringlet
_____     a. inornata W. H. Edwards — Inornate Ringlet
_____     b. benjamini McDunnough — Prairie Ringlet
       4. ochracea W. H. Edwards — Ochre Ringlet
_____     a. ochracea W. H. Edwards — Ochre Ringlet
_____     b. mackenziei Davenport — Davenport's Ringlet
_____     c. subfusca Barnes & Benjamin — White Mountains Ringlet
_____     d. furcae Barnes & Benjamin — Grand Canyon Ringlet
_____     e. brenda W. H. Edwards — Great Basin Ringlet
_____     f. mono Burdick — Mono Ringlet
       5. ampelos W. H. Edwards — Ringless Ringlet
_____     a. ampelos W. H. Edwards — Ringless Ringlet
_____     b. eunomia Dornfeld — Dornfeld's Ringlet
_____     c. columbiana McDunnough — Columbian Ringlet
_____     d. insulana McDunnough — Vancouver Island Ringlet
_____     e. elko W. H. Edwards — Nevada Ringlet
       6. california Westwood — California Ringlet
_____     a. california Westwood — California Ringlet
_____     b. eryngii Hy. Edwards — Siskiyou Ringlet

**_Cercyonis_ Scudder**
       1. pegala (Fabricius) — Wood Nymph
        *a. pegala (Fabricius) — Southern Wood Nymph (Eastern U.S. and Canada)
_____     b. texana (W. H. Edwards) — Texas Wood Nymph
_____     c. olympus (W. H. Edwards) — Olympian Wood Nymph

_____     d. ino Hall — Hall's Wood Nymph
_____     e. boöpis (Behr) — Ox-eyed Satyr
_____     f. ariane (Boisduval) — Ariane Satyr
_____     g. damei (Barnes & Benjamin) — Grand Canyon Satyr
_____     h. blanca T. Emmel & Matoon — Light Satyr
        2. meadii (W. H. Edwards) — Mead's Satyr
_____     a. meadii (W. H. Edwards) — Mead's Satyr
_____     b. melania Wind — Wind's Satyr
_____     c. alamosa T. & J. Emmel — Alamosa Satyr
_____     d. mexicana R. Chermock — Chermock's Satyr
        3. sthenele (Boisduval) — Woodland Satyr
           a. sthenele (Boisduval) — Sthenele Satyr; extinct
_____     b. silvestris (W. H. Edwards) — Woodland Satyr
_____     c. paula (W. H. Edwards) — Little Satyr
_____     d. masoni Cross — Mason's Satyr
        4. oeta (Boisduval) — Least Satyr
_____     a. oeta (Boisduval) — Least Satyr
_____     b. charon (W. H. Edwards) — Charon Satyr
_____     c. phocus (W. H. Edwards) — Phocus Satyr
_____     d. pallescens T. & J. Emmel — Pale Satyr

**_Erebia_ Dalman**

_____     1. vidleri Elwes — Vidler's Alpine
        2. rossii (Curtis) — Ross's Alpine
_____     a. rossii (Curtis) — Ross's Alpine
_____     b. kuskokwimi Holland — Kuskokwim Alpine
_____     c. gabrieli dos Passos — Gabriel's Alpine
_____     d. ornata Leussler — Ornate Alpine
        3. disa (Thunberg) — Disa Alpine
        *a. disa (Thunberg) — Disa Alpine (Arctic Europe)
_____     b. mancina Doubleday — Mancina Alpine
_____     c. steckeri Holland — Stecker's Alpine
_____     d. subarctica McDunnough — Subarctic Alpine
_____     4. magdalena Strecker — Magdalena Alpine
_____     5. mckinleyensis Gunder — Mt. McKinley Alpine
        6. fasciata Butler — Banded Alpine
_____     a. fasciata Butler — Banded Alpine
_____     b. avinoffi Holland — Avinoff's Alpine
        7. discoidalis (W. Kirby) — Red-disked Alpine
_____     a. discoidalis (W. Kirby) — Red-disked Alpine
_____     b. mcdunnoughi dos Passos — McDunnough's Red-disked
           Alpine
        8. theano (Tauscher) — Theano Alpine
        *a. theano (Tauscher) — Theano Alpine (Siberia)
_____     b. sofia Strecker — Churchill Alpine
_____     c. alaskensis Holland — Holland's Theano Alpine
_____     d. ethela (W. H. Edwards) — Ethel's Alpine
_____     e. demmia Warren — Demmia Alpine
        9. youngi Holland — Young's Alpine
_____     a. youngi Holland — Young's Alpine

_____        b. herscheli Leussler — Herschel Island Alpine
_____        c. rileyi dos Passos — Riley's Alpine
        10. epipsodea Butler — Common Alpine
_____        a. epipsodea Butler — Common Alpine
_____        b. remingtoni Ehrlich — Remington's Alpine
_____        c. hopfingeri Ehrlich — Hopfinger's Alpine
_____        d. freemani Ehrlich — Freeman's Alpine
_____        e. rhodia W. H. Edwards — Common Alpine
_____    11. callias W. H. Edwards — Mead's Alpine

**Gyrocheilus Butler**
         1. patrobas (Hewitson) — Tritonia
         *a. patrobas (Hewitson) — Tritonia (Mexico)
_____        b. tritonia (W. H. Edwards) — Tritonia

**Neominois Scudder**
         1. ridingsii (W. H. Edwards) — Riding's Satyr
_____        a. ridingsii (W. H. Edwards) — Riding's Satyr
_____        b. stretchii (W. H. Edwards) — Stretch's Satyr
_____        c. dionysus Scudder — Dionysus Satyr

**Oeneis Huebner**
         1. nevadensis (C. & R. Felder) — Great Arctic
_____        a. nevadensis (C. & R. Felder) — Great Arctic
_____        b. gigas Butler — Giant Arctic
_____        c. iduna (W. H. Edwards) — Iduna Arctic
_____     2. macounii (W. H. Edwards) — Macoun's Arctic
         3. chryxus (Doubleday & Hewitson) — Chryxus Arctic
_____        a. chryxus (Doubleday & Hewitson) — Chryxus Arctic
_____        b. valerata Burdick — Olympic Arctic
_____        c. stanislaus Hovanitz — Hovanitz's Arctic
_____        d. caryi Dyar — Cary's Arctic
_____     4. ivallda (Mead) — Ivallda Arctic
         5. uhleri (Reakirt) — Uhler's Arctic
_____        a. uhleri (Reakirt) — Uhler's Arctic
_____        b. reinthali F. M. Brown — Reinthal's Arctic
_____        c. varuna (W. H. Edwards) — Varuna Arctic
_____        d. nahanni Dyar — Nahanni Mountains Arctic
_____        e. cairnesi Gibson — Cairnes' Arctic
         6. alberta Elwes — Alberta Arctic
_____        a. alberta Elwes — Alberta Arctic
_____        b. oslari Skinner — Oslar's Arctic
_____        c. daura (Strecker) — Daura Arctic
_____        d. capulinensis F. M. Brown — Capulin Arctic
_____     7. excubitor Troubridge — Sentinel Arctic
         8. taygete Geyer — White-veined Arctic
_____        a. taygete Geyer — White-veined Arctic
_____        b. edwardsi dos Passos — Edwards' Arctic
_____        c. fordi dos Passos — Ford's Arctic
         9. bore (Schneider) — Boreal Arctic
         *a. bore (Schneider) — Boreal Arctic (Eurasia)

——     b. hanburyi Watkins — Boreal Arctic
——     c. mckinleyensis dos Passos — Mt. McKinley Arctic
    10. jutta (Huebner) — Jutta Arctic
      *a. jutta (Huebner) — Jutta Arctic (Arctic Europe and Asia)
——     b. ridingiana F. & R. Chermock — Riding Mountains Arctic
——     c. leussleri Bryant — Leussler's Jutta Arctic
——     d. alaskensis Holland — Alaskan Jutta Arctic
——     e. reducta McDunnough — Rocky Mountain Jutta Arctic
    11. melissa (Fabricius) — Melissa Arctic
      *a. melissa (Fabricus) — Melissa Arctic (Arctic Europe and eastern U.S.)
——     b. assimilis Butler — Northern Melissa Arctic
——     c. gibsoni Holland — Gibson's Melissa Arctic
——     d. lucilla Barnes & Benjamin — Colorado Melissa Arctic
——     e. beanii Elwes — Bean's Melissa Arctic
    12. polixenes (Fabricius) — Polixenes Arctic
      *a. polixenes (Fabricius) — Polixenes Arctic (e. Arctic America)
——     b. subhyalina (Curtis) — Subhyaline Polixenes Arctic
——     c. peartiae (W. H. Edwards) — Peart's Polixenes Arctic
——     d. brucei (W. H. Edwards) — Bruce's Polixenes Arctic
——     e. yukonensis Gibson — Yukon Polixenes Arctic

# Family Danaidae — Milkweed Butterflies

*Danaus* **Kluk**
——     1. plexippus (Linnaeus) — Monarch
       2. gilippus (Cramer) — Queen
      *a. gilippus (Cramer) — Queen (Brazil)
——     b. strigosus (H. W. Bates) — Striated Queen

# Family Heliconiidae — Long-wings

*Heliconius* **Kluk**
       1. charitonius (Linnaeus) — Zebra
      *a. charitonius (Linnaeus) — Zebra (West Indies, Cen. America, and northern S. America)
——     b. vazquezae W. P. Comstock & F. M. Brown — Zebra
*Agraulis* **Boisduval & Le Conte**
       1. vanillae (Linnaeus) — Gulf Fritillary
      *a. vanillae (Linnaeus) — Gulf Fritillary (tropical America)
——     b. incarnata (Riley) — Gulf Fritillary

# Family Apaturidae — Leaf-wings and Emperors

## Subfamily Charaxinae — Charaxines

*Anaea* **Huebner**
  1. andria Scudder — Goatweed Butterfly
___ a. andria Scudder — Goatweed Butterfly
___ b. ops (H. Druce) — Arizona Goatweed Butterfly
  2. aidea (Guérin-Méneville) — Tropical Leaf-wing
___ a. aidea (Guérin-Méneville) — Tropical Leaf-wing
___ b. morrisoni (W. H. Edwards) — Morrison's Tropical Leaf-wing

## Subfamily Apaturinae — Emperors

*Asterocampa* **Roeber**
  1. celtis (Boisduval & Le Conte) — Hackberry Butterfly
___ a. celtis (Boisduval & Le Conte) — Hackberry Butterfly
___ b. antonia (W. H. Edwards) — Antonia's Hackberry Butterfly
___ c. montis (W. H. Edwards) — Mountain Hackberry Butterfly
  2. leilia (W. H. Edwards) — Empress Leilia
___ a. leilia (W. H. Edwards) — Empress Leilia
___ b. cocles (Lintner) — Cocles' Emperor
  3. clyton (Boisduval & Le Conte) — Tawny Emperor
___ a. clyton (Boisduval & Le Conte) — Tawny Emperor
___ b. texana (Skinner) — Texas Tawny Emperor
___ 4. subpallida (Barnes & McDunnough) — Pallid Emperor

# Family Nymphalidae — Brush-footed Butterflies

## Subfamily Marpesiinae — Dagger-wings

*Marpesia* **Huebner**
___ 1. chiron (Fabricius) — Many-banded Dagger-wing
___ 2. petreus (Cramer) — Ruddy Dagger-wing

## Subfamily Limenitidinae — Admirals and Relatives

*Biblis* **Fabricius**
  1. hyperia (Cramer) — Hyperia

   \*a. hyperia (Cramer) — Hyperia (tropical America)

_____ b. aganisa Boisduval — Hyperia

**Mestra** Huebner

_____ 1. amymone (Ménétriés) — Amymone

**Basilarchia** Scudder

   1. arthemis (Drury) — White Admiral

_____ a. arthemis (Drury) — White Admiral

_____ b. rubrofasciata Barnes & McDunnough — Northern White Admiral

_____ c. astyanax (Fabricius) — Red-spotted Purple

_____ d. arizonensis (W. H. Edwards) — Arizona Red-spotted Purple

   2. archippus (Cramer) — Viceroy

_____ a. archippus (Cramer) — Viceroy

_____ b. watsoni dos Passos — Watson's Viceroy

_____ c. obsoleta (W. H. Edwards) — Western Viceroy

_____ d. lahontani (Herlan) — Nevada Viceroy

   3. weidemeyerii (W. H. Edwards) — Weidemeyer's Admiral

_____ a. weidemeyerii (W. H. Edwards) — Weidemeyer's Admiral

_____ b. angustifascia Barnes & McDunnough — Narrow-banded Admiral

_____ c. nevadae Barnes & Benjamin — Nevada Admiral

_____ d. oberfoelli (F. M. Brown) — Oberfoell's Admiral

_____ e. latifascia (E. M. & S. F. Perkins) — Wide-banded Admiral

   4. lorquini (Boisduval) — Lorquin's Admiral

_____ a. lorquini (Boisduval) — Lorquin's Admiral

_____ b. burrisoni (Maynard) — Burrison's Admiral

**Adelpha** Huebner

   1. bredowii (Geyer) — Sister

   \*a. bredowi (Geyer) — Sister (Mexico)

_____ b. eulalia (Doubleday) — Arizona Sister

_____ c. californica (Butler) — California Sister

## Subfamily Nymphalinae — Tortoise-shells, Angle-wings, Ladies, and Peacocks

**Nymphalis** Kluk

   1. vau-album (Denis & Schiffermueller) — False Comma (in Europe)

   \*a. vau-album (Denis & Schiffermueller) — False Comma (Asia and Eastern Europe)

_____ b. j-album (Boisduval & Le Conte) — Compton Tortoise-shell

_____ c. watsoni (Hall) — Watson's Tortoise-shell

   2. californica (Boisduval) — California Tortoise-shell

_____ a. californica (Boisduval) — California Tortoise-shell

_____ b. herri Field — Herr's Tortoise-shell

   3. antiopa (Linnaeus) — Mourning Cloak

_____    a. antiopa (Linnaeus) — Mourning Cloak
_____    b. hyperborea (Seitz) — Northern Mourning Cloak

***Aglais* Dalman**
      1. milberti (Godart) — Milbert's Tortoise-shell
_____    a. milberti (Godart) — Milbert's Tortoise-shell
_____    b. furcillata (Say) — Western Milbert's Tortoise-shell

***Polygonia* Huebner**
_____   1. interrogationis (Fabricius) — Question Mark
_____   2. comma (Harris) — Hop Merchant or Comma
      3. satyrus (W. H. Edwards) — Satyr Angle-wing
_____    a. satyrus (W. H. Edwards) — Satyr Angle-wing
_____    b. neomarsyas dos Passos — Western Satyr Angle-wing
      4. faunus (W. H. Edwards) — Green Comma or Faun
_____    a. faunus (W. H. Edwards) — Green Comma or Faun
_____    b. rustica (W. H. Edwards) — Rustic Angle-wing
_____    c. arctica Leussler — Arctic Angle-wing
_____   5. hylas (W. H. Edwards) — Colorado Angle-wing
_____   6. silvius (W. H. Edwards) — Sylvan Angle-wing
_____   7. zephyrus (W. H. Edwards) — Zephyr Angle-wing
      8. oreas (W. H. Edwards) — Oreas Angle-wing
_____    a. oreas (W. H. Edwards) — Oreas Angle-wing
_____    b. silenus (W. H. Edwards) — Silenus Angle-wing
_____   9. gracilis (Grote & Robinson) — Hoary Comma
_____  10. progne (Cramer) — Gray Comma

***Vanessa* Fabricius**
      1. atalanta (Linnaeus) — Red Admiral
       *a. atalanta (Linnaeus) — (Europe, n. Africa, Middle
          East)
_____    b. rubria (Fruhstorfer) — Red Admiral
_____   2. tameamea (Eschscholtz) — Kamehameha
_____   3. cardui (Linnaeus) — Painted Lady
_____   4. virginiensis (Drury) — American Painted Lady
_____   5. annabella (Field) — West Coast Lady

***Junonia* Huebner**
_____   1. coenia (Huebner) — Buckeye or Peacock Butterfly
_____   2. nigrosuffusa Barnes & McDunnough — Dark Peacock

***Anartia* Huebner**
      1. jatrophae (Johannson) — White Peacock
       *a. jatrophae (Johannson) — (tropical America)
_____    b. luteipicta Fruhstorfer — White Peacock

## Subfamily Argynninae — Fritillaries

***Speyeria* Scudder**
      1. cybele (Fabricius) — Great Spangled Fritillary
_____    a. cybele (Fabricius) — Great Spangled Fritillary
_____    b. pseudocarpenteri (F. & R. Chermock) — Chermocks'
          Fritillary
_____    c. carpenterii (W. H. Edwards) — Carpenter's Fritillary

_____     d. charlottii (Barnes) — Charlott's Fritillary
_____     e. letona dos Passos & Grey — Letona Fritillary
_____     f. leto (Behr) — Leto Fritillary
_____     g. pugetensis F. Chermock & Frechin — Puget Sound Fritillary

2. aphrodite (Fabricius) — Aphrodite
   *a. aphrodite (Fabricius) — Aphrodite (eastern U.S.)
_____     b. alcestis (W. H. Edwards) — Alcestis Fritillary
_____     c. manitoba (F. & R. Chermock) — Manitoba Fritillary
_____     d. whitehousei (Gunder) — Whitehouse's Fritillary
_____     e. columbia (Hy. Edwards) — Columbian Fritillary
_____     f. ethne (Hemming) — Ethne Fritillary
_____     g. byblis (Barnes & Benjamin) — Byblis Fritillary

_____ 3. idalia (Drury) — Regal Fritillary

4. nokomis (W. H. Edwards) — Nokomis Fritillary
_____     a. nokomis (W. H. Edwards) — Nokomis Fritillary
_____     b. nitocris (W. H. Edwards) — Nitocris Fritillary
_____     c. apacheana (Skinner) — Apache Fritillary
_____     d. coerulescens (Holland) — Bluish Fritillary

_____ 5. edwardsi (Reakirt) — Edwards' Fritillary

6. coronis (Behr) — Crown Fritillary
_____     a. coronis (Behr) — Crown Fritillary
_____     b. hennei (Gunder) — Henne's Fritillary
_____     c. semiramis (W. H. Edwards) — Semiramis Fritillary
_____     d. simaetha dos Passos & Grey — Simaetha Fritillary
_____     e. snyderi (Skinner) — Snyder's Fritillary
_____     f. halcyone (W. H. Edwards) — Halcyone Fritillary

7. zerene (Boisduval) — Zerene Fritillary
_____     a. zerene (Boisduval) — Zerene Fritillary
_____     b. conchyliata (J. A Comstock) — Royal Fritillary
_____     c. gloriosa Moeck — Glorious Fritillary
_____     d. sordida (W. G. Wright) — Sordid Fritillary
_____     e. malcolmi (J. A. Comstock) — Malcolm's Fritillary
_____     f. carolae (dos Passos & Grey) — Carol's Fritillary
_____     g. hippolyta (W. H. Edwards) — Hippolyta Fritillary
_____     h. behrensii (W. H. Edwards) — Behren's Fritillary
_____     i. myrtleae dos Passos & Grey — Myrtle's Fritillary
_____     j. bremneri (W. H. Edwards) — Bremner's Fritillary
_____     k. picta (McDunnough) — Painted Fritillary
_____     l. garretti (Gunder) — Garrett's Fritillary
_____     m. sinope dos Passos & Grey — Sinope Fritillary
_____     n. platina (Skinner) — Platina Fritillary
_____     o. pfoutsi (Gunder) — Pfouts's Fritillary
_____     p. gunderi (J. A. Comstock) — Gunder's Fritillary
       cynna dos Passos & Grey

8. callippe (Boisduval) — Callippe Fritillary
_____     a. callippe (Boisduval) — Callippe Fritillary
_____     b. comstocki (Gunder) — Comstock's Fritillary
_____     c. liliana (Hy. Edwards) — Lilian's Fritillary

---　　　　d. semivirida (McDunnough) — Half-green Fritillary
---　　　　e. elaine dos Passos & Grey — Elaine's Fritillary
---　　　　f. rupestris (Behr) — Rupestris Fritillary
---　　　　g. juba (Boisduval) — Yuba Fritillary
---　　　　h. inornata (W. H. Edwards) — Plain Fritillary
---　　　　i. laura (W. H. Edwards) — Laura's Fritillary
---　　　　j. sierra dos Passos & Grey — Sierra Fritillary
---　　　　k. nevadensis (W. H. Edwards) — Nevada Fritillary
---　　　　l. macaria (W. H. Edwards) — Macaria Fritillary
---　　　　m. laurina (W. G. Wright) — Unsilvered Macaria Fritillary
---　　　　n. harmonia dos Passos & Grey — Mt. Wheeler Fritillary
---　　　　o. meadii (W. H. Edwards) — Mead's Fritillary
---　　　　p. gallatini (McDunnough) — Gallatin Fritillary
---　　　　q. calgariana (McDunnough) — Calgary Fritillary
　　　　9. adiaste (W. H. Edwards) — Lesser Unsilvered Fritillary
---　　　　a. adiaste (W. H. Edwards) — Lesser Unsilvered Fritillary
---　　　　b. clemencei (J. A. Comstock) — Clemence's Fritillary
---　　　　c. atossa (W. H. Edwards) — Unsilvered Fritillary
　　　　10. egleis (Behr) — Egleis Fritillary
---　　　　a. egleis (Behr) — Egleis Fritillary
---　　　　b. tehachapina (J. A. Comstock) — Tehachapi Fritillary
---　　　　c. oweni (W. H. Edwards) — Owen's Fritillary
---　　　　d. linda (dos Passos & Grey) — Linda Fritillary
---　　　　e. mcdunnoughi (Gunder) — McDunnough's Fritillary
---　　　　f. albrighti (Gunder) — Albright's Fritillary
---　　　　g. utahensis (Skinner) — Utah Fritillary
---　　　　h. secreta dos Passos & Grey — Secret Fritillary
---　　　　i. toiyabe Howe — Toiyabe Fritillary
　　　　11. atlantis (W. H. Edwards) — Atlantis Fritillary
---　　　　a. atlantis (W. H. Edwards) — Atlantis Fritillary
---　　　　b. hollandi (F. & R. Chermock) — Holland's Fritillary
---　　　　c. hesperis (W. H. Edwards) — Hesperis Fritillary
---　　　　d. nikias (Ehrmann) — Nikias Fritillary
---　　　　e. dorothea (Moeck) — Dorothy's Fritillary
---　　　　f. nausicaa (W. H. Edwards) — Nausicaa Fritillary
---　　　　g. schellbachi Garth — Schellbach's Fritillary
---　　　　h. chitone (W. H. Edwards) — Chitone Fritillary
---　　　　i. wasatchia dos Passos & Grey — Wasatch Fritillary
---　　　　j. greyi (Moeck) — Grey's Fritillary
---　　　　k. tetonia dos Passos & Grey — Teton Fritillary
---　　　　l. viola dos Passos & Grey — Viola Fritillary
---　　　　m. dodgei (Gunder) — Dodge's Fritillary
---　　　　n. irene (Boisduval) — Irene's Fritillary
---　　　　o. electa (W. H. Edwards) — Electa Fritillary
---　　　　p. lurana dos Passos & Grey — Lurana Fritillary

_____ q. hutchinsi dos Passos & Grey — Hutchins's Fritillary
_____ r. beani (Barnes & Benjamin) — Bean's Fritillary
_____ s. lais (W. H. Edwards) — Lais Fritillary
         *helena* dos Passos & Grey
_____ t. dennisi dos Passos & Gray — Dennis's Fritillary
12. hydaspe (Boisduval) — Hydaspe Fritillary
_____ a. hydaspe (Boisduval) — Hydaspe Fritillary
_____ b. viridicornis (J. A. Comstock) — Greenhorn Fritillary
_____ c. purpurascens (Hy. Edwards) — Purple Fritillary
_____ d. minor dos Passos & Grey — Minor Fritillary
_____ e. rhodope (W. H. Edwards) — Rhodope Fritillary
_____ f. sakuntala (Skinner) — Sakuntala Fritillary
_____ g. conquista dos Passos & Grey — New Mexico Fritillary
13. mormonia (Boisduval) — Mormon Fritillary
_____ a. mormonia (Boisduval) — Mormon Fritillary
_____ b. bischoffi (W. H. Edwards) — Bischoff's Fritillary
_____ c. opis (W. H. Edwards) — Opis Fritillary
_____ d. jesmondensis dos Passos & Grey — Jesmond Fritillary
_____ e. washingtonia (Barnes & McDunnough) — Washington Fritillary
_____ f. erinna (W. H. Edwards) — Erinna Fritillary
_____ g. arge (Strecker) — Arge Fritillary
_____ h. artonis (W. H. Edwards) — Artonis Fritillary
_____ i. eurynome (W. H. Edwards) — Eurynome Fritillary
_____ j. luski (Barnes & McDunnough) — Lusk's Fritillary

***Euptoieta* Doubleday**
1. claudia (Cramer) — Variegated Fritillary

***Boloria* Moore**
1. napaea (Hoffmannsegg) — Napaea Fritillary
   *a. napaea (Hoffmannsegg) — (Eurasia)
_____ b. alaskensis (Holland) — Alaskan Fritillary
_____ c. nearctica Verity — Nearctic Fritillary
_____ d. halli Klots — Hall's Fritillary

***Clossiana* Reuss**
1. selene (Denis & Schiffermueller) — Silver-bordered Fritillary
   *a. selene (Denis & Schiffermueller) — (Eurasia)
_____ b. atrocostalis (Huard) — Dark-bordered Fritillary
_____ c. nebraskensis (Holland) — Nebraska Fritillary
_____ d. tollandensis (Barnes & Benjamin) — Tolland Fritillary
_____ e. albequina (Holland) — Whitehorse Fritillary
_____ f. sabulicollis (Kohler) — Kohler's Fritillary
2. bellona (Fabricius) — Meadow Fritillary
_____ a. bellona (Fabricius) — Meadow Fritillary
_____ b. toddi (Holland) — Todd's Meadow Fritillary

_____       c. jenistai (D. Stallings & Turner) — Jenista's Meadow
              Fritillary
          3. frigga (Thunberg) — Frigga's Fritillary
            *a. frigga (Thunberg) — (n. Europe)
_____       b. alaskensis (Lehmann) — Frigga's Fritillary
_____       c. sagata (Barnes & Benjamin) — Sagata Fritillary
          4. improba (Butler) — Dingy Northern Fritillary
_____       a. improba (Butler) — Dingy Northern Fritillary
_____       b. youngi (Holland) — Young's Dingy Northern Fritil-
              lary
_____     5. acrocnema Gall & Sperling — Uncomphaghre Fritillary
_____     6. kriemhild (Strecker) — Strecker's Small Fritillary
          7. epithore (W. H. Edwards) — Western Meadow Fritillary
_____       a. epithore (W. H. Edwards) — Western Meadow
              Fritillary
_____       b. chermocki (E. & S. Perkins) — Chermock's Meadow
              Fritillary
_____       c. sierra (E. Perkins) — Sierra Meadow Fritillary
_____       d. borealis (E. Perkins) — Northern Meadow Fritillary
          8. titania (Esper) — Purple Lesser Fritillary
            *a. titania (Esper) — (w. Europe to Siberia)
_____       b. rainieri (Barnes & McDunnough) — Rainier Fritil-
              lary
_____       c. boisduvalii (Duponchel) — Boisduval's Fritillary
_____       d. grandis (Barnes & McDunnough) — Purple
              Fritillary
_____       e. ingens (Barnes & McDunnough) — Purple Fritillary
_____       f. helena (W. H. Edwards) — Colorado Purple Fritillary
          9. polaris (Boisduval) — Polaris Fritillary
            a. polaris (Boisduval) — Polaris Fritillary
_____       b. stellata (Masters) — Polaris Fritillary
         10. freija (Thunberg) — Freija's Fritillary
_____       a. freija (Thunberg) — Freija's Fritillary
_____       b. tarquinius (Curtis) — Tarquinius's Fritillary
_____       c. natazhati (Gibson) — Mt. Natazhat Fritillary
_____       d. nabokovi (D. Stallings & Turner) — Nabokov's
              Fritillary
_____       e. browni (Higgins) — Brown's Fritillary
_____    11. alberta (W. H. Edwards) — Alberta Fritillary
_____    12. astarte (Doubleday & Hewitson) — Astarte Fritillary
_____    13. distincta (Gibson) — Distinct Fritillary
         14. chariclea (Schneider) — Arctic Fritillary
            *a. chariclea (Schneider) — (Arctic Europe)
_____       b. arctica (Zetterstedt) — Arctic Fritillary
_____       c. butleri (W. H. Edwards) — Butler's Arctic Fritillary
***Proclossiana* Reuss**
          1. eunomia (Esper) — Bog Fritillary
            *a. eunomia (Esper) — (n. Europe to Siberia)

|      |     |                                                                          |
|------|-----|--------------------------------------------------------------------------|
| ____ | b.  | triclaris (Huebner) — Bog Fritillary                                     |
| ____ | c.  | caelestis (Hemming) — Celestial Bog Fritillary                           |
| ____ | d.  | nichollae (Barnes & Benjamin) — Nicholl's Bog Fritillary                 |
| ____ | e.  | laddi (Klots) — Ladd's Bog Fritillary                                     |
| ____ | f.  | ursadentis (Ferris & Groothuis) — Beartooth Bog Fritillary               |
| ____ | g.  | denali (Klots) — Denali Bog Fritillary                                    |

## Subfamily Melitaeinae — Checker-spots, Patches, and Crescents

*Anthanassa* **Scudder**
____ 1. texana (W. H. Edwards) — Texas Crescent
*Eresia* **Boisduval**
 1. frisia (Poey) — Cuban Crescent
 *a. frisia Poey — Cuban Crescent (Cuba)
____ b. tulcis (Bates) — Tulcis Crescent
*Phyciodes* **Huebner**
 1. pascoensis W. G. Wright — Northern Pearl Crescent
____ a. pascoensis W. G. Wright — Northern Pearl Crescent
____ b. distinctus Bauer — Distinct Crescent
____ c. arcticus dos Passos — Arctic Pearl Crescent
____ 2. batesii (Reakirt) — Tawny Crescent
____ 3. phaon (W. H. Edwards) — Phaon Crescent
 4. campestris (Behr) — Field Crescent
____ a. campestris (Behr) — Field Crescent
____ b. camillus W. H. Edwards — Camillus Crescent
____ c. montanus (Behr) — Mountain Crescent
 5. pictus W. H. Edwards — Painted Crescent
____ a. pictus W. H. Edwards — Painted Crescent
____ b. canace W. H. Edwards — Painted Crescent
 6. orseis W. H. Edwards — Orseis Crescent
____ a. orseis W. H. Edwards — Orseis Crescent
____ b. herlani Bauer — Herlan's Crescent
 7. mylitta (W. H. Edwards) — Mylitta Crescent
____ a. mylitta (W. H. Edwards) — Mylitta Crescent
____ b. arizonensis Bauer — Arizona Crescent
 8. pallidus (W. H. Edwards) — Pale Crescent
____ a. pallidus (W. H. Edwards) — Pale Crescent
____ b. barnesi Skinner — Barnes' Pale Crescent
____ 9. vesta (W. H. Edwards) — Vesta Crescent
*Charidryas* **Scudder**
 1. gorgone (Huebner) — Gorgone Checker-spot
 *a. gorgone (Huebner) — Gorgone Checker-spot
____ b. carlota (Reakirt) — Gorgone Checker-spot
 2. nycteis (Doubleday) — Silvery Checker-spot

_____ a. nycteis (Doubleday) — Silvery Checker-spot
_____ b. drusius (W. H. Edwards) — Dark Silvery Checker-spot
_____ c. reversa (F. & R. Chermock) — Chermocks' Checker-spot
_____ 3. gabbii (Behr) — Gabb's Checker-spot
4. acastus (W. H. Edwards) — Acastus Checker-spot
_____ a. acastus (W. H. Edwards) — Acastus Checker-spot
_____ b. dorothyae (Bauer) — Dorothy's Checker-spot
5. neumoegeni (Skinner) — Neumoegen's Checker-spot
_____ a. neumoegeni (Skinner) — Neumoegen's Checker-spot
_____ b. sabina (W. G. Wright) — Sabino Canyon Checker-spot
6. palla (Boisduval) — Northern Checker-spot
_____ a. palla (Boisduval) — Northern Checker-spot
_____ b. whitneyi (Behr) — Whitney's Checker-spot
_____ c. vallismortis (J. W. Johnson) — Death Valley Checker-spot
_____ d. flavula (Barnes & McDunnough) — Flavid Checker-spot
_____ e. calydon (Holland) — Calydon Checker-spot
_____ f. sterope (W. H. Edwards) — Sterope Checker-spot
7. hoffmanni (Behr) — Hoffmann's Checker-spot
_____ a. hoffmanni (Behr) — Hoffmann's Checker-spot
_____ b. segregata (Barnes & McDunnough) — Segregated Checker-spot
_____ c. manchada (Bauer) — Manchada Checker-spot
8. damoetas (Skinner) — Damoetas Checker-spot
_____ a. damoetas (Skinner) — Damoetas Checker-spot
_____ b. malcolmi (J. A. Comstock) — Malcolm's Checker-spot

*Chlosyne* **Butler**
_____ 1. definita (Aaron) — Aaron's Checker-spot
2. lacinia (Geyer) — Bordered Patch
    *a. lacinia (Geyer) — (Mexico to Argentina)
_____ b. adjutrix Scudder — Bordered Patch
_____ c. crocale (W. H. Edwards) — Crocale Patch
_____ 3. californica (W. G. Wright) — California Patch

*Thessalia* **Scudder**
1. leanira (C. & R. Felder) — Leanira Checker-spot
_____ a. leanira (C. & R. Felder) — Leanira Checker-spot
_____ b. oregonensis (Bauer) — Oregon Checker-spot
_____ c. daviesi (Wind) — Davies' Checker-spot
_____ d. wrighti (W. H. Edwards) — Wright's Checker-spot
_____ e. cerrita (W. G. Wright) — Cerrita Checker-spot
_____ f. alma (Strecker) — Alma Checker-spot
_____ 2. fulvia (W. H. Edwards) — Fulvous Checker-spot
_____ 3. cyneas (Godman & Salvin) — Cyneas Checker-spot
4. theona (Ménétriés) — Theona Checker-spot

\*a.   theona (Ménétriés) — (Mexico and Cen. America)
___    b.   bollii (W. H. Edwards) — Boll's Checker-spot
___    c.   thekla (W. H. Edwards) — Thekla Checker-spot
___    5.  chinatiensis (Tinkham) — Tinkham's Checker-spot
**Dymasia** Higgins
___    1.  dymas (W. H. Edwards) — Dymas Checker-spot
       2.  chara (W. H. Edwards) — Chara Checker-spot
___    a.   chara (W. H. Edwards) — Chara Checker-spot
___    b.   imperialis (Bauer) — Imperial Checker-spot
**Texola** Higgins
       1.  elada (Hewitson) — Elada Checker-spot
       \*a.  elada (Hewitson) — (Mexico)
___    b.   callina (Boisduval) — Callina Checker-spot
___    c.   perse (W. H. Edwards) — Perse Checker-spot
**Microtia** W. H. Bates
___    1.  elva W. H. Bates — Elva
**Poladryas** Bauer
___    1.  minuta (W. H. Edwards) — Small Checker-spot
       2.  arachne (W. H. Edwards) — Arachne Checker-spot
___    a.   arachne (W. H. Edwards) — Arachne Checker-spot
___    b.   nympha (W. H. Edwards) — Arizona Checker-spot
___    c.   monache (J. A. Comstock) — Monache Checker-spot
**Occidryas** Higgins
       1.  chalcedona (Doubleday) — Chalcedon Checker-spot
___    a.   chalcedona (Doubleday) — Chalcedon Checker-spot
___    b.   dwinellei (Hy. Edwards) — Dwinelle's Checker-spot
___    c.   hennei (Scott) — Henne's Checker-spot
            *quino* of authors, not Behr
___    d.   macglashanii (Rivers) — McGlashan's Checker-spot
___    e.   olancha (W. G. Wright) — Olancha Checker-spot
___    f.   sierra (W. G. Wright) — Sierra Checker-spot
___    g.   klotsi (dos Passos) — Klots' Checker-spot
___    h.   kingstonensis (T. & J. Emmel) — Kingston Checker-
            spot
___    i.   corralensis (T. & J. Emmel) — Corral Checker-spot
       2.  colon (W. H. Edwards) — Colon Checker-spot
___    a.   colon (W. H. Edwards) — Colon Checker-spot
___    b.   perdiccas (W. H. Edwards) — Perdiccas Checker-
            spot
___    c.   paradoxa (McDunnough) — Contrary Checker-spot
___    d.   wallacensis (Gunder) — Wallace Checker-spot
___    e.   nevadensis (Bauer) — Nevada Checker-spot
       3.  anicia (Doubleday) — Anicia Checker-spot
___    a.   anicia (Doubleday) — Anicia Checker-spot
___    b.   helvia (Scudder) — Helvia Checker-spot
___    c.   howlandi (D. Stallings & Turner) — Howland's
            Checker-spot
___    d.   capella (Barnes) — Capella Checker-spot
___    e.   hermosa (W. G. Wright) — Handsome Checker-spot

_____ f.  magdalena (Barnes & McDunnough) — Magdalena Checker-spot
_____ g.  alena (Barnes & Benjamin) — Alena Checker-spot
_____ h.  carmentis (Barnes & Benjamin) — Carmentis Checker-spot
_____ i.  windi (Gunder) — Wind's Checker-spot
_____ j.  eurytion (Mead) — Eurytion Checker-spot
          *brucei* (W. H. Edwards)
_____ k.  maria (Skinner) — Maria's Checker-spot
_____ l.  effi (D. Stallings & Turner) — Eff's Checker-spot
_____ m.  hopfingeri (Gunder) — Hopfinger's Checker-spot
_____ n.  bernadetta (Leussler) — Leussler's Checker-spot
_____ o.  veazieae (Fender & Jewett) — Veazie's Checker-spot
_____ p.  bakeri (D. Stallings & Turner) — Baker's Checker-spot
_____ q.  macyi (Fender & Jewett) — Macy's Checker-spot
_____ r.  wheeleri (Hy. Edwards) — Wheeler's Checker-spot
_____ s.  morandi (Gunder) — Morand's Checker-spot
_____ t.  chuskae Ferris & R. Holland — Chuska Mountains Checker-spot
_____ u.  cloudcrofti Ferris & R. Holland — Cloudcroft Checker-spot

4. editha (Boisduval) — Edith's Checker-spot
_____ a.  editha (Boisduval) — Edith's Checker-spot
_____ b.  quino (Behr) — Quino Checker-spot
          *augusta* (W. H. Edwards), *wrighti* (Gunder)
_____ c.  insularis (T. & J. Emmel) — Island Checker-spot
_____ d.  bayensis (Sternitzky) — Bay Region Checker-spot
_____ e.  leuestherae (Murphy & Ehrlich) — Leuesther's Checker-spot
_____ f.  taylori (W. H. Edwards) — Taylor's Checker-spot
_____ g.  beani (Skinner) — Bean's Checker-spot
_____ h.  hutchinsi (McDunnough) — Hutchins's Checker-spot
_____ i.  alebarki (Ferris) — Alebark's Checker-spot
_____ j.  gunnisonensis (F. M. Brown) — Gunnison Checker-spot
_____ k.  edithana (Strand) — Strand's Checker-spot
_____ l.  baroni (W. H. Edwards) — Baron's Checker-spot
_____ m.  rubicunda (Hy. Edwards) — Ruddy Checker-spot
_____ n.  monoensis (Gunder) — Mono Checker-spot
          *fridayi* (Gunder)
_____ o.  lehmani (Gunder) — Lehman Caves Checker-spot
_____ p.  augustina (W. G. Wright) — Augustina Checker-spot
          *augusta* of Authors, not W. H. Edwards
_____ q.  colonia (W. G. Wright) — Colonia Checker-spot
_____ r.  aurilacus (Gunder) — Gold Lake Checker-spot

_____ s.  remingtoni (Burdick) — Remington's Checker-spot
_____ t.  lawrencei (Gunder) — Lawrence's Checker-spot
_____ u.  nubigena (Behr) — Cloud-born Checker-spot
*Hypodryas* **Higgins**
_____ 11. gillettii (Barnes) — Gillette's Checker-spot

# Family Papilionidae — Swallowtails and Parnassians

## Subfamily Parnassiinae — Parnassians

*Parnassius* **Latreille**
    1. eversmanni Ménétriés — Eversmann's Parnassian
      *a.  eversmanni Ménétriés — (Russia, Siberia)
_____  b.  thor W. H. Edwards — Eversmann's Parnassian
    2. clodius Ménétriés — Clodius Parnassian
_____  a.  clodius Ménétriés — Clodius Parnassian
_____  b.  strohbeeni Sternitzky — Strohbeen's Parnassian
_____  c.  sol Bryk & Eisner — Sol Parnassian
_____  d.  baldur W. H. Edwards — Baldur Parnassian
_____  e.  claudianus Stichel — Claudianus Parnassian
_____  f.  pseudogallatinus Bryk — False Gallatin Parnassian
_____  g.  incredibilis Bryk — Incredible Parnassian
_____  h.  altaurus Dyar — Altaurus Parnassian
_____  i.  menetriesii Hy. Edwards — Ménétriés' Parnassian
_____  j.  gallatinus Stichel — Gallatin Parnassian
    3. phoebus (Fabricius) — Phoebus Parnassian, Small Apollo
      *a.  phoebus (Fabricius) — (Siberia, European Alps)
_____  b.  behrii W. H. Edwards — Behr's Parnassian
_____  c.  sternitzkyi McDunnough — Sternitzky's Parnassian
_____  d.  magnus W. G. Wright — Large Parnassian
_____  e.  olympianus Burdick — Olympian Parnassian
_____  f.  smintheus Doubleday — Smintheus Parnassian
_____  g.  xanthus Ehrmann — Xanthus Parnassian
_____  h.  sayii W. H. Edwards — Say's Parnassian
_____  i.  hollandi Bryk & Eisner — Holland's Parnassian
_____  j.  pseudorotgeri Eisner — False Rotger's Parnassian
_____  k.  apricatus Stichel — Sunny Parnassian
_____  l.  golovinus Holland — Golovin Bay Parnassian
_____  m.  alaskensis Eisner — Alaskan Parnassian
_____  n.  elias Bryk — Mt. St. Elias Parnassian
_____  o.  yukonensis Eisner — Yukon Parnassian

## Subfamily Papilioninae — Swallowtails

*Battus* **Scopoli**
    1. philenor (Linnaeus) — Pipe-vine Swallowtail

——     a.  philenor (Linnaeus) — Pipe-vine Swallowtail
——     b.  hirsuta (Skinner) — Hairy Swallowtail

***Papilio* Linnaeus**

    1.  polyxenes Fabricius — Black Swallowtail
      *a.  polyxenes Fabricius — (Cuba)
——     b.  asterius Stoll — Black Swallowtail
——     c.  coloro Wright — Wright's Swallowtail
——   2.  bairdii W. H. Edwards — Baird's Swallowtail
    3.  oregonius W. H. Edwards — Oregon Swallowtail
——     a.  oregonius W. H. Edwards — Oregon Swallowtail
——     b.  dodi McDunnough — Dod's Swallowtail
    4.  zelicaon Lucas — Zelicaon Swallowtail
——     a.  zelicaon Lucas — Zelicaon Swallowtail
——     b.  nitra W. H. Edwards — Nitra Swallowtail
          *gothica* Remington
——   5.  kahli F. & R. Chermock — Kahl's Swallowtail
    6.  machaon Linnaeus — Old World Swallowtail
      *a.  machaon Linnaeus — (Europe)
——     b.  aliaska Scudder — Alaskan Old World Swallowtail
——     c.  hudsonianus A. H. Clark — Hudsonian Swallowtail
    7.  indra Reakirt — Indra Swallowtail
——     a.  indra Reakirt — Short-tailed Swallowtail
——     b.  minori Cross — Minor's Swallowtail
——     c.  pergamus Hy. Edwards — Edwards' Swallowtail
——     d.  kaibabensis Bauer — Grand Canyon Swallowtail
——     e.  fordi J. A. Comstock & Martin — Ford's Swallowtail
——     f.  martini T. & J. Emmel — Martin's Swallowtail
——     g.  nevadensis T. & J. Emmel — Nevada Swallowtail
——     h.  phyllisae J. F. Emmel — Phyllis' Swallowtail
——     i.  panamintensis J. F. Emmel — Panamint Swallowtail
——   8.  xuthus Linnaeus — Xuthus Swallowtail
——   9.  cresphontes Cramer — Giant Swallowtail
  10.  glaucus Linnaeus — Eastern Tiger Swallowtail
——     a.  glaucus Linnaeus — Eastern Tiger Swallowtail
——     b.  canadensis Rothschild & Jordan — Canadian Tiger Swallowtail
——     c.  arcticus Skinner — Arctic Tiger Swallowtail
  11.  rutulus Lucas — Western Tiger Swallowtail
——     a.  rutulus Lucas — Western Tiger Swallowtail
——     b.  arizonensis W. H. Edwards — Arizona Tiger Swallowtail
——   12.  eurymedon Lucas — Pale Swallowtail
——   13.  multicaudatus Kirby — Two-tailed Swallowtail
——   14.  troilus Linnaeus — Spicebush Swallowtail

# Family Pieridae — Whites and Sulfurs

## Subfamily Pierinae — Whites

***Neophasia* Behr**
     1. terlootii Behr — Southern Pine White
     2. menapia (C. & R. Felder) — Pine White
_____      a. menapia (C. & R. Felder) — Pine White
_____      b. melanica Scott — Coastal Pine White

***Pontia* Fabricius**
     1. beckerii (W. H. Edwards) — Becker's White
_____      a. beckerii (W. H. Edwards) — Becker's White
_____      b. pseudochloridice (McDunnough) — Becker's White
     2. sisymbrii (Boisduval) — California White
_____      a. sisymbrii — California White
_____      b. flavitincta (J. A. Comstock) — Flavous White
_____      c. elivata (Barnes & Benjamin) — Alpine White
_____      d. nordini (K. Johnson) — Nordin's White
_____      3. protodice (Boisduval & Le Conte) — Checkered White
     4. occidentalis (Reakirt) — Western White
_____      a. occidentalis (Reakirt) — Western White
_____      b. nelsoni (W. H. Edwards) — Nelson's White

***Artogeia* Verity**
     1. napi (Linnaeus) — Mustard White
     *a. napi (Linnaeus) — (Europe)
_____      b. pseudobryoniae (Verity) — Alaskan Mustard White
_____      c. hulda (W. H. Edwards) — Coastal Alaskan White
_____      d. venosa (Scudder) — Veined White
_____      e. microstriata (J. A. Comstock) — Small-veined White
_____      f. marginalis (Scudder) — Margined White
_____      g. mcdunnoughi (Remington) — McDunnough's White
_____      h. mogollon (Burdick) — Mogollon White
     2. rapae (Linnaeus) — Cabbage Butterfly

***Ascia* Scopoli**
     1. monuste (Linnaeus) — Great Southern White
     *a. monuste (Linnaeus) — Great Southern White (S. America)
_____      b. phileta (Fabricius) — Great Southern White

***Ganyra* Billberg**
     1. josephina (Godart) — Giant White
     *a. josephina (Godart) — (Caribbean)
_____      b. josepha (Godman & Salvin) — Giant White

## Subfamily Coliadinae — Sulfurs and Yellows

***Colias* Fabricius**
     1. meadii W. H. Edwards — Mead's Sulfur

———     a. meadii W. H. Edwards — Mead's Sulfur
———     b. elis Strecker — Elis Sulfur
    2. hecla Lefebvre — Hecla Sulfur
      *a. hecla Lefebvre — Hecla Sulfur (Greenland to Baffin I.)
———     b. hela Strecker — Hecla Sulfur
———     3. boothii Curtis — Booth's Sulfur
———     4. eurytheme Boisduval — Orange Sulfur
    5. philodice Godart — Clouded Sulfur
———     a. philodice Godart — Clouded Sulfur
———     b. eriphyle W. H. Edwards — Western Clouded Sulfur
———     c. vitabunda Hovanitz — Lively Clouded Sulfur
———     6. harfordii Hy. Edwards — Harford's Sulfur
    7. occidentalis Scudder — Western Sulfur
———     a. occidentalis Scudder — Western Sulfur
———     b. chrysomelas Hy. Edwards — Gold-and-black Sulfur
———     8. interior Scudder — Pink-edged Sulfur
    9. alexandra W. H. Edwards — Queen Alexandra Sulfur
———     a. alexandra W. H. Edwards — Queen Alexandra Sulfur
———     b. edwardsii W. H. Edwards — Edwards' Sulfur
———     c. columbiensis Ferris — Columbian Sulfur
———     d. christina W. H. Edwards — Christina Sulfur
———     e. astraea W. H. Edwards — Astraea Sulfur
———     f. krauthii Klots — Krauth's Sulfur
———     g. kluanensis Ferris — Kluane Sulfur
   10. scudderii Reakirt — Scudder's Sulfur
———     a. scudderii Reakirt — Scudder's Sulfur
———     b. ruckesi Klots — Ruckes's Sulfur
   11. gigantea Strecker — Giant Sulfur
———     a. gigantea Strecker — Giant Sulfur
———     b. harroweri Klots — Harrower's Sulfur
   12. pelidne Boisduval & Le Conte — Pelidne Sulfur
———     a. pelidne Boisduval & Le Conte — Pelidne Sulfur
———     b. minisni Bean — Bean's Sulfur
———     c. skinneri Barnes — Skinner's Sulfur
   13. palaeno (Linnaeus) — Palaeno Sulfur
      *a. palaeno (Linnaeus) — (Europe)
———     b. chippewa W. H. Edwards — Palaeno Sulfur
———     14. behrii W. H. Edwards — Behr's Sulfur
   15. nastes Boisduval — Nastes Sulfur
———     a. nastes Boisduval — Nastes Sulfur
———     b. streckeri Grum-Grschimailo — Strecker's Sulfur
———     c. moina Strecker — Moina Sulfur
———     d. aliaska Bang-Haas — Alaskan Sulfur
———     16. thula Hovanitz — Thula Sulfur
***Zerene* Huebner**
———     1. eurydice (Boisduval) — California Dogface
———     2. cesonia (Stoll) — Southern Dogface

*Anteos* **Huebner**
    1. clorinde (Godart) — Clorinde
      *a. clorinde (Godart) — (Brazil)
\_\_\_\_\_    b. nivifera Fruhstorfer — Clorinde
    2. maerula (Fabricius) — Maerula
      *a. maerula (Fabricius) — (Jamaica)
\_\_\_\_\_    b. lacordairei (Boisduval — Maerula

*Phoebis* **Huebner**
    1. sennae (Linnaeus) — Cloudless Sulfur
      *a. sennae (Linnaeus) — (West Indies)
\_\_\_\_\_    b. eubule (Linnaeus) — Cloudless Sulfur
\_\_\_\_\_    c. marcellina (Cramer) — Cloudless Sulfur
\_\_\_\_\_    2. philea (Johannson) — Orange-barred Sulfur
\_\_\_\_\_    3. agarithe (Boisduval) — Large Orange Sulfur

*Aphrissa* **Butler**
    1. statira (Cramer) — Statira
      *a. statira (Cramer) — (S. America)
\_\_\_\_\_    b. jada (Butler) — Statira

*Kricogonia* **Reakirt**
\_\_\_\_\_    1. lyside (Godart) — Lyside

*Eurema* **Huebner**
\_\_\_\_\_    1. boisduvaliana (C. & R. Felder) — Boisduval's Sulfur
\_\_\_\_\_    2. mexicana (Boisduval) — Mexican Sulfur
    3. salome (C. Felder) — Salome Sulfur
      *a. salome (C. Felder) — (S. America)
\_\_\_\_\_    b. limoneus (C. & R. Felder) — Salome Sulfur
\_\_\_\_\_    4. proterpia (Fabricius) — Proterpia Orange
      *gundlachia* (Poey) — "Gundlach's Orange"
\_\_\_\_\_    5. lisa (Boisduval & Le Conte) — Little Sulfur
    6. nise (Cramer) — Nise Sulfur
      *a. nise (Cramer) — (Fla. and the Antilles)
\_\_\_\_\_    b. nelphe (R. Felder) — Nise Sulfur
    7. dina (Poey) — Dina Sulfur
      *a. dina (Poey) — (Cuba)
\_\_\_\_\_    b. westwoodi (Boisduval) — Dina Sulfur
\_\_\_\_\_    8. nicippe (Cramer) — Sleepy Orange

*Nathalis* **Boisduval**
\_\_\_\_\_    1. iole Boisduval — Dainty Sulfur

## Subfamily Anthocharinae —
## Orange-tips and Marbles

*Anthocharis* **Boisduval, Rambur, & Graslin**
    1. cethura (C. & R. Felder) — Felder's Orange-tip
\_\_\_\_\_    a. cethura (C. & R. Felder) — Felder's Orange-tip
\_\_\_\_\_    b. catalina Meadows — Catalina Orange-tip
\_\_\_\_\_    c. morrisoni W. H. Edwards — Morrison's Orange-tip
\_\_\_\_\_    2. pima W. H. Edwards — Pima Orange-tip

    3. sara Lucas — Sara Orange-tip
_____ a. sara Lucas — Sara Orange-tip
_____ b. flora W. G. Wright — Flora Orange-tip
_____ c. gunderi Ingham — Gunder's Orange-tip
_____ d. inghami Gunder — Ingham's Orange-tip
_____ e. stella W. H. Edwards — Stella Orange-tip
_____ f. julia W. H. Edwards — Julia Orange-tip
_____ g. thoosa (Scudder) — Thoosa Orange-tip
_____ h. browningi Skinner — Browning's Orange-tip
_____ i. alaskensis Gunder — Alaskan Orange-tip

*Falcapica* **Klots**
    1. lanceolata (Lucas) — Boisduval's Marble
_____ a. lanceolata (Lucas) — Boisduval's Marble
_____ b. australis (F. Grinnell) — Grinnell's Marble

*Euchloe* **Huebner**
_____ 1. creusa (Doubleday) — Creusa Marble
    2. hyantis (W. H. Edwards) — Edwards's Marble
_____ a. hyantis (W. H. Edwards) — Edwards's Marble
_____ b. andrewsi Martin — Andrew's Marble
_____ c. lotta (Beutenmueller) — Southern Marble
    3. ausonides (Lucas) — Large Marble
_____ a. ausonides (Lucas) — Large Marble
_____ b. coloradensis (Hy. Edwards) — Colorado Marble
_____ c. mayi F. & R. Chermock — May's Marble
_____ d. palaeoreios K. Johnson — Johnson's Marble
    4. olympia (W. H. Edwards) — Olympia Marble
_____ a. olympia (W. H. Edwards) — Olympia Marble
_____ b. rosa (W. H. Edwards) — Rosy Marble

# Family Libytheidae — Snout Butterflies

*Libytheana* **Michener**
    1. bachmannii (Kirtland) — Snout Butterfly
_____ a. bachmannii (Kirtland) — Snout Butterfly
_____ b. larvata (Strecker) — Snout Butterfly

# Family Riodinidae — Metalmarks

*Apodemia* **C. & R. Felder**
    1. mormo (C. & R. Felder) — Mormon Metalmark
_____ a. mormo (C. & R. Felder) — Mormon Metalmark
_____ b. langei J. A. Comstock — Lange's Metalmark
_____ c. virgulti (Behr) — Behr's Metalmark
_____ d. tuolumnensis Opler & Powell — Tuolumne Metalmark
_____ e. dialeuca Opler & Powell — Whitish Metalmark
_____ f. deserti Barnes & McDunnough — Desert Metalmark

_____     g. cythera (W. H. Edwards) — Cythera Metalmark
_____     h. mejicanus (Behr) — Mexican Metalmark
_____     i. duryi (W. H. Edwards) — Dury's Metalmark
          2. palmerii (W. H. Edwards) — Palmer's Metalmark
_____     a. palmerii (W. H. Edwards) — Palmer's Metalmark
_____     b. marginalis (Skinner) — Margined Metalmark
_____     3. hepburni Godman & Salvin — Hepburn's Metalmark
_____     4. phyciodoides Barnes & Benjamin — Chiricahua Metal-
             mark
_____     5. nais (W. H. Edwards) — Nais Metalmark
_____     6. chisosensis H. A. Freeman — Chisos Metalmark

*Calephelis* **Grote & Robinson**
          1. nemesis (W. H. Edwards) — Fatal Metalmark
_____     a. nemesis (W. H. Edwards) — Fatal Metalmark
_____     b. australis (W. H. Edwards) — Southern Metalmark
_____     c. dammersi McAlpine — Dammers' Metalmark
_____     d. californica McAlpine — Dusky Metalmark
_____     2. perditalis Barnes & McDunnough — Lost Metalmark
_____     3. wrighti Holland — Wright's Metalmark
_____     4. rawsoni McAlpine — Rawson's Metalmark
_____     5. freemani McAlpine — Freeman's Metalmark
_____     6. arizonensis McAlpine — Arizona Metalmark
_____     7. dreisbachi McAlpine — Dreisbach's Metalmark

*Emesis* **Fabricius**
_____     1. ares (W. H. Edwards) — Ares Metalmark
          2. zela Butler — Zela Metalmark
         *a. zela Butler — (S. America)
_____     b. cleis (W. H. Edwards) — Cleis Metalmark

# Family Lycaenidae —
# Gossamer-winged Butterflies

## Subfamily Theclinae — Hairstreaks

*Habrodais* **Scudder**
          1. grunus (Boisduval) — Boisduval's Hairstreak
_____     a. grunus (Boisduval) — Boisduval's Hairstreak
_____     b. lorquini Field — Lorquin's Hairstreak
_____     c. herri Field — Herr's Hairstreak

*Hypaurotis* **Scudder**
          1. crysalus (W. H. Edwards) — Colorado Hairstreak
_____     a. crysalus (W. H. Edwards) — Colorado Hairstreak
_____     b. citima (Hy. Edwards) — Citima Hairstreak

## Subfamily Eumaeinae — Hairstreaks

*Atlides* **Huebner**
          1. halesus (Cramer) — Great Purple Hairstreak

_____     a. halesus (Cramer) — Great Purple Hairstreak
_____     b. estesi Clench — Great Purple Hairstreak
*Chlorostrymon* **Clench**
    1. *simaethis* (Drury) — Simaethis Hairstreak
    *a. *simaethis* (Drury) — (Antilles)
_____     b. sarita (Skinner) — Sarita Hairstreak
*Phaeostrymon* **Clench**
    1. alcestis (W. H. Edwards) — Alcestis Hairstreak
_____     a. alcestis (W. H. Edwards) — Alcestis Hairstreak
_____     b. oslari (Dyar) — Oslar's Hairstreak
*Harkenclenus* **dos Passos**
    1. titus (Fabricius) — Coral Hairstreak
_____     a. titus (Fabricius) — Coral Hairstreak
_____     b. watsoni (Barnes & Benjamin) — Watson's Hairstreak
_____     c. immaculosus (W. P. Comstock) — Immaculate Hairstreak
*Satyrium* **Scudder**
    1. fuliginosum (W. H. Edwards) — Sooty Gossamer-wing
_____     a. fuliginosum (W. H. Edwards) — Sooty Gossamer-wing
_____     b. semiluna Klots — Half Moon Hairstreak
    2. behrii (W. H. Edwards) — Behr's Hairstreak
_____     a. behrii (W. H. Edwards) — Behr's Hairstreak
_____     b. crossi (Field) — Cross's Hairstreak
_____     c. columbia (McDunnough) — Columbian Hairstreak
    3. acadicum (W. H. Edwards) — Acadian Hairstreak
_____     a. acadicum (W. H. Edwards) — Acadian Hairstreak
_____     b. coolinense (Watson & W. P. Comstock) — Coolin Hairstreak
_____     c. montanense (Watson & W. P. Comstock) — Montana Hairstreak
_____     d. watrini (Dufrane) — Watrin's Hairstreak
_____     4. californicum (W. H. Edwards) — California Hairstreak
    5. sylvinum (Boisduval) — Sylvan Hairstreak
_____     a. sylvinum (Boisduval) — Sylvan Hairstreak
_____     b. desertorum (F. Grinnell) — Desert Hairstreak
_____     c. itys (W. H. Edwards) — Itys Hairstreak
_____     d. putnami (Hy. Edwards) — Putnam's Hairstreak
_____     6. dryope (W. H. Edwards) — Dryope Hairstreak
    7. calanus (Huebner) — Banded Hairstreak
    *a. calanus (Huebner) — (Florida)
_____     b. falacer (Godart) — Banded Hairstreak
_____     c. godarti (Field) — Godart's Hairstreak
    8. liparops (Le Conte) — Striped Hairstreak
_____     a. liparops (Le Conte) — Striped Hairstreak
_____     b. fletcheri (Michener & dos Passos) — Fletcher's Hairstreak

_____      c. aliparops (Michener & dos Passos) — Striped Hair-streak
      9. auretorum (Boisduval) — Gold-hunter's Hairstreak
_____      a. auretorum (Boisduval) — Gold-hunter's Hairstreak
_____      b. spadix (Hy. Edwards) — Nut-brown Hairstreak
_____   10. tetra (W. H. Edwards) — Gray Hairstreak
           *adenostomatis* (Hy. Edwards)
     11. saepium (Boisduval) — Hedgerow Hairstreak
_____      a. saepium (Boisduval) — Hedgerow Hairstreak
_____      b. chalcis (W. H. Edwards) — Bronzed Hairstreak
_____      c. fulvescens (Hy. Edwards) — Fulvous Hairstreak
_____      d. chlorophora (Watson & W.P. Comstock) — Purplish Brown Hairstreak
_____      e. provo (Watson & W. P. Comstock) — Provo Hair-streak
_____      f. okanaganum (McDunnough) — Okanagan Hairstreak

***Ministrymon* Clench**
_____     1. leda (W. H. Edwards) — Leda Hairstreak
          *ines* (W. H. Edwards) — form "ines," the Ines Hairstreak, was formerly a separate species

***Tmolus* Huebner**
_____     1. echion (Linnaeus) — Echion Hairstreak
_____      a. echiolus (Draudt) — Larger Lantana Butterfly
_____     2. azia (Hewitson) — Azia Hairstreak

***Callophrys* Billberg**
      1. affinis (W. H. Edwards) — Green-winged Hairstreak
_____      a. affinis (W. H. Edwards) — Green-winged Hairstreak
_____      b. washingtonia Clench — Washington Hairstreak
      2. sheridanii (W. H. Edwards) — Sheridan's Hairstreak
_____      a. sheridanii (W. H. Edwards) — Sheridan's Hairstreak
_____      b. neoperplexa Barnes & Benjamin
_____      c. newcomeri Clench — Newcomer's Hairstreak
      3. dumetorum (Boisduval) — Bramble Hairstreak
_____      a. dumetorum (Boisduval) — Bramble Hairstreak
_____      b. perplexa Barnes & Benjamin — Perplexing Hair-streak
_____      c. oregonensis Gorelick — Oregon Hairstreak
      4. apama (W. H. Edwards) — Apama Hairstreak
_____      a. apama (W. H. Edwards) — Apama Hairstreak
_____      b. homoperplexa Barnes & Benjamin
_____     5. comstocki Henne — Comstock's Green Hairstreak
_____     6. lemberti Tilden — Lembert's Hairstreak
_____     7. viridis (W. H. Edwards) — Green Hairstreak

***Mitoura* Scudder**
_____     1. spinetorum (Hewitson) — Thicket Hairstreak
_____     2. johnsoni (Skinner) — Johnson's Hairstreak
      3. barryi K. Johnson — Barry's Hairstreak
_____      a. barryi K. Johnson — Barry's Hairstreak

_____      b. acuminata K. Johnson — Acuminate Hairstreak
     4. rosneri K. Johnson — Rosner's Hairstreak
_____      a. rosneri K. Johnson — Rosner's Hairstreak
_____      b. plicataria K. Johnson — Pleated Hairstreak
_____      5. byrnei K. Johnson — Byrne's Hairstreak
_____      6. nelsoni (Boisduval) — Nelson's Hairstreak
_____      7. muiri (Hy. Edwards) — Muir's Hairstreak
     8. siva (W. H. Edwards) — Siva Hairstreak
_____      a. siva (W. H. Edwards) — Siva Hairstreak
_____      b. juniperaria J. A. Comstock — Juniper Hairstreak
_____      c. mansfieldi Tilden — Mansfield's Hairstreak
_____      d. chalcosiva Clench — Clench's Hairstreak
_____      9. loki (Skinner) — Skinner's Hairstreak
_____    10. thornei J. W. Brown — Thorne's Hairstreak
   11. gryneus (Huebner) — Olive Hairstreak
_____      a. gryneus (Huebner) — Olive Hairstreak
_____      b. castalis (W. H. Edwards) — Olive Hairstreak

*Xamia* **Clench**
_____      1. xami (Reakirt) — Xami Hairstreak

*Sandia* **Clench & Ehrlich**
_____      1. mcfarlandi Ehrlich & Clench — McFarland's Hairstreak

*Incisalia* **Scudder**
     1. polia Cook & Watson — Hoary Elfin
_____      a. polia Cook & Watson — Hoary Elfin
_____      b. obscura Ferris & Fisher — Obscure Elfin
     2. henrici (Grote & Robinson) — Henry's Elfin
_____      a. henrici (Grote & Robinson) — Henry's Elfin
_____      b. solata Cook & Watson — Henry's Elfin
_____      3. fotis (Strecker) — Strecker's Elfin
     4. mossii (Hy. Edwards) — Moss's Elfin
_____      a. mossii (Hy. Edwards) — Moss's Elfin
_____      b. schryveri Cross — Schryver's Elfin
_____      c. bayensis (R. M. Brown) — San Bruno Elfin
_____      d. doudoroffi dos Passos — Doudoroff's Elfin
_____      e. windi Clench — Wind's Elfin
     5. augusta (W. Kirby) — Brown Elfin
_____      a. augusta (W. Kirby) — Brown Elfin
_____      b. iroides (Boisduval) — Western Brown Elfin
_____      c. annetteae dos Passos — Annette's Elfin
_____      6. niphon (Huebner) — Eastern Banded Elfin
     7. eryphon (Boisduval) — Western Banded Elfin
_____      a. eryphon (Boisduval) — Western Banded Elfin
_____      b. sheltonensis F. Chermock & Frechin — Shelton Elfin

*Eurystrymon* **Clench**
_____      1. polingi (Barnes & Benjamin) — Poling's Hairstreak
     2. ontario (W. H. Edwards) — Northern Hairstreak
_____      a. ontario (W. H. Edwards) — Northern Hairstreak
_____      b. autolycus (W. H. Edwards) — Autolycus Hairstreak

_____      c. violae (D. Stallings & Turner) — Viola's Hairstreak
_____      d. ilavia (Beutenmueller) — Ilavia Hairstreak

**Strymon** Huebner
     1. melinus Huebner — Common Hairstreak
       *a. melinus Huebner — (eastern U.S. and Canada)
_____      b. franki Field — Frank's Common Hairstreak
_____      c. pudicus (Hy. Edwards) — Modest Hairstreak
_____      d. setonia McDunnough — Seton Lake Hairstreak
_____      e. atrofasciatus McDunnough — Black-banded Hairstreak
_____      2. avalona (W. G. Wright) — Avalon Hairstreak
     3. columella (Fabricius) — Columella Hairstreak
       *a. columella (Fabricius) — (Antilles and Cen. America)
_____      b. istapa (Reakirt) — Columella Hairstreak
_____      4. alea (Godman & Salvin) — Lacey's Hairstreak
       *laceyi* (Barnes & Benjamin) — Lacey's Hairstreak
_____      5. bazochii (Godart) — Bazochii Hairstreak

**Erora** Scudder
     1. quaderna (Hewitson) — Quaderna Hairstreak
       *a. quaderna (Hewitson) — (Mexico and Guatemala)
_____      b. sanfordi dos Passos — Sanford's Hairstreak

# Subfamily Lycaeninae — Coppers

**Tharsalea** Scudder
     1. arota (Boisduval) — Tailed Copper
_____      a. arota (Boisduval) — Tailed Copper
_____      b. nubila J. A. Comstock — Cloudy Copper
_____      c. virginiensis (W. H. Edwards) — Virginia City Copper
_____      d. schellbachi Tilden — Schellbach's Copper

**Lycaena** Fabricius
     1. phlaeas (Linnaeus) — Little Copper
       *a. phlaeas (Linnaeus) — (Europe)
_____      b. americana Harris — American Copper
_____      c. hypophlaeas (Boisduval) — Western American Copper
_____      d. arethusa (Wolley-Dod) — Arethusa Copper
_____      e. arctodon Ferris — Beartooth Copper
_____      f. feildeni (M'Lachlan) — Feilden's Copper
     2. cuprea (W. H. Edwards) — Lustrous Copper
_____      a. cuprea (W. H. Edwards) — Lustrous Copper
_____      b. snowi (W. H. Edwards) — Snow's Copper
_____      c. henryae (Cadbury) — Henry's Copper

**Gaeides** Scudder
     1. xanthoides (Boisduval) — Great Copper
_____      a. xanthoides (Boisduval) — Great Copper
_____      b. dione (Scudder) — Dione Copper
     2. editha (Mead) — Edith's Copper
_____      a. editha (Mead) — Edith's Copper

———       b. montana (Field) — Montana Copper
———       3. gorgon (Boisduval) — Gorgon Copper

***Hyllolycaena*** **L. Miller & F. M. Brown**
———       1. hyllus (Cramer) — Bronze Copper
         *thoe* (Guérin-Ménéville)

***Chalceria*** **Scudder**
         1. rubida (Behr) — Ruddy Copper
———       a. rubida (Behr) — Ruddy Copper
———       b. duofacies (K. Johnson & Balogh) — Idaho Copper
———       c. perkinsorum (K. Johnson & Balogh) — Perkins' Copper
———       d. longi (K. Johnson & Balogh) — Long's Copper
———       e. sirius (W. H. Edwards) — Sirius Copper
———       f. monachensis (K. Johnson & Balogh) — Monache Copper
———       2. ferrisi (K. Johnson & Balogh) — Ferris's Copper
         3. heteronea (Boisduval) — Varied Blue
———       a. heteronea (Boisduval) — Varied Blue
———       b. clara (Hy. Edwards) — Bright Blue Copper

***Epidemia*** **Scudder**
         1. dorcas (W. Kirby) — Dorcas Copper
———       a. dorcas (W. Kirby) — Dorcas Copper
———       b. castro (Reakirt) — Rocky Mountain Copper
———       c. florus (W. H. Edwards) — Florus Copper
———       d. megaloceras Ferris — Bighorn Copper
———       e. arcticus Ferris — Arctic Copper
———       2. helloides (Boisduval) — Purplish Copper
         3. nivalis (Boisduval) — Nivalis Copper
———       a. nivalis (Boisduval) — Nivalis Copper
———       b. browni (dos Passos) — Brown's Copper
         4. mariposa (Reakirt) — Mariposa Copper
———       a. mariposa (Reakirt) — Mariposa Copper
———       b. penrosae (Field) — Penrose's Copper
———       c. charlottensis (Holland) — Northern Copper

***Hermelycaena*** **L. Miller & F. M. Brown**
———       1. hermes (W. H. Edwards) — Hermes Copper

## Subfamily Polyommatinae — Blues

***Brephidium*** **Scudder**
         1. exile (Boisduval) — Pygmy Blue
***Zizula*** **Chapman**
         1. cyna (W. H. Edwards) — Cyna Blue
***Lampides*** **Huebner**
         1. boeticus (Linnaeus) — Long-tailed Blue
***Vaga*** **Zimmerman**
         1. blackburni (Tuely) — Blackburn's Blue
***Leptotes*** **Scudder**
         1. marina (Reakirt) — Marine Blue

*Hemiargus* **Huebner**
    1. ceraunus (Fabricius) — Ceraunus Blue
      *a. ceraunus (Fabricius) — (Antilles)
_____    b. zachaeina (Butler & H. Druce) — Zachaeina Blue
_____    c. gyas (W. H. Edwards) — Gyas Blue
    2. isola (Reakirt) — Reakirt's Blue
      *a. isola (Reakirt) — (Mexico)
_____    b. alce (W. H. Edwards) — Reakirt's Blue

*Lycaeides* **Huebner**
    1. idas (Linnaeus) — Northern Blue
      *a. idas (Linnaeus) — (Europe)
_____    b. anna (W. H. Edwards) — Anna Blue
_____    c. ricei (Cross) — Rice's Blue
_____    d. lotis (Lintner) — Lotis Blue
_____    e. alaskensis (F. Chermock) — Alaskan Blue
_____    f. scudderii (W. H. Edwards) — Scudder's Blue
_____    g. ferniensis (F. Chermock) — Fernie Blue
_____    h. atrapraetextus (Field) — Dark-edged Blue
_____    i. sublivens Nabokov — Dark Blue
_____    j. longinus Nabokov — Longinus Blue
    2. melissa (W. H. Edwards) — Melissa Blue
_____    a. melissa (W. H. Edwards) — Melissa Blue
_____    b. annetta (W. H. Edwards) — Annetta Blue
_____    c. fridayi (F. Chermock) — Friday's Blue
_____    d. paradoxa (F. Chermock) — Orange-margined Blue
        *inyoensis* Nabokov

*Plebejus* **(Kluk)**
    1. saepiolus (Boisduval) — Greenish Blue
_____    a. saepiolus (Boisduval) — Greenish Blue
_____    b. hilda (J. & F. Grinnell) — Hilda Blue
_____    c. insulanus Blackmore — Vancouver Island Blue
_____    d. amica (W. H. Edwards) — Amica Blue
_____    e. gertschi dos Passos — Gertsch's Blue
_____    f. whitmeri F. M. Brown — Whitmer's Blue

*Plebulina* **Nabokov**
_____    1. emigdionis (F. Grinnell) — San Emigdio Blue

*Icaricia* **Nabokov**
    1. icarioides (Boisduval) — Boisduval's Blue
_____    a. icarioides (Boisduval) — Boisduval's Blue
_____    b. fulla (W. H. Edwards) — Fulla Blue
_____    c. mintha (W. H. Edwards) — Mintha Blue
_____    d. helios (W. H. Edwards) — Helios Blue
_____    e. evius (Boisduval) — Evius Blue
_____    f. moroensis (Sternitzky) — Morro Blue
_____    g. missionensis (Hovanitz) — Mission Blue
_____    h. ardea (W. H. Edwards) — Ardea Blue
_____    i. lycea (W. H. Edwards) — Lycea Blue
_____    j. buchholzi (dos Passos) — Buchholz's Blue
_____    k. pembina (W. H. Edwards) — Pembina Blue

      l.  blackmorei (Barnes & McDunnough) — Blackmore's Blue

      m. montis (Blackmore) — Montis Blue

      n.  pardalis (Behr) — Paradalis Blue

      o.  pheres (Boisduval) — Pheres Blue

      p.  fenderi (Macy) — Fender's Blue

  2. shasta (W.-H. Edwards) — Shasta Blue

      a.  shasta (W. H. Edwards) — Shasta Blue

      b.  minnehaha (Scudder) — Minnehaha Blue

      c.  pitkinensis (Ferris) — Brown's Blue

  3. acmon (Westwood & Hewitson) — Acmon Blue

      a.  acmon (Westwood & Hewitson) — Acmon Blue

      b.  texana Goodpasture — Texas Blue

      c.  spangelatus (Burdick) — Spangled Blue

      d.  lutzi (dos Passos) — Lutz's Blue

  4. lupini (Boisduval) — Lupine Blue

      a.  lupini (Boisduval) — Lupine Blue

      b.  monticola (Clemence) — Clemence's Blue

      c.  chlorina (Skinner) — Green Blue

  5. neurona (Skinner) — Veined Blue

***Vacciniina* Tutt**

  1. optilete (Knoch) — Cranberry Blue

     *a. optilete (Knoch) — (Eurasia)

      b.  yukona (Holland) — Yukon Blue

***Agriades* Huebner**

  1. franklinii (Curtis) — Arctic Blue

      *glandon* of authors, *aquilo* of authors

      a.  franklinii (Curtis) — Arctic Blue

      b.  lacustris (T. N. Freeman) — Lake-side Blue

      c.  bryanti (Leussler) — Bryant's Blue

      d.  megalo (McDunnough) — Large-spotted Blue

      e.  rusticus (W. H. Edwards) — Rustic Blue

      f.  podarce (C. & R. Felder) — Gray Blue

***Everes* Huebner**

  1. comyntas (Godart) — Eastern Tailed Blue

      a.  comyntas (Godart) — Eastern Tailed Blue

      b.  texanus F. Chermock — Texas Tailed Blue

  2. amyntula (Boisduval) — Western Tailed Blue

      a.  amyntula (Boisduval) — Western Tailed Blue

      b.  valeriae Clench — Valerie's Tailed Blue

      c.  albrighti Clench — Albright's Tailed Blue

      d.  herri F. Grinnell — Herr's Tailed Blue

***Philotes* Scudder**

  1. sonorensis (C. & R. Felder) — Sonoran Blue

***Euphilotes* Mattoni**

  1. battoides (Behr) — Square-spotted Blue

      a.  battoides (Behr) — Square-spotted Blue

      b.  oregonensis (Barnes & McDunnough) — Oregon Blue

_____     c. intermedia (Barnes & McDunnough) — Intermediate Blue
_____     d. glaucon (W. H. Edwards) — Glaucous Blue
_____     e. bernardino (Barnes & McDunnough) — Bernardino Blue
_____     f. martini (Mattoni) — Martin's Blue
_____     g. centralis (Barnes & McDunnough) — Central Blue
_____     h. allyni (Shields) — El Segundo Blue
_____     i. comstocki (Shields) — Comstock's Blue
_____     j. ellisii (Shields) — Ellis's Blue
_____     k. baueri (Shields) — Bauer's Blue
     2. enoptes (Boisduval) — Dotted Blue
_____     a. enoptes (Boisduval) — Dotted Blue
_____     b. columbiae (Mattoni) — Columbian Blue
_____     c. dammersi (J. A. Comstock & Henne) — Dammers' Blue
_____     d. smithi (Mattoni) — Smith's Blue
_____     e. ancilla (Barnes & McDunnough) — Ancilla Blue
_____     f. tildeni (Langston) — Tilden's Blue
_____     g. bayensis (Langston) — Bay Region Blue
_____     h. langstoni (Shields) — Langston's Blue
     3. rita (Barnes & McDunnough) — Rita Blue
_____     a. rita (Barnes & McDunnough) — Rita Blue
_____     b. emmeli (Shields) — Emmel's Blue
_____     c. coloradensis (Mattoni) — Colorado Blue
_____     d. mattonii (Shields) — Mattoni's Blue
     4. pallescens (Tilden & Downey) — Pallid Blue
_____     a. pallescens (Tilden & Downey) — Pallid Blue
_____     b. elvirae (Mattoni) — Elvira's Blue
_____     5. spaldingi (Barnes & McDunnough) — Spaldings's Blue
_____     6. mojave (Watson & W. P. Comstock) — Mojave Blue

**_Philotiella_ Mattoni**
     1. speciosa (Hy. Edwards) — Small Blue
_____     a. speciosa (Hy. Edwards) — Small Blue
_____     b. bohartorum (Tilden) — Boharts' Blue

**_Glaucopsyche_ Scudder**
     1. piasus (Boisduval) — Arrowhead Blue
_____     a. piasus (Boisduval) — Arrowhead Blue
_____     b. catalina (Reakirt) — Southern Arrowhead Blue
_____     c. nevada F. M. Brown — Nevada Blue
_____     d. daunia (W. H. Edwards) — Daunia Blue
_____     e. toxeuma F. M. Brown — Brown's Arrowhead Blue
     2. lygdamus (Doubleday) — Silvery Blue
     *a. lygdamus (Doubleday) — Silvery Blue (e. U.S.)
_____     b. couperi Grote — Couper's Blue
_____     c. afra (W. H. Edwards) — Afra Blue
_____     d. oro (Scudder) — Oro Blue
_____     e. jacki D. Stallings & Turner — Jack's Blue

_____ f. arizonensis McDunnough — Arizona Silvery Blue
_____ g. australis F. Grinnell — Southern Blue
_____ h. incognita Tilden — Behr's Blue
  *behrii* of authors, not W. H. Edwards
_____ i. columbia (Skinner) — Skinner's Blue
  3. xerces (Boisduval) — Xerces Blue (extinct)
*Celastrina* **Tutt**
  1. ladon (Cramer) — Spring Azure
  *argiolus* of authors, not Linnaeus
  *a. *ladon* (Cramer) — Spring Azure
_____ b. cinerea (W. H. Edwards) — Cinereous Blue
_____ c. echo (W. H. Edwards) — Spring Azure or Echo Blue
_____ d. lucia (W. Kirby) — Common Blue
_____ e. argentata (Fletcher) — Fletcher's Blue
_____ f. nigrescens (Fletcher)
_____ g. sidara (Clench)

# *Superfamily Hesperioidea — Skippers*

## Family Megathymidae — Giant Skippers

*Stallingsia* **H. A. Freeman**
_____ 1. maculosa (H. A Freeman) — Manfreda Borer
*Megathymus* **Scudder**
  1. coloradensis C. V. Riley — Colorado Yucca Borer
_____ a. coloradensis C. V. Riley — Colorado Yucca Borer
_____ b. elidaensis D. Stallings, Turner, & J. Stallings — Elida Yucca Borer
_____ c. navajo Skinner — Navajo Yucca Borer
_____ d. browni D. Stallings & Turner — Brown's Yucca Borer
_____ e. martini D. Stallings & Turner — Martin's Yucca Borer
_____ f. maudae D. Stallings, Turner, & J. Stallings — Maud's Yucca Borer
_____ g. arizonae Tinkham — Arizona Yucca Borer
_____ h. albasuffusa R., J., & D. Wielgus — Whitish Yucca Borer
_____ i. reubeni D. Stallings, Turner, & J. Stallings — Reuben's Yucca Borer
_____ j. winkensis H. A. Freeman — Wink Yucca Borer
_____ k. louiseae H. A. Freeman — Louise's Yucca Borer
  2. streckeri (Skinner) — Strecker's Yucca Borer
  3. texanus Barnes & McDunnough — Texas Yucca Borer
_____ a. texanus Barnes & McDunnough — Texas Yucca Borer
_____ b. leussleri Holland — Leussler's Yucca Borer

_____ 4. ursus Poling — Ursus Yucca Borer
_____    a. ursus Poling — Ursus Yucca Borer
_____    b. deserti R., J., & D. Wielgus — Desert Yucca Borer
_____ 5. violae D. Stallings & Turner — Viola's Yucca Borer

*Agathymus* H. A. Freeman

_____ 1. neumoegeni (W. H. Edwards) — Neumoegen's Agave Borer
_____ 2. carlsbadensis (D. Stallings & Turner) — Carlsbad Agave Borer
_____ 3. florenceae (D. Stallings & Turner) — Florence's Agave Borer
_____ 4. judithae (D. Stallings & Turner) — Judith's Agave Borer
_____ 5. diabloensis H. A. Freeman — Diablo Mountains Agave Borer
_____ 6. mcalpinei (H. A. Freeman) — McAlpine's Agave Borer
_____ 7. chisosensis (H. A. Freeman) — Chisos Agave Borer
_____ 8. aryxna (Dyar) — Aryxna Agave Borer
_____ 9. baueri (D. Stallings & Turner) — Bauer's Agave Borer
_____ 10. freemani D. Stallings, Turner, & J. Stallings — Freeman's Agave Borer
_____ 11. evansi (H. A. Freeman) — Evans' Agave Borer
_____ 12. mariae (Barnes & Benjamin) — Marie's Agave Borer
_____ 13. chinatiensis H. A. Freeman — Chinati Mountains Agave Borer
_____ 14. lajitaensis H. A. Freeman — Lajitas Agave Borer
_____ 15. rindgei H. A. Freeman — Rindge's Agave Borer
_____ 16. gilberti H. A. Freeman — Gilbert's Agave Borer
_____ 17. valverdiensis H. A. Freeman — Val Verde Agave Borer
_____ 18. stephensi (Skinner) — Stephens' Agave Borer
_____ 19. polingi (Skinner) — Poling's Agave Borer
_____ 20. alliae (D. Stallings & Turner) — Allie's Agave Borer

# Family Hesperiidae — True Skippers

## Subfamily Hesperiinae — Branded Skippers

*Panoquina* Hemming
_____ 1. errans (Skinner) — Wandering Skipper
_____ 2. sylvicola (Herrich-Schaeffer) — Sylvan Skipper

*Calpodes* Huebner
_____ 1. ethlius (Stoll) — Brazilian Skipper

*Lerodea* Scudder
_____ 1. eufala (W. H. Edwards) — Eufala Skipper.
_____ 2. arabus (W. H. Edwards) — Arabus Skipper

*Amblyscirtes* Scudder
_____ 1. simius W. H. Edwards — Simius Roadside Skipper
_____ 2. exoteria (Herrich-Schaeffer) — Large Roadside Skipper

_____    3. cassus W. H. Edwards — Cassus Roadside Skipper
_____    4. oslari (Skinner) — Oslar's Roadside Skipper
_____    5. aenus W. H. Edwards — Bronze Roadside Skipper
_____    6. erna H. A. Freeman — Erna's Roadside Skipper
_____    7. texanae Bell — Texas Roadside Skipper
_____    8. prenda Evans — Prenda Roadside Skipper
           *tolteca* of authors, not Scudder
_____    9. nereus (W. H. Edwards) — Nereus Roadside Skipper
_____   10. eos (W. H. Edwards) — Eos Roadside Skipper
_____   11. nysa W. H. Edwards — Nysa Roadside Skipper
_____   12. vialis (W. H. Edwards) — Roadside Skipper
_____   13. phylace (W. H. Edwards) — Phylace Roadside Skipper
_____   14. fimbriata (Ploetz) — Bellus Roadside Skipper
           *bellus* (W. H. Edwards)

**Atrytonopsis** Godman
         1. hianna (Scudder) — Dusted Skipper
_____       a. hianna (Scudder) — Dusted Skipper
_____       b. turneri H. A. Freeman — Turner's Skipper
_____    2. deva (W. H. Edwards) — Deva Skipper
_____    3. lunus (W. H. Edwards) — Lunus Skipper
_____    4. vierecki (Skinner) — Viereck's Skipper
_____    5. pittacus (WH. Edwards) — Pittacus Skipper
         6. ovinia (Hewitson) — Ovinia Skipper
         *a. ovinia (Hewitson) — (Mexico)
_____       b. edwardsi Barnes & McDunnough — Ovinia Skipper
         7. python (W. H. Edwards) — Python Skipper
_____       a. python (W. H. Edwards) — Python Skipper
_____       b. margarita (Skinner) — Margarita's Skipper
_____    8. cestus (W. H. Edwards) — Cestus Skipper

**Euphyes** Scudder
         1. ruricola (Boisduval) — Dun Skipper
           *vestris* (Boisduval)
_____       a. ruricola (Boisduval) — Dun Skipper
_____       b. metacomet (Harris) — Dun Skipper
_____    2. bimacula (Grote & Robinson) — Two-spotted Skipper

**Atrytone** Scudder
         1. arogos (Boisduval & Le Conte) — Arogos Skipper
_____       a. arogos (Boisduval & Le Conte) — Arogos Skipper
_____       b. iowa (Scudder) — Iowa Skipper
         2. logan (W. H. Edwards) — Delaware Skipper
_____       a. logan (W. H. Edwards) — Delaware Skipper
_____       b. lagus (W. H. Edwards) — Lagus Skipper

**Paratrytone** Godman
         1. melane (W. H. Edwards) — Umber Skipper
_____       a. melane (W. H. Edwards) — Umber Skipper
_____       b. vitellina (Herrich-Schaeffer) — Vitelline Skipper

**Poanes** Scudder
_____    1. hobomok (Harris) — Hobomok Skipper

_____ 2. taxiles (W. H. Edwards) — Taxiles Skipper
*Wallengrenia* **Berg**
_____ 1. otho (J. E. Smith) — Broken-dash
*Ochlodes* **Scudder**
     1. sylvanoides (Boisduval) — Woodland Skipper
_____    a. sylvanoides (Boisduval) — Woodland Skipper
_____    b. napa (W. H. Edwards) — Napa Skipper
_____    c. bonnevilla Scott — Bonneville Skipper
_____    d. santacruza Scott — Santa Cruz Island Skipper
_____    e. orecoasta Scott — Oregon Coast Skipper
_____ 2. pratincola (Boisduval) — Meadow Skipper
     3. agricola (Boisduval) — Farmer
_____    a. agricola (Boisduval) — Farmer
_____    b. verus (W. H. Edwards) — Verus Skipper
_____ 4. yuma (W. H. Edwards) — Yuma Skipper
_____ 5. snowi (W. H. Edwards) — Snow's Skipper
*Atalopedes* **Scudder**
_____ 1. campestris (Boisduval) — Sachem, Field Skipper
*Hylephila* **Billberg**
_____ 1. phyleus (Drury) — Fiery Skipper
*Polites* **Scudder**
_____ 1. coras (Cramer) — Peck's Skipper
       *peckius* (W. Kirby)
     2. sabuleti (Boisduval) — Sandhill Skipper
_____    a. sabuleti (Boisduval) — Sandhill Skipper
_____    b. tecumseh (F. Grinnell) — Tecumseh Skipper
_____    c. chusca (W. H. Edwards) — Chusca Skipper
_____ 3. mardon (W. H. Edwards) — Mardon Skipper
_____ 4. draco (W. H. Edwards) — Draco Skipper
_____ 5. themistocles (Latreille) — Tawny-edged Skipper
     6. origenes (Fabricius) — Cross-line Skipper
       *manataaqua* (Scudder)
_____    a. origenes (Fabricius) — Cross-line Skipper
_____    b. rhena (W. H. Edwards) — Rhena Skipper
     7. mystic (W. H. Edwards) — Long Dash
_____    a. mystic (W. H. Edwards) — Long Dash
_____    b. dacotah (W. H. Edwards) — Dacotah Long Dash
     8. sonora (Scudder) — Sonora Skipper
_____    a. sonora (Scudder) — Sonora Skipper
_____    b. utahensis (Skinner) — Utah Skipper
_____    c. siris (W. H. Edwards) — Dog Star Skipper
     9. vibex (Geyer) — Whirlabout
_____    a. vibex (Geyer) — Whirlabout
_____    b. praeceps (Scudder) — Whirlabout
_____    c. brettoides (W. H. Edwards) — Whirlabout
*Hesperia* **Fabricius**
     1. uncas W. H. Edwards — Uncas Skipper
_____    a. uncas W. H. Edwards — Uncas Skipper

_____      b. lasus (W. H. Edwards) — Lasus Skipper
_____      c. macswaini–MacNeill — MacSwain's Skipper
       2. comma (Linnaeus) — Comma Skipper
       *a. comma (Linnaeus) — (Europe)
_____      b. manitoba (Scudder) — Manitoba Skipper
_____      c. borealis Lindsey — Boreal Skipper
_____      d. assiniboia (Lyman) — Assiniboia Skipper
_____      e. harpalus (W. H. Edwards) — Harpalus Skipper
           *idaho* (W. H. Edwards)
_____      f. yosemite Leussler — Yosemite Skipper
_____      g. leussleri Lindsey — Leussler's Skipper
_____      h. tildeni H. A. Freeman — Tilden's Skipper
_____      i. dodgei (Bell) — Dodge's Skipper
_____      j. oregonia (W. H. Edwards) — Oregon Skipper
_____      k. hulbirti Lindsey — Hulbirt's Skipper
_____      l. ochracea Lindsey — Ochraceous Skipper
_____      m. colorado (Scudder) — Colorado Skipper
_____      n. susanae L. Miller — Susan's Skipper
_____      3. juba (Scudder) — Yuba Skipper
_____      4. woodgatei (R. C. Williams) — Woodgate's Skipper
_____      5. ottoe W. H. Edwards — Ottoe Skipper
       6. pawnee Dodge — Pawnee Skipper
       7. pahaska Leussler — Pahaska Skipper
_____      a. pahaska Leussler — Pahaska Skipper
_____      b. williamsi Lindsey — William's Skipper
_____      c. martini MacNeill — Martin's Skipper
_____      8. viridis (W. H. Edwards) — Green Skipper
_____      9. columbia (Scudder) — Columbian Skipper
_____      10. lindseyi (Holland) — Lindsey's Skipper
_____      11. dacotae (Skinner) — Dakota Skipper
_____      12. miriamae MacNeill — Miriam's Skipper
_____      13. nevada (Scudder) — Nevada Skipper

***Stinga*** **Evans**
_____      1. morrisoni (W. H. Edwards) — Morrison's Skipper

***Pseudocopaeodes*** **Skinner & R. C. Williams**
_____      1. eunus (W. H. Edwards) — Eunus Skipper

***Yvretta*** **Hemming**
_____      1. rhesus (W. H. Edwards) — Rhesus Skipper
       2. carus (W. H. Edwards) — Carus Skipper
_____      a. carus (W. H. Edwards) — Carus Skipper
_____      b. subreticulata (Ploetz) — Subreticulate Skipper

***Adopaeoides*** **Godman**
_____      1. prittwitzi (Ploetz) — Prittwitz's Skipper

***Copaeodes*** **Speyer**
_____      1. aurantiacus (Hewitson) — Orange Skipperling
_____      2. minimus (W. H. Edwards) — Southern Skipperling

***Oarisma*** **Scudder**
_____      1. powesheik (Parker) — Powesheik Skipper

_____ 2. garita (Reakirt) — Garita Skipperling
_____ 3. edwardsii (Barnes) — Edwards' Skipperling
**Ancyloxypha C. Felder**
_____ 1. arene (W. H. Edwards) — Tropical Least Skipperling
**Lerema Scudder**
_____ 1. accius (J. E. Smith) — Clouded Skipper
**Nastra Evans**
_____ 1. neamathla (Skinner & R. C. Williams) — Neamathla
        Skipper
_____ 2. julia (H. A. Freeman) — Julia's Skipper
**Erionota Mabille**
_____ 1. thrax (Linnaeus) — Banana Skipper

## Subfamily Heteropterinae Aurivillius

**Piruna Evans**
_____ 1. pirus (W. H. Edwards) — Pirus Skipperling
_____ 2. microsticta (Godman) — Small-spotted Skipperling
_____ 3. polingii (Barnes) — Poling's Skipperling
_____ 4. haferniki H. A. Freeman — Hafernik's Skipperling
**Carterocephalus Lederer**
       1. palaemon (Pallas)
         *a. palaemon (Pallas) — (Eurasia)
_____    b. mandan (W. H. Edwards) — Arctic Skipper

## Subfamily Pyrginae — Dusky-wings, Checkered Skippers, and Allies

**Pholisora Scudder**
_____ 1. catullus (Fabricius) — Common Sooty-wing
_____ 2. mejicana (Reakirt) — Mexican Sooty-wing
       3. libya (Scudder) — Mojave Sooty-wing
_____    a. libya (Scudder) — Mojave Sooty-wing
_____    b. lena (W. H. Edwards) — Lena Sooty-wing
       4. alpheus (W. H. Edwards) — Alpheus Sooty-wing
_____    a. alpheus (W. H. Edwards) — Alpheus Sooty-wing
_____    b. texana Scott — Texas Sooty-wing
_____    c. oricus W. H. Edwards — Oricus Sooty-wing
_____ 5. gracielae MacNeill — MacNeill's Sooty-wing
**Celotes Godman & Salvin**
_____ 1. nessus (W. H. Edwards) — Streaky Skipper
_____ 2. limpia Burns — Burns' Skipper
**Heliopetes Billberg**
_____ 1. domicella (Erichson) — Erichson's Skipper
_____ 2. ericetorum (Boisduval) — Large White Skipper
_____ 3. laviana (Hewitson) — Laviana Skipper
_____ 4. macaira (Reakirt) — Macaira Skipper

***Pyrgus* Huebner**
 1. centaureae (Rambur) — Grizzled Skipper
   *a. centaureae (Rambur) — (n. Scandinavia and arctic Russia)
_____   b. freija (Warren) — Freija's Grizzled Skipper
_____   c. loki Evans — Loki's Grizzled Skipper
_____ 2. ruralis (Boisduval) — Two-banded Skipper
_____ 3. xanthus W. H. Edwards — Xanthus Skipper
_____ 4. scriptura (Boisduval) — Small Checkered Skipper
 5. communis (Grote) — Common Checkered Skipper
_____   a. communis (Grote) — Common Checkered Skipper
_____   b. albescens Ploetz — Southern Checkered Skipper
_____ 6. philetas W. H. Edwards — Philetas Skipper

***Erynnis* Schrank**
_____ 1. icelus (Scudder & Burgess) — Dreamy Dusky-wing
 2. brizo (Boisduval & LeConte) — Sleepy Dusky-wing
_____   a. brizo (Boisduval & LeConte) — Sleepy Dusky-wing
_____   b. burgessi (Skinner) — Burgess's Dusky-wing
_____   c. lacustra (W. G. Wright) — Lacustra Dusky-wing
_____ 3. afranius (Lintner) — Afranius Dusky-wing
 4. persius (Scudder) — Persius Dusky-wing
_____   a. persius (Scudder) — Persius Dusky-wing
_____   b. fredericki H. A. Freeman — Frederick's Dusky-wing
_____   c. borealis (Cary) — Boreal Dusky-wing
_____ 5. funeralis (Scudder & Burgess) — Funereal Dusky-wing
_____ 6. martialis (Scudder) — Mottled Dusky-wing
 7. pacuvius (Lintner) — Pacuvius Dusky-wing
_____   a. pacuvius (Lintner) — Pacuvius Dusky-wing
_____   b. lilius (Dyar) — Dyar's Dusky-wing
_____   c. callidus (F. Grinnell) — Artful Dusky-wing
_____   d. pernigra (F. Grinnell) — Grinnell's Dusky-wing
 8. tristis (Boisduval) — Mournful Dusky-wing
_____   a. tristis (Boisduval) — Mournful Dusky-wing
_____   b. tatius (W. H. Edwards) — Tatius Dusky-wing
_____ 9. horatius (Scudder & Burgess) — Horace's Dusky-wing
 10. juvenalis (Fabricius) — Juvenal's Dusky-wing
_____   a. juvenalis (Fabricius) — Juvenal's Dusky-wing
_____   b. clitus (W. H. Edwards) — Clitus Dusky-wing
_____ 11. telemachus Burns — Telemachus Dusky-wing
_____ 12. propertius (Scudder & Burgess) — Propertius Dusky-wing
_____ 13. meridianus Bell — Meridian Dusky-wing
_____ 14. scudderi (Skinner) — Scudder's Dusky-wing

***Gesta* Evans**
 1. gesta (Herrich-Schaeffer) — Gesta Dusky-wing
   *a. gesta (Herrich-Schaeffer) — (S. America)
_____   b. invisus (Butler & H. Druce) — Gesta Dusky-wing

***Chiomara* Godman & Salvin**
 1. asychis (Stoll) — Asychis Skipper

_____ *a. asychis (Stoll) — (S. America)
_____ b. georgina (Reakirt) — Asychis Skipper
**Systasea W. H. Edwards**
_____ 1. pulverulenta (R. Felder) — Powdered Skipper
_____ 2. zampa (W. H. Edwards) — Edwards's Powdered Skipper
**Staphylus Godman & Salvin**
_____ 1. ceos (W. H. Edwards) — Ceos Sooty-wing
_____ 2. hayhursti (W. H. Edwards) — Southern Sooty-wing
**Cogia Butler**
_____ 1. hippalus (W. H. Edwards) — Hippalus Skipper
_____ 2. outis (Skinner) — Outis Skipper
**Phoedinus Godman & Salvin**
_____ 1. caicus (Herrich-Schaeffer) — Caicus Skipper
_____ *a. caicus (Herrich-Schaeffer) — (Mexico and Guatemala)
_____ b. moschus (W. H. Edwards) — Caicus Skipper
_____ 2. mysie (Dyar) — Mysie Skipper
**Thorybes Scudder**
_____ 1. pylades (Scudder) — Northern Cloudy-wing
_____ a. pylades (Scudder) — Northern Cloudy-wing
_____ b. albosuffusa H. A. Freeman — Suffused Cloudy-wing
_____ 2. diversus Bell — Diverse Cloudy-wing
_____ 3. mexicanus (Herrich-Schaeffer) — Mexican Cloudy-wing
_____ *a. mexicanus (Herrich-Schaeffer) — (Mexico)
_____ b. dobra Evans — Dobra Cloudy-wing
_____ c. nevada Scudder — Nevada Cloudy-wing
_____ d. aemilea (Skinner) — Aemilea's Cloudy-wing
_____ e. blanco Scott — Scott's Cloudy-wing
_____ 4. drusius (W. H. Edwards) — Drusius Cloudy-wing
**Achalarus Scudder**
_____ 1. casica (Herrich-Schaeffer) — Casica Skipper
**Autochton Huebner**
_____ 1. cellus (Boisduval & Le Conte) — Golden-banded Skipper
_____ 2. pseudocellus (Coolidge & Clemence) — Arizona Banded Skipper
**Urbanus Huebner**
_____ 1. proteus (Linnaeus) — Long-tailed Skipper
_____ 2. dorantes (Stoll) — Dorantes Skipper
**Codatractus Lindsey**
_____ 1. arizonensis (Skinner) — Arizona Skipper
**Zestusa Lindsey**
_____ 1. dorus (W. H. Edwards) — Short-tailed Skipper
**Chioides Lindsey**
_____ 1. catillus (Cramer) — Catillus Longtail
_____ *a. catillus (Cramer) — (S. America)
_____ b. albofasciatus (Hewitson) — White-striped Longtail
**Polygonus Huebner**
_____ 1. leo (Gmelin) — Hammock Skipper

——    *a. leo (Gmelin) — (Florida)
——     b. arizonensis (Skinner) — Arizona Hammock Skipper
***Epargyreus* Huebner**
      1. clarus (Cramer) — Silver-spotted Skipper
——     a. clarus (Cramer) — Silver-spotted Skipper
——     b. huachuca Dixon — Arizona Silver-spotted Skipper

## Subfamily Pyrrhopyginae

***Pyrrhopyge* Huebner**
      1. araxes (Hewitson) — Araxes Skipper
       *a. araxes (Hewitson) — (Mexico)
——     b. arizonae Godman & Salvin — Arizona Araxes
          Skipper

# Collecting Guidelines

The authors' suggestions on proper conduct and procedures in collecting butterflies appear on p. 12.

Because of environmental concerns and implications of the Federal Endangered Species Act, and following a poll of the membership, The Lepidopterists' Society appointed a committee in 1980 to establish guidelines for the collecting of butterflies and moths, and related activities. The report prepared by this Committee under the chairmanship of Dave Winter was approved by the Executive Council and published in 1982.

## The Lepidopterists' Society Statement of the Committee on Collecting Policy

### PREAMBLE

Our ethical responsibility to assess and preserve natural resources, for the maintenance of biological diversity in perpetuity, and for the increase of knowledge, requires that lepidopterists examine the rationale and practices of collecting Lepidoptera, for the purpose of governing their own activities.

To this end, the following guidelines are outlined, based on these premises:

Lepidoptera are a renewable natural resource.

Any interaction with a natural resource should be in a manner not harmful to the perpetuation of that resource.

The collection of Lepidoptera

- is a means of introducing children and adults to awareness and study of their natural environment;
- has an essential role in the elucidation of scientific information, both for its own sake and as a basis from which to develop rational means for protecting the environment, its resources, human health and the world food supply;
- is a recreational activity which can generally be pursued in a manner not detrimental to the resource involved.

315

# GUIDELINES

## Purposes of Collecting (consistent with the above):

· To create a reference collection for study and appreciation.
· To document regional diversity, frequency, and variability of species, and as voucher material for published records.
· To document faunal representation in environments undergoing or threatened with alteration by man or natural forces.
· To participate in development of regional checklists and institutional reference collections.
· To complement a planned research endeavor.
· To aid in dissemination of educational information.
· To augment understanding of taxonomic and ecologic relationships for medical and economic purposes.

## Restraints as to Numbers:

· Collection (of adults or of immature stages) should be limited to sampling, not depleting, the population concerned; numbers collected should be consistent with, and not excessive for, the purpose of the collecting.
· When collecting where the extent and/or the fragility of the population is unknown, caution and restraint should be exercised.

## Collecting Methods:

· Field collecting should be selective. When consistent with the reasons for the particular collecting, males should be taken in preference to females.
· Bait or light traps should be live-traps and should be visited regularly; released material should be dispersed to reduce predation by birds.
· The use of Malaise or other killing traps should be limited to planned studies.

## Live Material:

· Rearing to elucidate life histories and to obtain series of immature stages and adults is to be encouraged, provided that collection of the rearing stock is in keeping with these guidelines.
· Reared material in excess of need should be released, but only in the region where it originated, and in suitable habitat.

## Environmental and Legal Considerations:

- Protection of the supporting habitat must be recognized as the *sine qua non* of protection of a species.
- Collecting should be performed in a manner such as to minimize trampling or other damage to the habitat or to specific foodplants.
- Property rights and sensibilities of others must be respected (including those of photographers and butterfly-watchers).
- Regulations relating to publicly controlled areas and to individual species and habitats must be complied with.
- Compliance with agricultural, customs, medical and other regulations should be attained prior to importing live material.

## Responsibility for Collected Material:

- All material should be preserved with full data attached, including parentage of immatures when known.
- All material should be protected from physical damage and deterioration, as by light, molds, and museum pests.
- Collections should be made available for examination by qualified researchers.
- Collections or specimens, and their associated written and photographic records, should be willed or offered to the care of an appropriate scientific institution, if the collector lacks space or loses interest, or in anticipation of death.
- Type specimens, especially holotype or allotype, should be deposited in appropriate scientific institutions.

## Related Activities of Collectors:

- Collecting should include permanently recorded field notes regarding habitat, conditions, and other pertinent information.
- Recording of observations of behavior and of biological interactions should receive as high priority as collecting.
- Photographic records, with full data, are to be encouraged.
- Education of the public regarding collecting and conservation, as reciprocally beneficial activities, should be undertaken whenever possible.

## Traffic in Lepidopteran Specimens:

- Collection of specimens for exchange or sale should be performed in accordance with these guidelines.
- Rearing of specimens for exchange or sale should be from

stock obtained in a manner consistent with these guidelines, and so documented.

- Mass collecting of Lepidoptera for commercial purposes, and collection or use of specimens for creation of saleable artifacts, are not included among the purposes of the Society.

(From the NEWS of the Lepidopterists' Society, No. 5, Sept./Oct. 1982. Reproduced with permission.)

# Casual and Stray Species;
# Questionable Records

This list includes eastern species that may occur occasionally along the eastern border of our region (at the 100th meridian) and species recorded only once or twice from our area. Most of these are illustrated in *A Field Guide to the Butterflies* by Alexander B. Klots. Misidentified species and those incorrectly attributed to the West are also included below. Evaluation of old and vague records presents certain problems: some dubious records have been based on mislabeled specimens sold as from the United States by dealers in the last century.

## Milkweed Butterflies (Danaidae)

**MONTEZUMA** *Danaus eresimus montezuma* Talbot. (See Klots, p. 79.) Regularly found in s. Texas; has also been recorded from w. Tex. and Ariz.

**CERES** *Lycorea cleobaea atergatis* Doubleday & Hewitson. Large; banded with black, brown, and yellow. Tropical. One record from w. Tex.

## Clear-wings (Ithomiidae)

**KLUG'S DIRCENNA** *Dircenna klugi* (Geyer). Reported from "Los Angelos," Calif., by Reakirt in 1865, on the basis of specimens purchased from Lorquin which seem to have been from Mexico. (Illustrated in Holland, *The Butterfly Book,* Pl. VIII, Fig. 1.)

**CALIFORNIA LONG-WING** *Mechanitis californica* Reakirt. TL: "Los Angelos," Calif. Probably based on Mexican specimens; seems to be a synonym of the tropical *M. polymnia* (Linnaeus). (Illustrated in Holland, *The Butterfly Book,* Pl. VIII, Fig. 2.)

**LYCASTE** *Ceratinia lycaste* (Fabricius). Tropical. Reported from "Los Angelos," Calif., by Reakirt in 1865, apparently on the basis of mislabeled Mexican specimens. (Illustrated in Holland, *The Butterfly Book,* Pl. VIII, Fig. 3.)

## Brush-footed Butterflies (Nymphalidae)

**MALACHITE** *Siproeta stelenes biplagiata* (Fruhstorfer). (See

Klots, pp. 144, 278.) Tropical; frequent in s. Tex. May occur rarely in our area. At least one valid record for w. Kans.

**DINGY PURPLE-WING** *Eunica monima* (Stoll). (See Klots, pp. 97, 111.) One Ariz. record: Tucson, July 28, 1941.

**EUROPEAN COMMA** *Polygonia marsyas* (W. H. Edwards). Erroneously described as from Calif.; it is a synonym of the European *P. c-album.* The subspecies of the Satyr *(Polygonia satyrus)* to which the name *P. marsyas* has been misapplied has been named *P. satyrus neomarsyas* dos Passos.

**HARRIS' CHECKER-SPOT** *Charidryas harrisii* (Scudder). (See Klots, p. 94.) May stray to our eastern border. The subspecies *hanhami* (Fletcher) is found in Manitoba and adjoining areas.

**POLA CHECKER-SPOT** *"Melitaea" pola* Boisduval. This name was formerly used for *Poladryas arachne* (W. H. Edwards), in error. The true *pola* is Mexican (TL: Sonora), and does not occur in the U.S.

**MAY'S CHECKER-SPOT** *"Melitaea" mayi* (Gunder). Described from Smithers, British Columbia; also reported from Banff, Alberta, but seems to be a synonym of *Mellicta athalia,* a Eurasian species. Gunder's specimens may have been mislabeled. At any rate, no subsequent N. American specimens have ever been taken.

**BALTIMORE** *Euphydryas phaeton* (Drury). (See Klots, p. 93.) This species and its subspecies, *E. p. ozarkae* Masters, may possibly stray to our eastern border.

**MEXICAN FRITILLARY** *Euptoieta hegesia hoffmanni* W. P. Comstock. (See Klots, p. 84.) North to s. Tex.; may reach our area.

## Long-wings (Heliconiidae)

**JULIA** *Dryas julia moderata* (Riley). (See Klots, p. 83.) Regular in s. Tex.; may stray across the 100th meridian.

## Snout Butterflies (Libytheidae)

**MEXICAN SNOUT BUTTERFLY** *Libytheana carinenta mexicana* Michener. Reported vaguely from our southern border; few records.

## Metalmarks (Riodinidae)

**EUSELASIA ABREAS** (W. H. Edwards); has no common name. The stated TL is Arizona, but the type specimen is either lost or no longer in existence. The identity of the insect to which this name was given cannot be ascertained.

**NILUS METALMARK** *Calephelis nilus* (R. Felder). TL: Venezuela. The Lost Metalmark, *Calephelis perditalis* (p. 152), was for a short time considered a subspecies of this S. American species.

CALEPHELIS ARGYRODINES (H. W. Bates); no common name. This Cen. American species is no longer believed to occur in the U.S.

## Gossamer-winged Butterflies (Lycaenidae)

TELEA HAIRSTREAK *Chlorostrymon telea* (Hewitson). Formerly *Strymon maesites telea* (see Klots, p. 140.). One specimen taken at Laredo, Tex.; also reported vaguely from Ariz. We know of no authentic records.

CLYTIE HAIRSTREAK *Ministrymon clytie* (W. H. Edwards). (See Klots, p. 140.) Common in s. Tex.; apparently absent from w. Tex. Unauthenticated reports from s. Ariz.

BEON HAIRSTREAK *Calycopis isobeon* (Butler & Druce). (See Klots, p 134.) Resembles the Red-banded Hairstreak of the eastern U.S., but the postmedian band on the underside is narrow. S. Tex.; casual in Kansas.

JADA HAIRSTREAK *Arawacus jada* (Hewitson). Upperside pale blue; HW longer than wide. At least one authentic record for s. Ariz.: Baboquiviri Mts., July 30, 1949 by L. M. Martin.

CRITOLA HAIRSTREAK *Hypostrymon critola* (Hewitson). Reported from Ariz., but very rarely.

CASSIUS BLUE *Leptotes cassius striata* (W. H. Edwards). (See Klots, p. 157.) Casual specimens taken just west of the 100th meridian, from s. Tex. north to Scott Co., w. Kans.

## Swallowtails and Parnassians (Papilionidae)

POLYDAMUS SWALLOWTAIL *Battus polydamus* (Linnaeus). (See Klots, p. 180.) Breeds in s. Tex. One Calif. record: Santa Monica, 1924.

THOAS SWALLOWTAIL *Papilio thoas autocles* Rothschild & Jordan. Occasional in s. Tex. One record from Scott Co., Kans.: July 18, 1935. Has also been reported from s. Ariz. Such records are usually doubtful because of confusion with the Giant Swallowtail, *P. cresphontes* (p. 121). (See Klots, pp. 161, 174.)

ORNYTHION SWALLOWTAIL *Papilio ornythion* Boisduval. Occasional in s. Tex. At least one authentic Ariz. record: lower Madera Canyon, Sept., 1951 by T. Davies.

ASTYALUS SWALLOWTAIL *Papilio astyalus pallas* G. R. Gray. Pattern similar to that of Giant Swallowtail (p. 121), but yellow band wider. Not uncommon in se. Tex. At least one valid record for Ariz.: Baboquiviri Mts., Pima Co. July 28, 1949, by L. M. Martin.

PILUMNUS SWALLOWTAIL *Papilio pilumnus* Boisduval. This Mexican species has been reported from Ariz., perhaps erroneously.

ANCHISIADES SWALLOWTAIL *Papilio anchisiades idaeus* Fabricius. (See Klots, pp. 161, 178.) Established in lower Rio Grande Valley, Tex. One record for Scott Co., Kans., and one for Marfa, Brewster Co., Tex.

## Whites and Sulfurs (Pieridae)

**Dammers' Orange-tip** *Anthocharis dammersi* J. A. Comstock. TL: Whitewater Canyon, Riverside Co., Calif. The type is unique; it may be an aberration, or a hybrid between a marble and an orange-tip. Apparently no population of this insect exists.

**Falcate Orange-tip** *Falcapica midea* (Huebner). (See Klots, pp. 181, 208.) Eastern; west to Kans. and cen. Tex.

**Florida White** *Appias drusilla neumoegenii* (Skinner). (See Klots, pp. 161, 199.) West to se. Tex.; casual in Kans. and Neb.

**Ponten's Sulfur** *Colias ponteni* Wallengren. Described with a TL of the Hawaiian Islands ("Sandwitsch Inseln"), but has never been retaken there. *C. ponteni* seems to be the same as *Colias imperialis* from the Straits of Magellan; the type was apparently mislabeled.

**Argante Sulfur** *Phoebis argante* (Fabricius). Reported from the U.S., but probably mistaken for the Large Orange Sulfur, *Phoebis agarithe* (p. 140). There seem to be no valid U.S. records for the Argante Sulfur.

**Damaris Sulfur** *Eurema damaris* (C. & R. Felder). This name was added to our lists when Holland's *The Butterfly Book* showed a specimen of Salome *(Eurema salome)* misidentified as *E. damaris* (p. 296, Pl. XXXVII, Figs. 9 and 10). *E. damaris* is currently considered a synonym of the Mexican Sulfur, *Eurema mexicana*.

## True Skippers (Hesperiidae)

**Dion Skipper** *Euphyes dion* (W. H. Edwards). (See Klots, p. 255.) Recorded westward to e. Neb.; may occur on the eastern boundary of our area.

**Black Dash** *Euphyes conspicua* (W. H. Edwards). (See Klots, p. 258.) Occurs west to e. Neb. as subspecies *buchholzi* (Ehrlich & Gilham). TL: Valley, Nebraska, east of the 100th meridian.

**Mulberry Wing** *Poanes massasoit* (Scudder). (See Klots, p. 249.) Recorded west to e. Neb. and e. S.D.; may enter our area.

**Zabulon Skipper** *Poanes zabulon* (Boisduval & Le Conte). (See Klots, p. 250.) A common eastern species, found west to e. Neb., e. Kans., cen. Tex.; may occur along the eastern edge of our area.

**Broad-winged Skipper** *Poanes viator* (W. H. Edwards). (See Klots, p. 249.) Occurs just east of our area, from e. Neb. to Tex. May also occur along the eastern edge of our area.

**Little Glassy-wing** *Pompeius verna* (W. H. Edwards). (See Klots, p. 245.) West to e. Neb., south to Tex.; may occur in our area.

**Least Skipper** *Ancyloxypha numitor* (Fabricius). (See Klots, p. 231.) Eastern states, Canada to Tex.; rarely recorded from w. Kans. (Scott Co.).

**COLUMBINE DUSKY-WING** *Erynnis lucilius* (Scudder & Burgess). (See Klots, p. 227.) Reported from the Dakotas, Neb., and Kans. Old records are untrustworthy due to confusion with other species. The larva feeds on columbine *(Aquilegia)*.

**WILD INDIGO DUSKY-WING** *Erynnis baptisiae* Forbes. (See Klots, p. 227.) Neb. south to Tex.; may stray into our area. The larva feeds on wild indigo *(Baptisia)*.

**GRAIS SKIPPER** *Grais stigmaticus* (Mabille). (See Klots, p. 229.) Occurs in se. Tex. Also recorded west to Gillespie Co., just east of the 100th meridian; may stray into our area.

**SICKLE-WINGED SKIPPER** *Achlyodes thraso tamenund* (W. H. Edwards). (See Klots, p. 219.) May stray westward into our area.

**SOUTHERN CLOUDY-WING** *Thorybes bathyllus* (Smith). (See Klots, p. 212.) Eastern; recorded from Scott Co., w. Kans. May occur elsewhere along the eastern boundary of our area.

**ZILPA LONGTAIL** *Chioides zilpa* (Butler). Resembles the White-striped Longtail (p. 270), but has an indefinite white patch on underside of HW instead of the long white stripe. Has been recorded from s. Tex. and at least once from s. Ariz.

**ZESTOS SKIPPER** *Epargyreus zestos* (Geyer). (See Klots, p. 206.) Occurs in s. Fla. Evans, in *American Hesperiidae* (Part 2, p. 45), cites a female of this species from Ariz.

**EXADEUS SKIPPER** *Epargyreus exadeus* (Cramer). Has been reported by Holland as a "straggler in southern California, New Mexico, and Arizona." There is one apparently authentic record for s. Ariz. Our subspecies is *E. e. cruza* Evans.

**NYCTELIUS SKIPPER** *Nyctelius nyctelius* (Latreille). Occurs in s. Tex. and from Mexico to S. America. One Calif. record: El Cajon, San Diego Co., Calif. (Oakley Shields).

**SIMPLICIUS SKIPPER** *Urbanus simplicius* (Stoll). One specimen has been reared on bean *(Phaseolus)* in San Diego Co., Calif.

# Hawaiian Butterflies

Only two species — the Kamehameha Butterfly and Blackburn's Blue — are native to Hawaii. Six more species became established by 1900, two were purposely introduced for biological control in 1902, and no others are known to have arrived until 1970. From that year through 1979 five new species have become established. Hawaiian lepidopterists and interested visitors should watch for additional new species, as it seems quite likely that they will arrive in due time.

## *List of Hawaiian Butterflies*

### Danaiidae — Milkweed Butterflies

**MONARCH** *Danaus plexippus* (Linnaeus), p. 56. Arrived from N. America between 1845 and 1850.

### Heliconiidae — Long-wings

**GULF FRITILLARY** *Agraulis vanillae* (Linnaeus), p. 58. Arrived from Calif. in 1977.

### Nymphalidae — Brush-footed Butterflies

**RED ADMIRAL** *Vanessa atalanta* (Linnaeus), p. 74. Native to N. America and Europe; arrived after 1882.
**KAMEHAMEHA** *Vanessa tameamea* Eschscholtz, p. 74. Endemic — native to Hawaii.
**PAINTED LADY** *Vanessa cardui* (Linnaeus), p. 74. A cosmopolitan species; found nearly worldwide. Place of origin and time of arrival unknown. Common by 1879.
**AMERICAN PAINTED LADY** *Vanessa virginiensis* (Drury), p. 75. Native to N. and S. America; first found in Hawaii in 1878.

### Papilionidae — Swallowtails and Parnassians

**XUTHUS SWALLOWTAIL** *Papilio xuthus* Linnaeus, p. 121. A native of Asia and the Pacific islands to Guam. First recorded in 1971.

## Pieridae — Whites and Sulfurs

**CABBAGE BUTTERFLY** *Artogeia rapae* (Linnaeus), p. 128. A European species, introduced from Calif. on cabbages in 1897.

## Lycaenidae — Gossamer-winged Butterflies

**SMALLER LANTANA BUTTERFLY** *Strymon bazochii* (Godart), p. 180. Introduced from Mexico in 1902 as a biological control of weeds (Lantana).

**LARGER LANTANA BUTTERFLY** *Tmolus echion* (Linnaeus), p. 164. Introduced from Mexico in 1902 as a biological control of weeds (Lantana).

**LONG-TAILED BLUE** *Lampides boeticus* (Linnaeus), p. 188. Origin uncertain; occurs in Africa, s. Europe, Asia, and Australia. Present in Hawaii before 1882.

**BLACKBURN'S BLUE** *Vaga blackburni* (Tuely), p. 188. Endemic — native to Hawaii.

**PYGMY BLUE** *Brephidium exile* (Boisduval), p. 187. Native from the U.S. to Venezuela; probably introduced from Calif. First recorded in 1978.

## Hesperiidae — True Skippers

**BANANA SKIPPER** *Erionota thrax* (Linnaeus), p. 246. A native of Southeast Asia. First recorded in 1973.

**FIERY SKIPPER** *Hylephila phyleus* (Drury), p. 229. A native of N. and S. America. First recorded in 1970.

# Alaskan Butterflies

It is often believed that few or no butterflies are found in Alaska. This is far from the case. Between 75 and 80 species of butterflies have been recorded from Alaska, and from time to time species are found there that had not previously been detected (see p. 329).

Butterflies are found throughout the Far North, but the number of species decreases at the northern limits of vegetation. Some butterflies of the north are holarctic, found in the northern parts of Europe, Asia, and North America, including Alaska. Others are found in both Alaska and Siberia, but not in Europe, having apparently migrated to Alaska across the land bridge that once connected Alaska to Asia. However, some species of northern butterflies are found only in North America.

The North is often quite warm during its brief summer, with long days of sunshine. Plants grow very rapidly at this time. There is a great variety of plant life, with numerous flowers that carpet the ground with color in some places. In southern Alaska, there are great forests. As one goes farther north, the trees are smaller, and this dwarf forest, made up mostly of spruce, is called taiga. Farther north, or at higher elevations, the vegetation is low, consisting mostly of perennial plants with extensive underground root systems. This low vegetation is called tundra. Tundra may be wet and boggy, or quite dry, depending on the elevation and topography. Extremely wet areas with standing water are referred to as muskeg. Muskeg is usually inaccessible and has many mosquitoes but few butterflies.

Certain groups of butterflies are dominant in the Arctic. The arctics (genus *Oeneis*), the alpines (genus *Erebia*), the lesser fritillaries (genera *Boloria, Clossiana,* and *Proclossiana*) and the sulfurs (genus *Colias*), are very well represented. These genera account for more than one-third of all butterfly species so far listed from Alaska.

Arctics are dull-colored and hard to see. They fly rapidly and often perch on rocks, downed logs, or the trunks of standing trees. They lean sideways after alighting. Alpines fly in the open at moderate speed; their dark coloration makes them conspicuous. Lesser fritillaries fly low over the ground, often visit flowers, and are usually not conspicuous. Sulfurs fly rapidly and are difficult to catch except when nectaring at flowers.

Some Alaskan butterflies are common to abundant; you may

see several at one time. Because of the many hours of daylight in summer, butterflies are active for long periods of time. Since there is little or no night, moths also fly by day. Butterflies and moths may be the most visible insects, and are preyed on extensively by birds. When walking across dry tundra, one may see robins, wheatears, and lapland longspurs waiting to catch the butterflies and moths that fly up ahead of them. Wasps and dragonflies also capture butterflies and moths.

## *List of Alaskan Butterflies*

(Note: Species that are stray or casual in Alaska are indicated by an asterisk.)

### Satyridae — Satyrs and Wood Nymphs

### Nymphalidae — Brush-footed Butterflies

## Papilionidae — Swallowtails and Parnassians

## Pieridae — Whites and Sulfurs

## Lycaenidae — Gossamer-winged Butterflies

## Hesperiidae — True Skippers

As field work is carried on in Alaska, new butterflies continue to be discovered. Two recently described alpines (in family Satyridae) are listed below.

*Erebia phellea* Philip & Troubridge. Yukon, Alaska and NE Siberia. TL: Alaska: Seward Peninsula, Km 66–68 Council Rd.
*Erebia lafontainei* Troubridge & Philip. Yukon and Alaska. TL: Yukon: St. Elias Mts., Mt. Decoeli, 1300 m.

# Glossary

**Abdomen:** The last (3rd) major division of an insect's body; contains the digestive and reproductive organs.

**Anal angle:** The tornus; the lower outer corner of the wing (see front endpapers).

**Anal margin:** See inner margin (front endpapers).

**Anal veins:** The 6th, 7th, and 8th veins of the wing (see front endpapers). In butterflies, the 1st anal vein (1A) is usually absent, the 2nd anal vein (2A) is present, and the 3rd anal vein (3A) is often reduced or absent.

**Androconia:** Specialized scent scales, found in patches or along veins in some male butterflies (see stigma).

**Antenna (*pl.*, antennae):** Feelers (see front endpapers).

**Apex:** The outer tip of the wing.

**Apical:** Pertaining to the apex.

**Aurora (*pl.*, aurorae):** An orange or buff submarginal crescent on the hind wing of blues in subfamily Polyommatinae.

**Basal:** Pertaining to the base.

**Base:** The part of the wing nearest the thorax.

**Cell:** The area between wing veins. If not stated otherwise, "cell" means the discal cell; other cells are named for the veins above them (see front endpapers).

**Conspecific:** Belonging to the same species.

**Costa:** The front margin of the wing (see front endpapers).

**Coxa:** The basal segment of the leg (see front endpapers).

**Cremaster:** Hooks at the anal end of pupa (see Fig. 6, p. 27).

**Crochets:** Hooks on prolegs of larva (see Fig. 4, p. 26).

**Cubitus (Cu):** The 5th wing vein, which usually ends in 2 branches (see front endpapers).

**Diapause:** A period of inactivity and suspended development.

**Dimorphic:** Having two forms within a species. Sexually dimorphic — a condition in which the form or color of the male differs from that of the female.

**Disc, discal area:** The central area of the wing (see front endpapers).

**Discal cell:** The large, central wing cell (see front endpapers).

**Diurnal:** Active by day.

**Exoskeleton:** The hard or tough outer covering of an insect.

**Femur:** The 3rd leg segment from the base (see front endpapers).
**Fringe:** Scales or hairs extending out from the membrane along the wing margin.

**Genitalia:** The external reproductive organs (see Fig. 8, p. 31).
**Girdle:** A supporting silken band around the pupa.
**Gregarious:** Living together in groups, but not truly colonial.
**Ground color:** The color occupying most of the wing area.

**Head:** The foremost major division of the insect body; it bears the antennae, eyes, and mouth parts.
**Humeral vein (H):** The short vein near the base of the HW (see front endpapers).
**Hyaline:** Clear; transparent or translucent.

**Inner margin:** The lower edge of the wing (see front endpapers).
**Instar:** The period between molts in the larval stage; for example, the first-instar larva is newly hatched and has not yet undergone the first molt.

**Larva (*pl.,* larvae):** The caterpillar; the growing stage of a butterfly.

**Macular band:** Wing markings made up of spots, blotches, or bars, particularly on the underside (HW) of skippers in the genus *Hesperia.*
**Marginal:** Pertaining to the outer margin of the wing; refers to wing markings.
**Maxillae:** In butterflies, the proboscis (tongue) and its supporting structures (see front endpapers).
**Media (M):** The 4th wing vein, which has 3 branches (see front endpapers).
**Median:** The area halfway between the base and apex of each wing; refers to wing markings (see front endpapers).
**Mesothorax:** The middle segment of the thorax; it bears the forewings and the middle pair of legs.
**Metathorax:** The rearmost segment of the thorax; it bears the hind wings and the last pair of legs.

**Nectaring:** The practice by most adult butterflies of visiting flowers to obtain their nectar as food.
**Nominate subspecies:** The subspecies containing the type specimen (the first formally described specimen) of the species; it bears the same name as the species.

**Osmaterium:** Scent gland, as in swallowtail larvae.

**Outer margin:** The wing edge between the apex and the tornus or anal angle of each wing (see front endpapers).

**Overscaling:** Scales of a different color that lie over the basic ground color of the wings; in some species seen best only in fresh specimens.

**Palpi (*sing.*, palpus):** Paired, 3-segmented organs projecting in front of the face of an adult butterfly (see front endpapers).

**Papillae (*sing.*, papilla):** Small, nipplelike projections.

**Postbasal:** Refers to markings just beyond the wing base (see front endpapers).

**Postmedian (pm.):** Refers to markings just beyond the middle of each wing.

**Proboscis:** The "tongue" of a butterfly; coiled between the palpi when not in use (see front endpapers).

**Proleg:** The fleshy, abdominal leg of a butterfly larva (see Fig. 4, p. 26).

**Prothorax:** The foremost segment of the thorax; bears the first pair of legs.

**Pupa (*pl.*, pupae):** The inactive stage of a butterfly; the chrysalis (see Fig. 6, p. 27).

**Radius (R):** The 3rd wing vein, which has 3 to 5 branches (see front endpapers).

**Scales:** Flat hairs covering the wings of butterflies.

**Segment:** A ringlike or tubular division of the body or of an appendage, bounded by sutures (see Fig. 4, p. 26).

**Sphragus:** A structure attached to the tip of the abdomen of female parnassians during copulation (see genus *Parnassius,* p. 114).

**Spiracles:** A series of openings along each side of the body through which insects breathe (see Fig. 4, p. 26).

**Spur vein:** The side branch of a main vein (see humeral vein, front endpapers).

**Stigma:** A compact patch of specialized scent scales on males of some species of butterflies, especially hairstreaks and skippers. Also called sex scales (see **androconia**).

**Striated:** Having many fine markings across the wings.

**Subcosta:** The 2nd wing vein; unbranched (see front endpapers).

**Submarginal:** Located just in from the wing margin.

**Submedian:** Between postbasal and median.

**Subterminal:** Not quite at the end.

**Sympatric:** Refers to organisms that occur in the same area.

**Taiga:** The open, often stunted, evergreen forest between the tundra and the true boreal forest in the subarctic. This term is used by some workers to describe the more extensive, taller, and denser boreal coniferous forest, known to many as the "North Woods."

**Tail:** One or more slender projections on the HW of a butterfly.

**Tarsus:** The last section of an insect's leg, consisting of 5 or fewer subsections; bears the claws (see front endpapers).

**Tawny:** Brownish yellow.

**Thecla spot:** A colored spot at the anal angle of the HW, found in hairstreaks and some blues.

**Thorax:** The 2nd main section of an insect's body; bears the legs and wings.

**Tibia:** The 4th section of an insect's leg, between the femur and the tarsus; usually slender (see front endpapers).

**Tornus:** The lower outer corner of a wing; the anal angle.

**Trochanter:** The 2nd segment of an insect's leg; usually short.

**Tundra:** The treeless area in the Arctic between the ice cap and the subarctic forest (taiga). Tundra has permanently frozen subsoil and low-growing plant life such as mosses, lichens, clumps of fast-growing annual and perennial flowers, and stunted shrubs.

**Vein:** One of the tubular supporting structures of an insect's wing.

**Wingspan:** The width of a mounted butterfly, measured from apex to apex of the forewings.

# Bibliography

This *Field Guide to Western Butterflies* will enable you to identify the butterflies you see or collect in the West. It will also provide you with the basic essential taxonomic, biological, and distributional information about the butterflies of this region. Some useful references are provided below to give you more detailed information about butterfly species, and to enable you to investigate other aspects of butterfly study. Your library may have many of the publications listed; others may be ordered or purchased at your local bookstore. Some books are more difficult to locate, especially those that are out-of-print or published in another country. Specialized sources for such books are listed under Supply Houses and Organizations, starting on p. 340.

## SELECTED REFERENCES

### *General*

Ehrlich, Paul R., and Anne H. Ehrlich. 1961. *How to Know the Butterflies.* Dubuque: Wm. C. Brown.

Hodges, Ronald W., Tatiana Dominick, *et al.* (eds.). 1983. *Check List of the Lepidoptera of America North of Mexico.* London: E.W. Classey and Wedge Entomological Research Foundation.

Holland, W.J. 1931. *The Butterfly Book,* 2nd. ed. Garden City: Doubleday.

Howe, William H. (ed.). 1975. *The Butterflies of North America.* Garden City: Doubleday.

Miller, Lee D., and F. Martin Brown. 1981. *A Catalogue/Checklist of the Butterflies of America, North of Mexico.* The Lepidopterists' Society, Memoir No. 2.

### *Regional*

Austin, George T., and Anna T. Austin. 1980(81). Butterflies of Clark County, Nevada. Journal of Research on the Lepidoptera. 19(1):1–63.

Brown, F. Martin, Donald Eff, and Bernard Rotger. 1957. *Colo-*

*rado Butterflies.* Denver: Denver Museum of Natural History.

Christensen, James R. 1981. *A Field Guide to the Butterflies of the Pacific Northwest.* Moscow, Idaho: University Press of Idaho.

Comstock, John Adams. 1927. *Butterflies of California.* Los Angeles: published by the author.

Dornfeld, Ernst J. 1980. *The Butterflies of Oregon.* Forest Grove, Oregon: Timber Press.

Emmel, Thomas C., and John F. Emmel. 1973. *The Butterflies of Southern California.* Los Angeles: Natural History Museum of Los Angeles Co.

Field, William D. 1938. *A Manual of the Butterflies and Skippers of Kansas.* Lawrence, Kans.: Bulletin of the University of Kansas. 39(10): 1–328.

Ferris, Clifford D., and F. Martin Brown. 1981. *Butterflies of the Rocky Mountain States.* Norman: University of Oklahoma Press.

Garth, John S. 1950. *Butterflies of Grand Canyon National Park.* Grand Canyon Natural History Association Bulletin No. 11.

Garth, John S., and J.W. Tilden. In press. *California Butterflies.* Berkeley and Los Angeles: University of California Press.

―――. 1963. Yosemite Butterflies: An Ecological Survey of the Butterflies of the Yosemite Sector of the Sierra Nevada, California. Journal of Research on the Lepidoptera. 2(1): 1–96.

Hooper, Ronald R. 1973. *The Butterflies of Saskatchewan.* Regina, Sask.: Museum of Natural History.

Johnson, Kurt. 1972(73). The Butterflies of Nebraska. Journal of Research on the Lepidoptera. 11(1): 1–64.

Neill, William A., and Douglas J. Hepburn. 1976. *Butterflies Afield in the Pacific Northwest.* Seattle: Pacific Search Books.

Opler, Paul A., and George O. Krizek. 1984. *Butterflies East of the Great Plains.* Baltimore: Johns Hopkins University Press.

Orsak, Larry J. 1978. *The Butterflies of Orange County, California.* University of California at Irvine, Museum of Systematic Biology, Research Series No. 4.

Shapiro, Arthur M., Cheryl Ann Palm, and Karen L. Wcislo. 1979(81). The Ecology and Biogeography of the Butterflies of the Trinity Alps and Mount Eddy, Northern California. Journal of Research on the Lepidoptera. 18(2): 69–152.

Tilden, J.W. 1965. *Butterflies of the San Francisco Bay Region.* Berkeley and Los Angeles: University of California Press, Calif. Natural History Guides: 12.

Tilden, J.W., and David H. Huntzinger. 1977. The Butterflies of Crater Lake National Park, Oregon. Journal of Research on the Lepidoptera. 16(3): 176–192.

## Specific Groups or Species

Burns, John M. 1964. *Evolution in Skipper Butterflies of the Genus* Erynnis. University of California Publications in Entomology, Vol. 37.

Freeman, H. A. 1969. Systematic Review of the Megathymidae. Journal of the Lepidopterists' Society. Vol. 23, Supplement 1.

Hafernik, John E., Jr. 1982. *Phenetics and Ecology of Hybridization in Buckeye Butterflies.* Berkley, Calif.: University of California Press. University of California Publications in Entomology, Vol. 96.

MacNeill, C. Don. 1964. *The Skippers of the Genus* Hesperia *in Western North America With Special Reference to California.* University of California Publications in Entomology, Vol. 35.

Tyler, Hamilton A. 1975. *The Swallowtail Butterflies of North America.* Happy Camp, Calif.: Naturegraph Publishers.

Urquhart, F. A. 1960. *The Monarch Butterfly.* Toronto: University of Toronto Press.

## Collecting Butterflies

Arnett, Ross H. and Mary E. Ross. *The Naturalists' Directory and Almanac (International).* 1985. 44th edition. Flora & Fauna Books, 4300 N.W. 23rd Ave., Suite 100, Gainesville, Fla. 32606. The standard reference for locating persons with similar interests, this book lists many butterfly collectors who wish to exchange information, photographs, or butterfly specimens.

Arnett, Ross H. and Richard L. Jacques. 1985. *Insect Life: A Field Entomology Manual for the Amateur Naturalist.* Gainesville: Flora and Fauna Publications.

Barker, Paul C., *et al.* 1970. *A Study of Insects.* University of California Agricultural Extension.*

Beirne, B. P. 1955. *Collecting, Preparing, and Preserving Insects.* Canadian Dept. of Agricultural Entomology, Publication 932.*

Harman, Ian. 1954. *Collecting Butterflies and Moths.* New York: John de Graff.

Lehker, G.E., and H.O. Deay. 1964. *How to Collect, Preserve and Identify Insects.* Purdue University, Cooperative Extension Service, Extension Circular 509.*

---

*These publications are periodically updated or revised and re-issued.

Oldroyd, Harold. 1958. *Collecting, Preserving and Studying Insects*. New York: Macmillan.

Oman, P.W., and Arthur D. Cushman. 1948. *Collection and Preservation of Insects*. U.S. Dept. of Agriculture, Misc. Publication No. 601.*

Ross, H.H. 1962. *How to Collect and Preserve Insects*. Illinois Natural History Survey, Circular 39.*

Siggs, L.W. 1956. *Killing, Setting and Storing Butterflies and Moths*. The Amateur Entomologists' Society, Leaflet No. 28 (see List of Organizations, p. 341).

In addition, most State Agricultural Extension organizations publish other booklets on insect collecting and related aspects of insect study. These can be obtained from your County Extension Agent or your State Extension Office.

## *Watching Butterflies*

Measures, David G. 1976. *Bright Wings of Summer*. Englewood Cliffs, N.J.: Prentice-Hall.

Newman, L. Hugh. 1977. *Looking at Butterflies*. London: Collins.

Pyle, Robert Michael. 1974. *Watching Washington Butterflies*. Seattle: Seattle Audubon Society, Trailside Series.

———. 1981. *The Audubon Society Field Guide to North American Butterflies*. New York: Alfred A. Knopf.

———. 1984. *The Audubon Society Handbook for Butterfly Watchers*. New York: Charles Scribner's Sons.

*Sunset* Magazine. The Pleasure of Bug-watching. May 1962, pp. 262–266.

Whalley, Paul. 1980. *Butterfly Watching*. London: Severn House.

## *Photographing Butterflies*

Angel, Heather. 1975. *Photographing Nature: Insects*. Dobbs Ferry: Morgan & Morgan.

———. 1972. *Nature Photography: Its art and techniques*. London: Fountain Press.

Blaker, Alfred A. 1976. *Field Photography*. San Francisco: W.H. Freeman.

*These publications are periodically updated or revised and re-issued.

————. 1977. *Handbook for Scientific Photography*. San Francisco: W.H. Freeman.

Cott, Hugh B. 1956. *Zoological Photography in Practice*. London: Fountain Press.

Cruickshank, Allan D. (ed.). 1957. *Hunting with the Camera: Insects* by Edward S. Ross, pp. 108–134. New York: Harper & Brothers.

Cruise, John, and A. A. Newman (eds.). 1973. *Photographic Techniques in Scientific Research*. Vol. I., *Photography of Insects* by Douglas Lawson, pp. 111–218. London & New York: Academic Press.

Dalton, Stephen. 1975. *Borne on the Wind: The Extraordinary World of Insects in Flight*. New York: Reader's Digest/ Dutton.

Ettlinger, D.M. Turner (ed.). 1974. *Natural History Photography: Insects and other Invertebrates* by Sam Beaufoy. London–New York–San Francisco: Academic Press.

Linssen, E.F. 1953. *Entomological Photography in Practice*. London: Fountain Press.

Shaw, John. 1984. *The Nature Photographer's Complete Guide to Professional Field Techniques*. New York: Amphoto.

## *Painting and Drawing Butterflies*

Barlowe, Dorothea and Sy. 1982. *Illustrating Nature: How to Paint and Draw Plants and Animals*. New York: Viking Press.

Papp, Charles S. 1968. *Scientific Illustration: Theory and Practice*. Dubuque, Iowa: Wm. C. Brown.

————. 1976. *Manual of Scientific Illustration*. Sacramento, Calif.: American Visual Aid Books, distributed by Entomography Publications.

Wood, Phyllis. 1979. *Scientific Illustration: A Guide to Biological, Zoological, and Medical Rendering Techniques, Design, Printing, and Display*. New York: Van Nostrand Reinhold.

Zweifel, Frances. 1961. *A Handbook of Biological Illustration*. Chicago: University of Chicago Press.

## *Attracting and Rearing Butterflies*

Brewer, Jo.–1982. *Butterfly Gardening*. Xerces Society Self-Help Sheet 7: 1–12 (see list of organizations, p. 341).

Damrosch, Barbara. 1982. *A Butterfly Garden*. In *Theme Gardens,* New York: Workman Publishing.

Dickson, Richard. 1976. *A Lepidopterist's Handbook*. The Amateur Entomologists' Society. See Organizations (p. 341) for information.

Donahue, Julian P. *Take a Butterfly to Lunch: A Guide to Butterfly Gardening in Los Angeles*. Includes a portfolio and poster of caterpillars and a planting guide. Terra. 14(3): 3–20. California: Los Angeles County Natural History Museum.

Newman, L. Hugh. 1967. *Create a Butterfly Garden*. London: John Baker Ltd.

Rothschild, Miriam, and Clive Farrel. 1983. *The Butterfly Gardener*. London: Michael Joseph/Rainbird.

Stone, John L.S., and H.J. Midwinter. 1975. *Butterfly Culture*. Poole, Dorset, England: Blandford Press.

# *Butterfly Conservation*

Arnold, Richard A. 1983. *Ecological Studies of Six Endangered Butterflies (Lepidoptera, Lycaenidae): Island Biogeography, Patch Dynamics, and the Design of Habitat Preserves*. Berkeley: University of California Press. U.C. Publications in Entomology. Vol. 99.

Ehrlich, Paul R., and Anne H. Ehrlich. 1981. *Extinction: the Causes and Consequences of the Disappearance of Species*. New York: Random House.

Pyle, Robert M. 1976. Conservation of Lepidoptera in the United States. Biological Conservation. 9:55–75. England: Elsevier Applied Science Publishers.

Pyle, R., M. Bentzien, and P. Opler. 1981. Insect Conservation. Annual Review of Entomology. 26:223–258. Palo Alto, Calif.

Soule, Michael E., and Bruce A. Wilcox (eds.). 1980. *Conservation Biology*. Sunderland, Mass.: Sinauer.

Wells, Susan M., Robert M. Pyle, and N. Mark Collins. 1983. *The IUCN Invertebrate Red Data Book*. Gland, Switzerland: IUCN.

Xerces Society. All publications (see Organizations, p. 341).

# Directory of Entomological Equipment, Materials, Publications, and Services

## SUPPLY HOUSES

BioQuip Products, P.O. Box 61, Santa Monica, Calif. 90406. Extensive line of equipment, supplies, and books; insect labels printed to order.

Carolina Biological Supply Co., Powell Laboratories Division, Gladstone, Ore. 97027. Wide range of equipment, supplies, and books.

Clo Wind Company, 827 Congress Avenue, Pacific Grove, Calif. 93950. Aerial butterfly nets, sweeping nets, and insect pins.

Combined Scientific Supplies, P.O. Box 1446, Ft. Davis, Tex. 79734. Limited to insect boxes, glassine envelopes, spreading boards, pins, vials, and specimens.

Complete Scientific Supplies, P.O. Box 307, Round Lake, Ill. 60073. Insect cases, boxes, envelopes, Riker mounts, insect pins, and specimens.

E. W. Classey, Ltd., P.O. Box 93, Faringdon, Oxon. SN7 7DR, England. Limited to publications. Excellent inventory of new and used books and pamphlets, many on butterflies.

Entomological Reprint Specialists, P.O. Box 77224, Dockweiler Station, Los Angeles, Calif. 90007. Wide range of entomological publications.

Flora & Fauna Books, P.O. Box 3004, Seattle, WA 98114. New and used books in all fields of natural history.

Flora & Fauna Publications, 4300 NW 23rd Ave., Suite 100, Gainesville, Fla. 32606. Publishes books on entomology, zoology, botany, and ecology. Sells books on a great variety of natural history subjects, with selected titles available at a pre-publication discount. Write for details.

Ianni Butterfly Enterprises, P.O. Box 81171, Cleveland, Ohio 44181. Limited to insect pins, envelopes, exhibit cases, Riker mounts, fumigant boxes, books, and specimens.

Nasco, 901 Janesville Ave., Ft. Atkinson, WI 53538. Nasco West, 1524 Princeton Ave., Modesto, Calif. 95352. Carries a good variety of entomological supplies and equipment as well as items used in the physical sciences and other life sciences.

Scientific Products, Div. of American Hospital Supply Corp., 17111 Red Hill Ave., Irvine, Calif. 92714. General supplies and equipment for biologists.

Student Science Service, 622 W. Colorado St., Glendale, Calif. 91204. Chemicals, dissection instruments, forceps, fumigants, killing jars, pinning blocks, spreading boards, vials, etc.

Ward's Natural Science Establishment, Inc., 11850 Florence Ave., Santa Fe Springs, Calif. 90670. Wide range of equipment, supplies, and books.

Wildlife Publications, Inc., 1014 NW 14th Ave., Gainesville, Fla. 32601. Publishes a quarterly, *Wildlife Publications Review,* which includes an annual Catalog issue. Devoted to natural history literature of all kinds, including butterflies and other insects. On request, this publisher will try to obtain any natural history title in print anywhere in the world.

# ORGANIZATIONS

## *Devoted to Lepidoptera*

The British Butterfly Conservation Society. Tudor House, Quorn, Loughborough, Leicestershire, England, LE12 8AD.

The Lepidopterists' Society, c/o Ron Leuschner, 1900 John St., Manhattan Beach, Calif. 90266. Publishes *Journal of the Lepidopterists' Society, News of the Lepidopterists' Society, Memoirs,* and a commemorative volume.

The Lepidoptera Research Foundation, c/o Santa Barbara Museum of Natural History, 2559 Puesta del Sol Rd., Santa Barbara, Calif. 93105. Publishes *The Journal of Research on the Lepidoptera.*

The Xerces Society, c/o Dr. Karolis Bagdonas, 110 Biochemistry Bldg., University of Wyoming, Laramie, Wyo. 82071. Dedicated to habitat protection for rare and endangered butterflies and other terrestrial arthropods. Conducts an annual 4th of July Butterfly Count. Publishes *Wings, Atala,* educational leaflets, self-help sheets.

## *Devoted to Insects, including the Lepidoptera*

The Amateur Entomologists' Society, c/o Mrs. Wendy Fry, Registrar, 8 Heather Close, New Haw, Weybridge, Surrey

KT15 3PF, England, or AES Publications Agent, 137 Gleneldon Road, Streatham, London, SW16, England. Publishes *Bulletin of the Amateur Entomologists' Society,* AES leaflets, *A Lepidopterists' Handbook,* and other manuals.

Entomological Society of Alberta, Dept. of Entomology, University of Alberta, Edmonton, Alberta T6G 2E3, Canada.

Entomological Society of America, 4603 Calvert Rd., College Park, Md. 20740. Publishes *Bulletin of the Entomological Society of America, Annals of the Entomological Society of America, Environmental Entomology, Journal of Economic Entomology, ESA Newsletter,* and ESA Miscellaneous Publications.

Entomological Society of Canada, 1320 Carling Ave., Ottawa, Ontario K1Z 7K9, Canada. Publishes *Canadian Entomologist.*

Lorquin Entomological Society, Natural History Museum of Los Angeles County, 900 Exposition Blvd., Los Angeles, Calif. 90007.

Pacific Coast Entomological Society, California Academy of Sciences, Golden Gate Park, San Francisco, Calif. 94118. Publishes *Pan-Pacific Entomologist* and Memoirs.

Teen International Entomology Group (TIEG), Dept. of Entomology, Michigan State University, East Lansing, Mich. 48824. Publishes a newsletter, *TIEG News.* Primarily for teenagers, but membership extended to interested adults.

4-H Clubs. For teenagers and younger children. University Agricultural Extension (through county offices) sponsors local 4-H Clubs. Entomology project study sections can be organized if interest is shown and a leader can be found. Ask your County Farm Advisor for information.

# Index to Host Plants
# (Larval Food Plants)

This index includes common and scientific names of the food plants eaten by the caterpillars of the western butterflies. Scientific names of plants are indexed by genus and species, and by family when specific names are not given. Common names are indexed for species, some genera, and some general names applied to agricultural crops and garden plants.

# Index to Butterflies

This index includes common names and scientific names (genus, species, and subspecies where appropriate) of all the butterflies described in this book, and the common names of subfamilies. Cross references are provided for certain scientific names familiar to many, but no longer in approved use. Not indexed are subspecies listed in the Checklist (pp. 275–314), but not discussed in species accounts, and nominate species that are mentioned in the text but not found in our area. The photographic illustrations are indexed by plate numbers after the common names.

INDEX TO BUTTERFLIES        367

Satyrium, contd.
  calanus falacer, 162
  calanus godarti, 162
  californicum, 160
  dryope, 161
  fuliginosum, 159
  fuliginosum fuliginosum, 159
  fuliginosum semiluna, 159
  liparops, 162
  liparops aliparops, 162
  liparops fletcheri, 162
  liparops liparops, 162
  saepium, 163
  sylvinum, 161
  sylvinum desertorum, 161
  sylvinum itys, 161
  sylvinum putnami, 161
  sylvinum sylvinum, 161
  tetra, 163
Satyrodes eurydice, 37
  eurydice eurydice, 38
  eurydice fumosus, 38
Scolitantides. See Glaucopsyche
      piasus, 201
Siproeta stelenes biplagiata,
  319
Sister(s), 67, Pl. 10
  Arizona, 67
  California, 67
Skipper(s), Arabus, 215, Pl. 40
  Araxes, 272
  Arctic, 248, 329, Pl. 48
  Arizona, 269, Pl. 47
  Arizona Araxes, 272, Pl. 47
  Arizona Banded, 268, Pl. 47
  Arizona Hammock, 271, Pl. 47
  Arizona Silver-spotted, 271
  Arogos, 224, Pl. 41
  Assiniboia, 235, Pl. 43
  Asychis, 263, Pl. 46
  Banana, 246, 325, Pl. 44
  Bellus Roadside, 220, Pl. 41
  Bonneville, 227
  Boreal, 235, 329
  branded, 213
  Brazilian, 215, Pl. 40
  Broad-winged, 322
  Bronze Roadside, 217, Pl. 39
  Burns', 252
  Caicus, 265, Pl. 46
  Carus, 243, Pl. 44
  Casica, 268, Pl. 46
  Cassus Roadside, 216, Pl. 40
  Cestus, 223, Pl. 41
  Chusca, 230
  Clouded, 245, Pl. 44
  Colorado, 237, Pl. 43
  Columbian, 240, Pl. 43
  Comma, 234
  Common Checkered, 255, Pl. 48
  Cross-line, 232, Pls. 41, 42
  Dakota, 240, Pl. 43
  Delaware, 224, Pl. 41
  Deva, 221, Pl. 39

Skippers, contd.
  Dion, 322
  Dodge's, 236, Pl. 43
  Dog-star, 233, Pl. 42
  Dorantes, 269, Pl. 48
  Draco, 231, Pl. 42
  Dun, 223, Pl. 39
  Dusted, 220, Pl. 41
  Edwards' Powdered, 263, Pl. 46
  Eos Roadside, 219, Pl. 41
  Erichson's, 252, Pl. 45
  Erna's Roadside, 217, Pl. 40
  Eufala, 215, Pl. 39
  Eunus, 242, Pl. 44
  Exadeus, 323
  Field. See Sachem, 229
  Fiery, 229, 325, Pl. 48
  Freija's Grizzled, 254
  Golden-banded, 268, Pl. 47
  Grais, 323
  Green, 239, Pl. 43
  Grizzled, 254, 329, Pl. 45
  Hammock, 270
  Harpalus, 235, Pl. 48
  Hippalus, 264, Pl. 46
  Hobomok, 225, Pl. 42
  Hulbirt's, 237, Pl. 43
  Idaho. See Skipper, Harpalus, 235
  Iowa, 224
  Julia's, 246, Pl. 44
  Lagus, 225
  Large Roadside, 216, Pl. 40
  Large White, 253, Pl. 48
  Lasus, 234
  Laviana, 253, Pl. 45
  Least, 322
  Leussler's, 236, Pl. 43
  Lindsey's, 240, Pl. 43
  Loki's Grizzled, 254
  Long-tailed, 269, Pl. 48
  Lunus, 221, Pl. 41
  Macaira, 253, Pl. 45
  MacSwain's, 234
  Manitoba, 234, Pl. 43
  Mardon, 231, Pl. 42
  Margarita's, 223
  Martin's, 239
  Meadow, 227, Pl. 42
  Miriam's, 241, Pl. 43
  Morrison's, 241, Pl. 44
  Mysie, 266, Pl. 46
  Napa, 227
  Neamathla, 246, Pl. 44
  Nereus Roadside, 218, Pl. 41
  Nevada, 241, Pl. 43
  Nyctelius, 323
  Nysa Roadside, 219, Pl. 41
  Ochraceous, 237, Pl. 43
  Oregon, 237, Pl. 43
  Oregon Coast, 227
  Oslar's Roadside, 217, Pl. 40
  Ottoe, 238, Pl. 43
  Outis, 265, Pl. 46
  Ovinia, 222, Pl. 41

WOOD NYMPH, p. 43
*Cercyonis*
(Satyridae)

RINGLET, p. 40
*Coenonympha*
(Satyridae)

ARCTIC, p. 51
*Oeneis*
(Satyridae)

MILKWEED BUTTERFLY, p. 56
*Danaus*
(Danaidae)

LONG-WING, p. 57
*Heliconius*
(Heliconiidae)

LEAF-WING, p. 59
*Anaea*
(Apaturidae)

EMPEROR, p. 60
*Asterocampa*
(Apaturidae)

METALMARK, p. 150
*Apodemia*
(Riodinidae)

ADMIRAL, p. 64
*Basilarchia*
(Nymphalidae)

ANGLE-WING, p. 69
*Polygonia*
(Nymphalidae)

CRESCENT, p. 94
*Phyciodes*
(Nymphalidae)